CURRIER & IVES

PRINTS

An Illustrated Check List

New, Updated Edition

By FREDERIC A. CONNINGHAM

CROWN PUBLISHERS, INC.   NEW YORK

Foreword copyright © 1983 by Crown Publishers, Inc.
Copyright © 1970 by Mary Barton Conningham

Published by Crown Publishers, Inc., One Park Avenue, New York, N.Y. 10016
and simultaneously in Canada by General Publishing Company Limited.

Library of Congress Cataloging in Publication Data
Conningham, Frederic A. (Frederic Arthur), 1890–
    Currier & Ives prints.
    Includes index.
    1. Currier & Ives—Catalogs.   2. Lithography,
American—Catalogs.   I. Title.
NE2312.C8A4   1983   769.92′4   83-14346
ISBN 0-517-55115-2
ISBN 0-517-55116-0 (pbk.)

Library of Congress Catalog Card Number: 77–105958
Printed in the U.S.A.
First Revised Edition

FOREWORD

This book is meant to provide an up-to-date accurate list of the known N. Currier and Currier & Ives prints, giving the exact title, size, date of publication (if any), description when necessary, and approximate valuation of each print.* For further information about Currier and Ives, there are the books by the late Harry T. Peters who did a tremendous amount of research and gathered a great deal of information at first hand through his talks with Louis Maurer and Thomas Worth, two of the artists employed by Currier & Ives. Incidentally, he more than anyone else was responsible for the widespread interest in the prints as a result of his exhibitions, lectures, articles and books.

In 1828 Nathaniel Currier began his lithographic career as an apprentice in one of the earliest American lithographic firms, William and John Pendleton of Boston. Currier remained there for five years, then left to work for M. E. D. Brown of Philadelphia where he stayed only one year. Later he came to New York to form a partnership with Stodart, about whom very little is known. This venture also was short lived. Most of the work of these two at this time was done in conjunction with music and book publishers although they did publish one very important print under their own name—*Dartmouth College* (No. 1446). It is impossible to say which was the earliest print published by N. Currier but it could have been this view of Dartmouth. It is strange that Currier did not publish other decorative views of American Colleges.

Currier started his own establishment in 1835 at 1 Wall Street where he continued to work for various other publishers, among them J. H. Bufford and J. Disturnell. Some of the prints published at this time were: *Ruins of the Planter's Hotel, New Orleans* (No.5254), *Ruins of the Merchant's Exchange, N. Y.* (No. 5253) and *View of the Great Conflagration of Dec. 16 and 17, 1835* (No. 6413). Most of these early prints were marked, "N. Currier's Lith. N. Y." Shortly after Currier moved to 2 Spruce Street. From then on his work rooms were located either at 2 Spruce Street or 33 Spruce Street until the firm went out of business. For many years the retail store was just around the corner at 152 Nassau Street. Subsequently the store was moved to 125 Nassau Street and still later to 115 Nassau Street. Currier never went very far from Spruce Street except for a brief period in 1842 when he had a store at 169 Broadway, near Cortlandt Street. Since so few prints are marked with this address, it was evidently not maintained very long. Currier published one print *The Ressurection* (No. 5122) marked "N. Currier, Tract House, N. Y." dated 1849, but I think he was not actually located there.

Some of the small folio prints sold were uncolored, or "Plain" as Currier listed them, but most of those sold were colored. The coloring was done by a group of girls using assembly line methods. Each girl applied a single color, then passed the print on to the next girl and so on until the coloring was completed. The wholesale price for these small folio prints was $6.00

* Because prices fluctuate so much today, they have been eliminated from this new, updated edition (1983).

[v]

per hundred or any part of a hundred (according to Currier's Order Lists—see illustration). The retail price was 20¢ each. It is not surprising that the colors ran over the borders occasionally and sometimes inadequately covered the spaces allotted to them when one considers the speed at which the girls had to work in order to enable Mr. Currier to profit from a 6¢ item.

The large folio prints, however, were colored by more expert colorists. More time and care were used in applying the colors, and tempera or opaque colors were used to accentuate the highlights. These prints retailed from $1.00 to $3.00 each.

Not all Currier prints were colored entirely by hand. Many of the large folio prints were printed partially in color—even in the early days of the firm. I have seen an example of this printed as early as 1848. I have a number of these partially colored prints and in every instance the sky is printed in color and on some the foreground is also printed in color. The rest of the print was finished by hand. This was a method used by many of the print publishers, both here and abroad. Many fine prints were produced this way.

I have often been asked the reason for the sheen found on many of the prints. This sheen, found on the darkest portions of the composition, was used to make the shadows more luminous, thereby giving the print more brilliance and life.

In 1857 James Ives was made a partner of the firm. All prints made after that date and many of the prints previously published by N. Currier were marked Currier & Ives. Ives appears to have done little of the completed art work, judging by the credit on the prints. However, his name does appear on the set of prints, *Four Seasons of Life* (Nos. 2096-2097-2098-2099-2100), *Haying Time—The First Load* (No. 2760), *Haying Time—The Last Load* (No. 2761) and *Across the Continent* (No. 33).

Currier & Ives was undoubtedly the most prolific firm of lithographers, and its output was greater than that of all the other firms combined. The prints constitute practically our only source of colored pictures of every phase of American life and history of their period. The collector has an almost unlimited selection of groups to choose from—hunting, fishing, whaling, views of cities, rural scenes, historical, clipper ships, yachts, steamboats, Mississippi River scenes, Hudson River scenes, railroads, religion, comics—white and colored—gold mining, western scenes, advertising, sentimental, foreign views, trotting, temperance, winter scenes, portraits, and numerous other categories. Currier also published a number of flower and fruit prints which are becoming increasingly popular. Many of the early name prints, such as, *Mary, Susan, Elizabeth,* etc., are extremely decorative. The most ardent Currier fan will admit that everything produced by the firm is not a masterpiece but the fact remains that Currier employed or used the work of many of the celebrated artists of the day—J. F. Butterworth, Atwater, John Cameron, George Inness, Louis Maurer, A. F. Tait, Thomas Worth, Thomas Nast, C. H. Moore, F. F. Palmer, George Durrie, Charles Parsons, Eastman Johnson, Otto Knirsch, Venino, Napoleon Sarony and many, many others. Credit was usually given for their work on the large folios but only occasionally on the small folios, although a great many of the small ones were drawn by the same artists.

Nathaniel Currier retired in 1880 and died eight years later; James Ives died in 1895. The business was carried on by the sons of each. It was during this period that most of the famous Darktown subjects were produced, large bird's-eye views of New York, Boston, Chicago, Washington, etc., and a number of large folio horse prints, including reprints of many of their earlier horse prints, usually with a changed title and the elimination of portions of the background. This was done by the transfer method. The subject was printed on a special type of transfer paper, with a special transfer ink. The paper was placed face down on a prepared lithographic stone, using great pressure to insure perfect contact, then the paper was moistened and stripped from the stone leaving the inked impression. In principle it was similar to the old decalcomanias. Thereafter the stone was prepared for printing as in ordinary lithography.

Sometime in 1892 the old high-wheeled sulkies were supplanted by the new low-wheeled, pneumatic-tired "bikes" and this necessitated a change in composition of some of the earlier trotting prints. A very good example of this can be seen in the two prints, *A Race for Blood* which are illustrated.

The last prints published by the firm, of which I can find any record, are those pertaining to the Spanish-American War: *Our Victorious Fleets in Cuban Waters* (No. 4658), *Col. Theodore Roosevelt* (No. 1202) and others. With the introduction of new methods of printing, chromolithography, photo engraving, etc., and the increased use of illustrations in magazines and newspapers, which supplanted the older manual methods, Currier & Ives began to go out of fashion. Strangely enough a great many of the ideas which helped the new photoengraving process, including the invention of the shading screen known by his name, were invented by Ben Day, one of the artists who did work for Currier & Ives.

The firm carried on in a desultory fashion until 1907 when the equipment, prints, and lithographic stones were sold at auction. Mr. Joseph Koehler bought some of the large and small stones including the *Darktown Comics* and the *Lincoln Portrait* (No. 24) which he published under his name. Some of these stones were offered to me many years later but, in my opinion, at too high a price. After Mr. Koehler died I lost track of the stones. They would have made interesting collectors' items. I know several collectors who are the proud possessors of original Currier & Ives lithographic stones.

Lithography was invented by Alois Senefelder of Bavaria in the latter part of the 18th century. The principle on which it was based was that grease and water do not mix. The best lithographic stone was also discovered by Senefelder in the village of Solenhofen. This particular grade of carbonaceous limestone was of the highest quality having a very even texture and just the right porosity and density to receive grease and water with sufficient readiness. The method used in preparing a stone for printing was first to cut the stone to the required size, i.e. slightly larger than the overall size of the print to be reproduced and several inches thick. The surface to be drawn upon was then very carefully ground with either sand or finely ground glass until perfectly smooth. The picture to be reproduced was drawn in reverse on the stone with greasy crayons. When the drawing was completed, the stone

The interior of an early lithograph shop.
Not a Currier & Ives print, this is a rare view.

was subjected to a bath of gum arabic and nitric acid. This solution attacked and ate away the portions of the stone which had not been drawn upon, leaving the drawing in slight relief. When the stone was washed to stop the action, it was ready for printing. It was put in a press, wetted thoroughly and a special lithographic ink was applied with a roller, the ink adhering to the drawing on the stone but repelled by the untouched portions. A sheet of paper was placed on the stone, pressure applied and the print "pulled," that is, taken off the press, and colored. While we are on the subject, the sizes given in the checklist are subject to slight variations because of the fact that moisture was always present during the printing, and when the paper dried, the contraction was not always the same.

All of the original Currier prints were printed from stones on which the drawing was done entirely by hand. Today most lithographs, etc., are produced by mechanical means. If the reproductions in the book, for instance, are examined with a magnifying glass it will be seen that the image is made up of a geometrical design of dots. Similar dot patterns may be found on most reproductions although this isn't an infallible rule. A collector can soon learn to distinguish between the real thing and a reproduction. Furthermore, any reputable dealer will be glad to teach him.

Around 1915, a print dealer named Max Williams made impressions from the original stones of the Clipper Ship prints (Nos. 1143, 1144, 1145, 1160,

1168, 1169). These may not rightfully be called reproductions; yet since coloring, printing and paper are of inferior quality, their value is a small fraction of that of the originals.

If you object to stains on prints, do not attempt to clean them yourself. The use of strong bleaches takes out the original color and may weaken the basic image, damaging your print irreparably. Leave this work to the expert. Cleaning prints requires a thorough knowledge of the subject.

When our earlier book on Currier & Ives was published in 1930, we stated that we had not actually seen all of the prints listed. Many titles were obtained from auction catalogues, dealers lists and from several original Currier & Ives Order Lists, on which the titles were necessarily shortened. We asked the co-operation of our readers to help us find errors and make corrections. This was given most generously. From these sources we acquired new and unusual material.

In the interim I have had the privilege of checking many of the large Currier & Ives collections, including the extensive one at the Library of Congress in Washington, D. C., where I also examined the copyright records. The assistance of Mr. Hirst Milhollen of the Library was very helpful. I can now say the vast majority of the prints listed in this book has been seen by me, and I can guarantee the accuracy of their listing.

The method of listing these prints in the 1930 edition was easy to understand and practical; therefore I shall retain that method, with one important exception, the elimination of the prices obtained at auction. The auction galleries in New York and elsewhere have had a great many sales since 1930. The Plaza Auction Galleries, for instance, have conducted over fifty sales. There is no point in listing (in many instances) forty or fifty different prices obtained for any particular print. Many collectors have asked me to put a value on the prints in this book. I hesitated to do this because in my opinion no one person can place an accurate and unbiased valuation on all the prints. Therefore, let me state that these are my personal valuations and that I do not expect everyone to agree with me. My quotations apply to prints in good condition with reasonably wide margins. Since many of the popular prints were made over a period of years, there is some variation in the quality of the impression, coloring, etc.

How to use the method of listing:

      a   b   c   d
703. Brook Trout Fishing / "An Anxious Moment" / Painted by A. F. Tait.

     e   f   g
On stone by Ch. Parsons.   18.10x27.2   (Fisherman kneeling against rock

                                   h   i   j
in stream hooking trout.   More trout on bank.)   1862   L   C&I

a. First line of title on print.
b. / symbol indicates end of line.
c. Second line of title.

d. Artist of original painting.
e. Artist who drew the picture on the lithographic stone.
f. Size of picture (exclusive of margins) in inches and sixteenths of an inch.
g. Explanatory data in reference to the print is placed in parentheses.
h. Date of copyright (if any).
i. Size. For convenience four sizes are given:
> V.S.   very small—up to about 7″ x 9″
> S.   small—approximately 8.8″ x 12.8″
> M.   medium—approximately 9″ x 14″ to 14″ x 20″
> L.   large—anything over 14″ x 20″
j. Publisher's name:
> C&I—Currier & Ives
> N.C.—Nathaniel Currier
> C.C.—Charles Currier, brother of N. Currier

A word used very often is *vignette* to signify that the background of the print shades off instead of being confined by a border.

There are approximately 6,900 different titles listed in this book, which exceeds by nearly 1,200 the listings in the 1930 edition. Checking brought to light many duplications and errors in all books. This list is not complete and more titles will be found, but from the number of new subjects which have turned up in the last few years, I doubt if there will be many.

As this book was about to go to press, a story was published in the newspaper about an auction sale held in Ohio, where a man bought a frame for 80¢ to fit a picture he had at home. There was a worthless picture in the frame, but when he removed it he found *The Life of a Hunter—A Tight Fix,* valued at $4,000. I wish every reader the same luck.

> FREDERIC A. CONNINGHAM
> Sea Cliff, N.Y.   September 1949

FOREWORD TO THE 1983 EDITION

In 1970 Colin Simkin presented his foreword on the changes and collecting trends in Currier & Ives prints since the 1949 edition. Most of these trends are still true today.

In 72 years of publishing, Currier & Ives issued about 8,000 different prints of all subjects. No other American firm even approached this output! A few prints, other than those listed in this volume, are being discovered every year.

Certain subjects have appreciated more than others. The gay American Clipper Ships, attractive winter scenes, rare railroad prints, dramatic sporting prints, and the popular "American Homestead" set of four seem to have appreciated the most.

It is interesting to trace the appreciation of Currier & Ives prints over the years. One of my favorite small folio prints is "A Home on the Mississippi." Currier's astute combination of the home, carriages, steamboats and people makes for a very desirable lithograph—then and now.

Currier was selling the print in 1871 for about 15¢. In 1925 Warren A. Weaver's *Lithographs of N. Currier and Currier & Ives,* Holport Publishing Co., N.Y., lists it at $12.50. In October, 1930, it was sold at an important New York City auction of Currier & Ives prints for $21.00. Frederic A. Conningham lists it at $50.00 in his *Currier & Ives Prints/An Illustrated Check List,* Crown Publishers, 1949. The revised price of this print in the 1970 edition of this book was $150.00. At a large print auction I attended in Pennsylvania in 1976 this same print brought $250.00. It is currently selling in fine condition for about $400.00—when you can find it offered for sale.

The charm of Currier & Ives is ever expanding. Many books have been written about them. Their illustrations appear on Christmas decorations and cards, plates, calendars, place mats and the thousands of other reproductions that have been produced. Americans have undoubtedly spent much more on all of these "Currier tangibles" than Currier & Ives received from their total output of prints!

Currier & Ives left us an irreplaceable legacy of pictorial 19th-century America. Many of their works are certainly not masterpieces of art, nor were they intended to be. Currier advertised them as "Colored Engravings For The People." They now form a picture—a most complete image—of the wide variety of American city and country life in the 1800's.

The past decade has seen a growing scarcity of these charming treasures. Prices for the most desired prints have escalated sharply as more and more of them fall into the hands of large collectors, galleries and museums. Few unexplored attics and barns remain. Years may pass between sales of certain prints.

Values of rare and desirable Currier & Ives prints will certainly continue to rise sharply in the next decade. Certain other categories, such as religion and documents, will probably remain fairly stable. This diversified rate of appreciation makes quotation of specific prices today questionable and, in many cases, quickly obsolete.

Who would have predicted that Currier's "American Homestead Winter" (C-172), selling for about $250.00 in 1970, would be selling for about $750.00 in 1983? The other three prints in this most desirable set have done equally well. The "Spring" (C-170) and "Summer" (C-171), listed at $75.00 each in 1970, are each selling for about $250.00 today. The "Autumn" (C-168) is actually the most difficult of the four to find. It listed at $75.00 in 1970 and is currently bringing about $300.00. The various "In Memory Of" documents, on the other hand, are selling for little more than their 1970 listed prices of $10.00 to $25.00.

The future will continue to hold great promise for Currier & Ives lithographs. Collectors will still seek to obtain those prints which are within their means and appeal to them for decorative display in their home or office.

Collecting trends will probably not change. The quest for attractive scenes, railroad, firemen, nautical and sporting prints will continue to lead the way.

Whatever prints you collect in the world of Currier & Ives, your choice can be a joy, a diversion from the rigors of everyday life, and a source of investment and appreciation—as they have been to collectors for well over fifty years.

ROBERT L. SEARJEANT
Rochester, N.Y. February 1983

SUGGESTIONS FOR COLLECTORS
from COLIN SIMKIN

It would be impossible today, even with unlimited time and money, to build a collection of every N. Currier and Currier & Ives print. If it were possible, it probably would not be desirable. The serious collector finds it an interesting challenge to concentrate on one category. He has a wide variety from which to choose. If he likes farm, village, and countryside scenes, there are about 350; game animals and game birds, about 100; hunting, 100; fishing, 30. If he is interested in the history of wars, there are Revolutionary War subjects, 60; Mexican War, 50; Civil War, 100. Marine titles offer this variety: steamships, 200; sailing ships, 70; yachts, 70; U.S. Navy, 70; whaling, 15. For decorative subjects there are about 100 each of fruits and flowers. One of the major categories is horse racing, of which there are approximately 550 prints.

There are some 400 views, representing 25 states, Washington, D.C., Mexico, Cuba, and Canada. More than one half of these are of New York City and New York State. There is a strong interest in Western subjects, with some 80 excellent subjects available. Railroad items are limited to about 30, with most of them quite scarce and valuable. Early political campaigns offer a great variety of prints at moderate prices and are not as difficult to collect as some other categories: cartoons lampooning the issues of the day, 150; elaborate campaign portraits of candidates, 30. There are some 600 portraits, including the Presidential series but not the personalized girls' heads. It comes as a surprise to many persons that there was such a well-developed sense of humor a century ago, as revealed by the more than 500 comic prints.

Other specialties may be of interest: music sheets, 60; temperance, 30; Barnum's freaks, 25; religious subjects, 350; pets, such as kittens, dogs, chicks, 200; display cards, chiefly for merchants, such as *Fork Over What You Owe, Poor Trust is Dead, Delicious Ice Cream,* 25; name prints—glamorized pictures of girls with such quaint names as Abigail, Amelia, Fanny, Matilda, Minnie—250. The largest category is the sentimentals. Typical titles: *First at the Rendezvous, The Lovers' Adieu, Popping the Question,* and so on, for about 700 titles.

One category that seems to have been overlooked by collectors is that of trade cards. These are seldom, if ever, offered by major print dealers. In size they are about the same as today's postcards. The artwork is not of the quality of that in the folio prints, but they do provide an interesting example of a merchandising device widely used in the early 1880's. Of the slightly more than 100 that have been discovered to date, about 50 are comic, 40 are serious horseracing subjects, 20 relate to smoking, a few are views of steamships, railroads, the Statue of Liberty, the Brooklyn Bridge. In most cases the illustration is a reduction in size of a scene that had previously been printed in small folio (10" x 14") or very small folio (approximately 7" x 10"). The most noticeable difference is that an area in the sky or in the foreground has intentionally been left without drawing so that the merchant might imprint his name and business thereon. They are found with and without imprints. These cards were presented to customers and, hopefully, to prospective customers. The words "trade card" may be subject to two interpretations: to advertise the merchant's trade, or to be swapped or traded with other collectors. Today they are most likely to be found in those scrapbooks into which young people so diligently pasted Sunday school attendance stamps, labels, and every other colorful card that attracted their attention. They all bear the Currier & Ives imprint below the lower right corner of the illustration. Most of them are dated 1880, but there are a few before and a few after that date, and some are undated. Prices in 1983 range from about $45.00 to $75.00 each.

CURRIER & IVES: QUALITY GUIDELINES FOR COLLECTORS
by ROBERT L. SEARJEANT

What is an acceptable old print?

Much has been written about Mr. Currier, Mr. Ives, their business, the artists, their success, their decline. Seldom has anyone written more than a page on what constitutes an acceptable Currier print today. This is a very arbitrary subject and probably the reason so little has been written about it.

Many collectors and dealers will not agree with the guidelines that I set for myself some years ago. There are an infinite number of individual standards and levels of individual quality acceptance. Each collector has to decide on these levels for himself.

If you are a relatively new collector—or even an old-timer—and you wish to build your collection into 100 or more prints in only "mint" or "pristine" condition, my advice is—forget it! You will have much more success collecting some sort of 20th-century limited edition prints.

The average Currier is now about 125 years old. For a piece of paper to survive that long, in sizable quantities, is in itself quite a feat. It speaks well for Currier's paper—not so well for those who have handled it during the past century.

I would estimate that 95 percent of all Curriers in existence today have had their borders shaved or trimmed to some extent. Their value today depends a great deal on the amount of surgery performed.

It is a rare print that can boast that it has no stains, tears, time tone, foxing, trimming, or any one of many other defects. Yet thousands have survived despite human apathy and ignorance. How many other mass-produced tangible objects have withstood the same test of time as well?

Small folio prints were produced on sheets of paper up to about 13¼" x 17½". They were not a standard frame size.

When they were new, no one thought about matting them or making their frames fit their "cheap" prints. Thousands were simply trimmed by their new owners to fit their more expensive frames.

There are so many Curriers that measure about 10" x 14" that many persons think they have full margins!

Thousands of others were tacked, glued, or nailed to posts and walls.

Not long ago I was shown a horse stall in northern New York. It was lined "solid" on three sides with Currier's original horse prints—all glued down. Anyone can imagine their condition in this place. I estimated the value of that stall in the thousands if the prints had been at all decent. My feelings were intense.

The following are my print quality guidelines. They have not been impossible for me to attain. They are not lenient or rigid.

Width of Margins

1. Any small folio should have about ¾″ or more. Accept narrower margins if the print is rare or very desirable.

2. A medium folio print should have 1″ or wider margins except as noted above.

3. Large folio prints should have 1½″ or wider margins except as noted above.

Original Currier & Ives prints should not be "wet" or "dry mounted" in any way. An exception may be made for badly torn prints that are extremely rare. Other proper framing and storage procedures should be followed.

Stains

Years ago I frowned upon water or other stains as something horrid, and I avoided them at all costs. I soon found, however, that if I were to accumulate a quantity of prints for my collection and do it by the desired means, I had to be willing to accept a stained print. I had to learn to live with it or find a way to remove the stain.

Rounding up perfect, rare, or even the more desirable prints at auctions, antique shops, antique shows, and from my travels in the countryside (the various means I selected to acquire prints) has become virtually impossible. A good deal of luck is required. Almost without exception, any print acquired this way in recent years requires some help one way or another.

The virgin supply has all but disappeared.

The vast majority of mint, or pristine, prints has been carefully scavenged and plucked over the years from our cities, towns, countryside and dealers' inventories.

Most of them are resting quietly on the walls of our museums, galleries, and in large private collections.

Years may pass between sales of a rare print in such condition.

The last mint print I can recall finding in all of my travels was in 1977. It was at a small country auction. The print was "Little Brothers." Unframed, it must have rested for 100 years in between the pile of papers where I found it.

I do not advocate the purchase of any old stained print. Some discretion must be used.

It is surprising, however, just how much staining can be satisfactorily removed from a "dirty old print." After a well-done professional job, there isn't a trained eye that could tell exactly what was done.

Many "purists" will argue this point. Many would advocate doing nothing.

I have seen several fine collections where individuals and institutions do nothing—for years. Their prints just slowly deteriorate. Eventually deterioration will reach a point where restoration is no longer possible. These prints will go the way of those "saved" by Charles Currier in his damp basement.

A sorry loss. Negligence.

Those prints remaining have appreciated just a little bit more.

Tears

Any tear into the plate itself is a serious defect. Unless the print is quite rare, or one that cannot be "lived without," it should be avoided.

Margin tears are acceptable.

Three or four minor repaired margin nicks should not be allowed to quench the sale of any desirable print.

Any print, however, having more than one or two tears that come close to the image should be avoided, no matter how good any repair may be. Allowances may be made for extremely scarce prints, and they should be priced accordingly.

It never ceases to amaze me while attending good-quality antique shows that some dealers attempt to extract good dollars for virtually worthless prints. Many of them are torn, trimmed or stained beyond recognition and with outrageous prices.

I wonder, will these same mutilated prints fit general collecting guidelines for an acceptable print in the year 2000?

P. T. Barnum was certainly correct. There is, for old prints, one born every minute!

Other Defects

Moderate defects include foxing, acid mat burn, excessive time tone, and brown lines caused by wooden backing boards in old frames.

Unless these defects are extreme they should not deter one from a purchase.

More serious defects include knothole stains, worm holes, and silverfish damage. If this damage is extensive and in the plate itself, the print should be avoided.

Original or Reproduction

The question frequently asked is how do you determine an original Currier & Ives print from a reprint? There is no easy answer to this question.

There are a number of excellent reproductions on the market today, many made by the photoengraving process. These are relatively easy to pick out. They will all have the common geometric "dot pattern" throughout the entire print. Many times this can be seen clearly with a seven- or eight-power glass. Original Curriers made from their original stone plates do not have this fine dot pattern.

Size can also be a determining factor. This volume gives the sizes to $\frac{1}{16}''$ of many Currier prints. If a print varies more than about $\frac{1}{4}''$ from those sizes indicated, it should be suspect.

Upgrading

This process has been, for me, a primary method of building my collection.

No serious collector should set his original print acquisition sights above reasonable expectations.

I have known several collectors to pass up an opportunity to obtain a relatively fine print, one they were seeking and really wanted, because it was not mint or did not meet their private fastidious standards. Very seldom do they ever get another similar chance.

Some I have known pass on, still waiting, still looking.

A young collector may have more time to seek out a desired print in near mint condition. Many never have enough time.

Some may surmise from this that all of the prints in my collection are not perfect.

They are not.

Often I will locate a desirable old print in better condition than the one I have, at a price I am willing to pay. In most cases, the first print can be disposed of—and even at a small profit.

I have not suggested the purchase of just any old print. There must be certain limits.

Only the individual collector can establish his own level of quality.

It is surprising how quickly these levels can be determined at the moment of potential acquisition—to pass or not, to bid or not—the moment of decision!

CURRIER & IVES: AN ESSAY IN COLOR
by ROBERT L. SEARJEANT

Color was a prime ingredient contributing to the success of Currier & Ives prints and largely accounts for their continuing popularity today. No other American firm produced as many different-colored lithographs, the vast majority having been colored by hand. What emphasis Mr. Currier and Mr. Ives placed on this word in the infancy of its use! Their prints were advertised as "Fine Colored Prints," "Colored Engravings For The People," "Elegant Colored Pictures," "Hand Colored Prints," and so forth. Always the emphasis was on "colored." Imagine how these prints were greeted in a world so lacking in material color! No color TV, no color magazines or papers, no color movies, no color photos, little color packaging, little color period!

In 1952 Mr. Colin Simkin summed up this period as follows: "In any analysis of the popularity of Currier & Ives prints when they were published, color stands out as an important factor. There was very little color in the furnishings of the average home. One has only to look at a collection of New England colonial furniture and kitchen equipment to see how lacking in color it was. . . . In the rural areas, serviceable clothing materials were often of somber homespun. Any spot of color was the more conspicuous because of the background against which it showed. Bright materials were sought for a patchwork quilt; a paisley shawl was a treasured possession. . . . Into this color-void came the Currier & Ives prints with their bright splotches of color. Very few of them were without that cheerful color, red. The city-dwellers had more color in their costumes and their carriages but they, too, welcomed the colorful prints to brighten up their homes."

Another prominent collector, Roy King, later observed, "So long as the hand-colored lithograph remained the most effective—and cheapest—means of depicting glimpses of American life, the firm remained supreme." Modern machinery—and color printing—ended their reign.

THE BEST FIFTY

The word "best" seems to have a peculiar fascination for most people in this country. It is widely used by corporations in describing products or services. The word, however significant, is much more difficult to apply in the field of collecting rare or valuable items. Every collector aspires to possess the best, but finds that there are few criteria, other than price, to help substantiate such a judgment.

To a great extent this problem was solved for collectors of Currier & Ives prints when, in 1932, the late Harry Shaw Newman, proprietor of The Old Print Shop, suggested that a jury of fellow enthusiasts be polled as to their choice of the best fifty large folios published by the famous lithographers. The project was endorsed wholeheartedly by Charles Messer Stow, then antiques editor of The New York *Sun,* and by Harry T. Peters, outstanding collector and author. The jury was made up of twelve discriminating collectors whose studies and wide experience made them eminently qualified for the task.

Since each juror's list represented a personal choice, it was not expected that there would be absolute agreement on the titles. By computing the frequency of the appearance on the lists of a given title, it was possible to compile a selection that is just as authoritative today as it was in 1932. Starting in January 1933, The New York *Sun* reproduced the fifty prints, one each night for fifty issues. Although printings of these editions were substantially increased, all the papers were sold out. It should be noted that, nearly a century earlier, it was this same newspaper which helped establish Nathaniel Currier's reputation as a lithographer. Early in 1840 the *Sun* published an extra devoted to the burning of the steamship *Lexington.* The half-page illustration was by Currier.

Mr. Peters, from his extensive collection, loaned the fifty prints for exhibition at The Old Print Shop. To meet the demand for a list, Mr. Newman published an illustrated booklet in a limited edition. Today, dealers and collectors, in referring to a particular print, often identify it as one of The Best Fifty.

The publication of the list of The Best Fifty large folios created a tremendous interest in Currier & Ives lithographs. One year later, the same procedure was followed in determining The Best Fifty small folios. Again, the list was made available by The Old Print Shop. It was enthusiastically welcomed by collectors, particularly those who had recently become aware of the artistic and historical merit of the prints. Among the small prints there was a great variety of subjects, they were more plentiful, and they could be acquired at much lower cost.

Neither of these lists should be construed as being the only good prints or the only subjects worth collecting. There are hundreds of subjects that would have received mention if the lists had been longer. The choice of category is optional with the collector. Suggestions may be found on other pages in this volume.

COLIN SIMKIN
1970

THE BEST FIFTY
(Large Folio)

THE BEST FIFTY
(Small Folio)

CHRONOLOGY OF THE FIRM

Since a great many original N. Currier and Currier & Ives prints do not carry a publication date but do have an address at the bottom, the following list of addresses will assist the collector in dating undated prints.

Stodart & Currier:	1834–35	137 Broadway
N. Currier	1835–36	1 Wall St.
N. Currier	1836–37	148 Nassau St.
N. Currier	1838–56	{ 152 Nassau St. Cor. Spruce
		2 Spruce St.
Currier & Ives	1857–72	152 Nassau St.
Currier & Ives	1872–74	125 Nassau St.
Currier & Ives	1874–77	123 Nassau St.
Currier & Ives	1877–94	115 Nassau St.
Currier & Ives	1894–96	108 Fulton St.
Currier & Ives	1896–1907	33 Spruce St.

LIST OF ILLUSTRATIONS

[1]

LIST OF ILLUSTRATIONS (CONTINUED)

AARON CLARK

1 Aaron Clark / Published by Riley & Heidemans, 129 William St., N. Y. Lithographed by N. Currier. Henri Heidemans, 1838, on stone (Facsimile signature above title — tinted background. Mayor of New York. Upright vignette portrait, seated.)
und S N.C.

2 Abbey, The / 5.8x7.8 (Printed on the same sheet with "The Waterfall" No. 6571) und VS C&I

3 Abbey of Clare Galway, The / (Ireland) und S C&I

4 Abbey of the Holy Cross, The / Tipperary, Ireland / und S C&I

Abdallah Chief (Horse) See: No. 939.

5 Abbottsford (sic) / The Seat of Sir Walter Scott / (Four people in rowboat in foreground.) und M C&I

6 Abigail / (¾ length, white dress, window at left.) und S C.C.

7 Abigail / (¾ length, light dress, black lace gloves, left arm resting on table.)
und S N.C.

8 Abigail / (Bust portrait, vignette.)
und S C&I

9 Abigail / #270 (Half length, slightly to left, rose in hair, green curtain on left, rounded corners.) 1846 S N. C.

10 Aboriginal / Portfolio /, The / Published by J. O. Lewis 1853. On stone by J. Cameron. (Title page—portrait of an Indian.) und S C.C.

11 Abraham Lincoln / (Bearded portrait slightly to left, half length, vignette.)
1862 L C&I

12 Abraham Lincoln / Assassinated April 14th, 1865 / (Bearded bust portrait, slightly to right. Same stone as "Lincoln" No. 3543. Mourning border and second line of title added.)
und M C&I

13 Abraham Lincoln / Sixteenth President of the United States / 11.8x8.12 (Beardless, half length, seated, slightly to left.) 1860 S C&I

14 Abraham Lincoln / Sixteenth President of the United States / (Vignette, ¾ length standing, left hand on book, bearded, slightly to right.)
und S C&I

15 Abraham Lincoln / Sixteenth President of the United States / (Bearded bust, portrait to right.) und S C&I

16 Abraham Lincoln / Sixteenth President of the United States / #207 (Bust portrait, slightly to right, bearded, facsimile signature, vignette.)
und S C&I

17 Abraham Lincoln / Sixteenth President of the United States / 11.10x8.4 (Half length, slightly to left.)
und S C&I

18 Abraham Lincoln / Sixteenth President of the United States / Facsimile signature. (¾ length to right, oval.)
und S C&I

19 Abraham Lincoln / Sixteenth President of the United States / 12.8x7.8.
und S C&I

20 Abraham Lincoln / Sixteenth President of the United States / #720 / 11.6x8.8 (Bearded, seated, book in left hand. Red curtain.) 1861 S C&I

21 Abraham Lincoln / Sixteenth President of the United States / Assassinated April 14th, 1865 / 11.7x8.9 (Bearded, half length, seated.)
1861 S C&I

22 Abraham Lincoln / Sixteenth Presi-

dent of the United States / Assassinated April 14th, 1865 / 11.8x8.12 (Same stone as No. 13, beard and 3rd line added.) und S C&I

23 Abraham Lincoln / The Martyr President / Assassinated April 14th, 1865 / (Same stone as "Hon. Abraham Lincoln, etc." No. 2890 Black line added and title changed.) 1860 L C&I

24 Abraham Lincoln / The Martyr President / Assassinated April 14th, 1865 / Vignette, bearded, bust slightly to left. Joseph Koehler, Publisher, New York.) 1865 L C&I
(Joseph Koehler bought a number of the lithographic stones, prints, etc. from Currier & Ives when they went out of business and republished them with his name added.)

25 Abraham Lincoln / The Martyr President / Assassinated April 14th, 1865 / 17.6x10 (¾ length, vignette, in oval.) 1865 M C&I

26 Abraham Lincoln / The Nation's Martyr / Assassinated April 14th, 1865 / (Bust, slightly to right, beard, upright.) und S C&I

27 Abraham Lincoln / The Nation's Martyr / Assassinated April 14th, 1865 / Published by Golden & Sammons, #1 Clark St., Chicago. (Same as preceding.) und S C&I

28 Abraham Lincoln / The Nation's Martyr / Assassinated April 14th, 1865 / (Vignette, bust to right, bearded.) und L C&I

29 Abraham's Dream! / "Coming events cast their shadows before" / (Lincoln dreaming he is being driven from White House by "Columbia" while George B. McClellan enters. Vignette.) 1864 S C&I

30 Academy Waltz / Composed & Respectfully Dedicated to / Alonzo Crittenton, Esqur / By / John C. Andrews / Albany. Published by R. S. Measham / (View of Academy.) und S N.C.

31 Accepted, The / 11.12x8.9 (Upright.) und S C&I

32 Accommodation Train, The / Thos. Worth on stone. (Train waiting for large lady loaded down with bird cage, bags, kittens, etc. Vignette.) 1876 S C&I

33 Across the Continent / "Westward the Course of Empire takes its way" /

17.14x27.6 J. M. Ives, Del. Drawn by F. F. Palmer. 1868 L C&I

34 Actress, The / #486 (Full length.) und S N.C.

35 Ada / #426. und S N.C.

36 Adam and Eve Driven out of Paradise / #302 / 11.5x8.9 (Full length figures, snake at left.) und S N.C.

37 Adam and Eve Driven out of Paradise / #302 / 12.8x8.2 (Different composition from preceding.) und S N.C.

38 Adam and Eve in the Garden of Eden / #301. 1848 S N.C.

39 Adam naming the Creatures / Adam Llamo Los Animales / #545 (Adam on right, animals in foreground.) 1847 S N.C.
Adams, Charles F. See: No. 2478.
Adams, John See: Nos. 1530, 3251.
Adams, John Q. See: Nos. 1490, 2176-8, 3276-8.

40 Adams Express Co., The / (at top) This Company has facilities unsurpassed by those of any other express line in the world, for the safe expeditious forwarding & Prompt delivery of / Bank Notes, Gold & silver coin, etc. / 2 additional lines. C. Parsons, Del. 16.4x25.12 (Same stone as American "Express" Train, No. 129. Title changed and first car lettered "Adams Express Cos. Car.") 1855 L C&I
Addie V (Yacht) See: No. 4450.

41 Adelaide / #421 (¾ length, oval with ornamental borders, upright. Sometimes spelled Adalaide.) 1846 S N.C.

42 Adelaide / #421 (Oval in rectangular, floral border, roses in hair. Different composition from preceding.) 1847 S N.C.
Adelaide (Clipper Ship) See: Nos. 1139, 2962.

43 Adeline / 11.14x8.8 (¾ length, red dress, resting arm on chair, green curtain.) und S N.C.

44 Adeline / (Vignette, upright, slightly to right, holding fan.) und S N.C.

45 Adeline / #86 / 11.15x8.6 (Full length, standing in doorway, purple skirt, roses in hair and on dress.) 1848 S N.C.

46 Adeline / (Left arm resting on fur piece, ¾ length.) und S N.C.

47 Adeline / #131 / 11.13x8.10 (Half length, elbows on table.)
1849 S N.C.

48 Adeline / #131 / 11.13x8.7 (Full length seated, right hand on piano.)
und S N.C.

49 Adieu at Fontain-bleau / In Judustrie-Comptoir in Hersfeld / H. Vernet, Pinx. (Napoleon.) und L N.C.

Adirondacks See: Nos 173-4, 209-13, 323, 773-4, 1539, 2424, 2865, 2982, 2993-4, 3003, 3070, 3086, 3091, 4787-8, 5049, 5395-8, 5627.

50 Admiral Farragut's Fleet engaging the Rebel Batteries at Port Hudson, March 14th 1863 / Hartford, Richmond, Albatross, Monongahela, Kined, Mississippi, [aground and on fire] 18.2x12.10 (Three additional lines.)
und S C&I

51 Admiral Porter's Fleet Running the Rebel Blockade of the Mississippi at Vicksburg, April 16th, 1863 / Three additional lines. 8.2x12.9 (11 vessels keyed.) 1863 S C&I

Adriatic (Steamship) See: Nos. 5740-1, 6312.

52 Aesthetic Craze, The / "What's de Matter wid de Nigga? Why Oscar, you's gone wild" / (Colored Comic, Vignette.) 1882 S C&I

53 Affair of Honor, An — The Critical Moment / "Now den Brace em up, one! Two!" / King & Murphy, Dels. on stone. (Vignette.)
1884 S C&I

54 Affair of Honor, An—A Stray Shot / "Whar yer gwine, nigga yer done shot old sawbones" / King & Murphy, Dels. on stone. (Vignette.)
1884 S C&I

55 Africa / (Half-length vignette of dusky belle, not upright.)
1870 S C&I

56 Africa / Lith. and Pub. by N. Currier, 2 Spruce St. and 169 Broadway. (Upright vignette.) und S N.C.

Africa See: Nos. 600, 648.

57 African Jungle, The / (Puzzle print.)
und S C&I

58 After Marriage / Experience / Linder, pinxt. (Companion to "Before Marriage" No. 475 Blasé couple.)
und L N.C.

59 After the Bath / und S N.C.

60 Age of Brass, The / or the triumphs of Women's rights / Poster reading

"Vote for / Celebrated / Man / Tamer / Susan Sharp Tongue" / (Group of women in men's clothes, one smoking cigar, in polling place. Lone man carrying baby and being scolded. Vignette.)
1869 S C&I

61 Age of Iron, The / Man as he expects to be / (Horse and carriage with mannish female coachman and footman. Another mannish and extravagantly dressed woman about to enter carriage. At center, man sewing and rocking cradle; another washing clothes. Vignette.) 1869 S C&I

62 Agnes / #209 (¾ length, seated, head against green upholstery, hair dressed plain.) und S N.C.

63 Agnes / (¾ length, standing, left arm on coping, hand to cheek, hair in curls.)
und S N.C.

64 Agnes / On stone by H. Grevedon, Paris, 1840. Lith. by L. Litrenne, 17 Rue de Bac. Pub. by N. Currier. (Half-length vignette.) 1846 S N.C.

65 A. Goldsmith's B. G. Driver, by volunteer / Record 2:20 (Vignette, Broad side to right.) 1879 S C&I

66 Agricultural Hall / Grand United States Centennial Exhibition, 1876 / Fairmount Park, Philadelphia / one additional line dimensions / 7.13x12.15.
und S C&I

67 Agricultural Society, The / Awarded this Diploma / To .... 18.... / 14.15x 19.10 (Seven views around center.)
1877 M C&I

68 Ahead of the World / The Great American Four Track Railroad / Lightning Passenger and Freight Trains; Always on time / (The rarest railroad print.) 1875 L C&I

69 Ain't I Some / After Vernet / R. A. Clark on stone. #223 (Comic horse and rider, vignette.) und S N.C.

70 Ain't They Cunning? / 8.10x12.6 (Child with two pups.)
und S C&I

Alabama (State) See: No. 71.

71 Alabama State March, The / W. K. Hewitt on stone. (View of the State House.) und S N.C.

72 Alarm, The / F. Jones & A. F. Tait, 1861, on stone. Chromo in oil colors from the original painting by A. F. Tait 10x14. 1868 S C&I

Alaska See: Steamship No. 5742.

Albany. See: Steamship No. 5660.

Albany. (Sloop) See: No. 6336.
Albino family. See: Nos. 6762-4.
Alcryon (Horse). See: No. 6201.
Aldine (Horse). See: Nos. 732, 757, 925, 4256.

73 Alexander / 8.1 x 11.2 (Spirited white horse, rearing and being held by Arab.) und S C&I

Alexander (Horse). See: No. 926.

74 Alice / #252 (Full length, seated, back to spinet.) 1844 S N.C.

75 Alice / 11x7.14 (¾ length, standing by piano, slightly to right.) und S N.C.

76 Alice / (Vignette.) und S C&I

Alice Grey (Horse). See: Nos. 5811, 6170.

Alix (Horse). See: Nos. 979-80, 6196-7.

77 All Broke Up / "He'd a won de money, if it hadn't been for de odder dog" / King & Murphy, Dels. on stone. (Negro, very badly beaten up, wheeling a nearly dead white dog in a wheelbarrow, other negroes following. Upright vignette. Companion to "A Sure Thing" No. 5899.) 1884 S C&I

78 "All Hail the power of Christ's name" / und S C&I

79 All nice and hot / #58 12.2x8.13 (Upright, man cooking Frankfurters. Companion to "Hurry up the Cakes" No. 3006.) und S N.C.

80 All Primed / und S C&I

81 All Right! / 12.5x8.14 (Dog smoking pipe. Companion to "All Wrong" No. 84. Upright.) und S N.C.

82 All so Tired / und S C&I

83 All the World is Scheming / or / Oh, Times are really very hard / A comic song / Written by / J. E. Carpenter / sung by / Mr. Fitzwilliam / Published by James L. Hewitt & Co. / N. Currier's Lith. W. K. Hewitt on stone. (Full length figure, vignette.) und S N.C.

84 All Wrong / 12.5x8.14 (Upright. Companion to "All Right" No. 81.) und S N.C.

Allen, Richard Rev. See: No. 5135.
Allen, William H. See: No. 4398.
Aller (Steamship) See: Nos. 3035, 5743.
Allerton (Horse) See: No. 2524.
Alley (Horse) See: No. 440.

85 Almira / #338 (Seated full length, writing letter. Scratches on background.) 1845 S N.C.

86 Almira / (Same composition as preceding, with slight changes. Evidently made to replace defective stone of preceding.) und S N.C.

87 Alnwick Castle, Scotland / und M C&I

88 Alonzo and Cora / Destruction of the Temple of the Sun — Conquest of Mexico / und S N.C.

Alpha (Yacht) See: No. 5105.

Alps. See: Nos. 4367-8, 6082, 3784.

89 Amanda / #396 (Half length, letter in hand, dog looking up at girl.) und S N.C.

90 Amanda / 11.12x8.11 (¾ length, oval in rectangle, ornamental, not floral border.) 1846 S N.C.

91 Amanda / #396 (¾ length seated, Mantilla around head, roses in hair— upright vignette.) und S N.C.

92 Amateur Muscle in the shell / 11.2x 15.11 Thos. Worth on stone. 1876 M C&I

93 Amateur Muscle in the shell / 1879 S C&I

94 Amateur muscle in the shell / (Postcard size.) 1880 VS C&I

Amazon (Bark) See: No. 3994.

95 Ambuscade, The / 11.6x15.7 (Winter scene copied from an English print. und M C&I

96 Amelia / (Full length upright, seated, at closed spinet.) 1845 S N.C.

97 Amelia / (¾ length seated, marine scene through window, upright.) und S N.C.

98 Amelia / 12.3x8.10 (Full length seated, facing left, white dress, ermine trimmed coat.) 1845 S N.C.

99 Amelia / 12.2x8.10 (Full length red dress, seated to left. Table with vase of flowers at left. Picture of Washington's Reception on wall.) 1845 S N.C.

100 Amelia / (Half length, large Sleeves on dress. Exterior scene. Vignette upright.) und S N.C.

101 Amelia / #44 (Bust portrait, upright vignette.) und S C&I

102 America / (Half length, scenery in background. Upright.) und S N.C.

103 America / (Half length, not upright, girl's head Indian dress.)
1870 S C&I

104 America / Lith. and Pub. by N. Currier 2 Spruce St. & 169 Broadway. (¾ length vignette, upright. Bow (archery) in hand.)   und S N.C.
America (Yacht) **See:** Nos. 944, 1173-6, 2625.
America (Steamship) **See:** Nos. 5662, 5744.

105 American Autumn Fruits / (Vignette.)   1875 S C&I

106 American Autumn Fruits / F. F. Palmer, Del. 20x27.14 (Tinted background, highly colored group of fruits about white vase in center.)
1865 L C&I

107 American Beauty, The / (Half length vignette, girl's head.)   und S C&I

108 American Brook Trout / 8.7x12.7 (Still life, stream in background at right.)   1872 S C&I

109 American Buffaloes /
und S C&I

110 American Champion, The / Yacht "Puritan" / Modelled by Edward Burgess, of Boston, Mass. / Winner of the two races for the "America's Cup" against the English Cutter "Genesta" at New York, Sept. 14th and 16th, 1885 / Two columns, 4 lines of dimensions. 9.12x14.1   1885 S C&I

111 American Choice Fruits / 17x24. (Large bowl with various kinds of fruit, bird's nest, pitcher and wine glass.)   1869 L C&I

112 American Choice Fruits /
und L C&I

113 American Clipper Ship, An / Off Sandy Hook Light in a Snow Storm / #357 / 8.4x12.12 (Very rare.)
und S C&I

114 American Clipper Ship "Brewer" 4th Ship, The / of the American Packet Line for Australia. J. C. Erler, Agent / (First line of title in Plate. Ship sailing to right.) (Only one copy known.)   und S N.C.

115 American Clipper Ship Witch of the Wave, The / #476 / 8.14x12.14 (Title in Plate, Broadside to right.)
und S N.C.

116 American Club Hunt / Halt on the Scent / (Colored Comic.)
1884 S C&I

117 American Club Hunt / Taking a Header / (Colored Comic.)
1884 S C&I

118 American Coast Scene / Desert Rock Light House, Maine / und S C&I

119 American Coast Scene / Desert Rock Light House, Maine / 14.13x20.5.
und L C&I

120 American Cottage No. 1 / N. Currier's Lith. N. Y. 8.2x5.5 (With plan of floor under view. From "Rural Residences" by A. J. Davis, Architect, 1837.)   und VS N.C.

121 American Country Life / May Morning / F. F. Palmer, Del. 16.14x23.15.
1855 L N.C.

122 American Country Life / October Afternoon / F. F. Palmer, Del. 16.11x 23.14.   1855 L N.C.

123 American Country Life / Pleasures of Winter / F. F. Palmer, Del. 16.14x 24.   1855 L N.C.

124 American Country Life / Summer's Evening / F. F. Palmer, Del. 16.11x 23.14.   1855 L N.C.

125 American Dead Game / F. F. Palmer, Del. 19.11x27.11 (Same stone as "American Game" No. 163.)
1866 L C&I

126 American Eclipse / 1879 S C&I

127 American Eclipse / The Celebrated Race Horse and Sire of Racers / 4 additional lines. J. Cameron on stone. (Vignette, standing, profile to left.)
1880 S C&I

128 American Express Train /
1853 S N.C.

129 American "Express" Train / C. Parsons, Del. 16.4x25.12 (This plate was used as an "Ad" later for the Adams Express Co. Title changed completely and some changes in composition. **See:** No. 40.) (Train to left, four cars. Depot at right. Extremely rare and desirable.)
1855 L N.C.

130 American Express Train / F. F. Palmer, Del. 18x31 (Entirely different composition from preceding. Engine, tender, baggage car, and seven coaches to right, Hudson River Steamer in right background.) (Another pleasing and colorful print.) 1864 L C&I

131 American Farm Life / From a painting by A. O. Willes. 1868 M C&I

132 American Farm Scene, An / In the Olden Time /   und S C&I

AMERICAN FARM SCENES.

133 American Farm Scenes / No. 3 (Autumn) F. F. Palmer, Del. 16.15x24.1. (Farm yard scene, horses, cows, pigs, and chickens.)   1853 L N.C.

134 American Farm Scenes / No. 1 (Spring) F. F. Palmer, Del. 16.15x24.2 (Farmer behind plow drawn by two oxen.)   1853 L N.C.

135 American Farm Scenes / No. 2 (Summer) F. F. Palmer, Del. 16.15x 24.1 (Woman feeding chickens. turkeys, etc.)   1853 L N.C.

136 American Farm Scenes / No. 4 (Winter) F. F. Palmer, Del. 16.13x23.15. (Sleigh in foreground, loaded with milk cans, skating on pond in background.) 1853 L N.C.

137 American Farm, Winter / 2.11x4.3 (House on left, couple on path, barn and cows on right) (One of views on sheet of Landscape Cards, No. 3438.) und VS C&I

138 American Farm Yard—Evening / F. F. Palmer, Del. 16.13x23.14
1857 L C&I

139 American Farm Yard—Morning / F. F. Palmer, Del. 16.13x23.15
1857 L C&I

140 American Feathered Game / Mallard and Canvas Back Ducks / A. F. Tait on stone. (Upright vignette, still life. First state.)   und M N.C.

141 American Feathered Game / Mallard and Canvas Back Ducks / A. F. Tait, N. Y. on stone. O. Knirsch on stone. 16.4x13.8 (Second state. Oval background. Shading has been added to preceding. Although these are second states they are more attractive.)
1854 M N.C.

142 American Feathered Game / Partridges / A. F. Tait, N. Y., on stone. First state. Upright vignette, still life.) und M N.C.

143 American Feathered Game / Partridges / A. F. Tait, N. Y. on stone. 16.5x13.8 (Second state. Oval background. Shading has been added to preceding.)   1854 M N.C.

144 American Feathered Game / Wood Duck and Golden Eye / A. F. Tait, N. Y., on stone. (Upright vignette, still life, first state.)   und M N.C.

145 American Feathered Game / Wood Duck and Golden Eye / A. F. Tait,

[8]

N. Y., on stone. 16.4x13.7 (Upright. Oval background and shading added to preceding print. Second state.)
1854 M N.C.

146 American Feathered Game / Woodcock and Snipe / A. F. Tait, on stone. (First state, upright vignette, still life.)   und M N.C.

147 American Feathered Game / Woodcock and Snipe / A. F. Tait on stone. 16.7x13.8 (Second state. Oval background and shading added to preceding print.)   1854 M N.C.

148 American Field Sports / "A Chance for Both Barrels" / Painted by A. F. Tait. On stone by Ch. Parsons. 18.10x 26.12. (Second state of this is "A Chance for Both Barrels" No. 994.)
1857 L C&I

149 American Field Sports / "Flush'd" / Painted by A. F. Tait. On stone by Ch. Parsons 18.9x26.14.
1857 L C&I

150 American Field Sports / "On a Point" / Painted by A. F. Tait. On stone by Ch. Parsons. 18.12x26.12.
1857 L C&I

151 American Field Sports / "Retrieving" / Painted by A. F. Tait. On stone by Ch. Parsons. 18.9x26.12.
1857 L C&I

152 American Fireman, The / Always Ready / L. Maurer on stone. 17.4x13.4. (Upright.)   1858 M C&I

153 American Fireman, The / Facing the Enemy / L. Maurer on stone. 17.2x 13.7. (Upright.)   1858 M C&I

154 American Fireman, The / Prompt to the Rescue / L. Maurer on stone. 17.5x13.12. (Upright.)
1858 M C&I

155 American Fireman, The / Rushing to the Conflict / L. Maurer on stone. 17.7x13.6. (Upright.)
1858 M C&I

156 American Forest Game / F. F. Palmer, Del. 19.11x27.14 (Companion to "American Game" No. 163. Buck, turkey, grouse, etc.)   1866 L C&I

157 American Forest Scene / Maple Sugaring / A. F. Tait, Del. 18.11x27 (The only other print pertaining to maple sugaring is No. 3975.)
1856 L N.C.

158 American Frontier Life / "The Hunter's Strategem" / Painted by A. F. Tait and signed on stone. 19x27.6.
1862 L C&I

159 American Frontier Life / On the War Path / Painted by A. F. Tait. 18.9x27.6.   1863 L C&I

160 American Fruit Piece / 8.7x12.7 (Still life group. Various fruits including watermelon.)
und S C&I

161 American Fruit Piece / 20.5x27.5. (Tinted background, watermelon, peaches, apples, pineapple, cherries, grapes, etc.)   1859 L C&I

162 American Fruits / (Apples, pears, peaches, plums.)   1861 S C&I

163 American Game / F. F. Palmer, Del. 19.7x27.10. (Still life, grouse, woodcock, snipe, rabbit, etc. Same composition as "American Dead Game" No. 125.)   1866 L C&I

164 American Game Fish / F. F. Palmer, Del. 19.10x27.12 (Still life. Various types of fish, rod and reel, mountain lake in left background.)
1866 L C&I

165 American Girl / By Amos' Cassius M. Clay, Jr. dam Mr. Travis' Virginia Mare, pedigree unknown. / Record 2:16½ / J. Cameron on stone. (Vignette.)   1871 S C&I

166 American Girl / Record 2:16½ / J. Cameron 1871 on stone. (Vignette.)
1871 S C&I

167 American Girl and Lady Thorn / In their great match for $2,000 mile heats best 3 in 5 to wagons / Over the Fashion Course, L. I. May 10th, 1869 / J. Cameron 1869 on stone. 3 additional lines. 17.6x26.14 (¾ broadside to right, grandstand in rear.)
1869 L C&I

American Girl (Horse) See: Nos. 711, 923, 2420, 2448, 5708, 6183-5, 6189, 6761.

168 American Homestead — Autumn / 7.15x12.8   1869 S C&I

169 American Homestead — Autumn / (Five trees shown, house faces right, and other changes in composition.) Note: This is the only copy of this print I have ever seen. (See illustration.)   und S C&I

170 American Homestead — Spring / 7.15x12.8.   1869 S C&I

AMERICAN HOMESTEAD—AUTUMN.

AMERICAN HOMESTEAD—SPRING.

[10]

AMERICAN HOMESTEAD—SUMMER.

AMERICAN HOMESTEAD—WINTER.

[11]

AMERICAN HOMESTEAD AUTUMN.

171 American Homestead — Summer / 7.15x12.8.   1868 S C&I

172 American Homestead — Winter / 8x12.8.   1868 S C&I
(Undoubtedly the most popular set of small folios ever published by Currier & Ives.)

173 American Hunting Scenes / "An Early Start" / Painted by A. F. Tait. 18.15x27.11.   1863 L C&I

174 American Hunting Scenes / "A Good Chance" / Painted by A. F. Tait. 18.10x 27.11. (Republished as "A Good Chance" No. 2424.)
1863 L C&I

175 American Jockey Club Races, Jerome Park / Tom Bowling Winning the Jerome Stakes for 3 year olds. Value $5,500, Dash two miles, October 4th, 1873. [Unofficial time 3:40.] Merodac-Springbok - Fellowcraft - Count D'Orsay - Tom Bowling keyed above title. J. Cameron on stone. 16.6x26.4. (Horses under saddle, broadside to right. Clubhouse in rear.)   1873 L C&I

176 American Landscape / Early Morn-

ing. / F. F. Palmer, Del. 15.12x23.4.
1866 L C&I

177 American Landscape / Sacandaga Creek /   und VS C&I

178 American Landscapes / Moonlight— Summer / October Landscape / By the Seashore / Winter Twilight / (4 views on one sheet.)   und S C&I

179 American Mountain Scenery / 9.9x 16.12 (Deer at foot of waterfall, brilliant autumn scenery.)
1868 M C&I

180 American National Game of Baseball, The / Grand Match for the Championship at the Elysian Fields, Hoboken, N. J. / 19.14x29.14 (This is the only large print published by the firm pertaining to baseball.)
1866 L C&I

181 American Patriot's Dream, The / The Night before the battle / 2 columns, 4 lines of verse. 10.14x15.2 (Vision shows soldier returning to family after war. Top corners round.)
1861 M C&I

182 American Privateer "General Armstrong" Capt. Sam C. Reid / In the

AMERICAN JOCKEY CLUB RACES, JEROME PARK.

THE AMERICAN NATIONAL GAME OF BASEBALL.

AMERICAN RAILROAD SCENE.

harbour of Fayal [Azores] Oct. 26th, 1814. Repulsing the attack of 14 boats containing 400 men from the British ships "Plantagenet" 74 "Rota" 44 and "Carnation" 18 guns, / 3 additional lines #558 / 8.1x12.12.
        und S N.C.

183 American Prize Fruit / (Melons, Grapes, Peaches, Cherries, Apples, etc. Tinted background.)
        1862 L C&I

184 American Prize Fruit / #736 (Plate with knife and cut melon, basket of grapes, apples, pears, cherries, pine-apples, etc.)
        und S C&I

185 American Railroad Scene / Lightning Express Trains leaving the Junction / Parsons & Atwater, Del. 19.5x32.4 (First state. Group of people shown at left of print. Brakeman at right faces left, no advertising shown on engines, cars, or building.) One of the rarest railroad prints.
        1874 L C&I

186 American Railroad Scene / Lightning Express Trains Leaving the Junction / Tickets to all points West / Erie / Railway / Parsons & Atwater, Del. 19.5x32.5 (Second state.)
        1874 L C&I

187 American Railroad Scene / Snow-bound / 8.8x12.7 (Train stalled at night, group of passengers with shovels clearing track.)   1871 S C&I

188 American Railroad Scene / Snow-bound / (Identical to preceding in size and composition. Have no idea why this print was published but have seen a copy with this date.)
        1872 S C&I

189 American Railway Scene, at Hor-nellsville, Erie Railway / Great Trunk Line and United States Mail Route between New York City and the Western States and Territories, renowned for its beautiful scenery, etc. 2 lines. (At top) Purchase Tickets / Via Erie Railway / Parsons & Atwater, Del. 19x29. (Composition similar to "American Railroad Scene Lightning Express Trains, etc." No. 185 except that brakeman on car at right faces right, passengers at left eliminated, and less of building shown. Shape of car at right altered and advertising added to locomotives, cars, etc.)
        1874 L C&I

190 American River Scenery / View on the Androscoggin, Me. / 9.10x16.14. (2 men in foreground, fishing.)
        und M C&I

THE AMERICAN TROTTING STUD.

191 American Scenery / Palenville, N. Y. / #492 / 8.1x12.5 (Creek on right, cows on left bank.) und S C&I

192 American Ship rescuing the officers and crew of a British Man of War, An / 11.9x16.6. 1863 M C&I

193 American Sloop Yacht Mayflower / Winner of the American Cup, 1886 / 1886 L C&I

194 American Sloop Yacht "Volunteer" /Winning her second and final race for the "America's Cup" against Thistle, 1887 / 19.8x28.
1888 L C&I

195 American Speckled Brook Trout / Painted by A. F. Tait. Chromolithograph by C. Parsons. 16x22 (Still life, fish, rod, reel, flies, basket, etc.)
1864 L C&I

196 American Steamboats on the Hudson / Passing the Highlands / Parsons & Atwater, Del. 19.5x33.2 (Shows Steamers "Drew," "St. John," and "Excelsior".) 1874 L C&I

197 American Summer Fruits / (Vignette.) 1875 S C&I

198 American Tar, The / "Don't Give up

the Ship" / 11.14x8.8 (Upright, full length, seated on deck.)
1845 S N.C.

199 American Thoroughbreds / 7.14x12.5 (4 horses being exercised.)
und S C&I

200 American Trotting Stud, The / Ethan Allen—Pocahontas / J. Cameron on stone. 16.13x26.2 (2 columns, 3 and 4 lines of description. In field to left.)
1866 L C&I

201 American Trotting Stud / Mambrino Pilot-Flora Temple / J. Cameron on stone. 16.12x25.11 (2 columns, 3 and 2 lines.) 1866 L C&I

202 American Trotting Stud, The / Widow McChree-Hambletonian / J. Cameron on stone. 16.12x25.15 (2 columns, 5 lines of description.) (These three prints are extremely rare.)
1867 L C&I

203 American Views / (4 on one sheet).
und S C&I

204 American Whaler / #304. 8.9x12.13 (Title in plate. Three row boats leaving mother ship to chase whale.)
und S N.C.

[15]

AN AMERICAN WINTER SCENE.

205 American Whalers crushed in the ice / "Burning the Wrecks to avoid danger to other Vessels" / 8.8x12.8.
und S C&I

206 American Winter Scene, An / 5.8x7.8 (Oval, sleigh in foreground, farm house in rear.) Very rare. und VS C&I

207 American Winter Scenes / Evening / F. F. Palmer, Del. 16.12x24.2 (Companion to following. Sleighs on way to inn where party is being held.)
1854 L N.C.

208 American Winter Scenes / Morning / F. F. Palmer, Del. 16.8x24.1 (Skaters and children on sleds in foreground.)
1854 L N.C.

209 American Winter Sports / Deer shooting "On the Shattagee" [Northern New York]/ L. Maurer, Del. 17.14x 25.14. 1855 L N.C.

210 American Winter Sports / Trout Fishing "On Chateaugay Lake" [Franklin Co. N. Y.] A. F. Tait, 1856 on stone. C. Parsons, Del. 17.14x25.14 Printed by Endicott & Co. 1856 L N.C.

211 American Winter Sports / Trout Fishing, etc. / (Title, size same, and same stone as preceding. Printed by Endicott & Co. removed. Second state.)
1856 L N.C.

212 American Winter Sports / Same size, title, same stone as preceding. N. Currier removed and Currier & Ives substituted. Third state.)
1856 L C&I

213 Among the Hills / View on Ausable River / 9.14x16.14 (Early impressions of this subject were erroneously entitled "Ansafle" instead of "Ausable." New York State view.)
und S C&I
Among the Hills. See: "Gems of American Scenery' No. 2230.

214 Among the Pines / A First Settlement / 8.8x12.8. und S C&I
Ampudia See: No. 2231.
Amsterdam (Steamship) See: No. 5234.

215 Ancient Cross, The / Clonmacnoise, Ireland /. und S C&I
Anderson, Maj. Robert See: Nos. 683, 3940.
Andre See: Nos. 804-6.

216 Andrew Jackson / Seventh President of the United States / 11.8x9.2 (Upright, green curtain.) und S N.C.

217 Andrew Jackson / The Union "It must and shall be preserved" / (Upright, vignette bust portrait. Facsimile signature.) und M C&I

218 Andrew Johnson / Seventeenth President of the United States / (Upright vignette. Facsimile signature. Portrait.) und M C&I
Androscoggin See: "American River Scenery" No. 190.

219 Angel Footsteps / "Hark! I hear an angel's footsteps / coming down the shining stairs" / (Comic. Woman playing piano disturbed by slavey with tremendous feet, noisily coming down stairs. Vignette.) 1878 S C&I

220 Angel Gabriel, The / L'ange Gabriel, El arch. Sn. Gabriel / und S C&I

221 Angel of Prayer, The / Holy and pure the blest angel, etc. / 4 lines verse. (Oval.) und S C&I

222 Angel of Prayer, The / 4 lines of verse. 12x9.4 (¾ length.) 1875 S C&I

223 Angel of the Battlefield, The / 1865 S C&I

224 Angel of the Covenant, The / 4 lines of verse. 12.2x9.5 (Oval upright.) und S C&I

225 Angel voices sweetly calling / In responsive echoes falling, etc. / 4 lines in all. 9.12x12.12 (Man pushing cart filled with bottles, bags, etc., being jeered by rough looking characters in bar room. Comic.) und S C&I

226 Angeline / #414 (Half length, flowers under brim of bonnet.) und S N.C.

227 Angeline / #414 / 11.12x8.10 (¾ length, flowing gown, playing harp.) 1846 S N.C.

228 Angels of the Battlefield, The / 14.10x17.6 (Nurse and angel helping wounded, battle scene in background. Oval in rectangle, stars, and shield in corners.) 1865 M C&I

229 Animal Creation, The / J. C. (Cameron) on stone. 8.10x12.3 (Assorted animals.) 1875 S C&I

230 Ann / #82 / 12x8.3 (Full length with red cloak. Plain background.) 1848 S N.C.

231 Ann / #129 / 11.11x8.4 (¾ length, to right, red dress, floral wreath in hand; under tree, river in background.) und S N.C.

232 Ann / #129 (Same general composition as preceding except ¾ figure to left.) und S N.C.

233 Ann / 11.8x8 (Different composition from preceding.) und S N.C.

234 Ann Maria / #97 (¾ length lady in decolleté dress, roses in hand. Round corners.) 1846 S N.C.

235 Ann Maria / (Half length, vignette, holding parrot and bouquet.) und S N.C.

236 Ann Maria / (¾ length, on balcony.) 1849 S N.C.

237 Ann Maria / (Half length, vignette.) und S C&I

238 Annie / 11x9 (Half length, vignette.) und S C&I
Annie (Yacht) See: No. 4450.

239 Annunciation, The / 1844 S N.C.
Antarctic (Steamship) See: No. 5492.

240 Antelope Shooting / Fatal Curiosity / Catlin, Del. 12.14x18.4. und M C&I
Anthracite (Yacht) See: Nos. 5721, 5745.
Antietam, Md. See: Nos. 384, 3905.

241 Anxious Moment, An / "A Three Pounder Sure" / 14x18.8 (Composition very similar to "Brook Trout Fishing" No. 703. More fish on bank. Other slight changes.) 1874 M C&I

242 Anxious Mother, The / 8.8x12.8 (Hen watching young ducklings swimming.) und S C&I

243 Anxious Nurse, The / (Dog rocking infant in crib.) und S C&I

244 Any Port in a Storm / und S C&I

245 Any Port in a Storm / Thos. Worth on stone. (Men, women, and children clinging to barrels of Port, shipwreck scene. Vignette, comic.) 1884 S C&I

246 Apollo / Sired by Seneca Chief, by Rysdyk's Hambletonian, dam and G.D. by Sons of Hills Black Hawk / G.G.D. a Messenger Mare / Bred by Jacob Hathaway, now owned at Steuben County Breeding stables, Hornellsville, N. Y. / J. Cameron on stone. 1884 S C&I

247 Apollo / Sired by Seneca Chief, by Rysdyk's Hambletonian, / dam and G.D. by Sons of Hills Black Hawk / G.G.D. a Messenger Mare / Bred by Jacob Hathaway, now owned at Steuben County Breeding Stables, Hornellsville, N. Y. / J. Cameron on stone. (Vignette.) 1885 M C&I

248 Apples / Painted by W. M. Brown.
1868 S C&I

249 Apples and Plums / First Premium / (Upright, no plate line.)
1870 S C&I

Appomattox See: Nos. 2554, 5909-11.

250 April Shower, The / Louis Maurer. (3 children and dog.) und M C&I

251 Aquarium, The / und S C&I

Arabia (Steamship) See: No. 5235.

252 Arabian / (Horse, profile to left, held by Arab groom.)
1846 S N.C.

253 Arab's Bride, The / #645 / 12x8.15 (On black horse. Upright.)
und S N.C.

254 Araby's Daughter / #648 / 12.6x8.10 (Upright.) und S N.C.

255 Araby's Daughter / (Full length.)
und S C&I

256 Arched Bridge, The / 2.8x4.11.
und VS C&I

Archer (Jockey Who Rode Iroquois) See: Nos. 3131-3, 3555-6, 4255.

Archery See: Nos. 498, 2218.

257 Architectural Designs / Plan of Capitol of Indiana by I. Town & A. J. Davis, Architects / (Four Chamber Floors, similar to this above the principal Floor. 6 in all. Stodart & Currier.
und S N.C.

258 Architectural Designs / Temple of Thesus / Temple of Diana Propylea / Ionic Temple / Temple of Jupiter / Stodart and Currier. A. J. Davis, Architect. und S N.C.

259 Architectural Designs Pyonstyle Doric — Eustyle — Ionic — Diastyle — Corinthian. / Stodart and Currier. A. J. Davis, Architect (View of Parthenon in distance.) und S N.C.

260 Architectural Designs of Doric Anta Capitals / Two Capitals of Columns / with Doric Anta Capitals / 3 additional lines. Stodart and Currier. A. J. Davis, Architect. und S N.C.

261 Architectural Designs of Doric Capitals / A Parallel of Doric Capitals / 8 additional lines. Stodart and Currier. A. J. Davis, Architect.
und S N.C.

262 Architectural Plan / Astor's Hotel Basement, or Plan of stores / Stodart and Currier. A. J. Davis, Architect.
und S N.C.

263 Architectural Plan for Astor's Hotel / Plan by Ithiel Town, Arch't / for Astor's Hotel, New York, 1832 / Stodart and Currier. und S N.C.

264 Arctic Exploring Yacht Jeannette (exact title) to James Gordon Bennett this print of his / Arctic exploring yacht Jeannette / is respectfully dedicated by the Publisher / C. R. Parsons, Del. 1881 L C&I

Arctic (Steamship) See: Nos. 3781, 6313-4, 6791.

265 Arguing the Point / L. Maurer on stone. Painted by A. F. Tait. 18.5x23.14.
1855 L N.C.

266 Arion / By Electioneer / dam Manette by Nutwood / two year old / Record 2:10¾ / J. Cameron on stone. (Vignette, high-wheeled sulky to right.) 1892 S C&I

267 Aristocracy of Color, The /
und S N.C.

268 Aristotle (Low-wheeled sulky to left. vignette.) 1893 M C&I

269 Aristotle Byariostos / As a producer and Stock horse / Marie Frank by Charlie Wilkes / with her suckling colt, Red Virgil, by Aristotle / Red Virgil, by Aristotle, dam Marie Frank / in his yearling form / (3 vignette sketches on one sheet, each about 5x5.)
1893 M C&I

Arizona (Steamship) See: No. 2679.

Arkansas (State) See: Nos. 270, 591, 4159, 6248.

Arkansas (Battles) See: Nos. 404, 420-1.

270 Arkansas Traveller, The / Scene in the backwods of Arkansas / 3 additional lines. J. Cameron on stone. 7.14x 12.8 (Companion to "The Turn of the Tune" No. 6248. (Sometimes listed as "Arkansaw Traveller.")
1870 S C&I

271 Armoured Steel Cruiser Brooklyn, United States Navy / 1893 M C&I

272 Armoured Steel Cruiser Brooklyn,

United States Navy / (Different composition from preceding.)
und M C&I

273 Armoured Steel Cruiser New York, United States Navy / 9.15x15.
1893 M C&I

Arrow (Horse) See: No. 5936.

274 Art Gallery / Grand United States Centennial Exhibition, 1876 / Fairmount Park, Philadelphia / 1 additional line. 7.12x12.12.   und S C&I

275 Art of Making Money Plenty / in every man's pocket by / Doctor Franklin / (Portrait of Franklin and 13 line rebus, upright.)   und S N.C.

Arthur, Chester A. See: Nos. 1024, 2245-6, 2505-6.

276 Arthur Chambers / Light Weight Champion / (Upright) und M C&I

277 Artist in Hair, An / 12.11x8.1 (Upright. Barber combing lady's hair, full length.)   1872 S C&I

278 Artists Creek / North Conway / 10.6x15 (Rural scene, bridge over stream, farm house in background.)
und M C&I

279 As he was / A young man of fashion / (Full length, upright.)
und S C&I

280 As Kind as a Kitten / Thos. Worth on stone. (Vignette.)   1879 S C&I

281 As kind as a kitten / Thos. Worth on stone. (Man on horse, shooting pistols, darkies pulling horse's tail, banging cymbals, etc. while horse remains unconcerned. (Vignette.)
und S C&I

282 Ascension, The / #163 / 11.14x8.11 (Upright.)   1844 S N.C.

283 Ascension, The / La ascencion / #163.   und S N.C.

284 Ascension of Christ, The /
und S C&I

285 Ascension of the Virgin, The / Na Sa Del Transito / #559 / 12.13x8.10 Title in plate, ornamental borders.)
1848 S N.C.

286 Asia / (Vignette, upright. Oriental type girl.)   1870 S C&I

287 Asia / (¾ length, vignette, not upright.)   und S C&I

288 Asia / (Vignette, half length, different composition from preceding.)
und S N.C.

Asia (Steamship) See: No. 5236.
Ashland chief See: No. 896.

289 Asking a Hand / 'Leff me be de Possessah ob dat lubly number seven" (Vignette, colored comic. Darky proposing to girl. Companion to "Getting a Foot.")   1887 S C&I

290 Asleep / #594 / 8.10x12.13. (Woman asleep. Companion to "Awake" No. 326.)   1848 S N.C.

291 Assassination of President Lincoln, The / At Ford's Theatre, Washington, D. C., April 14th, 1865 / Keyed: Maj. Rathbone, Miss Harris, Mrs. Lincoln, President, Assassin / 7.15x12.5.
1865 S C&I

292 Assumption of the Holy Virgin /
und S C&I

Assyrian Monarch (Steamship) See: No. 5746.

Astor Place Opera House, N. Y., See: No. 2647.

293 Astoria Institute / For the Education of Young Ladies, Astoria, L. I. /
und S N.C.

294 At the Fair Grounds / L. Maurer on stone. 19.2x28.4 (General view: produce, cattle, horses in foreground. Horse race in progress with 5 horses and high-wheeled sulkies.)
1890 L C&I

295 At the Fair Grounds / L. Maurer on stone. 19.2x28.4 (Identical to preceding except low-wheeled sulkies have been substituted.)   1894 L C&I

296 At the Foot of the Cross /
und S C&I

297 Ataliba Receiving the last embraces of his Family / Conquest of Mexico / #374 (Upright.)   und S N.C.

Atalanta (Yacht) See: No. 5562.
Atlanta, Georgia See: No. 807.
Atlantic (Steamship) See: Nos. 330, 6315-19, 6786-7.

298 Atlantic, Mississippi and Ohio Railroad / F. F. Palmer, Del. 17.12x27.12 (Same stone as "American Express Train" No. 130.)   1864 L C&I

299 Attack and Massacre of Crew of Ship Tonquin by the Savages of the N. W. Coast / Frontispiece of Fanning's "Voyages" 2nd edition N.Y. 1838 / 7.7x3.7 (The Tonquin was built in New York City and while under the ownership of J. J. Astor was attacked and part of her crew massacred by

AT THE FAIR GROUNDS.

Indians at Vancouver Island. Lieutenant **J.** Thorn of the U. S. Navy, her Captain, then blew up the ship.)
und VS N.C.

300 Attack of the Gun Boats upon the City & Castle of San Juan de Ulloa / Commanded by Josiah Tatnall, Esq. U.S.N. / From a sketch taken on board the Steamer "Spitfiire" during the action by J. M. Ladd, U.S.N. 7 boats keyed. #467. / 8x13.
1847 S N.C.

301 Attack of the Lion / #56 / 11.11x8.8 (Knight and woman on white horse. Upright.)
und S N.C.

302 Attack on the Castle of Chapultepec / by Gens. Quitman & Shields Divisions, Sept. 13th, 1847 / Title repeated in Spanish. #629 / 7.10x12.4.
1848 S N.C.

303 Attack on the Home Guard, The / Th. Nast 9 / 63 on stone. 22x18 (5 children and dog playing war. Companion to "Domestic Blockade" No. 1598. Upright.)   1864 L C&I

304 Attack on the Widow M'Cormack's House / on Boulagh Common, Ireland, July 29th, 1848 / #619 / 8.3x12.5.
1848 S N.C.

305 Attacking the Badger / 8.6x12.11 (Dog attacking a badger.)
und S N.C.

306 Auburn Horse, The / Driven by his owner, Robert Bonner, Esq., to whom this print is respectfully dedicated by / the publishers / J. Cameron on stone. 16.11x25.15 (¾ broadside wagon to right.)   1866 L C&I

Auburn Horse, **See:** No. 6168.

307 Augusta / #80 / 12.1x8.2 (Sealed letter in hand, vases of flowers on right and left, upright.)
1848 S N.C.

308 Augusta / (¾ length seated, curtain on right, picture of girl on wall at left. Upright.)   und S N.C.

309 Augusta / In the role of Bayadere / (Facsimile signature) Pub. by W. A. Colman, 205 Broadway / Henri Heidemans on stone. N. Currier's lith. (Vignette, full length, upright.)
1837 S N.C.

Augusta: (Madlle) **See:** Nos. 309, 3855-6.

Augusta Victoria: (Steamship) **See:** Nos. 1787, 5747.

Australasian: (Steamship) **See:** No. 5237.

[20]

Austria: (Burning of S. S. Austria)
See: No. 748.

310 Author, The / (Frontispiece to "Osceola, or Fact and Fiction" by a Southerner. Seymour R. Duke, New York 1838. 1838 VS N.C.

311 Autumn / #455 / 8x12.8 (Group of men and horses, harvest scene, from an English print, companion to Nos. 5672, 5849, 6729.) und S N.C.

312 Autumn / (Vignette of a girl's head —cherries, grapes and leaves in hair. Companion to Nos. 5673, 5851, 6732.) 1871 S C&I

313 Autumn / #455 (¾ length, vignette —grapes in girl's hair, holding fruit. Companion to Nos. 5674, 5849A, 6730.) und S C&I

314 Autumn / (Vignette of girl with grapes, peaches and cherries in arms. Upright.) und M C&I

315 Autumn Cross, The / (Cross covered with holly, ferns, acorns, etc. Upright, vignette.) und S C&I

316 Autumn Foliage / und S C&I

317 Autumn Fruits / 12.8x17.10 (Still life — grapes, blackberries, peaches, melon, pears, etc. Companion to No. 5856.) 1861 M C&I

318 Autumn Fruits / und S C&I

319 Autumn Fruits / 5.8x7.8 (Oval, printed on same sheet with "Autumn Flowers" No. 320.) und S C&I

320 Autumn Flowers / 5.8x7.8 (Oval, printed on same sheet with "Autumn Fruits" No. 319.) und S C&I

321 Autumn Gift, The / 7.15x12.8 (Group of assorted fruits.) 1870 S C&I

322 Autumn in New England / Cider Making / Painted by G. H. Durrie. 14.13x25.4. 1866 L C&I

323 Autumn in the Adirondacks / Lake Harrison / 7.15x12.7 (Brilliant autumn foliage, 2 herds of deer.) und S C&I

324 Autumn on Lake George / 8.7x12.8 (Highly colored foliage, deer and young in center, deer and doe at side.) und S C&I

325 Available Candidate, An / The one qualification for a Whig President / (Gen. Zachary Taylor, Whig nominee for Pres. sitting on a pile of skulls. Military uniform, sword in hand. For sale at No. 2 Spruce Street. Vignette.) und S N.C.

326 Awake / #595 / 8.10x12.13 (Woman awakening. Companion to "Asleep" No. 290.) 1848 S N.C.

327 Awful Conflagration of the Steam Boat Lexington in Long Island Sound on Monday / Eve'g Jan. 13th, 1840, by which melancholy occurence; over 100 persons perished / Drawn by W. K. Hewitt. N. Currier Lith. & Pub. (Published first at The Sun office, with the headline "The Extra Sun" and a map of Long Island Sound showing the location of the disaster. 7 columns of newspaper text giving an account of the accident. First state. 8.7x12 size of picture alone.) und S N.C.

328 Awful Conflagration of the Steam Boat Lexington in Long Island Sound on Monday / Eve'g Jan. 13th, 1840, by which melancholy occurence; over 100 persons perished / Drawn by W. K. Hewitt. N. Currier Lith. & Pub., 2 Spruce St., N. Y. (Map of Long Island Sound showing location of disaster. 4 columns of passengers and boat's company. 2 long columns of Capt. Hilliard's testimony. W. Applegate, printer. 17 Ann St. The illustration itself is 8.7x12.) und S N.C.

329 Awful Explosion of the "Peacemaker" on Board the U. S. Steam Frigate "Princeton" on Wednesday 28th, Feb., 1844 / By which melancholy accident the Secy of State Mr. Upshur, the Secy of the Navy Mr. Gilmer, Com. Kennon, Mr. Gardner of N. Y., & Mr. Marcy were instantly killed, Capt. Stockton & 12 of the Ship's company wounded / 11 Names keyed. 8x12.13.) 1844 S N.C.

330 Awful Wreck of the Magnificent Steamer Atlantic on Fisher's Island in the Furious Gale on Friday, Nov. 27th, at 4½ o'clock, etc. (2 additional lines. 7.14x12.13.) 1846 S N.C.

331 Axtell / Record 2:12 / und S C&I

332 Axtell / Record 2:12 / J. Cameron on stone. 1890 L C&I
Axtell: (Horse) **See:** Nos. 2532, 2540.

333 Aztec Children, The / Patronized by Queen Victoria, Prince Albert, etc. 2 lines, and seven lines of testimonials / These wonderful children are on exhibition at Barnum's American Museum, N. Y., etc. (At top) Barnum's Gallery of Wonders No. 25 (Upright, vignette.) und S C&I

B

334 Babes in the Woods / Young Partridges / (Same composition as "The Infant Brood," Nos. 3099-3100. Also published as imitation oil painting.)
1868 S C&I

335 Baby's First Visit / 8.4x12.12 (Group of small children.)
und S C&I

336 Backed to Win / (Garfield astride eagle flying over White House, upright, vignette.)   1880 S C&I

337 Bad Break, A / J. Cameron on stone. (Vignette, comic horse race.)
1879 S C&I

338 Bad Break, A / Going it like Bricks / (Vignette, driver thrown back of sulky.)   und S N.C.

339 Bad Case of Heaves, A / Thos. Worth on stone. (2 sulkies, leaders shafts broken.)   1875 S C&I

340 Bad Dream, A / Going it like Bricks / #243.   und S N.C.

341 Bad Egg, A / 12.5x8.8. (Old man holding half an egg in each hand.)
und S N.C.

342 Bad Egg, A / Fuss and Feathers / (Full-length figure of rooster with human head, facing right. Egg on ground labelled "Free Soil Egg Hatched at Baltimore, June 21st, 1852." Vignette.) Entered 1852 by P. Smith.
1852 S N.C.

343 Bad Husband, The / The Fruits of Intemperance and Idleness / 8x12.5 (First state, later published as "The Fruits of Intemperance" No. 2193. Family of four on road with their few belongings.)   1870 S C&I

344 Bad Man at the Hour of Death, The / The Wages of sin is Death / #242 / 2 columns, 2 lines of verse. 11.8x8.10 (Figure of Death at bedside of dying man.)   und S N.C.

345 Bad Point, on a Good Pointer, A / Thos. Worth on stone. (Vignette, dog gets shot intended for game.)
1879 S C&I

346 Bad Point, on a Good Pointer, A / (Composition similar to preceding.)
1879 V.S. C&I

Bair, W. W. See: Nos. 5708, 6765.

347 Bad Streak, A /   1879 S C&I

Bainbridge, Wm. See: No. 4397.

Baker, Col. Edward D. (Death) See: Nos. 1187, 1475.

348 "Balk" on a sweepstake, A / Thos. Worth on stone. (Vignette, comic, horse frightened and thrown.)
1881 S C&I

349 Ball Play Dance / By the Choctaw Indians west of the Mississippi / 12.2x 17.14 Catlin, del.   und M C&I

350 Balls are Rolling, The—Clear the Track / (At left, man seated on Kansas Bogus Laws, holding rolls marked "Fugitive Slave Bill" and "Albany Speech." Another figure weighed down by Maine, Vermont and Cincinnati Platform. Atlantic and Pacific Oceans divided by Rocky Mountains, over which is rainbow marked "Free Soil, Free Speech, Free Men & Fremont." Eagle with scroll "Fremont, Dayton, Pierce, Douglas, Choate's Dying Confession" etc.)   und S N.C.

Balls Bluff, Va. See: No. 1475.

351 Ballynahinch / Ireland / (Lake with castle in center.)   und S C&I 8x20.

Baltic (Steamship) See: Nos. 6297, 6320-1.

352 Baltimore Bakery / Thomas Ritchie & Co / From Richmond / Bakers and Confectioners to his Democratic Majesty / 5 additional lines of description. 17.8x11.1. Pub. by Peter Smith, 2 Spruce St., N. Y. (Head of Lewis Cass on scoop about to be placed in oven.)
1848 M N.C.

353 Baltimore Clipper, A / Laying to / #489 / 8.9x12.15 From the original painting by J. B. Smith. (Extremely rare print of an early Clipper Ship.)
und S N.C.

354 Baltimore in 1880 / 1880 S C&I
Baltimore See: Nos. 1090, 3484, 6389.

Baltimore Course See: No. 2642.

355 Baltimore Oriole / 7.14x4.14 (Published on same sheet with "Scarlet Tanager" No. 5409.) und V.S. C&I

356 Banks of Doon, The / Burn's Monument / F. F. Palmer, Del. 14.15x20.4.
und M C&I

Banks, Maj. Genl. See: No. 3924.

357 Baptism of Christ / #150 / 11.14x 8.10 (1 additional line Biblical quotation.)   und S N.C.

358 Baptism of Jesus Christ / 11.12x8.7

(1 additional line Biblical quotation.)
und S N.C.

359 Baptism of Jesus Christ / 11.6 x 8.5 (1 additional line Biblical quotation. Different composition from preceding.)
und S C&I

360 Baptism of Jesus Christ, The / 24.2x 18.2 (1 additional line Biblical quotation. Christ in stream, spectators on bank.) 1893 L C&I

361 Baptism of Pocohantus, The / und S C&I

362 Baptismal Certificate / und S C&I

THE BARBER.

363 Barber, The / #573 / 12x8.10 (Full length of barber dressing woman's hair, upright.) und S N.C.
Barbering See: Nos. 277, 363, 2690, 2775, 3963, 5435, 6114.

364 Bard, The / By Longfellow, dam Bradamante by War Dance / (Vignette, under saddle.) 1887 S C&I

365 Bare Chance, A / Thos. Worth on stone. (Vignette, comic sporting print. Bear on bank threatening hunter in water with his own gun.) 1879 S C&I

366 Bare Chance, A / (Same general composition as preceding.)
und V.S. C&I

367 Barefaced Cheek / Thos. Worth on

stone (Fisherman on stump of tree over stream, bear on either side; one eating fish, the other drinking whisky.) 1881 S C&I

368 Barefoot Boy, The / 11.14x8.6. Stone signed FFP (Full length of boy, brown dog, no fishing pole.) 1872 S C&I

369 Barefoot Boy, The / 11.9x8 (Entirely different composition, full length of boy, white dog, and with fishing pole.) 1873 S C&I

370 Barefoot Girl, The / 11.9x8.1 (Full length, at seashore with pail and shovel.) und S C&I

371 Bark "Theoxena," The / 3rd ship of the "Australian Packet Line" Capt. A. Pelletier, Proprietor, 98 Wall St. / Consignees Overman & Gruner, 28 South St., N. Y. / Capt. T. De Latour, Del. On stone by J. Cameron. 17x24.6 (Extremely Rare.) und L C.C.
Barney, Joshua See: No. 4398.
Barnum, P. T. See: No. 3963.
Barnum's Gallery of Wonders No. 1 —The original Tom Thumb, etc. See: Nos. 2302, 2309, 4627.
Barnum's Gallery of Wonders No. 10 —Comm. Nutt, etc. See: Nos. 1226-7, 2307.
Barnum's Gallery of Wonders No. 4 —Lancashire Bell Ringers, etc. See: No. 3425.
Barnum's Gallery of Wonders No. 6 —Miss Susan Barton See: No. 4157.
Barnum's Gallery of Wonders No. 10 —The Maine Giantess See: No. 3894.
Barnum's Gallery of Wonders No. 14 —The Wonderful Albino Family See: No. 6762-3 and Wonderful Eliophobus Family No. 6764.
Barnum's Gallery of Wonders No. 17 —Chang and Eng See: No. 996.
Barnum's Gallery of Wonders No. 25 —Aztec Children See: No. 333.
Barnum's Gallery of Wonders No. 26 —What is it? See: No. 6628A.

372 Baron's Castle, The / #143 / 7.15x 12.5 (4 knights on horseback.)
und S C&I
Barry (John) See: No. 4399.

373 Barsqualdi's Statue / Liberty Frightening the World / Bedbug's Island, N. Y. Harbor / (Only authorized edition) / Thos. Worth on stone. (Colored

[23]

woman, representing "Liberty" holding book entitled "New York Port Charges" in hand, rooster at her side. Upright," vignette. Same composition as "Brer Thuldi's Statue" No. 655.)
1884 S C&I

Barton (Miss Susan) See: No. 4157.

Baseball See: Nos. 180, 374, 987-8, 2090, 4388.

374 Base Hit, A / Thos. Worth on stone. (Vignette.) 1882 S C&I
Bashaw, Jr. (Horse) See: No. 711.

375 Bass Fishing / at Macomb's Dam, Harlem River, N. Y. / From Nature and on stone by F. F. Palmer. 12.8x 20.2. (First State, later published as "View on the Harlem River," etc. No. 6441. 3 men in row boat in foreground.) 1852 L N.C.

376 Bass Fishing / 7.15x12.7 (Man and boy in boat in foreground.)
und S C&I
Baton Rouge (Battle) See: No. 385.

377 Battery, New York, The / By Moonlight / #10 / 8.1x12.4.
1850 S N.C.

378 Battle at Bunker's Hill / Fought June 17th, 1775 / #76 / 7.15x12.3 (Taken from Trumbull's famous painting.) und S N.C.

379 Battle at Bunker's Hill / Fought June 17th, 1775 / "The Path to Liberty is Bloody" Franklin. 7.15x12.4 (Same composition as preceding.)
und S C&I

380 Battle at Cedar Mountain, Aug. 9th, 1862, The / Between the Corps d'Armee of Genl. Banks, constituting a part of the army of Virginia, under Genl. Pope and a vastly superior number of the rebels under Elwell and Stonewall Jackson, etc. 2 lines. 9x11.3.
und S C&I

381 Battle at Cedar Mountain, Aug. 9th, 1862, The / Charge of Crawford's Brigade on the right / 2 additional lines. 8.1x12.10 (Entirely different composition from preceding.)
und S C&I

382 Battle of Five Forks, Va. / April 1st, 1865, The / 3 additional lines. 8.3x12.9.
und S C&I

383 Battle at Missionary Ridge, Ga., The / und S C&I

384 Battle of Antietam, Md., Sept. 17th, 1862, The / 7.15x12.7 (2 additional lines.) und S C&I

385 Battle of Baton Rouge, La., Aug. 4th, 1862, The / 3 additional lines. 8x 12.8 (Shows battle ships.)
und S C&I

386 Battle of Bentonville, N. C., The / March 19th, 1865 / und S C&I

387 Battle of Boonville—Or, The Great Missouri "Lyon" Hunt / (Cartoon of Gen. Nathaniel Lyon.)
und M C&I

388 Battle of Bunker's Hill / Fought June 17th, 1775 / "The Path to Liberty is Bloody" Franklin. 6.2x12.7.
und S N.C.

389 Battle of Buena Vista / Fought Feby. 23rd, 1847 / In which the American Army under Genl. Taylor were completely victorious / American Losses 264 killed, 450 wounded, 26 missing / #452 / 8.4x12.10 (Taylor's back to observer.) 1847 S N.C.

390 Battle of Buena Vista / Fought Feby. 23rd, 1847 / In which the American Army under Genl. Taylor were completely victorious / American Losses 272 killed, 387 wounded, 6 missing. J. Cameron on stone. 8.3x12.13 (Taylor facing the Mexicans and other changes in composition—much better drawing than preceding.) 1847 S N.C.

391 Battle of Bull Run, Va., July 21st, 1861. / Gallant charge of the Zouaves and defeat of the rebel Black Horse Cavalry / 7.13x12.5. und S C&I

392 Battle of Cedar Creek, Va., Oct. 19th, 1864, The / 3 additional lines. 7.13x 12.10. und S C&I

393 Battle of Cerro Gordo, April 18th, 1847 / #464 / 3 additional lines. 8.4x 12.11 (2 columns at each side of title giving American and Mexican losses. J. Cameron on stone.)
1847 S N.C.

394 Battle of Champion Hills, Miss., May 16th, 1863, The / und S C&I

395 Battle of Chancellorsville, Va., May 3rd, 1863 / 3 additional lines. 8.1x12.8.
und S C&I

396 Battle of Chattanooga, Tenn., Novr. 24th & 25th, 1863, The / Between the Union Forces under Genl. Grant, and the Rebel Army under Genl. Bragg / 4 additional lines. 7.15x12.7.
und S C&I

397 Battle of Chickamauga, Geo, The / Fought on the 19th and 20th of Sep-

tember 1863 / 3 additional lines. 8.2x 12.10.   und S C&I

398 Battle of Churubusco / Fought / Near the City of Mexico, 20th of Aug., 1847 / 2 additional lines of description / #534 / J. Cameron, 1847, on stone. 7.14x12.11 (2 columns American and Mexican losses.)   1847 S N.C.

399 Battle of Clontarf, A.D. 1014, The / Ireland.   und S N.C.

400 Battle of Coal Harbor, Va., June 1st, 1864 / 3 additional lines.
                              und S C&I

401 Battle of Corinth, Miss., Oct. 4th, 1862 / 2 additional lines. 8.3x12.11.
                              und S C&I

402 Battle of Fair Oaks, Va., May 31st, 1862, The / 4 additional lines. 8.1x12.8 (Shows an observation balloon used for the first time in America in warfare.)   1862 S C&I

403 Battle of Fair Oaks, Va., May 31st, 1862, The / 3 additional lines and Genl. Sumner and staff keyed. 15.7x21.15.
                              1862 L C&I

404 Battle of Fort Douglas (Arkansas.)
                              und S C&I

405 Battle of Fredericksburg. Va., Der. 13th, 1862 / 4 additional lines. 7.15x 12.13.   1862 S C&I

406 Battle of Gettysburg, Pa., July 3rd, 1863, The / 3 additional lines. 15.10x 22.7.   1863 L C&I

407 Battle of Gettysburg, Pa., July 3rd, 1863, The / 4 additional lines. 8x12.8.
                              und S C&I

408 Battle of Jonesboro, Georgia. Sept. 1st, 1864, The / #852 / 5 additional lines.   1864 S C&I

409 Battle of Lexington, Ky., 1861, The / und S C&I

410 Battle of Malvern Hill, Va., July 1st, 1862, The / Terrific bayonet charge of the Federal troops and final repulse of the Rebel Army /
                              und S C&I

411 Battle of Mexico, The / Attack on the Gate San Cosme Sept. 13th, 1847 / #562 / J. Cameron on stone. 8.4x13.
                              1847 S N.C.

412 Battle of Mill Spring, Ky., Jan. 19th, 1862 / Terrific bayonet charge, etc. / 8.5 x 12.13
                              und S C&I

413 Battle of Mill Spring, Ky., Jan. 19th, 1862 / Total rout of the rebel army by

the gallant soldiers of the west under Genls. Thomas and Schoepff / 8.2x 12.9 (Entirely different from preceding.)   und S C&I

414 Battle of Monterey / The Americans forcing their way to the main plaza, Sept. 23rd, 1846 / #360 / 8.7x12.11.
                              1846 S N.C.

415 Battle of Murfreesboro, Tenn., Dec. 31st, 1862 /   1862 L C&I

416 Battle of New Orleans Fought Jany. 8th, 1815, The / (Demolished cannon in right foreground.) 1842 S N.C.

417 Battle of New Orleans Fought Jany. 8th, 1815, The / 8.10x12.11 (Different from preceding. 2 men on right moving bale of cotton.) Published at 2 Spruce St. & 169 Broadway.
                              1842 S N.C.

418 Battle of New Orleans Fought Jany. 8th, 1815, The / (Cannon facing left and other changes in composition from the 2 previously listed prints.)
                              1842 S N.C.

419 Battle of Newburn, N. C., March 14th, 1862 / Brilliant victory of the Union Forces under Genl. A. E. Burnside and Total rout of the rebels. etc. / 8.2x12.6.   1862 S C.I

420 Battle of Pea Ridge, Arkansas, March 8th, 1862 / 2 additional lines.
                              1862 S C&I

421 Battle of Pea Ridge, Arkansas, March 8th, 1862, The / F. Crow on stone. 15.14x22.9.   1862 L C&I

422 Battle of Petersburg, Va., April 2nd, 1865, The / 3 additional lines. 8.2x12.8.
                              und S C&I

423 Battle of Pittsburg, Tenn., April 7th, 1862, The / 3 additional lines. (Union troops on right.)   1862 S C&I

424 Battle of Pittsburg, Tenn., April 7th, 1862. The / #791 / 3 additional lines. (Radically different composition from preceding. Union troops on left.)
                              1862 S C&I

425 Battle of Pittsburg, Tenn., April 7th. 1862. The / 2 additional lines. 15.12 x22.2 (Genls. Crittenden. Wallace, Buell, Sherman, Grant keyed.)
                              1862 L C&I

426 Battle of Resaca de la Palma, May 9th, 1846 / Capture of Genl. Vega by the Gallant Capt. May / #440 / 7.14x 12.12.   1846 S N.C.

427 Battle of Sacramento, The / Fought Feb. 28th, 1847 / Defeat of the Mexi

can Army under Major Genl. Hendea, by the United States Volunteers under Col. Alexander G. Doniphan / #482 / 2 additional lines. J. Cameron on stone. 8.6x12.9. (Americans charging Mexicans at right.)   1847 S N.C.

428 Battle of Sacremento, Feb. 28th, 1847, The / Terrific charge of the Mexican Lancers / Drawn from a sketch taken on the battle ground by E. B. Thomas, U.S.N. / #539 / R. Telfer, Del. on stone. 8.7x12.10 (Mexicans on the left, mountain background.)   1847 S N.C.

429 Battle of Sharpsburg, Md., Sept. 16th, 1862, The / U. S. troops under McClellan against troops commanded by Genls. Lee, Stonewall Jackson, Hill and Longstreet. / 3 lines description. 8.3x12.11.   und S C&I

430 Battle of Spottsylvania, Va., May 12th, 1864, The / 3 additional lines.   und S C&I

431 Battle of the Boyne / July 1st, 1690 / #723 / 4 columns, 4 lines of verse 12.4x8.1. (Upright.)   und S C&I

432 Battle of the Giants / Buffalo Bulls of the American Prairies / 8.14x12.8. (2 buffalo fighting.)   und S C&I

433 Battle of the Kings (exact title is— 2:11¼ — The Battle of the Kings — 2:10¾) / J. Cameron on stone. 18.6x 27.2 (St. Julien and Jay Eye See, three-quarter broadside to right, high-wheel sulkies.)   1884 L C&I

434 Battle of the Kings, The / St. Julien and Jay Eye See in their great match race, in harness Sept. 29th, 1883, at the Gentlemen's Driving Park, Morrisania, N. Y. / J. Cameron on stone. 18.7x27.1.   1884 L C&I

435 Battle of the Wilderness, Va., May 5th & 6th, 1864, The / 3 additional lines.   und L C&I

436 Battle of the Wilderness, Va., May 5th & 6th, 1864, The / 7.12 x 12.13. 3 additional lines.   und S C&I

437 Battle of Waterloo, June 18th, 1815 / (Shows Napoleon on white horse.)   und S N.C.

438 Battle of Williamsburg, Va., May 5th, 1862 / Victorious charge of the gallant soldiers of the north and east, under Genl. McClellan. the invincible leader of the Army of the Potomac /   und S C&I

439 Battle of Williamsburg, Va., May 5th, 1862, The / 16x22.14.   (3 addi-

tional lines of details. Shows McClellan leading troops.)
          1862 L C&I

440 Bay Gelding Alley, by Volunteer / Record 2:19 / (Vignette, three-quarter broadside, high-wheel sulky to right.)
          1879 S C&I

441 Bay Gelding Frank by Pathfinder 2nd / Driven by A. J. Feek of Syracuse / Record 2:20 / (Vignette.)
          1877 S C&I
Bay Line See: No. 2652.

442 Bay of Annapolis, The / Nova Scotia / 8.8x12.8.   und S C&I
Bay Ridge See: Nos. 4435-6.

443 Bay Stallion Hambrino, by Edward Everett / Dam Mambrino, by Mambrino Chief / Record 2:21¼ / (Broadside, high-wheel sulky to left, vignette.)   1879 S C&I

444 Be not wise in thine own eyes / 12.8x8.7 (Owl in oval surrounded by floral border.)   1872 S C&I

445 Beach Snipe Shooting / 11.14x15.
          1869 M C&I
Beacon Course, N. J. See: Nos. 1639-40.
Beacon Park (Boston) See: Nos. 3304, 4409.

446 Bear Hunting / Close Quarters / 8.6x12.4 (Bear has one hunter down in snow, dogs harassing bear; another hunter is about to shoot bear. This print is sometimes called the little "Tight Fix" because of the similarity to the large folio.)   und S C&I

447 Bear Hunting / Close Quarters / 8.8x12.10. (Entirely different composition from preceding. Summer scene, one hunter with two colored helpers about to shoot bear under tree at right.)   und S C&I

448 Beatrice Cenci / (Half-length vignette, tinted background, round top.)
          und S C&I

449 Beau Awake / 8.2x12.7.
          und S C&I
Beauregard (Genl.) See: Nos. 2256, 4551.

450 Beauties of Billiards, The / "A Carom off the Dark Red." 16.6x24.14. (Companion to "The Chances of Billiards" No. 995.)   1869 L C&I

451 Beauties of the Ballet /
          und S N.C.

452 Beautiful Blonde / 12x15.
          und M C&I

453 Beautiful Brunette / (Vignette.)
          und S C&I

[26]

BEAR HUNTING.
CLOSE QUARTERS

454 Beautiful Dreamer, The /
             und S C&I
455 Beautiful Empress, The / (Oval.
Empress Eugenie, Empress of France
—head and shoulders.)
           und S C&I
456 Beautiful Pair, A / 12.10x8. (Full-
length figure of woman admiring
shoes, interior scene with shoe clerk.
Evidently intended for advertisement.)
           1872 S C&I
457 Beautiful Persian, The / #112. (Oval
in rectangle.)   und S C&I
458 Beautiful Persian, The / 9x11.
(Oval. Girl with dog.)
           und S C&I
459 Beautiful Quadroon, The /
           und S C&I
460 Beauty Asleep / 8.4x12.7.
           und S C&I
461 Beauty Awake / 8x12.4.
           und S C&I
462 Beauty of New England /
           und S C&I
463 Beauty of the Atlantic / (Vignette.
Girl wearing hat decorated with flowers.)   und S C&I

464 Beauty of the Atlantic / (Portrait
of Jennie Cramer; vignette.)
           und S C&I
465 Beauty of the Mississippi / (Vignette.)   und S C&I
466 Beauty of the North, The / (Oval.)
           und L C&I
467 Beauty of the North West / 11x15.
           und M C&I
468 Beauty of the Pacific, The / (Vignette, head and shoulders.)
           und S C&I
469 Beauty of the Rhine /
           und S C&I
470 Beauty of the South, The / (¾
length figure, vignette.)
           und S C&I
471 Beauty of the South, The / (Oval.)
           und L C&I
472 Beauty of the South West /
           und S C&I
473 Beauty of Virginia / (Upright, vignette.)   und S C&I
474 Bed Time /   und S C&I
    Beecher: See: Nos. 628-9, 2641, 3009,
4273.

475 Before Marriage / Anticipation / Linder, Pinxt. (Companion to "After Marriage," No. 58.)   und L N.C.

476 Beg Sir! / 8.4x11.8. (Upright, child and dog.)   und S C&I

477 Begging a Bite / 8.11x11.10. (Upright, boy and dog.)   und S C&I

478 Begging a Crust / 13.9x10.13. (Upright, full length girl with lace pantalettes, dog waiting.)   und S C&I

479 Behold! How Brightly Breaks the Morning / The Celebrated Barcarolle / As sung by / Mr. Braham / the Music by D. F. E. Auber / Lith. by Stodart & Currier.   und S N.C.
    Belgenland (Steamship) See: No. 5748.

480 Belgian Royal and United States Mail Steamer / Westernland / of the Red Star Line /   und S C&I

481 Belgian Royal and United States Mail Steamer / Noordland / of the Red Star Line /   und S C&I

482 Believer's Vision, The / (Round Top, upright.)   und M C&I

483 Believer's Vision, The / 11x8.10. (4 lines of verse, in 2 columns, round top.)   und S C&I

484 Bell Ringers, The / #709 /   und S N.C.
    Bell, John / See: Nos. 2509, 2911-13, 4388, 4820, 4823, 5828, 5962, 6279.

485 Bella / By Rysdyk's Hambletonian, dam by Jupiter Abdallah / Record 2:22 / 8.6x14.15. (Vignette, high-wheeled sulky to left, broadside.)
        1876 S C&I

486 Belle Hamlin / Scott Leighton on stone. (Vignette.)   1889 S C&I

487 Belle Hamlin and Justina driven by J. C. Hamlin / J. Cameron on stone.
        1877 S C&I
    Belle Hamlin See: Nos. 486-7. 2639, 6186-8.
    Belle of Brooklyn See: No. 5436.

488 Belle of Chicago, The / (Vignette.)   und S C&I

489 Belle of New York, The / (Upright, vignette, half length holding fan.)   und S C&I

490 Belle of New York, The / #446 (¾ length, not vignette, entirely different composition.)   und S C&I

490A Belle of Saratoga, The /   und M C&I

491 Belle of the East / #466 / 8.6x12. (Half length, blue fur-trimmed cape, rose in hair, red curtain to right, rounded corners.)   1846 S N.C.

492 Belle of the East /   und M C&I

493 Belle of the Sea, The /   und S C&I

494 Belle of the West, The / #447 / 8.6x12.1 (¾ length, in riding costume, woodland background, rounded corners.)   1846 S N.C.

495 Belle of the Winter, The / (Vignette, full length, woman skating.)   und M C&I

496 Bell-y Punch, The / The conductor when he collects a fare / Must punch in the presence of the passinjare / Thos. Worth on stone. 8.9x12.9. (Conductor punching passenger in the stomach.)   1876 S C&I
    Belmont, August See: No. 4249.
    Belmont Park, Phila. See: No. 5574.

497 Belted Will's Tower—Naworth, Ireland /   und S C&I
    Ben Wade See: No. 5050.

498 Bending Her Beau / (Comic, vignette, archery.)   1880 S C&I
    Benicia Boy (Heenan) See: Nos. 2613, 3261-5.

499 Benjamin Franklin / The Statesman and Philosopher / #152 / (Oval with ornate frame surmounted by eagle.)   1847 S N.C.
    Bennett (James G.) See: Nos. 1550, 4273.

500 Benja. Franklin / (Half length bust, facsimile signature.)   und S C&I
    Bentonville See: No. 386.
    Bernhardt See: No. 5387.

501 Bessie / (Vignette head.)   1872 S C&I

502 Best Horse, The /   und S C&I

503 Best in the Market, The / #421 / (Used as an "ad" for "Perrin & McClune, Lawrence Street, Denver, Colorado" imprinted.)   1879 S C&I

504 Best in the Market, The / (Upright, vignette. Lady holding cigars. Tobacco advertisement. Same composition as preceding.)   1880 S C&I

505 Best Likeness, The / L. Maurer,

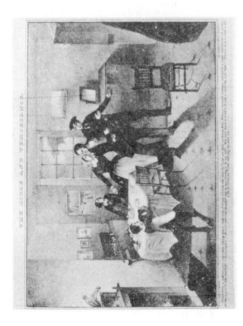

[29]

Del. 14.10x10.7. (Upright, girl looking through empty frame, dog alongside.)
1858 M C&I

506 Best Scholar, The / (¾ length, vignette, girl with books under arm, floral wreath in hair.)
und S C&I

507 Best Time on Record, three heats in 2:19¾-2:16½-2:16 / Goldsmith Maid and Judge Fullerton, in their Great Trot at East Saginaw, Mich., July 16th, 1874. / 2 additional lines / J. Cameron, Del. (Vignette, ¾ broadside, high-wheeled sulky to right, 2 horses keyed above title.)
1874 S C&I

508 Bethesda Fountain / Central Park, N. Y. / 8.8x12.5.
und S C&I

509 Betrothed, The / (¾ length girl seated on couch holding portrait of man.)
und S N.C.

510 Betrothed, The / #506 / (2 portraits of girl and man in rectangle.)
1848 S N.C.

511 Between Two Fires / Thos. Worth on stone. (Vignette, Fisherman on tree stump, dog on one bank, irate farmer on other.)
1879 S C&I

512 Between Two Fires /(Vignette, similar to preceding, postcard size.)
1879 V.S. C&I

513 Bewildered Hunter, The / "Puzzle Picture" / 8.7x12.8.
1877 S C&I

514 Bewildered Hunter. The / "Puzzle Picture" / 8.7x12.8. (Hunter and dog.)
1872 S C&I

515 B. F. Proctor / (Vignette portrait.)
und S C&I

516 B. F. Proctor / (Oval, vignette portrait.)
und S C&I

Bianca (Cutter) See: No. 1336.

Bibb, Henry See: No. 2782.

517 Bible and Temperance, The / (title at top) (at bottom) William White, a mechanic, and single man, having had a small sum of money left him calls upon his friend and fellow-workman, Harry Brown, a respectable mechanic, married to a steady industrious wife, persuades / him to go with him to make a merry night of it. Brown's wife and daughter seem to say—pointing to the tea-table "How much better it would be to take a cup of tea with them!" However, he is so weak as not / to like to refuse his friend and goes out with him / #409 / 8.3x12.7.
und S N.C.

518 Bible and Temperance, The / (title at top) (at bottom) From once going out with White, he goes again a second and a third time, and so on, until he loses his situation, and his character as a steady workman, and becoming careless in person, and idle and dissolute in manners, / brings his family to want and extreme wretchedness, his wife, still dainty, has just washed her small remaining stock of clothes, and he is lying down, trying to sleep the day away. The parish minister stops in and reads from the BIBLE / to the mother and daughter. / #410 / 8.4x12.6.
und S N.C.

519 Bible and Temperance, The / (title at top) (at bottom) The words of the Sacred volume touched the heart of Brown, who, waiting the departure of the minister, a feeling of shame for being seen in his present condition, having passed across his mind, jumps up, & taking / the Bible the minister had left, swears, upon the Book of Salvation, to reform and lead a new life. His wife and children, overpowered by the joyful event prays Heaven that THE WORD has already borne fruit / #411 / 8.4x12.6.
und S N.C.

520 Bible and Temperance, The / (title at top) (at bottom) Brown now being reformed, becomes steady, sober, and industrious, finds constant employment, which enables him to save a little money, he is thus enabled to take a small cottage and / gradually gets his furniture again, grateful to his Maker for the happy change he regularly attends his church to return thanks for his conversion, and to pray for that of others. The Minister and his wife, / who know his tale have just met him, and are congratulating him, upon his conversion, and his own and family's cleanly and decent appearance / #412 / 8.4x12.6.
und S N. C.

Bicycling See: Nos. 1374-9, 2466-7, 6365, 6633.

Biddle, Nicholas See: No. 4399.

521 Big Thing on Ice, A / B. Day on stone. (Man falling down, breaking ice, skaters in background. Upright, vignette.)
1862 M C&I

Bigler, William See: No. 6686.

522 Billiards—"A Double Carom" / J. C. (Cameron) on stone. 8.6x12.13. (Couple kissing surreptitiously while older man lights cigar.)
1874 S C&I

A BIG THING ON ICE.

523 Billiards—"Froze Together" / J. C.
(Cameron) on stone. 8.6x12.14.
1874 S C&I

524 Billiards—"Played Out" / J. C.
(Cameron) on stone. 8.6x12.14.
1874 S C&I
Billiards See: Nos. 450, 522-4, 995,
2453-4, 6272-4.
Billy Boyce (Horse) See: No. 4679.
Billy D (Horse) See: No. 6172.

525 Billy Edwards / Light Weight Champion of the World / J. Cameron on
stone. 14.13x12.4. (Upright.)
und M C&I
Bingham See: No. 5567.

526 Bird to Bet on, The / (Rooster with
head of W. S. Hancock standing on
hand, upright, vignette.)
und S C&I

527 Birdie and Pet / 7x5.7 (Girl in
woods, feeding birds, upright. Printed
on same sheet with "A Pretty Story."
und V.S. C&I

528 Bird's Eye view of / Mount Vernon
/ The Home of Washington / On stone
by J. Cameron, entered 1852 by R. Yale
and T. M. Evans. 13.2x17.15.
1852 M C.C.

529 Bird's Eye View of Philadelphia /
(12 points keyed.) 1875 S C&I

530 Bird's Eye View of the Centennial
Exhibition buildings / Fairmount Park,
Philadelphia, Pa. / Art Gallery, length
365 feet, width 210 feet. Main building, length 1,880 feet, width 464 feet,
area ground floor 20.12 acres. / 1 additional line. 8.12x12.14.
1875 S C&I

531 Bird's Eye view of the City of New York / 4x6.14 (From the southeast, over Brooklyn.) 1881 VS C&I

532 Bird's Eye view of the Pauper Lunatic Asylum / Blackwell's Island, New York / A. J. Davis, Archt.
und S N.C.

533 Bird's Nest, The /. und S C&I
Birney, James. See: Nos. 3154-5.

534 Birth of our Saviour, The / 1 additional line. 12.11x8.3 (Slightly round corners, upright.) 1867 S C&I

535 Birth of our Saviour, The / El Nac Imiento del Senor / one line Biblical quotation. und S N.C.

536 Birthplace of Genl. Frank Pierce / Hillsboro, New Hampshire / 7 9x12.11. From a daguerreotype by Cutting.
1852 S N.C.

537 Birthplace of Henry Clay, The / Hanover County, Virginia /.
und S N.C.

538 Birthplace of Shakespeare, The / Stratford on Avon / #840.
und M C&I

539 Birthplace of Washington, The / At Bridge's Creek, Westmoreland Co., Va. |Feb. 22nd, 1732.| This house commanded a view of the Potomac and the opposite shore of Maryland, etc. / 8.8 x12.8. und S C&I
Bismark, See: No. 2469.

540 Bite all Around, A /
1879 S C&I
Bither, E. D. See: No. 5708.

541 Bite all Around, A / (Postcard size.)
1880 VS C&I

542 Biting Lively! / Thos. Worth on stone (Vignette, comic fishing scene, 2 men in boat.) 1882 S C&I

543 Black Bass Spearing, / On the Restigouche, New Brunswick. / 11.6x 15.14 (Night scene, 2 men in boat with jacklight.) und M C&I

544 Bishop Allen of the African Church /
und S C&I

545 Black Blonde, The /
1882 S C&I

546 Black Cloud / By Ashland Chief, dam by Captain Walker / Record 2:17¼ / (Vignette, high-wheeled sulky to right.) 1882 S C&I
Black Cloud, (Horse) See: No. 896.
Black Diamond (Horse) See: No. 880-1.
Black Douglas (Horse) See: No. 956.

547 Black Duck Shooting / Thos. Worth on stone (Comic, vignette.)
1879 S C&I

548 Black Duck Shooting / (Postcard size.) 1880 VS C&I
Black Ethan Allen See: No. 880.

549 Black Eyed Beauty, The / Vignette.
und S C&I

550 Black Eyed Susan / (¾ length seated, moonlight scene, ship on lake in background.) und S N.C.

551 Black Eyed Susan / #102 / 11.11x 8.13 (6 lines of verse. Full length of girl and sailor on deck of ship.)
1848 S N.C.

552 Black Eyed Susan / (Vignette, head and shoulders.) und S C&I

553 Black Eyed Susan /. und S C&I

554 Black Gelding Frank, by Pathfinder 2nd, The / Driven by A. J. Feek of Syracuse / Record 2:20 / (Broadside to right, high-wheeled sulky, vignette.)
1877 S C&I

555 Black Hawk / Union Course, L. I., Tuesday, September 25th, 1849 / 4 additional lines. 12.14x20.13 (Broadside to right.) 1850 M N.C.

556 Black Hawk and Jenny Lind / Union Course, L. I., Nov. 17th, 1847 / Match for $500. Mile heats / 4 additional lines / R. A. Clarke on stone. 18.1x 26.11 (Broadside to left, skeleton wagons.) 1850 L N.C.
Black Mountain See: Lake George, No. 3406.

557 Black Rock Castle / Cork River, Ireland /. und S C&I

558 Black Persian, The / (Oval.)
und S C&I

559 Black Squall, A / (Colored comic, man overboard, wife at tiller. Companion to "A Lovely Calm" No. 3804. Vignette.) 1879 S C&I

560 Blackberry Dell / 11.6x15.14 (Group picking blackberries at right.)
und M C&I

561 Blackfish Nibble, A. / Hush! I Feel him! — Golly! You Got Him! (2 views on one sheet, colored comic fishing print.) 1880 S C&I

562 Blackwells Island, East River / From Eighty Sixth Street, New York / F. F. Palmer, Del. 11.1x15.11.
1862 M C&I
Blackwells Island See: Nos. 532, 562.

563 Blackwood, Jr. / Black Stallion by Blackwood, dam Belle Sheridan, by Blood's Black Hawk / 1 additional line and Record 2:22½ / J. Cameron on stone. (Vignette.)   und S C&I

Blaine, J. G. See: Nos. 621, 2907-8, 4821-2.

Blair, Frank P. See: Nos. 1191, 2251, 4387, 5490.

Blakely, Johnston See: "Naval Heroes No. 1" No. 4397.

Blanc Negre See: No. 1353.

564 Blarney Castle / County Cork / (2 columns, 2 lines of verse.)
                             und S C&I

Blenker, Brig. Gen. Louis See: No. 676.

565 Blessed Shepherdess, The / Divini Rergere — Divina Pastora de las Almas / (Upright — slightly rounded corners.)   und S C&I

566 Blessed Shepherdess, The / La Pastora Bendita / 11.15x8.8 (Different composition from preceding.)
                             und S C&I

567 Blessed Virgin Mary /.
                             und S C&I

568 Blessing of a Wife, The / (Same as "A Raal Convanience" No. 5033. Companion to "Miseries of a Bachelor" No. 4151.)   und S C&I

569 Blessing of Liberty, The /
                             und S N.C.

570 Blockade on the "Connecticut Plan" The / Respectfully dedicated to the Secretary of the Navy / (Two tubs marked "Cambridge" and "Gemsbok" attempting capture of the ship "Nashville," vignette.)   1862 S C&I

Blondine (Horse) See: No. 874, 4122.

571 Blood will Tell / (Horse and rider racing railroad train. Vignette. Similar composition to "Some Pumpkins" No. 5613 but reversed and some changes in drawing.) 1879 S C&I

572 Blood will Tell / (Postcard size.)
                             1880 VS C&I

573 Bloomer Costume, The / 11.10x8.5 (Upright, full length, shrubbery background, roses on left.)1851 S N.C.

574 Bloomer Costume, The / #645 /(Full-length, holding parasol, open rural background.)   und S N.C.

575 Blower / The King of the Road / Going his mile inside of 2:5 and never was trained a minute in all his life —

he is a spring colt, coming 4:— and is sound in wind, limb and — all over / Price, including halter and 1 blanket $2,500 / (Vignette.)   und S N.C.
Blower See: No. 882.

576 Blue Eyed Beauty /
                             und S C&I

577 Blue Eyed Mary / 11.12x8.10 (Upright.)   und S C&I

578 Blue Fishing / 8x12.8 (Composition similar to "Trolling for Blue Fish" No. 6158 but reversed.) und S C&I

579 Blue Monday / 8.3x12.8 (Wife beating husband. Companion to "Victory Doubtful", No. 6374.) und S C&I

580 Boatswain, The / 11.15x8.8. 2 columns, 2 lines of verse. (Upright.)
                             und S N.C.

581 Bodine / The Trotting Whirlwind of the West / By Volunteer, dam a Harry Clay Mare / Record 2:19¼ / (Vignette, broadside, high-wheeled sulky to left.)   1876 S C&I

582 Body of Gen. Robert E. Lee Lying in State, The /   und S C&I

583 Body of His Holiness Pope Pius IX / Lying in state / Before the High Altar of St. Peter's at Rome, Feby 12th, 1878 / 1 additional line.   1878 S C&I

584 Body of the Martyr President, Abraham Lincoln / Lying in State at the

THE BLOOMER COSTUME.

City Hall, N. Y., April 24th & 25th, 1865 / 12.x8.4 (Upright.)
1865 S C&I

585 Body of the Most Rev. Archbishop Hughes, lying in state / at St. Patrick's Cathedral N. Y., Jany 1864, The/ #835 / 7.14x12.5 (Top corners slightly round.) 1864 S C&I

586 Body of the Most Revd Archbishop Hughes lying in state / before the high Altar of St. Peter's in Rome, Feby 12th, 1864 / with his guard of honor, from the Noble Guard /
1864 S C&I

587 Bolted! / Thos. Worth on stone. (Horse running away, companion to "Unbolted" No. 6278.) und S C&I

588 Bolted! / (Postcard size.)
und VS C&I

589 Bombardment and Capture of Fort Fisher, N.C., Jany. 15th, 1865, The / 3 additional lines. 7.15x12.7 (Naval battle shown, troops in foreground.)
und S C&I

590 Bombardment and Capture of Fort Henry, Tenn. / By the Federal Gunboats, under command of Commodore Andrew H. Foote, Feby. 6th, 1862 / 7.10x12.3 (6 Boats keyed "Cincinnati." "St. Louis," "Carondelet," "Essex," "Conestoga," "Tyler.") und S C&I

591 Bombardment and Capture of Fort Hindman. Arkansas Post. Ark. Janv. 11th, 1863 / 2 additional lines. 8.1x12.8.
und S C&I

592 Bombardment and Capture of Fredericksburg, Va. Dec. 11th, 1862 / By the army of the Potomac under Genl Burnside / 3 additional lines. 7.15x 12.15. und S C&I

593 Bombardment and Capture of Island "Number Ten" / on the Mississippi River. April 7th, 1862 by the Gunboat and Mortar fleet under Com. A. H. Foote / 2 additional lines. 15.10x22.2.
1862 L C&I

594 Bombardment and Capture of the Forts at Hatteras Inlet, N.C. / by the U.S. Fleet under Commodore Stringham and the forces under Genl. Butler Aug. 27th, 1861 / 7.10x12.4.
und S C&I

595 Bombardment of Fort Pulaski Cockspur Island, Geo. 10th & 11th of April, 1862 / 2 additional lines. 7.14x11.14.
1862 S C&I

596 Bombardment of Fort Sumter, Charlestown Harbor / 12th & 13th of April 1861 / Ft. Moultrie Cummings Pt. (above title) / 7.14x11.13.
und S C&I

597 Bombardment of Fort Sumter, Charlestown Harbor / 12th & 13th of April 1861 / Cummings Pt. — Ft. Moultrie — Ft. Sumter (Above title.) 8x12. und S C&I

598 Bombardment of Island "Number Ten" in the Mississippi River / By the Gunboat and Mortar fleet, under the Command of Flag Officer A. H. Foote / 2 additional lines. 7.10x12.4.
1862 S C&I

599 Bombardment of Sebastopol / The Allied Fleet taking up their position / Deroy & V. Adam, Del. from official documents. 33 keys in 6 columns.
und S N.C.

600 Bombardment of Tripoli / August 1804 (Above title) #415 / 7.12x12.15.
1846 S N.C.

601 Bombardment of Vera Cruz / March 25th, 1847 / #458 / 2 additional lines. 8.5x12.12 (Genl Scott on white horse at left, soldiers sighting cannon at right.)
1847 S N.C.

602 Bombardment of Vera Cruz, March 25th, 1847 / Attack of the Gun boats upon the city & castle of San Juan de Ulloa / #467 / 8.6x12.13 (2 additional lines of description and 7 keys. Entirely different composition from preceding.) 1847 S N.C.

603 Bonefaced Cheek / und S C&I
Bon Homme Richard See: No. 4399.

604 Bonesetter / By the Brook's Horse, he by Pilot, Jr. / Record 2:20 / (Broadside to left, high-wheel sulky, vignette.) 1879 S C&I
Bonner, Robert See: Nos. 306, 1907, 2941, 2946, 3336, 3338, 3965, 4250, 4945.

605 Bonesetter Record 2:19 / (Not vignette.) 1881 V.S. C&I
Bonesetter See: Nos. 2533-4.

606 "Bonnie" Young Chieftain, The / 14.7x10.13 (Upright, full length, round top corners.) und M N.C.

607 Bonnington Linn / 5.6x7.6 (Printed on same sheet with "Bothwell Castle" No. 626, oval.) und V.S. C&I

608 Boomerang, A / From / Ohio and Indiana !! / (Vignette, man being hit on head by club marked #329 — same as "Shut the Door" No. 5502.)
1880 S C&I
Boonville, Mo. See: No. 387.

609 Boquet of Fruit, A / (Melons, etc., in bowls.)   1875 S C&I

610 Boquet, The / #383 (Pink and white roses in vase, blue and yellow flowers, butterfly, peacock decoration on vase. Upright vignette.)   1845 S N.C.

611 Boquet of Roses / #202 (Upright vignette.)   1862 S C&I
   Borussia (Steamship) See: No. 5749.

612 Boss Horse. The — Driven by the King Pin / Thos. Worth on stone. (Caricature of Comm. Vanderbilt driving on Riverside Drive, Palisades in background, vignette.)
                      1884 S C&I

613 Boss of the Market, The / (Bull bucking two tobacco salesmen, probably intended for a "Bull Durham Ad" — vignette.)   1880 S C&I

614 Boss of the Ring, The / (Caricature of William M. Tweed, vignette.)
                      und S C&I

615 Boss of the Road, The / Thos. Worth on stone. 8x12.6 (Colored comic.)
                      und S C&I

616 Boss of the Road, The / 2.14x4.12.
                      1880 V.S. C&I

617 Boss of the Road / (White comic, vignette.)   1883 S C&I

618 Boss of the Road, The / Thos. Worth on stone. 16.4x24 (Colored man with demijohn and opened umbrella riding on mule. Other horses frightened off road.)   1884 L C&I

619 Boss of the Track, The (Caricature of a horse with very long legs. Vignette, comic.)   1881 S C&I

620 Boss Rooster, De / Thos. Worth on stone. (Companion to "Copped at a Cock Fight" #1249.)   1882 S C&I

621 Boss State Carrier, The / Blaine! "I Can't Carry New York, Eh — Well, I should smile." / T. W. on stone. (J. G. Blaine carrying loaded ballot box on his back, Capitol in background, vignette.)   1884 S C&I

622 Boss Team. The! / Deadwood and Swiggler / Thos. Worth on stone. "Beatwood Track" on sign. (Caricature of Frank Work with team "Edward" and "Swiveller" — vignette.)
                      1882 S C&I
   Boston See: Nos. 623, 1091, 1571, 2614, 5714, 6399-1.

623 Boston Harbor / The Rocky Point of Boston / (At left) Edmond's Band / Day and Evening / Illuminated with twenty Electric lights / (At right) Clam Bakes / Every Day / Steamers "Gov. Andrew" / & "Gen. Lincoln" from India Wharf. / (At top) Melville Garden / Downer Landing / Open every Day / Except Monday / 8.11x13.
                      und S C&I
   Boston Tea Party See: No. 1571.
   Bothnia (Steamship) See: Nos. 5238, 5750.

624 Bothwell Bridge on the Clyde / 11.9 x17.   und M C&I

625 Bothwell Castle, on the Clyde / 11.10 x 16.15.   und M C&I

626 Bothwell Castle on the Clyde / 5.8x 7.8 (On same sheet with "Bonnington Linn" No. 607.)   und V.S. C&I

627 Bound down the River / 7.14x12.7 (Group on top deck of barge in foreground, steamers in background, Mississippi scene.)   1870 S C&I

628 Bound to hear Beecher / (Man jumping to catch ferry boat leaving slip.)
                      1881 S C&I

629 Bound to hear Beecher / 5.8x7.8 (Same composition as preceding.)
                      und V.S. C&I

630 Bound to Shine!! / Or a [Blacking] Brush on the Road / Thos. Worth on stone. 8.15x13.8 (Colored comic, companion to "Bound to Smash" No. 633.)
                      1870 S C&I

631 Bound to Shine /   1880 S C&I

632 Bound to Shine /
                      1880 V.S. C&I

633 Bound to Smash !! / or caught by the Wool / Thos. Worth on stone 8.15x 13.8 (Colored comic, companion to "Bound to Shine" No. 630.)
                      1877 S C&I

634 Bouquet, The /   1846 S N.C.

635 Bouquet of Fruit /
                      1875 S C&I

636 Bouquet of Roses, The / (Upright vignette.)   und S C&I

637 Bouquet of the Vase, The /
                      1875 S C&I
   Boutwell See: "The Smelling Committee" No. 5567.

638 Bower of Beauty /   und S C&I

639 Bower of Roses, The / 12x20.5 (Sleeping girl, awakened by lover.)
                      und L C&I
   Bowling Green, N.Y. See: No. 6415.

640 Boy and Dog /   und S C&I

641 Boy of the Period, Stirring up the Animals, The / (Caricature of Jay Gould with "Erie Railroad" in his pocket "Opera House" for stick pin, and "Bristol" and "Providence" for epaulets. Gould is shown annoying animals with pole labelled "N.Y. Gold Room" while Grant is seen running from U.S. Treasury with 5 Millions Gold. (Vignette.) 1869 S C&I

642 Boyne Water, The / This obelisk is "Sacred to the glorious memory of King William III, who with his army crossed the river July 1st, 1690 and fought the famous "Battle of the Boyne." (Obelisk and castle silhouetted by setting sun.) und S C&I
   Boyne See: King William.

643 Boz (Charles Dickens) D. Lawrence, Del. E. Brown, Jr. lith. Published 1839 by E. Brown, Jr., Broadway.
   und S N.C.

644 Brace of Meadow Larks, A (Two hunters, asleep by haycock, in water up to waists — vignette, comic.)
   1879 S C&I

645 Brack dog Wins, De / (Vignette, colored comic, companion to "De White Dog's Got Him!" No. 6641.)
   1889 S C&I
   Bragg (General) See: Nos. 396, 2577, 3679-80.
   Bramble (Horse) See: "The Race for the American Derby" No. 5037.

646 Branch and the Vine, The /
   und S C&I

647 Branch Cannot Bear Fruit, The / Except it abide in the vine / 8.7x12.7 (Motto—steamer with grape design.)
   1872 S C&I

648 Branding Slaves / On the coast of Africa previous to embarkation / #371 / 11.15x8.8 Drawn by "Roorabeck." (Upright.) 1845 S N.C.

649 Brandy Smash! / Thos. Worth on stone. (Upright vignette, colored waiter dropping bottle.) 1884 S C&I

650 Brave Boy of the Waxhaws, The / Andrew Jackson the 7th President of the U.S. In 1780 when a boy of 13 enlisted in the cause of his country and was / taken prisoner by the British. Being ordered by an officer to clean his boots he indignantly refused and received a sword cut for his temerity / 8.8x12.4. 1876 S C&I

651 Brave Wife, The / #620 / 11.12x8.10 (2 columns, 4 lines each. George B. McClellan, wife and son.)
   und S C&I

652 "Breaking In" / A Black Imposition / Thos. Worth on stone. (Horse tied to fence, annoyed by colored children, vignette, colored comic.)
   1881 S C&I

653 "Breaking Out" / A Lively Scrimmage / Thos. Worth on stone. (Horse kicking down fence, scattering tormentors. Vignette, colored comic, companion to preceding.) 1881 S C&I

654 Breaking that "Backbone" / B. Day on stone. (Political cartoon — Halleck and McClellan with mallets marked "Skill" and "Strategy" beating beast with Stanton "Draft", Lincoln axe "Emancipation Proclamation," while Davis holds animal. Vignette.)
   und M C&I
   Breckinridge, John See: 2283, 2495-6, 2627, 2914-6, 3258, 4385. 4388, 4820, 4823, 4960, 5828, 5962, 6279.

655 Brer Thuldy's Statue / Liberty frightenin de World / To be stuck up on Bedbug's Island — Jarsey Flats, Opposit de United States / Only Authorized Edition / Thos. Worth on stone. (This was also used as an "Ad" for "Turnbulls Famous Hats" 39 & 41 Fulton St., Brooklyn. Vignette, same composition as "Barsqualdi's Statue" No. 373, upright.) 1884 S C&I
   Brewer (Clipper Ship) See: No. 119.

656 Brian Borue / At the Battle of Clontarf / 2 columns, 1 line.
   und S N.C.

657 Bric-A-Brac Mania, The / Dat's fine piece "Broke Yerback" Missis Jonsing, Whar You got Him? / (Colored comic, vignette.) 1882 S C&I

658 Bridal Bouquet, The /
   und S C&I

659 "Bridal Veil" Fall / Yo-Semite Valley, California / (Bear in foreground.) 8.8x12.8. und S C&I

660 Bridal Wreath, The / (Orange blossoms on pillow, vignette.)
   und S C&I

661 Bride, The / #125 / 12.1x8.6 (¾ length, upright, round corners.)
   1847 S N.C.

662 Bride, The / #125 (Half-length vignette, upright.) und S C&I

663 Bride, The / und S N.C.

664 Bride & Bridegroom, The / (Upright.) und S N.C.

665 Bride of Lammermoor, The / #162 / 12x8.14. und S N.C.

666 Bride of the White House, The / Mrs. Grover Cleveland, formerly Miss Frankie C. Folsom / Married at the Presidential Mansion, Washington, June 2nd, 1886 / (Vignette.)
und S C&I

667 Bridesmaid, The / 1857 S C&I

668 Bridesmaid, The / 17.5x23 (Vignette, half length, rose in hair and neck of dress.) 1857 L C&I

669 Bridge, The / (Printed on same sheet with "The Cottages". No. 1269, about 5x7.) und V.S. C&I

670 Bridge at the Outlet, The / Lake Memphremagog (Vt.) / 7.14x12.8 (Also See: No. 3412.) und S C&I

Bridge's Creek, Va. See: "The Birth-Place of Washington" No. 539.

671 Bridget / #420 (¾ length seated.)
und S N.C.

672 Bridget / #420 (Full length, white dress, blue shawl.) 1845 S N.C.

673 Brig / #282 (To right.)
und S N.C.

674 Brig. Gen. Franz Sigel / U.S. Army / From a photograph by J. A. Scholton, St. Louis, Mo. (¾ length vignette.) 1861 S C&I

675 Brig. Gen. Irwin McDowell / U.S. Army (¾ length in uniform.)
und S C&I

676 Brig. Gen. Louis Blenker / First Regiment German Rifles / (¾ length vignette.) und S C&I

677 Brig. General Nathl. Lyon / Commanding the United States Army in Missouri / (¾ length vignette.)
1861 S C&I

678 Brig. General W. T. Sherman, U.S.A. / Commanding the Union forces, at the taking of Port Royal, November 7th, 1861 / (¾ length vignette.)
und S C&I

679 Brig. Genl. Ambrose E. Burnside / U.S. Army / (¾ length standing, sword resting on left arm.)
und S C&I

680 Brig. Genl. Michael Corcoran / At the Head of his Gallant Irish Brigade / 11.7x8.9 (Upright.) und S C&I

681 Brig. Genl. Michael Corcoran / of the Irish Brigade, late Colonel of the N.Y. "Sixty-Ninth" / (¾ length vignette portrait.) und S C&I

682 Brig. Genl. Nathl. Lyon, United States Army / Killed at the head of his troops fighting in defence of the Union at the Battle of Wilson's Creek, Mo., Aug. 10th, 1861 / (Half-length vignette.) 1861 S C&I

683 Brig. Genl. Robert Anderson / The Hero of Fort Sumter / (¾ length vignette.) und S C&I

684 Brig. Genl. Thomas Francis Meagher / "Irish Brigade" / (Vignette, upright.)
und S C&I

685 Brig. Genl. Wm. Sprague, U.S.A. / Governor of Rhode Island / (¾ length, upright, vignette.) und S C&I

686 Brig. Genl. W. S. Rosecrans / U.S. Army / (¾ length vignette.)
und S C&I

687 Brig Vision, Capt. Donovan / on her maiden voyage from New York to London, 1864 / #720 (2 additional lines. 2 men on deck with dog.)
und S C&I

688 Brigand, The / 7.15x10.2 (Band of brigands holding up stagecoach, and abducting unconscious girl.)
und S N.C.

689 Brigham Young (facsimile signature) / President of the Church of Jesus Christ of the Latter Day Saints / Born June 1, 1801. Died August 29th, 1877 / und M C&I

690 Brilliant Charge of Capt. May, The / At the battle of Resaca de la Palma [Palm Ravine] 9th of May, 1846. In which gallant exploit he captured the whole of the enemy's cannon and took Genl. La Vega prisoner of war / #438 / 8.8x12.12 (Cannon at right, Capt. May charging Mexicans at right.)
1846 S N.C.

691 Brilliant Charge of Capt. May, The / #438 / 8.8x12 (Balance of title identical to preceding, composition radically different — cannon at left, American troops at right, and other changes.)
1846 S N.C.

692 Brilliant Naval Victory on the Mississippi River near Fort Wright. May 10th, 1862 / Mallory, Louisiana [Ram], Cincinnati, Benton, Cairo, Carondelet, St. Louis, Conestoga [Wooden](Keyed) (2 additional lines.) 7.14x12.8.
1862 S C&I

693 Bring Up Your Horses / Thos. Worth on stone. 18.2x27.3 (Same composition as "Ready for the Trot" No. 5085.)
1886 L C&I

Bristol (Steamer) **See:** Nos. 2980, 4376, 5731.

Bristol College **See:** Nos. 1136, 4744, 6643.

Britannic (Steamship) **See:** No. 3878.

Broad Street **See:** No. 6416.

694 Broadway Belle, A / (¾ length vignette.) und S C&I

695 Broadway Fashions. New York / For Spring & Summer 1865, published by E. Butterick, 192 Broadway, N.Y. / Copyright by E. Butterick. 17.12x23.4 (2 views on 1 sheet, each the full width and half the height.)
1865 L C.C.

696 Broadway Fashions, New York / For Spring & Summer 1866, Published by E. Butterick, 192 Broadway N.Y. / Copyright by E. Butterick. 17.8x24.4 (2 views on 1 sheet as above.)
1866 L C.C.

697 Broadway, New York / From the Western Union Telegraph Building, Looking North / 16.6x24.
1875 L C&I

698 Broadway, New York / South from the Park / #599 / 8.1x12.13 (Shows Astor House and Barnum's Museum.)
und S N.C.

699 Broadway, New York South from the Park / und S C&I

700 Bronze Statue of Andrew Jackson, Washington, D.C. / by Clark Mills / J. Cameron on stone. und S C.C.

701 Brook, The / und S C&I

702 Brook, Summer, The / 12x9 (Upright, children on bridge, cows in stream.) und S C&I

703 Brook Trout Fishing / "An Anxious Moment" / Painted by A. F. Tait. On stone by Ch. Parsons. 18.10x27.2 (Fisherman kneeling against rock in stream, hooking trout, trout on bank.)
1862 L C&I

704 Brook Trout Fishing/8.8x12.7 (Fisherman on left bank of stream about to pull trout from water. Composition copied from large folio and similar.)
1872 S C&I

705 Brook Trout—Just Caught / 11x16.14

BROADWAY, NEW YORK.
FROM THE WESTERN UNION TELEGRAPH BUILDING LOOKING NORTH

(Still-life, waterfall in background.)
und M C&I

Brooklyn See: Nos. 1092-3, 1262, 1809, 1955, 3203, 4445, 4449, 6432.

Brooklyn, U.S. Cruiser See: Nos. 271-2.

Brooks, Sen. See: No. 1550.

706 Brother and Sister / 11.13x8.10 (Upright, under tree, brook alongside.)
und S N.C.

707 Brother and Sister / (Upright, similar composition to preceding, oval.)
1842 S N.C.

708 Brother and Sister / #169 (Rose arbor in background.) und S N.C.

709 Brother and Sister / #169 / 11.13x8.13 (Interior scene, red curtain.)
und S C&I

Brown, Dick See: Nos. 2344, 3383, 6170.

Brown, John See: Nos. 3253-5.

Brown, Gratz See: Nos. 2501, 4121, 5664.

Brown, Walter See: No. 3153.

710 Brush for the Lead, A / New York "Flyers" on the snow / From a sketch and signed on stone by Thos. Worth. 19.8x29.8.   1867 L C&I

711 Brush on the Homestretch, The / Between American Girl, Lucy, Bashaw, Jr., Goldsmith Maid, Rhode Island, and George Wilkes / In the last heat of their great trot on Prospect Park Fair Grounds, May 29th, 1869 / 8 additional lines. J. Cameron on stone. 17.3x27.2 (High-wheeled sulkies to right.)
1869 L C&I

712 Brush on the Road, A / Best 2 in 3 / J. Cameron on stone. 7.8x13 (Vignette, 2 boys in delivery truck, beating a fashionable rig.)   1872 S C&I

713 Brush on the Road. A / Mile heats, best 2 in 3 /   1853 M N.C.

714 Brush on the Road, A / Mile Heats, Best 2 in 3 / #712 / Thos. Worth on stone. (Vignette.)   1855 S N.C.

715 Brush on the Road, etc. / (Same as preceding.)   1855 S C&I

716 "Brush" on the Snow, A / J. Cameron on stone. 10.7x15.3 (2 sleighs to left, 4 people.)   1871 M C&I

717 Brush with Webster Carts, A / J. Cameron on stone. (2 couples, team and single horse rigs to right. Designed and printed in oil colors by Currier & Ives.)   1884 L C&I

A BRUSH WITH WEBSTER CARTS.

Buchanan, James **See**: Nos, 2495, 2564, 2627, 3149-52, 4632, 4820, 4960, 5141, 5464, 5628, 5828, 5962, 6279.

718 "Buck" taking the "Pot" / (Vignette.) und S N.C.

Buckner (Gen.) **See**: No. 2565.

Bud Crooke **See**: "A Celebrated Stallion Trio" No. 896.

719 "Budd" of the Driving Park, The / Thos. Worth on stone. (Full length of Budd Doble Holding Bag marked "Goldsmith Maid" 2:14-2:14½, vignette, upright.) 1876 M C&I

720 Buds of Promise / 12.1x8.10 (Mother holding back bed curtain to show two sleeping children, upright.) und S N.C.

Buell, Gen. **See**: No. 425.

Beuna Vista **See**: Nos. 389-90, 2009-11, 5382-3.

721 Buffalo & Chicago / Steam Packet Empire State / Commander M. Hazard / #692 / 8.2x13.2 (2 columns, 4 lines.) und S N.C.

722 Buffalo Bull, Chasing Back / "Turn about is Fair Play" / Catlin, Del. 11.15x17.8. und M C&I

723 Buffalo Chase, The / "Singling Out" / Catlin, Del. 12x17.14. und M C&I

724 Buffalo Dance, The / "To make the Buffaloes come" / Catlin, Del. 12.2x17.14. und M C&I

725 Buffalo Hunt on Snow Shoes / Winter on the Northern Prairies / Catlin, Del. 12.12x17.14. und M C&I

726 Buffalo Hunt, The / Surrounding the Herd / Catlin, Del. 12.13x18.8. und M C&I

727 Buffalo Hunt on the Banks of the upper Missouri / The Surprise / Catlin, Del. 12.2x17.14. und M C&I

728 Buffalo Hunt under the White Wolf Skin / An Indian stratagem on the level prairies / Catlin, Del. 12.2x17.14. und M C&I

Buffalo Track **See**: Nos. 884, 901, 914, 921, 3304, 4679, 5093, 6189.

Bull, John **See**: Nos. 870, 1586, 2371, 2607, 3256-7.

729 Bull Dozed!! / Thos. Worth on stone. 8x12.7 (Bull attacking mule and colored man.) 1877 S C&I

730 Bull Dozed!! / Thos. Worth on stone. (Postcard size.) 1877 V.S. C&I

731 Bull-Dozed / 1875 S C&I

Bull Run **See**: Nos. 391, 2213.

732 Bully Team, The / Scaldine and Early Nose / Thos. Worth on stone. (Caricature of Comm. W. H. Vanderbilt leaving "Charter Hoax" Park with his team "Aldine" and "Early Rose"—vignette.) 1882 S C&I

Bunker's Hill **See**: Nos. 378-9, 388, 6391.

Burgoyne **See**: No. 5907.

733 Burial of Christ, The / 9.6x7.2. und S N.C.

734 Burial of Christ, The / 9.6x7.2. und S N.C.

735 Burial of DeSoto / 2 additional lines 8.13x12.13 (Moonlight Scene.) 1876 S C&I

736 Burial of the Bird, The / (5 children burying bird.) und S C&I

737 Burning Glass, The / Painted by J. G. Brown. 16.14x13.11 (Boy and girl under tree, upright.) 1860 M C&I

738 Burning of Chicago, The / 3 additional lines. 8x12.10 (Bird's-eye view.) 1871 S C&I

739 Burning of the City Hall, New York / On the night of the 17th August, 1858 / Supposed to have taken fire from the fireworks exhibited in commemoration of the successful laying of the Atlantic telegraph cable / #597 / 8.1x12.4. und S C&I

740 Burning of the Clipper Ship "Golden Light" / Sailed from Boston to San Francisco, Feb. 12th, 1853, etc. / #548 (Title in plate.) 8.8 x 12.7. und S N.C.

741 Burning of the Henry Clay Near Yonkers / While on her trip from Albany to New York, on Wednesday afternoon, July 28th, 1852 / #720 / 2 additional lines. 7.9x13.8 1852 S N.C.

742 Burning of the Inman Line Steamship City of Montreal / On her voyage from New York to Liverpool, Aug. 10th, 1887 / 2 additional lines. 9x13.12. 1887 S C&I

743 Burning of the New York Crystal Palace / On Tuesday, Oct. 5th, 1858 / During its occupation for the Annual Fair of the American Institute / 16.12x25.4. und L C&I

744 Burning of the New York Crystal Palace / On Tuesday, Oct. 5th, 1858 / During its occupancy for the Annual Fair of the American Institute / #598 / 8x12.10 (Similar composition to preceding.) und S C&I

745 Burning of the Ocean Monarch of Boston, in the English Channel, August 24th, 1848 / #625 / 8,3x12.9 (4 additional lines of description.)
1848 S N.C.

746 Burning of the Palace Steamer Robert E. Lee / Off Yucatan Point, 35 miles below Vicksburg, on the Mississippi River at 3 o'clock A.M. September 30, 1882, while on her first trip of the season from Vicksburg / to New Orleans by which calamity 21 lives were lost / 2 additional lines. 8.8x13.9.
1882 S C&I

747 Burning of the Splendid Steamer "Erie" off Silver Creek, Lake Erie, Aug. 9th, 1841 / 8.4x12.8.
und S N.C.

748 Burning of the Steamship Austria Sept. 13th, 1858 / On her voyage from Hamburg to New York / By which appalling disaster over 500 persons were suffocated or drowned / 8.2x12.6.
und S C&I

749 Burning of the Steamship "Golden Gate" / July 27th, 1862 / On her voyage from San Francisco to Panama, having on board $1,400,000 in treasure / #548 / 8.3x12.9 (Broadside of ship to right.)
und S C&I

750 Burning of the Steamship "Golden Gate" / July 27th, 1862 / On her voyage from San Francisco to Panama, having on board 242 passengers and a crew / of 95 persons of whom about a hundred are known to have been saved / #548 / 8.3x12.9 (Same as preceding except change in title.)
und S C&I

751 Burning of the Steamship Naragansett/
und S C&I

752 Burning of the Throne, The / Paris, 25th February 1848 / #577 / Title repeated in French. 5 additional lines. 8x12.9.
1848 S N.C.

753 Burning of the U.S. Ship of the line Pennsylvania, 140 guns / and other vessels at the Gosport Navy Yard, Norfolk, Va. on the night of April 20th, 1861 / 8.8x12.10.
1861 S C&I

754 Burning of Warwick Castle, Dec. 3rd, 1871, The / 8.7x12.8.
und S C&I

Burnside (Gen. A. E.) See: Nos. 419, 679, 3901-2.

755 Bustin' a Picnic / Go away from dar. Sumfin fall on You head, Shuah! / Thos. Worth on stone. (White man and colored man clinging to overturned canoe, crocodiles in the water. Companion to "Sure of a Bite" No. 5898.)
1881 S C&I

756 "Busting the Pool" / Thos. Worth on stone. (Colored comic, companion to "A Clean Sweep" No. 1129.)
1889 S C&I

757 Bustin the Record / "Time Knocked Out" / J. Cameron on stone. (Comic showing Maud S and Aldine, wagon and driver and Record 2:15½. Father Time falling from high wheel bicycle, record 2:15¾ underfoot. vignette.)
1883 S C&I

Butler (Gen. Benj. F.) See: Nos. 3903, 4013, 4165, 5567.

Butler (Col. Pierce) See: No. 1478.

Butler (Wm. O.) See: Nos. 2492, 5050, 6695.

758 Butt of the Jokers, The / (Vignette, comic, horse print, companion to "Point of the Joke" #4814.)
1879 S C&I

759 Buttermilk Falls / 5.7x7.7 (Printed on same sheet with "The Pocanteco".)
und V.S. C&I

760 By the Seashore / Painted by J. P. Rossiter.
1868 M C&I

By the Seashore See: No. 178.

761 Byron and Marianna / #165 / 2 additional lines. Upright.
und S N.C.

762 Byron in the Highlands / #348 / 11.9x8 (Highland costume and dead stag in foreground.)
und S C&I

763 Byron's First Love / #504 (Couple in arbor, moonlight, upright.)
und S N.C.

Byron, Lord See: Residence No. 5118.

C

Cairns See: No. 801.

764 Cairn's Quick Step / Most Respectfully Dedicated to / Captn. John T. Cairns / of the / Independence Guards/ by / Dodsworth's National Brass Band / 4 additional lines. Published by James L. Hewitt & Co., 239 Broadway and entered, Etc. 1843.
und S N.C.

765 Cake Walk, De / For Beauty, Grace

and Style, de Wimmen takes de Cake / Thos. Worth on stone. (Vignette, colored comic.) 1883 S C&I

Calhoun, John C. **See:** Nos. 3259, 4165.

California (State) **See:** Nos. 659, 768, 1118-20, 1681, 3767, 4598, 5522, 6409, 6520, 6829-30.

766 California Beauty, The /
und S N.C.

767 California Gold / und S N.C.

768 California Scenery / Seal Rocks — Point Lobos / 8x12.8 (Moonlight scene, carriages, horsemen in foreground.)
und S C&I

769 California Wonder Occident, owned by Gov. L. Stanford, The / Time in harness, a private trial of speed / 2:19, 2:19, 2:19 / J. Cameron on stone. (Vignette, broadside to right.)
1873 S C&I

770 California Wonder Occident owned by Gov. L. Stanford, The / Record 2:16¾ / J. Cameron on stone. (Vignette, broadside to right.)
1873 S C&I

771 California Wonder, The / Hinda Rose / By Electioneer, dam Beautiful Bells by the Moor. Bred by Gov. Leland Stanford at Palo Alto, Cal. / 3 additional lines. (¾ broadside to right, high-wheeled sulky, vignette.)
1883 S C&I

California. (Steamship) **See:** Nos. 5751, 6322.

772 Californian Seeking the Elephant /
und S N.C.

Calvin (Death of) **See:** No. 1473.

Cambria (Sloop Yacht) **See:** Nos. 2625, 5245, 5431.

Cambria (Steamship) **See:** No. 6789.

Cambridge (Mass.) **See:** Nos. 2740, 6545-6.

Cambridge Course (Mass.) **See:** No. 3387.

Camors (Horse) **See:** No. 901.

Campania (Steamship) **See:** No. 6258.

Campbell, (Jane) **See:** No. 4154.

773 Camping in the Woods / "A Good Time Coming" / Painted by A. F. Tait. 18.12x27.8 (Group preparing dinner.)
1863 L C&I

774 Camping in the Woods / "Laying Off" / Painted by A. F. Tait. 18.12x 27.9. 1863 L C&I

775 Camping Out / "A Life in the Woods for Me" / (Moonlight scene, hunter and dog frightened by owls, comic, vignette.) 1879 S C&I

776 Camping Out—Life in the Woods /
1879 M C&I

777 Camping Out / "Some of the right sort" / L. Maurer, Del. 19x27.6.
1856 L N.C.

778 Can you keep a secret? (Vignette, head.) 1872 S C&I

779 Canadian Voyageurs / Walking a Canoe up the Rapid / 7.15x12.8.
und S C&I

780 Canadian Winter Scene / 9.15x16.12 (Showing skaters on pond at right.)
und M C&I

Canada **See:** Nos. 543, 779-80, 1826, 1828-30, 2319, 2616, 2650, 3094, 3412, 3418, 3540, 4519. 4609. 5051. 5329, 5663, 5927, 6352, 6396, 6420, 6452.

181 Canal Scene / Moonlight / #196 8.7x12.10 (Man and horse on bank pulling barge.) und S C&I

782 Canary Bird, The / und S C&I

783 Candidate on the stump, A / The Secesh Democratic Pirate sunk by the U.S. Gun Boat Union / (Seven Men, Belmont, Brick Pomeroy, Marble, Wade Hampton, Blair, Seymour, and Johnson are clinging to sinking ship. The "Union Gunboat" has five guns labelled "Indiana" "Ohio" "Penna" "Vermont" and "Maine." Vignette — political cartoon.) und M C&I

784 Can't be Beat! (Vignette. Knight on horse smoking cigar, smoke forming the word "Champion." Evidently published for an ad.) 1880 S C&I

785 Can't Play / (Companion to "Domino" No. 1599.) und S N.C.

786 Can't Play / 11.9x8.3 (Same idea as "Stocks Up" and "Stocks Down".)
und S N.C.

787 Can't you talk? / 12.8x9 (Upright, child with dog.) und S C&I

788 Canvas-Backs / 8.8x12 8.
und S C&I

789 Capability and Availability / 9.15x 16.15 (Political cartoon showing Houston, Crittenden, Benton, Fillmore, Bell, Cass, Douglas, and Webster. Scott and Pierce holding hand of symbolical figure "America." und M C&I

790 Capital Cigar, A / (Cigar advertising card.) 1880 V.S. C&I

791 Capital Joke, A ! / (Minister laughing heartily, vignette portrait, upright.) und S C&I

792 Capitol at Washington / und S N.C.

793 Capitol at Washington / #612 / 8.1x 12.8 (¾ front view, people in foreground.) und S N.C.

794 Capitol at Washington, The / 8.1x 11.8 (Almost direct front view, 7 people and dog in foreground.) und S C.C.

795 Capitol, Indiana. Plan of Principal Floor. A. J. Davis, Architect. / Stodart and Currier. (Vignette.) und S N.C.

796 Capitol of the State of Indiana / I. Town & A. J. Davis, Architects / 1834 Stodart & Currier (vignette.) und S N.C.

797 Capitulation of Vera Cruz / The Mexican Soldiers Marching Out and surrendering their arms to Genl. Scott, March 29th, 1847 / #457 / 7.12x12.9. 1847 S N.C.

798 Capt. Charles Wilkes, U.S.N. / Commanding U.S. Steam Frigate "San Jacinto" / The Man who dares to take the responsibility and arrest traitors wherever he finds them. / (Vignette.) und S C&I

Capt. Lewis (Horse) See: No. 894.

799 Capt. Thomas Francis Meagher / Zouave Corps of the "Sixty Ninth" / (¾ length, vignette.) und S C&I

800 Captive Knight, The / Sung by Mrs. Hemans. Published by James L. Hewitt. / (Music sheet.) und S N.C.

801 Captn. John T. Cairns / und V.S. N.C.

802 Capture and Fall of Charleston, S.C., Feby. 18th, 1865 / #857 / 3 additional lines. und S C&I

803 Capture of an unprotected female, or the close of the rebellion, the / J. Cameron on stone. (Jeff Davis disguised as a woman, and captured by Union Soldiers — vignette.) und M C&I

804 Capture of Andre, 1780 / David Williams, Isaac Van Wart, John Paulding / #368 / 8x11.12. 1845 S N.C.

805 Capture of Andre, The / By John Paulding, David Williams, and Isaac Van Wart, at Tarrytown, N.Y. Sept. 23rd, 1780 / 8.12x12.11 (Andre in center, right shoe and stocking off. Captor on left is talking to another on right, who is reading document.) 1876 S C&I

806 Capture of Andre, The / By John Paulding, David Williams, and Isaac Van Wart, at Tarrytown, N.Y., Sept. 23rd, 1780 / und S C&I

807 Capture of Atlanta, Georgia, Sept. 2nd, 1864 by the Union Army, under Major Gen. Sherman, The / 3 additional lines. und S C&I

808 Capture of Genl. La Vega by the Gallant Capt. May / at the battle of Resaca De La Palma, May 9th, 1846 / #440 / 8.8x12.10. / (Cannon in center foreground, Capt. May in back of cannon, on horseback.) 1846 S N.C.

809 Capture of Jeff Davis, The / His last official act "The Adoption of a new rebel uniform" / He attempts to "Clear his Skirts" but finds it "All up in Dixie." (Vignette.) und M C&I

810 Capture of Roanoke Island. Feby. 8th, 1862 / By the Federal Forces, under command of Genl. Ambrose E. Burnside, and Gunboats under Commodore L. M. Goldsborough / 8.2x12.4. und S C&I

811 Capturing a Wild Horse / Indian method of "Breaking Him down" Catlin, Del. 12.2x17.14. und M C&I

812 Capturing The Whale / (Title in plate. 3 boats and iceberg in background, ship on left.) und S N.C.

813 Cardinal James Gibbons / und S C&I

814 Cares of a Family, The / 18.6x22.12 Painted by A. F. Tait. (Companion to "A Rising Family" No. 5151 and "The Happy Family" No. 2712. Republished by Currier & Ives. 1856 L N.C.

815 Cares of a Family, The / A. F. Tait on stone. 8.12x12.8 (Companion to "The Infant Brood" No. 3099.) und S C&I

816 Cares of a Family, The / A. F. Tait on stone, 9.11x12.5 (Oval, companion to "The Infant Brood" No. 3100.) 1865 S C&I

817 Cares of a Family / #568 (Child feeding nest full of young birds.)
und S C&I

818 Carlo's ABC / und S C&I

819 Carlo's First Lesson / L. Maurer on stone. 14.11x10.8. 1858 M C&I
Carnation (British ship) See: No. 182.

820 Caroline / (Seated at table, wrap over arm, Hudson River scene on wall. ¾ length, same composition as "Emily" No. 1724, upright.)
und S N.C.

821 Caroline / (Half-length vignette, fan in hand, flowering bushes in background, roses in hair.)
und S N.C.

822 Caroline / (Slight changes in composition from preceding, 2 trees in back, 4 roses in hair.) und S N.C.

823 Caroline / (Slight changes to 2 preceding prints — in background, hair, and hair ornaments.) und S N.C.

824 Caroline / 11.14x8.7 (¾ length, seated at table, red dress, green curtain.)
und S N.C.

825 Caroline / (Full length, seated facing left, green curtain.)
1844 S N.C.

826 Caroline / #42 / 11.14x8.5 (Half length, rounded corners, rose in bodice, plain background, upright.)
1846 S N.C.

827 Caroline / #42 / 11.15x8.6 (Half length, seated on porch reading book, head turned to face observer.)
1847 S N.C.

828 Caroline / #84 / 11.15x8.2 (Full length, red dress, black lace shawl, fountain in background.)
1848 S N.C.

829 Caroline / (Half length vignette, plain buttoned dress.)
und S C&I

830 Carrie / (Half length vignette.)
und S C&I

831 Carrier Dove, The — The Departure / und S N.C.

832 Carrier Dove, The — The Departure (Vignette.) und S C&I

833 Carrier Dove, The — The Return / #351 / (¾ length, with 2 women, upright.) und S N.C.

834 Carrier Dove, The — The Return /

(Vignette.) und S C&I
Carroll Island See: No. 2757.

835 "Carry Me Back to Old Virginny" (Full length of darky playing banjo.)
und S C&I

C. O. D.

836 Cash on Delivery C.O.D. / Thos. Worth on stone. 8.14x12 (Bartender waiting for payment for drink.)
1868 S C&I

837 Cash System, The / 12.12x8.3 (Six column rebus.) 1877 S C&I
Cass (Lewis) See: Nos. 2288, 2492, 3364, 3481-2, 4165, 4520, 4884, 5227, 5569.

838 Cassius M. Clay / Of Kentucky / The Champion of Liberty / From a daguerreotype by Plumbe / #387 / 11.8x8.10 (Upright.)
1846 S N.C.

839 Castle Blarney, Ireland, The /
und S C&I

840 Castle Garden, New York / From the Battery / #624 / 8.1x12.9.
1848 S N.C.

841 Castle Howard / Vale of Avoka / (Ireland.) und M C&I

842 Castle of Chillon, Lake of Geneva / (2 columns, 3 lines of verse.)
und S C&I

843 Castle of Chillon, Lake of Geneva /
(2 columns, 3 lines of verse.)
und M C&I

Catalpa (Bark) See: No. 3993.

844 Cat-astrophe, The / #513 (Cat caught
in trap.) und S N.C.

845 Catching a Trout / "We hab you
now, sar!" / Painted by A. F. Tait.
18.5x25.12. 1854 L N.C.

846 Catherine / (Half length, holding
closed fan in hand, exterior scene, vignette.) und S N.C.

847 Catherine / (¾ length seated, with
pad and pencil.) und S N.C.

848 Catherine / #115 (¾ length, holding
bird and cage.) und S N.C.

849 Catherine / #115 / 11.13x8.4 (Full
length, red dress, seated, bouquet in
hand, roses in large vase on table.)
1845 S N.C.

850 Catherine / #115 / 11.13x8.4 (Composition similar to preceding but white
dress, urn on table, and other slight
changes.) 1845 S N.C.

851 Catherine / #83 / 11.15x8.5 (Full
length by shore, poke bonnet and red
dress.) 1848 S N.C.

852 Catherine Hayes / The Swan of
Erin / #710. und S N.C.

853 Catholic Memory /
und S N.C.

854 Cat Nap, A / L. Maurer on stone.
(Mother asleep, youngsters playing.)
1859 M C&I

855 Cat Nap, A / L. Maurer on stone.
(Three children playing, mother a-
sleep.) 1858 L C&I

856 Cat's Paw, The / #480 / 11.12x8.14
(Monkey compelling cat to pull chest-
nuts from fire.) und S N.C.

857 Catterskill Fall, The / at Catskill
Mountains / #197 / 8.7x12.11 (Figure
of man on rock in center, stream to
right.) und S C&I

858 Catterskill Falls / 7.15x12.8 (Different view, Falls in center, no figure in
foreground.) und S C&I

859 Cattskill Creek / (Vignette. Printed
on same sheet with "The Hill side" and
"The Ruins" about 5x7.)
und V.S. C&I

860 Catskill Mountains, The / From the
Eastern Shore of the Hudson / F. F.
Palmer, Del. 14.14x20 (Hudson River
Steamer "Aleda" shown.)
1860 L C&I

Catskills See: Nos. 191, 857-60, 1648,
1932-3, 3327, 5144, 5418-20.

861 Caught in the Act / (Vignette.)
und S C&I

862 Caught Napping / Thos. Worth on
stone. (Vignette, hunter asleep, fox
stealing dead game.) 1879 S C&I

863 Caught Napping / (Postcard size.)
1880 V.S. C&I

864 Caught on the Fly / Thos. Worth
on stone. (White comic, vignette. 2
fishermen hooked, while dog steals
their fish. Boy on opposite bank with
large catch. Companion to No. 3426.)
1879 S C&I

865 Caught on the Fly / (Postcard size,
similar to preceding but with slight
changes.) 1880 V.S. C&I

866 Cause and Effect. A Natural Result
/ "Dar, I Tole yer so! Now yous done
gone spile a little nigger" / (Soap suds
all over floor and darkie's face. Upright vignette.) 1887 S C&I

867 Cause and Effect. A Timely Warn-
ing / "Yous jess done leff dat soap
alone" / "Dat soap wash all de butiful
brack outen you" / (Colored boy about
to wash, upright vignette.)
1887 S C&I

868 Cavalry Tactics, by the Darktown
Horse Guards / "Now, win your spurs
to-day" (Vignette, companion to "Infantry Maneuvers," etc. No. 3111.)
1887 S C&I

869 Caved in — The Busted Sculler /
Thos. Worth on stone. 11x15.3.
1876 M C&I

870 Caving In, or a Rebel "Deeply Hu-
miliated" / Ben Day, Del., on stone.
(Lincoln and Jeff Davis boxing, spectators are various European powers.
John Bull fears Lincoln will take him
on next. Blows are marked on the
opponents faces as battles lost by each.
Vignette.) und M C&I

871 Cecelia / #438 (Full length, seated
at table, red dress, upright.)
1844 S N.C.

Cedar Creek, Battle of See: No. 392.

Cedar Mountain, Va., Battle of See:
Nos. 380-1.

872 Cedars of Lebanon, The / See: Foreign Views. und S C&I

873 Cela Winder / 1883 S C&I

874 Celebrated Boston Team Mill Boy
and Blondine, owned and driven by
John Shepard, Esq., The / Record 2:22

/ From the original painting by Scott Leighton, in possession of Mrs. J. Shepard. 20.8x33 (Four-wheel wagon to left.) 1882 L C&I

875 Celebrated Clipper Bark Grapeshot Belonging to Geo. Law, Esq. N.Y., The / (Broadside to left.) und S N.C.

876 Celebrated Clipper Ship "Dreadnought," The / und S C&I

877 Celebrated Clipper Ship "Dreadnought", The / Off Tuskar Light, on her passage into dock at Liverpool in 13 days 11 hours, from New York, December, 1854 / (Vignette, Broadside to left.) und S C&I

878 Celebrated Ethiopian Melodies, The/. und S N.C.

879 Celebrated Fighting Pig "Pape," Th. / Weighing only 34 Lbs. / As he fought the 46½ Lb. dog "Crib", on the evening of the 18th of March, 1849 / The pig won in 37 minutes, the dog was drawn and soon after died / "Pape" had previously fought the 38 Lb. dog "Imp" for $100 a side, the pig won, killing the dog in 1 minute, 37½ seconds / Carter & Hamilton Proprietors. / und M N.C.

880 Celebrated "Four in Hand" Stallion Team, The / Superb and his three sons / Nightshade, dam a well bred Virginia mare — Black Diamond, dam by Vermont Black Hawk. Superb by Ethan Allen, dam by Harris' Hambletonian — Black Ethan Allen, dam by Old Washington, he by Mambrino Paymaster / J. Cameron on stone. 18.2x28. 1875 L C&I

881 Celebrated "Four in Hand" Stallion Team, The / 18.2x28 (Balance of title identical to preceding, except "Black Ethan Allen" changed to "Success.") J. Cameron on stone. 1875 L C&I

882 Celebrated Horse "Blower" King of the Road. The / In his Great Match against time / Driven by one of the Bo-hoys & won in 2:10 1/16 / (Vignette, white comic, broadside to right.) und S N.C.

883 Celebrated Horse "Dexter," — "The King of the Turf", The / In his Great Match against time, Oct. 10th, 1865 / Trotting a mile under the saddle, in the unparalleled time of / 2:18 1/5 / 2 columns; 4 lines. J. Cameron on stone. 16.14x26.10 (Broadside to right, stands in right background.) 1865 L C&I

884 Celebrated Horse "Dexter," — "The King of the World" Driven by Budd Doble, The / As he passed the Judge's Stand on the Buffalo Fair-Grounds, Buffalo, N.Y. Aug. 14th 1867 / 14 additional lines and 2 columns, 30 and 29 lines of turf records. J. Cameron 1867 on stone. 17.2x26.13 (¾ to right, high-wheeled sulky.) 1867 L C&I

885 Celebrated Horse George M. Patchen, — "The Champion of the Turf," The / The property of Wm. Waltermire, Esq. 10 additional lines, 2 colums — 9 and 8 lines. L. Maurer on stone. 17.2x26.14 (Broadside to left, high-wheeled sulky.) 1860 L C&I

886 Celebrated Trotting Horse "John Stewart," as he appeared on the Twentieth Mile, The / In his great match against time over the Fashion Course, L.I. Tuesday Sept. 22nd, 1868 / when he performed the unparalleled feat of trotting to wagon / 20 miles in 59 minutes and 23 seconds / J. Cameron & Thos. Worth on stone. 16.8x25.8 (Broadside to left.) 1869 L C&I

887 Celebrated Horse Lexington |5 yrs. old| by "Boston" Out of "Alice Carneal," The / Bred by Dr. Warfield, owned by R. TenBroeck, Esq. / Winner of the great 4 mile match for against "Lecomte's" time of 7:26 / Over the Metairie Course, New Orleans, April 2nd, 1855 / Won in 7:19¾ !! / 2 columns, 7 lines each. L. Maurer. Del., and signed on stone. 18.13x26.6 (Standing, profile to right.) 1855 L N.C.

888 Celebrated Horse "Lexington" |5 yrs. old| by "Boston" Out of "Alice Carneal" etc. / (Balance of title, same as preceding.) und L C&I

889 Celebrated Kook Family, The / J. Cameron on stone. 13.11x10.4 (Upright.) und S C.C.

890 Celebrated Mare Flora Temple — "The Queen of the Turf," The / 9 additional lines, 2 columns, 13 lines. (Broadside to right, skeleton wagon.) 1853 L N.C.

891 Celebrated Mare Flora Temple — "The Queen of the Turf." The / 8 additional lines. (¾ to left.) und L C&I

892 Celebrated Mare Flora Temple — "The Queen of the Turf." The / The property of Wm. MacDonald, Esq. Baltimore / L. Maurer on stone. 8 additional lines, 2 columns, 14 lines. 17.4

x27.3 (Broadside to right, sulky.)
1860 L N.C.

893 Celebrated Pacing Mare "Pocahontas" driven by James McMann, Esq., The / Performing her wonderful feat of pacing a mile in the unprecedented time of / 2:17½ / 4 additional lines. L. Maurer on stone. 1855 L N.C.

894 Celebrated "Plough Horse" Captain Lewis, The Great Sensational Trotter. The / By Spink, dam Lucy Long / Record 2:20¼ / (Vignette, ¾, high-wheeled sulky to left.)
1882 S C&I

Celebrated Running Horse "Harry Bassett". The / See: "Ready for the Signal" No. 5082.

895 Celebrated / Spring-Flower Polka, The / For the Piano Forte. / C. Currier, Lith., 33 Spruce St., N.Y. / Composed and presented / to the Ladies of New York / Before his departure / For Europe / By / Sebastian Emile Cook, / ten years of age. / New York, Published by S. Cook, 423 6th Ave. Jaques & Brother, 385 Broadway, W. M. Hall & Son, 239 Broadway / (Music sheet.)   und S C.C.

896 Celebrated Stallion Trio, A / Wamba 1:44½ Running / Bud Crooke 2:15½ Pacing / Black Cloud 2:17¼ Trotting / By Waverly — By George Wilkes — By Ashland Chief. The Pride of Meyer's Lake Side Horse Farm, Canton, Ohio / Property of Ed. J. Meyer. 15.15x20.   und M C&I

897 Celebrated Stallions "George Wilkes" and "Commodore Vanderbilt", The / Trotting "A Dead Heat" match to wagons, best three in five / over the Union Course, L.I., Nov. 6th, 1865 / J. Cameron on stone. 17x26.8.
1866 L C&I

898 Celebrated Terrier Dog Major performing his wonderful feat of killing 100 rats in 8m — 58 sec, The / 14.2x 20.6. Entered according to act of Congress. 1846, by H. R. Robinson Published by N. Currier. und L N.C.

899 Celebrated Trotter Jay Eye See Driven by E. D. Bither, The / By Dictator, dam Midnight by Pilot Jr. / Record 2:10¾ / Jno. Cameron 1883 on stone. 17.12x27.3.
1883 L C&I

900 Celebrated Trotter Moose, by the Washburn Horse, The / Record 2:19½ / Scott Leighton on stone. (Vignette, ¾ to left, high-wheeled sulky.)
1881 S C&I

901 Celebrated Trotting Horse "Camors," by Gen. Knox, dam by Black Hawk, The / Won the first 2 heats in the contest for $7500 purse at Buffalo, N.Y., Aug. 7th, 1874 / time 2:20½ — 2:19¾ / J. Cameron on stone. (Vignette, ¾ to right.) 1874 S C&I

902 Celebrated Trotting Horse Gloster, by Volunteer, dam by Stockbridge Chief, The / Winner of the first prize in the $6000 purse for 2:20 horses at Rochester, N.Y., Aug. 14th, 1874 / J. Cameron on stone. (Broadside to right, high-wheeled sulky.) 1874 S C&I

903 Celebrated Trotting Horse Henry, driven by John Murphy, The / as he appeared at Prospect Park, L.I., June 27th, 1872 in his trot with Goldsmith Maid and Lucy / Best time in Harness 2:20¼ made at Beacon Park, Boston, June 25th, 1871 / R. Kluth on stone. (Vignette broadside to right, high-wheeled sulky.)   1872 S C&I

904 Celebrated Trotting Horse Henry, driven by John Murphy, The / Balance of title exactly the same as preceding. J. Cameron 1874 on stone. (Changes in composition, 2 additional lines of track records, vignette.) 1874 S C&I

905 Celebrated Trotting Horse Hopeful, by Godfrey's Patchen, The / driven by his owner A. W. Richmond Esq./ Record 2:14¾ / Scott Leighton on stone. 18.6x28 (¾ view, 4-wheeled rig to left, country road in background.)
1881 L C&I

906 Celebrated Trotting Horse Hopeful, By Godfrey's Patchen, The / Record 2:14¾ / Painted by Scott Leighton and signed on stone. 18.6x28 (Identical to preceding except for title change, ¾ view to wagon to left.)
1881 L C&I

907 Celebrated Trotting Horse "John Stewart" as he appeared on the Twentieth mile, The / in his great match against time over the Fashion Course, L.I., Tuesday Sept. 22nd, 1868 / driven by young Hiram Woodruff / 6 additional lines, 2 columns, 22 lines. Sketched from life by Thos. Worth. J. Cameron and Thos. Worth on stone. 16.10x25.8.   1868 L C&I

908 Celebrated Trotting Horse "John Stewart" as he appeared on the Twentieth mile, The. / In his great match against time over the Fashion Course, L.I., Tuesday Sept. 22nd, 1868 / When he performed the unparalleled feat of trotting to wagon / 20 miles in 59 min-

utes and 23 seconds / Thos. Worth and J. Cameron on stone. 16 8x25.8.

1869 L C&I

909 Celebrated Trotting Horse Judge Fullerton, as he Appeared, Driven by Dan Mace, The / at Utica, New York, August 25th, 1873, beating Lucille Golddust, Camors, and Sensation on which occasion he made in the third heat, a quarter / mile in 31½ seconds! and a half mile in 1:04¾! etc. / second heat in 2:19¼!! / 2 additional lines. J. Cameron, Del. on stone. 16.10x26.1 (High-wheeled sulky to right, passing judges stand.)

1874 L C&I

910 Celebrated Trotting Horse "Prospero" by Messenger Duroc, By Henry Clay, The / Driven by Dan Mace / Record 2:20 / Vignette, high-wheeled sulky, broadside to right.)

1877 S C&I

911 Celebrated Trotting Horse Trustee As he Appeared in his Twentieth Mile, The / in his great match against time of trotting in harness / 20 miles in 1 hour / over the Union Course, L.I., Oct. 20th, 1848 / 5 additional lines, 2 columns, 13 and 12 lines. From life by Samuel Jones. J. Cameron on stone. 18.6x27 (High-wheeled sulky broadside to right. This is the earliest print I have seen printed in more than one color.)

1848 L N.C.

912 Celebrated Trotting Mare "Daisy Dale" by Thornedale, The / Record 2:19¾ / Scott Leighton on stone. (Vignette, ¾ to left.) 1881 S C&I

913 Celebrated Trotting Mare Flora Temple Driven by James D. McMann, The / She entered in 95 races winning 75; received forfeit 5; and 2 drawn / best time in harness mile heat 2:19¾; 2 mile heats 4:50½ to wagon: Mile heats 2:25 / (Vignette, broadside to right.) 1872 S C&I

914 Celebrated Trotting Mare Goldsmith Maid driven by Budd Doble, The / Trotting in Harness at Buffalo, August 11th, 1871. Mile heats, best three in five — time 2:19¾ 2:19¼; 2:19, beating "Lucy" and "American Girl" / J. Cameron on stone. (Vignette, ¾ to right, high-wheeled sulky.) 1871 S C&I

915 Celebrated Trotting Mare "Goldsmith Maid" driven by Budd Doble, The / Trotting in harness in Milwaukee, Wisconsin, Sept. 6th. 1871. Mile heats, best three in five, time 2:20½;

2:17; 2:20¼ beating "Lucy" and also "Dexter's" best time / J. Cameron on stone. (¾, to right, vignette.)

1871 S C&I

916 Celebrated Trotting Mare Hattie Woodward by Aberdeen, dam by Henry Clay, The / Driven by Gus Wilson / record 2:15½ / From a sketch by France & Gates, St. Louis, and signed on stone. 18.6x27.12 (Broadside to right, high-wheeled sulky.)

1881 L C&I

917 Celebrated Trotting Mare Huntress beating Dutchman's 3 Mile Time, The / 1872 Sept. 23rd, Prospect Fair Grounds, L.I. Purse $1250 — 3 miles with $1000 added to the horse beating Dutchman's time 7:32½ / J. Cameron on stone. (Vignette, high-wheeled sulky, broadside to right.)

1873 S C&I

918 Celebrated Trotting Mare Lady Thorn, Formerly "Maid of Ashland," The / 4 additional lines, 10 additional lines of pedigree and best performances. J. Cameron on stone. 16.13x 26.4 (Skeleton wagon to left, broadside; grandstand in rear.)

1866 L C&I

919 Celebrated Trotting Mare Lady Thorn Formerly "Maid of Ashland," The / (Same as preceding, 4 additional lines and 9 lines of best performances and pedigrees.) 1866 L C&I

920 Celebrated Trotting Mare Lucille Golddust Driven by Chas. S. Greene, The/by Golddust dam by Bald Hornet/ record 2:16¼ / J. Cameron on stone. (Vignette, ¾ to right.)

1877 S C&I

921 Celebrated Trotting Mare Lucy Passing the Judges' Stand, The / In the fourth heat. Winning the prize at Buffalo, N.Y., August 9th, 1872 / 6 additional lines. 16.12x26.8 (¾ view to right, high-wheeled sulky.)

1872 L C&I

922 Celebrated Trotting Mare Lula owned by Mr. Joseph Harker, The / By Alexander's Norman. dam Thoroughbred / J. Cameron on stone. (Vignette.) 1874 S C&I

923 Celebrated Trotting Mare Lula, owned by Mr. Joseph Harker, The / By Alexander's Norman dam Thoroughbred / winner of the first prize $2000 of the Purse $4500 in the Free-for-all mile heats in harness, at the Rochester Driving Park, Aug. 14, 1875, beating Goldsmith Maid, American

Girl and Nettie. The Maid winning the first heat, time 2:15½; 2:16½; 2:15½; 2:17 / Rochester Driving Park, Oct. 14th, 1875, match against time 2:14 Lula to have three trials; purse mile heats in harness. Time 2:16½; 2:14¾; 2:16. This data consists of 2 columns, 4 and 3 lines. (Vignette, ¾ view to right.)   1877 S C&I

924 Celebrated Trotting Mare "Widow McChree" Formerly called "Mary Hoyt", The / Owned by Capt. Isaiah Rynders N. Y. / 5 additional lines. J. Cameron on stone. 16.7x25.10 (Broadside to right, high-wheeled sulky.)   1867 L C&I

925 Celebrated Trotting Mares Maud S. and Aldine, as They Appeared June 15th, 1883, The / at the Gentlemen's Driving Park, Morrisania, N.Y. Driven by their owner William H. Vanderbilt, Esq. / 2 additional lines and record 2:15½. 20.12x33.10 (¾ view, carriage to right.)   1883 L C&I

926 Celebrated Trotting Stallion Alexander by Ben Patchen. dam by Canada Jack, The / Record 2:19 / Painted by Scott Leighton and signed on stone. 18.4x27.12 (High-wheeled sulky to left.)   1882 L C&I

926A Celebrated Trotting Stallion Col. Upton, will, The / Make the season of 1882, at Middleburgh, Schoharie Co., N.Y. Freemyer House Stables / Terms of service $15.00 for the Season; to insure / 3 additional lines and 2 columns 22 and 20 lines description and pedigree & 4 additional lines. (At top) Col. Upton (Above title) 2:31½ (Vignette.)   1881 L C&I

927 Celebrated Trotting Stallion Ethan Allen in Double Harness with Running Mate, The / Driven by Dan Mace trotting against Dexter to sulky on the Fashion Course, L.I., June 21st, 1867 / J. Cameron on stone. (Vignette.)
        1872 S C&I

928 Celebrated Trotting Stallion "France's Alexander" by Ben Patchen, dam by Canada Jack, The / Record 2:19 / Scott Leighton on stone. (Broadside to right, vignette.)
        1882 S C&I

929 Celebrated Trotting Stallion "France's Alexander", The / driven by Gus Wilson / Record 2:19 / Scott Leighton on stone. (High-wheeled sulky to right.)   1882 L C&I

930 Celebrated Trotting Stallion George Wilkes by Rysdyk's Hambletonian,

The / J. Cameron on stone (Vignette.)
        1885 M C&I

931 Celebrated Trotting Stallion George Wilkes by Rysdyk's Hambletonian, The / J. Cameron on stone.
        1885 S C&I

932 Celebrated Trotting Stallion George Wilkes, Formerly "Robert Fillingham", The / by Hambletonian, dam Dolly Spanker, by Mambrino as he appeared in his great race against Lady Thorne / over the Union Course, L.I., June 14th, 1866 / 4 additional lines. J. Cameron on stone. 17.4x26.15 (Broadside to right, skeleton wagon, grandstand and judges stand at right.)
        1866 L C&I

933 Celebrated Trotting Stallion Jay Gould. the Property of H. N. Smith Esq., The / Fashion Stud Farm, Trenton, N. J. / Record 2:21½ / J. Cameron on stone. (Vignette, high-wheeled sulky to left.)   1877 S C&I

934 Celebrated Trotting Stallion Patron by Pancoast, dam by Cuyler, The / record 2:14¼ /.
        1887 S C&I

935 Celebrated Trotting Stallion Smuggler Owned by H. S. Russell, Milton, Mass., The / by Blanco, dam by Herod's Tuckahoe / on the back stretch of the third heat "Coming on" and winning the great stallion race for the championship of the United States / in the presence of [estimated] spectators at Mystic Park, Medford, Mass. Sept. 15th, 1875 / 3 additional lines. J. Cameron on stone. (Horse and rig broadside.)   1875 L C&I

936 Celebrated Trotting Stallion Smuggler Owned by H. S. Russell, Milton, Mass., The / by Blanco, dam by Herod's Tuckahoe / Record 2:16¼ / J. Cameron on stone. (¾ view of horse and rig.)   1876 L C&I

937 Celebrated Trotting Stallion, The / "Woodford Mambrino" / sired by Mambrino Chief, dam Woodbine by Woodford, by Kosciusko / Record 2:21½ / 8.15x12.7 (Stable scene.)
        1878 S C&I

938 Celebrated Trotting Stallions "Ethan Allen" and "George M. Patchen", The / in the first quarter of their great match to wagons for $2000 — mile heats / over the Union Course, L.I. Oct. 28th, 1858 / Ethan Allen winning in the remarkable time of 2:28 / 2 columns of 5 lines. L. Maurer on stone. 17x27.4 (Broadside to right, skeleton

wagons, horses keyed above title.)
1858 L C&I

939 Celebrated Trotting S t a l l i o n s
"Young Woful" and "Abdallah Chief",
The / on the last quarter of their great
five mile race in harness over the Fashion Course, L.I. Nov. 4th, 1865 / time
13:53 / 2 columns of 8 and 7 lines. J.
Cameron on stone. 16.13x25.13 (Broadside to right, high-wheeled sulkies.)
1866 L C&I

940 Celebrated Trotting Team Edward
and Swiveller, Owned by Frank
Work, Esq., N.Y., The / Winning their
match for $1000 against time 2:20 to
wagon, driven by John Murphy / at
the Gentlemen's Driving Park, Morrisania, N.Y. July 18th, 1882 / Record
2:16¾ / Scott Leighton on stone.
Printed in oil colors. 20x34.2 (¾ to
left, skeleton wagon, grandstand in
rear.) 1882 L C&I

941 Celebrated Winning Horses and
Jockeys of the American Turf /
Painted by Chas. Zellinsky.
1888 L C&I

942 Celebrated Winning Horses and
Jockeys of the American Turf / C. L.
Zellinsky, Flatbush, L.I., 1888-9, on
stone. 20.4x34.2 (15 horses and 15
jockeys, keyed.) 1889 L C&I

943 Celebrated Winning Horses and
Jockeys of the American Turf / Painted by Chas. Zellinsky. 1891 L C&I

944 Celebrated Yacht "America," The /
Winner of the "Queens Cup" Value
100 Guineas / In the Royal Yacht
Squadron Match for all nations at
Cowes, England, Aug. 22, 1851 / 9.6x
13.7 (Sailing to left, shore in background.) und S C&I

945 Celebrated Yachts, The / Coronet
and Dauntless / Starting March 12th,
1887 on their great ocean yacht race
from New York / To Roche's Point
Ireland. Won by the Coronet arriving
March 27th. Time 14 days, 19 hours,
56 minutes. The Dauntless arrived
March 28th, Time 16 days, 1 hour, 43
minutes. / 9.8x13.14 (Yachts keyed.)
1887 M C&I

Celeste, Madam **See:** Nos. 3851, 3857.

Cenci, Beatrice **See:** No. 448.

Centennial Exhibition, Philadelphia
See: Nos. 66, 274, 530, 946-7, 978,
2476-7, 2537, 2950, 3850, 3892, 5843.

946 Centennial Bock Bier / The Best can
be had here / 12.6x16.11 (Shows allegorical figures representing different

nationalities drinking, border of print
formed of hops.) 1876 M C&I

947 Centennial Exhibition Buildings,
Philadelphia / 1875 S C&I

948 Central Park in Winter / 8.8x12.7
(Moonlight scene — sleighs in foreground, pond in background.)
und S C&I

949 Central Park — The Bridge / 8x12.9
(Boat in center foreground — 6 swans
on right.) und S C&I

950 Central Park, N.Y. / The Bridge /
8.2x12.10 (Couple on bank, boat in
middle distance, 5 swans.)
und S C&I

951 Central Park, The Drive / 11.2x15.8.
1862 M C&I

952 Central Park, The Lake / 11.2x15.7.
1862 M C&I

953 Central Park, Winter / The Skating
Carnival / 8.1x12.9. und S C&I

954 Central Park, Winter / The Skating
Pond / C. Parsons, Del. 18.6x26.12.
(A very decorative and interesting
New York City view, showing costumes
of the period in detail.)
1862 L C&I

Central Park **See:** Nos. 508, 948-54.

955 Centre Harbor / Lake Winnipiseogee, N.H. / F. F. Palmer, Del. 11.11x
20.7. und L C&I

956 Centreville and Black Douglas /
Centreville Course, L.I., July 21st,
1853 / L. Maurer on stone. 4 additional
lines. 17.3x26.14 (Broadside to right,
skeleton wagons.)
1853 L N.C.

Centreville Course, L.I. Nos. 956,
2015-16, 2018, 2661, 2800, 3380, 3388,
3391, 4742, 5150, 6526.

Cephalonia (Steamship) **See:** No.
5752.

Ceres (Yacht) **See:** No. 5105.

957 Cerito in the Sylphide / #502 / Copyright by Sarony & Major. 8.1x11.12
(Moonlight scene, girl floating over
water as a "butterfly.")
1846 S N.C.

Cerito, **See:** Three Graces, No. 6034.

Cerro Gordo, Mexico **See:** No. 393.

958 Certificate of Baptism /
und S C&I

959 Certificate of Baptism / 8.13x12.13
(In German). und S N.C.

960 Certificate of Honor / Awarded to
.... / Of Co.........., Regt............ /
For bravery and good conduct as a soldier / In the cause of his country /
8.14x12.7 (4 battle and 1 marine
scene.)
1863 S C&I
und V.S. C&I

961 Certificate of Marriage /
und S C&I

962 Ch. Maurice de Tallyrand (Facsimile
signature) / For the Philosophical
Library. Stodart & Currier.
und V.S. N.C.

Challenge (Clippership) See: No.
4439.

Chambers, Arthur See: No. 276.

Champe, Escape of Sergeant See:
No. 1754.

Champion Hills, (Miss.) See: No.
394.

963 Champion in Danger, The / "Golly!
he's got dis Nigga suah, less sumfin
happens" / Thos. Worth on stone.
(Vignette, comic, sculling match.)
1882 S C&I

964 Champion in Luck, The / "Dar — I
know'd sumfin 'ud happen" / Thos.
Worth on stone. (Vignette, comic,
sculling match.) 1882 S C&I

965 Champion Irish Setter Rover, by
Beauty, out of Grace / The property
of Rev. J. Cumming Macdona, England / 8.14x12.12 (Profile of dog to
right.) und S C&I

966 Champion Pacer Direct, by Director / Record 2:06 / J. Cameron on
stone. (¾, to right, high-wheeled sulky.) 1891 S C&I

967 Champion Pacer Direct, by Director / Record 2:05½ / J. Cameron on
stone. (Vignette.) 1891 L C&I

968 Champion Pacer Johnston, by
Bashaw Golddust, The. / Named for
and driven by Peter V. Johnston, of
Chicago / Record 2:10 / J. Cameron
on stone. 18.4x27 Printed in oil colors
by Currier & Ives (¾ broadside, high-
wheeled sulky to left, country road.)
1884 L C&I

969 Champion Pacer Mascot, Record
2:04 / J. C. (Cameron) on stone. (Vignette, ¾ to right, low-wheeled sulky.)
1892 S C&I

970 Champion Pacer Mascot, Record
2:04 / J. Cameron on stone.
und L C&I

971 Champion Race, A / J. Cameron '87

on stone. 18.14x27.14 (¾ view to right,
high-wheeled sulkies, 2 horses shown.)
1887 L C&I

972 Champion Race, A / J. Cameron on
stone. 18.4x27.15 (Small rubber-tired
sulkies, and other changes in composition from preceding, same horses
shown, ¾ to right.)
1894 L C&I

973 Champion Rowist, The Pride of the
Club, The / Thos. Worth on stone.
10.12x15.7. 1876 M C&I

974 Champion Slugger—Knocking Them
Out, The / Edw. D. Kemble, Del.
(White comic, vignette.)
1883 S C&I

975 Champion Stallion, Directum, by
Director, Record 2:05¼ / (¾, low-
wheeled sulky to right, vignette.)
1893 S C&I

976 Champion Stallion "George Wilkes,"
The Great Sire of Trotters, The / By
Rysdyk's Hambletonian, dam Dolly
Spanker by Old Henry Clay / Record
2:22 / J. Cameron on stone. Oleographed by Currier & Ives. 18.5x28.
1888 L C&I

977 Champion Stallion Maxy Cobb by
Happy Medium / Record 2:13¼ / 17.9
x26.8 (High-wheeled sulky to left.)
1885 L C&I

Champion Steer, The / See: "The
Queen of Cattle" No. 5000.

978 "Champion Steer" of the World,
The / Owned and Fattened by George
Ayrault, Po'keepsie, N.Y. / Exhibited
at the Centennial, Philadelphia. 1876 /
3 additional lines. E. F. (E. Forbes)
on stone. 12.12x18.12. 1877 M C&I

979 Champion Trotting Queen Alix,
by Patronage, Record 2:07¾ / L. M.
(Maurer) on stone. 2 additional lines.
(Broadside to left, low-wheeled sulky,
vignette.) 1893 S C&I

980 Champion Trotting Queen "Alix" /
Record 2:03¾ / J. Cameron on stone.
18.10x27.2 (Low wheeled-sulky.)
1894 L C&I

981 Champion Trotting Stallion Nelson, by Young Rolph, dam Gretchen
by Gideon / Owned and driven by C.
H. Nelson, Waterville, Me. / Record
2:10¾ / J. Cameron on stone. 19.10x
27 (High-wheeled sulky, ¾ to right.)
1891 L C&I

982 Champion Trotting Stallion Nelson, by Young Rolph, dam Gretchen
by Gideon, The / Bred, owned and
driven by C. H. Nelson, Waterville,

Maine / Record 2:09 / (Same stone as preceding with exception of change in title and record.)   1891 L C&I

983 Champion Trotting Stallion Smuggler, The / Owned by H. S. Russell, Milton, Mass. / By Blanco, dam by Herod's Tuckahoe / On the backstretch in the third heat "coming away" and winning the great stallion race for the championship of the United States / In the presence of [estimated] Forty Thousand spectators at Mystic Park, Medford, Mass. Sept. 15th, 1874 / 3 additional lines. J. Cameron on stone. 16.12x26.4 (Broadside view to right, 5 other rigs trailing on left, grandstand shown on right.)
1875 L C&I

984 Champion Trotting Stallion Smuggler, Owned by H. S. Russell, Milton, Mass., The / By Blanco, dam by Herod's Tuckahoe / Record 2:16¾ / J. Cameron on stone. 17x26.12 (¾ view to right, high-wheeled sulky. 4 other rigs shown at left.)   1876 L C&I

985 Champions at Close Quarters / J. Cameron on stone. 18.2x28.4 (4 high-wheeled sulkies and horses.)
1892 L C&I

986 Champion at Close Quarters / J. Cameron on stone. 18.2x28.4 (Similar composition to preceding, but sulkies have small rubber tires.)
1894 L C&I

987 Champions of the Ball Racket, The / "At the Close of the Season" / (Vignette, colored comic.)   1885 S C&I

988 Champions of the Ball Racket, The / "On the Diamond Field" / (vignette, colored comic.)   1886 S C&I

989 Champions of the Barn, The / W. M. Cary on stone. 9.3x13.2 (Group of cows, chickens, ducks, etc.)
1876 S C&I

990 Champions of the Barn Yard /
und S C&I

991 Champions of the Field, The / Steady on a Point / F. P. (Palmer) on stone. (Brown setter and white pointer, profile to right.)
und S C&I

992 Champions of the Mississippi, The / "A Race for the Buckhorns" F. F. Palmer, Del. 18.4x27.14 (Steamers "Queen of the West," "Morning Star," and two others in a close finish, moonlight scene, crowd on shore around fire.)   1866 L C&I

993 Champions of the Union, The / 14.2 x20 (General Scott, General McClellan, General Wool and 22 other officers, vignette, round top.) 1861 M C&I

Champlain, Lake See: No. 4398.

994 Chance for Both Barrels, A / Painted by A. F. Tait. 18.10x26.12 (Same stone as American Field Sports / "A Chance for Both Barrels" No. 148.)
1857 L C&I

Chancellorsville, Va. See: No. 395.

995 Chances of Billiards, The / "A Scratch All Around" / 16.6x24.14 (Dog and cat fight interrupts game. Companion to "The Beauties of Billiards" No. 450.   1869 L C&I

996 "Chang" and "Eng" / The World Renowned United Siamese Twins / Now Exhibiting at Barnum's American Museum, New York / (At top) "Barnum's Gallery of Wonders No. 17." 12x9 (Full-length portraits, surrounded by 7 small views. Plowing, chopping trees, fishing, rowing, riding, etc., upright.)   1860 S C&I

997 Change of Base, A / "I jist done got a call to anodder congregation" / Thos. Worth on stone. (Vignette, colored comic, winter scene, companion to "Surprise Party" #5901.)   1883 S C&I

998 Change of drivers under the Rule, A / (Above title) The Man who drives to win & the man who "pulls" his horse. Rule 28 — If the judges believe a horse has been "Pulled" they shall substitute a Competent and reliable driver / Thos. Worth on stone. 10.15x15.1 (Shows a man bribing a fat man to drive in place of a thin one.)   1876 M C&I

999 Changed Man, A / This Man by his wife's advice / Bought one of our suits so nice / Reader; his advice to you / is "Walk in, and do so too" / J. Cameron on stone. (2 views on 1 sheet, before and after. Clothier's ad.)
1880 S C&I

Chapultepec, Mexico See: Nos. 302, 2247.

1000 Chappaqua Farm / West Chester County, New York / The Residence of Hon. Horace Greeley / 8.8x12.8.
1872 S C&I

1001 Charles / #178 (Full-length figure, interior, river scene through window, upright.)   1845 S N.C.

1002 Charles / (Printed with black background and used as a fire screen.)
und L C&I

1003 Charles F. Adams / Free Soil Candidate for Vice President / From a daguerreotype by Plumbe #622 / 11.7x 8.15 (¾ length, book in hand, red curtain, upright.) 1848 S N.C.

1004 Charles Gavan Duffy / "Educate that you may be free" / #675 / 8.15x 11.6 (¾ length, seated, red curtain, open window at right, upright.) 1849 S N.C.

1005 Charles O. Scott. The Prize Baby in 1855 / Exhibited at Barnum's Museum /. 1855 V.S. N.C.

1006 Charles Rowell / The Celebrated Pedestrian / 4 additional lines. 12.13x 9.2 (Full length, upright.) 1879 S C&I

1007 Charles Stewart Parnell, M.P. / The great land agitator. President of the Irish Land League / und S C&I

1008 Charles Stewart Parnell, M.P. / President of the Irish Land League, addressing a meeting / J. G. Biggar, M.P., T. Sexton, M.P., J. W. Sullivan, M.P., Patrick Egan, M.P., T. M. Healy, M.P. 13.1x9.6 (Upright.) 1881 S C&I

1009 Charles Sumner / und S C&I

1010 Charles Wesley, A.M. / und S N.C.

Charleston See: Virginia.

1011 Charley Ford / By Ferguson's Grey Eagle / Record 2:16¾ / (¾ broadside to right, high-wheeled sulky, vignette.) 1880 S C&I

1012 Charley / The Prize Baby Boy / (Charles O. Scott.) 1857 S C&I

1013 "Charlie is my Darling" / 11.15x8 (Boy in Highland costume.) 1872 S C&I

1014 Charlotte / (Half length, back view, head turned to left, yellow shawl, red curtain.) und S N.C.

1015 Charlotte / #118 (¾ length, seated, bird resting on finger, round top corners.) und S N.C.

1016 Charlotte / #118 (¾ length seated, similar to preceding.) 1845 S N.C.

1017 Charlotte / #118 / 12.3x8.13 (Full length on balcony, bird on hand, marine scene.) 1845 S N.C.
Charter Oak, Hartford, Conn. See: No. 2930.

1018 Charter Oak! Charter Oak! Ancient and Fair! / An ancient American Ballad / written by / Mrs. Sigourney / 8 additional lines. Published by Hewitt & Jaques. (Music sheet, vignette scene.) und S N.C.

1019 Chase — In the Olden Time, The / und S N.C.
Chateau D'Eau / See: France.
Chateaugay Lake See: New York State.

1020 Chatham Square, New York / #609 / F. P. on stone. 8.1x12.10. und S N.C.
Chattanooga, Tenn. See: No. 396.
Chattanooga Railroad See: Railroad.

1021 Check, A / "Keep your distance" / Painted by A. F. Tait. O. Knirsch on stone. 14.4x20.7 (Companion to "The Prairie Hunter" No. 4861.) 1853 L N.C.
Chepstow Castle, (Eng.) See: Ruins.

1022 Chepstow Ruins / South Wales / (Winter scene, oval.) und V.S. C&I

1023 Cherry Time / F. F. Palmer, Del. 9.15x13.15 (Various kinds of birds eating cherries.) 1866 M C&I

1024 Chester A. Arthur / (Vignette, upright.) und S C&I

1025 Chestnut Hill / Sired by Strothmore, he by Rysdyk's Hambletonian / dam Polly Barbey, by Bully King, by Geo. M. Patchen / Record 2:22½ / J. C. (Cameron) on stone. (Broadside to right, high-wheel sulky. Vignette.) 1879 S C&I

1026 Chicago, as it was / 8.6x12.14 (Birds-eye view, 6 keys.) und S C&I

1027 Chicago in Flames / Scene at Randolph Street Bridge / 8.8x12.8. und S C&I
Chicago,(Ill.) See: Nos. 738, 1026-7, 1094-6, 2615, 6393.
Chicago (U.S. Cruiser) See: No. 6644.
Chicago Race Track See: No. 2933.

1028 Chicago Platform and Candidate, The / Union soldier, Jeff's Friend, Jeff, Vallandingham, Mac, Fernando, Peace Democrat / (Vignette.) und M C&I
Chickamauga See: No. 397.

1029 Chicky's Dinner / 8.8x11.8. und S C&I

1030 Chief Cook and Bottle Washers / #774 / 8.6x13 (Kitchen scene, monkeys working. Companion to "Power of Music" No. 4858.) und S N.C.

1031 Child Jesus, The /. und S C&I

1032 Childhood's Happy Days / 11.5x 15.12 (5 children by roadside, picking flowers, path in woods at left.) 1863 M C&I

1033 Children in the Woods, The / 11.14x 8.8 (Full length, boy and girl.) und S C&I

1034 Children in the Woods, The / 1867 S C&I

1035 Children's Pic-nic, The / 12.6x9.3 (Group of children at swing, upright.) und S C&I

1036 Chincha Islands, The / Distance 5 miles north west by W. Sketched by Mr. H. Herryman, June 21, 1860. Wm. B. Coville, Publisher, Callao. / 7.13x 13.14. 1860 S C&I

1037 Chinese Junk Keying, The / Capt. Kellett / As she appeared in New York Harbor, July 13th, 1847, 212 days from Canton — 720 tons burthen / #479 / 7.14x13.1 (2 columns, 6 lines each.) 1847 S N.C.

1038 Chip of the Old Block, A / 15x20.15 (Young pup showing a rat it caught to parent.) und L N.C.

1039 Choice Apples / (Vignette, basket on side.) und S C&I

1040 Choice Bouquet, A / 8.7x12.8(Roses, morning glories in basket, bird's nest with eggs, black background.) 1872 S C&I

1041 Choice Bouquet, A / (Vignette, entirely different composition, roses, tiger lilies, in openwork basket.) 1874 S C&I

1042 Choice Fruit / 1865 L C&I

1043 Choice Fruits / (Apples, peaches, pears, plums, grapes, etc., oval about 5x7, on same sheet with "Ripe Fruits" No. 5148.) und V.S. C&I

1044 Choice Segars and Fine Tobacco / (Tobacco ad.) und S C&I

1045 Christ and the Angels / Le Cristo A Los Angels — Le Christ aux Angels / 11.11x8.6 (Christ nailed to cross, 2 angels kneeling, 4 cherubs.) und S C&I

1046 Christ and the Woman of Samaria at Jacobs Well / Title repeated in French / #36 / 12.6x8.12. und S N.C.

1047 Christ and the Woman of Samaria at Jacobs Well / Title repeated in French / 12.4x8.13. und S C&I

1048 Christ at the Well / #33 / 11.14x 8:10 (Full length, rounded corners.) 1846 S N.C.

1049 Christ at the Well / "Whosoever shall drink of the water that I shall give him shall never thirst" / #38 / 12.1x7.13. und S N.C.

1050 Christ at the Well / und S C&I

1051 Christ Bearing His Cross / #196 / 10.2x7.15 (Men on sides pulling him with rope, and soldiers.) und S N.C.

1052 Christ Bearing His Cross / Title repeated in Spanish and French #196 / 12.11x8.12 / (Composition similar to preceding print, ornamental borders.) 1847 S N.C.

1053 Christ Before Pilate / #195 / 12.11x 8.15 (Ornamental border, upright.) 1847 S N.C.

1054 Christ Before Pilate / und S C&I

1055 Christ Before Pilate / "He delivers Him up to Be Crucified" / Passion 1st at top / 9.14x7.13. und S N.C.

1056 Christ Blessing Little Children / Title repeated in Spanish / #286 / 11.11 x8.5 (2 disciples, 5 children, other figures behind full-length figure of Christ.) und S N.C.

1057 Christ Blessing Little Children / Jesu Christo Benedeciendo Criatures / #266. und S N.C.

1058 Christ Blessing Little Children / Suffer little children, etc., / 11.15x8.9 (2 disciples, 5 children, no figures behind Christ.) und S N.C.

1059 Christ Blessing the Children / und S C&I

1060 Christ Healing the Sick / 2 line Biblical quotation. 12.11x8.3 (Full-length figure of Christ, woman and child, and disciples in group of sick to be healed.) und S C&I

1061 Christ in the Garden (At the top) / Of Gethsemane (At the bottom) / und S C&I

1062 Christ in the Garden of Olives / und S N.C.

1063 Christ is our Light / Our Star of / Redemption / this star is so constructed so that its motto may be read

258, 253, 326, different ways from the center to every point / #656 / 12.11x9.4 (Star fills entire print.)
1849 S N.C.

1064 Christ is our Light — Our Star of Redemption / (Star fills entire print, made up of letters in title.)
1866 S C&I

1065 Christ Restoreth The Blind / El Señor da Vista a un Ciego / 2 additional lines.   1846 S N.C.

1066 Christ Restoreth The Blind / 2 additional lines.   und S C&I

1067 Christ Restoreth The Blind / 2 additional lines of Biblical quotations / #36 / 12.1x8.9 (No Spanish.)
1846 S N.C.

1068 Christ Stilling the Tempest / "Then He arose and rebuked the winds and the sea and there was a great calm" / Matt. VIII:26 / 7.13x12.7.
1871 S C&I

1069 Christ the Consoler / One line quotation from the Bible / 8.12x11.18 (Full-length figure of Christ; Mary Magdalene, 2 figures kneeling, Negro, group of others.)   und S C&I

1070 Christ Walking on the Sea / 2 additional lines of Biblical quotation / #37.   und S N.C.

1071 Christ Walking on the Sea / "But when they saw Him walking upon the sea, they supposed it had been a Spirit and cried out." / St. Mark VI:49 / 7.14 x12.9.   und S C&I

1072 Christ Washing His Disciples' Feet / #162.   und S N.C.

1073 Christ Weeping Over Jerusalem / 1 line quotation from the Bible / 7.15x 12.7 (Full-length figure of Christ; 7 disciples, shepherd with flock, buildings of Jerusalem. Slightly rounded corners.)   und S C&I

1074 Christ Weeping Over Jerusalem / El Señor lament anpose de Jerusalem/ #211 /   1847 S N.C.

1075 Christ's Entry Into Jerusalem / and the Multitude that went before and that followed, cried saying "Hosanna to the Son of David: Blessed is He that cometh in the Name of the Lord." St. Matt. XXI: 9 / 7.14x12.6 (Jesus riding a donkey, crowds bearing palm leaves. Slightly rounded corners.)
und S C&I

1076 Christ's Sermon on the Mount / The Parable of the Lily / 2 additional

lines of Biblical quotation / 11.15x17.6 (Round top.)   1866 M C&I

1077 Christ's Sermon on the Mount / The Parable of the Lily /
1866 S C&I

1078 Christening, The / #590 / (Man and woman at font, priest holding baby.)
und S N.C.

1079 Christian's Hope, The / (Vignette, clinging to cross "Rock of Ages".)
1874 S C&I

1080 Christian's Refuge, The / 10.6x 14.6.   1868 M C&I

1081 Christmas Snow / 7.15x4.15 (3 boys carrying Christmas trees, a cottage in the distance. On same sheet with "Ride to School" No. 5140, upright.)   und V.S. C&I

1082 Christopher Columbus / Discoverer of America, 1492 / Painted by Emilie Chaese from the Yanez and Puebla portraits in the National Museum at Madrid (Vignette, hand resting on globe.)   1892 L C&I

1083 Christus Consolator / Come unto Me, all ye that labor, etc., / #531 / 8.6x12.6.   und S N.C.

1084 Christus Consolatus /
und S C&I

Churubusco See: No. 398.
Cider Making See: No. 322.
Cilley, John See: 2917.
Cimbria (Steamship) See: No. 3780.
Cincinnati, Ohio (Track) See: No. 6206.
"Circulating Medium", A / See: "A Wild-Cat Banker" No. 6663.

1085 City Hall and County Courthouse, Newark, N.J. / E. Brown Jr., Del. 7.4x 11.8.   und S N.C.

1086 City Hall, New York / #597 / 8x12.6 J. Schutz on stone. (View from southeast.)   und S N.C.

1087 City Hall, New York / #597 / 8.4x 12.8 (View from southwest.)
und S N.C.

1088 City Hall and Vicinity, New York City / New Court House, Staats Zietung, French's Hotel, Sun Building / 8.6x12.7.   und S C&I
City Hall See: New York City.

1089 City Hotel / Broadway, New York / Gardner & Packer, Proprietors / W. K. Hewitt, Del. 15.4x22.4.
und L N.C.

1090 City of Baltimore, The /
1880 L C&I
   City of Baltimore (Steamship)
No. 5753.
   City of Berlin (Steamship) No.
5754.

1091 City of Boston, The / Parsons &
Atwater, Del. (10 lines of keys.)
1873 L C&I

1092 City of Brooklyn /
1879 L C&I

1093 City of Brooklyn / This certifies
that —— having served for 7 years
——, etc. / (Fireman's certificate.)
und S N.C.

1094 City of Chicago, The / 20.11x32.7
(Bird's-eye view, 69 references. 6
lines.) 1892 L C&I

1095 City of Chicago, The / Sketched
and drawn on stone by Parsons & Atwater. (Bird's-eye view, 6 lines of
keys.) 1874 L C&I

1096 "City of Chicago" (Steamship.)
1892 L C&I

1097 City of Jungo / 1840 S N.C.

1098 City of Mexico — vista de Mexico /
from the convent of San Cosme — des
de el convento dela Cosme / #555 /
8.2x12.6. 1847 S N.C.
   City of Montreal (Steamship) See:
Nos. 742, 5755.

1099 City of New Orelans, The / And
the Mississippi River. Lake Pontchartrain in the distance / 21.4x35.4
(41 keys, bird's-eye view.)
1885 L C&I

1100 City of New Orleans / Levee, St.
Charles Hotel, Canal Street, Custom
House, Jackson Square, Market, Lake
Pontchartrain. 8x12.10 (Bird's-eye
view.) und S C&I

1101 City of New York / (Bird's-eye
view, Castle Garden, Battery, Gover-
nors Island.) 1844 S N.C.

1102 City of New York / 33 references
in 5 lines / Sketched and drawn on
stone by C. Parsons. 20.14x29. (Bird's-
eye view.) 1855 L N.C.

1103 City of New York / 33 references
in 5 lines / Sketched and drawn on
stone by C. Parsons. (Bird's-eye view
from south — Commonwealth, Metropolis, Plymouth Rock. Boats shown,
very similar to "View of New York,
Jersey City, etc." No. 6406.)
1856 L N.C.

1104 City of New York, The / 48 references / 20.6x32.13. 1870 L C&I

1105 City of New York, The / 40 references in 6 lines. 20.5x32.13 (Bird's-eye
view looking north from east of Gov-
ernors Island. Steamers: City of New
York, Bristol, Old Colony shown.)
1870 L C&I

1106 City of New York, The / 55 references. (Bird's-eye view.)
1884 L C&I

1107 City of New York, The / Sketched
and on stone by Parsons & Atwater.
75 references. (Bird's-eye from south.)
1876 L C&I

1108 City of New York, The /
1886 L C&I

1109 City of New York, The /
1889 L C&I

1110 City of New York, The /
1892 L C&I

1111 City of New York and Environs /
10 references in 2 lines. 8.9x13.2
(Bird's-eye view from Jersey City.)
1875 S C&I

1112 City of New York / From Jersey
City / #626 / 9 names of buildings.
8.2x12.10. 1849 S N.C.

1113 City of New York, The / showing
the Buildings of the Equitable Life
Assurance Society of the United
States, No. 120 Broadway #1108 / 21.8
x33.12. 1876 L C&I

1114 City of New York, The / Showing
the Building of / The Equitable Life
Assurance Society of the United
States, No. 120 Broadway. / 22.4x35.1
(Bird's-eye view.) 1876 L C&I

   City of New York (Steamship) See:
No. 3879.

   City of Paris (Steamship) See: No.
3880.

1115 "City of Peking," Pacific Mail
Steamship Co. / 1 additional line.
und S C&I

1116 City of Philadelphia, The / 60 keys
/ Sketched and Drawn by Parsons &
Atwater. 1876 L C&I

   City of Rome (Steamship) See:
Nos. 3876, 3881.

1117 City of St. Louis, The / 33 references in 4 lines. Sketched and drawn
on stone by Parsons & Atwater. 20.8x
32.10 (Bird's-eye view.)
1874 L C&I

1118 City of San Francisco / 23 references. 8.6x13.4 (Bird's-eye view.)
1877 S C&I

1119 City of San Francisco, The / (Bird's-eye view from the Bay looking southwest, keys.)   1889 L C&I

1120 The City of San Francisco Sketched and Drawn by C. R. Parsons / (Bird's-eye view from the Bay looking southwest.)   1878 L C&I

1121 City of Vera Cruz, — Vista de Vera Cruz / From the road to Mexico Por el camino do Mexico / 8.4x12.6.
1847 S N.C.

1122 City of Washington, The / Bird's-eye view from the Potomac — Looking North. / 54 keys in 7 lines. C. R. Parsons, Del.   1880 L C&I

1123 City of Washington, The / Bird's-eye view from the Potomac — Looking North / 59 references. 20.9x33.2.
1892 L C&I

City of Washington (Steamship) See: No. 5756.

1124 Clam Boy — On his Muscle /
und S C&I

1125 Clara / #254 (¾ length, seated, flowers in urn in right background.)
und S N.C.

1126 Clara / #254 / 12.4x8.11 (Full length in doorway, black lace shawl, white dress, moonlight scene, fountain in background, upright.)
1849 S N.C.

1127 Clara /   und S C&I

1128 Clarissa / Copyright Sarony and Major. (Full length.) 1846 S N.C.

Clark, Aaron See: No. 1.

Clay, Cassius See: No. 838.

Clay, Henry See: Nos. 537, 1488-9, 1491-2, 2511-2, 2783-97.

Clay, Death of Henry. See: Nos. 1491-2.

1129 "Clean Sweep, A" / Thos. Worth on stone. (Poolroom scene, colored comic, vignette. Companion to "Bustin the Pool" No. 756.)
1889 S C&I

1130 Clear Grit / (Dog and rat.)
und S C&I

1131 "Clearing, A" / On the American Frontier / 8.7x12.7.   und S C&I

1132 Clearing, The /   und S C&I

Cleveland, Grover See: Nos. 1133-5, 2143, 2457, 2673, 3256, 4637, 4821-2, 4873-5.

Cleveland, Mrs. Grover See: No. 666.

1133 Cleveland Family, The /
1893 S N.C.

1134 Cleveland Family, The / 18.5x23.12 (¾ length.)   1893 L C&I

1135 Cleveland Smile, The / (Caricature of Cleveland wearing tricorn hat and glasses, vignette.)   und S C&I

Cleveland Track (Ohio) See: Nos. 2663, 5930.

1136 Clifton Hall, Bristol Col., Pa. / W. K. Hewitt, Del. on stone. 10.2x13.10 (Front view, on same sheet as "Pennsylvania Hall, Bristol College, Pa." No. 4744.)   1835 S N.C.

Cliff Castle See: No. 4778.

1137 Clingstone — Record 2:14 / 2.13x 4.12.   1882 V.S. C&I

1138 Clingstone / By Rysdyk's dam Gretchen, by Hambletonian / driven by T. Dunbar (¾, to right, high-wheeled sulky.)   1882 S C&I

Clingstone (Horse) See: Nos. 1137-8, 2528-9, 6173.

Clinton, DeWitt See: No. 1576.

1139 Clipper Ship "Adelaide" / Off Sandy Hook "Hove to for a Pilot" / Sketched by J. Smith & Son, Brooklyn, L.I. / On stone by Parsons. 16x24.8. (First state, also published as "Hove to for A Pilot" No. 2962.)
1856 L C&I

1140 Clipper Ship "Comet" of New York / In a Hurricane off Bermuda, on her Voyage from New York to San Francisco, Oct. 2, 1852 / E. C. Gardner, Commander. / C. Parsons, Del. 16.2x 23.10.   1855 L N.C.

1141 "Clipper Ship Contest" / (Above title) To Danl. D. Westervelt, Esq., Builder of the New York / Clipper Ship Contest / (Below title) This print is respectfully dedicated by the Publisher / 2 columns, £ and 4 lines. F. F. Palmer, Lith. 16x23.2.
1853 L N.C.

1142 Clipper Ship "Cosmos", The / 10.4 x14.14.   und M C&I

1143 Clipper Ship "Dreadnought" (exact title) To David Ogden, Esq., this print of the / Clipper Ship Dreadnought / Off Sandy Hook, Feb. 23rd, 1854, nineteen days from Liverpool / is respectfully dedicated by the Publisher / 2 columns, 4 and 5 lines. C. Parsons, Del. 16.8x24.4 (Later impressions have been made from this stone.)
1854 L N.C.

1144 Clipper Ship Dreadnought — off Tuskar Light / 12½ days from New York on her celebrated Passage into dock at Liverpool in 13 days, 11 hours Decr. 1854 / To her Commander, S. Samuels, Esq. This Print is respectfully dedicated by the Publisher / C. H. Parsons, Del. D. McFarlane pinxt. 16.2x24.10 (Moonlight scene, later impressions were made from this stone.)
1856 L N.C.

1145 Clipper Ship "Flying Cloud" / (exact title) To Messrs. Grinnell Minturn & Co. This print of their splendid / Clipper Ship "Flying Cloud" / is respectfully dedicated by the publisher / 2 columns, 3 and 4 lines. E. Brown Jr., Del. / 16.8x23.15 (Later impressions were made from this print.)
1852 L N.C.

1146 Clipper Ship "Great Republic" / (exact title) To Donald McKay, Esq., Builder of the Leviathan / Clipper Ship "Great Republic" / This print is respectfully dedicated. / 2 columns, of 2 lines. Painted by J. E. Buttersworth. 16x23.6.
1853 L N.C.

1147 Clipper Ship "Great Republic" / Built by Donald McKay, Esq., at East Boston, Mass. 1853 — Capt. Limeburner / Burnt to water's edge at New York, Decr. 1853, rebuilt 1854. A.A. Low & Brothers, Owners, New York / 2 columns of 2 lines. Drawn by J. B. Smith & Son, Brooklyn. On stone by C. Parsons. 16.4x24.
1855 L N.C.

1148 Clipper Ship "Great Republic" #347 / 1 additional line dimensions. 8.5x12.9 (Ship broadside to left, not vignette.)
und S N.C.

1149 Clipper Ship "Great Republic" / #363 / 1 additional line dimensions. 8.15x12.7. (Slight changes in composition from preceding.)
und S N.C.

1150 Clipper Ship "Great Republic" / #347 / 1 additional line dimensions. (Sailing to left—vignette.)
und S C&I

1151 Clipper Ship "Great Republic" / 1 additional line of dimensions. (Vignette, sailing to right.)
und S C&I

1152 Clipper Ship "Great Republic" / 1 additional line dimensions. (Similar to preceding, but with changes in composition and ship in distance, under bowsprit—vignette.)
und S C&I

1153 Clipper Ship "Hurricane" / of New York / 2 columns, 4 and 3 lines. F. F. Palmer, Del. 14.8x21.12.
1852 L N.C.

1154 Clipper Ship In a Hurricane, A / 11.4x16. (The ship shown in this print is the clipper ship "Comet.")
1855 M C&I

1155 Clipper Ship in a Hurricane, A / 8.15x12.7. (Composition same as preceding, second state, plate has been cut down in size.)
und S C&I

1156 Clipper Ship in a Hurricane, A / 8.15x12.7. (Third state, composition identical to preceding but lifeboat in rear of ship has been removed.)
und S C&I

1157 Clipper Ship in a Snow Squall, A / 8.8x12.8.
und S C&I

1158 Clipper Ship "Lightning" (exact title) To James Baines & Co. This print of the / Clipper Ship "Lightning" / Built by Donald McKay, Boston, Mass. / is respectfully dedicated by the Publisher / C. Parsons, Del. 2 columns, 4 and 2 lines.
1854 L N.C.

1159 Clipper Ship "Nightingale" / Getting under weigh off the Battery, New York / C. Parsons, Del. 16.5x24.
1854 L N.C.

1160 Clipper Ship "Ocean Express" / Outward bound "Discharging The Pilot" / Sketched by J. Smith & Son, Brooklyn, L. I. On stone by C. Parsons. 16.3x24.4. (Same stone as "Discharging the Pilot" No. 1584.)
1856 L N.C.

1161 Clipper Ship Off Cape Horn, A / (Same as "A Squall Off Cape Horn" Nos. 5679-80.)
und S C&I

1162 Clipper Ship Off the Port / (Same as "Off the Port" No. 4544.)
und S C&I

1163 Clipper Ship "Queen of Clippers" / #386 / Title in plate.
und S N.C.

1164 Clipper Ship "Racer" / (exact title) To D. L. Lawrence, Esq. This print of the / Clipper Ship "Racer" / is respectfully dedicated by the Publisher. / 2 columns, 4 and 5 lines. C. Parsons, Del. 16.4x24.2.
1854 L N.C.

1165 Clipper Ship "Red Jacket" / in the ice off Cape Horn on her passage from Australia to Liverpool, August,

1854 / Built by Geo. Thomas, Esq., at Rockland, Me., 1853, for Messrs. Secomb & Taylor, Boston, Mass. / Drawn by J. B. Smith & Son, Brooklyn, L. I. On stone by C. Parsons. 16.4x23.12. (Ship broadside to left.)
1855 L N.C.

1166 Clipper Ship "Red Jacket" / In the ice off Cape Horn on her passage from Australia to Liverpool / (Vignette, composition reversed, ship broadside to right.) und S C&I

1167 Clipper Ship "Sovereign of the Seas" (exact title) / To Donald McKay, Esq., Builder of the Magnificent /Clipper Ship "Sovereign of the Seas" /This print is respectfully dedicated by the Publisher. / E. Brown Jr., Del. 2 columns, 3 and 4 lines. 15.12x23.12.
1852 L N.C.

1168 Clipper Ship "Sweepstakes" (exact title) To Aaron J. Westervelt, Esq., Builder of the New York / Clipper Ship "Sweepstakes" / This print is respectfully dedicated by the publisher. / W. A. MacGill, Comdr. / F. F. Palmer, Lith. 2 columns of 4 and 3 lines. 16.5x23.10. (Later impressions have been made from this stone.)
1853 L N.C.

1169 Clipper Ship "Three Brothers," 2972 tons / The largest sailing ship in the world / 2 columns, 2 lines (George Cumming, Captain) 18.6x 27.14. (There are later impressions from this stone.) 1875 L C&I

1170 Clipper Ship "Three Brothers" / Formerly Steamship "Vanderbilt" / 1 additional line of dimensions. 8.10x12.6. und S C&I

1171 Clipper Ship "Young America" / (exact title) To George Daniels, Esq., Owner of the New York / Clipper Ship "Young America" / This print is respectfully dedicated by the publisher / 2 columns, 3 and 4 lines. F. Palmer, Lith. 16x23.4. 1853 L N.C.

Clipper Ships See: Nos. 113-4, 119, 353, 740, 875-7, 1584, 2962, 4439, 4536, 4543-4, 4666.

1172 Clipper Ships Homeward Bound / 8x12.6. und S C&I

1173 Clipper Yacht "America", The / Built by George Steers of New York for John C. Stevens, Esq., and associates of the New York Yacht Club. F. F. Palmer, Lith. 2 columns, 7 lines of dimensions. (Sailing to right— Yachts "Capricorn" "Gipsey Queen" "Xarifa" and "Surprise" keyed.)
und M N.C.

1174 Clipper Yacht "America," The / Review of the Royal Yacht Squadron Cup, value £100, in the great match for all nations / (Sailing to left.)
und M N.C.

1175 Clipper Yacht "America," The / Winner of the Royal Yacht Squadron Cup, 1851. / Built by Mr. George Steers of New York for Jno. C. Stevens, Esq., and associates of the New York Yacht Club /
und M N.C.

1176 Clipper Yacht "America," The / Of New York / Winner of the "Cup" in the great match for all nations at Cowes, August 22nd, 1851 / 2 columns, 5 and 7 lines. (Sailing to left.)
und S N.C.

Clonmacnoise See: No. 5471.

Clonmel See: No. 6147.

Clontarf (Battle) See: No. 399.

1177 Close Calculation, A / Don't you wish you may get it?/ #461 / 8.7x12.14. (Monkey holding his tail just beyond reach of chained dog.)
und S N.C.

1178 Close Finish, A / J. Cameron on stone. (Vignette.) 1874 S C&I

1179 "Close Heat, A" / Judge Fullerton, Gazelle, and Huntress. / Trotting at Fleetwood Park, Morrisania, N. Y., June 26th, 1873 / 6 additional lines. (Above title) Bay Mare Gazelle, driven by J. Lovett—Bay Mare Huntress, driven by A. Goldsmith—Champion Gelding Judge Fullerton, driven by Dan Mace. J. Cameron on stone. 16.12x26. (¾ view, high-wheeled sulky to left.) 1873 L C&I

1180 Close Lap on the Run In, A / 18x27.9 (¾ broadside, 3 horses under saddle to right.) 1886 L C&I

1181 Close Quarters / F. F. Palmer, Del. 25x19.12. (Large head of dog, woodcock lower right, upright. Companion to "Pointing a Bevy" No. 4817.)
1866 L C&I

1182 Coaching—Four In Hand / A Swell turn out / 11x15.13.
1876 M C&I

Coal Harbor, Va. See: No. 400.

Cochrane, John See: No. 2470.

1183 Cock-a-Doodle-do / (Rooster)
und S C&I

Cock Fighting See: Nos. 620, 1249, 2214-6, 3893.

1184 Cock of the Walk, The / Who with endurance passing all creation / Beat

the best walkers of the British nation / Mile after mile rolled up in figures thrifty / Until the score stood five hundred and fifty / (above title) E. P. Weston, Long Distance Champion of the World. (Shows Weston carrying off the winning belt, crippled Englishman watching. Ship "First Ship for the U. S." in background.) T. W. (Worth) on stone. (Vignette.)
1879 S C&I

1185 Cod Fishing—Off Newfoundland / 8.7x12.7.   1872 S C&I
Coenties Slip, N. Y. See: Nos. 6413-4.

1186 Col. E. L. Snow / Drawn on stone by F. Davignon. 4 lines of verse. (Tinted background, vignette.)
und S C.C.

1187 Col. Edward D. Baker / U. S. Senator from Oregon Commanding the first California Regiment / Killed while fighting in defense of the Union at the battle of Ball's Bluff near / Leesburg, Va., Oct. 21st, 1861 / (¾ length, vignette.)   und S C&I

1188 Col. Elmer E. Ellsworth / 1st Regt. New York Fire Zouaves / Assassinated at the capture of Alexandria, May 24th, 1861 / 2 additional lines of quotation.)   und S C&I

1189 Col. Elmer E. Ellsworth / (Balance title same as preceding but changes in composition and vignetted.)
und S C&I

1190 Col. Elmer E. Ellsworth / 1st Regt. New York Fire Zouaves / Assassinated at the capture of Alexandria, May 24th, 1861 / "He who noteth even the fall of a sparrow will have some purpose even in the fate of one like me" —Elmer /   und S C&I

1191 Col. Frank P. Blair, Jr. / First Regiment Missouri Volunteers / (¾ length, vignette.)   1861 S C&I

1192 Col. Fremont's Last Grand Exploring Expedition in 1856 / (Fremont on "Abolition Nag" with head of man led by Seward; one figure with a number of rifles on back; another in frontier costume. Hills in background marked "Kansas" and "Nebraska." For sale at 2 Spruce Street. Vignette.)
und S N.C.

1193 Col. H. S. Russell's Smuggler, by Blanco, dam by Herod's Tuckahoe / The great champion Trotting Stallion of the World!! / Record 2:15¼ / J. Cameron on stone. (Vignette, high-

wheeled sulky to left.)
1876 S C&I

1194 Col. Harney at the dragoon fight at Medelin, near Vera Cruz / March 25th, 1847 / #456 / 8.6x12.8 (Harney in foreground on white horse, lance in left hand, sword in right.)
1847 S N.C.

1195 Col. John E. Wool /
1847 S N.C.

1196 Col. John O'Mahoney / Head center of the Fenian Brotherhood / (Vignette.)   und S C&I

1197 Col. James A. Mulligan / Of the Illinois "Irish Brigade" / (¾ length; telescope in left hand, vignette.)
und S C&I

1198 Col. Max Weber / Of the 20th |New York Turners| Rifle Regiment / (Vignette, ¾ length.)   und S C&I

1199 Col. Michael Corcoran / at the battle of Bull Run, Va., July 21st, 1861 / The desperate and bloody charge of the "Gallant Sixty-Ninth" on the rebel batteries / 8.2x12.8.
und S C&I

1200 Col. Michael Corcoran / Commanding the Sixty-Ninth |Irish| Regiment / Erin Go Bragh / (¾ length, in uniform, vignette.)   und S C&I

1201 Col. Richard M. Johnson /
1846 S N.C.

1202 Col. Theodore Roosevelt U. S. V. / Commander of the famous Rough Riders / (Equestrian portrait to left, upraised sword, vignette.)
1898 S C&I

Col. Upton See: Celebrated Trotting Stallion Col. Upton, etc. No. 926A.
Cold Spring, N. Y. See: Nos. 2972-4, 2977, 6617.
Cold Spring Course Mil. See: Nos. 915, 1908, 2422.
Colfax, Schuyler See: Nos. 2919, 4390, 5050.

1203 Colored Beauty, The / (Vignette, head of colored girl, slightly to right.)
1872 S C&I

1204 Colored Beauty, The / J. A. on stone. (Vignette, different girl from preceding, slightly to left.)
1877 S C&I

1205 Colored Belle, The /
und S C&I

1206 Colored / Engravings / for the / People / Published by / N. Currier /

Lithographer / 2 Spruce Street / nearly opposite the City Hall / New York / For Sale Here / (Store card prepared for stores, etc., selling the prints by the firm.) und M N.C.

1207 Colored Volunteer, The / (Young colored boy, marching, and using a broom for a musket, oval.)
1863 M C&I

1208 Colored Volunteer, The / Marching into Dixie / 12.4x8.3. (Upright vignette portrait of colored soldier, ¾ length.) und S C&I

1209 Coloring His Meerschaum /
1879 V.S. C&I

1210 Coloring His Meerschaum / (Full length figure of man standing on bale of tobacco, smoking. Smoke forms the words 'Smoke our tobacco." Vignette.) 1880 S C&I

1211 Coloring His Meerschaum (Monkey on settee.) und S C&I

1212 Columbia (Head of girl, emblematical.) und S C&I

Columbia (Steamship) See: Nos. 1788, 4421, 5072.

Columbia (Yacht) See: No. 6821.

Columbian Exposition, C h i c a g o See: Nos. 1892, 2472.

Columbus (Landing) See: Nos. 1972, 3428-9, 3430-1.

1213 Com. Andrew H. Foote / The Hero of Fort Henry / (¾ length portrait in uniform, vignette.) und S C&I

1214 Com. Farragut's Fleet, passing the forts on the Mississippi, April 24th, 1862 / The U. S. Frigate Mississippi destroying the rebel ram Manassas / Fort St. Philip, Fort Jackson keyed. 7.14x12.9. 1862 S C&I

1215 Combat at the Military Station / Of Chateau d'Eau, 24th February, 1848 / #577 / 4 additional lines description, title repeated in French. 8x12.10. 1848 S N.C.

1216 Come Gang Awa' Wi'me / Ballad / Written and composed / By / Edwin Hansford / Published by Hewitt & Jaques. und S N.C.

1217 Come Into The Garden, Maud / "By Tabby's son" /
und S C&I

1218 Come! Take a Drink (Full-length figure of man at bar, inviting observer to join him, upright vignette.)
1868 S C&I

Comet (Clipper Ship) See: Nos. 1140, 1154-6.

1219 Coming From the Trot / Sports on the home stretch / Thos. Worth on stone. 18.10x28.10. (Showing Hiram Woodruff's place. Companion to "Going to the Trot." No. 2409.)
1869 L C&I

1220 Coming Home With A Family / (Cat and kittens.) und S C&I

1221 Coming in "On His Ear" / Thos. Worth on stone. (Horse, driver, and rig covered with mud, vignette.)
1875 S C&I

1222 Coming Match / 1881 S C&I

1223 Coming the Putty / #465 / L. M. (Maurer) on stone. 8.3x12.6. (Customer in saloon says "Ah, Billy, my beauty, can you give us an eye opener?" Bartender answers "Yes, Siree." Companion to "Momentous Q u e s t i o n" No. 4168.) 1853 S N.C.

1224 Coming up Smiling / Thos. Worth on stone. (Vignette, boxing comic— Companion to 'A Little Groggy" No. 3636.) 1884 S C&I

1225 Commander in Chief, The /.
1863 S C&I

1226 Commodore Nutt as Hop O' My Thumb / in the play of / The Giant And His Seven League Boots / Now performing at / Barnum's American Museum / New York / In person / (Central picture shows him conquering his rival, 4 views on top, 2 on sides, and 4 on bottom,) Barnum's Gallery of Wonders No. 2.
und S N.C.

1227 Commodore Nutt, The $30,000 Nut / The smallest man alive, 18 years old, 29 inches high and weighs only 24 pounds. On exhibition at Barnum's Museum, New York / (Full-length figure standing beside P. T. Barnum.)
und S C&I

Commodore Vanderbilt (H o r s e) See: No. 6202.

1228 Common Lot, The / (2 columns, 5 lines of verse. Mother with daughter who has just died, vignette, about 8x8.) und S N.C.

Commonwealth (Steamboat) See: No. 6406.

1229 Compagne Generale Transatlantique Steamer / "La Bourgogne" 1 additional line. und S C&I

1230 Compagne Generale Transatlantique Steamer / "La Bretagne" / 1 additional line. und S C&I

COMING THE PUTTY.

1231 Compagne Generale Transatlantique Steamer / "La Champagne" / 1 additional line.   und S C&I

1232 Compagne Generale Transatlantique Steamer / "La Gascogne" / 1 additional line.   und S C&I

1233 Compagne Generale Transatlantique Steamer / "L'Aquitaine" / 1 additional line.   und S C&I

1234 Compagne Generale Transatlantique Steamer / "La Lorraine" / 1 additional line.   und S C&I

1235 Compagne Generale Transatlantique Steamer / "La Touraine" / 1 additional line.   und S C&I

1236 Confederacy—The Secession Movement/   und S C&I

1237 Congressional Scales / A True Balance (Zachary Taylor holding weights in each hand entitled "Wilmot Proviso" and "Southern Rights", each pan of scales filled with human figures.)
1850 M N.C.

Connecticut See: Nos. 1649, 1966, 2276-9, 2456, 2930, 4790, 6426, 6429, 6443.

Connemara See: Ireland.

1238 Constance /   und L C&I
Constantine See: Foreign Misc.
Constitution (U. S. Frigate) See: Nos. 4400, 6303-4.

1239 Constitution and Guerriere, The / Fought August 19th, 1812 / #232 / Copyright Sarony & Major (Broadside view, sail and spar in water to right of Guerriere.)
1846 S N.C.

1240 Constitution and Guerriere, The / Fought August 19, 1812 / The Guerriere had 15 men killed and 63 wounded. The Constitution had 7 men killed and 7 wounded / (¾ stern view of Constitution, entirely different composition from preceding.)
und S N.C.

Constitution and Guerriere, See: No. 4400.

1241 Constitution and Java / The Constitution had 9 killed and 25 wounded / Fought Dec. 29th, 1812. The Java had 60 killed and 170 wounded / #87 / Published at C. Curriers, 33 Spruce Street, N. Y.
1845 S N.C.

CONSTITUTION AND JAVA.

1242 Constitution and Java / Fought Dec. 29, 1812 / The Constitution had 9 killed and 25 wounded—The Java had 60 killed and 170 wounded / 1846 S N.C.

1243 Constitution and Java / #403 / 7.14 x13 (Second state, coarser lines.) 1846 N.C.&I

1244 Constitution and Java / Action fought Dec. 29, 1812 / 7.12x12.14. (Third state, b r i l l i a n t l y colored, coarser lines and usually with another subject on reverse side.) 1846 S N.C.

Contest (Clipper Ship) See: No. 1141.

1245 Contested Seat, A / For sale at No. 2 Spruce St., N. Y. (At right Pierce, who has just had the Presidential chair drawn from under him, is sprawled on floor saying: "Look out there! What you bout General? / Do you want to knock a feller's brains out ?" / While the "Gen." holding the back of the chair replies, "Sorry to disappoint you Pierce; / but the people wish me to take / this chair.") und S N.C.

Cook (Kook Family) See: No. 889.

1246 Cooling Stream, The / combined from paintings by T. Creswick, R. A., and T. S. Cooper, A.R.A. 11.3x15.14. (Cows in stream, thatched cottage on left.) und M C&I

1247 Coon Club Hunt, The / "Hot on the Scent" / (Vignette, colored comic. 1885 S C&I

1248 Coon Club Hunt, The / "Taking a Header" / (Vignette, couple thrown into pond, colored comic.) 1885 S C&I

1249 Copped at a Cock Fight / Parson,—Leff me go, Boss, I only jis done go dar to reconcile dem roosters / Thos. Worth on stone. (Vignette, companion to "Boss Rooster" #620.) 1884 S C&I

Corbett, James J. See: No. 3156.

Corcoran, Michael See: Nos. 680-1, 1199, 1200.

1250 Cordelia Howard as "Eva" in "Uncle Tom's Cabin," after J. L. Magee, New York. 1852 V.S. CC

Corinth, (Miss., Battle of) See: No. 401.

1251 Corinthian Race, A / A High-Toned Start / Thos. Worth on stone. (Vignette, colored comic, horse race.) 1883 S C&I

1252 Corinthian Race, A / A Low-Toned Finish. / Thos. Worth on stone. (Vignette, colored comic, horse race.) 1883 S C&I

1253 Cork Castle and Black Rock Castle, The / Near Glanmire, County Cork, Ireland / und S C&I

1254 Cork River, The / Near Glanmire, County Cork, Ireland /. und S C&I

1255 Corned Beef / "Mammy this here cattle is cotch'd the staggers eatin them are rum cherries" / "Dear me what beasts they make of themselves. This all comes of their keeping company with that drunken beast my Husband" / #650 / (Farmer's wife and son and inebriated cows.) und S N.C.

1256 Cornelia / #391 / 11.11x8.8. (¾ length, red dress, under tree on balcony, upright.) 1846 S N.C.

1257 Cornelia / #391 /. 1847 S N.C.
Cornelia (Yacht) See: No. 5105.
Corning Erastus See: No. 1938.

1258 Cornwallis is Taken! / Lieut. Col. Tighlman of Washington's Staff, announcing the Surrender of Cornwallis from / The steps of the State House |Independence Hall| at Midnight, October 23rd, 1781 / 8.12x12.11. 1876 S C&I
Coronet (Yacht) See: No. 945.

1259 Correct Likeness of H. Rockwell's Horse Alexander, Bowery Amphitheater, New York, March 17th, 1840. (4 men on horseback in background. 2 men standing at left.) und M N.C.

1260 Correct Likeness of Mr. H. Rockwell's Horse Alexander, Bowery Amphitheater, New York, March 17th, 1840, A / #75 / 8.2x12.11. und S N.C.
Corsair (Yacht) See: No. 5722.

1261 Corsairs Isle, The / und M C&I

1262 Cortelyou Mansion—Old Mansion House, Gowanus Road / und S N.C.
Cortelyou Mansion See: No. 4568.
Corwin, Thomas See: No. 6022.

1263 Cottage by the Cliff, The / 8.7x12.7. und S C&I

1264 Cottage by the Wayside, The / 8.8x12.6. (Thatched cottage, old man, boy and girl in front.) und S C&I

1265 Cottage Dooryard—Evening, The / F. Palmer, Del. 10.7x14.15. 1855 M N.C.

1266 Cottage Life—Spring / Copyright N. Currier. 10.10x15. (Group of five at right, house with rig and coachman.) 1856 M C&I

1267 Cottage Life—Summer/ #125 / 8.14 x 12 (Composition similar to following.) und S C&I

1268 Cottage Life—Summer / Copyright N. Currier, N. Y. 10.6x15. 1856 M C&I

1269 Cottages, The / (Vignette, 3 cottages, 2 red and center 1 white, stone wall, fence, trees, etc. Printed on the same sheet with the "Bridge." No. 669, about 5x7.) und V.S. C&I

1270 Cotter's Saturday Night, The / und S C&I

1271 Cotton Plantation on the Mississippi, A / W. A. Walker '83 on stone. 20x30.1. Printed in Oil Colors by Currier & Ives. 1884 L C&I
Count D'Orsay See: No. 175.
Countess of Dufferin (Yacht) See: No. 6795.

1272 Courageous Conduct of a Young Girl / Place de la Concorde, 24th February, 1848 / #580. 1848 S N.C.

1273 Course of True Love, The / 11.6x8.8. (Cat comic, upright.) 1875 S C&I
Court House, Troy See: No. 6157.
Courtney, Charles See: No. 2650.

1274 Courtship / The Happy Hour / #436. 1857 S N.C.

1275 Cousins, The / und S N.C.

1276 Cove of Cork, The / 8x12.8. und S C&I
Cove of Cork See: Ireland.

1277 Cozzen's Dock, West Point / Hudson River / F. F. Palmer, Del. 10.13x15.4. und M C&I
Cozzen's Dock See: No. 4245.

1278 Crack Shot, A / 1879 S C&I

1279 Crack Shot, A / 2.15x4.12. (Same composition reversed as "E Pluribus Unum," No. 1646.) 1880 V.S. C&I

1280 Crack Shots, in Position, The / Dollymount, Creedmoor, and Wimbledon / C. M. Vergnes, 1875, on stone.

(4 Figures: E Pluribus Unum, Erin Go Bragh, The Queen's Own, The Highland Fling, on 1 sheet. Comic shooting print.)   1875 S C&I

1281 "Crack" Sloop in a Race to Windward, A / Yacht "Gracie" of New York / C. R. Parsons, Del. 19x28.1. Printed in oil colors by Currier & Ives.   1882 L C&I

1282 "Crack Team" at a Smashing Gait, A / Thos. Worth on stone. 16.7x24.14. (Team breaking through a toll gate, upsetting people, etc.)
          1869 L C&I

1283 Crack Trotter, A — "Coming Around" / Thos. Worth on stone. (Vignette.)   1880 S C&I

1284 Crack Trotter, A—"A Little Off" / Thos. Worth on stone. (Handlers dosing and rubbing him down, vignette.)   1880 S C&I

1285 "Crack Trotter, A" — Between the Heats / 2.15x4.12.
          1880 V.S. C&I

1286 "Crack Trotter" — Between the Heats / Thos. Worth on stone. (Vignette.)   1875 M C&I

1287 "Crack Trotter" In the Harness of the Period, A / 2.14x4.12.
          1879 V.S. C&I

1288 "Crack Trotter" In the Harness of the Period, A / Thos. Worth on stone. (Vignette.)   1875 M C&I

1289 Cracovienne, The / Danced by Madlle. Elssler / In the Grand Ballet of the Gipsey / Published by Hewitt & Jaques, N. Y. (Full-length portrait of Fanny Elssler with village and houses in background, vignette.)
          und S N.C.

1290 Cracovienne, The / Danced by Madlle. Elssler / In the Grand Ballet of the Gipsey / (Rustic background and other changes in composition, upright, full-length, vignette.)
          und S N.C.

1291 Cradle of Liberty, The / 11.15x8.14. (Upright, allegorical figures of "Justice," "Columbia," baby, flag, eagle, etc.)   1876 S C&I

Craney Island See: "Destruction of the Rebel Monster," No. 1572.

1292 Craps—A Busted Game / "Sebben and Lebben—Scoops the Crowd!" / J. Cameron on stone. (Vignette, colored comic.)   1890 S C&I

1293 Craps—A Close Call / "Come you pretty sebben, gib my gal new shoes" / J. Cameron on stone. (Vignette, colored comic.)   1890 S C&I

Crathie (Steamship) See: No. 5531.

1294 Crayon Studies / #464 / (2 vignette scenes: 1 shows a path leading to cottages with 3 figures, other shows barrel in cart, small cottage, etc.)
          und S N.C.

1295 Crayon Studies / #472 / (Identical composition to "Toll-gate, Jamaica, L. I." No. 6089. Vignette.)
          und S N.C.

1296 Crayon Studies / #473 (2 views on 1 sheet—#1 shows a covered wagon, small house, chicken, pigs, pond—#2 shows cottage with picket fence, summer house, trees. View #2 is same as "Old Farm House, Williamsburg, L. I." Vignette.)   und S N.C.

1297 Crayon Studies / Old Mansion House, Gowanus Road / (Vignette.)
          und S N.C.

1298 Crayon Studies / Summer Noon / #465 (Shows cows, man fishing from wooden bridge, vignette.)
          und S N.C.

1299 Crayon Studies / View on Fulton Avenue, Brooklyn, L. I. / #464. See: No. 6432. (Vignette.)
          und S N.C.

1300 Cream of Love, The / (2 cherubs eating ice cream — roses. Probably used as an advertisement.)
          1879 S C&I

1301 Creating a Sensation / The "Bully Boy on a Bicycle" / Thos. Worth on stone. (Bicyclist upsets plasterer, horseman, etc., companion to "Spoiling a Sensation" No. 5665. Vignette, colored comic.)   1881 S C&I

Crittenden, J. J. See: Nos. 425, 789.

1302 Cromwell's Bridge / Glengariff, Ireland / 8x12.8.   und S C&I

Crook, Genl. See: No. 2553.

1303 Cross and Anchor of Roses /
          und S C&I

1304 Cross and Crown of Flowers /
          1871 S C&I

1305 Cross and the Crown, The / 14x 10.12. (Figure on rock, cross on back, reaching for crown in sky.)
          1870 M C&I

1306 Cross Matched Race, A / 12.2x18.13 (2 horses with high-wheeled sulkies,

¾ to right. Same composition as "Hero and Flora Temple" No. 2800.)
1891 M C&I

1307 "Cross Matched" Team, A / Thos. Worth on stone. (Vignette.)
1878 S C&I

1308 Crossed by a "Milk Train" / (Colored comic, vignette, cow on railroad track holding up traffic.)
1884 S C&I

1309 Crossed by a "Milk Train" / (Identical to preceding except for changed publication date.) 1885 S C&I

Croton Aqueduct See: Hydrographic Map, No. 3012.

Crouse, Hannah See: No. 4153.

1310 Crow / Quadrilles / The / (Consisting of 9 pieces published by John F. Nunn's, Phila., 1837. 8 small vignetted scenes, a music sheet.)
und S N.C.

1311 "Crowd" that "Scooped" the Pools. The / 2.15x4.12. 1878 V.S. C&I

1312 "Crowd" that "Scooped" the Pools, The / Thos. Worth on stone. (Vignette, companion to "The Sports who Lost Their Tin" No. 5668.)
1878 S C&I

1313 Crowing Match, A /
und V.S. C&I

1314 Crown of Thorns, The / Ecce Homo / 10.13x8.11. (Bust portrait of Christ in oval.) und S C&I

1315 Crow's Nest / North River / #517. (Man and woman in foreground, no Hudson River Steamers shown.)
und S N.C.

Crow's Nest See: Nos. 6444-5, 6447-8.

1316 "Croxie" / by Clark Chief / 2:19¼ / J. Cameron on stone. (¾ view, high-wheeled sulky to right, vignette.)
1878 S C&I

1317 Crucifixion, The / #31 / 13.1x8.14. (Title in plate, ornamental border, upright.) 1847 S N.C.

1318 Crucifixion, The /
1894 S N.C.

1319 Crucifixion, The / 11.14x8.8. (Upright, 33 Spruce St.) und S N.C.

1320 Crucifixion, The / Lith. and Pub. by N. Currier, 2 Spruce and 169 Broadway. 12.4x8.13. (Woman kneeling at Christ's right side.) und S N.C.

1321 Crucifixion, The / 12.2x16.2 (Christ and 2 thieves on crosses.)
und M C&I

1322 Crucifixion, The / Title repeated in French and Spanish. (Slightly rounded corners.) und S C&I

1323 Crucifixion, The / La Crucificazion —La Crucifixion / J. Cameron on stone. 18.2x12.15. 1849 M N.C.

1324 Cruiser "New York," The /
und S C&I

1325 Crystal Palace, The / (At top) The Magnificent Buildings, for the World's Fair of 1851 / Built of Iron and Glass, In Hyde Park, London / #105 / 2 additional lines of dimensions. 8x12.11.
und S N.C.

1326 Crystal Palace, The / The Magnificent Building for the World's Fair of 1851, Hyde Park, London / 8x12.8.
und S C&I

Crystal Palace, N. Y. See: New York City.

Cuba See: Nos. 2758, 5385, 6410.

Cumberland (Frigate) See: Nos. 5530, 6305-6.

1327 Cumberland Valley / From Bridgeport Heights opposite Harrisburg, Pa. F. F. Palmer, Del. 15.13x20.8.
1865 L C&I

1328 Cup that Cheers, A / (Vignette, upright, 3 old ladies drinking tea.)
1884 S C&I

1329 Cunard Steamship "Servia" / 1 additional line of dimensions.
und S C&I

1330 Cupid's Own / 1879 S C&I

1331 Cupid's Own / (Cigar advertising card.) 1880 V.S. C&I

1332 Curfew Bell, The /
und S C&I

Currier & Ives / Grand Illuminating Posters. See: "A Head and Head Finish," No. 2766.

1333 Custer's Last Charge / Brevet Major-General George A. Custer, Lieutenant-Colonel 7th U. S. Cavalry / Killed in the Battle with the Sioux, June 25th, 1876 / (Upright, vignette, equestrian portrait.)
1876 S C&I

1334 Custom House, New York / #611 / 8.5x12.10. und S N.C.

1335 Custom House, New York / Longitudinal section / Plan of front of Custom House from Pine to Wall Sts. / Designed by Ithiel Town and Alexander J. Davis, Architects. Lith. press of Stodart and Currier. (2 views on 1 sheet.) und M N.C.

1336 Cutter Yacht "Bianca" / C. Parsons. 1854 L C&I

1337 Cutter Yacht "Galatea" / Modelled by J. Beaver Webb. Owned by Lieut. Henn, R. N. / 2 columns of 4 lines. 9.8x13.12. 1886 S C&I

1338 Cutter Yacht "Genesta" R. Y. S. / C. R. Parsons '85 on stone. 2 columns of dimensions, 4 lines each. 15.4x21. (Printed in color, ship sailing to right.) 1885 L C&I

1339 Cutter Yacht "Genesta"—title is: Sir Richard Sutton's Celebrated Cutter Yacht "Genesta" / Modelled by J. Beaver Webb / 8 lines of description. 9.11x13.14. 1885 S C&I

1340 Cutter Yacht "Madge" /.
und S C&I

1341 Cutter Yacht "Maria" / In her trial of speed with the Clipper Yacht "America" in New York Bay, 1851 / After J. Buttersworth. 2 columns of 7 lines. 1852 L N.C.

1342 Cutter Yacht "Maria" / Modelled by R. E. Stevens, Esq. / Owned by the Messrs. Stevens in New York / After J. Buttersworth. F. F. Palmer, Del. 1852 M N.C.

1343 Cutter Yacht "Scud" / Of Philadelphia / Modelled by Robert L. Stevens, Esq., to whom this print with permission / is respectfully dedicated by the publisher. / After J. E. Buttersworth. C. Parsons, Del. 2 columns of 4 and 5 lines. 1855 L N.C.

1344 Cutter Yacht "Thistle" / Designed by G. L. Watson. Built by L. W. Henderson & Co., Glascow. Owned by Mr. James Bell, Glascow. 1 additional line of dimensions. 10x13.10.
1887 S C&I

C. Vanderbilt. See: "Terrific Collision Between the Steamboats Dean Richmond and C. Vanderbilt," No. 5994.

D

1345 Dairy Farm, The / (Couple near barn, cows, chickens, pigs, ducks, etc.)
und S C&I

1346 Daisy and Her Pets / 11.12x9.6 (Dogs, cat, horse—upright.)
1876 S C&I

Daisy Burns (Horse) See: Nos. 1907, 3952.

Daisydale (Horse) See: No. 912.

Dale, Richard See: No. 4399.

Dallas, Geo. M. See: Nos. 2340-3, 2490-1.

1347 "Dan Rice" / Driven by Budd Doble / J. Cameron on stone. 16.12x26.
1868 L C&I

1348 "Dan Rice" / Owned by T. M. Lyom, Portsmouth, Ohio / J. Cameron on stone. 16.14x26.4. (Broadside to right, skeleton wagon.) 1866 L C&I

Dan Rice (Horse) See: Nos. 1347-8, 6203.

Dana, C. A. See: No. 5664.

1349 Dancing Lesson, The / 11.12x8.12.
und S C&I

Dancing. See: Nos. 451, 1289-90, 1872-3, 2041, 2743-4, 3371, 3854-6, 3858-60, 4163, 4412, 4726, 4825-8, 4986-7, 5466-7, 5475, 5638-9, 5966.

Dandy (Horse) See: No. 6564.

1350 Danger Signal, The / Printed in oil colors by Currier & Ives. Engine is named "Jas. R. Pitcher." Tender "United States Mutual Accident Ass'n / 320 & 322 Broadway, N. Y." / 17.2x 28.15 (1st state.) 1884 L C&I

1351 Danger Signal, The / (Same as preceding except for 2 columns on each side of title, and 5 additional lines under main title advertising "United States Accident Association" (2nd state.) 1884 L C&I

1352 Danl. D. Tompkins / 2.13x3. (From Jenkins' "History of Political Parties in the State of New York," 1846.)
und V.S. N.C.

1353 "Daniel D. Tompkins" and "Blanc Negre" / Hunting Park Course, Phila., Oct. 26th, 1849 / Beating Golish and Snow Storm / 1851 L N.C.

1354 Daniel in the Lion's Den / #325 / 12.6x9.4 (1 additional line Biblical quotation, full length, upright.)
und S N.C.

1355 Daniel in the Lion's Den / 1 additional line. 11.14x8.7. und S C&I

1356 Daniel O'Connell / The Champion of Freedom / #164 / 11.14x8.10 (Seated, rolled paper in left hand, round corners, upright.) und S N.C.

1357 Daniel O'Connell / The Champion

[67]

of Freedom / 11.14x8.15 (Full length on heights, white dog on left.)
und S N.C.

1358 Daniel O'Connell / The Champion of Freedom / #724 (At left) Born August 6th, 1775 / (At right) Died May 15th, 1847 / 11.9x8.4 (Full length figure, black clothes and cape, dog, and man driving cow.) und S C&I

1359 Daniel O'Connell / The Champion of Freedom / Born August 6th, 1775— Died May 15th, 1847 / 11.13x8.9 (Upright.) und S C&I

1360 Daniel O'Connell — The Champion of Freedom / Drawn by permission from the large plate pub. by Turner & Fisher in 1837 (Full length, standing under tree, with dog.)
und S N.C.

1361 Daniel O'Connell / The Great Irish "Liberator" and Champion of Catholic Emancipation / 2 additional lines. 11.12 x8.10 (Full length with white dog.)
und S C&I

1362 Daniel Webster / 20x23.8 (Half length, vignette.) 1852 L N.C.

1363 Daniel Webster / Defender of the Constitution / #130 / From the original painting by Lawson in the possession of D. Bixby, Esq., Broadway, Hotel New York. 11.1x8.12 (Half length, white tie, slightly to right, upright.)
1851 S N.C.

1364 Daniel Webster / New England's Choice for / Twelfth President of the United States / #130 / 11.10x8.15 (Half length, black tie — red curtain in background. Oval in ornamental rectangular border.) 1847 S N.C.

1365 Daniel Webster / New England's Choice for / Twelfth President of the United States / (Bust, red curtain, ornamental border, eagle surrounded by stars.) 1847 S N.C.

1366 Daniel Webster / Secretary of State 1841 / J. L. McGee, Del. 11.14x9.1 (Seated, pen in hand, green curtain, upright.) und S N.C.
Darby (Horse) **See:** No. 6179.

1367 "Dargle" Glen, The / Ireland.
und M C&I

1368 Dark Eyed Beauty, The /
und S C&I

1369 Dark Foreshading, On a Flash Picture, A / "Take us Smilin or We'el lay yer out" / (Vignette, companion to "A Positive Process from a Negative Result" No. 4852.) 1890 S C&I
Darkness (Horse) **See:** No. 2583.

1370 Darktown Athletics — A Quarter Mile Dash / "One has de speed and de oder de bottom" / J. Cameron on stone. (Vignette.) 1893 S C&I

1371 Darktown Athletics — A Running High Jump / Match between the Darktown grasshopper and the Blackville frog / J. Cameron on stone. (Vignette.) 1893 S C&I

1372 Darktown Banjo Class — All in tune / "Thumb it, darkies thumb it — oh, how loose I feel" / (Vignette.)
1886 S C&I

1373 Darktown Banjo Class — Off the key / "If yous can't play de music jess leff de banjo go" / (Vignette.)
1886 S C&I

1374 Darktown Bicycle Club — Knocked Out / "Dar! I knowed dem odd fellers was a breedin mischief" / J. Cameron on stone. (Vignette.) 1892 S C&I

1375 Darktown Bicycle Club — On parade, The / "Hurray for de rumatic! Don't she glide lubly" / J. Cameron on stone. (Vignette.) 1892 S C&I

1376 Darktown Bicycle Race — A Sudden Halt, The / "I knowd we'd have busted de record if it hadnt been for dis misforchin" / J. Cameron on stone. (Vignette.) 1895 S C&I

1377 Darktown Bicycle Race — The Start, The / "Now for de Fastest record ever known" / J. Cameron on stone. (Vignette.) 1895 S C&I

1378 Darktown Bicycling — A tender Pair / "I'se gwine to git dat pear or bust sumfin" / (Colored boy on limb of tree above couple on bicycles, vignette.) 1897 S C&I

1379 Darktown Bicycling — Scooped de Pear / "And somfins busted" / (Limb breaks and boy falls on pair, vignette.)
1897 S C&I

1380 Darktown Bowling Club, The / Bowled Out / (Vignette.)
1888 S C&I

1381 Darktown Bowling Club, The / Watching for A Strike / (Vignette.)
1888 S C&I

1382 Darktown Donation Party, A — A Doubtful Acquisition / "Dare Parson you can see de debbil hisself in dat mirror" / (Vignette.) 1893 S C&I

1383 Darktown Donation Party, A — An object lesson / (Vignette.)
1893 S C&I

1384 Darktown Elopement, The / "Skip softly lub, don't 'sturb de ole man and

de bull pup!" / (Vignette.)
1885 S C&I

1385 Darktown Elopement, The / "Hurry Mr. Jonsing, dars dat chile 'loping wif de coachman" / (Vignette.)
1885 S C&I

1386 Darktown Fire Brigade, The — A Prize Squirt / "Now den! shake her up once moah for de Mug" / (Vignette, companion to 1395.) 1885 S C&I

1387 Darktown Fire Brigade, The — All on their Mettle / "Git dere fust if you's bust you trousers" / (Vignette.)
1889 S C&I

1388 Darktown Fire Brigade, The—Hook and Ladder Gymnastics / "Brace her up dar! and cotch her on de fly!" / (Vignette.) 1887 S C&I

1389 Darktown Fire Brigade, The — Investigating a Smoke / Parson — "No sah de meetin house aint afire, but de congregation am taking a smoke of de world's best terbakker" / (Vignette.) 1894 S C&I

1390 Darktown Fire Brigade, The — Taking a Rest / Foreman "Right you is Parson dis terbacker beats de deck"/ (Vignette.) 1894 S C&I

1391 Darktown Fire Brigade, The — Saved / Thos. Worth on stone. (Vignette.) 1884 S C&I

1392 Darktown Fire Brigade, The — Slightly Demoralized / "I knowed we'd make em take water!" / (Vignette.)
1889 S C&I

1393 Darktown Fire Brigade / The Chief on Duty / "Lite up dem hose dar — Yous heah me" / (Vignette.)
1885 S C&I

1394 Darktown Fire Brigade / The Foreman on Parade / "De gals all mire me so much dey make me blush" / (Upright, full-length figure, vignette.)
1885 S C&I

1395 Darktown Fire Brigade, The — The Last shake / "We's won de Mug but we's smashed de ole machine" / (Vignette, companion to No. 1386.)
1885 S C&I

1396 Darktown Fire Brigade — To the Rescue, The / Thos. Worth on stone. (Vignette.) 1884 S C&I

1397 Darktown Fire Brigade — Under Full Steam, The / "Now den squirt, for all she's wuff" / (Vignette.)
1887 S C&I

1398 Darktown Football Match — The Kick Off, The / (Vignette.)
und S C&I

1399 Darktown Football Match — The Scrimmage, The / (Vignette.)
und S C&I

1400 Darktown Glide, The / "Aint dis Jes lubly" / Murphy on stone. (Vignette, couple roller skating.)
1884 S C&I

1401 Darktown Hook and Ladder Corps / Going to the Front / King & Murphy, Dels. on stone. (Vignette.)
1884 S C&I

1402 Darktown Hook and Ladder Corps — Going to the Front / 25.8x38.
1891 L C&I

1403 Darktown Hook and Ladder Corps, The / In Action / King & Murphy, Dels. on stone. (Vignette.)
1884 S C&I

1404 Darktown Fire Brigade — Saved, The / 26x36.12 (Vignette.)
1891 L C&I

1405 Darktown Hunt — Presenting the Brush, The / "You done better keep it, Kurnel, to polish you cheek" / (Vignette.) 1892 S C&I

1406 Darktown Hunt — The Meet, The / "Keep you tempers ladies de one dat gits tother end fust gits de brush" / (Vignette.) 1892 S C&I

1407 Darktown Law Suit, A — Cheerful Milker / "De Plaintiff has de head and de defendant de tail but I get de cream all de time" / J. Cameron on stone. (Vignette.) 1886 S C&I

1408 Darktown Law Suit, A — Part second / The case dismissed with an extra allowance to the Attorney /(Cow kicking over 3 colored men and milk pail, vignette.) 1887 S C&I

1409 Darktown Lawn Party, A / A Bully Time / (Bull upsetting picnic table, vignette.) 1888 S C&I

1410 Darktown Lawn Party, A / Music in the air / (Bull in distance sees picnic table covered with red umbrella, vignette.) 1888 S C&I

1411 Darktown Opera — The Lover's Leap / "Whar yer gwine to, dis aint in de book" / (Vignette.)
1886 S C&I

1412 Darktown Opera — The Serenade / "Come lub, come de moon am in de sky" / (Vignette.) 1886 S C&I

1413 Darktown Othello, The / "I mashed

her on de dangers I had passed (driving an army muel") / 9.2x13 (Not vignette.)   1886 S C&I

1414 Darktown Race — Facing the Flag, A / Match between "His Lowness" and "The Stretcher" for de gate money / (2 horses at judge's stand — "Coony Island Jockey Club." Vignette.)   1892 S C&I

1415 Darktown Race — Won by a Neck, A / "Golly dat gyraffy neck does de bizness!" / (Vignette.)   1892 S C&I

1416 Darktown Riding Class, The — The Gallop / (Vignette.)   1890 S C&I

1417 Darktown Riding Class, The — The Trot / (Vignette.)   1890 S C&I

1418 Darktown Slide, The / "Golly! am dere an Erfquake?" / Murphy, Del. on stone. (Vignette, roller skating.)   1884 S C&I

1419 Darktown Slide, The / "Golly! Wot's Busted?" / Murphy, Del. on stone. (Man felling couple roller skating, vignette.)   1844 S C&I

1420 Darktown Sociables / A "Fancy Dress" Hoodoo / (Vignette.)   1890 S C&I

1421 Darktown Sociables / A "Fancy Dress" Surprise / (Vignette.)   1890 S C&I

1422 Darktown Society — On their Feed / (Vignette.)   1890 S C&I

1423 Darktown Society — On their Manners / (Vignette.)   1890 S C&I

1424 Darktown Sports — A Grand Spurt / "I'll Beat dat ole Pelter, or bust" / (Sulky and high-wheeled bicycle race, vignette.)   1885 S C&I

1425 Darktown Sports — Winning Easy / "I Knowed I'd send him in de air" / (Vignette.)   1885 S C&I

1426 Darktown Tally-Ho, The—Straightened out / Thos. Worth on stone. (Vignette.)   1889 S C&I

1427 Darktown Tally-Ho, The — Tangled Up / Thos. Worth on stone.   1889 S C&I

1428 Darktown Tourists — Coming back on their Dig / "Don't know common Niggahs" / (Vignette.)   1886 S C&I

1429 Darktown Tourists — Going off on their Blubber / "Nuffin but poor weak cullud pussons" / (Vignette.)   1886 S C&I

1430 Darktown Tournament, A — Close quarters / J. Cameron on stone. (Whitewashers fighting, vignette.)   1890 S C&I

1431 Darktown Tournament, A — First Tilt / J. Cameron on stone. (Vignette.)   1890 S C&I

1432 Darktown Trial, A — The Judge's Charge / 1 additional line. (Vignette.)   1887 S C&I

1433 Darktown Trial, A — The Verdict / 1 additional line. (Vignette.)   1887 S C&I

1434 Darktown Trolley — "Clar de track when de bell rings" / Popular line — Transfer every where / J. Cameron on stone. (Vignette.)   1896 S C&I

1435 Darktown Trolley — Through car in danger / "Go way from dar; de lightning strike you" / J. Cameron '95 on stone. (Vignette.)   1896 S C&I

1436 Darktown Trotter, Ready for the Word, A / "Now den say go! and see 'Fancy Pranks' bust de record wif dis ball bearin' bike" / Thos. Worth on stone. (Vignette.)   1892 S C&I

1437 Darktown Wedding — The Parting Salute, A / (Vignette.)   1892 S C&I

1438 Darktown Wedding — The Send Off, A / (Vignette.)   1892 S C&I

1439 Dark Town Yacht Club, The — Hard up for a Breeze / The Cup in danger / (Vignette.)   1885 S C&I

1440 Darktown Yacht Club — Ladies Day / "In cose I will, honey" / J. Cameron on stone. (Vignette, big woman falling in water.)   1896 S C&I

1441 Darktown Yacht Club — Ladies Day / "You'll just ballast de boat, Miss Tiny" / J. Cameron on stone. (Vignette.)   1896 S C&I

1442 Darktown Yacht Club, The — On the Winning Tack / The Cup Secure / (Vignette.)   1885 S C&I

1443 "Darling, I am Growing Old" / (Very small girl at piano playing "Silver Threads Among the Gold" although music sheet is upside down, small boy in large chair listening, vignette.)   und S C&I

1444 Darling Rosy / (¾ length, girl, roses in hand, vignette.)   und S C&I

DARTMOUTH COLLEGE.

1445 Darrynane Abbey, Ireland / The Home of O'Connell / (Sea in background.) 1869 M C&I

1446 Dartmouth College / Ami B. Young, Delt. Pub. by B. O. Tyler. A lith. of Stodart & Currier, N.Y. 8.5x 12.13 (One of the earliest Currier prints, pub. in 1834.) und S N.C.

1446A Dartmouth College / Ami B. Young, Delt. Tyler name removed. (Same size as preceding.)
und S N.C.

1447 Dartmouth College / 8.5x12.13 (Same as preceding. N. Currier, N.Y., Stodart & Tyler names removed.)
und S N.C.

1448 Dash for the Pole, A / L. Maurer on stone. 18x28 (6 horses and low-wheeled, rubber-tired sulkies, ¾ view to right.) 1893 L C&I

1449 Daughter of Erin, The / 12.7x9 (Half length, playing harp.)
und S N.C.

1450 Daughter of the North West, The / und S C&I

1451 Daughter of the Regiment, The / #663 / A.V. on stone. 11.7x8.10 (Full-length figure with drum, camp scene

in background, upright, the girl portrayed is Jenny Lind.)
1849 S N.C.

1452 Daughter of the South, A / und S C&I

1453 Daughters of Temperance / Virtue, Love, and Temperance / #702 / 11.11x 8.8 (Full length in regalia.)
und S N.C.

Dauntless (Yacht) See: Nos. 945, 2625, 4450, 6796-7.

1454 Davenport Brothers, The / 1864 S C&I

1455 David and Goliath / und S C&I

Davis, Genl. See: No. 5490.

Davis, Jefferson See: Nos. 803, 809, 870, 1594, 2909, 3134, 3191-4, 3444, 4551, 5712, 6236, 6873.

1456 Dawn of Love, The / (Postcard size, colored couple on boat.)
1880 V.S. C&I

1457 Dawn of Love, The / #529 / 2 columns, 2 lines of verse. 11.6x8.10 (Scottish scene, exterior, upright.)
und S N.C.

1458 Dawn of Love, The / #101 / 11.12x

8.3 (Full-length figure of girl, kissed by cupid — upright.) und S C&I

1459 Day before Marriage, The / #113 / 11.13x8.5 (Full length of bride seated before mirror, trying on jewelry, companion to 6825.) 1847 S N.C.

1460 Day Before Marriage, The / (Different composition from preceding, about 8x10.) und S N.C.

1461 Day Before Marriage, The / The Bride's Jewels / 11.8x8.8 (Companion to "A Year after Marriage" No. 6826, bride seated, pearls in hand, no mirror.) und S C&I

1462 Day Before the Wedding, The / und S N.C.

1463 Day of Rest, The / 9.10x16.13 (Family leaving home for church.) 1869 M C&I

Dayton See: W.L. No. 2502.

1464 Deacon's Mare, The / (Postcard size.) 1880 V.S. C&I

1465 Deacon's Mare, The / Getting the Word Go! from a bad little boy on Sunday morning / Thos. Worth on stone. (Vignette.) 1879 S C&I

1466 Dead Beat, A / und S C&I

DEAD BROKE.

1467 Dead Broke / Thos. Worth on stone. 11.12x8.15 (Dejected man in saloon sitting on barrel marked "Trade Mark M.T." Sign on wall "No Slate." Upright.) 1873 S C&I

1468 Dead Game / Quail / 12.6x8.12 (Black background, upright.) 1872 S C&I

1469 Dead Game / Woodcock & Partridge / 12.7x8.14 (Upright, black background.) 1872 S C&I

Deadhead (Horse) See: No. 6564.

Dean Richmond (Steamboat) See: Nos. 4748, 5994.

1470 "Dearest Spot on Earth to Me, The" / 9x12.10 (Owner burying horse, comic, same as "The Trotters Burial" No. 6164.) 1878 S C&I

1471 Death Bed of the Martyr President, Abraham Lincoln, The / Washington, Saturday morning April 15th, 1865 at 22 minutes past 7 o'clock / 13 keys. 11.1x16.4. 1865 M C&I

1472 Death of the Hon. Andrew Johnson / U.S. Senator from Tennessee and ex-President of the United States / Died at Greenville, Tenn. July 31st, 1875, aged, etc. / 7 keys. 8.5x12.7. 1875 S C&I

1473 Death of Calvin, The / #172 / 8.4x 12.6. 1846 S N.C.

1474 Death of Charles Sumner, The / At Washington, D.C., March 11th, 1874, aged 63 years, 2 month, and 5 days / "Do not let the Civil Rights Bill fail" / 7 keys. 8.5x12.7. 1874 S C&I

1475 Death of Col. Edward D. Baker / At the battle of Balls Bluff, near Leesburg, Va., Oct. 21st, 1861 / 8.6x 12.8. 1861 S C&I

1476 Death of Col. Ellsworth / After hauling down the rebel flag, at the taking of Alexandria, Va. May 24th, 1861. (Brownell and Jackson keyed, upright, vignette.) 1861 S C&I

1477 Death of Col. John J. Hardin / Of the 1st Regiment Illinois Volunteers / #461 / J. Cameron 1847 on stone. 8.5x 12.9. 1847 S N.C.

1478 Death of Col. Pierce M. Butler / Of the South Carolina [Palmetto Regiment] / At the battle of Churubusco [Mexico] Aug. 20th, 1847 / #537 / 3 additional lines. Cameron on stone. 8.3x12.13. 1847 S N.C.

1479 Death of Daniel O'Connell / At Genoa, Saturday May 15th, 1847. / His heart at Rome, his body in Ireland, and his soul in Heaven / #475 / 8.4x 12.8. 1847 S N.C.

1480 Death of Genl. Andrew Jackson / Born 15th March, 1767, President of the United States from 1829 to 1837— Died 8th June, 1845 / #346 / 8.9x11.13. 1845 S N.C.

1481 Death of General Grant, The / At Mount McGregor, Saratoga Co. New York July 23rd, 1885. / Keyed, left to right: Henry [The Nurse] — U. S. Grant, Jr. — Rev. Dr. Newman — Mrs. Grant, Dr. Douglas, Mrs. Sartoris [Nellie Grant], Jesse R. Grant, Harrison [The General's Body Servant], Col. Fred Grant. / 8.15x13.7.
1885 S C&I

1482 Death of General James A. Garfield / Twentieth President of the United States / 19 keys. 2 additional lines. 8.13x13.5. 1881 S C&I

1483 Death of General Lyon / At the head of his troops while successfully charging the rebel forces at the Battle of Wilson's Creek, Missouri, Aug. 10th, 1861 / 8.6x12.10. 1861 S C&I

1484 Death of General Robert E. Lee / At Lexington, Va. October 12th, 1870 / Aged 62 years, 8 months, and 6 days / 2 additional lines. 7.10x12.3.
1870 S C&I

1485 Death of Genl. Z. Taylor / 12th President of the United States / At the President's House, July 9th, 1850. 35 minutes past 10 o'clock, P.M. / 2 columns, 2 lines each, 12 references in plate. 8.4x12. 1850 S N.C.

1486 Death of Harrison, April 4, A.D. 1841 / "I wish you to understand the true principles of the Government. I wish them carried out. I ask nothing more." / 8 keys. 8.7x12.15.
1841 S N.C.

1487 Death of Harrison, April 4, A.D. 1841 / "I wish you to understand the true principles of the Government. I wish them carried out. I ask nothing more." / 8.8x12.14 (Very similar in composition to preceding, slight changes in size and draughtsmanship.)
1841 S N.C.

1488 Death of Honl. Henry Clay / "My son, I am going, sit by me" / #357 / 8 keys. 1852 S N.C.

1489 Death of Honl. Henry Clay / "My son, I am going, sit by me" / #357 / 1 additional line. 8.10x11.14 (Upright, 3 figures shown, no keys.)
1852 S N.C.

1490 Death of John Quincy Adams / At the U.S. Capitol Feby. 23d, 1848 /"This is the end of earth, I am content" / #567 / 8.4x12.13. 1848 S N.C.

1491 Death of Lieut. Col. Henry Clay, Jr. / Of the Second Regiment Kentucky Volunteers / At the battle of Buena Vista, Febr. 23rd, 1847 / #460 / J. Cameron on stone. 8.4x12.8 (Horse standing, Clay and orderly in center foreground, American troops on left.)
1847 S N.C.

1492 Death of Lieut. Col. Henry Clay, Jr. / Of the Second Regiment Kentucky Volunteers / At the battle of Buena Vista Feb. 23rd, 1847 / #460 / 1 additional line. 8.4x12.7 J. Cameron on stone. (Horse down and 3 others in foreground, American troops on right.) 1847 S N.C.

1493 Death of Maj. Genl. James B. M'Pherson / Commander of the Army and Department of Tennessee / At the battle near Atlanta, Ga. July 22nd, 1864 / und S C&I

1494 Death of Major Ringgold / Of the Flying Artillery / At the Battle of Palo Alto [Texas] May 8th, 1846 / #430 / 8.8x12.10 (Ringgold on black horse, facing right.) 1846 S N.C.

1495 Death of Major Ringgold / Of the flying Artillery / At the battle of Palo Alto [Texas] May 8th, 1846 / #430 / 8.9x12.12 (Ringgold on white horse, facing left, other changes in composition.) 1846 S N.C.

1496 Death of Minnehaha, The / J. Cameron on stone. 3 columns, 5 lines of verse from Longfellow. 14.10x20.14 (Winter scene.) 1867 L C&I

1497 Death of Montgomery / In the attack of Quebec, Dec. 1775 / #515 / 11.15x8.12 (Upright.) und S N.C.

1498 Death of Napoleon / 8.5x12.10.
und S N.C.

1499 Death of Pope Pius IXth. / At the Vatican, Rome, February 7th, 1878 / 3 additional lines. 7.15x12.5.
1878 S C&I

1500 Death of President Lincoln / At Washington, D.C., April 15th, 1865 / The Nation's Martyr / 12 key names. 8.10x12.15 (With full-length portrait of Genl. Halleck.) 1865 S C&I

1501 Death of President Lincoln / At Washington, D.C. April 15th, 1865 / The Nation's Martyr / #875 / 12 key names. 8.7x12.14 (Portrait of Vice-President Johnson, substituted for portrait of Genl. Halleck and other changes in composition.)
1865 S C&I

1502 Death of President Lincoln / 13x
15.8.   und M C&I

1503 Death of St. Joseph / 8.3x11.2.
                und S C.C.

1504 Death of St. Joseph /
                und S C&I

1505 Death of St. Patrick. The Apostle
of Ireland, The / At the Monastery of
Saul in Ulilia, March 17th, A.D. 465.
Aged 78 years / 8.8x12.
                1872 S C&I

1506 Death of "Stonewall" Jackson, The
/ 2 additional lines. 7.13x12.5.
                1872 S C&I

1507 Death of Tecumseh / Battle of the
Thames, Oct. 5th, 1813 / J. L. McGee,
Del. et lith. 11.8x9.1. 1841 S N.C.

1508 Death Of Tecumseh / Battle of the
Thames, Oct. 18, 1813 / Col. R. M.
Johnson — Tecumseh. / 12x8.14.
                1841 S N.C.

1509 Death of Tecumseh / Battle of the
Thames, Oct. 5, 1813 /
                1842 S N.C.

1510 Death of Tecumseh at the Battle
of the Thames /   1845 S N.C.

1511 Death of Tecumseh / Battle of the
Thames, Oct. 18, 1813 / Col. R. M.
Johnson, Tecumseh / #151 / 8.4x12.5
(Johnson in center on white horse.
Tecumseh on right.)
                1846 S N.C.
  Note: There is some doubt about
the exact date of Tecumseh's death,
hence difference in dates on prints.

1512 Death of the Blessed Virgin /
                und S C&I

1513 Death of the Just, The / Title repeated in Spanish and French. 8.4x
12.10 (Man on death bed, crucifix,
rosary, priest, angels, etc.)
                und S C&I

1514 Death of the Sinner, The / Title
repeated in French and Spanish. 8.3x
12.11 (Man on death bed, crucifix,
priest, serpents, demons, hell fire, etc.)
                und S C&I

1515 Death of Warren at the Battle of
Bunker Hill, 1775 / #514 / 11.10x8.6.
                und S N.C.

1516 Death of Washington, Dec. 14, A.D.
1799 / 5 keys. 8.9x12.15 (Washington's
hand on bed spread, Quaker seated.)
                1841 S N.C.

1517 Death of Washington Dec. 14 A.D.
1799 / 5 keys. 8.7x12.13 (Composition
similar to preceding, but Mrs. Washington holding his hand, and Quaker
standing.)   und S N.C.

1518 Death of Washington, Dec. 14th,
A.D. 1799 / Quaker, an intimate friend
of Washington, Physician, Grandchildren, and Lady Washington, Domestics / (Head to left.) und S N.C.

1519 Death of Washington, Dec. 14, A.D.
1799 / 5 keys. 8.4x12.13.
                und S N.C.

1520 Death of Washington, Dec. 14, A.D.
1799 / 6 keys. 8.8x13 (Washington
facing right.)   und S N.C.

1521 Death of Washington, Dec. 14, A.D.
1799 / Grandchildren, Lady Washington, Physician, Quaker, an intimate
friend of Washington, Domestics /
#69 / 5 Keys. 8.5x12.12 (6 in room,
Washington's head to left.)
                1846 S N.C.

1522 Death of Washington, December 14,
A.D. 1799 / (8 keyed figures, 7 in room
beside Washington, taken from an old
wood cut.)   und M N.C.

1523 Death Shot, The / 8.7x12.8 (Buck.)
                und S C&I
  Decatur, Stephen See: No. 4397.

1524 Declaration, The / #107 / 11.15x8.6
(¾ length, round corners.)
                1846 S N.C.

1525 Declaration, The / #107 / 11.14x8.5
(¾ length, in grape arbor.)
                und S C&I

1526 Declaration, The / (Full length,
flowers in background.)
                und S C.C.

1527 Declaration, The / #107 / 11.14x8.7
(Full length.)   und S N.C.

1528 Declaration, The / (Full length, exterior scene, different composition from
preceding.)   und S N.C.

1529 Declaration, The / J. McGee, Del.
8.14x7.2 (Exterior, companion to "The
Wedding Day" No. 6597.)
                und S N.C.

1530 Declaration Committee, The / 5 additional lines. 8.10x12.8 (Thomas Jefferson, Roger Sherman, Benjamin
Franklin, Robert R. Livingston, John
Adams keyed.)   1876 S C&I

1531 Declaration of Independence, The
/ July 4th, 1776 / #385 / 8.2x12.7
(Table at which Washington sits to
right.)   und S N.C.

1532 Declaration of Independence, The /
July 4th, 1776 / 8.2x12.7 (Identical

composition to preceding except reversed.)   und S N.C.

1533 Declaration of Independence, The / July 4th, 1776 / 7.13x12.3.
und S C&I

1534 Decoration of the Casket of Gen. Lee at Lexington, Va. Oct. 15, 1870 /
und S C&I

1535 Deer and Faun / 8.6x12.6.
und S C&I

1536 Deer Hunting by Torchlight / 10.6 x15.3 (Somewhat similar composition to "Still Hunting on the Susquehanna" No. 5815, only one deer shown.)
und M C&I

1537 Deer Hunting on the Susquehanna/ 10.4x14.12 (Same stone as "Still Hunting on the Susquehanna" No. 5815.)
und M C&I

1538 Deer in the woods / 8.8x12.8 (Also published with the title "The King of the Forest" No. 3333.)
und S C&I

1539 Deer Shooting / In the Northern Woods / 8.8x12.8 (1 hunter shown, roughly the same composition as "American Winter Sports, Deer Shooting on the Shattagee" No. 209, only 1 man shown.)   und S C&I

1540 Defence of the Flag, The /
und S C&I

1541 Defiance! / 8.6x12.6 (Stag and 2 deer on shore of lake.) und S C&I
Delaware (River) See: Nos. 5054, 6439-40, 6521-5.
Delaware (U.S. Ship of the Line) See: No. 6331.

1542 Delaying A Start / "Come, quit fooling and bring up that horse" / Thos. Worth on stone. (Diminutive jockey trying unsuccessfully to manage spirited horse, vignette.)
1881 S C&I

1543 Delia /   und S N.C.

1544 Delicious Coffee! / (Half length of of man holding cup and saucer, vignette.)   1881 S C&I

1545 Delicious Fruit / 5.8x7.8.
1865 V.S. C&I

1546 Delicious Fruit / (Musk Melon in center, vignette.)   1875 S C&I

1547 Delicious Fruit / (Tinted background, watermelon, plums, peaches, grapes, cantaloup, etc., oval.)
1865 M C&I

1548 Delicious Fruit / (Same as preceding, but circle.)   1865 M C&I

1549 Delicious Ice Cream / (Advertising card.)   und S C&I
Dembinski, Gen. See: No. 2248.

1550 Democracy in Search of a Candidate, The / Brooks, Pendleton, Wood, Miles O'Reilley, Hancock, Johnson, Seymour, Hoffman, Rynders, Bennett, Farragut / (Vignette.)
1868 M C&I

1551 Democratic Platform, The / Old Bullion, Franklin and Prince Charles supporting Buchanan. Riding him is a southern planter and negro boy, Uncle Sam advising that supports of Buchanan may give way; Martin Van Buren, with animal body in cave marked "Kinderhook" (Vignette, for sale at No. 2 Spruce St. No publisher's name, but published by N. Currier.)
und M N.C.

1552 Democratic Reformers in Search of A Head / (Shows a free-for-all fight; only hands, feet, blackjacks, guns shown. Vignette.)   1876 S C&I
Denmark (Steamship) See: No. 5757.

1553 Departed Worth / (Mother, child and dog in cemetery.)
und S N.C.

1554 Depths of Despair, The / #517 / 11.7x8.4 (Man with mandolin falling in rain barrel, companion to "The Summit of Happiness" No. 5881.)
und S C&I

1555 Der Hugern vom Vaterland 1849 / The Hungarian's farewell to their native land / Perezel Klapka aulich Kossuth Dembinski Bem / #548 (Title also in French.)   und S N.C.

1556 Descent from the Cross, The /
und S C&I

1557 Descent from the Cross, The/#207/ 12.10x8.14.   1847 S N.C.

1558 Descent from the Cross, The / #290 / 12.2x8.9. (5 disciples lifting Christ from cross.)   und S C&I

1559 Descent from the Cross, The / Joseph places the body of Jesus in a shroud / Passion 13 (Top of print) / 9.13x7.14.   und S N.C.
Desert Rock Light House / See: Nos. 117-8.

1560 Design for a Model School House / By Alex. J. Davis, Architect, N. Y.
und S N.C.

1561 Design for Astor's Hotel. Transverse Section. East to West. / A. J.

Davis, Architect. Stodart & Currier. (Vignette.)   und S N.C.

1562 Design for Astor's Hotel, N. Y. Section through the Gothic Hall and Courts (North & South) / A. J. Davis, Architect. Stodart & Currier. (Vignette.)   und S N.C.

1563 Design for Paddle Wheel Steamer done for E. F. Aldrich / 13.13x14.12.
                und M N.C.

1564 Design made for Astor's Hotel / The great windows light three floors / By I. Town & A. J. Davis, Arch'ts 1832. (Vignette.)   und S N.C.

De Soto **See:** Nos. 735, 1585.

1565 Desperate Finish, A /
                1885 S C&I

1566 Desperate Finish, A / 18x28. (4 horses under saddle to right.)
                1895 L C&I

1567 Desperate Peace Man, A /
                und S C&I

1568 Dessert of Fruit, A / (Melons berries, etc., vignette.)
                und S C&I

1569 Dessert of Fruit, A / 16.12x23.12 (In low plate on table—bird's nest with 3 eggs in foreground.)
                1869 L C&I

1570 Destruction of Jerusalem By The Romans / Under the Command of Titus, A. D. 70 / 10 keys. O. Knirsch on stone. 19.7x29.   1853 L N.C.

1571 Destruction of Tea at Boston Harbor, The / #516 (Some prints have: "Entered by Sarony & Major.")
                1846 S N.C.

1572 Destruction of the Rebel Monster "Merrimac" off Craney Island, May 11th, 1862 / 8.2x12.2. und S C&I

1573 Destruction of the Rebel Ram "Arkansas" / By the United States Gunboat "Essex" on the Mississippi River, near Baton Rouge, August 4th, 1862. / 8.2x12.10. ("Arkansas" and "Essex" keyed.   und S C&I

Deutschland (Steamship) **See:** No. 6259.

1574 Devil's Glen, The / Killarney, Ireland /   und S C&I

A DESSERT OF FRUIT.

1575 Dewdrop / By Falsetto, dam by Explosion / J. Cameron on stone. (Under saddle, broadside to right, vignette.)   1886 S C&I

Dewees, Wm. P. See: No. 6696.

1576 De Witt Clinton / 2.13x3. (From Jenkin's "History of Political Parties in the State of New York.")   und V.S. C.C.

1577 "Dexter" / By Rysdyk's Hambletonian, dam Hawkin's mare, by American Star / J. Cameron on stone. (Vignette.)   1871 S C&I

1578 Dexter, Ethan Allen, and Mate / In their wonderful race over the Fashion Course, L. I., June 21st, 1867. Match for $2000 mile heats best 3 in 5 / 3 additional lines and time 2:15, 2:16, 2:19 / J. Cameron on stone. (Vignette, to right passing judges' stand.)   1874 S C&I

1578A Dexter, Ethan Allen and Mate / Fashion Course, L. I., June 21st, 1867. Won by Ethan Allen. Time 2:15, 2:16, 2:19 / J. Cameron on stone. (Vignette, identical composition to preceding but judges' stand removed.)   1874 S C&I

Dexter (Horse) See: Nos. 883-4, 927, 1577-8, 1578A, 1757, 1907, 2243-4, 2941, 2946, 3336-8, 5708, 6117, 6168.

1579 Dexterous Whip, A / 1 additional line.   1876 S C&I

Diana (Steamboat) See: No. 5042.

1580 Dick Swiveller / By Walkill Chief, dam a Clay Mare / As he appeared at Hartford, Aug. 20th, 1878, beating Proteine and four others / Record 2:19 / (2 high-wheeled sulkies shown, to right, vignette.)   1878 S C&I

Dickens, Charles See: No. 643, 3297.

Dickenson, D. S. See: No. 1938.

1581 Die Familie des Kaiser's van Deutschland /   und S C&I

1582 Direct, driven by Geo. Starr / Record 2:05½ /   1891 S C&I

Direct See: Nos. 966-7.

1583 Director / 2.12x4.12 (Title in plate.)   1882 V.S. C&I

Director See: No. 6163.

Directum (Horse) See: Nos. 975, 6204.

1584 Discharging The Pilot / Sketched by J. Smith & Son, Brooklyn, L. I. On stone by C. Parsons. 16.4x24.4. (Second state of "Clipper Ship Ocean Express" No. 1160.)   1856 L N.C.

1585 Discovery of the Mississippi, The / By Ferdinand De Soto, and his followers, May 1541 / 8.15x12.15.   1876 S C&I

1586 Disloyal British "Subject," A / John Bull "Now Pat, mind! If you enlist with either of the belligerents I shan't protect you if you are taken as a pirate" / Pat: "Be me sowl thin, I don't want your protectshun, Th' ould Stars and Stripes there that I'm fight'n for will protect me" / (Allegorical figure of John Bull and Irish sailor, vignette.)   und S C&I

1587 Disputed Heat, A / Claiming a Foul / L. Maurer, Lith. Printed by Heppenheimer & Maurer. Thos. Worth on stone. 17.13x26.15. (First state, later republished as "A Good Race, Well Won" No. 2444.)   1878 L C&I

1588 Disputed Prize, The / 8.8x12.8. (2 sparrows quarreling over apple.)   und S C&I

1589 Distanced !! / Thos. Worth on stone. (Vignette, comic horse race.)   1878 S C&I

1590 Distant Relations / 8.7x11.6 (Group of country children watching well-dressed city child.)   und S C&I

1591 Distinguished Militia Genl. During An Action, A /   und S C&I

Distinguished Vocalist, Miss Phillips See: No. 4156.

1592 Dis-United States, The / or the Southern Confederacy / (Gentleman from South Carolina, guns in belt, whip in hand sitting on negro boy. "Florida" seaman in row boat, Georgia, Mississippi, and Alabama seated on bales of cotton. "Louisiana" seated on barrel of syrup, vignette.)   und S C&I

1593 Do You Love Butter? / 11.12x9.1. (Boy holding buttercup under girl's chin, upright.)   1878 S C&I

Dobbins (Horse) See: No. 2628.

Doble, Budd See: Nos. 719, 2531, 3337, 4740-1, 5708, 6189.

Doctor Franklin See: "The Art of Making Money in Every Man's Pocket," etc. No. 275.)

1594 "Dodge" That Won't Work, A / J. Cameron on stone. (Greeley and Jeff Davis with whip and chain. Greeley asking colored men to vote for him. They say they are going to vote for General Grant, Mr. Lincoln's friend, vignette.)   1872 S C&I

DISTANT RELATIONS.

1595 Dodger — Carter H. Harrison against the Boodlers, The /
und S C&I

1596 Dolly Varden / (Full-length figure, dress has large bustle.)
1872 S C&I

1597 Domestic Bliss / The First Born / #639 (Upright, full-length.)
und S C&I

1598 Domestic Blockade, The / Thos. Nast 3/62 on stone. 22.13x18.8. (Kitchen scene, mother repulsing attack by boy and girl, companion to "Attack on the Home Guard" No. 303.)
1862 L C&I

1599 Domino / #517 (Companion to "Can't Play" No. 785.)
und S N.C.

Domino (Horse) See: No. 2628.

1600 Don Juan / Plate 1 # 145 / 8.7x13.1 (4 columns, 4 lines of verse.)
und S N.C.

1601 Don Juan / Plate 2 #146 / 8.8x13.2 (4 columns, 4 line verse.)
und S N.C.

1602 Don Juan and Lambro / Plate 3 #147 / (4 columns, 4 lines of verse.)
und S N.C.

1603 Don Juan separated from Haidee / Plate 4 #148 / (4 columns, 4 lines of verse.)
und S N.C.

1604 Done Gone Busted! / Thos. Worth on stone. (Companion to "De Tug Ob War" No. 6246, vignette.)
1883 S C&I

Donelson, Andrew See: No. 2489.

1605 Don't Hurt My Baby / 11.8x8.10. (Large dog trying to see puppy held by little girl.)
1872 S C&I

1606 Don't Say Nay /
1846 S N.C.

1607 Don't You Want Another Baby? /
und S C&I

1608 Don't You Wish You Might Get It? / J. Schutz, Del. 12.7x8.5.
und S N.C.

1609 Doremus, Suydams and Nixon, Importers and Jobbers of Dry Goods, 37 and 39 Nassau, corner of Liberty Street, opposite the Middle Dutch

Church, New York / J. H. Bufford, Del. et lith. Currier's Press. 9.12x15.4.
und S N.C.

Dorr, T. W. See: No. 6251.

1610 Dotty Dimple / 12x8.8 (Upright, vignette, bust of child.)
und S C&I

1611 Double-Barrelled Breech Loader, A / (Hunter's gun discharging at both ends, and shooting dog, vignette, comic.) 1880 S C&I

Douglas, Hon. Stephen See: Nos. 2627, 2920-4, 4386, 4388, 4820, 4823, 4960, 5812-3, 5828, 5962, 6279.

Douglass, F. D. See: No. 2130.

1612 Dove, The / 12.1x8.13 (Girls and dove, upright.) und S N.C.

1613 Dove's Refuge, The /
und S C&I

1614 Down, Charge! / 8.12x12.13 (2 hunters, 2 dogs at their feet.)
und S C&I

1615 Dr. Friedr. Hecker / "Auf der Rednerbuhne der Grosherz bad Ilten Kammer" / #628 (½ length portrait, standing on rostrum, battle scene seen through window.) und S N.C.

1616 Dr. William Valentine / In some of his Eccentric Characters / Sketched by Dr. Northall of Brooklyn / during an entertainment / 12.12x18.6 (Central portrait of Valentine, surrounded by 6 smaller ones as "Sourcrout" "Joab Squash" "Tabitha Tiptongue" "Old Woman of Eighty" "Billy Jones" and "Peleg Smooth"—very early print by N. Currier.) und M N.C.

1617 Draw Poker—Getting 'em Lively / "3 of a kind beat 2 pair" / (Vignette.) 1886 S C&I

1618 Draw Poker—Getting 'em Lively / "three of a kind beat two pair" / "Chew Pan Handle Scrap" Tobacco / (Advertisement.)
1886 M C&I

1619 Draw Poker—Laying for 'em Sharp / "See you and go three better." (Vignette.) 1886 S C&I

1620 Drawing Cards for Beginners (6 views on sheet.) und S C&I

1621 Drawing Cards for Beginners / (8 views on sheet.) und S C&I

1622 Drawing Studies/(4 views on sheet, vignette.) und S C&I

1623 Drawing Studies / [Second Series] / (4 rural scenes on sheet, vignette, about 5x7.) und S C&I

1624 Dreadful Wreck of the Mexico on Hempstead Beach, Jany. 2nd, 1837; As now exhibiting at / Hanington Dioramas / Published at the Sun office by B. H. Day. Drawn on the spot by H. Sewel. N. Currier's lith., cor. of Nassau & Spruce Sts. 6.13x10.4.
und S N.C.

Dreadnought (Clippership) See: Nos. 876-7, 1143-4.

Dreadnought (Yacht) See: No. 6821.

1625 Dreams of Youth, The / 9.10x16.13 (Boy lying on back, on bank overlooking river valley, vision of castle in the sky.) 1869 M C&I

1626 "Drew" and "St. John" of the People's Evening Line between New York and Albany / Drawn by C. R. Parsons. 1878 L C&I

Drew (Hudson River Steamer) See: Nos. 196, 1626, 2523, 2541, 4747-8, 5732-3.

Drink See: Nos. 244, 649, 946, 1629, 1797, 2142, 2769, 4168-9, 4612, 5274, 5670, 5953, 6242, 6489, 6497, 6606.

1627 Drive Through the Highlands, The / 10.4x14.12 (3 people in wagon, team of horses, country scene.)
und M C&I

Driver (Horse) See: Nos. 65, 2423.

1628 Driving Finish, A / L. Maurer on stone. 21.12x31.12 (3 horses heads, close up.) 1891 L C&I

1629 Drunkard's Progress, The / From the first glass to the grave / #431 / 8.7x12.12 (Shows 9 steps from 1st glass to death by suicide, bottom center oval of mother and child fleeing burning home.) 1846 S N.C.

1630 Dryburgh Abbey, Scotland /
und S C&I

1631 Dublin Bay / Ireland / (2 people shown on rocks at right.)
und S C&I

1632 Dublin Bay, Ireland / From Kingston Quarries / (4 people on rocks and changes in composition from preceding.) und S C&I

Dublin, See: Ireland.

Duc de Chatres (Horse) See: No. 4749.

1633 Duchess of Orleans, The / In the Chamber of Deputies, 24th February, 1848 / #579 / 8x12.12 (5 additional lines, title repeated in French.)
1848 S N.C.

1634 Dude Belle, A / Thos. Worth on stone. (Extravagantly dressed colored lady carrying dog, comic, upright, vignette.) 1883 S C&I

1635 Dude Swell, A / Thos. Worth on stone. (Full-length of colored man passing cafe, spectators admiring his "get-up," upright vignette, companion to preceding.) 1883 S C&I

Duelling See: Nos. 2927, 5399.

Duffy, Charles Gavan See: No. 2897.

1636 Duke and Duchess of Edinburgh, The / (Upright, 2 heads.) und S C&I

Duke See: No. 310.

Duke of Magenta (Horse) See: No. 5037.

Dunn, O. J., Lieut. Gov. Louisiana See: No. 4631.

1637 Dusted—and Disgusted / Thos. Worth on stone. (Vignette, horse comic.) 1878 S C&I

1638 "Dutchess" of Oneida / (Pedigreed cow.) und S C&I

1639 Dutchman / Beacon Course, N. J., August 1st, 1839. Match $1000, a side 3 miles under the saddle, against time 7 minutes, 49 seconds / 3 additional lines and 2 columns, 6 lines each. 12.13x20.15 (Broadside to left.) 1850 L N.C.

1640 "Dutchman" and "Hiram Woodruff" /As they appeared on the Beacon Course, N. J., August 1st, 1839, in the great performance by "Dutchman" of trotting with Hiram's weight, etc. / J. Cameron on stone. (Vignette, under saddle to right.) 1871 S C&I

1641 Dutchman / Three miles in 7:32½ under saddle / und S C&I

1642 Dwight L. Moody / The American Evangelist / Born in Northfield, Mass., February 5th, 1837 / (Vignette portrait.) und S C&I

Dwyer, John J. See: No. 3268.

1643 Dying Buffalo Bull / Deadly Effect of the Indian Arrow / Catlin, Del. 12.2x17.12. und M C&I

E

1644 E. Forrest as Metamora / #180 / 12.5x8.14 (Full-length figure as Indian Brave, upright, no hills or river in background.) und S N.C.

1645 E. Forrest as Metamora / 12.5x8.14 (Full-length figure, same as preceding except river and hills shown in background and other slight changes in composition.) und S N.C.

1646 E Pluribus Unum / The Great International Rifle Match, Dollymount, July, 1875 / C. M. Vergnes on stone. 11.4x16 (Companion to 1753, 2824, 5028.) 1875 S C&I

1647 Eager For The Race / L. Maurer on stone. 18.5x27.14 (Head on view of 7 horses under saddle.) 1893 L C&I

Eagle (Steamer) See: No. 5042.

1648 Early Autumn in the Cattskills / (Hunter and dog at foot of waterfall.) und M C&I

1649 Early Autumn / Salmon Brook, Granby, Connecticut / 1869 S C&I

1650 Early Piety / Remember thy Creator, etc. / #123 / 8.11x12.2 (Upright.) 1846 S N.C.

Early Rose (Horse) See: No. 732.

1651 Early Spring / (Farm wagon on road, cow, river in background, sailboats.) und M C&I

1652 Early Winter / 9.10x16.15 (Skating pond on right, cottage and road on left.) 1869 M C&I

East Saginaw Course, Mich. See: Nos. 507, 2421, 4741, 6009.

1653 Easter Cross, The / und S C&I

1654 Easter Cross, The / 22x16.12 (Upright, vignette, cross covered with flowers.) 1869 L C&I

1655 Easter Flowers / 12.7x8.7 (Cross covered with flowers, upright.) 1869 S C&I

1656 Easter Flowers / 12.6x8.8 (Cross covered with flowers, different composition.) 1874 S C&I

1657 Easter Flowers / und S C&I

1658 Easter Morning / 1 additional line Biblical quotation. 11.8x8.4. und S C&I

1659 Easter Offering, An / 12.2x8.8 (Cross covered with flowers, black background, upright.) 1871 S C&I

1660 Easter Offering, An / (Cross covered with flowers, vignette, upright, white background.)
und S C&I

1661 Eastern Beauty, The / (Vignette.)
und S C&I

1662 Eating Crow on a Wager / De fust brace. / Thos. Worth on stone. (Vignette.) 1883 S C&I

1663 Eating Crow on a Wager / De last lap / Thos. Worth on stone. (Vignette.) 1883 S C&I

1664 Echo Lake / White Mountains / 11.3x14.9 (Oval, row boat, 6 people to left, no people in foreground.)
und M C&I

1665 Echo Lake—White Mountains / 8.7x12 (Bright autumn foliage, row boat and people in foreground.)
und S C&I

1666 Eclipse and Sir Henry / A representation of the famous match race for 20,000 dollars a side between Mr. Van Ranst's horse, Eclipse and Mr. R. Johnson's horse, Henry. Run on the Long Island Union Course, May 27, 1823 / (3 ovals on large folio.)
und L C&I

Eclipse (Horse) See: No. 1666.

Eclipse (Mississippi Steamboat) See: Nos. 4116, 4607, 5730.

Eclipse Course, L. I. See: Nos. 2019-20.

Edison, Thomas See: No. 1685.

1667 Edith / (Vignette.)
und S C&I

1668 Edward / 1879 S C&I
Edward (Horse) See: Nos. 622, 940, 4251.

1669 Edward / By Fisk's Hambletonian / Record 2:19 / J. Cameron on stone. (Vignette, ¾ view, high-wheeled sulky.) 1879 S C&I

1670 Edward and Swiveller / Scott Leighton, Del. 1882 S C&I

Edwards, Billy See: No. 525.

1671 Edwin Forrest /
1860 S C&I

1672 Edwin Forrest / (Facsimile signature.) (Vignette, head and shoulders.)
1860 M C&I

1673 Edwin Forrest / E. Brown, Del. Published by Brown & Minot.
und S N.C.

1674 Edwin Forrest as Metamora / 12.5x8.14. und S N.C.

1675 Edwin Forrest / By Brannock's Ned Forrest, Jr., dam Fanny Mundy by Flight, son of Leviathan / Bred by Jas. H. Haddock at Harrisonville, Cass Co., Mo. Foaled April, 1871 / Record 2.18 (Broadside to right.)
1878 S C&I

1676 Edwin Forrest / Record 2:11¾ (Vignette.) 1878 S C&I

1677 Edwin Thorne / By Thornedale, dam by Ashland / Record 2:17½ / Scott Leighton on stone. (Vignette, high-wheeled sulky, ¾ view to left.)
1882 S C&I

Edwin Thorne See: No. 2530.

Egypt (Steamship) See: Nos. 2094, 3887, 5758.

1678 Egyptian Beauty, The / (Vignette.)
und M C&I

1679 Egyptian Beauty, The / (Vignette, head.) und S C&I

Egyptian Monarch (Steamship) See: No. 5759.

Eider (Steamship) See: No. 5760.

1680 (Eighteen Seventy Six) 1876—On Guard / Unceasing Vigilance is the Price of Liberty / 8.15x12.7 (Shows Union soldier holding off 3 allegorical figures.) 1876 S C&I

1681 El Capitan—From Mariposa Trail / 8.8x12.8. und S C&I

1682 El Dorado Pain Abstractor, The / And all healing Herb ointment.)
1846 S N.C.

1683 El Nino Cantivo /
und S C&I

1684 El Santo Nina de Atocha /
und S C&I

Elba (Italian Island) See: No. 5127.

Elbe (Steamship) See: Nos. 3036, 5531.

Electioneer (Horse) See: No. 2651.

1685 Electric Light, The / (Shows Edison standing on New York City and C. F. Brush, inventor of arc light, in Brooklyn touching lighted cigars. Vignette. New York, Brooklyn and New Jersey keyed.) 1880 S C&I

1686 Electric Light—Tobacco / (Advertising card.) und S C&I

1687 Elephant and His Keepers, The / J. Cameron on stone. (Vignette.)
und M C&I

Eliophobus Family See: Nos. 6762-4.

Elisha Kent Kane See: No. 2578.

THE ELECTRIC LIGHT.

1688 Eliza / #49 (On balcony, facing bird in cage at right, rose in hand, ¾ length.) und S N.C.

1689 Eliza / (On balcony, composition reversed, no rose in hand and other slight changes.) und S N.C.

1690 Eliza / (Full-length, facing left, paper in hand.) 1844 S N.C.

1691 Eliza / #49 (Bust portrait, vignette, large gold brooch.) und S C&I

1692 Eliza / #78 (Full-length, dressed for street, seated, flowers in vase at right.) 1844 S N.C.

1693 Eliza / 11.15x8.2 (Similar to preceding, with slight changes in composition.) 1848 S N.C.

1694 Eliza / (½ length.) und S C&I

1695 Eliza / (Seated, left arm over back of chair, cornucopia vase.) und S N.C.

1696 Eliza Jane / #98 / 11.9x8.8 (¾ length, holding roses in hand, oval in ornamental floral border.) 1847 S N.C.

1697 Elizabeth / (Full-length, vase flowers on table, window at left.) und S N.C.

1698 Elizabeth / 12.2x8.7 (½ length, red dress with blue piping, round corners.) 1846 S. N.C.

1699 Elizabeth / #69 / 12.3x8.7 (Full-length, blue shawl, poke bonnet, red dress, seated, exterior scene.) 1848 S N.C.

1700 Elizabeth / #45 / 12.5x9 (¾ length, seated, black shawl, chin resting on right hand.) und S C&I

1701 Elizabeth / (Bust portrait, young lady wearing tiara, vignette.) und S C&I

1702 Elizabeth / (Full-length, on chair, dog in center.) und S N.C.

1703 Elizabeth / #15 (Full-length, seated, red dress, window at right.) und S N.C.

1704 Elizabeth / #15 (¾ length, arm resting on back of chair.) und S N.C.

Elizabeth, Queen **See:** No. 5153.

1705 Ella / (Vignette.) und S C&I

1706 Ellen / #51 (½ length, Turkish scene.) und S N.C.

1707 Ellen / (¾ length, standing at dressing table.) 1844 S N.C.

1708 Ellen / (¾ length, standing at dressing table, similar to preceding with slight changes in composition.) 1848 S N.C.

1709 Ellen / #76 (Full-length, seated, book in hand.) 1848 S N.C.

1710 Ellen / #51 / Sarony on stone. (Oval in ornamental border, ½ length.) 1846 S N.C.

1711 Ellen / #51 / (¾ length.) 1845 S N.C.

1712 Ellen / #51 / (¾ length, different composition from preceding.) und S N.C.

1713 Ellen Tree (Facsimile) / In the character of Mariane in the Wrecker's Daughter / "Two months is a long time" / Henri Heidemans, 1837, on stone. Published by W. A. Colman, 205 Broadway. (Full-length, vignette.) 1837 S N.C.

1714 Ellen Tree as Hero in "Woman's Wit" / Henri Heidemans on stone. 1838 S N.C.

1715 Ellen Tree as Ion / und S N.C.

Elliott, Robert Brown **See:** No. 5177.

Elssler, Madlle. **See:** Nos. 1289-90, 1872-3, 3858, 6034.

Ellsworth, Elmer **See:** Nos. 1188-90, 1476.

1716 Elopement, The / 12.10x8.4 (Knight and lady on horseback, castle in background, companion to "The Pursuit" No. 4975.) und S N.C.

Elwell, Genl. **See:** No. 380.

1717 Emblem of Hope, The / (Group of flowers arranged in the shape of an anchor, vignette.)   und S C&I

1718 Emblem of Salvation, The / (Floral cross, ferns, etc., vignette.)
1874 S C&I

1719 Embracing An Opportunity / #468.
und S C&I

1720 Emeline / (¾ length, seated, arm on table.)   und S N.C.

1721 Emeline / #87 / 11.15x8.4 (Full-length, poke bonnet, red robe, church seen through window at right.)
1848 S N.C.

1722 Emeline / #253 (Vignette, ½ length.)   und S C&I

1723 Emily / (¾ length, seated in window.)   und S N.C.

1724 Emily / (¾ length, seated at table, wrap over arm, identical composition to "Caroline" No. 820.)
und S N.C.

1725 Emily / #52 (Firth & Hall, 1 Franklin Square, New York [name on piano], ¾ length of girl, seated at piano, decollete dress. Print has rounded corners.)   1846 S N.C.

1726 Emma / #258 (¾ length, standing at table to left, book in hand.)
und S N.C.

1727 Emma /   1849 S N.C.

1728 Emma / (Dog in arms, red dress.)
und S N.C.

1729 Emma / (Standing to right at table, open book, ¾ length.)
und S N.C.

1730 Emma / (Vignette.)
und S C&I
Emma B (Horse) See: No. 2662.
Emmet, Robert See: Nos. 5183-7.

1731 Emmet's Betrothed /
und S C&I

1732 Emperor, The /   und S N.C.

1733 Emperor of Norfolk / By Norfolk, dam Marian by Malcom / J. C. on stone (J. Cameron). (Vignette, under saddle, colored boy jockey to right, vignette.)   1888 S C&I
Empire (Steamboat) See: No. 5725.
Empire State (Steam Packet) See: No. 721.

1734 Empress, The / #124 (¾ length.)
und S C&I

1735 Empress Eugenie /
und S N.C.

1736 Empress Eugenie and Queen Victoria / (2 portraits on same sheet, about 5x8, vignette.)
und S C&I

1737 Empress Josephine / (Vignette, head and shoulders.)
und S C&I

1738 Empty Cradle, The / #223 (Mother crying beside crib, full-length.)
und S N.C.

1739 Enchanted Cave, The / 14.13x20.9.
1867 L C&I

1740 Enchanted Isles, The / 7.15x12.8.
1869 S C&I

1741 End of Long Branch, The / J. Cameron on stone. (Grant fishing in sea on "Long Branch," Greeley chopping down "Presidential Tree"—vignette.)
1872 S C&I
England See: Nos. 538, 1325-6, 1745, 2073, 2623-4, 2827, 2864, 3283, 3328, 3438, 3442, 3752, 3800, 3872, 4114, 4136, 4479, 4599, 5346, 5411, 5836, 6475, 6500, 6720.

1742 English Beauty, The / (Vignette, head.)   und S C&I

1743 English Snipe / 8.8x12.8 (Open country, birds in profile.)
und S N.C.

1744 English Snipe / 8.8x12.8 (2 snipe on left bank of woodland stream, 1 on right bank in rear, radically different composition from preceding.)
1871 S C&I
English, W. H. See: Nos. 2499-500, 2926.

1745 English Winter Scene, An / 8.8x12.8 (People on way to church, snow-covered cottage.)
und S C&I

1746 English Yacht Off Sandy Hook, An / 9x12.8.   und S C&I
Ennis, John See: No. 3266.

1747 Enoch Arden—The Hour of Trial / 14.14x22.14 (Enoch shown looking in window of his home.)
1869 L C&I

1748 Enoch Arden—The Hour of Trial / 2 columns, 6 lines of verse.
und S N.C.

1749 Enoch Arden—The Lonely Isle / 14.13x22.14 (2 columns, 6 lines of verse.)   1869 L C&I

1750 Enos T. Throop / 2.13x3 (From Jenkins' "History of Political Parties in the State of New York," 1846.)
und V.S. C.C.

1751 Entrance to the Highlands, The / Hudson River—Looking South / 1864 L C&I

1752 Entrance to the Holy Sepulchre, Jerusalem / Title repeated in Spanish / #641 / 8.6x12. 1849 S N.C.

Eole (Horse) See: No. 2764.

Epsom Downs, England See: No. 4599.

Erie (Burning Steamer) See: No. 747.

Erie Railroad See: Nos. 186, 189, 641, 2643, 5713, 5716.

1753 Erin Go Bragh / The Great International Rifle Match, Dollymount, July, 1875 / C. M. Vergnes on stone. 11.3x15.15 (Companion to "E Pluribus Unum" Nos. 1646, 2824, 5028.) 1875 M C&I

1754 Escape of Sergeant Champe, The / In the endeavor to carry out Washington's plan to capture Arnold and save the life of the traitor's victim, the gallant Major Andre, 1780, / 8.10x12.6. 1876 S C&I

Essex (U.S. Gunboat) See: No. 1573.

1755 Esther / #276 (Full-length, river in background.) und S N.C.

1756 Esther / (¾ length figure.) und S N.C.

1757 Ethan Allen and Mate and Dexter / In their wonderful race, over the Fashion Course, L. I., June 21st, 1867 / 4 additional lines and 2 columns of 6 lines. J. Cameron on stone. 17.6x27.6 (Skeleton wagon and sulky.) 1867 L C&I

1758 Ethan Allen & Mate and Lantern & mate / Crossing the Score "A Dead Heat" Time 2:24½ / In their great match for $10,000 over the Union Course, L. I., May 18th, 1859 / 4 additional lines. L. Maurer on stone. 17.6x27.12 (Skeleton wagons, ¾ to right, passing judge's stand.) 1859 L C&I

1759 Ethan Allen and Mate and Lantern and Mate / In their great match for $10,000 over the Union Course, L. I., 1859 / L. Maurer on stone. 1859 L C&I

1760 Ethan Allen and Mate to wagon / Driven by Dan Mace / 1874 S C&I

Ethan Allen (Horse) See: Nos. 927, 938, 1578, 1578A, 5708.

EUROPA.

THE EUROPEAN WAR DANCE!

Great Turko Muscovite jig, executed by the Cossacks and Bashi-Bazouks for the protection of Christianity and the advance of civilization.

Ethiopian Singers **See:** No. 878.
Etruria (Steamship) **See:** Nos. 4429, 5761.

1761 Etta / und S C&I

1762 "Euchered" / (Tearful old maid playing cards depicting babies, vignette, companion to "A Full Hand." No. 2204.) 1884 S C&I

1763 Eugenie / Empress Regent of France / (Vignette, head) und S C&I
Eugenie, Empress **See:** Nos. 455, 1735-6.

1764 Europa / und M C&I
Europa (Steamship) **See:** No. 5239.

1765 Europe / (Vignette, head.) 1870 S C&I

1766 Europe / Pub. by N. Currier, 2 Spruce St. & 169 Broadway (½ length, exterior scene, Marine background, vignette.) und S N.C.

1767 European Bowling Alley, The / King William — Jules Favre. / Die Europaische Kegelbahn / (King William using ball marked "Sedan" to knock down pins "Prince Imperial" "Napoleon" "Eugenie" "Pope." Jules Favre in charge of alley.) 1870 S C&I

1768 European War Dance, The / Great Turko Muscovite Jig executed by the Cossacks and Bashi-Bazouks for the protection of Christianity and the ancient civilization / 12.3x17.2 (Shows various European countries fighting, Uncle Sam in boat labelled "War Parties Served with Material, etc." A. W. on stone.) 1877 M C&I

1769 Evacuation of Richmond, Va. / By the government of the Southern Confederacy on the night of April 2nd, 1865. 1865 S C&I

1770 Evangeline / (2 lines of verse.) und S C&I

1771 Evangeline / Drawn by L. Maurer after the painting by Thomas Faed, A.R.A. 2 lines of verse. (½ length round top.) und L C&I
Evangeline **See:** No. 2863.

[85]

1772 Evening of Love, The / 11.8x8.4.
und S C & I

1773 Evening Prayer, The / "Defend us from all perils and dangers of this night." / 9.14x7.14 (Oval in rectangular floral border, upright, companion to No. 4206.)   und S C.C.

1774 Evening Prayer, The / "Defend us from all perils and dangers of this night" / #8 / 11.12x8.6.
und S N.C.

1775 Evening Prayer, The / #8 (2 columns, 2 lines of verse, companion to No. 4205.)   und S C&I

1776 Evening Star, The / (¾ length on balcony, stars in background.)
und S N.C.

1777 Evening Star, The / #500 (Girl asleep in bed, book in hand, slightly rounded corners.)   und S C&I

1778 Evening Star, The / (Vignette, head of girl.)   und S C&I

1779 Evening Star, The / #333 / Sarony on stone. (Oval in ornate rectangular border.)   1846 S N.C.

1780 Eventide—October / The Village Inn / Painted by B. Hess. 14.9x25.
1867 L C&I

1781 Eventide—The Curfew / (2 columns, 4 lines of verse.)
und S C&I
Everett, Edward See: Nos. 2509, 2899, 4820, 4823.

1782 Everybody's Friend / Thos. Worth on stone. 3 columns, 2 lines of verse. (Vignette, 3 men smoking, chewing, and taking snuff, evidently designed as a tobacco ad.)   1876 M C&I

1783 Every Thing Coming Down / (Balloon with the words "The Bottom Out" and basket marked "Gold Speculation." Clothes, beef, cheese, butter, etc., falling out and people below scrambling to pick them up, vignette.)
1870 S C&I

1784 Everything Lovely / (Mule in greenhouse knocking over flower pots and eating flowers, vignette.)
1880 S C&I
Excelsior (Hudson River Steamboat) See: No. 196.

1785 Exciting Finish, An /
1895 S C&I

1786 Exciting Finish, An / J. Cameron on stone. 18.12x27.12 (vignette, broadside of 3 horses, printed in oil colors.)
1884 L C&I

THE EXPRESS TRAIN.

[86]

1787 Express Steamship "Augusta Victoria" Hamburg American Packet Co. / 1 additional line of dimensions.
und S C&I

1788 Express Steamship "Columbia," The / Hamburg American Packet Co. / 1 additional line of dimensions.
und S C&I

1789 Express Steamship "Furst Bismark" Hamburg American Packet Co. / 1 additional line. 8.15x14.14.
und S C&I

1790 Express Train, The / J. Schutz, Del. 7.12x12.4 (Old style wood-burning locomotive, tender, baggage car and 3 coaches passing under bridge to left, group of people in costumes of the period to right. This is one of the earliest railroad prints by N. Currier.)
und S N.C.

1791 Express Train, The / Chas. Parsons, Del. 17.8x26.8 (¾ view, engine, tender, baggage car and 4 coaches to right.)   1859 L C&I

1792 Express Train, The / 8x12.8 (Engine, tender, baggage car, and 6 coaches passing under bridge at left.)
1870 S C&I

1793 Express Train, The / 8x12.7 (Engine, tender, baggage car and 7 passenger cars pulling to left around bend in road at right.)   1870 S C&I

1794 Express Train, The / #127 (Vignette, engine, tender, baggage car, and 7 cars to left.)   und S C&I

1795 Expulsion of Adam and Eve /
und S N.C.

1796 Exquisite, The / The "Pet of The Ladies." / (Oval caricature portrait of man with dog's head.)
und M C&I

1797 Extra Cool Lager Beer / (Store card.)   und S C&I

1798 Extraordinary Express Across the Atlantic / Pilot Boat Wm. J. Romer, Capt. McGuire / Leaving for England —Feb. 9th, 1846 / 2 columns, 2 additional lines. 8.4x12.11 (Shows fort on Governor's Island.)
1846 S N.C.

F

1799 Fair Beauteous Queen / A favorite song and trio written, composed and respectfully dedicated to St. George's Society by William Clifton / C. E. Lewis, Del. 10.7x8.7 (Portrait of Queen Victoria.)   und S N.C.

1800 Fair Equestrian / (¾ length, vignette.)   1857 L C&I

1801 Fair Equestrian, The / "Over the hills and far away" / (Woman on white horse, dog in foreground.)
und S N.C.

1802 "Fair Field and No Favor, A" / J. Cameron, '91, on stone. 18x28.2 (¾ view from rear of 6 horses passing grand stand and judge's stand.)
1891 L C&I

1803 "Fair Moon, To Thee I Sing" / (Comic stage scene from "Pinafore," vignette.)   1879 S C&I

1804 "Fair Moon, To Thee I Sing" / (Postcard size.)   1880 V.S. C&I

Fair Oaks, Va. See: Nos. 402-3, 2289.

1805 Fair Patrician, The / (Vignette.)
und S C&I

1806 Fair Patrician, The / (Vignette portrait, tinted background.)
und M C&I

1807 Fair Puritan, The / ½ length vignette.)   und S C&I

1808 Fair Start, A / "Take de water togedder when yous hear de shot!" / King & Murphy, Dels., on stone. Companion to "Result in Doubt" No. 5120.)
1884 S C&I

1808A Fair Start, A / "Take de water togedder when yous hear de shot!" / (Used as ad "Chew Pan Handle Scrap.")   1884 M C&I

1809 Fairest Flower So Palely Drooping / Greenwood Cemetery / Entrance to the grounds of the church of our Saviour / Poetry by / Mrs. Balmanno / Music composed by / Miss Augusta Browne / This song was occasioned by the recent deeply lamented demise of a lovely and accomplished lady, well known in this community / Mary Balmanno, Del. (Vignette, 7.8x5.15, published by C. Holt, Jr.)
1847 S C.C.

1810 Fairest of the Fair / (Vignette.)
und S C&I

1811 Fairies Home, The / 14.13x20.7.
und L C&I

1812 Fairies Home, The /
1868 M C&I

1813 Fairmount Water Works / From the Canal, showing Wire Bridge / F. F. Palmer, Del. 11x15.6.
und M C&I

1814 Fairy Grotto / 14.12x20.8.
1867 L C&I

1815 Fairy Grotto, The /
1867 S C&I

1816 Fairy Isle, The /
und S C&I

1817 Fairy Tales /
und S C&I

1818 Faith, Hope and Charity / (Scroll, flowers, angels, etc.)
1874 S C&I

1819 Fall and Winter Fashions for 1837 & 8 by Scott & Perkins, 164 Broadway, N. Y. / Entered according to Act of Congress, 1837. 2 columns, 7 and 8 lines. W. K. H. on stone. (Hewitt) 18.8x24.14 (Male and female figures.)
und L N.C.

1820 Fall from Grace, A / Thos. Worth on stone (Colored couple down in snow, kids running away—vignette, companion to "A Put Up Job" No. 4979.)
1883 S C&I

1821 Fall of Richmond, Virginia, The / On the night of April 2nd, 1865 / 16x22.4.
1865 L C&I

1822 Fall of Richmond, Virginia, The / On the night of April 2nd, 1865 /
1865 S C&I

1823 Fall of Richmond, Va., The / On the night of April 2nd, 1865. (Similar composition to preceding but with changes in pedestrians, carriages, etc., crossing bridge.)
1865 S C&I

1824 Falling Springs, Va. / Chromo in oil colors from the original painting by Saml. Colman. 1868 S C&I
Falling Springs, Va. See: "Picturesque Landscapes" No. 4778.
Falls, The See: No. 3439.

1825 Fall of Sebastopol, The / Capture of the Malakoff Tower by the French Division / Septembre 8th, 1855 / #705.
und S N.C.

1826 Falls "Des Chats" / Ottawa River, Canada / 8x12.8 (Group of canoeists at left.)
und S C&I

1827 Falls of Niagara / From Clifton House / 8.4 x 12.11.
und S N.C.

1828 Falls of Niagara, The / "From the Canada Side" / Painted by B. Hess. Parsons & Atwater, Dels. 18.4x27.13

(12 keys, rainbow shown.)
1859 L C&I

1829 Falls of Niagara / "From the Canada Side" / Painted by B. Hess. Parsons & Atwater, Dels. 18.2x28.2 (Printed in color, 13 keys, rainbow shown.)
1873 L C&I

1830 Falls of the Ottawa River / Canada / 7.15x12.7 (Moonlight scene, 4 men in canoe.)
und S C&I

1831 Falls of Tivoli, Italy /
und S C&I

1832 Falsetto / By Enquirer dam Farfaletta, by Imp Australian / (Vignette, under saddle, crowded stands in background.)
1879 S C&I

1833 Familien Register / #194.
1846 S N.C.

1834 Familien Register / (4 columns in German.)
1869 S C&I

1835 Family Devotion / Reading the Scriptures /
und S N.C.

1836 Family Devotion / 7.14x12.5 (Father reading to 4 members of family.)
1871 S C&I

1837 Family Garland / (Floral border, 3 columns, small view of marriage at top, spaces for photographs of mother and father, vignette.)
1874 S C&I

1838 Family Garland /
und S C&I

1839 Family of Louis Kossuth /
1851 S N.C.

1840 Family Pets, The / (Girl with dogs. Full length.)
und S N.C.

1841 Family Photograph Register / 8.13x12.13 (4 columns.)
und S C&I

1842 Family Photograph Register, The /
1864 M C&I

1843 Family Photograph Tree, The / 8.8x12 (12 oval spaces for photographs, village scene in background.)
1871 S C&I

1844 Family Record / Entered, etc. / 1846 by Wm. J. Bunce, J. R. Foster, Del. 4 columns.
und S C&I

1845 Family Register / (4 views.)
und S C.C.

1846 Family Register / (4 columns, 4 small views at top.) 1845 S N.C.

1847 Family Register / #73 (4 oval scenes.)
1850 S N.C.

1848 Family Register / #487 (4 columns surmounted by group scenes, and 4 views at bottom, 3 of which are marine. Copyright Sarony & Major.)
1846 S N.C.

1849 Family Register / (4 columns) #74.
1852 S C&I

1850 Family Register / #74 / 12.9x9 (Upright, 2 portraits of man and woman.)
1853 S N.C.

1851 Family Register / 12.13x8.14 (Female figures on each side.)
und S N.C.

1852 Family Register / #485 / 12.12x9 (4 scenes at top.)   1864 S C&I

1853 Family Register / #74.
1862 S C&I

1854 Family Register / 4 columns, heading in German.)   1869 S C&I

1855 Family Register /
1873 S C&I

1856 Family Register [A] / 11.13x9 (4 scenes showing angels.)
1874 S C&I

1857 Family Register [C] / 12.13x9.1 (2 oval spaces for photographs of parents, 4 columns, baskets of flowers on each side.)   1874 S C&I

1858 Family Register / For Colored People (4 scenes.)   1873 S C&I

1859 Family Register / 16.6x12.10 (4 columns with scenes at top of each.)
1864 M C&I

1860 Famous Double Trotting Team, The / Sir Mohawk and Nellie Sontag / Full brother and sister / Owned by Richard K. Fox, Proprietor of the Police Gazette, New York / Jno. Cameron on stone. 19.3x30. Copyright by Richard K. Fox, N. Y. Printed in oil colors (4-wheeled wagon to left.)
1889 L C&I

1861 Famous Trotter Majolica, by Bonner's "Startle," The / Owned by Nathan Straus, Esq., New York. Driven by John Murphy / Record 2:17 / Printed in oil colors. 19.1x27.10 (High-wheeled sulky broadside to right. This print is also published without the second line of title.) 1884 L C&I

1862 Famous Trotter Police Gazette, Formerly Emma B, The / The property of Richard K. Fox, Proprietor of the Police Gazette of New York / Record 2:22 / Printed in oil colors by Currier & Ives. 18.4x26.10 (High-wheeled sulky, stands seen in extreme rear, ¾ to left.)   1882 L C&I

1863 Famous Trotting Gelding Guy by Kentucky Prince, The / Record 2:10¾ / J. Cameron on stone (Vignette, ¾ to right, high-wheeled sulky.)
1888 S C&I

1864 Famous Trotting Mare Goldsmith Maid, Record 2:14 / J. Cameron on stone.   1871 S C&I

1865 Fancied Security, or The Rats on a Bender / ("Government Crib" in center. Farmer with club "Fillmore." 8 rats with human heads attempting to enter crib, vignette.)
und S N.C.

1866 Fannie / (Vignette, with fan.)
und S C&I

1867 Fannie / #132 (¾ length, white dress, red curtain.)   und S C&I
Fannie Witherspoon (Horse) See: No. 5708.

1868 Fanny / #132 (¾ length, bouquet in hand, pearls in hair.)
1846 S N.C.

1869 Fanny / #132 (Full length, white dress, rose in hand.) 1846 S N.C.

1870 Fanny / (¾ length. Exterior rural scene.)   und S N.C.

1871 Fanny / G. K. on stone. (Vignette, yellow shawl.)   und S N.C.

1872 Fanny Elssler in the Shadow Dance / #501 / 8.2x11.13 (Moonlight scene.)
1846 S N.C.

1873 Fanny Elssler / In the Favorite Dance / La Cachucha / #156 / 12.2x9.6.
und S N.C.

1874 Farewell, The / (Mother and child on sea wall, oval, companion to "The Return" No. 5125.)   und S C&I

1875 Farewell, The / (Oval.)
und M C&I

1876 Farewell A'while My Native Isle /
und S N.C.

1877 Farm and Fireside / Buckeye Grain Drive, P. P. Mast & Co., Springfield, Ohio. 9.2x15.7 (Exterior scene various farm activities.)
1878 M C&I

1878 Farm Life in Summer / The Cooling Stream / 16.12x24.14 (Cows in stream, farmer with load of hay, team of oxen, farm house in rear.)
1867 L C&I

FARM AND FIRESIDE.

1879 Farm Yard, The / No. 1 #717 / 9.9x13.10 (Cow and calf in manger.) und S N.C.

1880 Farm Yard, The / #717 (Man and boy feeding cows, winter scene.) und S N.C.

1881 Farm-Yard in Winter, The / Painted by G. H. Durrie. 16.4x23.9. 1861 L C&I

1882 Farm Yard Pets / 8.4x12.4. und S C&I

1883 Farm Yard Pets / 12.4x8.5 (Girl feeding horse.) und S C&I

1884 Farm Yard — Winter / und S C&I

1885 Farmer Garfield / Cutting a swath to the White House / (Garfield with scythe cutting heads from snakes "Fraud" "Calumny" "Malice" "Hatred" etc — vignette.) 1880 S C&I

1886 Farmer's Daughter, The / #242 / 12x8.10 (¾ length of girl holding sheaf of wheat, upright; companion to "Farmer's Son" No. 1895.) und S C&I

1887 Farmer's Friends, The / #689 / 12.12x8.14. und S N.C.

1888 Farmer's Friends, The / #689 / 8x 12.8 (Barnyard scene, similar to "The Old Homestead" No. 4562, but with no house shown.) und S C&I

1889 Farmer's Home — Autumn, The / F. F. Palmer, Del. 16.1x23.6 (Group picking apples and grapes.) 1864 L C&I

1890 Farmer's Home—Harvest, The / F. F. Palmer, Del. 16x23.6 (Loading wheat on oxcart.) 1864 L C&I

1891 Farmer's Home — Summer, The / F. F. Palmer, Del. 16x23.6 (Mother and daughter on porch awaiting carriage.) 1864 L C&I

1892 Farmer's Home — Winter, The / Painted by G. H. Durrie. 16.3x23.13. 1863 L C&I

1893 Farmer's House / with plans for basement, first floor, second floor, and attic. From "Rural residences" by A. J. Davis, 1837. 8.2x5.14. und S N.C.

1894 Farmer's Pride, The / 1852 S N.C.

1895 Farmer's Son, The / #241 / 12.4x8.8 (¾ length of boy, cask and bag over shoulder, dog at side, companion to

"Farmer's Daughter" No. 1886.)
und S C&I

Farragut, Commodore See: Nos. 50, 1214.

Fashion Course, L.I. See: Nos. 167, 886, 907-8, 927, 939, 1578-78A, 1757, 2243-4, 3379, 6117, 6205, 6225.

Fashion (Horse) See: No. 4763.

1896 Fashionable "Turn-Outs" in Central Park. / Sketched from life and signed on stone by Thos. Worth. 18.10x28.14.
1869 L C&I

1897 Fashions / For Fall & Winter 1854 & 5. Published by H. Clay No. 8 Barclay St., N.Y. / On stone by J. Cameron. (2 columns, male and female figures.)   1854 L C.C.

1898 Fast Heat, A / J. Cameron 1887 on stone. 18.4x27.5 (5 horses, ¾, high-wheeled sulkies to right, horse "breaking" on extreme right.)
1887 L C&I

1899 Fast Heat, A / J. Cameron on stone. 18.3x28.4 (4 horses, ¾, low-wheeled, rubber-tired sulkies to right, radically different composition from preceding.)   1894 L C&I

1900 Fast Team — Out on the Loose, The / (Vignette.)   und S C&I

1901 Fast Team, A /"Out on the Loose"/ Thos. Worth 1859 on stone. 10.7x15.1 (Broadside to left, different from preceding, companion to No. 1904.)
1859 M C&I

1902 Fast Team, A / "Out on the Loose" / J. Cameron on stone. 8.3x12.8.
1871 S C&I

1903 Fast Team, "Taking a Smash," A /
und S C&I

1904 Fast Team, A / "Taking a Smash" / Thos. Worth on stone. (Companion to No. 1901.)   1859 M C&I

1905 Fast Team Taking a Smash, A / #307 / Thos. Worth on stone.
und S C&I

1906 Fast Trotters on a Fast Track / L. Maurer on stone. 17.3x27.15 (Composition similar to "Lady Woodruff Miller's Damsel," Etc. No. 3399 but horses not named.)   1889 L C&I

1907 Fast Trotters on Harlem Lane, N.Y. / Com. Vanderbilt with Myron Perry and Daisy Burns-Bonner with Dexter / J. Cameron on stone. 18.10x 28.11.   1870 L C&I

1908 Fast Trotting in the West / Lucy and Goldsmith Maid / Trotting their closely-contested race over the Cold Spring Course, Milwaukee, Wis. Sept. 6th, 1871 / 5 additional lines. J. Cameron on stone. 16.11x25.14 (2 high-wheeled sulkies to right.)
1871 L C&I

1909 Fast Trotting to Fast Wheels / J. Cameron on stone. 18.5x28.2 (3 horses, low-wheeled rubber-tired s u l k i e s , broadside to right.) 1893 L C&I

1910 Fate of the Radical Party /
und S C&I

1911 Father and Child / # 665 / 12.2x8.1 (Full length, child asleep on father's knee.)   1849 S N.C.

1912 Father, Into Thy Hands, I Commend My Spirit / #484 / 13.13x10.2 (Christ on the cross, black background.)   1850 S N.C.

1913 Father Mathew / Administering the Temperance Pledge /
1848 S N.C.

1914 Father Mathew / Administering The Temperance Pledge / "May God Bless you and enable you to keep your promise" / 9.1x7.13 (¾ length.)
und S N.C.

1915 Father's Pet /   1851 S N.C.

1916 Father's Pet /   und S C&I

1917 Father's Pride / (Boy and dog, conventional border, oval.)
1846 S N.C.

1918 Father's Pride /(Father and son, ¾ length vignette.)   1859 S C&I

1919 Father's Pride / #400 (Upright, vignette.)   1859 S N.C.

1920 Father's Pride / 10.4x8.4 (Father letting boy listen to tick of his watch, oval.)   und S C&I

1921 Favorite Cat, The / #244 / 12.3x8 (Head, upright.)   und S N.C.

1922 Favorite Horse, The / (2 dogs, 1 with riding crop in mouth.)
und S N.C.

1923 Favorite Horse, The / J. Schutz on stone. (Similar to preceding, but with changes in composition.)
und S N.C.

1924 Favorite Horse, The / 8.12x12.7 (To left.)   und S C&I

1925 Favorite Horse, The / 8.7x12.11 (To right.)   und S C&I

1926 "Favorite" in the Pools, The / "A Mutual Understanding" / Thos. Worth on stone. 11.1x15.6 (Driver talking to horse.)   1876 M C&I

1927 Favorite Jerseys / (2 cows.)
und M C&I

1928 Favorite Jerseys / 12.12x9.14 (Girl with 2 cows, upright.) und S C&I

1929 Favorite Pony, A / J. Schutz on stone. 13.3x8.13 (White pony and 2 dogs.) und S N.C.

1930 Favorite set of Quadrilles for the Piano, A / Composed and respectfully Dedicated to the members of the American Boat Club, / By Antonio C. Martinez, 1839. (Shows a view of the Battery, N.Y.) und S N.C.

1931 Favorites, The / (Boy with dog, girl with cat.) und S N.C.

1932 Fawn's Leap, The / 2.9x4 (Oval, companion to "Sacandaga Creek" No. 5275.) und V.S. C&I

1933 Fawn's Leap, The / Catskills / 5.7x 7.7. und V.S. C&I

1934 Feast of Fruits, A / (Group of grapes, apples, etc., oval.)
und S C&I

1935 Feast of Roses, A / (Upright, vignette, vase on table.) 1873 S C&I

1936 Feast of Strawberries, A / (Upright, basket.) und S C&I

1937 Feather Weight Mounting A Scalper, A / "It's only a little playful he is" / Thos. Worth on stone. (Vignette.) 1881 S C&I
Federal Hall N.Y. See: New York City Views.

1938 Federal Pap! Cass-Taylor-Cresswell-Propaganda / Corning-Dickenson-Foster-John Van Buren-Martin Van Buren-Goddess of Liberty / Excerpt from a speech by Daniel Washburn, Esq. at the Utica Convention. Pub. by Peter Smith, 2 Spruce St. 16.12x10.8.
und M N.C.

1939 Feeding the Swans / 7.14x12.5 (2 children.) und S C&I
Fellowcraft (Horse) See: No. 175.

1940 Fenian Volunteer, The / (Figure trampling England and carrying Irish flag, verses under title.)
1866 S C&I

1941 Ferns / In red pot, upright, vignette. und S C&I

1942 Ferry Boat, The / F. F. Palmer, Del. 10.9x15 (Rural scene, horse and passengers in flat-bottomed boat.)
und M N.C.
Fessenden See: No. 5258.

1943 Fido's Lesson / 11.7x8.5 (Child with book, teaching dog.) und S C&I

1944 Fidele / #45 (Spaniel sitting on stool, upright.) und S N.C.

1945 Fiend of the Road, The / Painted by Scott Leighton and signed on stone. Printed in oil colors. 15.13x24 (Winter Scene.) 1881 L C&I

1946 Fifth Avenue Belle, A / (Half length, vignette.) und S C&I
Fifth Avenue See: New York City Views.
Fillmore, Millard See: Nos. 1865, 2489, 2513-4, 2564, 2641, 4128-9, 4130-1, 4694, 5141.

1947 Finest in the World / Jay Eye See — Maud S — St. Julien. 16.3x27.8 (3 large heads to left.)
1885 L C&I

1948 Finest in the World / Jay Eye See — Maud S — St. Julien. (Same as preceding, but with the words "R. B. Crouch" on the reins, adv.)
1885 L C&I

1949 Finish in the Great Match race for $5000 a side and $5000 added money one mile and a quarter / at Sheepshead Bay, N.Y. June 25th, 1890 between / Salvator and Tenny / J. B. Haggin's Ch.C. Salvator by Prince Charlie Murphy — D. F. Pulsifor's B. C. Tenny by Rayon D'Or Garrison won by a neck / Time 2:05. 1890 S C&I
Fire See: Nos. 738-54, 1950-6, 2614-9, 5253-4.

1950 Fire Department Certificate /
1877 S C&I

1951 Fire Department Certificate /
1889 M C&I

1952 Fire Department Certificate /
und S C&I

1953 Fire Department Certificate / This Certifies — 20.4x15 (Upright, fire scenes on margin.) 1877 M C&I

1954 Fire Engine No. .... /
und S N.C.

1955 Fire Engine "Pacific" Brooklyn. N.Y. / und S C&I
Fireman See: Nos. 152-5, 3515-20, 3622.

1956 Firemen's Certificate /
1889 M C&I

1957 First Appearance of Jenny Lind in America / At Castle Garden, Sept. 11th, 1850. Total receipts $26,238 / 9.3x14.1. 1850 S N.C.

1958 First at the Rendezvous / Why don't he Come! / #366 (Woman on horseback, dog alongside.)
und S N.C.

1959 First Bird of the Season, The / Thos. Worth on stone. (Vignette, hunting comic, 10 hunters shooting at 1 bird.)   1879 S C&I

1960 First Bird of the Season, The / (Vignette, same general composition as preceding, postcard size.)
1880 V.S. C&I

1961 First Blood /   1882 S C&I

1962 First Care, The / The Young Mother / #409 (Oval, mother by bed, baby and dog on floor.)
und S C&I

1963 First Care, The / The Young Mother / 11x8.15 (Oval, composition similar to preceding with slight changes and composition reversed, exterior scene.)
und S C&I

1964 First Christmas Morn, The /
und S C&I

1965 First Colored Senator and Representatives in the 41st & 42nd Congress of the United States, The / (7 kevs. vignette.)   1872 S C&I

1966 First Company, Government Foot Guards of Connecticut /
und S C&I

1967 First Duchess of Oneida / (Pedigreed cow.)   und S C&I

1968 First Easter Dawn, The / (2 angels flying.)   und S C&I

1969 First Fight between Iron Clad Ships of War, The / Terrific Combat between the "Monitor" 2 guns and "Merrimac" 10 guns / In Hampton Roads, March 9th, 1862 / 1 additional line. 7.13x12.12 (Minnesota and Rebel Steamer keyed above title, Monitor in foreground.)   1862 S C&I

1970 First Flirtation, The / 11.2x8.4 (Upright, girl on chair, boy with rose behind his back.)   und S C&I

1971 First Game / (White bulldog and greyhound racing, companion to "Revenge" No. 5133.)   und S N.C.

1972 First Landing of Columbus, The / On the shores of the New World / At San Salvador W.I., Oct. 12th, 1492 / 18.1x28.   1892 L C&I

1973 First Lesson, The / 12.8x20.8 (Terrier teaching her pups how to catch rats. Part of this print forms the composition of "Who's Afraid of You" No.

6648, companion to "Not caught Yet" No. 4513.)   und L N.C.

1974 First Love #2 /   und S N.C.

1975 First Meeting of Washington and Lafayette, The / Philadelphia, August 3rd, 1777 / 8.12x12.12.
1876 S C&I

1976 First Pants, The / (Vignette, upright, full length.)   und M C&I

1977 First Parting. The / 2 columns, 2 lines of verse. (Full length, shepherd, girl and dog, upright.)
und S C&I

1978 First Party, The / 10x8.3 (Child on stairs, mother adding finishing touches to party dress, upright.)
und S C&I

1979 First Playmate, The /
und S C&I

1980 First Prayer, The / (4 lines of prayer, oval.)   1870 S C&I

1981 First Prayer, The / (Oval.)
und M C&I

1982 First Premium Grapes / A Royal Cluster / 17.15x14.13 (Companion to "Prize Black Hamburg Grapes" Nos. 1983, 4934, 4939.)   1865 M C&I

1983 First Premium Muscat Grapes / A Royal Cluster / (Companion to preceding and "Prize Black Hamburg Grapes" No. 4934 and "Prize Grapes" No. 4939.)   1861 M C&I

1984 First Premium Poultry / (Hen and rooster in foreground, house, barn, ducks, chickens, etc.) und S C&I

1985 First President of the Mormons (Joseph Smith) /   1879 S C&I

1986 First Presidents / of the / Church / of / Jesus Christ / of / the / Latter day Saints / John Lind, Agent, Utah. (Portraits of Orson Pratt, John Taylor, Orson Hyde, Charles C. Rich, Joseph Smith, Hyram Smith, Wilford Woodruff, Joseph F. Smith, Brigham Young, Heber C. Kimball, George Q. Canon, F. D. Richards, Daniel H. Wells, George A. Smith, Erastus Snow, Albert Carrington, Brigham Young, Jr., Lorenzo Snow. 14.6x10 (Upright.)
1879 S C&I

1987 First Ride, The / #669 / 12.8x9 (Boy on pony, 3 white dogs alongside.)
1849 S N.C.

1988 First Ride, The / 12.1x8.12 (Scots costume, girl on horse, dog alongside, upright.)   und S C&I

1989 First Scholar, The /
    und S C&I

1990 First Smoke, The / All Right /
(Boy on barrel, smoking cigar, ¾
length, vignette, upright.)
    1870 S C&I

1991 First Smoke, The / All Wrong /
(Boy on barrel, sick after smoking —
full length vignette, upright.)
    1870 S C&I

1992 First Snow, The / 15.3x12.11 (Old
lady holding baby. Young girl, mother,
rabbits in front of house — upright.)
    und S C&I

1993 First Step, The / #410 / 10.13x8.13
(Oval, mother to left, baby, dog, and
puppy, 1 bird, upright, exterior scene.)
    und S C&I

1994 First Step, The / #410 / 10.15x8.15
(Composition reversed, and changes in
composition, 3 birds shown.)
    und S C&I

1995 First Step, The / "Come to Mama" /   1859 S C&I

1996 First Step, The / "Come to Mama" / L. Maurer on stone. 14.11x
10.10.   1859 M C&I

1997 First Toilet, The / J. C. (Cameron)
on stone. 11.8x8.3 (Upright, girl at
mirror.)   1873 S C&I

1998 First Trot of the Season, The /
"Free-for-all horses go as they please"
/ 18.8x28.14 (Sulkies, skeleton wagons,
horses under saddle passing stand —
undoubtedly by Thos. Worth but not
signed.)   1870 L C&I

1999 First Violet, The /
    und S C&I

2000 First under the Wire / Thos. Worth
on stone. (Vignette.)   1878 S C&I
    Fish, Hamilton **See:** No. 4121.

2001 Fish out of water, A / 11.12x15.10
(Weed and Seward fishing in political
pool.)   und M N.C.

2002 Fisherman's Cot, The / (1 of 4
scenes on 1 sheet: The Pool, The Fisherman's Cot, The Windmill, and Winter Morning.)   und V.S. C&I

2003 Fisherman's Dog, The / (Dog and
little girl retrieving fisherman's hat.)
    und S N.C.

    Fishing **See:** Nos. 108, 164, 195, 241,
367, 375-6, 511-2, 540-3, 561, 578, 703-5,
845, 864-5, 1185, 2072, 2856, 2928,
3001-2, 3007, 3014, 3320, 3426, 4777,
4951, 5049, 5372, 5478, 5670, 5844,
5898, 5981, 6158, 6227-31, 6488, 6747.

    Fisk, Jim **See:** Nos. 2643, 5716.
    Five Forks, Va. **See:** No. 382.

2004 Flag of our Union, The / 2 columns,
2 lines of verse. (Soldier with flag
and sword.)   1861 M C&I
    Fleet Wing (Yacht) **See:** Nos.
2634, 4450, 6798.
    Fleetwood Park Track, Morrisania
See: Nos. 1179, 2448, 5063, 6616.

2005 Fleety Golddust / By Old Golddust,
dam a Morgan Mare / Winner of the
first prize [2000] in the $4000 purse
for 2:30 horses, at Buffalo, N.Y., Aug.
7th, 1874 / Time 2:23½, 2:20½, 2:22¼
/ J. Cameron on stone. (Broadside to
right, vignette.)   1874 S C&I

2006 Fleety Golddust, Record 2:10½,
driven by Chas. S. Green / J. C. (Cameron) 1875 on stone. und S C&I

2007 Flight into Egypt /
    und S N.C.

2008 Flight of Eliza, The /
    und S C&I

2009 Flight of the Mexican Army / at
the Battle of Buena Vista, Febr. 23rd,
1847 / 8.5x12.8 (Artillery wheel to
left.)   1847 S N.C.

2010 Flight of the Mexican Army / At
the Battle of Buena Vista, Febr. 23rd,
1847 / #455 / 8.6x12.9 (Changes from
preceding, drum to left.)
    1847 S N.C.

2011 Flight of the Stakeholder / (Vignette, colored man fleeing menacing
crowd.)   1889 S C&I

2012 Floating down to Market / 7.15x
12.7 (Colored family on barge.)
    1870 S C&I

2013 Flora / #408 / 11.8x8.8 (Oval in
rectangle, ornate border, floral wreath
in hand.)   1846 S N.C.

2014 Flora / (Head of girl, floral
wreath.)   und V.S. C&I

2015 Flora Temple / June 28th, 1853.
In a match with Highland Maid, for
$2000 over the Centreville Course, L.I./
5 additional lines, 2 columns 7 and 5
lines.   1853 L N.C.

2016 "Flora Temple" and "Highland
Maid" / Centreville Course, L.I. June
15th, 1853 / 4 additional lines. L.
Maurer on stone. 17.6x26.13.
    1853 L N.C.

2017 Flora Temple and Lancet / In their
great match for $2000, mile heats

best 3 in 5 / Sept. 30, 1856 / L. Maurer, Del.   1856 L N.C.

2018 Flora Temple and Lancet / In their great match for $2000, mile heats best 3 in 5 / Over the Centreville Course, L.I. Sept. 30th, 1856 / Time 2:28, 2:28, 2:25½. / L. Maurer on stone. 16.12x 25.14 (Sulky versus horse under saddle.)   1856 L N.C.

2019 Flora Temple and Princess / The Competitors in the four great matches over the Eclipse Course, L.I. 1859 / 4 columns, 8 lines of records. 17.8x26.13 (Broadside to right, high-wheeled sulkies.)   1859 L C&I

2020 Flora Temple and Princess / In their great match for $5000 over the Eclipse Course, L.I. June 23rd, 1859 / two mile heats in harness / J. Eoff named B. M. Princess . . . 1:1: / D. Tallman named B. M. Flora Temple . . . 2:2: / 17.7x26.15 (Broadside to right-sulkies.)   1859 L C&I

Flora Temple See: Nos. 201, 890, 913, 2800, 5620, 5708, 6170.

2021 Floral Beauties / (Upright vignette, bouquet with bird.)
                    und S C&I

2022 Floral Bouquet /
                    und S C&I

2023 Floral Cross / (Cross decorated with autumn flowers.)
                    und S C&I

2024 Floral Gems / (Upright vignette.)
                    und S C&I

2025 Floral Gift / (Bouquet of roses, lilies, bleeding hearts.)
                    und S C&I

2026 Floral Gift / 5.8x7.8.
                    und V.S. C&I

2027 Floral Group /
                    und S C&I

2028 Floral Offering / (Upright vignette.)   und S C&I

2029 Floral Treasure / 5.8x7.8.
                    und V.S. C&I

2030 Floral Tribute / (Upright vignette, bouquet.)   und S C&I

2031 Flora's Bouquet / (Vignette, hand holding flowers.)   und S C&I

2032 Flora's Gift / (Upright vignette, bouquet roses, lilies, etc.)
                    und V.S. C&I

2033 Flora's Treasure / (Upright vignette, bouquet flowers.)
                    und V.S. C&I

2034 Flora's Treasures / (Vignette, bouquet flowers.)   und S C&I

2035 Florence / #683 (¾ length, holding bouquet in lap, red dress.)
                    und S N.C.

2036 Florida / By Rysdyk's Hambletonian, dam Florida Maid by Goldsmith's Volunteer / A. H. Taylor's Stock Farm, Central Valley Orange Co. N.Y. / Painted by J. H. Wright and signed on stone 1874. Jos. Abrams, Lith. 19.2x27.2 (Profile to left.)
                    1877 L C&I

2037 Florida Coast, The / 8.8x12.7.
                    und S C&I

Florida (Horse) See: No. 2036.
Florida (Steamboat) See: Nos. 2652, 5762.
Florida (State) See: Nos. 2037, 2088, 3404.

2038 Flower Basket, A / 12.8x8.8 (Upright, black background.)
                    1872 S C&I

2039 Flower Basket, A / (Vignette, tiger lilies.)   1874 S C&I

2040 Flower Basket, The / (Basket with roses, pansies, fuchsia.)
                    und S C&I

2041 Flower Dance, The / By the Vienna Children / #415 / 8.5x12 (Companion to "The Harvest Dance" No. 2743, round corners.)   1846 S N.C.

2042 Flower Girl, The / #359 / 11.15x8.11 (¾ length to left, green curtain, water background, upright.)
                    1845 S N.C.

2043 Flower of the Harem, The / #534 / 11.12x8.10 (Upright, half length.)
                    und S N.C.

2044 Flower Piece / A choice Bouquet /
                    und S C&I

2045 Flower Stand, The /
                    und S C&I

2046 Flower-Strewn Grave, The / 12.14 x8.9 (Widow and child.)
                    1867 S C&I

2047 Flower Vase, The / #249 (Vignette, portrait of girl on vase.)
                    1848 S N.C.

2048 Flower Vase, The / (Silhouette, head of girl on Empire vase.)
                    und S N.C.

2049 Flower Vase, The /
                    1859 S C&I

2050 Flower Vase, The / (Upright vignette, white ornamental vase, roses, pansies, morning glories, etc.)
1870 S C&I

2051 Flower Vase, The / (Upright vignette, 6-sided base on vase, tiger lilies predominating.)   1875 S C&I

2052 Flower Vase, The / (Passion flower, yellow rose, tulip, gloxiana, carnation, tulip, rose (pink), rose (red) Keyed.)
1859 M C&I

2053 Flower Vase, The / (Vignette, upright, assorted flowers, different from preceding.)   und L C&I

2054 Flower Vase, The /
und S C&I

2055 Flower Vase, The / #249 (Vignette, upright vase.)   und S C&I

2056 Flowers / (Roses, bluebells, hummingbird, fuchsia, petunias.)
und S N.C.

2057 Flowers / (Roses, bluebells, fuchsia, petunia, hummingbird.)
und S C&I

2058 Flowers / (3 roses, 10 buds.)
und S N.C.

2059 Flowers / (4 roses, 6 buds.)
und M N.C.

2060 Flowers / (3 roses, 7 buds, sweet peas, daisies, etc.)
und S C&I

2061 Flowers No. 1 / #565 (3 roses, 9 buds, upright vignette.)
und S N.C.

2062 Flowers No. 1 / J. Schutz, Del. on stone.   und S N.C.

2063 Flowers No. 1 / #565 (Exterior scene in background.)
1848 S N.C.

2064 Flowers No. 1 / #569 (Bouquet, no exterior scene in background.)
und S N.C.

2065 Flowers No. 2 / J. Schutz, Del. on stone.   und S N.C.

2066 Flowers No. 2 / (Basket on porch, bird's nest, hummingbird.)
1848 S N.C.

2067 Flowers — Roses and Bluebells / (Vignette, upright hummingbird.)
1870 S C&I

2068 Flowers — Roses and Bluebells /
und M C&I

2069 Flowers / Roses and Buds /
und S C&I

2070 Flowers / Roses and Buds / (Different from preceding.)
und S C&I

2071 Flushing a Woodcock / 8x12.8 (2 dogs and 1 bird.)
und S C&I

2072 Fly Fishing / (Vignette, fishing comic, line snarled in tree, fisherman bothered with insects.)
1879 S C&I

Flying Cloud (Clipper Ship) See: No. 1145.

2073 Flying Dutchman C. Marlow and Voltigeur N. Flatman, The / Running the great match at York on the 13th of May, 1851, for 1000 sovereigns a side / 1 additional line and time 3:55. Printed by J. F. Herring, Senr. from an engraving by J. Harris. 12.6x20.10.
und L N.C.

Flying Jib (Horse) See: No. 2517.

2074 Foliage /   und V.S. C&I

2075 Foliage /   und V.S. C&I

2076 Foliage /   und V.S. C&I

2077 Foliage /   und V.S. C&I
(These 4 prints are all of different composition and printed on 1 sheet.)
und M C&I

2078 Folly of Secession, The /
1861 S C&I

Folsom, Abbe See: No. 4165.

2079 Font at Easter, The / (Altar covered with flowers.)
und S C&I

2080 Font at Easter, The /
1869 S C&I

Fontainebleau See: France.
Football See: Nos. 2483-4.
Foote, Andrew See: No. 1213.

2081 Fording the River / F. F. Palmer, Del. 10.6x14.15 (Boy driving goats, man and boy crossing stream on horse.)   und M N.C.

2082 Fording the River /
und S C&I

2083 Fords of the Jordan, The /
und S C&I

Foreign, Misc. See: Nos. 600, 1752, 2083, 2220, 3206-7, 4465-6, 4625, 4710, 4837, 5067, 5126-7, 5442, 5509, 5977-9, 6082, 6106, 6118, 6382.

2084 Forest Scene on the Lehigh / F. F. Palmer, Del. 14.15x20.3.
und M C&I

[97]

2085 Forest Scene, Summer / (Ducks in stream and overhead, no other life shown.) und S C&I

2086 Forest Scene, Summer / 7.15x12.8 (Large tree in center, 4 deer in left background.) und S C&I

Forfarshire (Steamship) See: No. 2464.

2087 Fork over what you owe / 12.15x 8.14 (Rebus — letters formed of human figures, slightly rounded corners.) 1868 S C&I

Forrest, Edwin See: Nos. 1671-4, 2647.

Forrest (General) See: No. 3488.

Fort Donelson See: Nos. 5822, 5823, 5824.

Fort Douglas, Ark. See: No. 404.

Fort Fisher See: Nos. 589, 6372.

Fort Hamilton See: Nos. 4379-82, 5715.

Fort Henry, Tenn. See: No. 590.

Fort Hindman, Ark. See: No. 591.

Fort Moultrie See: Nos. 596, 2089.

2088 Fort Pickens / Pensacola Harbor, Florida / 7.15x12.5 (Fort McRay keyed.) und S C&I

Fort Pulaski See: No. 595.

Fort Putnam See: Nos. 6378, 6379, 6380.

2089 Fort Sumter / Charleston Harbor, S.C. / Fort Moultrie — Morris Island Batteries / (Marine view — sailboat in foreground.) 7.13x12.7. und S C&I

Fort Sumter, S.C. See: Nos. 2089, 3118, 5508.

Foster, J. G. See: No. 1938.

2090 Foul Tip, A / Thos. Worth on stone. (Baseball, colored comic.) 1882 S C&I

2091 "Four-In-Hand" / L. Maurer on stone. 17.9x27.14 (Open barouche, 2 men on front seat, 3 ladies in back.) 1861 L C&I

2092 "Four-In-Hand" / L. Maurer on stone. 17.9x27.14 (Used as an ad by Miner, Stevens & Co.) 1861 L C&I

2093 "Four-In-Hand" / J. Cameron on stone. 19.2x28.15 (Closed coach, 5 people on top, also 2 footmen. Entirely different composition from preceding.) 1887 L C&I

2094 Four Masted Steamship "Egypt" of the National Line / running between New York and Liverpool / und S N.C.

2095 Four Oared Shell Race, A / 18.8x 28.1 (Shows race between Harvard and Yale crews on the Thames at New London.) 1884 L C&I

2096 Four Seasons of Life, Childhood, The / "The Seasons of Joy" / J. M. Ives, Del. Drawn by F. F. Palmer and J. Cameron. 2 columns, 4 lines of verse. 15.13x23.12. 1868 L C&I

2097 Four Seasons of Life, Middle Age, The / "The Season of Strength" / J. M. Ives, Del. Drawn by F. F. Palmer and J. Cameron. 2 columns, 4 lines of verse. 15.14x23.14 (Exterior scene — Father greeting wife and 3 children at door of cottage, lake background.) 1868 L C&I

2098 Four Seasons of Life, The Middle Age / "The Season of Strength" / J. M. Ives, Del. on stone. 15.6x23.10 (Interior scene.) 1868 L C&I

2099 Four Seasons of life. Old Age, The/ "The Season of Rest" / J. M. Ives, Del. Drawn by Parsons & Atwater. 15.10x 23.10 (Interior scene, winter landscape through window.) 1868 L C&I

2100 Four Seasons of Life. Youth, The / "The Season of Love" / J. M. Ives, Del. Drawn by F. F. Palmer and J. Cameron on stone. 15.13x23.14. 1868 L C&I

2101 Fourth of July / (Upright, full length of boy shooting fire crackers.) 1867 S C&I

2102 Fourth of July / Young America Celebrating / L. Maurer on stone. (Full length, boy shooting firecrackers, vignette.) 1858 L C&I

2103 Fox Chase / Gone Away, No. 2 / #410 / 8.8x12.11. 1846 S N.C.

2104 Fox Chase / In Full Cry, No. 3 / #411 / 8.8x12.10. 1846 S N.C.

2105 Fox Chase / The Death, No. 4 / #412 / 8.8x12.11. 1846 S N.C.

2106 Fox Chase / Throwing Off, No. 1 / #409 / 8.8x12.10. 1846 S N.C.

(There is supposed to be another state of these four subjects with no publication date, but I have never seen them.)

2107 Fox Hounds / #444 (Group of 9 dogs in inner court, copied from an

"FOUR-IN-HAND."

"FOUR-IN-HAND."

[99]

English print published by Ackerman.)
1846 S N.C.

2108 Fox-Hunter, The / 8.4x12.12 (2 columns, 4 lines of verse, horseman hurdling stream.) und S N.C.

2109 Fox-Hunter, The / 8.4x12.12 (2 columns, 4 lines of verse, horseman and hounds at the death.)
und S N.C.

2110 Fox Hunting, Full Cry / 11.7x15.14.
und M C&I

2111 Fox Hunting, The Death / 11.7x12.12. und M C&I

2112 Fox Hunting, The Find / 11.7x15.15. und M C&I

2113 Fox Hunting, The Meet / 11.6x15.15. und M C&I

2114 Fox without a tail — or the Southern Confederacy /
1861 S C&I

2115 Foxhall / By King Alphonso, dam Jamaica, by Lexington / Winner of the "Grand Prize" of June 12th, 1881 / J. Cameron on stone. 17.4x25.13 (Broadside to left.)
1882 L C&I

2116 Foxhall / Mr. Jas. R. Keene's bay colt—3 years, by Alphonso, dam Jamaica, by Lexington / Ridden by the celebrated English jockey, Geo. Fordham / Winner of the Grand Prize of Paris, June 12th, 1881 / (Under saddle.) und S C&I

2117 Foxhall — Winner of the Grand Prize of Paris 1881 / (Vignette.)
1882 V.S. C&I

Foxhall (Horse) See: No. 4253.

2118 Fox's Old Bowery Theatre / The last scene in G. L. Fox's pantomine / "The House that Jack built" /
und M C.C.

2119 Fragrant and Fair / (Vignette, glass vase, flowers and hummingbird.)
und S C&I

2120 Fragrant Cup, A / (Vignette, man, woman and child at table. 4 lines of verse.) 1884 M C&I

France's Alexander (Horse) See: Nos. 928-9.

2121 Frances / #89 (Full length, standing, back to chair, river scene through window.) und S N.C.

2122 Francis R. Shunk / Governor of Pennsylvania / 11.9x8.11 Turner & Fisher, Phila. (¾ length, red curtain.)
1844 S N.C.

Francis Skiddy (Hudson River Steamer) See: No. 4474.

France See: Nos. 49, 752, 1215, 1272, 1633, 2139-40, 2486, 3365, 3438, 4610, 4746, 6463.

Frank (Horse) See: Nos. 441, 554.

2123 Frankie and Tip /
und S C&I

2124 Franklin / (Upright vignette.)
und S C&I

2125 Franklin / (Vignette, bust portrait.)
und M C&I

2126 Franklin Pierce / Democratic Candidate for / Fourteenth President of the United States / From a daguerreotype by T. Dunlap. 11.1x8.14 (Half length portrait, red curtain.)
1852 S N.C.

2127 Franklin Pierce / Fourteenth President of the United States / From daguerreotype by T. Dunlap (Same as preceding, except for title change.)
1852 S N.C.

Franklin, Benjamin See: Nos. 275, 499, 500, 1530, 2124-5, 2128.

Franklin (Steamship) See: No. 5763.

2128 Franklin's Experiment, June 1752 / Demonstrating the identity of lightning and electricity, from which he invented the lightning rod / 8.7x12.7 (Franklin and a boy with key and kite.) 1876 S C&I

2129 Fraud against Truth / T.C. on stone. (Knight on horse "Truth" striking down "Misrepresentation" on dragon "Tyranny.") 1872 S C&I

Fraunce's Tavern See: New York City Views.

Frederick Karl See: "Unser Karl" No. 6348.

2130 Frederick Douglass (Facsimile) / The Colored Champion of Freedom / (Vignette.) und S C&I

Frederiksted See: No. 6427.

Fredericksburg, Va. See: No. 405.

2131 Free For All / "Now den Bossy han down a yaller cap and you'll see de best muell time on record." / Thos. Worth on stone. 10.5x16.4 (Darky with patched up rig asking judge's permission to race.) 1875 M C&I

2132 Free Lunch, A / W. A. Walker on stone. 10.4x14 (Mice eating food on table.) 1872 M C&I

2133 Free Soil Banner / #618 / From daguerreotype by Plumbe. (Martin Van Buren & Charles F. Adams in 2 circles surmounted by flags and eagles.)
1848 S N.C.

2134 Free Trade and Protection / (2 views poor and well-to-do families. In 1, father says, "Alas my children I cannot give you food. Free trade has ruined my occupation. I have no work and we must beg or starve." In the other view the father says, "Here, wife is provisions for a week, and money to put in the bank; thanks to protective tariff, I have plenty of work and good wages.")   1888 M C&I

2135 Freedmen's Bureau, The / 11.15x 8.12 (Upright, darky dressing, Lincoln's picture on the wall.) 1868 S C&I

2136 Freedom to Ireland / (Vignette, female figure in armor, 2 columns, 6 lines of verse.)   1866 M C&I

2137 Freedom to the Slaves / Proclaimed January 1st, 1863, by Abraham Lincoln, President of the United States / #878 / 1 line Biblical quotation. 11.13x 8.11 (Full length of Lincoln, kneeling negro with broken shackles on the ground, upright.)   und S C&I

2138 Freeland / By Longfellow, dam Belle Knight, by Knightwood / (Walking to right, under saddle, colored jockey, vignette.)   1885 S C&I

Frelinghuysen, T. See: Nos. 2512, 6005-6.

Fremont, Col. See: Nos. 1192, 2470, 2502, 2564, 2641, 2646, 3260, 3896, 3916, 5141.

2139 French Revolution, The / Burning the Royal Carriages at the Chateau D'eu, Feby. 24th, 1848 / No. 2 #575 / 8.5x12.11 (Second line repeated in French.)   1848 S N.C.

2140 French Revolution, The / Scene in the Throne-Room of the Tuileries, Feby. 24th, 1848 / No. 1 #574 / 8.5x 12.10 (Second line repeated in French.) 1848 S N.C.

French Revolution See: France.

2141 Fresh Bouquet, A / (Roses, etc., in cornucopia-shaped vase, upright, vignette.)   und S C&I

2142 Fresh Cool / Lager Beer / (Large glass in center, factory view and wreath.)   und S C&I

2143 Friend Cleveland / 1881 S C&I

2144 Friend In Need, A / 8x12.8 (Dog rescuing child from water.)   und S C&I

2145 Friends of Flowers / #359 (2 children, roses, and butterflies.)   und S C&I

2146 Friendship, Love, and Truth / 13x 9.1 (On banner, flowers.)   1874 S C&I

Friesland (Steamship) See: No. 5764.

2147 Frightened Brood, The / (Dog chasing chickens.)   und S C&I

2148 Frightened Brood, The / #413 / 8.2x11.12 (Hen attacking boy and girl who are holding chicks.)   und S C&I

Frisia (Steamship) See: No. 2697.

2149 Frolicsome Kits / 8.3x11.3.   und S N.C.

2150 Frolicksome Kits / (Postcard size.) 1880 V.S. C&I

2151 Frolicksome Pets / 12.3x8.3 (Girl on bench with doll, kittens playing, basket of roses.)   und S C&I

2152 From Shore to Shore / 2 columns, 4 lines of verse. (Allegorical scene, group of people from infancy to old age in rowboat.)   und S C&I

2153 Frontier Lake, The / 8x12.8.   und S C&I

2154 Frontier Settlement, A / 11.2x16.12.   und M C&I

2155 Frozen Up / 8.8x12.8 (Grist mill in background, 2 sleighs, oxen and horse drawn.)   1872 S C&I

2156 Fruit /   1861 M C&I

2157 Fruit / #358 (Peaches, grapes, and butterflies, upright, vignette.)   und S C&I

2158 Fruit / #359 (Apples, plums, grapes, and butterflies, vignette.)   und S C&I

2159 Fruit, The, No. 1 / #604 / 12.1x8.8 (Cherries, grapes, peaches, and flowers, upright.)   1848 S N.C.

2160 Fruit and Flower Piece / F. F. Palmer, Del. 11.2x15.8 (Vase with strawberries, cherries, flowers.)   1863 M C&I

2161 Fruit and Flower Piece / (Vase of strawberries, cherries, currants, roses, pansies, etc.)   und S C&I

2162 Fruit and Flower Piece / 1870 S C&I

2163 Fruit and Flowers / (Roses, grapes, poppy, morning-glory.)   1848 S N.C.

2164 Fruit and Flowers. No. 1 / #604 (Roses, bluebells, peach, white and black grapes, cherries, etc.)   1848 S N.C.

2165 Fruit and Flowers. No. 2 / #605 (Roses, basket of peaches, cherries, pineapple, etc.) 1848 S N.C.

2166 Fruit and Flowers / (Basket of strawberries, roses, apple blossoms, fuchsia, anemone.) 1870 S C&I

2167 Fruit and Flowers / Grapes, Peaches, and Rose / und S C&I

2168 Fruit and Flowers / Grapes, Peaches, and Roses / 12 x 8.12 (Vase of bleeding hearts.) 1870 S C&I

2169 Fruit and Flowers / Cherries, Strawberries, & Rose / 12x8.12 (Flowers around basket of strawberries.) und S C&I

2170 Fruit and Flowers in Summer / und S C&I

2171 Fruit and Flowers of Autumn / 12.12x14.4. und M C&I

2172 Fruit and Flowers of Autumn / (Tinted background, roses, dahlia, peaches, pear, berries, oval. Companion to No. 2191.) 1865 M C&I

2173 Fruit Girl, The / #358 / 11.12x8.7 (Girl holding bowl of pears.) 1845 S N.C.

2174 Fruit Girl, The / (¾ length, red dress, green curtain.) 1847 S N.C.

2175 Fruit Girl, The / #358 (¾ length, similar to preceding with slight changes.) 1845 S N.C.

2176 Fruit Piece, The / 1845 S N.C.

2177 Fruit Piece, The / (Upright, fruit in dish and flowers in vase in background.) 1859 M C&I

2178 Fruit Piece, The / 10.14x15.7 (Grapes, blackberries, pears, etc. in glass dish, flowers under dish.) 1867 M C&I

2179 Fruit Piece / 8x12.8. 1870 S C&I

2180 Fruit Piece / #607 (3 pears, blackberries, plums, apples, grapes.) und S C&I

2181 Fruit Piece / und V.S. C&I

2182 Fruit Piece / Summer Gift (Apples, pears, plums.) und S C&I

2183 Fruit Piece / Autumn Gift / und S C&I

2184 Fruit Vase / #451 (Vignette, white and black grapes in vase, dancing figure on vase.) 1847 S N.C.

2185 Fruit Vase / (Upright, different composition from preceding.) 1847 S N.C.

2186 Fruit Vase / (Vignette, ornate white vase, round base.) 1870 S C&I

2187 Fruit Vase, The / #451 (Upright, vignette, cherries, grapes, pears, peaches, apples, and plum.) und S C&I

2188 Fruits and Flowers / 11.14x8.12 (Flowers, grapes, peaches, roses.) und S C&I

2189 Fruits, Autumn Varieties / 8.7x 12.7 (Watermelon, blackberries, grapes, pears, and peaches, black background.) 1871 S C&I

2190 Fruits, Summer Varieties / 8.8x 12.7 (Bluebird pecking cherry, strawberries, gooseberries, apples, pears.) 1871 S C&I

2191 Fruits and Flowers of Summer / 12.4x14.8 (Oval, strawberries, lemon, Easter lily, roses, etc. tinted background. Companion to "Fruits and Flowers Of Autumn," No. 2172.) 1865 M C&I

2192 Fruits of Intemperance, The / 1848 S N.C.

2193 Fruits of Intemperance, The/8x12.6 (Family on road with their few belongings. Evidently evicted.) 1870 S C&I

2194 Fruits of Temperance, The / Behold the Son of Temperance / 8.3x12.13 (Exterior scene, Father arriving home, family greeting him.) 1848 S N.C.

2195 Fruits of Temperance, The / 7.15 x 12.11 (Interior scene, happy family, same as "The Good Husband" No. 2432.) 1870 S C&I

2196 Fruits of the Garden / und S C&I

2197 Fruits of the Golden Land / 8.8x 12.8 (Peaches, plums, grapes, etc. black background.) 1871 S C&I

2198 Fruits of the Season / 7.14x12.7 (Apples, peaches, grapes, blackberries, cherries.) 1870 S C&I

2199 Fruits of the Season / #569 (Baskets of currants, peach, pear, apple, strawberries, blackberries.) und S C&I

2200 Fruits of the Season — Autumn / und S C&I

2201 Fruits of the Seasons / 8 x 12.8. (Grapes, apples, peaches, pears, berries, etc.) 1872 S C&I

2202 Fruits of the Seasons / #569 / 8.4x 12.3 (Same fruits as preceding, different arrangement.) und S C&I

2203 Fruits of the Tropics / 8.7x12.7 (Bananas, pineapples, oranges, lemons, grapes.) 1871 S C&I

Fulda (Steamship) See: No. 3037.

2204 "Full Hand, A" / F. C. on stone. (Man holding 2 babies, another 2 on chair, vignette, upright. Companion to No. 1762.) 1884 S C&I

2205 Funeral of Daniel O'Connell, The / Thursday, August 5th, 1847 / The hearse passing Mr. O'Connell's house in Merrion Sq. / #531 / 7.15x12.12. 1847 S N.C.

2206 Funeral of President Lincoln, New York, April 25th, 1865, The / Passing Union Square / #877 / 8.3x13. 1865 S C&I

Furst Bismark (Steamship) See: No. 1789.

2207 "Fust Blood, De" / Thos. Worth on stone. (Vignette, boxing comic, companion to 2208.) 1882 S C&I

2208 "Fust Knock-Down, De" / Thos. Worth on stone. (Vignette, boxing comic.) 1882 S C&I

2209 Futurity Race at Sheepshead Bay, The / Proctor Knott [Barnes]—Salvator [Hamilton] — Galen [Turner] / Sept. 3, 1888. Value $50,000. Won by Proctor Knott / Painted by L. Maurer, and signed L. Maurer 1888 on stone. 20.4x34.2. 1889 L C&I

G

Gaandam (Steamship) See: No. 5766.

Galatea (Yacht) See: Nos. 1337, 4091.

Galen (Horse) See: No. 2209.

Galileo (Steamship) See: No. 5767.

2210 Gallant Charge of the Fifty-Fourth Massachusetts [Colored] Regiment, The / On the relief works at Fort Wagner, Morris Island near Charleston / July 18, 1863, and death of Colonel Robert Shaw / 8.4x12.8. 1865 S C&I

2211 Gallant Charge of the Kentucky Cavalry under Col. Marshall, The / At the Battle of Buena Vista, Febr. 23d, 1847 / #454 / 8.6x12.15. 1847 S N.C.

2212 Gallant Charge of the Kentuckians at the Battle of Buena Vista, Feby. 23rd, 1847 and complete defeat of the Mexicans / American Army 4500 men, Mexican Army 20,000 men. American loss 264 killed, 450 wounded, 26 missing. Mexican loss, killed & wounded 4000 / #5 / 8.2x12.12. 1847 S N.C.

2213 Gallant Charge of the "Sixty-Ninth" / On the rebel batteries at the battle of Bull Run, Va. July 21st, 1861 / und S C&I

Game See: Nos. 334, 788, 814, 1468-9, 1523, 1535, 1538, 1541, 1743-4, 2712, 2865-7, 3099-100, 4079, 4988, 4991-2, 5036, 5151, 5248, 5468, 5581, 6866.

2214 Game Cock, The — El Gallo De Pelea / In Full Feather / #640 (Upright, vignette to left, head to right, cocks fighting in background.) 1849 S N.C.

2215 Game Cock, The — El Gallo De Pelea / Trimmed / #601 (Vignette, upright, full length, to right.) 1849 S N.C.

2216 Game Cock, The / #601 (Same as preceding, except for title change.) 1848 S N.C.

2217 Game Dog, A / Thos. Worth on stone. (Vignette, watch dog has treed hunter and eaten his game.) 1879 S C&I

2218 Game of the Arrow / Archery of the Mandan Indians. Headwaters of the Missouri / Painted by Catlin. 12.2 x17.14. und M C&I

2219 Gap of Dunloe, The / Ireland / und S C&I

2220 Garden of Gethsemane, The / #112/ 1 line Biblical quotation. 8.6x12.4. 1846 S N.C.

2221 Garden, Orchard and Vine / F. F. Palmer, Del. 15x20.5 (Group of fruits, berries, nuts, watermelon, tinted background.) 1867 M C&I

2222 Garfield Family, The / Little Abe, Mrs. Garfield, Miss Mollie, President Garfield, Irving, Harry, Mother Garfield, James / 8.9x12.11. 1882 S C&I

Garfield, James A. See: Nos. 1482. 1885, 2222, 2280-1, 3148, 4121, 4489, 5091, 5664, 6068, 6244, 6544, 6782.

Garfield, Mrs. **See**: Nos. 3832, 4263.

Garibaldi, Gen. **See**: Nos. 2257-8.

2223 Garnet Pool, The / White Mountains / 10.7x14.15 (Group of 4 on rocks at left.)   und M C&I

2224 Garrett Davis / By Glencoe, dam by Sir Leslie / From the original painting in possession of his owner W. W. Boyden, Esq. / President of the National Jockey Club of New York / To whom this print is respectfully dedicated by the Publisher / Paint. by R. A. Clarke. 18.12x36.4 (Profile to left, standing, first line of title in plate.) 1854 L N.C.

2225 Gate of Belen / Mexico, the 13th September, 1847 / #630 / 7.11x11.10 (Title repeated in Spanish.) 1848 S N.C.

2226 Gay Deceiver, The / J. Cameron on stone. 10.3x14.13 (Dogs in court room, breach of promise suit.) 1872 M C&I

Gazelle (Horse) **See**: No. 1179.

Geary, Gen. **See**: No. 5490.

2227 Geburts und Taufschein / 12.9x8.11 (Certificate in German, religious pictures, Last Supper, Biblical quotations, etc.)   und S C&I

2228 Gem of the Atlantic, The / #693 / 8.12x12.15 (Title in plate, view of New York Harbor in the background, 1 of the New York Packet Ships under sail to right, companion to "The Gem of the Pacific" No. 2229.) 1849 S N.C.

2229 Gem of the Pacific, The / #694 / 8.13x12.15 (Title in plate, ship under full sail to left, companion to preceding.)   1849 S N.C.

2230 Gems of American Scenery / (4 small views on 1 sheet: Silver Cascade, Northern Scenery, Among the Hills, The River Road.)   und S C&I

2231 General Ampudia treating for the capitulation of Monterey, with General Taylor, 24th Sept. 1846 / 1846 S N.C.

2232 General and Mrs. Washington / 1876 S C&I

2233 General Andrew Jackson / The Hero, the Sage, and the Patriot / "We mourn our Loss" / (Line at each side of title) Born 15th March, 1767 — Died 8th June, 1845 / #73 / 12.2x8.9 (Full length, under tree, White House in background, black border.) 1845 S N.C.

2234 General Andrew Jackson / Balance of title same as preceding. #347 / 12.2 x8.7 (Round corners.) 1846 S N.C.

2235 Gen. Andrew Jackson / The Hero of New Orleans / 12.2x8.9 (Horse to left, Jackson's head to right.) 1845 S N.C.

2236 Gen. Andrew Jackson / The Hero of New Orleans / #61 (Jackson facing left, equestrian portrait, vignette.)   und S N.C.

2237 Gen. Andrew Jackson / The Hero of New Orleans /   und S C&I

2238 General Andrew Jackson / At New Orleans, Jan. 8th, 1815 / 11.15x8.7 (Sword in right hand, equestrian, battle in background.)   und S N.C.

2239 General Andrew Jackson / Born 15th March, 1767 — The Hero, the Sage, and the Patriot — Died 8th June, 1845. "We mourn our Loss" / und S N.C.

2240 Genl. Andrew Jackson / "The Union must and shall be preserved." / #61 (Vignette equestrian portrait, upright, troops in background.)   und S C&I

General Armstrong (Privateer) **See**: No. 182.

Genl. Banks **See**: No. 380.

2241 Gen. Bem, the Hungarian Hero / 1849 S N.C.

2242 Gen. Benj. F. Butler / Greenback Labor Candidate for President of the United States /   und S C&I

2243 General Butler and Dexter / In their great match for $2000, two mile heats, to wagons. / Over the Fashion Course, L.I. Oct. 27th, 1865 / 6 additional lines. J. Cameron on stone. 16.10 x26.12 (Broadside to right, skeleton wagons.)   1866 L C&I

2244 General Butler and Dexter / Match for $2000, two mile heats, to wagons, over the Fashion Course, L.I. Oct. 27th, 1865 / H. Woodruff's B. R. G. Dexter 1. 1. 1. — D Tallman's BL. G. General Butler 2. 2. 2. / Time 5:00¾, 4:56¼ / J. Cameron on stone. (Vignette.)   1874 S C&I

General Butler (Horse) **See**: No. 3379.

General Benj. Butler **See**: No. 2242.

2245 Gen. Chester A. Arthur / Republican Candidate for Vice-President of the United States / (Vignette, half length.) 1880 M C&I

2246 Gen. Chester A. Arthur / Twenty-first President of the United States / (Vignette, same as preceding, except change in title.)   1880 M C&I

2247 Gen. D. E. Twiggs / at the Storming of the Fortress of Chapuletepec / #550 / 11.8x8.8 (Upright, vignette, equestrian.)   1847 S N.C.
   General Darcy (Horse) See: Nos. 3399, 6170.

2248 Genl. Dembinsky / The Polish Champion of Liberty / Hungary 1849 / (Vignette, upright, equestrian.)   1849 S N.C.

2249 Genl. E. Cavaignac / Appointed Provisional President of the French Republic with the powers of a dictator, June 23d, 1848 / #600 / 12x8.15 (Horseback, troops fighting in background.)   1848 S N.C.

2250 General Francis Marion, of South Carolina in his Swamp Encampment / Inviting a British officer to share his dinner of sweet potatoes and cold water / 8.8x12.8.   1876 S C&I

2251 Genl. Frank P. Blair, Jr. / The Nation's Choice for / Vice President of the U.S. / (Vignette, bust slightly to left.)   und S C&I

2252 Genl. Franklin Pierce / From a daguerreotype in possession of Messrs. Dunlap & Libby (Full face, half length vignette.)   1852 L N.C.

2253 Genl. Franklin Pierce / Fourteenth President of the United States / #628 (Full face, seated, quill in hand, red curtain.)   und S N.C.

2254 Genl. Franz Sigel / (Vignette, half length.)   1862 S C&I

2255 Genl. Franz Sigel / At the battle of Pea-Ridge, Ark. March 8th, 1862 / 11.10x8.13 (Upright, on white horse, 2 Union soldiers on ground.)   1862 S C&I

2256 Genl. G. T. Beauregard (Facsimile) / (Bust, head to left.)   und S C&I

2257 General Garibaldi / The Hero of Italy / #17 / 11.13x8.12 (Standing by white horse, upright.)   und S C&I

2258 General Garibaldi / The Hero of Italy / 12x8.15.   und S C&I

2259 Genl. Geo. B. McClellan and Staff / At the battle of Williamsburg, Va., May 5th, 1862 / (On horseback.)   1862 S C&I

2260 Genl. Geo. B. McClellan and Staff / before Yorktown, Va., April 1862 / 11.14x9.1 (Upright, equestrian.)   1862 S C&I

2261 Gen. George Washington / The Father of his Country / (Equestrian, hat raised, troops in background.)   und S N.C.

2262 Gen. George Washington / The Father of his Country / (Equestrian, hat in hand, vignette.)   und S N.C.

2263 Gen. George Washington / The Father of his Country / #60 / 11.2x9 (Holding hat over head, marching troops in rear, vignette.)   und S N.C.

2264 General George Washington / The Father of his Country / 11.2x8.12 (Washington on horse, sword in right hand, hat in right, soldiers in background.)   und S C&I

2265 Genl. George Washington / The Father of his Country / L.M. (Maurer) on stone. (On white horse, to left, hat in right hand, no troops, vignette.)   und M C&I

2266 Genl. George Washington / The Father of his Country / #60 / 11.1x6.10 (Horseback, vignette, sword in right hand, held straight ahead.)   und S C&I

2267 Genl. George Washington Morrison Nutt / 16 years old 29 inches in height, and weighing only 25 lbs. / (Top corners round.)   und S C&I

2268 Genl. Gorgey / The Hungarian Patriot / #617 (Vignette, upright, on horseback.)   1849 S N.C.

2269 General Grant /   1884 S C&I

2270 General Grant / (Military uniform, vignette profile to right.)   1885 L C&I

2271 General Grant, U. S. / (Vignette, in military uniform, full face.)   1885 L C&I

2272 General Grant / In his library, writing his memoirs / 16x21 (Grant, seated, facing left, civilian clothes. Portrait by permission of A. Bogardus & Co. from their splendid photograph, the last and best taken of General Grant.)   1885 L C&I

2273 General Grant and Family / Genl. Grant — Jesse Root Grant — Ulysses Simpson Grant — Frederick Dent

Grant — Ellen Wrenshall Grant —
Mrs. Grant / 8.2x12.5.
1867 S C&I

2274 General Grant at / The Tomb of
Abraham Lincoln / Oak Ridge Cemetary. Springfield, Illinois / 8x12.8.
1868 S C&I

2275 General Helmuth Von Moltke von
Preussen / 11x10.   und S C&I

2276 General Israel Putnam / The Iron
son of '76 Effecting his Escape from
the British Dragoons /.
und S C.C.

2277 Genl. Israel Putnam / The Iron son
of '76 effecting his escape from the
British dragoons / #367 / (Upright,
riding down steps on horseback.)
1845 S N.C.

2278 Genl. Israel Putnam / The Iron son
of '76 / Effecting his escape from the
British dragoons / 11.12x8.9.
und S N.C.

2279 General Israel Putnam / The Iron
son of '76 / Effecting his escape from
the British dragoons, at Rocky Neck,
Conn. /   und S C&I

2280 Gen. James A. Garfield / Twentieth
President of the United States /
1880 S C&I

2281 General James A. Garfield / Twentieth President of the United States /
1880 M C&I

2282 Genl. James Irvin / Whig Candidate for / Governor of Pennsylvania /
#480 / 11.6x8.10 (Half length, seated.)
1847 S N.C.

2283 Gen. John C. Breckinridge /
und S C&I

2284 Genl. John E. Wool / At the battle
of Buena Vista Febr. 23rd, 1847 / #540
(Equestrian upright vignette, battle
in background.)   1847 S N.C.

2285 Gen. Joseph E. Johnston /
1861 S C&I

2286 General Lafayette / The Compan-
ion-in-Arms of Washington /
und S N.C.

2287 General Lafayette / The Compan-
ion-in-Arms of Washington / Born
Sept. 6th, 1757 — Died May 20th, 1834
/ 12x8.9 (Full length, upright, hat and
cane in right hand.)
und S N.C.

2288 Genl. Lewis Cass / Of Michigan /
#384 / 11.10x8.11 (Seated, red curtain,
fort seen through open window.)
1846 S N.C.

2289 Genl. Meagher at the battle of Fair
Oaks, Va. June 1st, 1862 / 3 additional
lines. 7.15x12.7.   1862 S C&I

2290 General Philip Kearney / 3 additional lines. (Upright, equestrian portrait, top corners round.)
und S C&I

2291 General Robert E. Lee / (Facsimile
signature, vignette.)
und S C&I

2292 Gen. Robert E. Lee at the grave of
"Stonewall" Jackson /
und S C&I

2293 General Scott's Victorious Entry
into the City of Mexico, Sept. 14th,
1847 / #549 / 12.11x8.5 (Full-length
figures: Scott and staff on horseback.)
1847 S N.C.

2294 General Shields at the battle of
Winchester, Va., 1862 / 3 additional
lines. 7.15x12.8.   1862 S C&I

2295 General Stoneman's Great Cavalry
Raid, May 1863 / 3 additional lines.
8x12.14.   und S C&I

2296 General Taylor and Staff / The
Heroes of Palo Alto, Resaca de la
Palma, Monterey, and Buena Vista /
#463 / 12.2x8.8 (Upright, reviewing
troops.)   1847 S N.C.

2297 Genl. Taylor at the battle of Palo
Alto / May 8th, 1846 / #439 / C. S.
on stone. 8.8x12.8 (Taylor on black
horse at left, American troops charging Mexicans, cannon at right, no
Mexican flag.)   1846 S. N.C.

2298 Genl. Taylor at the battle of Palo
Alto / May 8th, 1846 / #439 (Different
composition to preceding. Taylor on
white horse, Mexican flag at right.)
1846 S N.C.

2299 Genl. Taylor at the battle of Resaca
de la Palma / Capt. May receiving his
orders to charge the Mexican Batteries,
May 9th, 1846 / #436 / 8.7x12.11 (Capt.
May on black horse, cannon on right,
wounded soldier at extreme left.)
1846 S N.C.

2300 Genl. Taylor at the battle of
Resaca de la Palma / Capt. May receiving his orders to charge the Mexican batteries, May 9th, 1846 / #436 /
8.9x12.11 (Capt. May on white horse,
and other changes in composition,
wounded in center foreground.)
1846 S N.C.

2301 Genl. Thomas Francis Meagher at
the battle of Fredericksburg, Va., Dec.

13th, 1862 / 11.14x8.7 (General Meagher on white horse, Irish flag.)
und S C&I

2302 General Tom Thumb / 11.13x8.10 (Thumb standing on chair, 6 views on each side, upright.)
1849 S N.C.

2303 General Tom Thumb / Born in 1832, is 28 inches high, and weighs only 15 pounds / From a daguerreotype by Plumbe. Barnum's Gallery of Wonders No. 1 (at top) (13 inset portraits) 12.4x8.8.
1849 S N.C.

2304 General Tom Thumb / Born in 1832, is 28 inches high and / weighs only 15 pounds / #680 / From a daguerreotype by Plumbe. 12.13x8.9 (Equipage across top, 6 inserts on each side, upright.)
1849 S N.C.

2305 General Tom Thumb / The smallest man alive, 22 years old, 33 inches high. 12.8x8.8 (at top) Barnum's Gallery of Wonders No. 1 (9 of his portraits on sides of print, upright.)
1849 S N.C.

2306 Genl. Tom Thumb / Standing by the side of an ordinary sized man. The wonderful dwarf is 11 years old, 22 inches high, and weighs only 15 lbs / C. Capelli, F. on stone. (Upright, vignette, full length. This print was published about 1843.)
und S N.C.

2307 Genl. Tom Thumb & Wife, Com. Nutt & Minnie Warren / Four Wondrously Formed & Strangely Beautiful Ladies & Gentlemen in miniature, nature's smallest editions of her choicest works / The greatest wonders in the world / 2 additional lines. (1 central group, surrounded by 10 small views.)
1863 S C&I

2308 Genl. Tom Thumb as Hop O' My Thumb / In the play of / The Giant and his Seven League Boots / Now performing at / Barnum's Museum / Philadelphia / Barnum's Gallery of Wonders No. 2 (at top) 13x8.15 (Thumb in center defeating giant, surrounded by 11 smaller scenes.)
und S N.C.

2309 Genl. Tom Thumb's Marriage at Grace Church, N.Y. Feby. 10th, 1863 / 10 small scenes around center view.)
1863 S C&I

2310 General Transatlantic Company's Steamer Normandie / Between New York and Havre /   und S C&I

2311 General Trochu / Gouverneur de Paris et Ministre de Guerre / Provisoire de la Republic Francaise / (Vignette.)
und S C&I

2312 Gen. U. S. Grant /
1884 S C&I

2313 Gen. U. S. Grant / 1885 / 9.9x12.4 (Half-length portrait.)
1885 S C&I

2314 Gen. U. S. Grant / 1885 / 8.1x6.13 (Same portrait as preceding but just head and shoulders shown.)
1885 S C&I $30.

2315 General U. S. Grant / General-in-Chief of the Armies of the United States /   und S C&I

2316 Gen. U. S. Grant / The Nation's Choice for / President Of The U.S. / (Vignette.)   und S C&I

2317 General U. S. Grant / President of the U.S. / (Vignette.)
und S C&I

2318 General U. S. Grant /
und S C&I

2319 General View of the City of Toronto, N.C. / T. Young, Arct. Delt. Toronto, N.C. / J. H. Bufford, Del. on stone. 11.14x17.14.
1835 M N.C.

2320 Genl. Von Steinmetz / Von Preussen / (Vignette.)   und S C&I

2321 Genl. William F. Packer / Governor of Pennsylvania / 11.6x8.10.
und S C&I

2322 General William H. Harrison / Hero of Tippecanoe, Fort Meigs, & Thames / 12x8.15 (Full length, standing to left of white horse.)
und S C&I

2323 General William H. Harrison / Hero of Tippecanoe, Fort Meigs & Thames / 12x10.1 (Sword in left hand, facing right.)   und S N.C.

2324 Gen. William H. Harrison / At the / Battle of Tippecanoe / #57 / 11.10x9.11 (2 additional lines. Harrison on charger, troops, slain Indian.)
und S N.C.

2325 General William H. Harrison / at the / Battle of Tippecanoe / # 57 / 2 additional lines. 11.2x8.11 (Harrison on white horse, 2 dead Indians.)
und S N.C.

2326 Genl. William J. Worth / At the storming of the Bishop's Palace, Monterey, Sept. 22nd, 1846 / #471 (Upright, vignette, equestrian.)

1847 S N.C.

2327 Genl. William T. Sherman / U.S. Army / (Facsimile signature.)
und S C&I

2328 Gen. Winfield S. Hancock / Democratic Candidate for President of the United States / (Vignette.)
und S C&I

2329 Gen. Z. Taylor / The Hero of the Rio Grande / #437 (Black horse, vignette to right.)   1846 S N.C.

2330 Gen. Z. Taylor / ["Rough and Ready"] #541 / 12.3x8.13 (Full length, military uniform.)
1846 S N.C.

2331 General Z. Taylor / "Rough and Ready" / The Hero of Palo Alto, Resaca de la Palma, Monterey and Buena Vista / 11.15x8.8.
1847 S N.C.

Genesta (Yacht) See: Nos. 1338-9, 4973, 5536.

2332 Genteel Stepper, A. /
und V.S. C&I

2333 Genteel Stepper, A / (Used as an "ad" for Gemmill, Burnham & Co., Hartford, Conn.)   und V.S. C&I

Gentleman's Driving Park, Morrisania See: Nos. 434, 925, 940, 4251, 4256.

2334 Genuine Havana, A /
und S C&I

2335 George /   und S C&I

2336 George and Lucy /
und S C&I

2337 George and Martha Washington / (2 portraits on same sheet, vignette.)
und S C&I

2338 George B. McClellan / (Facsimile signature, vignette.)
und M C&I

2339 George Clinton / 2.13x3 (From Jenkin's "History of Political Parties in the State of New York" 1846.)
und V.S. C.C.

2340 George M. Dallas /
1846 S N.C.

2341 George M. Dallas / The People's Candidate for / Vice-President of the United States / (Seated to right, full face, green curtain.)
und S N.C.

2342 George M. Dallas / The People's Candidate for Vice-President / Of the United

States / 11.11 x 8.12 (Profile, ship seen through window.)   und S N.C.

2343 George M. Dallas / Vice-President of the United States / 11.10x8.11 (Profile, seated, red curtain, ship seen through window.)   1844 S N.C.

2344 George M. Patchen, Brown Dick and Miller's Damsel / In their splendid trotting contest for a purse of over the Union Course, L.I., July 7th, 1859 / L. Maurer on stone. 5 additional lines. 17.8x27.8 (High-wheeled sulkies to left.)   1859 L C&I

George M. Patchen (Horse) See: Nos. 885, 938.

George M. Patchen, Jr. (Horse) See: No. 6205.

George Palmer (Horse) See: Nos. 6180, 6184-5, 6189.

2345 George W. Williams / (Negro soldier and historian.)
und S C&I

2346 George Washington / (Head and shoulders, slightly to left, vignette.)
und M N.C.

2347 Go. Washington / (Bust to right, lace jabot, vignette.)
und M C&I

2348 Go. Washington / (Bust to right, plain jabot, vignette.)
und M C&I

2349 Go. Washington / (Bust to right, lace jabot.)   und S C&I

2350 Go. Washington / (Facsimile signature, ¾ length in military uniform.)
und S C&I

2351 George Washington / (Full length, in uniform.)   und S N.C.

2352 George Washington / First President of the United States / 11.6x9 (Seated, half length to left, right arm on table.)   und S N.C.

2353 George Washington / First President of the United States / 11.16x8.12 (Seated, half length to left, sword resting in left arm, curtained background. The Stuart type, red curtain, slight changes in composition from preceding.)   und S N.C.

2354 George Washington / First President of the United States / 11.2x8.8 (Half length seated to left, sword in left arm, curtained background.)
und S N.C.

2355 George Washington / First President of the United States /
und S C&I

2356 George Washington and His Family
J. Cameron, Del.
und L C&I

George. Wilkes (Horse) See: Nos.
711, 897, 930-2, 976, 3379.

Georgia (State) See: Nos. 383, 397,
408, 595, 807, 5965.

2357 Georgiana / 11.9x8.7 (Oval in
ornate border, ½ length, lace gloves,
decollete dress and fan.)
1846 S N.C.

2358 Georgiana / 10.14x8.10 (Upright
oval.)   und S C&I

2359 Georgie / Quite tired / #704 (Vignette.)   und S C&I

2360 Georgie / Quite tired / #704 (Half
length.)   und S N.C.

Geraldine (Yacht) See: No. 4450.

2361 German Beauty, The / (Vignette.)
und S C&I

Germanic (Steamship) See: No.
3882.

Germany See: Nos. 6450, 6485,
6560.

2362 Gertrude / #397 / 11.12x8.4 (½
length in bridal costume.)
1846 S N.C.

Gertrude (Yacht) See: No. 5105.

Gessler See: Nos. 6706, 6709.

2363 Getting a Boost / Thos. Worth on
stone. (Vignette, drunken driver helped
into rig, companion to "On the Homestretch" No. 4600.)   1882 S C&I

2364 Getting A Foot / "Guess youse
done got de ole man's number — foa-
teen" / (Colored suitor getting kicked
out of house by girl's father.)
1887 S C&I

2365 Getting a Hoist / A Bad Case of
Heaves / Thos. Worth on stone. (Vignette, horse kicking blacksmith.)
1875 S C&I

2366 Getting A Hoist /
1879 V.S. C&I

2367 Getting Down / #40 (2 men fighting, woman throwing water on them,
companion to No. 2370.)
und S N.C.

2368 Getting In / (Companion to No.
2369.)   und S N.C.

2369 Getting Out / #707 (Soldier hiding
under shelf, found by woman and dog,
companion to No. 2368.)
und S N.C.

2370 Getting Up /   und S N.C.

Gettysburg, Pa. See: Nos. 406-7,
3911.

2371 Ghost, The / A new spectral illu-
sion, lately discovered in Europe, and
now causing a great commotion in
America / (Napoleon with crown
raised from his head, dropping crown
of Mexico from his hand; John Bull
holding horns of 2 rams, vignette.)
1863 S C&I

2372 Giant's Causeway, The / County
Antrim — Ireland / 8.8x12.9.
und S C&I

2373 Gift of Autumn, A / (Assorted
fruits in glass vase and at base of
vase, vignette.)   1875 S C&I

Gilbert's Dry Dock See: No. 4789.

Gillmore, Gen. Q. A. See: No. 3927.

2374 Gipsie's Camp, The / 11.8x16.6
(Camp at side of stream, ruined castle
in background.)   und M C&I

2375 Girard Avenue Bridge / Fairmount
Park, Philadelphia / 8.8x12.8.
und S C&I

2376 Girl I Love, The / (Bust portrait,
vignette.)   1870 S C&I

2377 Girl of my Heart, The / (Vignette.)
und S C&I

2378 Girl of the Period, The / (Full-
length figure, young girl with bustle,
riding whip, and cigarette, vignette.)
und S C&I

2379 "Give me Liberty, or Give me
Death!" / Patrick Henry delivering
his great speech on the rights of the
colonies before the Virginia Assembly /
Convened at Richmond March 23rd,
1775 / 8.13x12.11.   1876 S C&I

2380 Give us this day / Our Daily Bread
/ (Scroll with bread, wheat, and flowers, vignette.)   1872 S C&I

2381 Give Us This Day Our Daily
Bread /   1878 S C&I

2382 Giving Him Taffy /
1881 S C&I

Glen, The See: "Landscape Cards"
No. 3439.

2383 Glen at Newport, The / 8.8x12.8
(Picnic scene in foreground.)
und S C&I

2384 Glengariff Inn, / Ireland / 8x12.12
(Lake in foreground, boats, people,
etc.)   und S C&I

Glengariff See: ''Cromwell's
Bridge'' No. 1302.

2385 Glimpse of the Homestead, A / F.
F. Palmer, Del.   1863 M C&I

2386 Glimpse of the Homestead, A / F.
F. Palmer, Del. 11.7x16.2 (White house
on left, chickens, ducks, cows, etc. Cottage on right.)   1865 M C&I

2387 Glimpse of the Homestead, A /
11.2x15.8.   1859 M C&I

2388 Glorious Charge of Hancock's Divi-
sion [2nd] of the Army of the Potomac
/ At the battle near Spottssylvania
Court House, Va., May 12th, 1864 /
#846 / 8.1x12.9.   und S C&I

Gloster (Horse) See: No. 902.

Go Ahead Principle See: No. 5566.

2389 Go As You Please /
1879 S C&I

2390 Go In and Win / Thos. Worth on
stone. (Vignette, trainer instructing
colored jockey.)   1880 S C&I

2391 God Bless / Father and Mother /
(Vignette, motto and flowers.)
1876 S C&I

2392 God Bless Our Home / (Motto and
flowers, vignette.)   und S C&I

2393 God Bless Our School / (Scroll
surrounded by books, globe, etc.)
1874 S C&I

2394 God Bless Thee and Keep Thee /
und S C&I

2395 "God is Love" / (Banner, flowers,
fruits, vegetables — vignette.)
1874 S C&I

2396 God Save My Father's Life / #342
(¾ length, girl and old man, vignette.)
und S N.C.

2397 God Spake All These Words /
(Vignette, 10 commandments in 3 columns.)   1876 S C&I

2398 Going Against the Stream / 2 lines
of verse at sides of title. 10.10x15
(Symbolical view of couple in rowboat on stream of life, companion to
No. 2410.)
und M N.C.

2399 Going for a Shine / "He kin knock
de stuffin outen a mule" / (Vignette,
comic, companion to No. 4818.)
1888 S C&I

2400 Going for Him / J. C. (Cameron)
on stone. 8.4x12.3 (4 puppies after rat,
slightly rounded corners, identical composition as "You will, will you?" No.
6832. Companion to "Who's Afraid of
You?" No. 6648.)   1868 S C&I

2401 Going for the Money / 18x28 (2
horses, high-wheel sulkies to right.)
1891 L C&I

2402 Going it Blind / "Give me a good
pair of wheels and I'll go it blind" /
R. A. Clarke, Del.
und S N.C.

2403 Going to Pasture / Early Morning
/ (Girl driving flock of cattle through
stream.)   und S C&I

2404 Going to the Front! / Thos. Worth
on stone. (Vignette, 3 rigs and horses.)
1878 S C&I

2405 Going to the Front /
1880 S C&I

2406 Going to the Front /
1880 V.S. C&I

2407 Going to the Mill /
und S N.C.

2408 Going to the Mill / 11.1x15.6.
1859 M C&I

2409 Going to the Trot / A Good day and
Good Track / Thos. Worth on stone.
Companion to 1219. 18.13x28.12.
1869 L C&I

2410 Going With the Stream / 2 lines
of verse at sides of title. 10.11x15
(Symbolical view, young married couple in row boat. Companion to "Going
against the Stream" No. 2398.)
und M N.C.

2411 Gold Dust / J. Cameron on stone.
(Profile of horse, standing to left, vignette.)   1875 S C&I

2412 Gold Mining in California / 8.8x
12.8.   1871 S C&I

2413 Gold Seekers, The /
1851 S N.C.

2414 Golden Fruits of California / 14.15
x20.7 (Tinted background.)
1869 L C&I

Golden Gate (Steamship) See: Nos.
749-50.

Golden, James See: No. 5708.

Golden Light (Clipper Ship) See:
No. 740.

2415 Golden Morning, A /
und M N.C.

2416 Golden Morning, The /
und M C&I

2417 Golden Morning, The / 12.8x8.8
(View through window, roses, bluebells, butterflies, humming bird.)
und S C&I

2418 Goldsmith Maid, 2:14 / 2.12x4.12.
1881 S C&I

2419 Goldsmith Maid / Record 2:14 / (¾ view to right, vignette.)
1871 S C&I

2420 Goldsmith Maid and American Girl / In the "Brush Home" of their capital race of six closely contested heats / over the Union Course, L.I., July 4th, 1868 / 17.11x27.11 (Broadside to right, passing judge's stand.)
1868 L C&I

2421 Goldsmith Maid and Judge Fullerton / In their great trot at East Saginaw, Mich., July 17th, 1874 / Purse $5000. $2500 to first, $1500 to second, and $1000 to the horse which beats 2:16½, mile heats, 3 in 5 in harness. Budd Doble's b.m. Goldsmith Maid 1-1-1. B. Mace's schg. Judge Fullerton 2-2-2 / J. Cameron on stone. 8x13.4.
1874 S C&I

2422 Goldsmith Maid and Lucy / Cold Spring Course, Milwaukee, Wis., Sept. 6th, 1871 — Purse $4000 mile heats 3 in 5 in harness / 2 additional lines. J. Cameron on stone. (To right high-wheeled sulkies.) 1874 S C&I
Goldsmith Maid See: Nos. 507, 711, 914-5, 923, 1864, 1908, 2419-22, 2448, 4740-1, 5479, 5708, 6009, 6163, 6184-5, 6189, 6761.

2423 was a duplicate of 65.

2424 Good Chance, A / Painted by A. F. Tait. 19.4x28.4 (Same composition as "American Hunting Scenes — A Good Chance." No. 174, slightly enlarged.)
1863 L C&I

2425 Good Day's Sport, A / Homeward Bound / L. Maurer on stone. 18x25.12 (Companion to "Out for a Day's Shooting" No. 4661.)
1869 L C&I

2426 Good Enough! / (Vignette, head of minister with Bible.)
und S C&I

2427 Good Evening / (Child and dog.)
und S C&I

2428 Good little Fido and Naughty Kittie / 8.8x12.3 (Kitten on table, eating, dog watching.) und S C&I

2429 Good for a Cold /
und S C&I

2430 Good for Nothing / 15.14x12.14 (Interior of school room, teacher telling mother that her boy is bad.)
und M C&I

2431 Good Friends, The /
und S C&I

2432 Good Husband, The / The Fruits of Temperance and Industry / 7.14x12.10 (Same as "Fruits of Temperance" No. 2195.) 1870 S C&I

2433 Good Little Brother / 11.11x8.11 (Carrying sister across stream.)
1872 S C&I

2434 Good Little Girl / (Vignette, holding book.) 1871 S C&I

2435 Good little Sisters, The / 11.9x8.8 (1 removing thorn from boy's foot while the other dries his eyes.)
und S C&I

2436 Good Luck to Ye / (Cigar ad, Irish woman holding horseshoe, postcard size.) 1880 V.S. C&I

2437 Good Man at the Hour of Death, The / #241. und S N.C.

2438 Good Morning / (Child and dog.)
und S C&I

2439 Good Morning! Little Favorite! / 12.7x8.12 (Upright, baby and dog awake, companion to No. 2441.)
und S C&I

2440 Good Natured Man, The /
und S N.C.

2441 Good Night! Little Playfellow / 12.8x8.11 (Baby in crib, dog at side, upright, companion to No. 2439.)
und S C&I

2442 "Good old Doggie" / L. M. (Maurer) on stone. 11.12x15.6 (Child in cart, petting dog.) und M C&I

2443 Good Old Rover and Kittie / (Girl feeding birds, dog and cat by her side.)
und S C&I

2444 Good Race, Well Won, A / Thos. Worth on stone. 18.1x27.1 (Same composition as "A Disputed Heat" No. 1587.) 1887 L C&I

2445 Good Samaritan, The / #677 / 12x 8.10 (4 additional lines.)
1849 S N.C.

2446 Good Samaritan, The /
und S C&I

2447 Good Send Off, Go!, A / J. Cameron on stone. 17.10x26.14 (Same composition as following, no names of horses given, judge's stand altered.)
1888 L C&I

2448 Good Send Off, Go!, A / Goldsmith Maid, American Girl, Lucy, and Henry / Trotting at Fleetwood Park, Morrisania, N.Y., July 9th, 1872 / 6 additional lines. J. Cameron on stone. 17.3x26.7. (4 high-wheeled sulkies passing stand to right, ¾ view from rear.) 1872 L C&I

2449 Good Shepherd, The /
und S C&I

2450 Good Shepherdess, The / #418 / 11.14x8.8. 1846 S N.C.

2451 Good Times on the old Plantation / 8.9x12.9 (Darkies in front of cottage on bank of river.) und S C&I

Gorgey, General See: No 2268.

2452 Gospel Ordinance / #568 / 2 additional lines of Biblical quotation. (Baptismal scene, column on each side entitled "Passages of Scripture on Baptism.") 1846 S N.C.

Gosport Navy Yard See: No. 753.

2453 Got 'em Both! / Thos. Worth on stone. (Colored comic, billiards. Companion to "Two To Go," Nos. 6272-4.) 1882 S C&I

2454 Got 'em Both! / 23x36 (Vignette.) 1892 L C&I

2455 "Got the Drop on Him" / Thos. Worth on stone. (Vignette, tiger after hunter on end of cracking limb of tree, Indian in canoe. Companion to "Tumbled To It" No. 6247, vignette.) 1881 S C&I

2456 Government Guards — Conn. / 1st Company / und S C&I
Gould, Jay See: No. 641.

2457 Gov. Grover Cleveland / 22nd President of the United States / (at top) Cleveland and Reform. / 7 excerpts printed in background. Copyright by Elnathan Gardner.
1885 M C&I

2458 Government House / From the original drawing by W. J. Condit / Copyright 1847 by H. R. Robinson / From an original drawing in the possession of Thomas N. Campbell, Esq. Printed in colors by C. Currier. C. Melbourne Delint et Excud, 1797. 14.12 x21.5 1847 L C.C.

2459 Governor Rutherford B. Hayes /
und S C&I

2460 Gov. Samuel J. Tilden / Of New York / Democratic Candidate for President of the United States /
und S C&I

2461 Governor Sprague / Black Trotting Stallion, bred by Amasa Sprague, Providence, R.I. / By Rhode Island / Record 2:20½ Po'keepsie, N.Y. Aug. 22nd, 1876 / und S C&I

2462 Gov. Thomas A. Hendricks / Of Indiana / National Democratic Candidate for Vice-President of the United States / (Vignette.)
und S C&I

2463 Governor Wade Hampton / Published by Chas. C. Richter, Charleston, S.C. / (Vignette.)
und S C&I

Governor's Guard See: No. 6067.

Governor's Island See: No. 4636.

2464 Grace Darling / (View of wreck of Forfarshire Steamship.)
und S N.C.

2465 Grace, Mercy and Peace / (Motto.)
und S C&I

2466 Graces of the Bicycle, The / (Women on high-wheeled bicycles, vignette.) 1880 S C&I

2467 Graces of the Bicycle, The / (Postcard size.) 1880 V.S. C&I

2468 Gracie / (Vignette, head.)
und S C&I

Gracie (Yacht) See: No. 1281.

2469 Graf von Bismark / Preussicher Premier Minister / (Vignette.)
und S C&I

Grafton (Horse) See: No. 2946.

Graham, Wm. A. See: Nos. 2515, 6684.

2470 Grand Banner of the Radical Democracy / for 1864 / 11.14x8.13 (Portraits of Gen. John C. Fremont and Gen. John Cochrane, candidates for President and Vice-President of the United States, horns of plenty, flag, eagle, etc.) 1864 S C&I

2471 Grand Bird's Eye view of / The Great East River Suspension Bridge / Connecting the cities of New York and Brooklyn / Showing the splendid panorama of / The Bay and Port of New York / (View looking Southeast, 12 keys.) 1885 L C&I

2472 Grand Bird's Eye view of the grounds and buildings of the great Columbian Exhibition at Chicago, Illinois, 1892-3 / In commemoration of the four hundredth anniversary of the discovery of America by Christopher Columbus / Oct. 12th, 1492 / 19 buildings keyed. 19.4x35.14.
1892 L C&I

2473 Grand California Filly, Sunol, Record 2:10½ at 3 yrs. old, The / By Electioneer, dam Waxane, Grandam Waxy by Lexington / L.M. on stone.

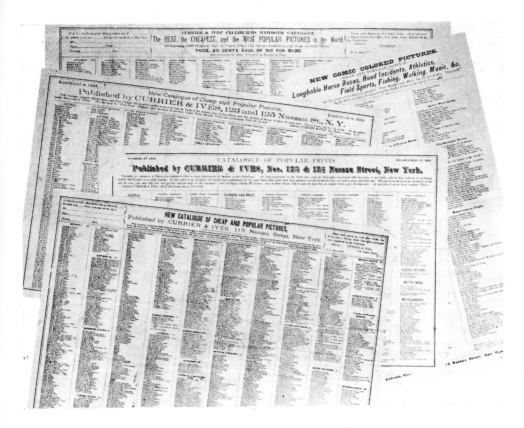

Group of Original Currier Order Lists

(Vignette, ¾ to left, high-wheeled sulky.)   1889 S C&I

2474 Grand California Filly, The / Wildflower / by Electioneer, dam by St. Clair. Bred by Gov. Leland Stanford, at Palo Alto, Cal. / J. Cameron on stone. (Vignette, ¾ to left, high-wheeled sulky.)   1883 S C&I

2475 Grand California Trotting Mare Sunol, Record 2:10½ at 3 years old, The / By Electioneer, dam Waxana by Gen'l Benton, Grandam Waxy by Lexington / Record 2:08¼ / Drawn by L. Maurer and on stone. 18.6x28.3 (Broadside to right, sound in background.)   1890 L C&I

2476 Grand Centennial Smoke, A / History in Vapor / (Figures representing Turkey, Germany, Russia, England, United States, France, Italy, and Spain — all smoking. Each figure has vision over his head formed with smoke: Russia—"Bear," Germany—"Sedan," Eng-

land—"King William," U. S.—"Washington and Cherry Tree," France—"At Keyhole," Italy—"The Pope," Spain—"Cuban Woman Burning at Stake.")   1876 M C&I

2477 Grand Centennial Wedding, The / Of Uncle Sam and Liberty / 12.7x15.14 Spirit of Washington says "Bless you my children." Uncle Sam lifting roof from Main Building Philadelphia.)   1876 M C&I

2478 Grand Democratic Free Soil Banner / From a daguerreotype by Plumbe / #616 / 12.3x9.1 (Martin Van Buren and Charles F. Adams — Free Soil, Free Labor, Free Speech.)   1848 S N.C.

2479 Grand Display of Fireworks and Illuminations, The / At the opening of the Great East River Bridge / Between New York and Brooklyn /   1883 S C&I

2480 Grand Display of Fireworks and

[113]

Illuminations, The / At the Opening of the great Suspension Bridge between New York and Brooklyn / On the evening of May 24th, 1883 / View from New York, looking towards Brooklyn / 2 columns, 7 lines. 12x17.9.
1883 M C&I

2481 Grand Drive, Central Park, N.Y. The / 17.7x27.15. 1869 L C&I

2482 Grand Fight for the Champion's Belt between Granite Pierce & Old Chapultepec / J. L. Magee, Pub. by P. Smith. (Pierce, Cass, Seward, Gen. Scott.) und S N.C.

2483 Grand Football Match — Darktown against Blackville / A Kick Off / (Vignette.) 1881 S C&I

2484 Grand Football Match — Darktown against Blackville / A Scrimmage / (Vignette.) 1888 S C&I

2485 Grand Funeral Procession in Memory of General Jackson as it started from the City Hall, New York, June 24, 1845 / 8.12x12.8.
und S N.C.

2486 Grand Funeral Procession of the victims of the Revolution / #581 / Title repeated in French. 8.6x12.13 (French Revolution.)
1848 S N.C.

2487 Grand Horse St. Julien, The "King of Trotters", The / by Volunteer, dam by Sayre's Harry Clay / As he appears when at full speed, handled by his celebrated trainer and driver, Orrin A. Hickok / Record 2:11¼ / J. Cameron on stone (Vignette, ¾ view to right.) 1880 S C&I

2488 Grand horse St. Julien, the "King of Trotters", The / by Volunteer, dam by Sayre's Harry Clay / As he appears when at full speed, handled by his celebrated trainer Orrin A. Hickok / Record 2:11¼ / Scott Leighton on stone. (Different composition and artist from preceding, vignette, ¾ to right.) 1881 S C&I

2489 Grand National American Banner / Millard Fillmore and Andrew J. Donelson, the American's Choice for President and Vice-President of the United States / 11.13x8.5.
1856 S N.C.

2490 Grand National Democratic Banner / Polk the young Hickory — Dallas and Victory / President and Vice-President / Press Onward / 11.12x8.5 (2 ovals under row of stars.)
1844 S N.C.

2491 Grand National Democratic Banner / Polk the young Hickory — Dallas and Victory / The People's Candidates for President and Vice-President / Press Onward / 11.12x8.5 (2 ovals under flags, eagle.)
1844 S N.C.

2492 Grand National Democratic Banner / Press Onward / Lewis Cass and Wm. D. Butler, The Democrat's Choice for President and Vice-President / #585 / 11.10x8.3.
1848 S N.C.

2493 Grand National Democratic Banner / Press Onward / Franklin Pierce and Wm. R. King / For President and Vice-President / The Union Now and Forever / Portraits from daguerreotypes by Plumbe / #585 (Also head of Washington.) 1852 S N.C.

2494 Grand National Democratic Banner / Press Onward / 11.10x8.2 (Balance of title as above, changes in composition and no portrait of Washington.)
1852 S N.C.

2495 Grand National Democratic Banner / Press Onward / James Buchanan and John C. Breckinridge, The Democrat's choice for President and Vice-President of the United States /
1856 S N.C.

2496 Grand National Democratic Banner for 1860 / (Breckinridge and Lane.)
1860 S C&I

2497 Grand National Democratic Banner / Peace! Union! and Victory! / 11.15x 8.14 (Portraits of Geo. B. McClellan and Geo. H. Pendleton. Eagle, flags, horns of plenty, figure of "Liberty" and view of a city on a harbor.)
1864 S C&I

2498 Grand National Democratic Banner/ (Gov. Samuel J. Tilden and Gov. Thos. A. Hendricks.) 1876 S C&I

2499 Grand National Democratic Banner / 1880 / For President / Home Rule & Honest Money Gen. W. S. Hancock / of Penna. For Vice-President Hon. W. H. English of Indiana. English Free men for a free Ballot — Union is Strength / 1880 L C&I

2500 Grand National Democratic Banner / Home Rule and Honest Money / Gen. W. S. Hancock and Hon. W. H. English / 1880 S C&I

2501 Grand National / Liberal Republican Banner for 1872 / For President Horace Greeley of New York and Benjn. Gratz Brown of Missouri for Vice-President / 1872 S C&I

2502 Grand National Republican Banner / Free Labor, Free Speech, Free Territory / 13.3x8.11 (John C. Fremont and Wm. L. Dayton.)   1856 S N.C.

2503 Grand National Republican Banner for 1872 / U. S. Grant and Horace Greeley /   1872 S C&I

2504 Grand National Republican Banner / Liberty and Union / General Rutherford B. Hayes for President. Hon. Wm. A. Wheeler for Vice-President /
1876 S C&I

2505 Grand National Republican Banner 1880 / Garfield & Arthur /
1880 S C&I

2506 Grand National Republican Banner 1880 / Gen. James A. Garfield of Ohio for President, Gen. Chester A. Arthur of New York for Vice-President / (2 oval portraits surmounted by eagle.) 20.4x28.12.   1880 L C&I

2507 Grand National Temperance Banner / Dedicated to every son & daughter of temperance throughout the Union / 11.14x8.10 #59.
1851 S N.C.

2508 Grand National Temperance Banner /   und S C&I

2509 Grand National Union Banner for 1860 / The Candidates and their Platform / (Hon. John Bell of Tennessee and Hon. Edward Everett of Massachusetts both resting hands on scroll "Constitution of the United States".) 12.4x8.10.   1860 S C&I

2510 Grand National Union Banner for 1864 / Liberty, Union and Victory / Portraits of Abraham Lincoln and Andrew Johnson / 12x8.13.
1864 S C&I

2511 Grand National Whig Banner / Onward / Justice to Harry of the West / (Portrait of Henry Clay, surmounted by eagle and flags.)
1844 S N.C.

2512 Grand National Whig Banner / Onward / The Nation's Choice, etc. / Henry Clay and T. Frelinghausen / 11.11x8.3.   1844 S N.C.

2513 Grand National Whig Banner / Zachary Taylor and Millard Fillmore / The People's Choice for President and Vice-President from 1849 to 1853 / #587.   1848 S N.C.

2514 Grand National Whig Banner / Press Onward / "If we all pull together we can't be beat" / 11.12x8.4 (Taylor and Fillmore.)   1848 S N.C.

2515 Grand, National, Whig Banner / 12.4x8.2 (Winfield Scott and William A. Graham.)   1852 S N.C.

2516 Grand New Steamboat Pilgrim, the Largest in the World, The / Flagship of the Fall River Line — Running between New York and Boston via Newport and Fall River. Commander Capt. Benj. M. Simmons / 2 additional lines. C. R. Parsons, Del. 20.12x35.
1883 L C&I

2517 Grand Pacer Flying Jib, Record 2:04, The / L. M. (Maurer) on stone. (Vignette, low-wheeled sulky to right.)
1892 S C&I

2518 Grand Pacer Mascot by Deceiver / Record 2:04 / Guy 2:06¾ Flying Jib 2:05¾ / 18.2x28 J. C. (Cameron) on stone (Composition identical to "Pacing in the Latest Style" No. 4680. 3 low-wheeled sulkies to right.)
1893 L C&I

2519 Grand Pacer Richball, Record 2:12½, The / Owned by D. L. Hughes, Keokuk, Iowa. Driven by James M. Allen / (Vignette, broadside to right, high-wheeled sulky.)
1890 S C&I

2520 Grand Patent India — Rubber Air Line Railway to California / Competition Defied / From the Atlantic to the Pacific, Through in no time / 2 additional lines. 10.12x17.7.
1849 M N.C.

2521 Grand Racer Kingston, by Spendthrift, The / Dam imp. Kapanga, by Victorious 2nd, dam Kapunda, by Stockwell / J. Cameron on stone. Sketched from life by Charles L. Zellinsky. 19.15x27.2 (Standing, to right, under saddle with jockey.)
1891 L C&I

2522 Grand Reception of Kossuth / "The Champion of Hungarian Independence" at the City Hall, New York, December 6th, 1851 / Title repeated in Hungarian / #472 / 8.2x12.2.   1851 S N.C.

2523 Grand Saloon of the Palace Steamer Drew / Of the People's Evening Line between New York & Albany, The / 1 additional line, 2 columns 6 lines. C. R. Parsons, Del. 20.15x34.12 (Interesting scene showing costumes of the period.)   1878 L C&I

2524 Grand Stallion Allerton, by Jay Bird, The / Record 2:09½ / J Cameron on stone. (Vignette, ¾ to right, high-wheeled sulky.)   1891 S C&I

2525 Grand Stallion Maxy Cobb, by

Happy Medium, The / Driven by John Murphy / Record 2:13¼ / J. Cameron on stone. (Vignette, high-wheeled sulky to right.)   1884 S C&I

2526 Grand Stallion Maxy Cobb, by Happy Medium, The / Record 2:13¼ / J. Cameron on stone. (Vignette, different from preceding.)
        1884 S C&I

2527 Grand Through Route Between North and South /
        1878 S C&I

2528 Grand Trotter Clingstone, driven by G. H. Saunders, The / By Rysdyks dam Gretchen, by Hambletonian / Record 2:14 / J. Cameron on stone. 17.13x 26.9 (¾ view to right, high-wheeled sulky.)   1883 L C&I

2529 Grand Trotter "Clingstone" by Rysdyk's dam "Gretchen," The / Record 2:14.   1882 S C&I

2530 Grand Trotter Edwin Thorne, driven by John E. Turner, The / By Thornedale dam by Ashland / Record 2:16½ / 18.2x26.9 (¾ view, high-wheeled sulky to left.)
        1883 L C&I

2531 Grand Trotting Queen Nancy Hanks driven by Budd Doble, The / To a bicycle sulky built by the Chas. Caffrey Co. Camden, N.J. / Record 2:04 / J. Cameron on stone. 19.12x27.15 (Broadside to right. Despite title 3 horses are shown.)
        1892 L C&I

2532 Grand Trotting Stallion Axtell by William L. by George Wilkes / Record at 3 yrs. old 2:12 / Driven by C. W. Williams / L. Maurer on stone. 18.4x28.2 (Nearly broadside to right.)
        1889 L C&I

2533 Grand Trotting Stallion Boneset- ter, by the Brook's horse by Pilot, Jr., The / Record 2:19 / Scott Leighton on stone. (¾ view to left, high-wheeled sulky, vignette.)   1881 S C&I

2534 Grand Trotting Stallion Boneset- ter by the Brook's horse, by Pilot, Jr., The / As he appeared at Oakland Park, Cal. Oct. 25th, 1879 / (Vignette.)
        1881 S C&I

2535 Grand Trotting Stallion St. Ju- lien driven by Orrin A. Hickok, The / By Volunteer, dam by Sayre's Henry Clay / 1 additional line / Record 2:12¾ / Jno. Cameron on stone. 16.14x26.2 (Broadside to right.)
        1880 L C&I

2536 Grand United Order of Odd-Fellows / Chart / 13.6x10 (27 small pictures of emblems, etc.)   1881 S C&I

2537 Grand United States Centennial Exhibition 1876 / Main Building / Fair- mount Park, Philadelphia / (2 columns, 2 lines each. 7.12x12.12.)
        und S C&I

Grand United States Centennial Exhibition See: Centennial Exhibition, etc.

2538 Grand Young Trotter Jay Eye See, The / Record 2:10 / (Vignette.)
        1883 S C&I

2539 Grand Young Trotting Mare Nan- cy Hanks by "Happy Medium," dam by Dictator, The / 4 year old Record 2:14½ / J. Cameron on stone. (Vig- nette, standing in front of stable, white dog by side.)   1890 S C&I

2540 Grand Young Trotting Stallion "Axtell" by William L, by George Wilkes, The / Record at 3 yrs. old 2:12 the champion of the world / 1 addi- tional line. L. M. on stone. (Vignette, ¾ to right, high-wheeled sulky.)
        1889 S C&I

2541 Grandest Palace Drawing Room Steamers in the World, The / Drew and St. John / Of the People's New York & Albany Evening Line / Pass- ing on the Hudson / 2 columns, 7 lines. Sketched and drawn by C. R. Parsons. 21x34.11.   1878 L C&I

2542 Grandfather's Advice / "Honor thy Father and Mother." /
        und S N.C.

2543 Grandma's "Specs" / (¾ length, lit- tle girl knitting, wearing glasses.)
        1877 S C&I

2544 Grandma's "Specs" / #272 (¾ length, entirely different from preced- ing, holding glasses to eyes.)
        und S C&I

2545 Grandma's Treasures / (Children at bedside.)   und S C&I

2546 Grandmother's Present, The / The Bible: Remember thou keep Holy the Sabbath day / 9.12x7.10.
        und S N.C.

2547 Grandpa's "Specs" / #287 (Vig- nette, little girl with specs on nose, reading.)   und S C&I

2548 "Grandpa's Specs" / #287 / 12x9.7.
        und S C&I

2549 Grandpa's Cane / (Vignette, child with cane.)   und M C&I

2550 Grandpapa's Cane /
und S C&I

2551 Grandpapa's Cane /
und S N.C.

2552 Grandpapa's Ride / 15.14x11.10 (2 girls and boy hitched to grandfather's chair.)
und M C&I

Grant, U. S. See: Nos. 396, 425, 1481, 1741, 2269, 2270-4, 2312-8, 2503, 2553-7, 2565, 3489, 3490-2, 3928, 3962, 4121, 4390, 4463, 4489, 5050, 5091, 5664, 6068, 6244, 6544, 6782.

2553 Grant and His Generals / Distinguished Commanders in the Campaign against Richmond / Grant, Sheridan, Meade, Weitzel, Terry, Crook, Rawlins, Parke, Wright, Hancock, Warren, Humphrey. (Vignette.)
1865 M C&I

2554 Grant & Lee Meeting near Appomattox Courthouse, Va. April 10th, 1865, The day after the surrender of Lee's army / From the original picture by Lieut. Col. Otto Botticher /
1868 S C&I

2555 Grant at Home /
1869 S C&I

2556 Grant at Home / E. Blinner on stone. 16.7x24.7 (7 keys, Capitol seen through window at right.)
1869 L C&I

2557 Grant in Peace /
und S C&I

Grapeshot (Clipper Bark) See: No. 875.

2558 Grass Hopper Strut, The / Which shews the Present Passion / Of the Butterflies of Fashion / (Full-length figure of woman in foreground, man walking in opposite direction, vignette.)
und S C&I

2559 Grave of Stonewall Jackson, The / Lexington, Virginia / 8x12.8 (Woman and child placing flowers on grave.)
1870 S C&I

2560 Gray Eagle / J. Cameron on stone. (Broadside to left, skeleton wagon.)
1866 L C&I

Gray Eagle See: No. 6169, 6206.

2561 Gray Gelding Jack by Pilot Medium / Record 2:19¾ / J. Cameron on stone. (Vignette, broadside to left, high-wheeled sulky.)
1888 S C&I

2562 Gray's Elegy — In a Country Churchyard / F. F. Palmer, Del. 16x 23.2.
1864 L C&I

2563 Grazing Farm, The / 16.12x24.14 (Horses, ducks, pigs, etc.)
1867 L C&I

2564 Great American Buck Hunt of 1856, The / (Stag with head of Buchanan running toward the White House, Fillmore at right, standing on "Union Rock" aiming rifle at "Buck" Fremont with gun which has exploded. Published at No. 2 Spruce St.)
und M N.C.

2565 Great American Tanner, The / Great Sachem of Tammany, Seymour, Blair, Grant, Lee, Pemberton, Buckner / J.M.I. (Ives) and Thos. Worth sketch. J. Cameron on stone. (Grant has "tanned" Lee, Pemberton, and Buckner. Sachem is presenting the others for the same treatment, vignette.)
1868 S C&I

2566 Great Bartholdi Statue, The / 3x 5.12 (Moonlight scene from the south, New York in background.)
1884 V.S. C&I

2567 Great Bartholdi Statue, The / 2.15x 5.9 (Daylight scene from the south, New York in background.)
1884 V.S. C&I

2568 Great Bartholdi Statue, The / Liberty Enlightening the World /
und V.S. C&I

2569 Great Bartholdi Statue, The / Liberty Enlightening the World / 6 additional lines. 12.8x9.3 (View from the south, New York in background.)
1883 S C&I

2570 Great Bartholdi Statue, The / Liberty Enlightening the World / The Gift of France to the American people / To be erected on Bedloe's Island / 6 references. 25.8x21.2.
1882 L C&I

2571 Great Bartholdi Statue, The / Liberty Enlightening the World / The gift of France to the American People /
1884 L C&I

2572 Great Bartholdi Statue, The / Liberty Enlightening the World / The gift of France to the American People / To be erected on Bedloe's Island, New York Harbor / 25.8x21.2.
1883 L C&I

2573 Great Bartholdi Statue, The / Liberty enlightening the world / The gift of France to the American people / Erected on Bedloe's Island, New York Harbor / 1 additional line. 13.9x9.11.
1885 M C&I

2574 Great Bartholdi Statue, The / Liberty enlightening the World / The gift of France to the American People / to be / Erected on Bedloe's Island, New

York Harbor / 3 additional lines. 15.13 x9.11. 1885 M C&I

2574A Great Bartholdi Statue, The / Liberty Enlightening the world / The gift of France to the American people/ Erected on Bedloe's Island, New York Harbor / 20.14x27 — 6 keys. (View from south, New York City in background.) 1885 L C&I

THE GREAT BARTHOLDI STATUE,
LIBERTY ENLIGHTENING THE WORLD.
WITH THE WORLD RENOWNED AND BEAUTIFUL
STAR LAMP.

2575 Great Bartholdi Statue, The / Liberty enlightening the world / The gift of France to the American people / Erected on Bedloe's Island, New York Harbor / Unveiled Oct. 28th, 1886 / 6 additional lines. (New York sky line and Brooklyn Bridge in background.) 1886 L C&I

2576 Great Bartholdi Statue, The / Liberty enlightening the world / With the world renowned and beautiful / Star Lamp / 19.11x15.14 (View showing the Russian Corvette "Strelok," British Warships "Garnet" and "Cana," U.S. Frigates "Minnesota" and "Omaha"

which saluted the French Frigate "Isere" New York in background, "Liberty" holding "Star Lamp" instead of the customary torch.) 1885 M C&I

2577 Great Battle of Murfreesboro, Tenn. Jany. 2nd, 1862 / Between the Union forces under Genl. Rosecrans and the rebel army under General Bragg / 3 additional lines. 1863 S C&I

2578 Great Black Sea Lion, The / The Monarch of the Artic (sic) Seas / (Portrait of Elisha Kent Kane, standing by seal, other seals in water, vignette.) und S C&I

Great Britain (Steamship) See: No. 3129.

2579 Great Command, The / 4 additional lines. 17.5x12 (Round top, shows Christ preaching.) 1866 M C&I

2580 Great Conflagration at Pittsburgh, Pa. April, 10th, 1845 / Nearly 1200 houses destroyed—Estimated loss of property $9,000,000. / Published by Turner & Fisher, 15 North 6th St., Phila., and N. Currier, N.Y. 8.3x12.8 (First state.) und S N.C.

2581 Great Conflagration at Pittsburgh, Pa. April 10th, 1845 / Nearly 1200 houses destroyed — Estimated loss of property $9,000,000. Pub. by Turner & Fisher 15 North 6th St., Phila. and N. Currier N.Y. 8.3x12.8 (2nd state.) und S N.C.

2582 Great Double Team Trot, A / 17.7x 28.2 (¾ view to right, skeleton wagons, judge's stand in rear.) 1891 L C&I

2583 Great Double Team Trot, The / Darkness and Jessie Wales — Honest Allen and Kirkwood / Trotting at the Prospect Park Fair Grounds, Brooklyn, L.I. July 21st, 1870 / 4 additional lines. J. Cameron 1870 on stone. 16.13x 27.5 (2 teams to skeleton wagons to right, passing judge's stand.) 1870 L C&I

2584 Great East River Bridge, The / To connect the Cities of New York & Brooklyn / 2 columns of 6 lines. 8.7x 12.6 (View looking Southeast from New York.) 1872 S C&I

2585 Great East River Bridge, The / Connecting the Cities of New York and Brooklyn / 1882 S C&I

2586 Great East River Suspension Bridge / No. 1 — Connecting the Cities of New York & Brooklyn / 2 additional lines dimensions. (Postcard size.) 1883 V.S. C&I

2587 Great East River Suspension Bridge / No. 2 — Connecting the Cities of New York & Brooklyn / 2 additional lines dimensions. (Postcard size, different angle from preceding.)
1883 V.S. C&I

2588 Great East River Suspension Bridge / No. 3 — Connecting the Cities of New York & Brooklyn / 2 additional lines of dimensions (Postcard size, different angle from 2 preceding prints.) 1883 V.S. C&I

2589 Great East River Suspension Bridge, The / Connecting the Cities of New York & Brooklyn / 2 additional lines. 3.4x5.8 (View from Brooklyn; looking southwest.)
1883 V.S. C&I

2590 Great East River Suspension Bridge, The / Connecting the Cities of New York and Brooklyn / 6 additional lines. 4.6x7 (View from Brooklyn looking West.) 1883 V.S. C&I

2591 Great East River Suspension Bridge, The / Connecting the Cities of New York and Brooklyn / From New York looking northeast / 6 additional lines. 4.6x7. 1883 V.S. C&I

2592 Great East River Suspension Bridge, The / Connecting the Cities of New York and Brooklyn / 3 additional lines and 2 columns, 6 and 5 lines. Parsons & Atwater, Del. 20.7x32.13 (View looking southwest.)
1874 L C&I

2593 Great East River Suspension Bridge, The / Connecting the Cities of New York & Brooklyn — From New York, looking southeast / 3 additional lines. Parsons & Atwater, Del. 20.12x33.
1877 L C&I

2594 Great East River Suspension Bridge, The / Connecting the Cities of New York and Brooklyn / 3 additional lines. 9x12.14 (Southwest from Brooklyn.) 1881 S C&I

2595 Great East River Suspension Bridge, The / Connecting the Cities of New York and Brooklyn / 3 additional lines. 9x12.14 (Same view as preceding, night scene, lights added on bridge.)
1881 S C&I

2596 Great East River Suspension Bridge, The / Connecting the Cities of New York and Brooklyn. View from Brooklyn, looking West / 4 additional lines. 20x26.12 (Several Sound steamers shown.) 1883 L C&I

2597 Great East River Suspension Bridge, The / Connecting the Cities of New York and Brooklyn. View from Brooklyn, looking West / 18.4x33(Very similar to above but closer view of bridge. Ferry boats instead of Sound steamers shown.)
1883 L C&I

2598 Great East River Suspension Bridge, The / Connecting the Cities of New York and Brooklyn. View from Brooklyn, looking West / 6 additional lines description. 8.15x4.11.
1883 V.S. C&I

2599 Great East River Suspension Bridge, The / Connecting the Cities of New York and Brooklyn /
1885 L C&I

2600 Great East River Suspension Bridge, The / Connecting the Cities of New York and Brooklyn /
1886 L C&I

2601 Great East River Suspension Bridge, The / Connecting the Cities of New York and Brooklyn / From New York looking South / Bird's eye view showing the complete system of the bridge. The Promenade, Cable Car Tracks, and Carriage Roadway / 3 additional lines. 18.3x25.4.
1890 L C&I

2602 Great East River Suspension Bridge, The / Connecting the Cities of New York and Brooklyn /
1892 L C&I

2603 Great Eastern / The Mammoth Trotting Gelding, 17.2 high / By Walkill Chief, by Rysdyk's Hambletonian, dam Dolly Mills by Seeley's American Star / Record 2:19 to harness / J. Cameron on stone. (Vignette, ¾ view to left, high-wheeled sulky.)
1877 S C&I

Great Eastern (Horse) See: No. 5063.

2604 "Great Eastern," The / 22,500 tons, 3000 horse power [nominal] / Constructed under the direction of I. K. Brunel, F.R.S. — D.C.L. / Commanded by Capt. William Harrison / 2 columns, 9 and 11 lines. C. Parsons, Del. 10.11x 17.7 (Broadside to right.)
1859 M C&I

2605 "Great Eastern", The / 22,500 Tons, 3000 horse power [nominal] / Constructed under the direction of I. K. Brunel F.R.S. — D.C.L. / Commanded by Capt. Vine Hall / 2 columns of 4 lines. #369 (¾ view from stern.)
und S C&I

2606 "Great Eastern" / The Iron Steamship "Leviathan" 22,500 Tons / Constructed under the direction of I. K. Brunel, F.R.S. — D.C.L. / Commanded by Capt. William Harrison / 2 columns. C. Parsons, Del. 17.12x28.14.
1868 L C&I
Great Eastern (Steamship) See: Nos. 3130, 3957-9.

2607 Great Exhibition of 1851, The / American Department / 2 additional lines and 4 lines each end of title. 9.14x16.14 (Yankee showing John Bull Cunard liner, Clipper ship, Collins Line boat, agricultural machinery.)
und M N.C.

2608 Great Exhibition of 1860, The / Greeley playing hand organ marked "New York Tribune," Lincoln playing hobby horse with rail marked "Republican Platform" / (Vignette.)
und M C&I

2609 Great Fair on a Grand Scale, A / 13x19.1 (Scene showing fair grounds, race track, cattle, horses, pigs, balloon, etc.)
1894 M C&I

2610 Great Field in a Grand Rush, A / (19 horses head on.)
1888 L C&I

2611 Great Fight at Charlestown, S.C., April 7th, 1863, The / 4 additional lines. 8.1x12.9 (5 keys, naval battle.)
1863 S C&I

2612 Great Fight between the "Merrimac" & "Monitor" March 9th, 1862, The / The first battle between Ironclad ships of War / From a sketch furnished by F. Newman of Norfolk, Va. 8.3x12.10 / (Merrimac in foreground.)
1862 S C&I

2613 Great Fight for the Championship, The / Between John C. Heenan "The Benicia Boy" & Tom Sayers "Champion of England" / Which took place April 17th, 1860 at Farnborough, England / 2 additional lines. (Vignette. This print was later copyrighted in 1860, and published with that date.)
und S C&I

2614 Great Fire at Boston, The / November 9th & 10th, 1872 / 2 additional lines. 8x12.11.
1872 S C&I

A GREAT FAIR ON A GRAND SCALE.

THE GREAT FIRE AT CHICAGO. OCTR. 8TH 1871.

2615 Great Fire at Chicago, Octr. 8th, 1871, The / The Fire commenced on Sunday evening, Oct. 8th, and continued until Tuesday, Oct. 10th, consuming the business portion of the City, Public Buildings, Hotels, Newspaper Offices, Railroad Depots / And extending over an area of five square miles. About 500 lives were lost, and property valued at 200,000,000 of dollars was destroyed / 14 keys. 16.14x24.8. 1871 L C&I

2616 Great Fire at St. John, N.B., June 20th, 1877, The / 3 additional lines description. 8.1x12.11.
1877 S C&I

2617 Great Fire at St. Louis, Mo. / Thursday night, May 17th, 1849 / Total amount of property destroyed estimated at $3,000,000 / #682 / 8.3x12.13.
1849 S N.C.

2618 Great Fire of 1835, The / "The Fire" Dec. 17th, 1835 /
1835 L C&I

2619 Great Fire of 1835, The / "The Ruins" /
und L C&I

2620 Great Five Mile Rowing Match for $4000 / See: "James Hammill," etc. No. 3153. 1867 L C&I

2621 Great Footrace for the Presidential Purse [100,000 and picking] over the Union Course 1852, The / 10.4x15.13.
und M N.C.

2622 Great Horses in a Great Race / The Finish in the Great match race for $5000 a side and $5000 added money one mile and a quarter / at Sheepshead Bay, N.Y., June 25th, 1890 between / Salvator and Tenny / 2 additional lines. J. Cameron on stone. 18.1x28 (Broadside to right, under saddle.)
1891 L C&I

2623 Great International Boat Race, Aug. 27th, 1869, The / Between Oxford and Harvard on the river Thames near London, 4 miles 2 furlongs / Won by Oxfords by a half length clear water. Time 22 min. 20 sec. / 8x12.7.
und S C&I

2624 Great International University Boat Race, The / On the River Thames [England] from Putney to Mortlake 4

miles 2 furlongs August 27th, 1869 /
Between the picked crews of the Harvard [American] and Oxford [English]
Universities / Won by Oxford / 4 additional lines, 2 columns, 11 and 10
lines. 1869 L C&I

2625 Great International Yacht Race,
August 8, 1870, The / For the Queens
Cup won by the America at Cowes, in
1851 / From the Club House, Staten
Island, N.Y. around the S. W. Spit, to,
and around, / The Light Ship off Sandy
Hook and back, forty miles / 17.12x
27.12 (Magic, Dauntless, Idler, Cambria, America keyed.)
1870 L C&I

2626 Great International Yacht Race,
August 8, 1870, The / From the Club
House, Staten Island, around the S. W.
Spit, to, and around / The Lightship
and back, 40 miles / 8.3x12.10 (2 columns 7 and 10 lines.)
1870 S C&I

2627 Great Match at Baltimore, The /
Between the "Illinois Bantam" and the
"Old Cock" of the White House /
Buchanan, beaten by Douglas "Illinois
Bantam" another cock "Breckinridge"
being readied in background (Vignette.) 1860 M C&I

2628 Great Match Race [A Dead Heat]
between Dobbins and Domino for
$10,000 a side, The / Over the Coney
Island Futurity Course, Sheepshead
Bay, Long Island, August 31st, 1893 /
3 additional lines (Under saddle).
und M C&I

2629 Great Mississippi Steamboat Race,
The / From New Orleans to St. Louis,
July 1870 / Between the R. E. Lee,
Capt. John W. Cannon and Natchez,
Capt. Leathers / Won by the R. E.
Lee, Arriving at St. Louis, July 4th
at 11:20 A.M. / Time 3 days, 18 hours,
and 14 minutes / 8x12.8.
1870 S C&I

2630 Great Mississippi Steamboat Race,
The / From New Orleans to St. Louis
July 1870 / Between the R. E. Lee,
Capt. John W. Cannon and Natchez,
Capt. Leathers / Won by the R. E. Lee.
Arriving at St. Louis July 4th at 11:20
A.M. / Time 3 days, 18 hours, and 14
minutes / 8x12.7 (Moonlight scene.)
und S C&I

2631 Great Mississippi Steamboat Race,
The / From New Orleans to St. Louis
July 1870 / 2 columns. (Daylight
scene.) und S C&I

THE GREAT RACE ON THE MISSISSIPPI.

2632 Great Naval Blockade of Round Island, The / Showing the immense importance of having an efficient right arm of national defence / 11x17.7.
und M C&I

2633 Great Naval Victory in Mobile Bay, Aug. 5th, 1864, The / #851 / 8x12.9 4 additional lines.　und S C&I
　Great Northern (Steamship) **See:** No. 5768.

2634 Great Ocean Yacht Race, The / Between the Henrietta, Fleetwing, & Vesta / The "Goodbye" to the Yacht Club Steamer "River Queen" 4 miles east of Sandy Hook Light ship, Decr. 11th, 1866 / Sketched by Charles Parsons from the Yacht Club Steamer "River Queen"/ 2 additional lines. 17.12 x28 (3 keys: Fleetwing, 212 tons. Vesta, 201 tons. Henrietta, 205 tons.)
1867 L C&I

2635 Great Oyster Eating Match between the Darktown Cormorant and the Blackville Buster / The Finish — "You's is a tie-de one dat gags fust, am a gone crow" / (Vignette.)
1886 S C&I

2636 Great Oyster Eating Match between the Darktown Cormorant and the Blackville Buster / The Start — "Now den don't yous be too fresh, wait for de word — Gulp" / (Vignette.)
1886 S C&I

2637 Great Pacer Johnston, driven by P. V. Johnston, Record 2:10, The / J. Cameron on stone. (Vignette, ¾ to right, high-wheeled sulky.)
1883 S C&I

2638 Great Pacer Sorrel Dan, driven by Dan Mace, The / Record 2:14 / (Vignette, ¾ view to right, high-wheeled sulky.)　1880 S C&I

2639 Great Pole Mares Belle Hamlin and "Justina" Trotting to skeleton wagon, The / At Independence, Iowa Oct. 24th, 1890 driven by their owner C. J. Hamlin, Esq. / Making the fastest team time on record 2:13¼ / Which was reduced Oct. 27 driven by their trainer Mr. Andrews to 2:13 / J. Cameron on stone. (¾ to left.)
1890 S C&I

2640 Great Pontoon Drawbridge, The / Over the Missouri River at Nebraska City [Neb.] the largest in the world / 4 additional lines. 9.5x13.7 (Small view at lower right, train on trestle.)
und S C&I

2641 Great Presidential Sweepstakes of 1856, The / Free for all ages "Go as they please" / "Young America" enters "Fillmore" by Honesty out of Experience [trained on the Union Track]/ "Democrat" enters "Old Buck" [Alias Platform] by "Filibuster" out of "Federalist" exercised on the Ostend Course / Greeley, Weed, Beecher & Co. enter "Canuck Pony" "Fremont" by "Wooly Head" out of "Wooly Horse" from the Mariposa Stable / (Vignette.)
und M N.C.

2642 Great Race at Baltimore, Oct. 24th, 1877, The / Between the three grand Champions of the American Turf / Parole, Ten Broeck, and Tom Ochiltree / (Above title) Tom Ochiltree, ridden by Barbee — Ten Broeck, ridden by Walters — Parole, ridden by Barrett. (Vignette, under saddle to right.)
1877 S C&I

2643 Great Race for the Western Stakes 1870, The / (On the left Commodore Vanderbilt straddling engines of "Hudson River R.R." and "N.Y. Central R.R." and racing Jim Fisk astride locomotive "Erie RR." Vanderbilt saying "Now then, Jim, no jockeying." Fisk answers "Let em Rip, Commodore, but don't stop to water or you'll be beat." Vignette.)　1870 S C&I

2644 Great Race on the Mississippi, The / From New Orleans to St. Louis 1210 miles / Between the Steamers Robt. E. Lee, Capt. J. W. Cannon and Natchez, Capt. T. P. Leathers. Won by the R. E. Lee — Time 3 days, 18 hours, 30 minutes/2 columns, 6 and 5 lines. 18.9x29.6 (Daylight scene.)
1870 L C&I

2645 Great Racing Crack Hindoo, by Virgil, Dam Florence, by Lexington, The/ (Vignette, under saddle to left.)
1881 S C&I

　Great Republic (Clipper ship) **See:** Nos. 1146-52.

　Great Republic (Steamship) **See:** No. 4673.

2646 Great Republican Reform Party, The / Calling on their Candidate / (Fremont addressing 6 callers, vignette.)　und S N.C.

2647 Great Riot at the Astor Place Opera House, New York / On Thursday Evening, May 10th, 1849 / 8.4x 12.11 (Forrest Macready Riot.)
1849 S N.C.

2648 Great St. Louis Bridge, The / Across the Mississippi River / 2 columns of 5 lines. (Vignette.)
und S C&I

2649 Great Salt Lake, Utah / 8.8x12.8 (View of city from heights, lake in distance.) und S C&I

2650 Great "Scullers Race" on the St. Lawrence, The / Between Chas. E. Courtney of New York and Edward Hanlan of Toronto / At Lachine, Canada, Oct. 3rd, 1878 — Distance Five miles / For $1000 a side, — The Championship of America and a purse of $6000. Contributed by the citizens of Montreal / Won by Hanlan by one length and a quarter: Time 36m. 22s. / 1 Line above title. 8.2x13.4.
1878 S C&I

2651 Great Sire of Trotters Electioneer by Rysdyk's Hambletonian, The / L.M. on stone. (Profile to left, vignette.)
1891 S C&I

2652 Great Through Route between the / North and South, The / (at top) Baltimore, Norfolk, & Portsmouth / Bay Line / C. R. Parsons on stone. 17.2x 27.4 (Boat "Florida" shown, broadside to right.) 1878 L C&I

2653 Great Victory in the Shenendoah Valley, Va., Sept. 19th, 1864, The / Genl. Sherman's Cavalry charging and routing the rebel horsemen / 3 addi-

tional lines. 7.12x12.8.
und S C&I

2654 Great Walk — Come in as You can, The / The Finish / Thos. Worth on stone. (Vignette.)
1879 S C&I

2655 Great Walk — Go as You Please, The / The Start / Thos. Worth on stone. (Vignette.) 1879 S C&I

2656 Great Walk — Come in as You Can, The / 1879 V.S. C&I $20.

2657 Great Walk — Go as You Please, The / 1879 V.S. C&I

2658 Great West, The / 7.15x12.8 (Engine, tender, 4 cars, mountain scenery.)
1870 S C&I

Great Western (Steamship) See: No. 4594.

2659 Grecian Bend, The / Thos. Worth on stone. (Caricature of young woman with grotesque costume, and large bustle, full length, upright, vignette.)
1868 S C&I

Greeley, Horace See: Nos. 1594, 1741, 2501, 2503, 2608, 2641, 2776, 2904, 2936-7, 3033, 3134, 3445, 3479, 3967, 4121, 4273, 4413, 4423, 4464, 4694, 4770, 4820, 4823, 5050, 5052, 5095, 5114, 5664.

GREY EAGLE.

GULICK GUARD.

Greeley (Home) **See:** No. 1000.

Greensboro **See:** No. 5908.

Greenwood Cemetery **See:** No. 1809, 4445, 4449.

Gregg Battery **See:** No. 5508.

2660 Grey Eagle / Driven by / Hiram Woodruff, Esq. / 2 columns, 5 lines. 12.12x21.1 (Sulky, broadside to left.) 1850 L N.C.

Grey Eagle **See:** No. 6169.

2661 Grey Eddy / Centreville Course, L.I. Sept. 26th, 1854/2 columns records, 7 and 5 lines, 3 additional lines. L.

Maurer on stone. 16.15x26.6 (Broadside to left.) 1855 L N.C.

Grey Eddy (Horse) **See:** No. 6170.

2662 Grey Mare Emma B by Bayard / Record 2:22½ / E. Forbes on stone. (¾ view, high-wheeled sulky, vignette.) und S C&I

2663 Grey Mare Lucy, the Pacing Queen, The / of the Famous Quartette of 1879 / Sired by Tom Crowder / Winner at Cleveland, O. July 31st, 1879 purse $1000, beating Sleepy Tom, Rowdy Boy, and Mattie Hunter / Record 2:15 /

[125]

(Vignette, high-wheeled sulky to right.)   1879 S C&I

2664 Grey Mare Police Gazette, formerly Emma B. / By Bayard, Purchased by Richard K. Fox, May 1st, 1882, for $10,000 / Record 2:22 / E. Forbes on stone. (Vignette.)
1879 S C&I

2665 Grey Trotting Wonder Hopeful / Record 2:14¾ / (Vignette.)
1877 S C&I

2666 Grottoes of the Sea, The /
1865 S C&I

2667 Grottoes of the Sea, The / 7.15x12.7 (Similar to "The Fairy Isle," etc. No. 1816.)   1869 S C&I

2168 Group of Fruit / (Vignette—pears, apples, peaches, and plums.)
1875 S C&I

2669 Group of Flowers / (Upright, vignette.)   und S C&I

2670 Group of Lilies / (Upright, in white glass bowl.)   und S C&I

2671 Group of Lilies / (Upright, vignette, entirely different composition from preceding.)
und S C&I

2672 Group of Lilies / (Upright vignette different from 2 preceding.)
und S C&I

2673 Grover Cleveland / President of the United States /   und S C&I

2674 Growling Match, A / (Advertising card.)   und S C&I

2675 Guardian Angel, The / 11.12x8.4

(Children and Angel.)
und S N.C.

2676 Guardian Angel, The / #328 11.12 x8.4 (Changes in composition.)
und S N.C.

2677 Guardian Angel, The / #358 11.7x 8 (Title repeated in Spanish, 2 children.)   und S C&I

2678 Guardian Angel, The / Title repeated in French and Spanish. 11.12x 8.15 (Full-length Angel walking with little girl.)   und S C&I
Guerriere See: Nos. 1239-40, 4400.

2679 Guion Line Steamship "Arizona" of the "Greyhound Fleet" / Making safe, short, sure, and reliable passages across the Atlantic /
und S C&I

2680 Gulick Guard / Firemen with Pleasure — Soldiers at Leisure / W. K. Hewitt, Del. on stone. 14.7x11 (Full-length vignette, but with plate line.)
1838 M N.C.

2681 Gunboat Candidate, The / At the Battle of Malvern Hill /
1864 S C&I

2682 Gunboat Candidate, The / At the Battle of Malvern Hill / (Vignette.)
und S C&I

2683 Gustav Struve / (Facsimile signature) Title repeated in German. 11.12 x8.10 #635 (¾ length, battle scene through window.)
1848 S N.C.

2684 Guy by Kentucky Prince / Record 2:10¾ /   1888 S C&I
Guy (Horse) See: No. 1863.

H

2685 Hadley Falls / Massachusetts /
und M C&I

2686 Hague Street Explosion / Awful Explosion of a Steam Boiler / Belonging to A. B. Taylor & Co., Machinist, No. 5 and 7 Hague St., / On Monday, February 4th, at a quarter to 8 o'clock / Wounding and killing about 120 persons / 11.12x9.9 (Those killed listed in 4 columns) Copyright 1850 by C. E. Lewis & Co.   und S C.C.

2687 Haidee / #425 (Half length of Turkish girl, rose in hand.)
und S N.C.

2688 Haidee / (Different composition from preceding.)   und S N.C.

2689 Hail Mary, Mother of God /
und S C&I

2690 Hair Tonic Explosion, A / "O! Hans, vot for you put dot tonic on dat red haired mans" / Thos. Worth on stone. 9x13.12 (Customers rushing from barber shop, man with hair afire, vignette.)   1884 S C&I
Hal Pointer (Horse) See: No. 4681.
Hale, J. P. See: No. 4884.
Hall, Oakley See: No. 5664.
Halleck, Maj. (Genl. Henry) See: Nos. 3913-5.

2691 Halls of Justice, New York / Designed by John Haviland, Archt. 7.8x 11.12 (¾ view.)   und S N.C.

2692 Halls of Justice, New York / Designed and Erecting by John Haviland, Architect / 7.8x11.12.
und S N. C.

2693 Halls of Justice, New York / (View from directly in front, no pedestrians.)
und S N.C.

2694 Halt by the Wayside, A / 8x12.7 (Covered wagon and family of 9 under tree.)
und S C&I

2695 Hambletonian /
1871 S C&I
Hambletonian See: Nos. 5269-73.
Hambletonian Mambrino See: No. 6207.

2696 Hambrino / Bay Stallion by Edward Everett, dam Mambrino Chief / Driven by John E. Turner, Record 2:21½ /
1879 S C&I
Hambrino (Horse) See: Nos. 443, 2696.

2697 Hamburg — American Line Mail Steamer / Frisia / 8x13.11.
und S C&I
Hamilton, Alexander See: No. 6509.
Hamlin, Hannibal See: Nos. 2900-2, 4389, 4960, 5113A.
Hammill, James See: Nos. 2620, 3153.
Hammonia (Steamship) See: No. 5769.
Hampton, Wade See: No. 2463.
Hancock, John See: Nos. 3237, 3937.
Hancock, Winfield See: Nos. 2328, 2388, 2499-500, 2553.

2698 Handsome Man, The / Comic Song / Written by / John Francis, Esq. / Author of "They Don't Propose" / Sung by, etc. / 3 additional lines, and 2 columns, 2 lines of verse. Published by Wm. Hall and Son, 239 Broadway, E. Brown, Sr.
und S N.C.

2699 Hand-Writing on the Wall, The / or the modern Belshazzar / (Vignette.)
und S C&I
Hanlan, Edward See: No. 2650.

2700 Hannah / #136 / 8.6x11.13 (½ length, thin shawl around neck, rose in hair, rounded corners.)
1846 S N.C.

2701 Hannah / (¾ length, on balcony, red dress.)
und S N.C.

2702 Hannah / (Half length, red dress, vignette.)
und S N.C.

2703 Hannis / Record 2:17¼, Driven by John E. Turner /
1879 S C&I

2704 Hannis /
1881 S C&I
Hannis (Horse) See: Nos. 6208-9.

2705 Hanover / By Hindoo Bourbon Belle by Bonnie Scotland / (Under saddle, to left, spectators in rear, vignette.)
1887 S C&I
Hanover, N.H. See: Nos. 1446-7.

2706 Happy Faces / A Ballad / Published by James L. Hewitt, 239 Broadway.
und S N.C.

2707 Happy Family, A /(Family group.)
und S N.C.

2708 Happy Family, The / 8x13.3 (3 puppies.)
und S N.C.

2709 Happy Family, The / 7.15x12.7 (Farm scene, dog, cat, chickens, rabbits, and pigeons, having dinner, kennel on left.)
1869 S C&I

2710 Happy Family, The / 8.1x12.3 (Many more animals than in above, kennel on right.)
1874 S C&I

2711 Happy Family, The /
und S C&I

2712 Happy Family, The / Ruffed Grouse and Young / F. F. Palmer Del. 19.13x 27.13 (Companion to Nos. 814, 5151. The most attractive game print published by Currier.)
1866 L C&I

2713 Happy Home, The / # 521 / Sarony on stone. 11.14x8.8 (Mother, father, 4 children.)
und S N.C.

2714 Happy Hour, The /
und S N.C.

2715 Happy Land / 10.12x8.15 (Oval.)
und S C&I

2716 Happy Little Chicks / From nature by F. F. Palmer. 9.14x13.15.
1866 M C&I

2717 Happy Little Pups / 10x8 (Upright, 4 pups.)
und S C&I

2718 Happy Mother, The / 11.14x8.12 (Holding 2 children.)
und S N.C.

2719 Happy Mother / 11.13x15 (Playing with baby.)
und M C&I

2720 Happy Mother, The / 8.8x12.7 (Doe and fawn, same general composition as "The Home of the Deer," No. 2865.)
und S C&I

2721 Happy New Year / #122 (Winter Scene, man under tree with club, with hand out for gift, companion to "Merry Christmas.")
und S N.C.

2722 Happy New Year / (Vignette, rustic scroll, holly, flowers, etc.)
1876 S C&I

2723 Happy New Year, A / (Entirely different type, and flowers.)
und S C&I

2724 Harbor for the Night, A / 8.9x12.8 (Group of 4 at left by fire.)
und S C&I

2725 Harbor of New York, The / From the Brooklyn Bridge Tower — Looking Southwest. / 9 references. 9x12.15 (Shows Statue of Liberty.)
und S C&I

2726 Harbor of New York, The / From the Brooklyn Bridge Tower — Looking Southwest / (No Statue of Liberty, and other changes in composition.)
und S C&I

2727 Hard Road to Travel, A / Thos. Worth on stone. 8.4x12.14 (3 men walking beside wrecked rig.)
1862 S C&I

2728 Hard Road to Travel / 8.4x12.10 (Different composition, 2 men beside damaged 4-wheeled rig, broadside to left.)
und S C&I

Hardin, John J. See: No. 1477.

Hardy (Miss Sylva) See: No. 3894.

Harlem Lane See: No. 1907.

Harlem River, Macomb's Dam See: Nos. 375, 5644, 6441.

Harney, Col. See: No. 1194.

Harpers Ferry, Va. See: No. 6395, 6449.

2729 Harriet / (½ length, vignette, rural background.)
und S N.C.

2730 Harriet / #116 (White shawl over head, ½ length, vignette.)
und S C&I

2731 Harriet / (Head, facing right.)
und S C&I

2732 Harriet / #116 (Seated, white dress, book in hand.)
1845 S N.C.

2733 Harrisburg and the Susquehanna / from Bridgeport Heights / F. F. Palmer Del. 14.15x20.10.
1865 M C&I

Harrison, Carter H. See: No. 1595.

Harrison, W. H. See: Nos. 1486-7, 2322-5, 4876, 6077-8, 6101-2, 6690-3.

2734 Harry Bassett / By "Lexington," dam "Canary Bird." The property of Col. M. McDaniels, winner in 1870 of the "Kentucky Stakes" at Saratoga,
etc. / 1 additional line. (Horse under saddle to right, J. Cameron 1871 on stone.)
1871 S C&I

2735 Harry Bassett and Longfellow / in Their great races at Long Branch, N.J., July 2nd, and Saratoga, N.Y., July 16th, 1872 / 2 columns, 6 lines each of description. 16.15x26.12 (Broadside to right, under saddle, passing judges' stand.
1872 L C&I

2736 Harry Bassett and Longfellow / at Saratoga, N.Y., July 16, 1872. Saratoga Cup for all ages, 2¼ miles Harry Bassett by Lexington; Longfellow by Leamington, 5 yrs. J. Cameron on stone. (Vignette, broadside to right.)
1874 S C&I

Harry Bassett See: Nos. 2734-6, 5082.

2737 Harry Bluff / #393 (Vignette, verses under title.)
und S N.C.

2738 Harry Wilkes / By George Wilkes, Dam Molly Walker by Capt. Walker / Driven By Frank Van Ness / Record 2:13½ / Scott Leighton on stone. 18.2x27.2. Printed in oil color. (Broadside to left.)
1885 L C&I

2739 Harry Wilkes / 2.12x4.12.
1886 V.S. C&I

Harry Wilkes See: Nos. 5708, 6163, 6175.

Harte, Bret See: No. 2773.

Hartford, Conn. (Racetrack) See: No. 5931.

2740 Harvard College, Cambridge, Mass. / A. J. Davis Del.
und S N.C.

Harvard See: Nos. 2095, 2623-4, 2968.

2741 Harvest / #688 / 8.5x12.11 (Group of 4 in foreground, others gathering sheaves of wheat, companion to "Spring" No. 5671.)
1849 S N.C.

2742 Harvest / (Group of 3 on road on right, haywagon hitched to oxen crossing bridge on left.)
und S C&I

2743 Harvest Dance, The / By The Vienna Children / #212 / 8.5x11.14 (Companion to "Flower Dance" No. 2041, round corners.)
1846 S N.C.

2744 Harvest Dance, The / By The Vienna Children / (Composition reversed and 2 figures eliminated.)
1847 S N.C.

2745 Harvest Field, The / 11.6x15 (Oval in rectangle, companion to "The Roadside" No. 5172.)
und M N.C.

2746 Harvest Moon, The / 11.11x16.3
(Group harvesting by moonlight.)
und M C&I

2747 Harvest Queen, The / (Vignette.)
und S C&I

2748 Harvester, The /
und M C&I

2749 Harvesting / 8.8x12.5 (Hay-wagon,
load of hay, 2 horses, group of farm
people, dog — country scene.)
und S C&I

2750 Harvesting / The Last Load / 8.7x
12.8 (Same description as above, cottage on right.)   und S C&I

2751 Hat That Makes The Man /
1869 S C&I

2752 Hat That Makes The Man, The /
When first in the town my old hat was
seen, the boys cried "shoot it old
verdant green." But now the girls ask
"What young man is that? Who wears
such a nobby and genteel hat" / (2
views on 1 sheet, before and after.)
1880 S C&I

2753 Hat That Makes The Man, The /
(2 views — old and new hat on man.

Hatters advertising card.)
1880 V.S. C&I
Hatteras Inlet See: No. 594.

2754 Hattie / (Girls head, vignette.)
und S C&I

2755 Hattie Woodward / Record 2:15½
(Not vignette.)   1881 V.S. C&I
Hattie Woodward (Horse) See: No.
916.

2756 Haunted Castle / 7.14x12.6 (3 figures, wooden bridge, stream, old castle on hill.)   und S C&I

2757 Haunts of the Wild Swan, The /
Carroll Island — Chesapeake Bay /
8.7x12.8 (7 swans shown close-up,
others in rear.)   1872 S C&I

2758 Havana / View from the Lower
Batteries / 1 additional line. (Custom
house, Capt. Generals House, Cathedral, entrance to the Harbor, Jail and
Hospital, Morro Castle Fortress, ca-
bana.)   und S C&I

2759 Have A Peach /
und S C&I
Havel (Steamship) See: No. 3038.

HAYING-TIME. THE FIRST LOAD.

Hayes, Rutherford B. **See:** Nos. 2459, 2504, 4878, 5268.

Hayes, Catherine **See:** No. 852.

2760 Haying-Time — The First Load / J. M. Ives, Del. Drawn by F. F. Palmer and J. Cameron. 15.14x23.14.
1868 L C&I

2761 Haying-Time — The Last Load / J. M. Ives, Del. Drawn by F. F. Palmer and J. Cameron. 15.15x23.15.
1868 L C&I

Haze (Yacht) **See:** Nos. 5105, 6799.

Hazen, Genl. **See:** No. 5490.

2762 He Is Saved / 8.14x12.7 (Dog with rescued child.)
und S C&I

2763 He Loves Me! / 9.7x12.4 (¾ length, girl reading letter.)
und S C&I

2764 Head and Head at the Winning Post / Eole-Monitor-Parole / (Vignette, 3 large heads.)
1884 L C&I

2765 Head and Head Finish, A / 13x 15.14 (Upright, 3 horses head on;

also used as an advertisement. Low-wheeled sulkies.)
1893 M C&I

2766 Head and Head Finish, A / Currier & Ives / Grand Illuminated Posters / Size Sheet, 30x42 / For Races, Trotting Meetings and Fairs / Your Advertising Matter / Printed in this Style / In Alternate / Red and Black Type / Address / Currier & Ives / 115 Nassau Street / New York / J. Cameron Del. (8 horses under saddle, ¾ view to right.)
1892 L C&I

2767 Head and Head Finish, A / 18x28 (Same illustration as preceding, no advertising.)   1892 L C&I

2768 Heads of the Democracy /
und S C&I

2769 Health to the King and Bismarck / J. Cameron on stone. (Uncle Sam and German shaking hands, drinking beer, vignette, title repeated in German.)
1870 S C&I

2770 Heart of Divine Love /
und S C&I

THE "HEATHEN CHINEE."

"But the hands that were played by that heathen Chinee
And the points that he made were quite frightful to see
Till at last he put down a right bower
Which the same Nye had dealt unto me."

2771 Heart of Jesus / Reign Thou / Ever in my Heart / (Portrait of Jesus surrounded by floral scroll, vignette.) 1876 S C&I

2772 Heart of the Wilderness, The / 11.7x16.8 (Brilliant autumn foliage.) und M C&I

2773 Heathen Chinee, The / "But the hands that were played by that heathen Chinee / And the points that he made were quite frightful to see / Till at last he put down a right bower / Which the same Nye had dealt unto me" / 7.15 x 12.7 (Chinaman beating 2 westerners at card game. From Bret Harte.) 1871 S C&I

2774 Hebe / (Head of a girl.) und V.S. C &I

Hecker, Dr. Friedr. See: No. 1615.

Heenan, John C. See: Nos. 2613, 3261-5.

2775 Height of Impudence, The / "Is my face good for a shave" / und S C&I

2776 Heir to the Throne, An / Or the next Republican Candidate / (Group of 3 figures, Greeley on the left, Lincoln on the right, Negro in the center whom Lincoln and Greeley propose to run as the next Candidate of Black Republicanism for President — vignette.) 1860 M C&I

2777 Helen / #439 (Vignette, blue ribbon in hair, red dress.) 1855 S N.C.

2778 Helen / (Vignette, bust — rose in hair, red cape.) und S C&I

Hendricks, Thomas See: Nos. 2462, 2498, 6349.

2779 Henrietta / #231 (¾ length, seated on couch, red drape.) und S N.C.

Henrietta (Yacht) See: Nos. 2634, 4450, 6800-2.

2780 Henry / #369 / 8.12x12.2 (Full length, standing, red curtain.) 1845 S N.C.

2781 Henry / Record 2:20½, Driven by John Murphy / (Vignette.) 1874 S C&I

Henry (Horse) See: Nos. 903-4, 2448.

2782 Henry Bibb / Lord deliver me from slavery / And I will ever serve Thee! / Stop the runaway! Where is he? / $50 reward for him / Daniel Lane after Henry Bibb / In Louisville, Kentucky, June 1838 / The object was to sell Bibb in the slave market, but Bibb turned the corner too quick for him and escaped / Copyright by H. Bibb, 1847. (Portrait of a runaway slave — upright.) und S N.C.

2783 Henry Clay / (Vignette, head and shoulders.) 1853 L N.C.

2784 Henry Clay / Justice to Harry of the West (Oval portrait surrounded by wreath and banner.) und S N.C.

2785 Henry Clay / Nominated for Eleventh President of the United States / und S N.C.

2786 Henry Clay / Of Kentucky / 12.4x 8.15 (Full length, left arm on table, quill in right hand.) 1842 S N.C.

2787 Henry Clay / Of Kentucky / 12.2x 8.13 (Full length right hand on table, scroll in left, Capitol seen on right.) 1844 S N.C.

2788 Henry Clay / Of Kentucky / 11.11x 8.8 (Full length, right arm on table.) 1844 S N.C.

2789 Henry Clay / Of Kentucky / #189 (Composition similar to No. 2786 with slight changes.) und S N.C.

2790 Henry Clay / Of Kentucky / (Seated, half length, slightly to right, right hand on book, green curtain.) und S N.C.

2791 Henry Clay / Of Kentucky / J. L. McGee, Del. 12.13x8.13 (Seated, green curtain.) und S N.C.

2792 Henry Clay / Of Kentucky / 12.1x 8.10 (Full-length portrait in library, bookcases, etc.) und S N.C.

2793 Henry Clay / Of Kentucky / From a daguerreotype by Plumbe. 11.8x8.13 #126 (Half length, seated, hand on book.) 1848 S N.C.

2794 Henry Clay / Painted and Engraved by A. H. Ritchie. 1852 S N.C.

2795 Henry Clay / The Farmer of Ashland / (Upright, seated on horse, right hand extended holding high hat.) und S N.C.

2796 Henry Clay / The Nation's Choice for Eleventh President of the United States / (Exterior scene, red-lined robe, ¾ length, slightly to left.) und S N.C.

2797 Henry Clay / The Nation's choice for Eleventh President of the United States / (Composition similar to pre-

ceding, slight changes and reversed.)
und S N.C.

Henry Clay (Burning of Steamship) **See:** No. 741.

Henry, Patrick **See:** No. 2379.

2798 Henry Wilkes /
1884 S C&I

2799 Hercules of the Nation Slaying the Great Dragon of Secession, The /
und S C&I

Hermann (Steamship) **See:** Nos. 5770-1.

2800 Hero and Flora Temple / "Swinging on the Homestretch" / In their great match for $2000 over the Centreville Course, L.I., Oct. 17th, 1855. Two mile heats / 6 additional lines. L. Maurer on stone. 17.2x26.2 (¾ head on view, high-wheeled sulky and skeleton wagon.) 1856 L N.C.

2801 Heroes of "76" Marching to the Fight / 8.12x12.11 (Led by fife and drum corps.) 1876 S C&I

2802 Heroine of Monmouth, The / Molly Pitcher, the wife of a gunner in the American army, who when her husband / was killed took his place at the gun and served throughout the battle [June 28th, 1778] / 8.9x12.
1876 S C&I

2803 Heroine of the Lighthouse, The /
und S C&I

2804 Hewitt's Quick Step /
1840 S N.C.

2805 Hiawatha's Departure / 3 columns, 5 lines of verse. 15x20.5.
1868 L C&I

2806 Hiawatha's Wedding / 2 columns, 4 lines of verse. 8.8x12.8.
und S C&I

2807 Hiawatha's Wedding / L. Maurer, Del. 1858 L C&I

2808 Hiawatha's Wooing / 2 columns, 4 lines of verse.
und S C&I

2809 Hiawatha's Wooing / 2 columns of verse. 14.14x20.14. Hoomer, Del.
1860 L C&I

Hickok, Orrin **See:** Nos. 2487-8, 3339, 5708.

2810 High Bridge at Harlem, N.Y., The / 2 additional lines. 8.3x12.11 (Horse and buggy in foreground.)
1849 S N.C.

2811 High Bridge at Harlem, N.Y., The / #699 / 2 additional lines and 2 columns,

2 lines. 8.2x12.10 (Broadside view of bridge, no life in foreground, rowboat with 2 figures.) 1849 S N.C.

2812 High Old Smoke, A / Go in fellers / "Dese am de best in de market." / J. Cameron on stone. (Vignette, colored comic.) 1881 S C&I

2813 High Pressure Steamboat Mayflower Capt. Joseph Brown / First Class Packet between St. Louis and New Orleans on the Mississippi River / Ch. Parsons, Del. 16.4x28.2 (Broadside to left.) 1855 L N.C.

2814 High Speed Steam Yacht Stiletto, the Fastest Vessel in the World / In her race with the Steamboat Mary Powell on the Hudson River. June, 1885 / 1885 S C&I

2815 High Toned / 2.15x4.12 (Cigar advertising card.) 1880 V.S. C&I

2816 High Toned / 3.7x4.9 (Cigar advertising card.) 1880 V.S. C&I

2817 High Toned / 4.7x7.3 (Dude with monocle, smoking cigar. Smoke forms word "Exquisite." (Not vignette.)
1880 V.S. C&I

2818 High Toned / (Same description as before, vignette.)
1880 S C&I

2819 "High Water" in the Mississippi / J. M. Ives, Del. Painted by F. F. Palmer. 18.1x28 (Steamer "Stonewall Jackson" shown. Companion to "Low Water in the Mississippi" No. 3824.)
1868 L C&I

2820 Highland Beauty, The / (Vignette.)
und S C&I

2821 Highland Boy, The /
und S C&I

2822 Highland Girl, The /
und S N.C.

2823 Highland Fling / #503 (Copyright by Sarony & Major. Oval within ornamental border, title in plate.)
1846 S N.C.

2824 Highland Fling, The / A Bonny Shot for a Canny Scot / C. M. Vergnes on stone. 11.4x16 (Companion to Nos. 1646, 1753, 5028.)
1876 M C&I

2825 Highland Lovers, The /
1846 S N.C.

Highland Maid (Horse) **See:** Nos. 2015-6.

2826 Highland Mary /
1876 S C&I

By GLENCOE, Dam CASTANET, By MONARCH.

2827 Highland Waterfall / (Oval, published on same sheet with St. Mary's Abbey No. 5346.)
und V.S. C&I

2828 Highlander / By Glencoe, dam Castanet by Monarch / From the original painting in possession of his owner W. W. Boyden, Esq. / President of the National Jockey Club of New York / Painted by R. A. Clarke. O. Knirsch on stone. 19.1x26.5 (Profile standing in field to left. The name "Highlander" in plate.) 1854 L N.C.

2829 Highlander's Return, The / 14.6x 11.4 und M C&I

Highlands in Winter, The / See: Landscape Cards, No. 3438.

Hill, Genl. See: No. 429.

Hillsboro, N.H. See: No. 536.

2830 Hillside Pastures — Cattle / 10.12 x14.4. Rosa Bonheur, Pinxt.
und M C&I

2831 Hillside Pastures — Sheep / Rosa Bonheur, Pinxt.
und M C&I

2832 Hillside, The / (Printed on same sheet with "Cattskill Creek" and "The Ruins." Vignette, about 5x7.)
und V.S. C&I

Hinda Rose (Horse) See: No. 771.

2833 Hindoo, Winner of the Kentucky Derby, 1881 / (Vignette, under saddle, postcard size.) 1881 V.S. C&I

Hindoo (Horse) See: Nos. 2645, 2833.

Hiram Woodruff (Horse) See: No. 1640.

2834 His Eminence / Cardinal McCloskey / (¾ length, vignette, upright.)
1875 M C&I

2835 His Mother-In-Law / Thos. Worth on stone. (Full-length figure of woman arriving at home of son-in-law with parrot, trunks, etc. Dismayed son-in-law peeks out of window, upright, vignette.) 1877 S C&I

Hoboken, N.J. See: Nos. 180, 3203.

Hoffman, John See: No. 5664.

2836 Hold the Fort / 2 columns 4 lines

[133]

of verse. 8.10x12.8 (Righteous people singing hymns and holding devils at bay.) 1875 S C&I

2837 Hold Your Horse, Bossy? / Horse Shed Stakes / Free for All / 8.7x12.12. 1877 S C&I

2838 Holidays in the Country. / Troublesome Flies / 15.14x23.15 (Barn Scene; 2 children tickling sleeping darky, while another youngster watches from the door.) 1868 L C&I

Holland, Stewart **See:** No. 3446.

Holly, Right Reverend **See:** No. 5143.

Holt's Hotel, N.Y. **See:** No. 6296.

2839 Holy Bible, The /
und S C&I

2840 Holy Catholic Faith, The /
und S C&I

2841 Holy Communion, The / Hoc est Enim corpus Meum / 11.12x8.9 (Upright.) 1873 S C&I

2842 Holy Cross, The / (Vignette—I H S on cross, with floral wreath.)
und S C&I

2843 Holy Cross Abbey on the Suir/(Ireland) /
und S C&I

2844 Holy Eucharist, The / #558 / 11.14x 8.7 (Ornamental borders.)
1848 S N.C.

2845 Holy Eucharist, The /
und S C&I

2846 Holy Face, The /
und S C&I

2847 Holy Family / #77
und S N.C.

2848 Holy Family /
und S C.C.

2849 Holy Family / #227 / 11.13x8.3 Title repeated in Spanish. (Mary, Jesus, and child.)
und S N.C.

2850 Holy Family, The /
und S C&I

2851 Holy Sacrament of the Altar /
und S C&I

2852 Holy Sepulchre, The / El Santo Sepulchre / 12.4x 8.8.
und S C&I

2853 Holy Virgin / Pray for Us / (Vignette, figure surrounded by flowers.)
1876 S C&I

2854 Holy Well, The / 12.8x8.7.
und S C&I

2855 Home and Friends /
und S C&I

2856 Home from the Brook / The Lucky Fisherman / 16.12x24.14 (Companion to "Home from the Woods. The Successful Sportsmen" No. 2859.)
1867 L C&I

2857 Home From The War / (Officer shown at left.) 1862 S C&I

2858 Home From the War / The Soldier's Return / (Composition similar to preceding, enlisted man shown and reversed, companion to No. 4539.)
1861 S C&I

2859 Home From the Woods / The Successful Sportsmen / 16.13x24.15 (Companion to No. 2856.)
1867 L C&I

2860 Home in the Country, A / From Nature and on stone by F. F. Palmer. 12.9x17.5 (5 figures on lawn and 2 on porch.) und M C&I

2861 Home in the Wilderness, A / 8x12.8 (Winter scene.) 1870 S C&I

2862 Home in the Woods, A /
1870 S C&I

2863 Home of Evangeline, The / "In the Acadian Land" / 2 columns, 11 lines of verse. F. F. Palmer, Del. 16.1x23.6.
1864 L C&I

2864 Home of Florence Nightingale, The / Lea Hurst, Derbyshire, England / 11.4x15.7. und M C&I

2865 Home of the Deer, The / Morning in the Adirondacks / Painted by A. F. Tait. On stone by Ch. Parsons. 18.7x 23.13 (Doe and 2 young deer on shore of lake.) 1862 L C&I

2866 Home of the Deer, The / 10x15.6 (Trees in back of deer extend to top plate line, small bush to right of rock in center foreground on which deer stands, no similarity to preceding.)
1870 M C&I

2867 Home of the Deer, The / 9.15x15.7 (No bush to right of rock in foreground, foliage does not extend to upper plate line, tree on right bank leans at angle of 45 degrees and other changes in composition from preceding.) und M C&I

2868 Home of the Seal / (Coast scene, seals on rocks in foreground.)
und S C&I

2869 Home of the Soul, The / 2 columns, 4 lines of verse. 8.9x12 (Vision of angels, castle, etc.)
1876 S C&I

2870 Home of Washington, Mount Vernon, The / On stone by J. Cameron. Published by R. Yale and T. Evans. 1852 M C.C.

2871 Home of Washington, The / Mount Vernon, Va. / 8.9x12.8.
und S C&I

2872 Home of Washington, The / Mount Vernon, Va. / 14.12x20.1 (Male figure on lawn, facing observer on lawn at right center, round top corners.)
und M C&I

2873 Home of Washington, Mount Vernon, Va., The /
und L C&I

2874 Home of Washington, The / Mount Vernon, Va. / 11.8x15.13 (Figure on lawn, 2 groups of 4 and 5, 2 couples on verandah, round tops.)
und M C&I

2875 Home on "Sick Leave" / Edw. J. Mullen on stone.   1863 S C&I

2876 Home on the Mississippi, A / 8.7x 12.7.   1871 S C&I

2877 Home Sweet Home / 2 columns, 2 lines verse. 15.14x23.7.
1869 L C&I

2878 Home, Sweet Home / (Motto, flowers and scroll — vignette.)
1874 S C&I

2879 Home Sweet Home / 8.8x12.9 (Cattle in brook on right, house on left, sheep on lawn.)   und S C&I

2880 Home Sweet Home /
und M C&I

2881 Home Sweet Home / (Motto.)
und S C&I

2882 Home To Thanksgiving / Painted by G. H. Durrie. Jno. Schutler, Del. 14.12x25.1.   1867 L C&I

2883 Home Treasures / (Upright vignette, 2 small children.)
und S C&I

2884 Homeward Bound / #378.
und S N.C.

2885 Homeward Bound / #378 / 8x12.9. 1845 S N.C.

2886 Homeward Bound / (Vignette.)
und S C&I

2887 Honest Abe Taking Them on the Half Shell / (Lincoln holding oyster shells in each hand, 1 containing Douglas, the other Breckinridge — vignette.)   und M C&I
Honest Allen (Horse) See: No. 2583.

2888 Honor the Lord / (Fruit piece.)
und S C&I

2889 Honor the Lord / With thy Substance / And the first fruits of all thine increase / (Motto, dish of fruit, vignette.)   1872 S C&I

2890 Hon. Abraham Lincoln / Of Illinois / National Republican Candidate for / Sixteenth President of the United States / From a photograph by Brady. 1860 L C&I

2891 Hon. Abraham Lincoln / "Our Next President" / From a photograph by Brady. (Above title, facsimile signature A. Lincoln. ¾ length vignette, no buttons shown on vest, beardless.)
1860 S C&I

2892 Hon. Abraham Lincoln / "Our Next President" / From a photograph by Brady. (Slightly smaller, vest shows 4 buttons, vignette.)   1860 S C&I

2893 Hon. Abraham Lincoln / "Our President" / From a photograph by Brady. (Full face, vignette.)
1860 S C&I

2894 Hon. Abraham Lincoln / (Facsimile Signature) Republican Candidate for / Sixteenth President of the United States / From a photograph by Brady. (Beardless, vignette.)
1860 M C&I

2895 Hon. Abraham Lincoln / (Facsimile signature) Republican Candidate for / Sixteenth President o f the United States / 12.4x9 (Oval, bust to right, beardless.)   1860 S C&I

2896 Hon. Abraham Lincoln / Sixteenth President of the United States / From a photograph by Brady. (Vignette, bust to right, beard.)
1860 M C&I

2897 Hon. Charles Gavan Duffy / The Irish Patriot /   1849 S N.C.

2898 Hon. Daniel Webster / The days of our years are three score and ten / (Above title) Aged 70 years / born Jany. 18th, 1782. Died Oct. 24, 1852 / #130 / (¾ length, seated, red curtain.)
und S N.C.

2899 Hon. Edward Everett of Massachusetts / National Union Candidate for Vice-President of the United States / 14.10x12.4 (Full face, head to left.)
und M C&I

2900 Hon. Hannibal Hamlin / "Our Next Vice President" / From a photograph by J. E. McClees, Phila.
1860 S C&I

2901 Hon. Hannibal Hamlin / Republican Candidate for / Vice-President of the

United States / (Half length, oval, red curtain.) 1860 S C&I

2902 Hon. Hannibal Hamlin / (Facsimile H. Hamlin) / Republican Candidate for / Vice-President of the United States / (Head and shoulders, vignette.) 1860 M C&I

2903 Hon. Herschel V. Johnson / Democratic Candidate for President 1860 / 1860 S C&I

2904 Hon. Horace Greeley / Our Next President / (Vignette, head and shoulders.) 1872 S C&I

2905 Hon. Horatio Seymour / The Nation's Choice for / President of the United States / (Vignette, bust, slightly to right.) und S C&I

2906 Hon. Horatio Seymour / The Nation's Choice for / President of the United States / und M C&I

2907 Hon. James G. Blaine / (Facsimile signature) Republican Candidate for / 22nd President of the United States / (Vignette.) und L C&I

2908 Hon. Jas. G. Blaine / The Great American Statesman / And Republican Parliamentary Leader / (Vignette.) und S C&I

2909 Hon. Jefferson Davis / 12x8.8. und S C&I

2910 Hon. John A. Logan / Republican Candidate for / Vice-President of the United States / (Vignette, facsimile signature.) und S C&I

2911 Hon. John Bell / Of Tennessee / National Union Candidate for Sixteenth President of the United States / (Vignette, facsimile signature, head and shoulders.) 1860 M C&I

2912 Hon. John Bell / Of Tennessee / National Union Candidate for Sixteenth President of the United States / From a photograph by J. McClees, Phila. (Vignette, tinted background.) 1860 L C&I

2913 Hon. John Bell / "Our Next President" / From a photograph by J. E. McClees, Phila. (Vignette.) 1860 S C&I

2914 Hon. John C. Breckinridge / Democratic Candidate for / Sixteenth President of the United States / (Facsimile signature above title, vignette, ½ length.) 1860 S C&I

2915 Hon. John C. Breckinridge / Democratic Candidate for / Sixteenth Presi-

dent of the United States / (Facsimile signature, vignette.) 1860 M C&I

2916 Hon. John C. Breckinridge / Of Kentucky / National Democratic Candidate for Sixteenth President of the United States / (Vignette, tinted background.) 1860 L C&I

2917 Hon. John Cilley / J. H. Colen, Delt. / Entered 1838 by J. B. Sears / (Vignette, upright, head and shoulders.) 1838 L N.C.

2918 Hon. Joseph Lane / Democratic Candidate for / Sixteenth Vice-President of the United States / (Facsimile signature, vignette, ½ length.) 1860 S C&I

2919 Hon. Schuyler Colfax / The Nation's Choice for / Vice-President of the United States / 10.8x9. und S C&I

2920 Hon. Stephen A. Douglas / Democratic Candidate for / Sixteenth President of the United States / und S C&I

2921 Hon. Stephen A. Douglas / From a Photograph / (Bust portrait, slightly to right, vignette.) 1860 L C&I

2922 Hon. Stephen A. Douglas of Illinois / National Democratic Candidate for Sixteenth President of the United States / 1860 S C&I

2923 Hon. Stephen A. Douglas / Of Illinois / National Democratic Candidate for Sixteenth President of the United States / (Vignette.) 1860 L C&I

2924 Hon. Stephen A. Douglas / U.S. Senator from Illinois / Born April 23rd, 1818 — Died June 3d, 1861 / (Facsimile signature, vignette, half length, slightly to right.) und S C&I

2925 Hon. Wm. A. Wheeler / Of New York / National Republican Candidate for Vice-President of the United States / (Vignette, bust portrait.) und S C&I

2926 Hon. William H. English / Democratic Candidate for Vice-President of the United States / (Vignette.) und M C&I

2927 Honour! / J. Schutz, Del. 7.7x11.15 (Duelling scene, 4 monkeys. Companion to "Satisfaction" No. 5399.) und S N.C.

2928 Hooked! / 8.8x12.8 (Fishing scene
— trout. Companion to "Tempted"
No. 5981.)   1874 S C&I
     Hooker See: Maj. Jos. Nos. 3921-3.

2929 Hopeful / Grey gelding by Godfrey's Patchen, dam unknown /.
                    und S C&I

2930 Hopeful / Grey gelding by Godfrey's Patchen, dam unknown / Owned
by Mr. Gillender, trained by "Benny"
Mace, driven by Dan Mace / At
Charter Oak, Hartford, Conn. Sept.
3rd, 1875 in the "Free for All" Purse
$4000. Hopeful beat American Girl
three straight mile heats in harness in
2:17¼, 2:18¼, 2:18¼ / Record 2:14¾
/ Thos. Worth on stone. 16.7x25.1
(Broadside, high-wheeled sulky broadside to left.)
                 1876 L C&I

2931 Hopeful / Grey gelding, by Godfrey's Patchen, dam unknown / Record
2:17¼, Sept. 3, 1875 / (¾ view to left,
high-wheeled sulky, vignette.)
                 1877 S C&I

2932 Hopeful / Grey gelding by Godfrey's Patchen, dam unknown / Record
2:17¼ Sept. 3, 1875 (Broadside to left,
high-wheeled sulky.)
                 1876 S C&I

2933 Hopeful / By Godfrey's Patchen,
dam by the Bridham horse / Winner
of all the "Free for All" races in the
grand circuit of 1878 / Beating the
most celebrated horses of the day and
gaining at Chicago Oct. 12th, 1878 a
wagon record of 2:16½, 2:17, 2:17 /
Record 2:14¾ / J. Cameron 1879 on
stone. 17.1x26.2 (Skeleton wagon, ¾
view to right, passing the judge's
stand.)   1879 L C&I

2934 Hopeful / Record 2:16½ to wagon /
(Postcard size.)   1881 V.S. C&I
     Hopeful See: Nos. 905-6, 2665, 2929,
2930-4.

2935 Hopeful Driver, A / You Can Bet
Your Life On Me /
                    und S C&I

2936 Horace Greeley 14.8x12.8 (Facsimile signature.)
                    und M C&I

2937 Horace Greeley / Our Next President /   1872 M C&I
     Hornellsville, N.Y. See: Nos. 185-6,
189.

2938 Horse Car Sports Going To a
Chicken Show / All Flush / (Colored
comic, vignette.)   1886 S C&I

2939 Horse Car Sport on the Back Track
/ Dead Broke / (Colored comic, vignette.)   1886 S C&I

2940 Horse Fair, The / Rosa Bonheur,
pinxt. 7.14x12.12.   und S C&I

2941 Horse for the Money, The / Dexter
in Danger / J. Cameron on stone. (Boy
with decrepit horse pointing to sign
"$100,000 for a horse to equal Dexter
whether he be old or young, sound or
unsound, etc. Robert Bonner." Sign on
opposite side says "The New York
Ledger," Circulation 275,000 weekly,
new story by Beecher-Tyng-Bryant
"Romance of a Horse" by Sylvanus
Cobb, etc. Vignette.)
                  1869 S C&I

2942 Horse Shed Stakes, Free For All,
The / Thos. Worth on stone. 8.7x12.12
(Driver besieged by porters.)
                     1877 S C&I

2943 Horse Shed Stakes, The / (Postcard size.)   1880 V.S. C&I

2944 Horse That Died on the Man's
Hands, The / Moral "Don't hold your
trotter too high" / 9.2x13.1 (Comic.)
                  1878 S C&I

2945 Horse That Took the Pole, The /
(Rig smashed after colliding with post,
vignette.)   1875 M C&I

2946 Horse-man of the Period, The /
Beating time on the road / Thos. Worth
on Stone. 10.14x17.4 (Names of horses
on their blankets "Pocohantus," "Joe
Elliott," "Dexter," "Grafton," "Lady
Stout," "Wellesley Boy," "Music."
Commodore Vanderbilt at side with
stopwatch, Bonner driving, Dan Mace,
Budd Doble watching.)
                  1876 M C&I

2947 Horse-Man of the period, The /
9.15x16.5 (Entirely different composition. Driver with 2 spirited horses
chasing chickens and dog, other rigs
in background.)   1877 M C&I

2948 Horses at the Ford / 15x20.11 (Boy
driving 3 horses and colt, farm scene
in background.)   1867 L C&I

2949 Horses in a Thunderstorm / F. P.
(Palmer) on stone.
                    und S C&I

2950 Horticultural Hall / Grand United
States Centennial Exhibition, 1876 /
Fairmount Park, Philadelphia / 1 ad-
ditional line dimensions 7.14x13.
                    und S C&I

2951 Hot Race from the Start, A / L.
Maurer on stone. (10 horses under

[137]

HORSES AT THE FORD.

saddle to right, stands in background.)
1893 L C&I

2952 Hot Race to the Wire, A /
1876 S C&I

2953 Hot Race to the Wire, A / (¾ view, 2 horses, high-wheeled sulkies to right — same as "Smuggler and Judge Fullerton" No. 5574.)
1887 S C&I

2954 Hour of Victory, The / "Zouaves, remember Ellsworth" / (Full length figure with flag, upright, vignette, troops in background.)
1861 M C&I

Housatonic (River) **See:** No. 6443.

2955 House in Roxbury, Mass, The / As it now stands August 1840 / In which Joseph Warren was born / In the year 1741 / 2 additional lines (Vignette.)
und S N.C.

2956 House, Kennel and Field / 18.1x 28.1 (Group of various breeds of dogs.)
1892 L C&I

2957 Household Pets / 12.1 x 8.11 (Child with 2 dogs, upright.)
1845 S N.C.

2958 Household Pets / #493 / (Mother, baby, cat, and dog. Round top.)
und S C&I

2959 Household Pets, The / #334 / 12x 8.10 (Mother holding young girl, puppy and cat on lap.)
1857 S N.C.

2960 Household Treasures / #493 / 12.2 x 8.8 (Child in crib, sister and 2 dogs at side, and round top.)
und S C&I

2961 Household Treasures / (Baby in crib, sister, dog, and kitten at side. Similar to preceding with changes and round top.)
1874 S C&I

Houston, Sam **See:** No. 789.

2962 Hove To For a Pilot / Sketched by J. Smith & Son, Brooklyn, L.I. On stone by C. Parsons. 16.11x25 (2nd state of "Clipper Ship Adelaide" No. 1139.)
1856 L N.C.

2963 How Pretty! / (Upright.)
und S C&I

2964 How Sweet! / (Girl smelling rose, vignette.)
und S C&I

Howard **See:** Cordelia No. 1250.

Howard, Gen. **See:** No. 5490.

2965 Howling Swell, A / On the War Path / Aw! I say, Billy pour us a snifter and bring on your injuns" / (Vignette.)   1890 S C&I

2966 Howling Swell, A / With his scalp in danger / Aw! I don't want to hunt injuns anymore, I want to go home / (Vignette.)   1890 S C&I

2967 Howth Castle / Ireland / und S C&I

2968 H—Oxford's, You Know / (2 full length figures, representing Harvard man and Oxford man, vignette.) und S C&I

2969 H R H Albert / Prince of Wales / (Vignette, head and shoulders.) und S C&I

2970 H R H Princess Louise / Consort to Marquis of Lorne Governor-General of Canada / (Vignette, head.) und S C&I

2971 Hudson at Peekskil, The / 8.1x12.10. und S C&I

2972 Hudson, From West Point, The / Grounds of the U.S. Military Academy / (Above title — Brass Mortars taken in the Mexican War — Cold Spring — Constitution Island — F. F. Palmer, Del. 11.3x15.11.   1862 M C&I

2973 Hudson Highlands, The / From the Peekskill and Cold Spring Road, near Garrison's Landing / F. F. Palmer, Del. (Cows on road, porch on house, 4 windows above porch.) 1857 L C&I

2974 Hudson Highlands, The / From the Peekskill and Cold Spring Road, near Garrison's Landing / F. F. Palmer, Del. 15x20.7 (Horse and wagon on road, no cows, porch removed from house, roof slopes to left, and barn to left of house.)   1867 L C&I

2975 Hudson Highlands, The / 8.7x12.7 (2 trees with overhanging branches, 2 people under tree.) 1871 S C&I

2976 Hudson Highlands, The / Near Newburg, N.Y. / 8.2 x 12.6. und S C&I

2977 Hudson Near Coldspring, The / Chapel of Our Lady / 7.15x12.8 (3 men in rowboat, 2 sailboats to right.) und S C&I

2978 Hudson River — Crow's Nest / 8x12.7 (No figures on rock in foreground, river steamer and 5 sailboats shown.)   und S C&I

2979 Hudson River — Crow's Nest / und S C&I

Hudson River See: New York State — Hudson River scenes.

Hudson River R.R. See: No. 2643.

2980 Hudson River Steamboat "Bristol" / und S C&I

2981 Hudson River Steamboat "St. John" / F. F. Palmer, Del. 2 columns, 4 lines of description.   1864 L C&I

2982 Hues of Autumn, The / On Racquet (sic) River / 8.7x12.8 (2 men in boat, fisherman on shore.) und S C&I

2983 Hug Me Closer, George! / (Girl hugged by bear. She thinks it's her beau, but he is up tree — vignette.) 1886 S C&I

Hughes, Archbishop See: Nos. 585-6, 4224-5.

Hull, Isaac See: No. 4398.

2984 Humming Trot, A / 12.3x19.5 (Two low-wheel, rubber-tired sulkies to right.)   1893 M C&I

Humphrey, Genl. See: No. 2553.

2985 Hundred Leaf Rose / J. Schutz on stone.   und S N.C.

2986 Hundred Leaf Rose / (Upright, vignette, 5 roses, 4 buds.) und S C&I

2987 Hundred Leaf Rose / #564 / (5 roses, 5 buds.)   und S N.C.

2988 Hundred Leaf Rose, The / (Upright, vignette, 6 roses, 5 buds.) 1870 S C&I

2989 "Hung Up" — With the Starch Out / Thos. Worth on stone. (Driver and rig wrecked by a beer truck, vignette.) 1878 S C&I

2990 "Hung Up" — With the Starch Out / (Postcard size.) 1878 V.S. C&I

Hungarian's Farewell See: Der Hugern, etc. No. 1555.

Hungary See: Nos. 1555, 3448.

2991 Hungry Little Kitties / (Upright, mother cat feeding mouse to 5 kittens.) und S C&I

2992 Hunter's Dog, The / 8x12.4 (Dog protecting his master from an angry eagle, winter scene.) und S N.C.

2993 Hunter's Shanty, The / In the Adirondacks / 14.10x20.12. 1861 L C&I

2994 Hunter's Shanty, The / (Printed on same sheet with Sunnyside, Sluice Gate, and Riverside.)
und V.S. C&I

Hunting **See:** Nos. 173-4, 240, 446, 773-7, 994, 1536-7, 1539, 1614, 2071, 2424-5, 2859, 2992-3005, 3084-5, 3096, 3507, 3511-4, 3521-5, 3527, 3554, 4139, 4185, 4187, 4189, 4196-7, 4472, 4592, 4714-9, 4780, 4816-7, 5034-5, 5131, 5478, 5496-8, 5577-8, 5670, 5681-2, 5815, 6562, 6567-9, 6665-73, 6677, 6772-5.

Hunting (Comic) **See:** Nos. 345-6, 365-6, 644, 862-3, 1247-8, 1611, 1959-60, 2455, 4425-6, 4484, 4593, 5587.

Hunting, Fox **See:** Nos. 2103-14.

Hunting (Puzzles) **See:** Nos. 513-4.

Hunting(Miscellaneous Shooting) **See:** Nos. 445, 547-8, 4989-90, 5053-4.

2995 Hunting Casualties / A turn of speed over the Flats / The result of be'ng broke in a grazing country / #575 / 8.2x12.8. und S N.C.

2996 Hunting Casualties / A Strange Country / Only give him his head and he'll bring you in at the death / #576 / 8.1x12.6. und S N.C.

2997 Hunting Casualties / Dispatched to Headquarters / Taking it up with a military seat / #577 / 8x12.7.
und S N.C.

2998 Hunting Casualties, up to Sixteen Stone / Master of my weight but would rather my weight was master of him / #578 / 8.3x12.7. und S N.C.

2999 Hunting Casualties / A rare sort for the Downs / They told me he'd leave every thing behind him / #579 / 8.3x12.6. und S N.C.

3000 Hunting Casualties / A Mutual Determination / If he goes on at this rate I am afraid I must part with him/ #580 / 8.3x12.7. und S N.C.

3001 Hunting, Fishing and Forest Scenes / Good Luck all around / 16.13x25 (Companion to following.)
1867 L C&I

3002 Hunting, Fishing, and Forest Scenes / Shantying on the Lake Shore / 16.14 x24.15 (Companion to preceding & **See:** No. 5478.) 1867 L C&I

3003 Hunting in the Northern Woods / 8.8x12.7 (Almost identical to "The Hunter's Shanty" Nos. 2993-4.)
und S C&I

3004 Hunting on the Plains / 8.7x12.7 (Portion of the composition of this print taken from "Life on the Prairie / The Buffalo Hunt" No. 3527.)
1871 S C&I

3005 Hunting on the Susquehanna / 10.5 x14.11 (2nd State. Originally published as "Still Hunting on the Susquehanna" No. 5815.) und M C&I

Hunting Park Course, Phila. **See:** Nos. 3390, 3848, 5943.

Huntress (Horse) **See:** Nos. 917, 1179, 6616.

Hurricane (Clipper Ship) **See:** No. 1153.

3006 Hurry up the Cakes / #57 / Companion to No. 79. und S N.C.

3007 Hush! I've a Nibble / 8.8x12.8 (3 children fishing on bank of stream.)
und S C&I

3008 Husking / Painted by Eastman Johnson. On stone by C. Severin. E. Johnson 1860 on stone. 21.1x27.6.
1861 L C&I

3009 H. W. Beecher / (Facsimile signature, vignette, head and shoulders.)
1860 M C&I

3010 Hyde Park, Hudson River / #260 / 8.4x11.10 (2 figures right foreground.)
und S N.C.

3011 Hyde Park / On the Hudson River / #232 / (2 women, 2 children. Different composition from preceding.)
und S C&I

Hyde, Orson **See:** No. 1986.

3012 Hydrographic Map / of the Counties of / New York, Westchester and Putnam / and also showing the line of the / Croton Aqueduct / 6.12x20.3.
und M N.C.

3013 Hydrographic Map Showing the distribution of Rain over the Surface of the Globe Arranged by Berghans by E. W. Griffin / On stone by J. Cameron. 16x23.6. und L C.C.

3014 I Am As Dry As A Fish / 12.15x 8.15 (Rebus. Male human figures in various poses forming the letters of the title, plus a picture of a large fish.) 1868 S C&I

3015 I Canna Bid Him Gang, Mither / Ballad / Written by / Andrew Mc-Mekin, Esq., etc. / W. K. Hewitt on stone. Entered 1839 by Geo. W. Hewitt & Co. und S N.C.

3016 I See You / #434 / 12.11x8.7.
und S N.C.
I Get Trusted — I Pay, etc. See:
"The Wrong Way" No. 6793.

3017 I Told You So /.   1860 S C&I

3018 I Told You So / Painted by W. H.
Beard. 15.13x19.11 (Bear hugging dog
while donkey watches over fence. Also
published as "In a Tight Place" No.
3044.)   1860 M C&I

3019 I Will Not Ask to Press That
Cheek / (Young man serenading young
lady with the mumps, comic vignette.)
1875 S C&I

3020 I Will Not Ask to Press That
Cheek / (Postcard size.)
1880 V.S. C&I

3021 Ice-Boat Race on the Hudson / (Ice
boat racing passenger train, Hudson
River Scene.)   und S C&I

3022 Ice Cold Soda Water / (Vignette.)
1879 S C&I

3023 Ice Cream Racket, An — Freezing
In / "Oh dat lubly cream! seems as I
could nebber git enuf." / (Colored
comic, vignette.)
1889 S C&I

3024 Ice Cream Racket, An — Thawing
Out / "Golly! Guess yous done got
enuf dis time."/(Colored girl sitting on
stove to get thawed out, vignette.)
1889 S C&I

3025 Iced Lemonade / Cool and Refreshing / (Lemon, squeezer, sugar, glass,
etc., vignette.)   1879 M C&I
Idler (Yacht) See: No. 2625.

3026 Idlewild — On the Hudson / The
Glen /   8.8 x 12.9.   und S C&I
Illinois See: Nos. 2274, 2472, 6105.

3027 Illuminated Cards / For Schools /
(4 on the sheet.)   und S C&I

3028 Illuminated Cards / For Schools /
(16 on the sheet.)   und S C&I

3029 Immaculate Conception, The /
und S C&I

3030 Impeachment of Dame Butler, Fessenden, Butler, and Ben Wade /
und S C&I

3031 Impending Catastrophe, An /
und S C&I

3032 Impending Catastrophe, An /
1868 S C&I

3033 Impending Crisis, The, or Caught
in the Act / (Policeman with club
marked "New York Daily Times" about

to arrest Greeley with copy of "The
Tribune" in his pocket. Another man
with "The Courier & Enquirer" under
his arm urging arrest. Another man
in the water holding "Greeley's Letter" in his hand — vignette.)
1860 M C&I

3034 Imperial Beauty, The / (Vignette,
girl's head.)   und S C&I

3035 Imperial German Mail Steamer
Aller / of the North German Lloyd
Line / 1 additional line of dimensions.
und S C&I

3036 Imperial German Mail Steamer
Elbe / of the North German Lloyd
Line / 1 additional line of dimensions.
und S C&I

3037 Imperial German Mail Steamer
Fulda / of the North German Lloyd
Line / 1 additional line of dimensions.
und S C&I

3038 Imperial German Mail Steamer
Havel, The / of the North German
Lloyd Line / 1 additional line of di-
mensions.   und S C&I

3039 Imperial German Mail Steamer
Trave, The / of the North German
Lloyd Line / 1 additional line of di-
mensions.   und S C&I

3040 Imperial German Mail Steamer
Werra, The / of the North German
Lloyd Line / 1 additional line of di-
mensions.   und S C&I

3041 Imported Messenger /
1879 S C&I

3042 Imported Messenger / The Great
Fountainhead in America of the "Messenger Blood" / 3 additional lines. J.
Cameron on stone. (Profile to right,
vignette.)   1880 S C&I

3043 Imposing the Cardinal's Beretta /
Upon His Grace Archbishop McCloskey
of New York by His Grace Bayley of
Baltimore at St. Patrick's Cathedral
N.Y. April 27th, 1875 / 8x12.5.
1875 S C&I

3044 In a Tight Place / Getting Squeezed
/ Painted by W. H. Beard. 19.12x15.10
(Bear squeezing dog, donkey watching
over fence. Also published as "I Told
You So" No. 3018.)
1860 M C&I

3045 In and Out of Condition / Thos.
Worth on stone. 9x13.7 (1 man fat
and healthy, with well-fed cattle, dog,
and horse talking to another man who
is underfed, cattle, dog, and horse the
same.)   1877 S C&I

[141]

3046 In and Out of Condition / (Same general idea as preceding but changes in composition; more cattle and horses shown, vignette.)
1879 L C&I

3047 In and Out of Condition / (Post-card size.) 1880 V.S. C&I

3048 In Full Bloom / (Vignette, girl with floral wreath in hair.)
1870 S C&I

3049 In Full Dress / (Girl's head.)
und S C&I

3050 In God is Our Trust / (Vignette, flowers and birds.)
1874 S C&I

3051 In Memoriam /
und S N.C.

3052 In Memory Of / 13x8.3 (Man, wo-man, and boy.) und S N.C.

3053 In Memory Of / #280 / 12.12x8.10 (Man and woman, church in back-ground, tomb on left.)
und S N.C.

3054 In Memory Of / #318 / 12.12x8.12.
und S N.C.

3055 In Memory Of / #370 / (3 children at tomb.) 1845 S N.C.

3056 In Memory Of / (Warship in back-ground.) und S N.C.

3057 In Memory Of / #184. 12.10x8.9 (Woman and boy.)
1846 S N.C.

3058 In Memory Of / #191 / 12.8x8.7.
1846 S N.C.

3059 In Memory Of / #280. 12.7x8.7 (Young couple, tomb, church, weeping willow.) und S N.C.

3060 In Memory Of / #153. 12.14x8.12 (Couple and boy to right, churchyard.)
1846 S N.C.

3061 In Memory Of / 12.13x8.13 (Couple and girl with pantalettes at left, 2 roses on top of tombstone.)
1845 S N.C.

3062 In Memory Of / (Couple and child at right, tomb and willow tree.)
und M N.C.

3063 In Memory Of / (Vignette, upright cross with flowers, motto entwined.)
1872 S C&I

3064 In / Memory / Of / 13.2x9.3 (Man, woman and child at right, church in back, tomb at left; woman with poke bonnet, child in pantalettes. A very early Currier print, but undated.)
und S N.C.

3065 In Memory Of / (St. Paul's.)
1847 S N.C.

3066 In Memory Of / (St. Paul's) / J. Schutz, Del. 12.12x8.10.
1849 S N.C.

3067 In Memory Of / (St. Paul's) / 12.13 x10.14 (Couple and child at Cooke's Tomb.) und S N.C.

3068 In Memory Of / (St. Paul's) / 12.12 x10.13 (3 figures at right, church in rear, tomb at left.)
und S N.C.

3069 In the Harbor / 8.9x12.12 (View looking south, showing Governor's Is-land and Fort, sailing boats in harbor.)
und S C&I

3070 In the Indian Pass / Adirondacks /
und S C&I

3071 In the Mountains / 7.15x12.7 (Stream and waterfall, deer in fore-ground.) und S C&I

3072 In the Mountains /
und M C&I

3073 In the Northern Wilds / Trapping Beaver / 7.15x12.8.
und S C&I

3074 In the Springtime /(2 children pick-ing flowers.) und S C&I
In the Summertime See: Pictur-esque Landscapes No. 4778.

3075 In the Woods / (Group on bank of stream, child wading.)
und S C&I

3076 In the Woods / 12.7x7.15 (4 chil-dren on bank, 2 climbing tree, no child wading.) und S C&I

3077 Inauguration of Washington, The / First President of the United States, April 30th, 1789, at the Old City Hall, New York / (8 keys.)
1876 S C&I

3078 Increase in Family, An / 15.14x 12.14 (Little girl showing basket of kittens to grandmother, mother, and child.) 1863 M C&I
Independence (Frigate) See: No. 6307.
Independence, Iowa — Horse Race See: No. 2639.

3079 Independence Hall, Philadelphia 1776 / 8.3x12.8 (¾ view, carriages and people.) und S C&I

3080 Independent Gold Hunter on His Way to California, The / I neither bor-row nor lend / 12.8x8.7. Full length figure, man loaded down with pots,

pans, tea kettle, shovels, scales, etc.)
und S N.C.

3081 Indian Ball Players / Tul-lock
Chish-ko, a Chocktaw; We-Chus-Ta-
Doo-Ta, a Sioux; Ah-Wo-Je-Nahge, a
Sioux / Catlin, Del. 12.8x8.7.
und M C&I

3082 Indian Bear Dance, The / Invoking
the aid and protection of the bear
spirit / Catlin, Del. 12.2x17.14.
und M C&I

3083 Indian Beauty, The / (Vignette, ½
length.)   und S C&I

3084 Indian Buffalo Hunt / "Close Quarters" / Catlin, Del. 12.2x17.14.
und M C&I

3085 Indian Buffalo Hunt / On the
"Prairie Bluffs" / Catlin, Del.
und M C&I

3086 Indian Falls / New York / (Brilliant autumn colors.)
und S C&I

3087 Indian Family / 12.4x8.8 (Full
length boy and girl under tree at
waterside.)   und S N.C.

3088 Indian Family, The / #303. 12x9
(Indian, squaw, and baby, another baby
in hammock in background.)
und S N.C.

3089 Indian Hunter / #373. 12.1x8.8
(Full length with foot on bear he has
killed.)   1845 S N.C.

3090 Indian Hunter, The /
und S C&I

3091 Indian Lake — Sunset / Painted by
B. Hess. 14.12x22.13 (New York State.)
1860 L C&I

3092 Indian Pass, The / Rocky Mountains / 9.13x16.14.   und M C&I
    Indian Pass — Adirondacks See:
Source of the Hudson No. 5627.

3093 Indian Summer / Squam Lake,
N.H. / 9.9x16.14.
1868 M C&I

3094 Indian Town / River St. John, N.B.
/ 8.8x12.8.   und S C&I

3095 Indian Warrior, The / 12.1x8.9
(Full length, Indian advancing on
fort.)   1845 S N.C.
    Indiana See: Nos. 795-6.
    Indianapolis See: Nos. 257, 795-6.

3096 Indians Attacking the Grizzly Bear
/ The most savage and ferocious animal of North America / Catlin, Del.
12.2x17.14.   und M C&I

3097 Infancy of Jesus / #143. 12.2x8.9
(Title repeated in Latin and Spanish.)
1849 S N.C.

3098 Infancy of the Virgin / #144. 12.11
x8.11 (Title repeated in Latin and
Spanish.)   1849 S N.C.

3099 Infant Brood, The / A. F. Tait '56
N.Y. on stone. 8.12x12.6 (Companion
to "Cares of a Family" No. 815.)
und S C&I

3100 Infant Brood, The / A. F. Tait '56
N.Y. on stone. 9.5x13.3 (Oval, companion to "Cares of a Family" No.
816.)   1865 S C&I

3101 Infant Jesus Preaching in the Temple, The / #701. (Title in French,
Spanish, Italian, and Latin.)
und S N.C.

3102 Infant St. John, The /.
1845 S N.C.

3103 Infant St. John, The / #84. (Full
length, upright.)   und S C&I

3104 Infant St. John, The / El Chiquito
Sn. Juan — Le Petit St. Jean / #61.
12.1x8.3.   und S N.C.

3105 Infant Saviour, The /
und S C&I

3106 Infant Saviour, The / El Salvator
del Mundo — La Sauveur du Monde /
12x8.2 (Ornate border.)
und S N.C.

3107 Infant Saviour & St. John / #67
11.8x8.7.   und S C&I

3108 Infant Saviour and Saint John /
11.7x8.8 (Changes in composition.)
und S C&I

3109 Infant Saviour with Mary and Joseph /   und S C&I

3110 Infant Toilet / 11.7x8.7 (Full
length, 2 young girls at dressing table.)
und S N.C.

3111 Infantry Manoeuvers by the Darktown Volunteers / "In the Front Rank
He Fell" / (Vignette, pig upsetting
leader. Companion to "Cavalry Tactics" No. 868.)   1887 S C&I

3112 Ingleside Winter, The / 8x12.9
(Group with faggots crossing bridge
to house. Winter scene.)
und S C&I

3113 Initiation Ceremonies of the Darktown Lodge — Part First / The Grand
Boss Charging the Candidate / (Vignette.)   1887 S C&I

3114 Initiation Ceremonies of the Darktown Lodge — Part Second / The Can-

didate Charging the Grand Boss / (Vignette.) 1887 S C&I

3115 Innisfallen / Ireland / (Woodland lake scene.) und M C&I

3116 Innocence / 1848 S N.C.

3117 Innocence / (Black background.) und L C&I

Intemperance See: Nos. 343, 1629, 2192, 2193, 4952-8, 6132, 6133.

3118 Interior of Fort Sumter / During the Bambardment, April 12th, 1861 / 8.7x11.15. und S C&I

3119 Into Mischief / 1857 S C&I

3120 Into Mischief / (Little girl washing doll's clothes in high hat, doll upset in pitcher.) 1857 M C&I

3121 Into Mischief / L. Maurer on stone. 24.5x18.13 (Same composition as preceding, tinted background, round corners.) 1857 L C&I

3122 Inundation, The / und S N.C.

3123 Inundation, The / #635 / 8.4x12.4 (Dog and 2 puppies on overturned doghouse, 1 puppy in water.) und S C&I

3124 Inviting Dish, An / (Peaches, grapes, etc.) 1870 S C&I

3125 Inviting Gift, An / 1870 S C&I

3126 Ira D. Sankey / The Evangelist of Song / (Vignette portrait.) und S C&I

Ireland See: Nos. 3-4, 215, 304, 351, 399, 431, 497, 557, 564, 642, 656, 839, 841, 1253-4, 1276, 1302, 1367, 1445, 1505, 1574, 1631-2, 1753, 2219, 2372, 2384, 2843, 2967, 3115, 3329-31, 3340-5, 3421-2, 3557, 3753-5, 3825, 3839, 4101-2, 4136, 4265, 4590, 4633, 4635, 4689-90, 4726, 5030-1, 5058, 5159, 5183-5, 5218, 5221-2, 5322, 5371-2, 5412, 5416-7, 5424, 5471, 5510-1, 5517, 5690, 6147, 6353, 6356, 6656.

Irene (Yacht) See: Nos. 5103-5.

3127 Irish Beauty, The / (Vignette, head.) und S C&I

3128 Iron R. M. Steamship "Persia" — Cunard Line / 2 columns, 3 lines dimensions. 8.4x12.13 (Broadside to right.) und S N.C.

3129 Iron Steamship Great Britain, The / Largest in the World / Off Sandy Hook, May 14th, 1852 / #354 — 2 columns, 4 and 5 lines (Broadside to left.) und S N.C.

3130 Iron Steamship "Great Eastern," 22,500 Tons, The / Constructed under the direction of I. K. Brunel F.R.S.-D.C.L. / 2 columns, 9 & 11 lines. (Broadside to left, many row boats with people in foreground.) C. Parsons, Del. 1858 L C&I

3131 Iroquois / By Imp Leamington, dam Maggie, B.B. by Australian / 17.10x 26.14 (Under saddle, profile to left.) 1882 L C&I

3132 Iroquois — Winner of the Derby / (Vignette about 3.8x5.) 1881 V.S. C&I

3133 Iroquois Winning the Derby / Epsom Downs, England, June 1st, 1881 / Town Moor-Peregrine-Iroquois (above title) (Under saddle to right, vignette.) 1881 S C&I

Iroquois See: Nos. 3555-6, 4255.

3134 Irrepressible Conflict, The / (Group of 10 in sinking lifeboat. Negro wearing "Discord's Patent Life Preserver," Lincoln at helm, Greeley throwing man overboard (Seward), Jeff Davis on shore.) 1860 M C&I

Irvin, Genl. James See: No. 2282.

Irving, Washington See: Nos. 5891-3.

Isaac Newton (Steamboat) See: Nos. 3823, 4474, 5726, 6405.

3135 Isabella / #25 / (¾ length, lace dress, poke bonnet.) und S C.C.

3136 Isabella / #150 / 11.9x8.4 (¾ length, lace dress, poke bonnet, facing right.) 1845 S N.C.

3137 Isabella / 11.12x8.7 (Composition nearly the same as preceding, but reversed. Figure faces left.) 1844 S N.C.

3138 Isabella / (Vignette portrait.) und S C&I

3139 Italian Landscape / 7.15x12.8 (Cattle in foreground, lake and ruins in background.) und S C&I

Italy See: Nos. 586, 1831, 3410-1, 4241, 5118, 6366, 6367, 6572.

3140 Ivanhoe / Interview of the Templar, and Rebecca / #537. 2 columns, 2 lines. und S N.C.

3141 Ivy Bridge, The / und S C&I

3142 Ivy Clad Ruins, The /.
und S C&I

3143 Ivy Clad Ruins, The / F. F. Palmer, Del.
und M C&I

3144 Ivy Clad Ruins, The / (Road and stream in foreground, man resting on bank by road.) und M N.C.

J

J. O. Nay (Horse) **See:** No. 6174.
Jack (Horse) **See:** No. 2561.

3145 Jack Rossiter / Saratoga Course 2:28 — 1849 / 12.13x20.12. 2 columns, 5 lines (Broadside to right.)
1850 L N.C.

3146 Jack Rossiter / Union Course, L.I. Tuesday, Sept. 9th, 1851. Purse and stake $1000. Mile heats best 3 in 5 in harness / 4 additional lines, 2 columns, 4 and 5 lines. 12.12x20.15 (Broadside to right, high-wheeled sulky.)
1850 L N.C.

Jackson, Andrew **See:** Nos. 216-7, 650, 1480, 2233, 2234-40, 2485.

Jackson, Stonewall **See:** Nos. 380, 429, 1506, 2559, 6065.

3147 James / 11.8x8.4 (Full length, standing against wall, river in background.) 1845 S N.C.

3148 James A. Garfield / (Facsimile signature) (Half length vignette.)
und S C&I

3149 James Buchanan / Democratic Candidate for / Fifteenth President of the United States / #716 / 8.10x11.5 (¾ length, slightly to right, red curtain.)
und S N.C.

3150 James Buchanan / Democratic Candidate for Fifteenth President of the United States / From a photograph by M. B. Brady, N.Y. (Vignette, slightly to right.) 1856 L N.C.

3151 James Buchanan / Fifteenth President of the United States / #627 — 11.2x8.8. und S N.C.

3152 James Buchanan / Fifteenth President of the United States / #597.
und S C&I

3153 James Hammill and Walter Brown in Their / Great Five Mile Rowing Match for $4000 & the Championship of America / At Newburg Bay, Hudson River Sept. 9th, 1867 / 2 additional lines and 2 columns, 2 lines. 16.12x 24.12 (Won by Hammill — time 41 minutes, 56 seconds.)
1867 L C&I

3154 James G. Birney / From a daguerreotype by Chilton. (¾ length, green curtain.) 1844 S N.C

3155 James G. Birney / Nominated by the Liberty Party for Eleventh President of the United States / #319. guerreotype by Chilton. 12.1x8.11.
1844 S N.C.

James Howard (Steamboat) **See:** No. 4117.

3156 James J. Corbett — Champion Heavyweight / J. Cameron on stone.
und M C&I

3157 James K. Polk / #29 / (Seated, full face, slightly to right. Red curtain, no view of Capitol through window.)
1846 S N.C.

3158 James K. Polk / Eleventh President of the United States / 11.9x8.13 (Seated to left, Capitol in right background.)
und S C.C.

3159 James K. Polk / Eleventh President of the United States / #319 From a daguerreotype by Plumbe. 11.11x8.10 (Oval in rectangle, sur-

rounded by 13 stars, cannon, flags, etc.)
1846 S N.C.

3160 James K. Polk / Eleventh President
of the United States / 11.9x8.12
(Seated to right, Capitol through window at left.) und S N.C.

3161 James K. Polk / Eleventh President
of the United States / (Seated to right,
Capitol through window at left.)
und S C.C.

3162 James K. Polk / Eleventh President
of the United States / 11.10x8.14
(Seated to left, Capitol in back.)
und S N.C.

3163 James K. Polk / Eleventh President of the United States / 11.8x8.9
(Seated, Capitol through window at right.) und S N.C.

3164 James K. Polk / Nominated for /
Eleventh President of the United
States / 11.10x8.12 (Seated, right arm
resting on table, full face, no Capitol
in back.) und S N.C.

3165 James K. Polk / President Elect
of the United States / 12.1x8.11 (Full
length, left hand on table, right arm
extended.) 1844 S N.C.

3166 James K. Polk / The People's Candidate for President / Of the United
States / 12.1x8.11 (Full length, left
hand on table, green curtain.)
1844 S N.C.

3167 James K. Polk / The People's
Choice for President / Of the United
States / (Vignette, on white horse.)
und S N.C.

3168 James K. Polk / Union Course,
L. I., Friday, Oct. 15th, 1847. Purse
$250, 2 mile heats / 2 columns, 5 lines
12.15x20.13 (Broadside to left, skeleton wagon.) 1850 M N.C.

3169 James L. Hewitt & Co. / Music
Publishers / No. 137 Broadway, New
York / Orders from any part of the
country, for music or musical instruments, executed with care and dispatch / Lith. of Stodart & Currier.
11.4x6.13 (Landscape with female
figures, one playing lyre, and boy with
flageolet.) und S N.C.

3170 James L. Hewitt & Co. / (Same as
preceding. Stodart's name removed
and change of address.)
und S N.C.

3171 James Madison / Fourth President
of the United States / 11.12x9.5
(Seated, slightly to right, papers in
right hand, green curtain.)
und S N.C.

3172 James Monroe / Fifth President of
the United States / #23 — 11.6x9.1
(Papers in hand.)
und S N.C.

3173 James Myers / Samuel Lewis —
Chas. C. Merchant / (Names on store
located at 243 Broadway, N. Y.) W.
K. H. (Hewitt) on stone. 8.15x7.15
(This is a very early Currier print.)
und S N.C.

3174 James Stephens / Head Center of
the Irish Republican Brotherhood / (2
additional lines description.)
und S C&I

3175 Jane / #19 (¾ length, fan in hand.)
und S N.C.

3176 Jane / #47 (½ length, oval ornamental borders.)
1847 S N.C.

3177 Jane / #47 (¾ length, shawl and
flowers in hand.)
und S N.C.

3178 Jane / #47 (Full length, seated,
red dress, window at left.)
1845 S N.C.

3179 Jane / #47 (Full length, seated,
red dress. Changes in scenery seen
through window.)
1845 S N.C.

3180 Jane / #71 (Full length, red cape,
yellow dress, standing at mirror.)
12x8.12. 1848 S N.C.

3181 Jane / (Vignette, head and shoulders.) und S C&I
Jasper, Sergeant See: No. 5463.
Java See: Nos. 1241-3.
Jay, John See: No. 3269.

3182 Jay Eye See / By Dictator / Record 2:10¾ / J. Cameron on stone.
(Vignette, ¾, high-wheeled sulky to
right.) 1883 S C&I

3183 Jay Eye See / Record 2:01 / Scott
Leighton on stone. 17.10x26.14 (¾
view to left.) 1883 L C&I

3184 Jay Eye See / Record 2:1 / J. Cameron on stone. (¾ to left, high-wheeled
sulky.) 1883 L C&I

3185 Jay Eye See / The Phenomenal
Trotting Gelding / Driven by E. D.
Bithers. 1884 L C&I

3186 Jay Eye See, 2:10 / 2.12x4.12.
1886 V.S. C&I
Jay Eye See See: Nos. 433-4, 899,
1947-8, 2538, 3182-3-4-5-6-7, 3471, 4405,
5708, 6163.

3187 Jay Eye Sore, De Great World Beater / "When dat colt am warmed up he kin lay em all out" / (Vignette, colored comic, patched-up rig and horse.) 1885 S C&I
Jay Gould (Horse) See: No. 933.

3188 Jeanette / #400 / 11.12x8.10 (¾ length, fur-trimmed dress. Round corners.) 1846 S N.C.

3189 Jeanette / #400 / (¾ length on terrace, facing right, head turned to observer, roses in hair, bouquet in hand, hair in ringlets.) 1846 S N.C.
Jeanette (Arctic exploring yacht) See: No. 264.

3190 Jeanie / #400 (¾ length, Scotch girl seated in arm chair on porch, highlands and lake in background.) 1850 S N.C.

3191 Jeff D. Hung on a "Sour Apple Tree" or Treason made Odious / (Jeff Davis hanging off ground, arms around Greeley's neck. Greeley holding prison door open. Vignette.) 1867 S C&I

3192 Jeff Davis on His Own Platform / or The Last Act of Secession / und S C&I

3193 Jefferson Davis / (Profile to right, portrait, vignette.) und S C&I

3194 Jeff's Last Shift / (Davis dressed as a woman. Soldiers lifting skirt, vignette.) 1865 S C&I
Jefferson, Thomas See: Nos. 1530, 6026, 6509.

3195 Jem Mace / Born at Beeston, near Swaffham, in Norfolk, England, April, 1831. / Height 5 feet, 8½ inches; weight 160 lbs. / 14.14x12. 2 columns, 12 lines. 1870 M C&I

3196 Jennie / (½ length vignette.) und S C&I

3197 Jennie Cramer / (Vignette, head and shoulders.) und S C&I

3198 Jenny Lind / Facsimile, signature / #194 (Off-shoulder dress, roses in hair—vignette.) und S N.C.

3199 Jenny Lind / Als Tochter des Regiments / #309 / (Full length, soldiers in background.) und S N.C.

3200 Jenny Lind / From the bust by J. Durham. #194 (Facsimile signature in lower margin.) und S N.C.

3201 Jenny Lind / The Swedish Nightingale's / Greeting to America / (Full length, white dress, top corners round.) und M N.C.
Jenny Lind Also See: Nos. 1451, 1957.
Jenny Lind (Horse) See: No. 556.

3202 Jerome Eddy (Horse.) 1882 S C&I
Jerome Park Track See: No. 175, 5037, 6092, 6564.

3203 Jersey City, Hoboken and Brooklyn /. 1858 S C&I

3204 Jersey Litchfield Bull / Centennial Prize / Owned by Ratchford Starr Echo Farm, Litchfield, Conn. / und S C&I

3205 Jersey Prize Niobe / und S C&I

3206 Jerusalem / From the Mount of Olives / #5 (Title repeated in French and Spanish.) 1846 S N.C.

3207 Jerusalem From the Mount of Olives / Jerusalem desde el Monte de Olivar / 1849 S N.C.
Jerusalem See: No. 1752.
Jessie Wales (Horse) See: No. 2583, 5436.

3208 Jesus and the Cyrenian / Jesus aju dado pelo Cirineo / #51 12.15x9.3 (Border of Stations of the Cross.) 1848 S N.C.

3209 Jesus and the Cyrenian / 1 additional line Biblical quotation (at top) Passion 5th. 9.15x7.15.
und S N.C.

3210 Jesus / and the Twelve Apostles / #552 12.15x9.3 (Jesus in center, surrounded by 12 portraits.) 1847 S N.C.

3211 Jesus Ascendeth into Heaven / 11.12x8.7 (Title repeated in Spanish. Full length of Jesus, slightly rounded corners.) und S C&I

3212 Jesus Ascending into Heaven / 11.11x8.9 (Title repeated in Spanish. Full length figure of Jesus.) und S C&I

3213 Jesus Bearing His Cross / #196 12.12x8.12 (Title repeated in Spanish and French.) 1847 S N.C.

3214 Jesus Bearing His Cross / #48 12.15x9.3 (Title repeated in Spanish.) 1848 S N.C.

3215 Jesus Bearing his Cross / "They conduct Him to a place called Calvary"

/ #196 10.3x8 (At top) Passion 2nd. und S N.C.

3216 Jesus Blessing Little Children / 1 line Biblical quotation.
1866 S C&I

3217 Jesus Blessing Little Children / 1 line B i b l i c a l quotation. 12.11x8.2 (Slightly rounded corners.)
1867 S C&I

3218 Jesus Blessing Little Children / 3 additional lines Biblical quotation. 17.6x11.15. 1866 M C&I

3219 Jesus Condemned to Death / #47 13x9.2 (Title repeated in Spanish.) Border Station No. 1. (At Top.)
1848 S N.C.

3220 Jesus Consoles the Women of Jerusalem / 1 additional line Biblical quotation. 9.15x7.15 (At top) Passion 8th.
und S N.C.

3221 Jesus Consoles the Women of Jerusalem / 12.9x8.11 (Title repeated in Spanish. Jesus with crown of thorns.)
1848 S N.C.

3222 Jesus Crucified / "And crying aloud He gave up the Ghost" / (At top) Passion 12th. und S N.C.

3223 Jesus Crucified / #206 12.11x8.15 (Title repeated in Spanish and French. Border XII station.)
1847 S N.C.

3224 Jesus Despoiled of His Garments / #204. und S N.C.

3225 Jesus Despoiled of His Garments / 9.15x7.15 (At top) Passion 10th.
und S N.C.

3226 Jesus Despoiled of His Vestments / #56 12.14x9.2 (Title repeated in Spanish.) Border X Station.
1848 S N.C.

3227 Jesus Falls for the First Time / #49 13x9.4. Border III station.
1848 S N.C.

3228 Jesus Falls for the First Time / "He is overpowered by the weight of the Cross" / 9.14x7.15 (At top) Passion 3d. und S N.C.

3229 Jesus Falls for the / Second Time / #201 (Title repeated in Spanish and French. Ornamental border.) VII station at top. und S N.C.

3230 Jesus Falls for a Second Time / "My Knees have sunk under Me" / 9.13x7.14 (At top) Passion VII.
und S N.C.

3231 Jesus Falls For the Third Time / #55 Border IX station.
1848 S N.C.

3232 Jesus Fall for the Third Time / 9.14x7.14 (At top) Passion IX. und S N.C.

3233 Jesus Imprints His Face on a Cloth / #52 12.13x9.12 (Title repeated in Spanish.) Sta VI border.
1848 S N.C.

3234 Jesus is Nailed to the Cross / 1 additional line Biblical quotation. 9.15x7.14 (At top) Passion 11th.
und S N.C.

3235 Jesus is Nailed to the Cross / Jesus Posto im Cruz / Jesus Attache a la Croix / #205 (Conventional border of crosses, keys, etc.) und S N.C.

3236 Jesus is Placed in the / Sepulchre / #208 / 12.11x8.15 (Title repeated in Spanish and French.) Border Station XIV. 1847 S N.C.

3237 Jesus Laid in the Sepulchre / 12.9x 8.9 (Title Repeated in Spanish.) (At top) Station XIV. 1846 S N.C.

3238 Jesus Meeting his Mother / #198.
und S N.C.

3239 Jesus Meets his Mother / "Woman behold your son" / 9.15x7.15 (At top) Passion 4th. und S N.C.

3210 Jesus Meets St. Veronica / #200.
und S N.C.

3241 Jesus Nailed to the Cross / #57 / 13x9.3 (Title repeated in Spanish.) Station XI. 1848 S N.C.

3242 Jesus of Nazareth Passes By / und S C&I

3243 Jesus on the Cross / 15x11.4 (Rounded corners.)
und M C&I

3244 Jesus on the Cross / El Salvador del Mundo / 11.11x8.2.
und S C&I

3245 Jesus Put in the Sepulchre / #208.
und S N.C.

3246 Jesus Taken from the Cross / 12.10x8.12 (Title repeated in Spanish.) (At top) Station XIII.
1846 S N.C.

3247 Jib and Mainsail Race, A /
1882 L C&I

3248 Jockey Club / 4.7x7.3 (Cigar Ad.)
1880 V.S. C&I

3249 Jockey's Dream, The / 9.6x12.13 (Jockey sleeping in stall, dreaming.

Vision of winning race over his head.)
1880 S C&I

Joe Elliott (Horse) See: No. 2946, 4250.

Joe Patchen See: No. 885, 4684.

3250 John / #355 / 11.15x8.8. (Full length, seated.) 1845 S N.C.

3251 John Adams / Second President of the United States / 11.9x9.4 (Right hand resting on book, slightly to right, green curtain.) und S N.C.

3252 Jo. Anderson, My Jo / 2 lines of poetry / as sung by / Mr. Wilson / New York / Published by Atwill, 201 Broadway. / und S N.C.

3253 John Brown / Meeting the slave mother and her child on the steps of Charleston jail on his way to execution / Regarding them with a look of compassion Captain Brown stopped, stooped, and kissed the child / 11.10 x8.8. From the original painting by Louis Ransom. 1863 S C&I

3254 John Brown—The Martyr / 11.10 x8.8. (Upright.) 3 additional lines.
1870 S C&I

3255 John Brown / Leader of the Harper's Ferry Insurrection / (Vignette portrait.) und S C&I

3256 John Bull and His friend Cleveland / Column at left, John Bull Says: "That suits me, Mr. Cleveland, keep my / mills and factories going if the rest of / mankind starve. I am glad to see you / sport my colors the red Bandanna / Column at right, President Cleveland says: "I am proud of your approval, Mr. Bull / and am doing my best to serve you / as you say —I wear the real British Red / There isn't anything green about me / (Full length figures of John Bull on left with his factories and workmen busy. Cleveland on right holding document "Free Trade Message to Congress" and his factories and workmen idle. Vignette.) 1888 S C&I

3257 "John Bull" Makes a Discovery /
und S C&I

3258 John C. Breckinridge / Vice President of the United States / 11.3x8.10 (½ length, seated.)
und S N.C.

3259 John C. Calhoun / (½ length, slightly to left, vignette.)
1853 L N.C.

3260 John C. Fremont / Republican Candidate for / Fifteenth President of the United States / #717 / From a photograph by Brady, taken June, 1856 / (Red curtain.) und S N.C.

3261 John C. Heenan, Champion of the World / (Above title) "The Benicia Boy" / Born in West Troy, N. Y., May 2, 1835 / (Full length in fighting costume, exterior scene slightly to right. Vignette.) 1860 S C&I

3262 John C. Heenan, Champion of the World (Above title) "The Benicia Boy" / Born in West Troy, N. Y., May 2, 1835 / (½ length, vignette.)
1860 S C&I

3263 John C. Heenan "The Benicia Boy" / Champion of the World / 14.14x12.2 (Full length, exterior scene.)
1860 M C&I

3264 John C. Heenan, Champion of the World / (Above title) "The Benicia Boy" / L. M. on stone. 12x8.10 (¾ length, seated, dressed for the street.)
und S C&I

3265 John C. Heenan, Champion of the World / (Above title) "Benicia Boy" / Born in West Troy, New York, May 2, 1835. Height 6 feet, 1½ inches. Fighting weight from 192 to 195 lbs. / Beat the Champion of England in 42 rounds April 17th, 1860. Time 2 hours, 20 min. / #631 (Profile to left, full length fighting pose. Vignette.)
1860 S C&I

3266 John Ennis / The Celebrated Pedestrian / Born at Richmond Harbor, County Longford, Ireland, June 4th, 1842. Height 5 ft. 8 in. Weight 150 lbs. / 12.14x9.3. 1879 S C&I

3267 John Hancock's Defiance / July 4th, 1776 / 3 additional lines, 9 keys. 12.6x9. 1876 S C&I

3268 John J. Dwyer, Champion of America / J. Cameron, Del.
und M C&I

3269 John Jay / 2.13x3 (From Jenkins "History of Political Parties in the State of New York" N. Y.)
und V.S. C&I

3270 John L. Sullivan / Champion Pugilist of the World / (Above Title) Copied by permission of the "New York Illustrated Times" from their only genuine portrait. J. Cameron on stone. 8 additional lines. 15.15x12.7 (Full length in fighting costume.)
1883 M C&I

3271 John Milton / (Facsimile signature) (Vignette portrait.)
und M C&I

John Minturn (Steamship) See:
No. 6788.

3272 John Mitchell / The First Martyr
of Ireland in her Revolution of 1848 /
/ #589 / 11.8x9 (Full face, slightly
to right, ship seen through window
at right.)   1848 S N.C.

3273 John Mitchell / The First Martyr
of Ireland in her Revolution of 1848 /
#589 / 11.6x8.6. 4 additional lines of
description (Profile to right, ship
seen through window at right.)
                               1848 S N.C.

3274 John Mitchell / The First Martyr
of Ireland in her Revolution of 1848 /
(Facsimile signature) 2 columns, 5
lines. 11.1x8.12.   und S N.C.

3275 John Morrissey / Born February 5,
1831 / Height 6 ft. Weight 170 lbs /
2 columns, 4 and 3 lines. 14.14x11.15
(Full length, in fighting togs.)
                               1860 M C&I

3276 John Quincy Adams / Sixth President of the United States / #24 /
11.10x9 (Seated slightly to left, small
book in left hand, red curtain.)
                               und S N.C.

3277 John Quincy Adams / Sixth President of the United States / N. Currier's Lith. Pub. by Case & Skinner,
Hartford, Conn. 11.14x9.14 (Seated,
slightly to left, similar composition to
preceding, white jabot. A much earlier
print.)   und S N.C.

3278 John Quincy Adams / Sketched by
Arthur J. Stansbury, Esqr. / A Few
hours previous to the death of Mr.
Adams / Entered 1848 by A. J. Stansbury. Lith. by Sarony & Major, sold
by N. Currier / 14.3x10.2.
                               1848 S N.C.

3279 John R. Gentry / Record 2:00½
(Vignette, ¾ view to right, rubber-
tired, low-wheeled sulky.)
                          und S C&I
    John Stewart (Horse) See: Nos.
886, 907-8.

3280 John Straus! John Straus! / "The
Girls are all Mad" / Comic Ballad /
Published by Hewitt & Jaques, 239
Broadway / N. Currier's Lith. (5 small
scenes.)   und S N.C.

3281 John Tyler / Tenth President of
the United States / 11.8x9.1 (Seated,
slightly to right, left hand on papers.)
                          und S N.C.

3282 John Wesley / (½ length.)
                          und S N.C.

John W. Conley (Horse) See: No.
6616.

3283 John Wesley Preaching on his
Father's Grave / In the Church Yard
at Epworth, Sunday, June 6th, 1742 /
3 line quotation. 8.4x12.3.
                          und S C&I

3284 Johnny and Lily /
                          und S C&I
    Johnson, Andrew See: Nos. 218,
1472, 2510, 4960, 5567.
    Johnson, Herschel See: Nos. 2903,
4386.
    Johnson See: Col. R. No. 1201.

3285 Johnson's Hotel, kept on the European Plan / No. 2, 4, 6, & 8 Warren
St. New York / Cheap, Elegant, and
Commodious / 5 additional lines. On
stone by J. Probst. 18.1x16.2 (Upright.)   1854 M C.C.
    Johnston See: Gen. Joseph Nos.
2285, 5908.
    Johnston See: William F. No. 6688.

3286 Johnston, Pacer — Record 2:06¼ /
2.12x4.12.   1881 V.S. C&I
    Johnston (Horse) See: No. 968,
2637, 3286, 5708, 6163.

3287 Jolly Dog, A / 12.10x8.15 (Dog
standing, cigar in mouth, champagne
and box of cigars alongside.)
                          1878 S C&I

3288 Jolly Hunters, The / 7.15x12.7
(Monkeys riding dogs and chasing rabbits.)   und S C&I

3289 Jolly Jumper, A / "Come along
Bismark, I bet you don't got me left" /
(German with child in cart, pulled by
dog, about to board ferry boat at last
minute. Companion to "A Sorry Dog"
No. 5625. Vignette.)
                          1888 S C&I

3290 Jolly Smoker, The / (Full length,
bundle of cigars beside him, vignette.)
                          1880 S C&I

3291 Jolly Smoker, The /
                          1880 L C&I

3292 Jolly Smoker, The / 2.15x4.12.
                          1880 V.S. C&I

3293 Jolly Smoker, The / 3.7x4.8 (Oval,
full length man smoking cigar. Smoke
forms the word "Capital.")
                          1880 V.S. C&I

3294 Jolly Smoker, The / 4.7x7.3 (Man
smoking. Smoke forms the word
"Capital.")   1880 V.S. C&I

[150]

3295 Jolly Young Ducks / 9.12x14. From nature by F. F. Palmer.
1866 M C&I

Jones, Jacob **See:** No. 4398.

Jones, John Paul **See:** Nos. 4398-9.

Jones, Miss Martha **See:** No. 4155.

Jones, Miss Martha **See:** Lilliputian No. 4155.

Jonesboro, Ga. Battle of **See:** No. 408.

Jordan **See:** Foreign views, misc.

3296 Joseph C. Yates / 2.13x3. From Jenkin's "History of Political Parties in the state of New York" N.Y.
und V.S. C.C.

3297 Joseph Grimaldi / Pub. by W. H. Colyer, 1838 (Vignette, ½ length portrait about 4x6. Frontispiece of Memoirs of Joseph Grimaldi, edited by "Boz.") und V.S. N.C.

3298 Josephine / #81 / 11.15x8.6 (Full length, red dress, plain background.)
1848 S N.C.

3299 Josephine / #251 / 11.6x8.7 (¾ length, oval in floral rectangle, exterior scene.) 1847 S N.C.

3300 Josephine / #251 (Seated on sofa, holding bouquet.)
und S N.C.

3301 Josephine / 11.10x8.8 (¾ length, interior, arms on table.)
und S N.C.

3302 Josephine / (Vignette.)
und S C&I

3303 Josie / (Vignette, head.)
und S C&I

3304 Judge Fullerton / As he appeared in harness, driven by Dan Mace / Winner of first prize $5000 in the contest for the $10,000 purse at Buffalo, N.Y. August 9th, 1872, time 2:25, 2:24¾ 2:33¾ at / Beacon Park, Boston August 29th, 1873 beat Camors and Sensation trotting the second heat in 2:19¼ and at Utica, N.Y. Aug. 25th, 1873 beat Lucille Golddust, Camors, Sensation trotting in the third heat a half mile in the extraordinary time 1:04¾ / J. Cameron on stone. (Broadside to left, high-wheeled sulky, vignette.) 1873 S C&I

Judge Fullerton **See:** Nos. 507, 909, 1179, 2421, 5479, 5574, 6009, 6181.

3305 Julia / (Full length, white dress, blue shawl.) 1845 S N.C.

3306 Julia / W. K. Hewitt on stone. (Slightly to left, ½ length, vignette.)
und S N.C.

3307 Julia / G. Kramm on stone. (Exterior scene, yellow dress, roses in hair, red shawl, vignette.)
und S N.C.

3308 Julia / #48 / 12.2x8.7 (Bust portrait, round corners, red dress, wide white collar.) 1846 S N.C.

3309 Julia / #67 / (Full length, interior, red dress, curtain on left, picture of girl on wall at right.)
1848 S N.C.

3310 Julia / 12.1x8.10 (¾, seated, music on table.) und S N.C.

3311 Julia / (Vignette.)
und S C&I

3312 Julia / "I should like to be treated like a dog" / #43 / 11.14x8.12 (¾ length girl holding dog in lap, decollete dress.) 1848 S N.C.

3313 Juliet / und S C&I

3314 Juliette / und S C&I

3315 June / und S C&I

Juniata, Pa. **See:** No. 4603.

3316 Juno / (Girl's head.)
und V.S. C&I

3317 Juno / A celebrated setter / 8.9x7.2 (Profile, head to left.)
und S N.C.

3318 Juno / 12.1x8.7 (Setter resting, gun and game in front.)
und S N.C.

3319 Juno / 11.15x9.12 (Setter resting, gun and game in front — more top ground than preceding.)
und S N.C.

3320 Just caught / Trout and Pickerel / 12.8x9 (Upright, still life, black background.) 1872 S C&I

3321 Just Married / (Vignette, head with jewels.) und S C&I

3322 Just My Style / (½ length vignette of girl.) 1871 S C&I

Justina (Horse) **See:** Nos. 487, 2639.

K

3323 Kaiser Wilhelm der Grosse / Of the North German Lloyd Line / und S C&I

3324 Kate / (Vignette, bust portrait.) und M C&I

3325 Kate / (Vignette, rural background.) und S C&I

3326 Kate / 8.8x11.6 (½ length, oval in conventional rectangular border, Scots costume.) 1846 S N.C.

3327 Katz-Kills in Winter, The / Bastion Falls / 8.7x12.8. und S C&I

Kearney, Philip See: No. 2290.

Kearsarge See: Nos. 6338-9.

3328 Kenilworth Castle / F. F. Palmer, Del. und L C&I

Kensington (Steamship) See: 6257.

Kentucky See: Nos. 409, 412-3.

Keying (Chinese Junk) See: No. 1037.

3329 Kilkenny Castle / Ireland / und S C&I

Killarney See: Ireland.

Keene, Jas. R. See: No. 4253.

Kilby (Bark) See: No. 5492.

3330 Killeries, The / Connemara / 8x12.7 (Fishing scene.) und S C&I

3331 Killeney Hill / Dublin / und S C&I

Kilpatrick, Gen. See: No. 5490.

Kimball, Heber C. See: No. 1986.

3332 Kind, Kind and Gentle Is She / Published by Hewitt & Jaques. (Music sheet.) und S N.C.

King, Wm. R. See: Nos. 2493-4, 6701-2.

3333 King of the Forest, The / 8.8x12.9 (Same composition as "Deer in Woods" No. 1538.) und S C&I

3334 King of the House / (Baby in crib.) und S C&I

3335 King of the House, The. / (Companion to "Queen of the House" No. 5012.) 1875 S C&I

3336 King of the Road, The / Dexter, driven by his owner, Mr. Robt. Bonner of the New York Ledger / at Prospect Park, Brooklyn, August 31st, 1869 trotting a mile to a road wagon weighing with driver 319 lbs. in the unprece-

dented time of / 2 minutes 21¾ seconds / 2 columns, 5 and 14 lines. Cameron on stone. 16.12x25.14 (¾ view to right.) 1869 L C&I

3337 King of the Turf "Dexter" Driven by Budd Doble, The / Best Time Mile Heats to Saddle 2:18 in Harness 2:17¼ to Wagon 2:24 to Road Wagon Driven by / Mr. Bonner, Wagon and Driver Weighing 319 lbs. 2:21¾ / J. Cameron on stone. (Vignette to left, high-wheeled sulky.) 1871 S C&I

3338 King of the Road, The / Dexter driven by his owner Mr. Robert Bonner / 1870 S C&I

3339 King of the Turf St. Julien Driven by Orrin A. Hickok / By Volunteer, dam by Sayre's Harry Clay / Record 2:11¼ / Scott Leighton on stone. (¾ view to right.) 18.4x28. 1880 L C&I

3340 King William III / Crossing the Boyne July 1st, 1690 / 2 columns, 4 lines of verse. Pub. by J. Fisher 71 Court St., Boston. (Equestrian portrait, head turned to left.) 1845 S N.C.

3341 King William III / Crossing the Boyne, July 1st, 1690 / 2 columns, 4 lines of verse. (Equestrian portrait, troops in background.) 1863 S C&I

3342 King William III / Crossing the Boyne July 1st, 1690 / (2 columns, 4 lines of verse.) und S C&I

3343 King William III / Crossing the Boyne, July 1st, 1690 / J. Schutz on stone. 2 columns, 8 lines of verse. und S C&I

3344 King William III / Prince of Orange / Born November 4th, 1650 Died March 8th, 1701 / 4 additional lines and 4 lines of verse. (Vignette, head and shoulders.) und S C&I

3345 King William of Orange / (Vignette, ½ length.) und S C&I

3346 Kingston / By Spendthrift — Dam imp. Kapanga / (Standing, profile, portrait to left, vignette and running horse.) 1891 S C&I

Kingston (Horse) See: No. 2521.

Kirkwood (Horse) See: No. 2583.

3347 Kiss in the Dark, A / Mischievous Conductor "Dark Tunnel, Through in Half an Hour" Scene—When the train struck the light in just three minutes. / (2 views on 1 sheet: Minister taking drink and dude kissing colored woman. Railroad print.)   1881 S C&I

3347A Kiss Me Quick /
                    und S N.C.

3348 Kiss Me Quick / 8.14x11.9 (¾ length portrait, young couple.) 125 Nassau St.   und S C&I

3349 Kiss Me Quick / "Children: This is the third time within an hour that I have placed your hats properly on your heads — there!" / #700 (Young man kisses nurse while she pushes hats down on children's heads to prevent their seeing.) 8.14x11.9. 152 Nassau St.
                    und S C&I

3350 Kitch-Ee-I-Aa-Ba — Or the Big Buck / A Chippewa Chief / Taken at the Treaty of Prairie du Chien by J. O. Lewis 1852. (Vignette.)
                    und S N.C.

3351 Kitties Among the Clover /
                    1873 S C&I

3352 Kitties Among the Roses / 8.11x12.9 (2 white kittens in and out of basket.)
                    1873 S C&I

3353 Kitties' Breakfast / L. Maurer on stone. 17.13x22.11 (Little girl feeding kittens, vignette, upright.)
                    1857 L C&I

3354 Kittie's Lesson / 8.8x12.1 (With alphabet book.)   1877 S C&I

3355 Kitties on a Frolic / The New Hat/
                    und S C&I

3356 Kitties on a Frolic / The New Hat/ 8.2x12.6.   1877 S C&I

3357 Kitty / (Girl's head.)
                    und V.S. C&I

3358 Kitty / (Gray kitten — doll in cradle in background, vignette.)
                    und S N.C.

3359 Kitty and Polly / Dividing the Spoils / (Companion to "Polly and Kitty" No. 4829.)
                    und M C&I

3360 Kitty and Rover /
                    und S C&I

3361 Kitty in Clover / 8.6x11.7 (Girl with white kitten in arms, upright.)
                    1872 S C&I

3362 Kitty's Dinner / #717 / 8.8x11.9 (Full-length figure, girl with cat.)
                    und S C&I

Knickerbocker (Steamboat) See: No. 5727.

3363 Knitting Lesson, The / (Interior scene, woman teaching young girl, upright.)   und M C&I

3364 Knocked Into a Cocked Hat / (Cass struck by cannon ball labelled "Z. Taylor," Cannon named "Philadelphia" Convention.) Pub. by P. Smith.
                    1848 M N.C.

Knox, Henry See: No. 6509.

3365 Konig Wilhehm Von Preussen in der Schlact Von Sedan in Frankreich am 1. September 1870 / 3 additional lines of description. 8.14x12.7.
                    und S C&I

Kook Family See: No. 889.
Kosciusko See: Nos. 6103-4.

3366 Kossuth / Hungary's Champion & America's Guest / #695 8.10x11.3 (¾ length portrait, standing at table, battle scene in background, red curtain.)
                    und S N.C.

Kossuth See: Nos. 2522, 3787-8, 3838.

3367 Kremlin / Record 2:07¾ / (¾ view, high-wheeled sulkey to right, vignette.)
                    1893 S C&I

L

3368 La Alemada de Mexico — The Public Park of Mexico / #631 / 8.6x12.12.
                    1848 S N.C.

La Aquitaine See: No. 1233.
La Bourgogne See: No. 1229.

La Bretagne See: No. 1230.
La Champagne See: No. 1231.

3369 La Cigarita / (Woman smoking, advertising card.)
                    1880 V.S. C&I

La Gascogne See: No. 1232.

3370 La Gitana /   und S N.C.
La Lorraine / See: No. 1234.

3371 La Muzurka / Danced in / "La Gitana" / by / Madame Taglioni / published by Hewitt & Jaques. (Vignette portrait of Taglioni — music sheet.)   und S N.C.

3372 La Reine des Anges /
                    und S N.C.

La Touraine **See:** No. 1235.

3373 Ladder of Fortune, The / 1 additional line. 11.10x8.13 (Good people in foreground climbing ladder "Morality, Honesty, Industry, Etc. to get apples "Success" "Riches" etc. Others in background playing races, lotteries, policy games — upright.)   1875 S C&I

3374 Ladies Boquet, The / (Vase with narrow shaft, upright, vignette.)
und S C&I

3375 Ladies Boquet, The / (Upright, vignette, flowers in vase.)
1870 S C&I

3376 Ladies Bouquet, The / (Flowers in vase.)   und S C&I

3377 Ladies Loyal Union League, The / 9x12.8 (Portraits of Martha Washington and Florence Nightingale.)
1863 S C&I

3378 Lady and Moor / 7.14x9.12 (Similar composition to "Attack of the Lion" No. 301, white horse.)
und S N.C.

3379 Lady Emma, George Wilkes, and General Butler / Trotting for a purse of $1000, mile heats, best 3 in 5 / over the Fashion Course, L.I. Sept. 28th, 1865 / 4 additional lines. J. Cameron on stone. 16.14x26.8 (3 skeleton wagons to right.)
1865 L C&I

3380 Lady Fulton / Winner of the great match against time of trotting in harness twenty miles within one hour / Over the Centreville Course, L.I. July 18th, 1855. Driven by Mr. Jas. D. McMann / 5 additional lines. L. Maurer on stone. (Vignette, riderless horse running in field.)   1857 S C&I

Lady Mac **See:** Nos. 4258-9, 5565.

3381 Lady Maud / Bay Mare by General Knox, Pedigree, of Dam unknown / 2:18¼ / (Vignette, broadside, high-wheeled sulky to left.)
1876 S C&I

3382 Lady Moscow / Union Course, L.I. June 13th, 1849 / 2 columns of 6 lines. S. B. Jones, Del. on stone. 12.15x21.1 (High-wheeled sulky to right.)
1850 L N.C.

3383 Lady Moscow, Rocket, and Brown Dick / Trotting for a purse and stake of $2000 / Mile Heats best 3 in 5 / Over the Union Course, L.I. Sept. 15th, 1856 / L. Maurer, Del.
1857 L N.C.

Lady Moscow **See:** Nos. 3382-3, 3390.

3384 Lady of the Lake / #211 / 4 additional lines of verse. 11.9x8.9.
und S N.C.

3385 Lady of the Lake / (Full-length figure in boat, Scotsman on bank, no verse and radically different composition.)   und S C&I

3386 Lady of the Lake / 4 lines of verse 11.10x8.3 (Changes in composition, upright.)   1870 S C&I

Lady Stout (Horse) **See:** No. 2946.

3387 Lady Suffolk / 1 Mile in 2:26 June 14th, 1849 / Cambridge Course, Mass. / 2 columns, 2 and 1 line. 12.13x20.11 (Broadside to left, under saddle.)
1850 M N.C.

3388 Lady Suffolk / Centreville Course, L.I. Friday Aug. 3rd, 1849 / Purse $300. Mile Heats best 3 in 5 in harness / 4 additional lines and 2 columns, 10 and 12 lines. 17.10x26.12 (Broadside to right, high-wheeled sulky, grandstand in rear.)   1852 L N.C.

3389 Lady Suffolk. Record 2:26 /
und L C&I

3390 Lady Suffolk and Lady Moscow / Hunting Park Course, Phila. June 13th, 1850 / 4 additional lines. 17.12x26.7 (Broadside to right, skeleton wagons.)
1850 L N.C.

Lady Suffolk (Horse) **See:** No. 5708.

3391 Lady Sutton / Centreville Trotting Course, L.I. / Friday May 19th, 1848. Purse $300 mile heats in harness best 3 in 5. James Whelply Bn.M. Lady Sutton 1.1.3.3.3.1. / 1 additional line. 2 columns of 7 lines. J. Cameron on stone. 13x21.1 (Broadside to right, high-wheeled sulky.)
1849 L N.C.

3392 Lady Sutton /   1850 S N.C.

3393 Lady Thorn / By Mambrino Chief, dam a thoroughbred mare by Gano. Best time in harness 2:18, to wagon 2:24 / J. Cameron, Del.
1871 S C&I

3394 Lady Thorn and Mountain Boy / In their great match for $2000, mile heats best 3 in 5 in harness / over the Union Course, L.I., Oct. 7th, 1867. / 3 additional lines, 2 columns of 6 and 7 lines. J. Cameron on stone. 16.15x 26.7 (Broadside to right, high-wheeled sulky.)   1867 L C&I

3395 Lady Thorn and Mountain Boy / Trotting for a Purse of $2000, mile heats best 3 in 5, in harness / on the

Prospect Park Fair Grounds, Brooklyn, L.I. Sept. 3rd, 1867 / 3 additional lines, 2 columns of 5 and 6 lines. J. Cameron 1867 on stone. (Despite difference in location of race, which I have carefully checked, this is evidently the same stone as preceding and date of publication was not changed.)   1867 L C&I

Lady Thorn (Horse) **See:** Nos. 918-9, 932, 5015, 5708, 6169, 6184-5, 6761.

3396 Lady Washington / (Vignette, portrait slightly to right, veil tied under chin.)   und L C&I

3397 Lady Washington /
                            und S N.C.

3398 Lady Washington / Drawn by John Cameron. (Bust to left, veil tied under chin.)   und M C&I

Lady Whitman (Horse) **See:** No. 5436.

3399 Lady Woodruff, Miller's Damsel, General Darcy, and Stella / Trotting for a purse of $800, mile heats. Best time 3 in 5 in harness / Over the Union Course, L.I. May 26th, 1857 / 5 additional lines. L. Maurer '57 on stone. 17x27.10 (¾, broadside to left, grandstand in background.)
                            1857 L C&I

Lady Woodruff (Horse) **See:** No. 6170.

3400 Lady's Bouquet, The / #203 (Vignette, flowers in vase.)
                            1862 S C&I

3401 Lady's Bouquet, The / (Vignette, bouquet in vase, entirely different composition.)   und S C&I

Lafayette, Marquis / **See:** Nos. 1975, 2286-7.

3402 Lafayette / (Bust portrait, military uniform.)   und S C&I

3403 Lafayette at / The Tomb of Washington / Mount Vernon, Va. / #77 / 11.14x8.8 (Upright.)
                            1845 S N.C.

3404 Lafayette Lake / Near Tallahassee, Florida / 8.7x12.7 (Autumn foliage, row boats on lake.)
                            und S C&I

Lahn (Steamship) **See:** No. 5773.

3405 Lake and Forest Scenery / 10x15.6 (Brilliant autumn foliage, hunter and dog in right foreground.)
                            und M C&I

Lake Champlain — Mc'Donough's Victory **See:** No. 4096.

Lake Erie **See:** Nos. 4397, 4754.

3406 Lake George / Black Mountain / 8.2x12.10 (Rowboat with 4 people left foreground, deer and dog in water, man and dog on shore in right foreground.)   und S C&I

3407 Lake George, N.Y. / 8x12.8 (2 deer in foreground.)   und S C&I

3408 Lake George, / White Mountains / 8.2x12.10 (Deer and rowboat.)
                            und S C&I

Lake George **See:** Nos. 324, 6435-6.

Lake Harrison **See:** "Autumn in the Adirondacks" No. 323.

3409 Lake in the Woods, The / 8.7x12.6 (Deer and doe in clearing.)
                            und S C&I

3410 Lake Lugano, Italy /
                            und S C&I

3411 Lake Lugano, Italy / (Group of peasants in right foreground.)
                            und L C&I

3412 Lake Memphremagog / Owl's Head / 8x12.8 (Shepherd and sheep in foreground.)   und S C&I

Lake Memphremagog, **See:** "Bridge at the Outlet" No. 670.

3413 Lake Mohonk / 8.8x12.6 (View from elevation, hotel on far shore.)
                            und S C&I

3414 Lake of the Dismal Swamp, The / (Virginia.)   und L C&I

3415 Lake of the Dismal Swamp, The / (Virginia) 8x12.8 (Crow on tree in right foreground, no other life shown.)
                            und S C&I

3416 Lake Thun — Near the Alps / (Oval.)   und V.S. C&I

3417 Lake Thun — Near the Alps /
                            und S C&I

3418 Lake Winneposgis, Manitoba, Canada /   und S C&I

3419 Lake Winnipiseogee / From Center Harbor, New Hampshire / Painted by F. F. Palmer. 14.6x20.6.
                            und L C&I

3420 Lake Winnipiseogee / (Published on a sheet of landscape views—New York State No. 3439.)   und V.S. C&I

Lake Winnipiseogee **See:** Nos. 955, 3439.

3421 Lakes of Killarney, The / (26 references in 5 columns, and 10 references at top of print.)   1868 S C&I

3422 Lakes of Killarney, The / 56 references of seven lines, 8 columns. 8 references at top of print. 14.11x20.7. 1867 L C&I

3423 Lakeside Home / 9.11x16.15 (Mansion at top of hill, rowboat, swans.) 1869 M C&I

3424 Lamb and the Linnet, The / 8.8 x12.5. und S C&I

Lamphey Palace, England See: No. 3438.

3425 Lancashire Bell Ringers, The / The Most talented and wonderful band of the kind in the world / Performing under the auspices of P. T. Barnum, Proprietor / (At top) Barnum's Gallery of Wonders No. 4.
und S C&I

Lancet (Horse) See: Nos. 2017-8, 6170.

3426 Landing a Trout / (Companion to No. 864, white comic, vignette.) 1879 S C&I

3427 Landing in the Woods, A / 8.8x12.8 (Couple alighting from rowboat.) und S C&I

3428 Landing of Columbus / #427 / 8.6 x12.10 (Boat about to land, Indians on shore.) und S N.C.

3429 Landing of Columbus, The / At San Salvador, Octr. 12th, 1492 / 9x12.15 1876 S C&I

3430 Landing of Columbus, Octr. 11th, 1492, The / 2 additional lines. 1846 S N.C.

3431 Landing of Columbus, Octr. 11th, 1492, The / Then, a broad bright Edenland burst on his raptured gaze / 1847 S N.C.

3432 Landing of the American Forces under Genl. Scott / At Vera Cruz, March 9th, 1847 / 1 additional line. 8.6x13.1. 1847 S N.C.

3433 Landing of the Pilgrims at Plymouth, 11th Dec., 1620 / 8.4x12.11 (Pilgrims around wood fire, others landing from boat, crawling Indian at extreme left.)
und S N.C.

3434 Landing of the Pilgrims at Plymouth, 11th Dec., 1620 O. S. / #235 (Scattered groups coming up hill, 3 men in right foreground, Mayflower in left background.) und S N.C.

3435 Landing of the Pilgrims at Plymouth, Mass., Dec. 22nd, 1620, The /

8.15x12.13 (Pilgrims standing at top of hill, Indian at tree on left, Mayflower in rear.) 1876 S C&I

3436 Landscape and Cattle / (Farm house on right, cattle in stream.) und M C&I

3437 Landscape and Ruins / F. F. Palmer, Del. und M C&I

3438 Landscape Cards / Moonlight and Winter Effects / Magic Lake—Magic Grottoes — Trenton Falls / Village Chapel near Paris—My Cottage Home —Ruins in Sussex, England / The Highlands in Winter—American Farm, Winter — Ruins of Lamphey Palace, England / 2.11x4.3 each (9 miniature views on one sheet.) und S C&I

3439 Landscape Cards / Sylvan Lake—View up the River—View down the River / Sunnyside—Lake Winnipiseogee—The Falls / The Glen—View on the Hudson—Saratoga Lake / 2.11x4.3 each (9 miniature views on one sheet.) und S C&I

3440 Landscape, Fruit and Flowers / F. F. Palmer, Del. 19.12x27.8 (View of the Hudson in background.) 1862 L C&I

3441 Landscape—Morning / about 36x9 (Upright, scene of mountain stream.) und L C&I

Lane, Joseph See: Nos. 2496, 2918.

3442 Lanercost Priory / England / F. F. Palmer, Del. und M C&I

Langham, Nat See: No. 4383.

Lantern (Horse) See: Nos. 1758-9, 4925, 5811, 5170.

3443 Lapped on the Last Quarter / Thos. Worth on stone. (Companion to "Mixed at the Finish" No. 4162 (Vignette, horse comic.) 1880 S C&I

L'Aquitaine (Steamship) See: No. 1233.

3444 Last Ditch of the Chivalry. The, or a President in Petticoats / (Jefferson Davis, disguised as a woman, chased by Union soldiers—vignette.) und M C&I

3445 "Last Ditch" of the Democratic Party, The / J. Cameron on stone. (Vignette, Greeley in water marked "Baltimore" clinging to a log marked "Cincinnati". Politicians trying to pull him out.) und M C&I

3446 Last Gun of the Arctic, The / Stewart Holland / September 27th.

Landscape, Fruit and Flowers.

1854 / The portrait from a daguerreotype of the young hero in possession
of his father / 13.13x10.7 (Upright.)
1855 M N.C.

3447 Last hit in the game, The / A
home run / (Colored comic, vignette.)
1886 S C&I

3448 Last Leaders of Hungary, The /
(5 portraits.)   und S N.C.

3449 Last Shake, The /
1885 S C&I

3450 Last Shot, The / L. Maurer, Del.
17.9x25.8 (Wounded scout shooting Indian about to tomahawk him.)
1858 L C&I

3451 Last Supper, The / Verily I say,
etc. / Apostles keyed.   11.7x16.12.
und M C&I

3452 Last Supper, The / Apostles keyed
in English and Spanish. 7.12x11.5.
und S N.C.

3453 Last Supper, The / Apostles keyed.
7.15x11.11. 33 Spruce Street (Slight
changes in composition.)
und S N.C.

3454 Last Supper, The / La Ultima Sena
/ 7.12x12.4 (1 additional line.)
und S C&I

3455 Last Supper, The / Verily I say
unto you, etc. / Apostles keyed. 8x12.8.
und S C&I

3456 Last Supper, The / Verily I say,
etc. / Apostles keyed. 8x11.8.
und S N.C.

3457 Last War-Whoop, The / Painted
by A. F. Tait. 18.3x25.9 (First state.)
1856 L N.C.

3458 Last War Whoop, The / Painted by
A. F. Tait. Published by Currier &
Ives. 18.3x25.9 (Second state.)
1856 L C&I

3459 Laugh No. 1, The / The Butt of the
Jokers / (Team of spirited horses passing old horse, vignette.)
1879 S C&I

3460 Laugh No. 2, The / The Point of
the Joke / (Decrepit horse passing
fine team, vignette.)
1879 S C&I

3461 Laura / #390 / 8.12x12.4 (¾ length seated, dark decollette dress, red curtain in rear.)   1846 S N.C.

3462 Laura / (½ length portrait, vignette.)   und S C&I

3463 Lawn Tennis at Darktown / A Scientific Player / (Vignette.)   1885 S C&I

3464 Lawn Tennis at Darktown / A Scientific Stroke / (Vignette.)   1885 S C&I

Lawrence, James See: No. 4397.

Lawrence (Frigate) See: No. 4754.

3465 "Laying Back"—Stiff for a Brush / Thos. Worth on stone. (Companion to "Hung Up," etc. No. 2989—vignette.)   1878 S C&I

3466 "Laying Back"—Stiff for a Brush / 2.14x4.12.   1878 V.S. C&I

3467 Le Marechal MacMahon / Grand Commandant / De L'Armee Francaise / 12x9.8 (Vignette, upright.)   und S C&I

3468 Le Petit St. Jean / The Infant St. John. El Chiquito St. Juan / 13x10.   1845 S N.C.

3469 Le Petit St. Jean / El Chiquito St. Juan / The Infant St. John / (Same general composition, larger figures.)   und S N.C.

3470 Le Sauveur Du Monde—El Salvador Del Mundo / The Saviour of the World / (Oval in floral border.)   und S N.C.

3471 Leaders, The / Jay Eye See 2:10; Maud S 2:08¾; St. Julien 2:11¼ / 17.15x27.8 (Heads of horses, printed in oil colors.)   1888 L C&I

Leander (Horse) See: No. 4257.

3472 Learn Something so that you can do something by which you can earn something and honestly possess something / (Vignette, entwined flowers.)   und S C&I

3473 Learning to Ride /   und S C&I

Lebanon (Shakers) See: No. 5475.

3474 Lee at the Grave of Stonewall Jackson /   1872 S C&I

Lee, Robert E. See: Nos. 429, 1484, 1534, 2291-2, 2554, 3962, 4551, 5909-11.

Lee, Robert E. (Steamboat) See: Nos. 2629-30.

Leesburg—Death of Baker See: No. 1475.

Lehigh—Forest Scene on the Lehigh See: No. 2084.

3475 Lend me Your Watch! / #158 (Same composition as "Merry Christmas" No. 4109, second state, upright.)   und S N.C.

3476 Leonora /   und S C&I

3477 Les Membres de Gouvernment Provisoire 24 Fevrier, 1848 / #582 (Lamartine center, surrounded by 12 portraits.)   1848 S N.C.

L'Esperance (Yacht) See: Nos. 5103-5.

3478 Let Not Mercy and / Truth / Forsake Thee / 8 7x12.7 (2 ovals: Good Samaritan helping injured man—open Bible surrounded by flowers.)   1872 S C&I

3479 Letting the Cat Out of the Bag / (Vignette, political cartoon showing Greeley, Lincoln and the editor of the New York Times, while Sumner lets a vicious cat out of the Republican bag.)   und M C&I

3480 Levee—New Orleans, The / W. Walker 1883 on stone. 19.15x29.14 (Printed in oil colors.)   1884 L C&I

Leviathan (Steamship) See: No. 3960.

3481 Lewis Cass / Democratic Candidate for / Twelfth President of the United States / From daguerreotype by Plumbe. #384 (Red curtain, seated.)   1848 S N.C.

3482 Lewis Cass / Democratic Candidate for / Twelfth President and Wm. O. Butler, Democratic Candidate for Vice-President / From daguerreotype by Plumbe. 8.12x12.8 (2 oval portraits in rectangle.)   1848 S N.C.

Lewis, Morgan. See: No. 4193.

3483 Lexington / The great Monarch of the Turf and Sire of Racers / 3 additional lines. (Vignette, profile portrait to right. Similar composition to large folios Nos. 887-8.)   und S C&I

Lexington (Horse) See: Nos. 887-8.

3484 Lexington of 1861, The / The Massachusetts Volunteers fighting their way through the Streets of Baltimore on their march to the defence of the National Capitol, April 19th, 1861. Hurrah for the glorious 6th / 8x12.5.   und S C&I

Lexington (Steamboat) See: No. 327-8.

Lexington, Va. See: No. 409.

3485 Liberty / (Vignette.)
und S C&I

3486 Liberty / (Vignette.)
1876 S C&I

3487 Liberty Frightening the World / (Colored woman as Statue of Liberty holding rooster.) 2.15x5.11 (Used as advertisement for Mansfield Medicine Co. and R. C. Brown & Co., West Broadway & Franklin St., N. Y.)
1884 V.S. C&I

3488 Lieut. Gen. N. B. Forrest /
und S C&I

3489 Lieut. General Ulysses S. Grant at the Siege of Vicksburg, July 4th, 1863 / und S C&I

3490 Lieut. Genl. Ulysses S. Grant / General-in-Chief of the Armies of the United States / #740 11.13x8.15 (Equestrian portrait, right arm at side. Border of stone slightly rounded at corners, upright.)
und S C&I

3491 Lieut. Genl. Ulysses S. Grant / General-in-Chief of the Armies of the United States / 11.11x9.1 (Equestrian on white horse portrait, right hand extended, no rounded corners, upright, other changes in composition.)
und S C&I

3492 Lieut. Genl. Ulysses S. Grant / General-in-Chief of the Armies of the United States / #754 (Vignette portrait.) und S C&I

3493 Lieut. Genl. William T. Sherman / U. S. Army / Facsimile signature above title. (½ length vignette.)
und S C&I

3494 Lieut. Gen. Winfield Scott / Commanding U. S. Army / Facsimile signature. (Vignette.)
1861 L C&I

3495 Lieut. Gen. Winfield Scott / General-in-Chief of the U. S. Army / #477 (¾ length, seated, to left, vignette.)
und S C&I

3496 Lieut. Gen. Winfield Scott / General-in-Chief of the U. S. Army / (½ length to right, vignette.)
und S C&I

3497 Lieut. Gen. Winfield Scott / General-in-Chief of the United States Army / 14x12 (Upright, vignette, full face portrait.) 1861 M C&I

3498 Life and Age of Man, The / Stages of man's life from the cradle to the grave / 8.15x12.12.   und S C&I

3499 Life & Age of Man, The / Stages of man's life from the cradle to the grave / #87 / 11 columns of 4 lines of verse. 8.14x12.13 (Title within plate. 152 Nassau St.)   und S N.C.

3500 Life & Age of Man, The / Stages of man's life, etc. / 2 Spruce St. 8.15x 13.2 (Composition similar to preceding but much finer drawing.)
und S N.C.

3501 Life & Age of Woman, The / Stages of woman's life from the cradle to the grave. / #262—8.14x12.10 (11 scenes.) 1850 S N.C.

3502 Life and Age of Woman, The / Stages of a woman's life from the cradle to the grave / #262 / 8.12x12.13 (About same as preceding with slight changes.) 1850 S N.C.

3503 Life and Death / Place the print at a distance and see a human skull / 11.14x9.14 (Young couple seated. upright.) und S C&I

3504 Life in New York—Cuffy dancing for eels / Catherine Market / #465 / Thos. Worth on stone. (Portrait of F. S. Chanfrau as "Mose.")
1857 S C&I

3505 Life in New York / The Breadth of Fashion—5th Avenue / #463 / Thos. Worth on stone. (Group of overdressed people, vignette.)
und S C&I

3506 Life in New York / That's so! / #464 / Thos. Worth on stone. (Vignette, horse-driven cart upsetting small dog-driven cart, man & woman.)
und S C&I

3507 Life in the camp—Preparing for Supper / Thos. Nast 12-61 on stone. 15.9x21.2. 1863 L C&I

3508 Life in the Country—Evening / F. F. Palmer, Del. 11.5x15.8 (Companion to "Life in the Country—Morning" No. 3509, a Hudson River scene.)
1862 M C&I

3509 Life in the Country—Morning / F. F. Palmer, Del. 11.3x15.7 (A Hudson River scene.) 1862 M C&I

3510 Life in the Country—Morning / und S C&I

3511 Life in the Country / Out for a Day's Shooting / L. Maurer, Del. 17.13 x25.15 (Team and buggy to right, 2 hunters, and 2 dogs running alongside. Later the composition was changed to "Out for a Day's Shooting" No. 4661.) 1859 L C&I

3512 Life in the Country / "The Morning Ride" / L. Maurer on stone. 17.12 x25.15 (Family of 5 in covered carriage.) 1859 L C&I

3513 Life in the Woods—"Returning to Camp" / 18.13x27.10. 1860 L C&I

3514 Life in the Woods—"Starting Out" L. Maurer, Del. 19.4x27.8. 1860 L C&I

3515 Life of a Fireman, The / The Fire —"Now, then with a will—Shake her up, boys!" / L. Maurer, Del. 17.2x25.14 (Republished later "N. Currier" changed to "Currier & Ives." Also used with main title eliminated and "Insured in the American Insurance Co. of Newark, N. J." substituted.) 1854 L N.C.

3516 Life of a Fireman, The / The Metropolitan System / J. Cameron, Del. 17x26.4. 1866 L C&I

3517 Life of a Fireman, The / The new era. Steam and Muscle / C. Parsons, Del. 17.1x25.14 (Scene at Murray and Church Streets. City Hall in background.) 1861 L C&I

3518 Life of a Fireman, The / The Night Alarm—"Start her Lively, boys." / L. Maurer, Del. 16.14x25.14 (Shows the Eagle Co. No. 2 Henry St., N. Y. Included in firemen shown are Nathaniel Currier, J. M. Ives, and George B. Ives. Republished later—"N. Currier" changed to "Currier & Ives.") 1854 L N.C.

3519 Life of a Fireman, The / The Race —"Jump her boys, jump her" / L. Maurer, Del. 16.15x25.13 (Republished later "N. Currier" changed to "Currier & Ives." View of City Hall in background.) 1854 L N.C.

3520 Life of a Fireman, The / The Ruins. "Take Up"—"Man your rope" / L. Maurer, Del. 16.15x26 (Republished later, "N. Currier" changed to "Currier & Ives.") 1854 L N.C.

3521 Life of a Hunter, The / Catching a Tartar / Painted by A. F. Tait. 18.10 x27.4 (Hunter attacked by a stag, companion to following.) 1861 L C&I

3522 Life of a Hunter / A Tight Fix / Painted by A. F. Tait. 18.12x27.1 (This

THE LIFE OF A HUNTER—A TIGHT FIX.

print brought the highest price ever obtained at auction.)
1861 L C&I

3523 Life of a Sportsman, The / Camping in the Woods / 8.7x12.7 (2 huntters, 2 dogs in front of log cabin.)
1872 S C&I

3524 Life of a Sportsman, The / Coming into Camp / 8.8x12.9 (Companion to preceding, 1 hunter, 1 dog in canoe, other hunter and dog on shore.)
1872 S C&I

3525 Life of a Sportsman, The / Going Out / 8.7x12.8 (Hunter & dog in canoe, other hunter pushing canoe from shore.)
1872 S C&I

3526 Life of a Trapper, The / A Sudden Halt / J. Cameron, Del. 17.3x26.4 (Same stone as "Taking The Back Track" No. 5961.)
1866 L C&I

3527 Life on the Prairie / The "Buffalo Hunt" / Painted by A. F. Tait. 18.7x 27.1 (3 hunters on horseback shown.)
1862 L C&I

3528 Life on the Prairie / The Trapper's Defence "Fire Fight Fire" / Painted by A. F. Tait. 18.7x27 2.
1862 L C&I

3529 Light and Shadow / After painting by Gilles. (Portrait of 2 girls, oval, companion to "Past and Future.")
und M C&I

3530 Light Artillery / Th. Nast 1863 on stone.
und M C&I

3531 Light of the Dwelling, The / 10.15 x 8.8 (¾ length, mother and child.)
und S C&I

3532 Lighthouse Point / 2.8x4.11.
und V.S. C&I

3533 Lightning Express, The. / (W. P. D. & G. R. R.)
und S C&I

3534 Lightning Express, The / (To right showing observation car, 3 coaches, tender, and engine going away. vignette.)
und S C&I

3535 "Lightning Express" Trans, The / "Leaving the Junction" F. F. Palmer, Del. 17.14x27.14. (Most dramatic of the railroad prints—moonlight scene.)
1863 L C&I

3536 Lightning Express Trains Leaving the Junction, The / (2 wood-burning engines and cars running to right, team and group of people at R. R. station in rear—daylight scene.)
1871 S C&I

Lightning (Clipper Ship) See: No. 1158.

3537 Lilliputian King / 28 inches high / 16 years old / weighing 35 lbs / Master R. W. Osborn. (Standing on large chair, rounded top corners.)
und S C&I

3538 Lilly / (Head of girl.)
und V.S. C&I

3539 Lily and her Kitty /
und S C&I

3540 Lily Lake / Near St. John, N. B. / 8.8x12.8.
und S C&I

3541 Lime Kiln Club, De / A Temperance Racket / Thos. Worth on stone. (Vignette.)
1883 S C&I

Limerick See: Ireland.

3542 "Limited Express," A / "Five seconds for refreshments" / Thos. Worth on stone. (Vignette.)
1884 S C&I

3543 Lincoln / (Bearded bust, slightly to right, vignette.)
und M C&I

3544 Lincoln At Home / (Mrs. Lincoln-Robert-Thaddeus-President Lincoln.)
1867 S C&I

3545 Lincoln at Home / Mrs. Lincoln-Robert-Thaddeus-President Lincoln / G. Thomas on stone. 16.14x23.13.
1867 L C&I

3546 Lincoln Family The / 8.2x12.8 (Same general composition as preceding.)
1867 S C&I

3547 Lincoln Family, The / 8.1x12.7 (1 line of keys.)
1867 S C&I

3548 Lincoln Statue, The / In Lincoln Square, Washington, D. C. / Unveiled April 14th, 1876 / 3 additional lines. (Vignette, upright.)
und S C&I

3549 Lincoln "Three in one Picture" / Made up of Portraits of Lincoln, Grant & Sherman. (Grant and Sherman are pasted back to back, cut in narrow strips & placed at regular intervals at right angles to the portrait of Lincoln. This enables the spectator to see Sherman from the left, Lincoln from the center, and Grant from the right.)
und S C&I

3550 Lincoln "Three in one Picture" / (Same description as preceding only Grant at left, Lincoln center, Sheridan right.)
und S C&I

Lincoln See: Nos. 11-29, 291, 584, 870, 1471, 1500-2, 2137, 2206, 2510, 2608, 2776, 2887, 2890-6, 3134, 3479,

3543-50, 3634, 4388-9, 4464, 4551, 4820, 4823, 4879, 4880-3, 4960, 5052, 5055, 5113A-4, 5258, 5828, 6105, 6236, 6279, 6510, 6873.

Lind, Jenny **See:** Nos. 1451, 1957, 3198-201.

3551 Line Shot, A—The Aim / Thos. Worth on stone. (Vignette, comic.)
1881 S C&I

3552 Line Shot, A—The Recoil / Thos. Worth on stone. (Vignette, comic.)
1881 S C&I

3553 Lion and the Lamb, The / #562 (Greyhound with rose in its mouth and Bulldog—rounded corners.)
und S N.C.

3554 Lion Hunter, The / #437 / 8.2x13.
und S N.C.

3555 Lions of the Derby, The / Thos. Worth on stone. (Lion riding horse, Uncle Sam waving banner "Iroquois" and Queen Victoria waving banner entitled "Archer"—vignette, comic.)
1881 S C&I

3556 Lions of the Derby, The / Iroquois and Archer / Thos. Worth on stone. (Same stone as preceding except banners are not labelled and title changed.)
1881 S C&I

3557 Lismore Castle / County Waterford / 8x12.6 (Cattle in stream in foreground.)
und S C&I

3558 Literary Debate in the Darktown Club, A / The Question Settled / (Vignette.)
1885 S C&I

3559 Literary Debate in the Darktown Club, A / Settling the Question / Thos. Worth on stone. (Vignette.)
1884 S C&I

3560 Little Alms-Giver, The / "The Lord loveth a cheerful giver" / 8.9x12.1 F. P. (Palmer) on stone. (Full-length figure, girl at poor box, upright.)
und S C&I

3561 Little Anna /
und S C&I

3562 Little Annie / #541 (Vignette, portrait with dog.)
und S C&I

3563 Little Annie / and her Kittie / 11.6x8.6 (Upright.)
1868 S C&I

3564 Little Annie and her Kitties /
und S C&I

3565 Little Arthur / By Glencoe, Dam Blue Bonnets / Painted by R. A. Clarke from the original painting in possession of the New York Jockey Club,

New York, to whom this print is dedicated by the publisher. ("Little Arthur" is also written in background.)
1854 L N.C.

3566 Little Astronomer, The / (Full-length figure, girl, moonlight scene, upright.)
und S C&I

3567 Little Barefoot / 8.8x11.7 (Girl crossing stream on stepping stones.)
1872 S C&I

3568 Little Bashful /
und S C&I

3569 Little Bear, The /
und S C&I

3570 Little Beau, The / 11.8x8.10 (Boy with 2 girls, upright.)
1872 S C&I

3571 Little Beauty, The / 11.9x8.9 (2 boys and girl, upright, girl accepting bouquet, exterior.)
1872 S C&I

3572 Little Beauty / (Vignette, tinted background.)
und M C&I

3573 Little Beggar, The / 8.7x12.15 (Bird and puppies.)
1873 S C&I

3574 Little Belle / (Vignette.)
und S C&I

3575 Little Blossom / 11.2x8.2 (Little girl among flowers, companion to Nos. 3593, 3719, 3721—upright.)
und S C&I

3576 Little Bluebell / (Vignette, girl with bluebells.)
und S C&I

3577 Little Bo-Peep /
und S C&I

3578 Little Bountiful / F. N. on stone. 11.14x8.10 (Little girl feeding pigeons at window.)
und S C&I

3579 Little Bouquet /
1872 S C&I

3580 Little Bouquets / (4 separate groups on one sheet, vignette.)
und S C&I

3581 Little Boy Blue /
und S C&I

3582 Little Brother / 11.6x8.2.
1865 S C&I

3583 Little Brother / (Vignette, bust portrait.)
und S C&I

3584 Little Brother / #586 (Vignette, ¾ length, boy holding puppy in arms, companion to No. 3708.)
und S C&I

3585 Little Brother and I /
und S C&I

3586 Little Brother and Sister / #702 (Slightly rounded corners.)
1863 S C&I

3587 Little Brother and Sister / (Boy with bird's nest.)
1875 S C&I

3588 Little Brother and Sister / (Full length, upright, vignette, children carrying birds.)
und S C&I

3589 Little Brothers / 11.7x8.6 (Full length, seated under trees, companion to No. 3710.)
1875 S C&I

3590 Little Brothers / 11.9x8.5 (Full length, under grape arbor.)
1863 S C&I

Little Brown Jug (Horse) **See:** Nos. 4685, 5708.

3591 Little Brunette / 15.7x12.
und M C&I

3592 Little Busy Bee / 11.9x8.7 (Girl sewing, doll by side.)
1872 S C&I

3593 Little Butterfly / 11.4x8.5 (Companion to Nos. 3575, 3719, 3721. Young child in wheat field, roses, butterflies, etc. Upright.)
und S C&I

3594 Little Caroline /
und S N. C.

3595 Little Carrie / (Vignette.)
und S C&I

3596 Little Cavalier, The /
und S C&I

3597 Little Charlie / (Upright.)
1872 S C&I

3598 Little Charlie and his Horse / Presented free to every subscriber to the White Winged Messenger /
1874 S C&I

3599 Little Charlie / "The Prize Boy" / #705 (Vignette. Entered, etc., 1855 by N. Currier.)
und S C&I

3600 Little Cherubs, The / 11.1x8 (Upright, detail from the "Sistine Madonna.")
und S C&I

3601 Little Chieftain /
und S C&I

3602 Little Children—Love One Another / (Motto.)
und S C&I

3603 Little Colored Pet /
1881 S C&I

3604 Little Daisy / (Vignette, girl carrying sheaf of flowers.)
und S C&I

3605 Little Dolly / (Vignette, upright, holding doll.)
1872 S C&I

3606 Little Dot / (Upright, vignette, head.)
1872 S C&I

3607 Little Dressmaker, The / 11.12x 8.12 (Upright, sewing clothes for doll.)
und S C&I

3608 Little Drummer Boy, The / Rub a Dub Dub / #611 (Vignette, upright, full length, playing Drum. Same composition as "Young America." Slight changes.)
und S C&I

3609 Little Emma / Going to School / (Upright, ¾ length, attractive.)
und S C&I

3610 Little Emmie / (Full length, seated on sofa.)
und S C&I

3611 Little Emmie / 11.15x8.1 (Upright, full length, standing on chair holding doll.)
1872 S C&I

3612 Little Emperor, The / #708 (Full length, Napoleon as a baby.)
und S C&I

3613 Little Ella / (Taken from the painting "Sunday Morning" by Sir John Everett Millais. Full-length figure sitting in church, slightly round corners.)
und S C&I

3614 Little Ellen / #558 (¾ length with flowers.)
und S C&I

3615 Little Eva /
und S C&I

3616 Little Fairy / 12x8.7 (Full length, wand in hand.)
und S C&I

3617 Little Fannie / (Holding doll.)
und S C&I

3618 Little Fanny /
und S N.C.

3619 Little Favorite, The / W. K. Hewitt on stone. 10x7.12 (Oval, child and bird.)
und S N.C.

3620 Little Favorite, The / 10x7.10 (Same composition as preceding with slight changes.)
und S N.C.

3621 Little Favorite, The / #103 / 11.13 x8.3 (Geometrical border, steeple top.)
und S N.C.

3622 Little Fireman, The / L. Maurer, Del. 25x18.4 ("Young America Chief Engineer" — full length tinted background, rounded corners.)
1857 L C&I

3623 Little Flora / (¾ length figure vignetted.)
1874 S C&I

3624 Little Flora / Presented to subscribers to "The Home," a monthly journal /
1879 S C&I

3625 Little Flower Gatherer /
und S C&I

3626 Little Flower Girl, The / #589 /
12.2x8.15 (This print is erroneously
dated 1853; it was really published in
1863 and is a companion to No. 3632
"Little Fruit Girl." Full-length figure,
slightly rounded corners.)
1853 S C&I

3627 Little Flower Girl, The / (Vignette.)   1863 S C&I

3628 Little Flower Girl / (Vignette.)
und S C&I

3629 Little Folks in the Country /
8.8 (5 children under tree.)
und S C&I
Little Fred See: No. 5436.

3630 Little Freddie /
und S C&I

3631 Little Fruit Bearer / (Upright,
vignette.)   1873 S C&I

3632 Little Fruit Girl, The / #590 / 12
x8.12 (Full length, slightly rounded
corners, companion to No. 3626.)
1863 S C&I

3633 Little Fruit Girl / (Vignette, bust
portrait, little girl holding peach and
cherries in right hand.)
und S C&I

3634 Little Game of Bagatelle between
Old Abe, the railsplitter, and Little
Mac, the gunboat general /
und S C&I

3635 Little Georgie / (Upright, vignette,
full-length figure.)
und S C&I

3636 Little Groggy, A / Thos. Worth on
stone. (Boxing comic, companion to
No. 1224.)   1884 S C&I

3637 Little Harry / #617 (¾, top corners
round.)   und S N.C.

3638 Little Harry / (Vignette, ½ length,
kitten on chair.)   und S C&I

3639 Little Hero / (¾ length, vignette.)
und S C&I

3640 Little "High Strung," A / Thos.
Worth on stone. (Horse rearing and
scattering buyers at auction sale,
comic.)   1879 S C&I

3641 Little Highlander, The / #709 /
11.13x8.12 (Upright.)
und S C&I

3642 Little Jamie /   und S C&I

3643 Little Jane /   und S C&I

3644 Little Jane / #615 (¾ length, top
corners rounded.)   und S N.C.

3645 Little Janice /   und S C&I

3646 Little Jennie / (Vignette, ¾ length,
holding bird.)   und S C&I

3647 Little Johnnie and Bessie /.
und S C&I

3648 Little Johnnie /
und S C&I

3649 Little Julia / #608 (Vignette.)
und S C&I

3650 Little Kate / #321 (¾ length, vignette portrait, red coat, rose in hair.)
1851 S N.C.

3651 Little Kate /   und S C&I

3652 Little Katie / (¾ length, vignette,
holding watch.)   und S C&I

3653 Little Kittie and Her Kits /
und S C&I

3654 Little Kitties among the Roses /
1873 S C&I

3655 Little Kitty / (Vignette, little girl
holding kitten.)   und S C&I

3656 Little Lily / (¾ length of child
holding flowers.)   und S C&I

3657 Little Lizzie / (Vignette, portrait,
roses in lap and hand.)
und S C&I

3658 Little Lizzy / #324 (Vignette, top
corners rounded.)   und S C&I

3659 Little Lulu / So Sleepy / (¾ length,
in church, companion to "Little Ella"
No. 3613.)   und S C&I

3660 Little Maggie / (Vignette.)
und S C&I

3661 Little Mamie / (½ length portrait,
rose in hand.)   1875 S C&I

3662 Little Mamma, The / #194 / 10.2
x7.12 (Full-length figures, boy and
girl.)   und S N.C.

3663 Little Manly / (Full length, seated,
upright, vignette.)
1874 S C&I

3664 Little Martha / #320 (Vignette.)
und S C&I

3665 Little Martha / #320 (Girl and dog,
top corners rounded.)
und S C&I

3666 Little Martha / (Vignette portrait,
shawl over head.)   1873 S C&I

3667 Little Mary / #322 (Vignette.)
und S N.C.

3668 Little Mary /   und S C&I

3669 Little Mary and Her Lamb /
und S C&I

3670 Little Mary and the Lamb / Mary
had a little lamb, its fleece was white
as snow, etc. / 11.8x8.8.
1877 S C&I

3671 Little May Blossom / (Vignette,
½ length, bouquet in hand.)
1874 S C&I

3672 Little May Blossom /
und S C&I

3673 Little May Queen / 11.10x8.4 (Child
sitting, holding flowers, flowers also
in hair, full length.)
und S C&I

3674 Little May Queen / (Vignette, full-length
figure, girl holding cornucopia filled with
flowers.)   und S C&I

3675 Little Mechanic, The / 12x8.6 (Upright, child on carpenter's bench.)
und S C&I

3676 Little Merry Boy /
und S C&I

3677 Little Minnie / (½ length with
black cat, vignette.)
1862 S C&I

3678 Little Minnie / "Taking Tea" /
und S C&I

3679 "Little More Grape Capt. Bragg,"
A / Gen. Taylor at the Battle of Buena
Vista, Feby 23rd, 1847 / #474 / 8.4
x12.11. J. Cameron on stone. (Taylor
at right on white horse, sword upraised.)   1847 S N.C.

3680 "Little More Grape Capt. Bragg,"
A / #474 / Same title as preceding. J.
Cameron on stone. 8x12.8 (Sword low-
ered and other changes in composition.)   1847 S N.C.

3681 Little Mother, The /
und S C&I

3682 Little Mourner / 8.8x11.6 (Girl with
dead bird in hand.)
1872 S C&I

3683 Little Nellie / 10.8x8.13 (Oval, full
length seated, blue curtain, window at
right.)   und S C&I

3684 Little Nelly / #614 (Seated, full
length open window at left.)
und S C&I

3685 Little Orphan Girl, The /
und S C&I

3686 Little Pets, The / #452 / 11.14x9
(Full-length portrait, girl on rustic

bench, white kitten and cat alongside,
vignette, slightly rounded corners.)
und S C&I

3687 Little Pilgrims, The. / 11.12x8.12
(Boy and girl bearing crosses.)
1873 S C&I

3688 Little Playfellow, The / #104 (Boy
and girl, ornamental border.)
und S N.C.

3689 Little Playmates, The / #173 / 11.13
x8.8.   und S N.C.

3690 Little Potato Bugs /
und S N.C.

3691 Little Protector, The / 2 Spruce St.
& 169 Broadway. 10.3x7.14 (Boy with
sword, and girl seated on bench.)
und S C&I

3692 Little Protector, The / 11.12x8.7
(Upright.)   1867 S C&I

3693 Little Prudy / (Vignette.)
und S C&I

3694 Little Recruit, The / 15.13x13
(Mother and young girl getting child
ready to join other children outside
playing war.)   1863 M C&I

3695 Little Red Riding Hood / Painted
by J. Sant, A.R.A.
und L C&I

3696 Little Red Riding Hood / 12x8.11
(With dog.)   und S C&I

3697 Little Rosebud / (Vignette.)
1870 S C&I

3698 Little Saint John Baptist / 11.9x8.8
(Staff with streamer "Ecce Agnus
Dei," upright.)   und S C&I

3699 Little Sarah / #183 (Vignette,
seated at table.)   und S N.C.

3700 Little Sarah / (Vignette, with cat.)
1862 S C&I

3701 Little Sarah / (¾ length, holding
kitten.)   1874 S C&I

3702 Little Sarah / (Full length, seated
on floor with doll, vignette.)
1876 S C&I

3703 Little Scholar, The / (Vignette, ½
length of girl at table.)
und S C&I

3704 Little "76" / (¾ length boy with
sword and military costume, upright.)
1876 S C&I

3705 Little Shore Bird /
und S C&I

3706 Little Sister /   1865 S C&I

3707 Little Sister / 11.12x8.5 (Full length, seated on sofa, not vignette.) 1878 S C&I

3708 Little Sister / #587 (Vignette, half length, holding puppy, companion to No. 3584.) und S C&I

3709 Little Sister / (Vignette, bust figure, with locket.) und S C&I

3710 Little Sisters / 11.9x8.10 (Full length, wearing pantalettes, under tree, companion to No. 3589.) 1875 S C&I

3711 Little Sisters / #610 (Full length, red dress, slightly rounded corners.) und S C&I

3712 Little Sister's First Step / 11.2x8.6 (Interior, older child teaching young one to walk. Full length, upright.) 1872 S C&I

3713 Little Sister's First Step / (Full length.) und S C&I

3714 Little Sisters Ride / (3 children on hobby horse, upright.) und S C&I

3715 Little Sisters, The / (Full length, not under tree, pantalettes.) und S C&I

3716 Little Sisters, The / 13.12x10.11 (Full length, upright, 1 with kitten, other with doll under arbor, pantalettes, slightly rounded corners.) 1865 M C&I

3717 Little Sisters, The / 15.8x12.12 (Group of 3, ¾ length vignette.) 1862 M C&I

3718 Little Sleepy / (Companion to "Wide Awake" No. 6657.) und S C&I

3719 Little Snowbird / 11.4x8.4 (Companion to Nos. 3575, 3593, 3721. Upright, full length, child feeding sparrow, snow scene.) und S C&I

3720 Little Students, The / 11.4x8.9 (Oval.) und S C&I

3721 Little Sunbeam / 11.2x8.2 (Companion to Nos. 3575, 3593, 3719. Full length.) und S C&I

3722 Little Sunshine / Brown, Del. 1868 S C&I

3723 Little Sweetheart / (Girl holding fan and flowers, vignette.) 1875 S C&I

3724 Little Tea Party, The / 12x8.8 (Exterior scene, upright, 2 children with doll.) und S C&I

3725 Little Teacher, The / R. Kluth on stone. 11.11x8.2 (Upright, full length, 2 girls.) und S C&I

3726 Little Thoughtful / und S C&I

3727 Little Violet / (½ length, flowers in hair, and holding bouquet.) 1874 S C&I

3728 Little Volunteer, The / 1861 S C&I

3729 Little Volunteers, The / und S C&I

3730 Little Wanderer, The / F. F. Palmer, Del. 13.14x9.15 (Chicken straying from brood.) 1867 S C&I

3731 Little White Doggies / Into Mischief / 8.2x12.8 (Pulling milk bottle from table.) 1877 S C&I

3732 Little White Kitties / Eating Cake / und S C&I

3733 Little White Kitties / Fishing / 8.5x12.4. 1871 S C&I

3734 Little White Kitties / Into Mischief / 8.1x12.10 (Overturned vase of flowers and milk.) 1871 S C&I

3735 Little White Kitties / Playing Ball / und S C&I

3736 Little Wildflower / #510 / 11.1x8.4 (Upright, full length figure of girl in flower-covered field.) und S C&I

3737 Little William and Mary / (Upright, vignette.) und S C&I

3738 Little Willie / (Vignette, Scotch costume.) und S C&I

3739 Little Yachtsman, The / 12.2x8.15 (Full length, standing on pier, leaning against stanchion.) 1875 S C&I

3740 Little Zouave, The / "Up boys, and at them" / #300 (Upright, vignette.) 1861 S C&I

3741 Living Chinese Family, The / Arrived in New York, April 1850. In the ship Lanthe, Capt. Johnson from Canton / Exhibited under the auspices of P. T. Barnum, Proprietor of American and Chinese museums New York and Barnum's Museum Philadelphia / #708/ 8.5x12.5 (3 lines, names, ages, etc. under figures within stone.) 1850 S N.C.

3742 Livingston Guards Quick Step / 1844 S N.C.

Livingston, Robert **See:** No. 1530.
Livonia (Yacht) **See:** No. 5040.

3743 Lizzie / 15x13.
und S C&I

3744 Llewellyn — The Great / 11.8x8.8
(Upright, knight on horseback, castle
in background.) und S N.C.

3745 Loading Cotton / (Same stone as
"On the Mississippi" No. 4607 showing
the New Orleans Packet "Eclipse.")
1870 S C&I

3746 Lobster Sauce /
und S N.C.

3747 Lobster Sauce / 15x21.
und M N.C.

Locke, G. E. **See:** No. 6823.

3748 Log Cabin or Tippecanoe Waltz /
Composed and Respectfully Dedicated
to General Wm. H. Harrison by Wm.
C. Raynor / und S N.C.

Logan, John A. **See:** Nos. 2910,
5490, 5567.

3749 Lola Montez / (½ length, red dress,
riding crop in hand.)
und S N.C.

3750 Lola Montez as Mariquita / In the
Ballet du Jour de Carneval of Seville /
#419 / 11.12x8.7 (Upright.)
und S N.C.

3751 Lola Montez, Belle of the West /
und S N.C.

3752 London from Kew Gardens (St.
Paul's in the distance) / 8.7x12.8.
und S C&I

London **See:** Nos. 1325-6.

3753 Londonderry, Ireland / 7.15x12.7.
und S C&I

3754 Londonderry / Ireland.
und L C&I

3755 Londonderry / On the River Foyle,
Ireland / 8.7x12.6.
und S C&I

Long Branch, N.J. (Track) **See:** No.
2735.

3756 Long Island Sound / 9.14x17
(Steamer and sailing boats shown,
rocky shore on right.)
1869 M C&I

3757 Long Live the Republic / We Swear
to Defend It and Die For It /
und M N.C.

3758 Longfellow / (Poet) (Vignette.)
1881 S C&I

3759 Longfellow / By Lexington, dam
Nantura by Brawner's Eclipse, / the

property of John Harper of Kentucky,
etc. / J. Cameron on stone. (Under saddle, vignette, profile to left.)
1871 S C&I

Longfellow (Horse) **See:** Nos.
2735-6.

Longfellow, H. W. — Steam Catamaran See: No. 5720.

Longstreet, Genl. **See:** No. 429.

3760 Look at Mama / #229 / 11.4x8.10
(Upright, mother showing portrait of
herself to boy.) und S N.C.

3761 Look at Mama / 11.10x8.9 (Upright,
mother showing boy portrait of herself.) 1872 S C&I

3762 Look at Mamma / (Upright, mother
showing daughter portrait of herself.)
und S N.C.

3763 Look at Papa / 12.1x8.11 (Upright,
mother holding boy up to picture on
wall, on left.) und S N.C.

3764 Look at Papa / 11.11x8.8 (Upright,
mother holding boy up to portrait of
father on wall, at right.)
und S C&I

3765 Look at Papa / 11.10x8.9 (Mother
showing young child portrait of father
in locket, no picture on wall.)
1872 S C&I

3766 Look at Papa / 11.12x8.10 (Picture
at left, mother holding child.)
und S N.C.

3767 Looking down the Yo-Semite / 8.8
x12.8. und S C&I

3768 Looking In / #494 / 8.7x12.2 (Man
reading "Spirit of the Times" which
shows advertisement by N. Currier.)
und S N.C.

3769 Looking Out / #495 (Brigand in
window with gun.)
und S N.C.

3770 Looking Unto Jesus / 8.10x10.9
(Oval portrait of woman.)
1870 S C&I

3771 Lookout Mountain, Tennessee / And
the Chattanooga Rail Road / F. F. Palmer, Del. 15x20.7.
1866 L C&I

3771A Lord be with You, The / (Motto.
Flowers in background, hummingbird,
no basket, vignette.)
und S C&I

3772 Lord be with You, The / (Motto —
basket of autumn fruits, vignette.)
1872 S C&I

3773 Lord be with You, The /
1878 S C&I

3774 Lord's Prayer, The / (Vignette of
"The Last Supper," the prayer in a
scroll.) und S N.C.

3775 Lord's Prayer, The /
und S C&I

3776 Lord's Prayer, The & The Angelical
Salutation / #300 (Ornate border,
group of religious pictures.)
und S N.C.

3777 Lord Byron / Published by Atwill,
201 Broadway / E. Brown, Del. (Vignette, full-length figure, ornamental
border.) und S N.C.

3778 Lord's Supper, The / Title repeated
in French and Spanish. 2 additional
lines Biblical quotation. 13 keys. Published by N. Currier Tract House, N.Y.
und S N.C.

Lorillard, Pierre See: No. 4255.

3779 Loss of the Steamboat Swallow /
While on her trip, from Albany / to
New York on Monday Evening, April
17th, 1845 / 1 additional line. 8.2x12.7.
1845 S N.C.

3780 Loss of the Steamer "Cimbria" /
On her voyage from Hamburg to New
York, January 19th, 1883 / The Cimbria was run down by the British Sultan, etc. / 8.5x13.11.
1883 S C&I

3781 Loss of the U.S.M. Steam Ship
Arctic / Off Cape Race, Wednesday
September 27th, 1854 / 2 additional
lines. #352. 8.6x12.13.
1854 S N.C.

3782 Lost / #672 / 8.10x12.10 (Domino
holding blank cards, dejected. Companion to "Won" See: No. 6756.
und S N.C.

3783 Lost Cause, The / 8.7x12.8 (Southern Soldier weeping at 2 graves, his
home in background, not vignette.)
1872 S C&I

3784 Lost in the Snow / Dogs of St.
Bernard / 8.8x12.8.
und S C&I

3785 Lottie / und S C&I

3786 Loue Soit A Jamais J. C. Dans le
tres Saint Sacrement de L' Autel /.
und S N.C.

3787 Louis Kossuth, / General in Chief
And President Of Hungarian States /
8.12x11.15. (Full length in military
uniform.) 1849 S N.C.

3788 Louis Kossuth and his Staff /
und S N.C.

3789 Louis Napoleon Bonaparte / Ne / à
Paris, le 20 avril, 1808 / Elected 1st
President of France, Dec. 10th, 1848 /
8.11x11.12 #645 (¾ length, Paris
through window, facsimile signature.)
1849 S N.C.

3790 Louisa / 1850 S N.C.

3791 Louisa / 8.12x12.8 (¾ length, flow-
ered dress, red cape over left shoulder,
plain background.)
1849 S N.C.

3792 Louisa / (Half length.)
und S N.C.

3793 Louisa / #135 (Full length, white
dress.) und S N.C.

3794 Louisa / (Full length, seated on
settee.) und S N.C.

3795 Louisa V. Parker as Eva in "Uncle
Tom's Cabin." / J. L. Magee, Del.
und S C.C.

Louisiana See: Nos. 50, 385, 1099-
100, 3480, 5254, 5915.

Louisiana (Battles) See: Nos. 417-
18, 3480, 5915.

3796 Love is the Lightest / 8.9x11.14
(Woman balancing Cupid and butterfly
in scales 4 rounded corners.)
1847 S N.C.

3797 Love is the Lightest / (Vignette,
same idea as above but changes in
composition.) und S C&I

3798 Love Letter, The / #210 / 12.1x8.6
(Full length, round corners, composition same as No. 4296.)
und S N.C.

3799 Love Letter, The / (Full-length figure girl, rounded corners.)
und S N.C.

3800 Love Life at Windsor Castle / Albert and Victoria in 1842 /
und S C&I

3801 Love's Light / Makes Home Bright/
(Motto, entwined flowers, vignette.)
1874 S C&I

3802 Love one Another / (Motto, bouquet of flowers, vignette.)
und S C&I

3803 Love the Old Dog, Too / (Girl with
dog and puppy.) und S C&I

3804 Lovely Calm, A / (Colored comic,
vignette, companion to No. 559.)
1879 S C&I

3805 Lovers, The / #435 / 11.11x8.8 (Full-length figures under tree.) 1846 S N.C.

3806 Lovers, The / #435 / 11.10x8.8 (Full-length figures under tree, slightly different composition and moonlight scene.) und S C&I

3807 Lover's Adieu, The / #525 / 11.9x 8.8 (Upright, ¾ length figures, marine scene thru window at left.) 1852 S N.C.

3808 Lover's Adieu, The / #525 / 11.15x 9.14 (Upright, ¾ length, window on right, red curtain.) und S N.C.

3809 Lover's Leap / 1886 S C&I

3810 Lover's Quarrel, The / #167. 1846 S N.C.

3811 Lover's Quarrel, The / #443 / 11.12 x9.8 (Slight changes in composition from preceding.) 1846 S N.C.

3812 Lover's Quarrel, The / #167 / 11.14 x8.9 (Clothes of man and woman changed from preceding.) und S C&I

3813 Lovers Reconciliation, The / #168 (Feather in girl's hair.) 1846 S N.C.

3814 Lovers Reconciliation, The / #442 / 11.12x8.8. 1846 S N.C.

3815 Lovers Reconciliation, The / #168 / 11.12x8.9 (Similar to No. 3813 rose in girl's hair and other changes in composition.) und S C&I

3816 Lovers Reconciliation, The / #442 (Girl has arms crossed, fan in right hand, feathers under hat, different from No. 3813.) 1846 S N.C.

3817 Lover's Return, The / #526 (¾ length.) 1852 S N.C.

3818 Lover's Return, The / #526 / 11.14x 8.9 (Girl with white dress, ribbon around waist, rose in hair, red curtain.) 1846 S N.C.

3819 Lover's Walk, The / #685 (Upright.) 1849 S N.C.

3820 Lover's Walk, The / 11.14x8.9. und S C&I

3821 Love's Light / Makes Home Bright/ (Vignette, motto entwined, flowers.) 1874 S C&I

3822 Love's Messenger / und S N.C.

3823 Low Pressure Steamboat "Isaac Newton", The / Passing the Palisades

on the Hudson / Ch. Parsons, Del. 16.4 x28.4 (1 of the most attractive Hudson River scenes.) 1855 L N.C.

3824 Low Water in the Mississippi / F. F. Palmer / 17.15x27.15 (R. E. Lee on steamer, companion to "High water in the Mississippi" No. 2819.) 1868 L C&I

3825 Lower Lake of Killarney, The / Kerry County, Ireland / #556 / 7.15x 12.7 (A very attractive view.) und S C&I

3826 Loyal Union League Certificate / 9x12.8. 1863 S C&I

Lucania (Steamship) See: No. 6260.

3827 Lucille / By Exchequer / Record 2:21 / (Vignette, high-wheeled sulky, broadside to left.) 1878 S C&I

3828 Lucille Golddust / Driven by Chas. S. Green / Record 2:16½ / J. Cameron on stone. 1871 S C&I

Lucille Golddust (Horse) See: No. 920.

3829 Lucky Escape, The / F. Palmer, Del. (Group of children beside stream trying to recapture fish and eels which have escaped from pail.) und M N.C.

3830 Lucretia / (¾ length, profile to right, seated, arm on table. red waist, white dress.) und S N.C.

3831 Lucretia / #268 (Full length, red dress, playing mandolin.) und S N.C.

3832 Lucretia R. Garfield / Wife of James A. Garfield / Twentieth President of the United States / und S C&I

3833 Lucy / (Half length, blue dress, white shawl, vignette.) und S N.C.

3834 Lucy / (¾ length seated, white dress, red curtain on right.) und S N.C.

3835 Lucy / #117 / Sarony on stone. 12.1 x 8.11 (Full length, seated on settee.) und S N.C.

3836 Lucy / By Geo. M. Patchen, dam by May Day, Son of Henry / Record 2:18¼ / Driven by Orrin Hickok / J. Cameron on stone. 1871 S C&I

3837 Lucy Record 2:15 Driven by Sam Keyes / und S C&I

Lucy (Horse) See: Nos. 711, 921,

1908, 2422, 2448, 2663, 5931, 6184-5, 6189-90.

3838 Ludvig Kossuth / The Hungarian Leader / 3 additional lines. #695 / 11.15 x9 (Upright, ¾ length, military uniform.)   1849 S N.C.

3839 Luggelaw / County Wicklaw-Ireland / 8.6x12.7.   und S C&I

3840 Luke Blackburn / By Bonnie Scotland, Dam Nevada / E. Forbes on stone. (Vignette, profile portrait to right, standing.)   1880 S C&I

3841 Luke Blackburn / (Vignette.)
                         1881 V.S. C&I

3842 Lula / Bay Mare, by Alexander's Norman, Dam by Imp. Hooten / Owned by Mr. Joseph Harker, of N.Y. Trained and Driven by Ch. S. Green, Babylon, L.I. / Record 2:15½ Aug. 14th, 1875 / Thos. Worth on stone. 2 columns of 2

lines. 16.9x24.13. (High-wheeled sulky, broadside to right.)
                         1876 L C&I

3843 Lula / Record 2:15 Driven by Chas. S. Green /   1877 S C&I
    Lula (Horse) See: Nos. 922-3.

3844 Luscious Peaches /
                         und S C&I

3845 Luxury of Tobacco, The / "To take an occasional chew" / Is a thing I delight to do. / Your chewing is well enough / but it isn't up to snuff / I get the cream of the joke / You chew and take snuff, and I smoke" / Thos. Worth on stone.   1876 S C&I

3846 Lydia / (¾ length, playing harp.)
                         und S N.C.
    Lyon, Brig. Gen. Nathaniel See: Nos. 387, 677, 682, 1483.
    Lysander (Horse) See: No. 4257.

M

3847 "Mac" / June 28th, 1853. In a match with "Tacony" over the Union Course, L.I. / 2 additional lines and 2 columns of 5 and 4 lines. L. Maurer '53 on stone. 17.5x26.4 (Broadside to right, high-wheeled sulky.)   1853 L C&I

3848 Mac and Zachery Taylor / In the great contest at Hunting Park Course, Phila. July 18th, 1849 / For the championship of the turf / Mac victorious / 1 additional line and 2 columns of 6 and 5 lines. Detailed description of Hunting Park contest at bottom left of 24 lines. Detailed description of Cambridge Park contest, July 14, 1849 at bottom right. H. Delattre, Del. 12.10x 20.13 (Broadside to right, under saddle, grandstand in rear.)
                         1851 L N.C.
    Mac (Horse See: No. 5943.

3849 Mac-cut-mish-e-ca-cu-cac / or / Black / Hawk / Celebrated Sac Chief / Painted from life by J. O. Lewis at Detroit 1833 / Entered 1836 by J. O. Lewis / (Vignette.)
                         und S C.C.
    MacMahon See: No. 3467.
    Mace, Dan See: Nos. 1760, 2638, 2930, 5469, 5649, 5708, 6225.
    Mace, Jem See: No. 3195.
    Macedonian, H. B. M. See: No. 6311.

3850 Machinery Hall / Grand United States Centennial Exhibition, 1876 / Fairmount Park, Philadelphia / 2 col-

umns, 2 lines of description. 7.15x12.15.
                         und S C&I

3851 Madame Celeste as "Miami" / In Buckstone's Celebrated Drama / Green Bushes / #606 / 8.14x12.2 (Full length figure as Indian huntress.)
                         1848 S N.C.

3852 Made. Vestris / published by J. & H. G. Langley — 57 Chatham Street, N.Y. Henry Heidemans 1838 on stone. (½ length figure, vignette.)
                         1838 S N.C.
    Madeleine (Yacht) See: Nos. 5432, 6803.
    Madison, James See: No. 3171.

3853 Madison, The Capitol of Wisconsin/ Taken from the Water Cure, South Side of Lake Menona, 1855 /
                         1855 S C.C.
    Madge, (Yacht) See: Nos. 1340, 5439.

3854 Madle Taglioni As La Bayadere / (Full length figure, top corners plate line rounded.)   1847 S N.C.

3855 Madlle Augusta In La Bayadere / Henri Heidemans 1837 on stone.
                         1837 S N.C.

3856 Madlle Augusta In La Bayadere / und S N.C.

3857 Madlle Celeste / As The / Wild Arab Boy /   und S N.C.

3858 Madlle Fanny Elssler In "La Taran-

tule" / W. K. H. (Hewitt) on stone.
#79 (Full length figure.)
und S N.C.

3859 Madlle Fanny Elssler In The Cracovienne / #80. und S N.C.

3860 Madlle Taglioni As La Bayadere / Sarony, Del. und S N.C.

3861 Madonna Di San Sisto /
und S C&I

3862 Madonna Of The Shawl /
und S C&I

3863 Magadino, Lake Maggiore / Canton Tessin, Switzerland /
und L C&I

3864 Maggie / (Vignette, head.)
und S C&I

Magic, (Yacht) See: Nos. 2625, 5433-4.

3865 Magic Cure, The / (2 views on 1 sheet, colored man revives at sight of Watermelon, vignette.)
1890 S C&I

3866 Magic Grottoes / 2.11x4.3 (Published on a sheet of landscape cards, No. 3438.) und V.S. C&I

3867 Magic Grottoes /
1870 S C&I

3868 Magic Grottoes, The / 10.7x14.15.
1870 M C&I

3869 Magic Lake / 2.11x4.3 (Published on a sheet of landscape cards, No. 3438.) und V.S. C&I

3870 Magic Lake / 10.8x14.8.
und M C&I

3871 Magic Lake, The / 10.9x15.1 (Slight changes in composition.)
und M C&I

3872 Magnificent Building For The World's Fair Of 1851 / Built of iron and glass, in Hyde Park, London / 2 additional lines. At top — The Crystal Palace / #105. und S N.C.

3873 Magnificent New Steamer "Priscilla" Built of Steel and Iron, The /.
und S C&I

3874 Magnificent New Steamer "Puritan" Built of Steel and Iron, The / 1 of the fleet forming the Fall River Line, etc. / At left 3 additional lines. 9.13x15.6. 1889 M C&I

3875 Magnificent New Steamer "Puritan" Built of Steel and Iron, The / 1 of the fleet forming the Fall River Line, etc. / At left 3 additional lines.
1889 S C&I

3876 Magnificent New Steamship "City of Rome" 8415 Tons Of The Anchor Line / 2 columns, 2 lines dimensions.
und S C&I

3877 Magnificent O'Connell Funeral Car, The / Passing the Park in New York City, on Wednesday, Sept. 22nd, 1847 / 1 additional line & 2 columns of 1 line/ #535, 7.15x12.12. 1847 S N.C.

3878 Magnificent Steamship "Britannic" Of the White Star Line / 1 additional line description. und S C&I

3879 Magnificent Steamship "City Of New York" / Of the Inman Line / 2 additional lines. 8 x 14.12. und S C&I

3880 Magnificent Steamship "City Of Paris", The / Of the Inman Line / 2 additional lines. und S C&I

3881 Magnificent Steamship "City Of Rome" 8415 Tons of the Anchor Line, The / Between New York and Liverpool / 2 additional columns of 2 lines.
und S C&I

3882 Magnificent Steamship "Germanic" of the White Star Line / 1 additional line. Length 468 ft. Breadth 45 ft. Tonnage 5004. Horsepower 4500. 7.8x14.4.
und S C&I

3883 Magnificent Steamship "Majestic" of the White Star Line, The /
und S C&I

3884 Magnificent Steamship "New York" of the American Line, The / 2 additional lines. und S C&I

3885 Magnificent Steamship "Paris" of the American Line, The / 2 additional lines. und S C&I

3886 Magnificent Steamship "St. Louis" of the American Line, The / 2 additional lines. und S C&I

3887 Magnificent Steamships, The / Egypt and Spain / Of the National Steamship Line between New York and Liverpool / Off Sandy Hook entering and leaving the Port of New York / Drawn and on stone by C. R. Parsons. 21.6x33.12. 1879 L C&I

3888 Maiden Rock / Mississippi River / 7.15x12.8 (2 steamers passing, daylight scene.) und S C&I

3889 Maiden Rock / Mississippi River / (Steamers large and slight changes in composition, moonlight scene.)
und S C&I

3890 Maiden's Prayer, The /
und S C&I

3891 Maiden's Rock / Mississippi River / (Identical composition to No. 3888 — with exception of title.) 7.15x12.8.
und S C&I

3892 Main Building / Grand United States Centennial Exhibition 1876 / Fairmount Park, Philadelphia / 2 additional lines. 7.14x12.14.
1876 S C&I

3893 Main of Cocks, A / The first battle / 10x14. (Vignette.)
und M C&I

Maine See: Nos. 117-8, 190, 4186.

Majestic (Steamship) See: Nos. 3883, 5774.

3894 Maine Giantess, The / Miss Silva Hardy, nearly 8 feet high / (at top) Barnum's Gallery of Wonders, No. 10.
und S C&I

3895 Maj. Gen. Franz Sigel / The hero of the west / und S C&I

3896 Maj. Gen. John C. Fremont / U.S. Army / (¾ length, vignette.)
und S C&I

3897 Maj. Gen. Philip H. Sheridan / U.S. Army / (Facsimile signature, vignette.) und S C&I

3898 Maj. Gen. Philip H. Sheridan / Rallying his troops at the battle of Cedar Creek, Va. after his famous ride from Winchester, October 19th, 1864 / (Equestrian portrait, right hand upraised with sword, top corners plate line slightly rounded.)
und S C&I

3899 Majolica / Owned by Nathan Straus, driven by John Murphy / Record 2:17 / 1885 L C&I

3900 Majolica — Record 2:15 / 2.12x4.12.
1885 V.S. C&I

Majolica See: Nos. 1861, 6163.

3901 Majr. Genl. Ambrose E. Burnside / Commander in Chief of the Army of the Potomac / (Full length equestrian portrait, head to right.)
1862 S C&I

3902 Majr. Genl. Ambrose E. Burnside / At the battle of Fredericksburg, Va., Decr. 13th, 1862 / (Equestrian portrait, upright.) 1863 S C&I

3903 Major Gen. Benj. F. Butler / Of Massachusetts / (Vignette portrait, in uniform.) und S C&I

3904 Maj. Genl. Franz Sigel / The Hero of the West / und S C&I

3905 Majr. Genl. George B. McClellan / At the Battle of Antietam, Md. Sept.

17th, 1862 / 11.15x8.10 (Upright, on horseback to left, sword in upraised right hand.) 1862 S C&I

3906 Majr. Genl. Geo. B. McClellan / General-in-Chief of the U.S. Army / und S C&I

3907 Majr. Genl. George B. McClellan / The people's choice for Seventeenth President of the United States / #753 / (Bust portrait slightly to left, vignette, facsimile signature "Geo. B. McClellan" over title.)
und S C&I

3908 Majr. Genl. George B. McClellan / U.S. Army / (Vignette, bust, slightly to right, in uniform.)
und S C&I

3909 Majr. Genl. George B. McClellan / U.S. Army / (Vignette bust slightly to right in uniform. Similar composition to preceding with slight changes and facsimile signature "Geo. B. McClellan" over title.)
und S C&I

3910 Majr. Genl. George B. McClellan / U.S. Army / (Vignette, ¾ length portrait, head slightly to right.)
und S C&I

3911 Majr. Genl. George G. Meade / At the Battle of Gettysburg, July 3rd, 1863 / 11.11x9.2 (On horseback, to right, sword upraised, top corners slightly round.) 1863 S C&I

3912 Majr. Genl. George G. Meade / Commander-in-Chief of the "Army of the Potomac" July 3rd, 1863 / (Bust portrait in uniform, facing right.)
und S C&I

3913 Major Genl. Henry W. Halleck / General-in-Chief of the Armies of the U.S. July 1862 / (Equestrian portrait to left.) und M C&I

3914 Major Genl. Henry W. Halleck / General-in-Chief of the Armies of the U.S. July 1862 / 11.13x9 (Equestrian full length, battle to left.)
1862 S C&I

3915 Major Genl. Henry W. Halleck, U.S.A. / (¾ length in uniform, vignette.) und S C&I

3916 Maj. Genl. John C. Fremont / U.S. Army / (¾ length, vignette.)
und S C&I

3917 Major Genl. John E. Wool / U.S. Army / und M C&I

3918 Major Genl. John E. Wool / U.S. Army / (¾ length in uniform, vignette.) und S C&I

3919 Majr. Genl. John Pope / Commanding United States Army of Virginia /
(Vignette.) und S C&I

3920 Major General John Pope / The
Hero of New Madrid, Miss. /
und S C&I

3921 Major Genl. Joseph Hooker / (Upright, on horseback.)
und S C&I

3922 Major Genl. Joseph Hooker / Commander-in-Chief of the "Army of the
Potomac" / und S C&I

3923 Major Genl. Joseph Hooker /
|Fighting Joe| at the Battle of Antie-
tam, Sept. 17th, 1862 / 11.3x8.11 (Upright, full length on horseback, profile
to left.) und S C&I

3924 Majr. Genl. Nathl. Banks / (Upright, on horse, to right.)
und S C&I

3925 Maj. Gen. Philip H. Sheridan /
Rallying his troops at the battle of
Cedar Creek, Va. after his Famous ride
from Winchester October 19th, 1864 /
(Equestrian portrait, right hand with
upraised sword, horse prancing, top
corners slightly rounded.)
und S C&I

3926 Maj. Gen. Philip H. Sheridan / U.S.
Army / (Facsimile signature, vignette.) und S C&I

3927 Majr. Genl. Q. A. Gilmore / U.S.
Army / (Vignette portrait.)
und S C&I

3928 Maj. Genl. U.S. Grant / At the
siege of Vicksburg July 4, 1863 /
(Equestrian.) und S C&I

3929 Major Genl. William S. Rosecrans /
At the Battle of Murfreesboro Jany.
2nd, 1863 / und S C&I

3930 Major General William S. Rosecrans / U.S. Army /
und S C&I

3931 Major Gen. William T. Sherman /
On his Victorious March through
Georgia and South Carolina / 11.12x8.6
(Equestrian portrait.)
und S C&I

3932 Majr. Genl. William T. Sherman /
U.S. Army / (Vignette, facsimile signature.) und S C&I

3933 Major Genl. Winfield Scott / At
Vera Cruz, March 25th, 1847 / #468 /
11.12x8.7 (Full length, harbor in background.) 1847 S N.C.

3934 Major Genl. Winfield Scott / From
a daguerreotype by Venino / (Vignette.) 1852 L N.C.

3935 Major General Winfield Scott /
General-in-Chief, United States Army/
#99 / 12.4x8.10. 1846 S N.C.

3936 Major General Winfield Scott /
General-in-Chief, United States Army/
The Hero of Chippewa, Lundy's Lane,
and Vera Cruz / (Upright, full length,
on horseback, troops in rear.)
1846 S N.C.

3937 Maj. Genl. Winfield Hancock / At
the Battle near Spottsylvania Court
House, Va. May 12th, 1864 / #847 /
11.6x8.12 (Equestrian portrait, on
white horse to right.)
und S C&I

3938 Major Genl. Z. Taylor before Monterey / Sept. 20, 1846 / #596 / 12.12x
8.5 (Vignette, equestrian, to left, leading troops.) 1846 S N.C.

3939 Major General Zachary Taylor /
"Rough and Ready" / The Hero who
never lost a battle / #437 / (Vignette,
on white horse, to left.)
1847 S N.C.

3940 Major Robert Anderson / The Hero
of Fort Sumter / (Vignette.)
und S C&I

3941 Major Samuel Ringgold / |Of the
Flying Artillery| at the Battle of
Palo Alto, Texas, May 8th, 1846 /
#450 / (Vignette, black horse to left.)
1846 S N.C.

3942 Ma-Ko-Me-Ta or Bear's Oil / A
Monomonic Chief / Sketch'd at the
Treaty at Green Bay, 1827 by J. O.
Lewis / J. Cameron, Lith, N.Y. (Pub-
lished in Lewis' "Aboriginal Port-
folio".) und S C.C.

Mallory (Yacht) See: No. 6804.

Malvern Hill, Va. See: No. 410.

3943 Mama's Darling / (Mother and
child.) und L C&I

3944 Mama's Darlings / (Vignette, ¾
length of 2 children, smaller holding
rose.) 1877 S C&I

3945 Mama's Jewel / und S C&I

3946 Mama's Pet / 11.14x8.8 (Upright,
child seated holding kitten, doll on
table.) 1878 S C&I

3947 Mama's Pet / (Half length girl
holding hen and chickens.)
und S C&I

3948 Mama's Pets / #17 / (Girl, dog,
and doll.) 1847 S N.C.

3949 Mama's Rosebud / L. Maurer on
stone. 14.8x10.9. 1858 M C&I

3950 Mambrino / 1879 S C&I

3951 Mambrino / The Sire of Imported Messenger / From the celebrated picture by the great English painter Stubb / (Vignette.)
und S C&I
Mambrino Champion (Horse) See: No. 6210.
Mambrino Gift (Horse) See: No. 6211-2.

3952 Mambrino Pilot, Daisy Burns, and Rosamond / Trotting for a purse, mile heats, best 3 in 5 in harness / Over the Union Course, L.I. May 15th, 1866 / 4 additional lines. J. Cameron on stone. 16.12x27 (Broadside to right, high-wheeled sulkies, grandstand and judge's stand in background.)
1866 L C&I
Mambrino Pilot (Horse) See: No. 201.

3953 Mamma's Darlings / (Vignette, 2 children with roses and butterflies.)
und S C&I

3954 Mamma's Pet / #544 / (Girl with birds and rooster.)
und S C&I

3955 Mamma's Pets / 9.6x7.6 (Oval, 2 children under tree with kitten.)
und S N.C.

3956 Mamma's Treasure /
und M C&I

3957 Mammoth Iron Steamship "Great Eastern," The / 22,500 Tons, 300 Horsepower / 2 columns 7 lines, 4 additional lines underneath / #466 / (To left, 4 smokestacks, vignette.)
und S C&I

3958 Mammoth Iron Steamship "Great Eastern," The / 3 columns, 4 lines (Vignette, to left, slight changes from preceding.) und S C&I

3959 Mammoth Iron Steamship "Great Eastern," The / 22,500 Tons 2,600 Horse-Power / 2 columns, 3 additional lines / #466 / (Vignette, to right, 5 stacks shown.) und S C&I

3960 Mammoth Iron Steamship "Leviathan" / 22,500 Tons, 3000 Horse-Power / 2 columns, 7 lines, 4 additional lines / #466 (Same stone as preceding, name changed, vignette.)
und S C&I

3961 Man of Words — The Man of Deeds Which Do You Think The Country Needs?, The /
1868 S C&I

3962 Man of Words, The — The Man of Deeds / Which do you think the Country Needs? / J. Cameron on stone. (2 views on 1 sheet; at left "The man of words," Seymour, surrounded by mob, negro being hanged on lamp post, colored orphan asylum in flames in rear, children jumping from windows. At right "The man of Deeds," Grant, accepting Lee's sword, and his foot resting on hydra-headed dragon "Rebellion." Vignette.)
und S C&I

3963 Man that gave Barnum his turn, The / (At Top) (At Bottom) Scene — Tom Higginson's Barber shop — Enter Barnum, "Tom, I am in a hurry," Sorry for it Mr. Barnum but it's that gentleman's turn next." / Barnum to gentleman from Ireland "My friend if you'll let me have your turn I'll pay for what you have done" — Gentleman consents, the above is what the "Gentleman" "has done" / 2 large oval portraits, the one at left "Before" shows a dirty, unshaven man. At right the same man shaved, washed, with his hair cut and curled "After" small oval below shows barber presenting a bill to Barnum for $1.60, the amount of the "Gentleman's work." 2 small views at sides of print showing barber's tools, ornamental border.)
und S C&I

3964 Man that Kept the Bridge, The / Thos. Worth on stone. (Vignette.)
1881 S C&I

3965 Man that Knows a Horse, The / Innocence only $55,000 cash / Man at right says "Never been beat, her bottom is one of her best pints and she can stay when the rest can't". Man at right is examining horse, bag in hand marked "N.Y. Ledger" / (Bonner) Thos. Worth on stone. 10.1x13.9.
1877 M C&I

3966 Man who Drives to Win, The /
1876 S C&I

3967 Managing a Candidate / (Salt River, Baltimore Bridge in foreground, Editor of "Times" at left, Greeley center, and Seward being carried on shoulders of Gen. Winfield Scott.) Entered in 1852 by P. Smith (nomdeplume for Currier.) 1852 M C& I

Manhattenville See: Reindeer Polka No. 5109.

3968 Manifestation of the Sacred Heart/
und S C&I

3969 Mansion of the Olden Time, A / 8.8x12.7 (Hudson River Scene.)
und S C&I

3970 Map of Centreville / County Seat of St. Joseph County, Michigan / 19.6 x25.12.　　　und L N.C.

3971 Map of Mt. Vernon / With printed references of the sub-divisions /
und S C.C.

3972 Map / of Property at / Jamaica, L.I. / Belonging to / Abrm. H. Van Wyck / 4 additional lines (From the land of Mrs. Stewart and the land of Johannes Lott. East of Van Wyck Avenue to the land of Abner Chichester and From Jamaica Turnpike to road to Jamaica) 20.12x32.8.
und L N.C.

3973 Map of the property / belonging to / the Prot. Ep. General Theol. Seminary / Chelsea New York / About 10x18.　　　　　　und M N.C.

3974 Map / Of the / Western Land District / Wisconsin / 3 notes certifying map Dated Nov. 19, 1836 / 26.2x37.14 Pub. by Leander Judson. Lith. & for sale by N. Currier's office, etc.
und L N.C.
　Maple Sugaring See: No. 157.

3975 Maple Sugaring / Early Spring in the Northern Woods / 8.7x12.8.
1872 S C&I

3976 March Away! March Away! Buckler and Bonnet Blue! / A Celebrated Scotch Ballad sung by / Mr. Wood. The Poetry and Melody by / George Croal / Pub. by James L. Hewitt & Co., 239 Broadway /
und S N.C.

3977 Marcus Morton / Governor of Massachusetts /　　und S N.C.
　Marcy, W. L. See: No. 4632, 6694.

3978 Margaret / #128 / 11.11x8.10 (¾ length, tending flowers.)
1846 S N.C.

3979 Margaret / #85 / 11.15x8.6 (Full length, seated, white dress, red curtain.)　　　　1848 S N.C.

3980 Margaret / #128 / 12x8.9 (¾ length on balcony, bird on hand.)
1849 S N.C.

3981 Margaret / #128 / (¾ length, drinking tea.)　　und S N.C.

3982 Margaret / (Vignette, bust portrait.)　　　　und S C&I

3983 Marguerite /　　und S. N.C.

3984 Maria / (Half-length, bridal veil and roses in hair.)
und S N.C.

3985 Maria / W. K. Hewitt on stone. (Vignette, half length, red dress, roses in hair.)　　und S N.C. $20.

3986 Maria / #48 / 11.11x8.11 (Oval in rectangular border of cherubs, ¾ length, bouquet in hand.)
1846 S N.C.

3987 Maria / 12.3x8.10 (Full length, white dress, marine view through window, miniature in hand.)
1845 S N.C.

3988 Maria / #48 / 11.11x8.11 (Oval, ornamental border, scroll and cherubs, ¾ length, bird on hand.)
1846 S N.C.

3989 Maria / #79 / 12x8.2 (Seated at fireplace, red cloak, blue dress.)
1848 S N.C.

3990 Maria / 12.2x8.8 / (¾ length, seated, light-colored dress, vase of flowers on mantle.)
und S N.C.

3991 Maria / (Vignette.)
und S C&I

3992 Maria / #48 / (¾ length, seated, castle in background.)
und S C&I
　Maria (Yacht) See: Nos. 1341-2, 6805.

3993 Marine Bark "Catalpa" /
und S N.C.

3994 Marine Bark "The Amazon" /
und S N.C.
　Marion, Francis See: No. 2250.

3995 Marion's Brigade Crossing the Pedee River, S.C. 1778 / On their way to attack the British forces under Tarleton / 12.7x8.14.
und S C&I

3996 Marriage, The / #140 / 11.12x8.12 (¾ length.)　　und S N.C.

3997 Marriage, The /　　und S N.C.

3998 Marriage, The /.　　und S C&I

3999 Marriage Certificate / At top — "Whom God Hath joined together, let no man put asunder" / #634 / 12.7x9.3 (Minister, bride, and groom; church interior.)　　　1848 S N.C.

4000 Marriage Certificate / At top — "Whom God hath joined together let no man put asunder" / #570 / (Same as preceding but minister has Bible in hand.)　　　1848 S N.C.

4001 Marriage Certificate /
1857 S C&I

4002 Marriage Certificate / #634 / (View at top shows group of 5 at wedding ceremony, vignette.)
1865 S C&I

4003 Marriage Certificate / (Vignette, 2 oval spaces for photographs.)
1875 S C&I

4004 Marriage Certificate / 10.3x13.5 (Marriage ceremony at top, oval picture of couple in rowboat.)
1877 S C&I

4005 Marriage Certificate / 8.8x9.3.
1869 S C&I

4006 Marriage Certificate /
und S C&I

4007 Marriage Certificate / For Colored People /　　　　und S C&I

4008 Marriage Evening, The / #317 / 11.5x8.8 (Full length, guests seen through door at left, top corners round.)　　　und S N.C.

4009 Marriage Evening / (¾ length of bride, red curtain.)
und S C&I

4010 Marriage Morning, The / #316 / 11.10 x 8.10.　　　　und S N.C.

4011 Marriage Morning / #316 / (Full length.)　　　und S C&I

4012 Marriage of Queen Victoria to Prince Albert /　　　und S C&I

4013 Marriage of the Free Soil and Liberty Parties / Barnburner-Matty-B.F.B. / (Matty (Martin Van Buren) marrying a colored woman. B.F.B. (Benjamin F. Butler) is the minister) Entered 1848 by Peter Smith, etc.
und S N.C.

4014 Marriage Vow, The /
und S N.C.

4015 Marriage Vow, The / #527 / 11.13x 8.6 (Full length of couple kneeling at altar.)　　　　1846 S N.C.

4016 Married / #342 / (Mother, father, and child open window in background.)
1845 S N.C.

4017 Martha / #134 / (¾ length, seated, hands in lap, river seen through window.)　　　und S N.C.

4018 Martha / #134 / (Half length, long curls, roses and leaves in hair.)
und S N.C.

4019 Martha / #134 / Sarony on stone. (¾ length, seated, red dress.)
und S N.C.

4020 Martha / (¾ length, seated, holding fan.)　　　und S N.C.

4021 Martha / (Vignette.)
und S C&I

4022 Martha Washington / 12.8x9.12 (Bust to left, veil tied under chin, wrap with band of fur.)
und S C&I

4023 Martha Washington / (Black paper background, bust to left, no veil.)
und M C&I

4024 Martha Washington / #832 / (Facsimile signature, white cap, dress edged with lace, white scarf.)
und S C&I

4025 Martha Washington / (Vignette — on same sheet with George Washington.)　　　und V.S. C&I

4026 Martha Washington / (Bust to left, no veil.)　　　und S C&I

4027 Martha Washington / (Vignette.)
und M C&I
Martha Wilkes (Horse) See: No. 6191.

4028 Martin Van Buren / From Jenkins "History of Political Parties in the State of New York" / 2.13x3.
und V.S. C.C.

4029 Martin Van Buren / The Champion of Democracy / (Vignette, on white horse, cutaway coat and silk hat, upright.)　　　und S C&I

4030 Martin Van Buren / The Champion of Democracy / And Free Soil Candidate for 12th President / #26 / (Red curtain.)　　　und S N.C.

4031 Martin Van Buren / Eighth President of the United States / 11.7x9.2 (Slightly to right, left hand on book, green curtain.)　　und S N.C.

4032 Martin Van Buren / Eighth President of the United States / (Slightly to left, book in left hand.)
und S N.C.

4033 Martin Van Buren / Eighth President of the United States / 17x12.8.
und M N.C.

4034 Martin Van Buren / Eighth President of the United States / 12.1x10.
und S N.C.

4035 Martin Van Buren / Free Soil Candidate for Twelfth President of the United States /
und S N.C.

4036 Mary / #41 / 12.2x8.11 (Full length, lace-trimmed dress, picture of S.S. Oregon on wall.)　　1845 S N.C.

4037 Mary / #41 / 12.1x8.11 (Full length, picture of S.S. Oregon on wall, changes in composition from preceding.)
1845 S N.C.

4038 Mary / (Similar composition to preceding 2 prints but reversed and picture of S.S. Swallow on wall.)
1845 S N.C.

4039 Mary / 11.14x8.7 (¾ length, flower basket, curtain background.)
und S N.C.

4040 Mary / (¾ length, dressed for the street.)
und S C&I

4041 Mary / #65 / 11.15x8.7 (Full length, seated, exterior scene, black lace parasol and shawl.)
1848 S N.C.

4042 Mary / (Half length, vignette, rural background, exterior.)
und S N.C.

4043 Mary / (Half length, vignette, rural background. Different from preceding.)
und S N.C.

4044 Mary / #97 / (Half length, vignette.)
und S C&I

4045 Mary / #41 / (Head and shoulders, vignette, red dress, roses in hair, to right.)
und S C&I

4046 Mary / (Head and shoulders, vignette, red dress, roses in hair, to left.)
und S C&I

4047 Mary / 14.5x10.8 (Head and shoulders, vignette, roses in hair, tinted background.)
und M C&I

4048 Mary / #41 / 12.1x8.11.
und S N.C.

4049 Mary and her Little Lamb /
und M C&I

4050 Mary Ann / #339 11.12x8.6 (¾ length, lace trimmed dress, flowers in hair, basket of flowers on arm.)
und S N.C.

4051 Mary Ann / (Similar in composition to preceding but reversed.)
und S C.C.

4052 Mary Ann / (¾ length.)
und S N.C.

4053 Mary Elizabeth / #64 / 12x8.8 (¾ length, standing at open window, dress with flaring sleeves.)
1846 S N.C.

4054 Mary Elizabeth / (Different composition from preceding.)
1846 S N.C.

4055 Mary Jane / #95 / (Half length, round corners.)
1846 S N.C.

4056 Mary Jane / #95 / (Full length, holding parasol.)
1850 S N.C.

4057 Mary Jane / 12.15x9.2 (Full length, flowers in 1 hand, parasol in the other, woods in background, title in plate, different from preceding.)
1850 S N.C.

Mary Powell (Steamer) See: No. 2814.

4058 Mary, Queen of Scots / (Bust portrait, vignette.)
1870 S C&I

4059 Mary, Queen of Scots / (Full length, blue dress, red curtain.)
1845 S N.C.

4060 Mary, Queen of Scots / #111 / 12x8.8.
und S N.C.

4061 Mary, Queen of Scots Leaving France / 11.8x8.8 (On shipboard, companion playing guitar, upright.)
1870 S C&I

Mary, Queen of Scots See: No. 5153.

Maryland See: Nos. 354, 384, 429, 1090, 3484, 3905, 6389.

4062 Mary's Little Lamb /
und S C&I

Mascot (Horse) See: Nos. 969-70, 2518.

Masher (Horse) See: No. 4249.

4063 Mashers, The / Thos. Worth on stone. (Vignette, 5 fops ogling passing girl, white comic.)
1884 S C&I

Mason, J. F. See: No. 4632.

4064 Masonic Chart, The / 13.7x9.12 (Upright group of small views.)
1876 S C&I

Massachusetts See: Nos. 378-9, 388, 623, 1091, 1571, 2685, 2955, 3304, 3433-35, 4240, 4415-6, 5571, 5714, 6390-1, 6545-6.

Massachusetts (U.S. Cruiser) See: No. 6644.

4065 Massachusetts / (Ship) 9x14.9.
1882 M C&I

Massachusetts (Steamboat) See: Nos. 4688, 4968-9, 5734.

4066 Master R. W. Osborn / The Lilliputian King. Col. Wood's Museum. / 11x8.6.
und S N.C.

4067 Match Against Time, A / Thos. Worth on stone. (Horse racing Father Time, on bicycle. Wheels are clock faces. Vignette.)
1878 S C&I

THE MASHERS.

4068 Mater Dolorosa /
und S N.C.

4069 Mater Dolorosa /
und S C&I

4070 Maternal Affection /
1845 S N.C.

4071 Maternal Affection / #749 / (¾ length, mother and baby.)
1846 S N.C.

4072 Maternal Affection / (¾ length.)
und S N.C.

4073 Maternal Happiness / #639 / 11.10x 8.9 (Mother and 2 children, exterior scene.)
1849 S N.C.

4074 Maternal Piety / #571 / 12.1x8.10 (Mother holding baby, boy kneeling in prayer.)
und S N.C.
Mathew (Father) See: Nos. 1913-4, 6369-70.

4075 Matilda / (¾ length, rounded corners.)
und S N.C.

4076 Matilda / (¾ length, urn on left, white dress, leaning on red robe.)
und S N.C.

4077 Matilda / #154 / 11.15x8.7 (Full length, pink dress, black lace shawl, round corners.)
1847 S N.C.

4078 Matilda / #154 / (Bouquet in hand, flowers in background, half length.)
und S N.C.

4079 Mating — in the Woods / "Ruffed Grouse" / 8.8x12.8 (Similar composition to "The Happy Family" No. 2712.)
1871 S C&I

4080 Mattie /
und S C&I

4081 Mattie Hunter, Record 2:12½ / Driven by Ed. Geers /
1881 S C&I

4082 Mattie Hunter, Pacer — Record 2:15 — 2.12x4.12.
1881 V.S. C&I

4083 Mattie Hunter / The sorrel beauty of the Pacing Quartette of 1879 / Sired by Prince Pulaski / Record 2:15 / (Vignette, high-wheeled sulky, ¾ to right.)
1879 S C&I
Mattie Hunter (Horse) See: No. 6163.

4084 Maud Muller / (¾ length, vignette.)
und L C&I

4085 Maud S. Record 2:09¾ / Scott Leighton on stone. (Vignette.)
1881 S C&I

4086 Maud S. and St. Julien /
1884 S C&I

Maud S. (Horse) **See:** Nos. 757, 925, 1947-8, 3471, 4085-6, 4256, 4266, 4405, 5016, 5708, 6163, 6198-9, 6765-7.

4087 Maxy Cobb / Record 2:13¼ / 2.12 x4.12.   1882 V.S. C&I

Maxy Cobb (Horse) **See:** Nos. 977, 2525, 5708, 6163.

May, Capt. **See:** Nos. 426, 690-1, 2299-300.

4088 May Queen / By Alexander's Norman, dam by Crockett's Arabian / Record 2:20. Aug. 17, 1875 / (Vignette, ¾ to left.)   1876 S C&I

4089 May Queen, The / (Placing a floral wreath on head of another girl, ¾ length.)   und S N.C.

4090 May Queen, The / (Half length, flowers in hair, plain background.)
                                         und S C&I

4091 Mayflower Saluted by the Fleet / Crossing the bow of "Galatea" in their first race for the "America's Cup" over the inside course, New York Bay, Sept. 7th, 1886 / Won by Mayflower. / Painted by Franklyn Bassford, '86 on stone. 19.5x28.   1886 L C&I

Mayflower (Sloop Yacht) **See:** Nos. 193, 4091, 5559.

Mayflower (Steamer) **See:** Nos. 2813, 4605.

4092 Mazeppa Pl. 1 / 4 columns, 4 lines / #91 / 8.2x12.6. (Bound to wild horse.)
                                    1846 S N.C.

4093 Mazeppa Pl. 2 / 4 columns, 4 lines each / #92 / 8.2x12.7. (Pursued by wolves.)   1846 S N.C.

4094 Mazeppa Pl. 3 / 4 columns, 4 lines each / #93 / 8.2x12.7 (Surrounded by wild horses.)   1846 S N.C.

4095 Mazeppa Pl. 4 / 2 columns, 4 lines each / #94 / 8.3x12.6 (Rescued.)
                                    1846 S N.C.

McAlister, Rev. **See:** No. 5136.

McCarthy, W. H. **See:** No. 5708.

McClellan, George B. **See:** Nos. 29, 429, 438-9, 651, 654, 993, 2259-60, 2338, 2497, 3905-10, 4551, 4824, 6236, 6543, 6873.

McClernand, Gen. **See:** No. 5824.

McCloskey, Cardinal **See:** No. 2834.

McCormack **See:** Ireland.

McCrea, Miss Jane **See:** No. 4269.

McDonough, Thomas **See:** Nos. 4096, 4398.

4096 M'Donough's Victory on Lake Champlain / # 389 / 7.15x13.2.
                                    1846 S N.C.

McDowell, Brig. **See:** No. 675.

McPherson **See:** Death Nos. 1493, 5490.

Meade, Gen. Geo. **See:** Nos. 2553, 3911-2.

4097 Meadow in Springtime, The / The Twin Lambs / 16.12x24.13.
                                    1867 L C&I

4098 Meadow, Springtime, The /
                                  und L C&I

4099 Meadowside Cottage /
                                  und M C&I

Meagher, Genl. Thomas, **See:** Nos. 799, 2289, 2301.

4100 Medalla Milagrosa — Medaille Miraguleuse — Miraculous Medal / #654/ 11.11x8.11 (Full length figure, oval, 2 columns, 3 lines, 4 scenes around border.)   1849 S N.C.

4101 Meeting of the Waters, The / In the Vale of Avoca, County Wicklow, Ireland / 8x12.8 (8 keys and 4 lines of verse.)   1868 S C&I

4102 Meeting of the Waters, The / In the Vale of Avoca, County Wicklow, Ireland / From a sketch by Fairland 16.13x24.14 (4 lines of verse by Moore, 7 keys.)   1867 L C&I

4103 Melrose Abbey / (3 figures in foreground, vignette.)
                                         und S C&I

4104 Melrose Abbey / 7.14x12.6 (Similar to above, no figures and not vignetted.)
                                         und S C&I

4105 Melrose Abbey / F. F. Palmer, Del. 11.4x15.10 (2 columns, 4 lines of verse, moonlight scene.)
                                    1862 M C&I

Memphis (Steamboat) **See:** No. 4117.

4106 Merchant's Exchange, New York / Wall Street / #613 / 8.6x12.8.
                                    1848 S N.C.

Merodac (Horse) **See:** No. 175.

Merrimac **See:** Nos. 1572, 1969, 2612, 5530, 5995-8.

4107 Merry Christmas / (Vignette, scroll and flowers.)
                                    1876 S C&I

4108 Merry Christmas / (Vignette, motto entwined with holly, different from preceding.)   und S C&I

4109 Merry Christmas / #123 / (Upright, rough-looking character accosting man on lonely road. First state — later published as "Lend Me Your Watch" No. 3475.)   und S N.C.

4110 Merry, Merry Maiden and the Tar, The / (Vignette, scene from "Pinafore.") 1879 S C&I

Messenger (Steamer) See: No. 5735.

Metairie Course, New Orleans See: Nos. 887-8.

Meteor (Yacht) See: Nos. 6806-7.

Metropolis (Steamer) See: No. 6406.

4111 Mexican Fandango, 1848 / (Music sheet.) 1848 S N.C.

Mexico See: Nos. 88, 297, 300, 302, 389-90, 393, 398, 411, 601, 797, 808, 1098, 1121, 2009-10, 2225, 2231, 2293, 3368, 3432, 3938, 4112-13, 4120, 4396, 4976, 5512-13, 5825-6, 5829-31, 5976, 6008, 6392.

Mexico City See: Nos. 1098, 3368.

4112 Mexican Guerrilleros / Mexico in 1848 / #632 / 8.7x12.12 (Guerrilla on horseback riding on road littered with dead, battle in background.) 1848 S N.C.

4113 Mexicans Evacuating Vera Cruz, The / And surrendering their arms to the U.S. Army under Genl. Scott / #485 / 8.7x12. 1847 S N.C.

Mexico (Ship) See: No. 1624.

4114 Middlesex Pauper Lunatic Asylum London England / Plan and elevation to a parallel scale engraved from the original plate in the possession of Dr. James MacDonald / (Vignette, front view, 2 on 1 sheet.) und M N.C.

Michigan See: No. 3970.

4115 Midnight / By Peacemaker, by Rysdyk's Hambletonian / Record 2:18¼ / (Broadside to right, high-wheeled sulky.) 1879 S C&I

4116 Midnight Race on the Mississippi, A / F. F. Palmer, Del. From a Sketch by H. D. Manning of the "Natchez" / 18.7x28.2 (Shows the steamboats "Natchez" and "Eclipse," moonlight scene, to left.) 1860 L C&I

4117 Midnight Race on the Mississippi / 9x13.3 (Steamboats "Memphis" and "James Howard," moonlight, 3 boats to left. Also used as an ad. See: Steamboat Race on the Mississippi No. 5730.) 1875 S C&I

4118 Midsummer-Night's Dream, A / Act IV Scene 1 (4 lines of verse.) und L C&I

4119 Miligrosa Imagen / de Sn. Francisco Javier Que Se Venera en la Iglesia Parroquial Dela Villa Magdalena, Sonora / und S C&I

4120 Military College of Chapultepec, The / The Ancient Site of the halls of the Montezumas / From a Sketch by Gualdi, and forewarded by Lieut. Larkin Smith, U.S.A. / #554 / 8.6x12.6. 1847 S N.C.

4121 Millitary Ring, The / (Grant at table, 5 army officers offering him chickens, liquor, and cigars from Greeley, Brown, and Smith. Vignette.) 1872 S C&I

4122 Mill Boy and Blondine / 1881 S C&I

Mill Boy (Horse) See: No. 874.

4123 Mill Cove Lake / "Near Po'keepsie-on-the-Hudson" / 8.8x12.8 (Location of the present campus of Vassar College. The small farm house in the middle distance is said to be the first building of Vassar.) und S C&I

4124 Mill Dam at "Sleepy Hollow", The / 17x22.8. und L C&I

4125 Mill in the Highlands / 9.10 x 17 (Man fishing from bank of stream below waterfall.) und M C&I

4126 Mill River Scenery / F. F. Palmer, Del. (Upright.) und L C&I

Mill Spring, Ky. See: Nos. 412-3.

4127 Mill-Stream, The / F. F. Palmer, Del. 11.1x15.10 (Grist mill on right, cattle and ducks in foreground.) und M C&I

4128 Millard Fillmore / Thirteenth President of the United States / and National Candidate for the Fifteenth President of the United States / 1856 S N.C.

4129 Millard Fillmore / Thirteenth President of the United States / And National American Candidate for the Fifteenth President of the United States / L. M. on stone. From a photograph by M. B. Brady. 18.11x23.1 (Vignette, slightly to left ½ length.) 1857 L N.C.

4130 Millard Fillmore / Thirteenth President of the United States /. 1856 S N.C.

4131 Millard Fillmore / Whig Candidate for / Vice-President of the United States / #590 / 11.14x8.14. From a daguerreotype by Plumbe (Holding letter in right hand, red curtain, ¾ length.) 1848 S N.C.

Miller, Warren See: No. 6499.

Miller's Damsel (Horse) **See:** Nos. 2344, 3399.

4132 Miller's Home, The / Painted by T. Creswick A.R.A. and exhibited at the British Art Institute, London. (Dog and children on stone bridge.)
und M C&I

4133 Mind Your Lesson, Fido /
und S C&I

Mineola, L.I. **See:** Permanent Fair Grounds of the Queens County Agricultural Society, Etc. No. 4753.

4134 Miner, Stevens & Co. / Manufacturers of / First Class Carriages and Light Wagons, / Warerooms No. 656 Broadway / (Same stone as "Four-In-Hand" No. 2092, title changed.)
1861 L C&I

4135 Miniature Landscapes / (10 small views, American scenes.)
und M C&I

4136 Miniature Landscapes No. 1 — The Trout Stream, The Bridge, Waterfall, Lighthouse near Holyhead, Ben Venue, Scotland, Niagara Falls, Falls near Tarrytown, N.Y., The Giant's Causeway /
und S C&I

4137 Miniature Ship "Red, White, and Blue" / On her voyage from New York to London, August 1866: with Capts. Hudson & Fitch & dog Fanny / Sailed from New York, July 9th, arrived at Margate, August 16th, 1866 / 1 additional line dimensions. (On side of boat "Ingersoll's Improved Metallic Life Boat.") 8x12.6.
und S C&I

4138 Miniature Ship "Red, White, and Blue," The / (Title exactly same as preceding, slight changes in composition and no lettering on side of boat. Vignette.)
und S C&I

4139 Mink Trapping / "Prime" / Painted by A. F. Tait. 19.1x27.12.
1862 L C&I

4140 Minnehaha / Laughing Water / (Vignette, upright.)
und S C&I

Minnehaha **See:** No. 1496.

4141 Minnehaha Falls / Minnesota / (Female Indian figure on ledge at foot of falls.) und M C&I

Minnesota (Steamship) **See:** No. 5775.

Minnesota **See:** Nos. 4141, 5519-20.

4142 Minnie / (Girl's head.)
und V.S. C&I

4143 Minnie / (Vignette.)
und S C&I

Minnie R. (Horse) **See:** No. 5708.

4144 "Minute-Men" of the Revolution, The / 8.14x12.12 (Men answering call of horseman, leaving farms to fight.)
1876 S C&I

4145 Miraculous Medal /
und S N.C.

4146 Miraculous Image of St. Francis Xavier / Milagroso Imagende de San Francisco / und S C&I

Mischief (Yacht) **See:** No. 5562.

4147 Mischief and Music / 12.6x8.1 (Girl playing piano, boy playing cello, smaller boy with horn.)
und S C&I

4148 Mischievous Little Doggie / 9.4x7.13 (Dog with rose in mouth, overturned vase.) und S C&I

4149 Mischievous Little Kittie / (Kitten on stool annoying 2 dogs.)
und S C&I

4150 Mischievous Little Kitties / 12.6x8.1 (Playing in woman's hat.)
1877 S C&I

4151 Miseries of a Bachelor, The / 12x9 (Companion to "Blessings of a Wife" No. 568. Same composition as "Onconvanience of Single Life" No. 4611. Man patching his own clothes, upright.) und S C&I

4152 Miss Elizabeth Reid — The Lilliputian Queen / und S C&I

4153 Miss Elizabeth Reid — Miss Hannah Crouse / The Smallest woman in the World — The Largest Woman in the World / Both at Barnum's American Museum / 11.12x8.14 (2 portraits on 1 sheet.) und S N.C.

4154 Miss Jane Campbell / The Great Connecticutt Giantess. 18 years old. Weighs 628 pounds. To be seen at Barnum's Museum at all hours every day and evening (At Top) Barnum's Gallery of Wonders / 11.3x8.11.
und S C&I

4155 Miss Martha Jones / The Lilliputian Queen / Twenty years old and only thirty Inches High. Weight less than 33 Pounds / Born in Mass. now Travelling and Exhibiting before the American People / 11.11x8.5.

und S N.C.

4156 Miss S. Phillips / The Distinguished Vocalist / Published at Atwill's Music Saloon. Entered 1835 by Joseph F. At-

will (On cover of music sheet: "Oh! tis sweet when the moon is beaming.")
und S N.C.

4157 Miss Susan Barton / The Mammoth Lady / as exhibited at / Barnum's American Museum, New York, 1849 / Weighs 576 pounds / (At Top) Barnum's Gallery of Wonders No. 6 / #666 / 12.1x8.12 (2 columns, 2 lines, full length seated, red curtain.)
1849 S N.C.

4158 Miss Woodford / By Billet, dam Fancy Jane by Niel Robinson, GD. by Imp. Knight of St. George / (Vignette, standing profile to left, under saddle.)
1884 S C&I
Missionary Ridge, Ga. **See:** No. 383.

4159 Missionary Stone Chapel at Wheelock, Choctaw Nation / C. Dickenson, Del. (Arkansas.)   und S C.C.

4160 Mississippi in Time of Peace, The/ F. F. Palmer, Del. 18.4x27.12 (5 Steamers shown, express train in foreground.)   1865 L C&I

4161 Mississippi in Time of War, The / F. F. Palmer, Del. 18.4x27.12 (Gunboats, river steamer at right in flames and sinking.)   1865 L C&I
Mississippi River **See:** Nos. 593, 598, 627, 992, 1271, 1573, 1585, 2012, 2629-31, 2644, 2813, 2819, 2876, 3480, 3745, 3824, 3888-9, 3891, 4116-7, 4160-1, 4180, 4605-7, 5042, 5223, 5414, 5422, 5659, 5730, 6776.
Mississippi (U.S. Steam Frigate) **See:** Nos. 6341-2.
Mississippi (Steamship) **See:** No. 5776.
Missouri **See:** Nos. 387, 1117, 2617, 2648.
Missouri (U.S. Steam Frigate) **See:** No. 6382.
Mitchell, John **See:** Nos. 3272-4.

4162 Mixed at the Finish / Thos. Worth on stone. (Vignette, horse print, companion to, "Lapped in the Last Quarter" No. 3443.)   1880 S C&I
Mobile Bay **See:** No. 2633.

4163 Model Artists as the three graces, as they appeared on the stage of the Apollo Rooms, New York City /
und S N.C.

4164 Modern College Scull, A / Graduating with all honors / Thos. Worth on stone. 10.15x15.9 (Boating comic, sculler with numerous cups, bridge in background marked "Pons Asinorum.")
1876 M C&I

4165 Modern Colossus, The / Eighth wonder of the World / Abby Folsum-Matty-Butler-Cass-Calhoun. Pub. by Peter Smith. 10.10x16.12. (Matty [Van Buren] attempting to stretch from right bank "Democratic Platform" to left bank "Whig Abolition Platform" over Salt River; Butler, Cass, and Calhoun in row boat.)
und M N.C.
Mohawk (Yacht) **See:** No. 6808.

4166 Mollie McCarthy / 2.12x4.12.
1881 V.S. C&I

4167 Molly McCarthy / The Racing Queen of the Pacific Slope / H.S. on stone. 3 additional lines. (To right, under saddle, vignette.)
1878 S C&I

4168 Momentous Question, The / "Ah, Billy, my beauty, can't you give us an Eye Opener? Yes Sir-ee." / L. M. on stone. (Saloon scene, companion to "Coming The Putty," No. 1223.)
1853 S N.C.

4169 Momentous Question, The / "Is my face good for a drink?" No Sir-ee" / #464 / L.M. on stone. 8.2x12.6.
1853 S N.C.

4170 Momentous Question, The /
1861 S C&I
Monitor, (Ironclad ship) **See:** Nos. 1969, 2612, 5995-8.
Monitor (Horse) **See:** No. 2764.
Monmouth, N.J. **See:** Nos. 2802, 4587, 6754-5.
Monroe, James **See:** No. 3172.

4171 Monroe Chief / Record 2:18¼ / 2.12x4.12.   1881 V.S. C&I
Monroe Chief (Horse) **See:** Nos. 4171, 6213.
Montauk (Ironclad) **See:** No. 6284.
Montefiori, Sir Moses **See:** No. 5535.
Monterey **See:** No. 414.
Montez, Lola **See:** Nos. 3749-51.
Montgomery, Gen. **See:** No. 1497.

4172 Monument / Seventy-five feet high containing 720 tons solid granite, erected in the National Cemetery near Fortress Monroe, by subscriptions of loyal citizens in the northern cities, in memory of Union soldiers, who perished in the War of the Rebellion / 8.4x12.7.
und S C&I
Moody, Dwight **See:** No. 1642.

IS MY FACE GOOD FOR A DRINK?

NO SIR-EE!

NO TRUST.

THE MOMENTOUS QUESTION.

4173 Moonlight / 5.8x7.8 (Companion to "Sunlight" No. 5887.)
und V.S. C&I

4174 Moonlight / 10x15.
und S C&I

4175 Moonlight in Fairyland /
und S C&I

4176 Moonlight in the Tropics / 8.7x12.9.
und S C&I

4177 Moonlight on Lake Catalpa, Va. /
und M C&I

4178 Moonlight on Long Island Sound / (Shows Steamers "Bristol" and "Massachusetts." Very smiliar to "Steamboats passing on Long Island Sound" No. 5731.) und S C&I

4179 Moonlight on the Lake / (2 deer in foreground.) und M C&I

4180 Moonlight on the Mississippi / G. M. on stone. 8.7x12.6 (Broadside of Steamer "Great Republic" to right.)
und S C&I

4181 Moonlight Promenade, The /
und S C&I

4182 Moonlight Promenade / 7.15x12.6 (3 couples, fountain, castle in background.) und S C&I

Moonlight — Summer See: American Landscapes No. 178.

4183 Moonlight / The Castle / #837 / 8.2x12.9 (Couple with dog.)
und S C&I

4184 Moonlight—The Ruins / 8.3 x 12.10 (2 figures at right foreground.)
und S C&I

Moose (Horse) See: No. 900.

4185 Moose and Wolves / A Narrow Escape / 8.6x12.7 (Winter scene, moose pursued through broken ice.)
und S C&I

4186 Moosehead Lake / 7.15x12.8 (Moose in center foreground.)
und S C&I

4187 More Free than Welcome / F.P. on stone. 8x12.8 (Fox and rabbits.)
und S C&I

4188 More Frightened than Hurt /(Child and geese.) und S C&I

4189 More Frightened than Hurt / #592 / 8.2x12.8 (Fox escaping trap. Probably companion to "Not Caught Yet" No. 4514.) und S N.C.

4190 More Plucky than Prudent / 8.15x

12.4 (Railroad comic, bull charging locomotive.) 1885 S C&I

4191 More Than Welcome /
und S C&I

4192 Morgan Lewis /
und S C.C.

4193 Morgan Lewis / 2.13x3 (From Jenkins "History of Political Parties in the State of New York.")
und V.S. C&I

4194 Morning / Erom the original Bas Relief by Thorwaldsen. 11x8.4.
und S C&I

4195 Morning Glories / (Girls' figures.)
und S C&I

4196 Morning in the Woods / F. F. Palmer, Del. 14.13x20.2 (Composition very similar to "Partridge Shooting" No. 4714. 2 hunters and 4 dogs, no dead game on the ground in foreground and foliage heightened.)
1852 L N.C.

4197 Morning in the Woods / F. F. Palmer, Del. 14.12x20.8 (2 hunters, 2 dogs, stream on left, costumes, locale, and dogs different from preceding.)
1865 L C&I

4198 Morning of Life, The / 8.9x12.8 (Child in flower-laden boat.)
und S C&I

4199 Morning of Life, The / Childhood / 8.7x12.8 (Changes in shape of boat, flowers in foreground.)
1874 S C&I

4200 Morning of Love, The / 11.7x8.5.
und S C&I

4201 Morning Prayer, The / 9.14x8 (Oval.) und S N.C.

4202 Morning Prayer, The / #7 / 11.12 x8.5 (3 additional lines.)
und S N.C.

4203 Morning Prayer, The / (Vignette, full length of boy kneeling at chair.)
1857 L C&I

4204 Morning Prayer, The / (Vignette, 4 lines of verse.) 1862 M C&I

4205 Morning Prayer, The / #7 / (2 columns, 2 lines verse, companion to No. 1775.) und S C&I

4206 Morning Prayer, The / "Defend us from all evil throughout this day" / 9.13x7.15 (Companion to "Evening Prayer" No. 1773.)
und S C.C.

4207 Morning Recreation, The / #523 / Sarony on stone. 11.14x8.9 (Full length

of man and woman, river in background.) und S N.C.

4208 Morning Ride, The / #681 / (Upright, 2 children on ponies.)
1849 S N.C.

4209 Morning Ride, The / #681 / (Upright, woman and boy.)
1849 S N.C.

4210 Morning Rose, The / #668 / 11.13x 8.10 (Full length, woman picking roses in garden.) 1849 S N.C.

4211 Morning Rose, The / #668 / 12x 8.10 (Full length.)
und S C&I

4212 Morning Roses / (Upright, vignette.) und S C&I

4213 Morning Star, The / (Vignette, head of girl.) und S C&I

4214 Morning Star, The /
1846 S N.C.

4215 Morning Star / #499 / 12.2x8.4 (Girl lying on bed, dog awakening her, slightly rounded corners.)
und S C&I

Morning Star (Steamboat) **See:** No. 5223.

Morris Island **See:** No. 2089, 2210, 5508.

Morrisania **See:** No. 2448.

Morrissey, John **See:** No. 3275.

Morton, Marcus **See:** No. 3977.

4216 Moses and the Decalogue /
und S N.C.

4217 Moss Rose, The /
und S C&I

4218 Moss Rose, The / #551 / (2 roses, 6 buds, spray of flowers entwined, vignette.) 1847 S N.C.

4219 Moss Rose, The / #551 / (Tinted background, round corners.)
1847 S N.C.

4220 Moss Roses and Buds / (Upright, vignette, 5 roses, 7 buds.)
1870 S C&I

4221 Moss Roses and Buds /
und S C&I

4222 Most Holy Catholic Faith, The / 11.15x8.8 (Upright, nun holding cross and Holy Eucharist.)
1872 S C&I

4223 Most Holy Sacrifice, The / A Precious gift for the faithful soul / 12.7 x8.5 (Lamb on altar, 2 angels with censors.) 1872 S C&I

4224 Most Rev. John Hughes, D.D., The / First Archbishop of New York /

(Vignette, upright, ½ length, 3 additional lines.)   1864 M C&I

4225 Most Rev. John Hughes, D.D., The / First Archbishop of New York / 11.10x8.2 (3 additional lines, ¾ length.)   und S C&I

4226 Most Rev. John McCloskey, D.D., The / Second Archbishop of New York /   und S C&I

4227 Most Reverend M. J. Spalding, D.D., The / Archbishop of Baltimore / 11.9 x8.6.   und S C&I

4228 Mother and Child / #1 / 11.10x8.10 (Under trees, teaching child ABC's.)   1846 S N.C.

4229 Motherless, The /   und S N.C.

4230 Motherless, The /   und S C&I

4231 Mother's Blessing, The / O. Starck on stone. 14.15x11.4. 2 columns, 2 lines of verse. (Mother at bedside of sleeping son, round top.)   und M C&I

4232 Mother's Dream, The / 11.15 x 8.14 (Round top.)   und S C&I

4233 Mother's Dream, The / 17.12x13.5. 2 columns, 2 lines of verse. (Baby on couch, mother asleep in chair. Vision of angel flying away with baby, round top.)   und M C&I

4234 Mother's Joy / #405 / 11.11x8.11 (¾ length, seated with girl on lap.)   1846 S N.C.

4235 Mother's Joy / (Upright vignette of mother, child with pantalettes.)   1859 S C&I

4236 Mother's Joy / 10.3x8.3 (Oval, mother holding children.)   und S C&I

4237 Mother's Pet / #544 / 11.14x8.10 (¾ length, girl and deer.)   und S N.C.

4238 Mother's Treasure, A / #542 / (Vignette bust of child.)   und S N.C.

4239 Mother's Wing / F. F. Palmer, Del. 9.15x14 (Hen and chickens.)   1866 M C&I

4240 Mt. Holyoke Female Seminary, South Hadley, Mass. / P. G. Thurston, Del.   und S N.C.

Mount Vernon, Va. See: Nos. 528, 2870-4, 3971, 6107-12, 6515.

4241 Mount Vesuvius, Italy /   und S C&I

4242 Mount Washington and the White Mountains / From the Valley of Conway / F. F. Palmer, Del. 14.15x20.6.   1860 L C&I

Mountain Boy (Horse) See: Nos. 3395, 6169.

4243 Mountain Pass, The / Sierra Nevada / F. F. Palmer, Del. 17.8x25.14 (Bear in foreground on felled tree.)   1867 L C&I

4244 Mountain Ramble, A / 8.7x12.6 (3 couples on path at left.)   und S C&I

4245 Mountain Spring, The / West Point, near Cozzen's Dock / F. F. Palmer, Del. 11.1x15.10.   1862 M C&I

4246 Mountain Stream, The / 9.11x16.12 (Boy fishing, stone bridge, man on horseback.)   und M C&I

4247 Mountaineer's Home, The / 9.10x 16.15 (Family group in front of cottage, sheep, waterfall.)   und M C&I

4248 Mountaineer's Return, The / The Evening song of the Alpine Peasants /   und S N.C.

4249 Mr. August Belmont's / Potomac |Hamilton Up| and Masher |Bergen Up| / By St. Blaise, dam Susquehanna by Lexington. By the Ill Used, dam Magnetism by Kingfisher / The Celebrated horses which ran first and second for the Great Futurity Stakes at Sheepshead Bay, N.Y. Aug. 30th, 1890/ Sketched from life by Chas. L. Zellinsky. 19.14x27.15 (See "Ready for the Race" No. 5081.)   1891 L C&I

4250 Mr. Bonner's Horse Joe Elliott, driven by J. Bowen / Trotting in harness at Mystic Park, Medford, Mass. June 28th, 1872 / The Fastest mile ever trotted either in public or private in / 2:15½ / J. Cameron on stone. 17x 26.10 (Broadside to right, high-wheeled sulky, printed in color.)   1873 L C&I

4251 Mr. Frank Work's Celebrated Team / Edward and Swiveller / To road wagons winning a wager of $1000 against time 2:20 at the Gentlemen's Driving Park, N.Y., July 13th, 1882 / Trotting a mile in 2:16¾ without a skip or break / (Vignette, ¾ to right.)   1882 S C&I

4252 Mr. J. Proctor / in his Great original Character / of the Jibbenainosay in |Nick of the Woods| / "Up then and follow on the track" / This Play was performed at the Bowery Thea-

tre, N.Y. May 1867. Mr. Proctor taking 6 parts / (Upright, vignette.)
und S C&I

4253 Mr. Jas. R. Keene's Bay Colt, 3 yrs., Foxhall, by King Alphonso, Dam Jamaica by Lexington / Ridden by the celebrated English jockey George Fordham / Winner of the "Grand Prize" of Paris June 12th, 1881 / J. Cameron on stone. (Vignette, under saddle, to left.) 1881 S C&I

4254 Mr. Placide / In the character of Frederick 2nd in / "St. Patrick's Eve"/ Published by Linen, Horn & Co. 389 Broadway, N.Y. Entered by Wm. Wilshire Riley. H. Heidemans, Del. On stone by Wm. K. Hewitt. N. Currier's Lith. (Full length vignette.)
1837 S N.C.

4255 Mr. Pierre Lorillard's Br. Colt, 3 yrs. Iroquois, by Leamington, dam Maggie B. by Australian / Ridden by Fred Archer / The American winner of the English Derby at Epsom June 1st, 1881 / (Vignette, under saddle, to right.) 1881 S C&I

4256 Mr. Wm. H. Vanderbilt driving his magnificent Team / Maud S and Aldine / At the Gentleman's Driving Park, Morrisania, N.Y. June 15th, 1883 to road wagons, weighing with driver 411 lbs. a mile in the unprecedented time of / 2:15½ / Jno. Cameron on stone. (Vignette, to left.)
1883 S C&I

4257 Mr. Wm. H. Vanderbilt's Celebrated Road Team / Lysander and Leander / Lysander, formerly Lysander Boy, Record 2:20¾. Leander, formerly Dr. Lewis, record 2:24 / (Vignette, ¾ to left.) 1879 S C&I

4258 Mr. William H. Vanderbilt's Celebrated Team / Small Hopes and Lady Mac / Driven by their owner to road-wagon time 2:23 / From the original painting by Edwin Forbes, etc. 20.9x34 (To left, country road.)
1878 L C&I

4259 Mr. Wm. H. Vanderbilt's Celebrated Road Team / Small Hopes and Lady Mac / Driven by their owner, trotting a mile to road wagon in the unparalleled time of 2:23 wagon & driver weighing 346½ lbs. Sept. 11th, 1877 / E. Forbes, Del. on stone. (Vignette, to right.) 1877 S C&I

4260 Mrs. Fish and the Misses Fox / The original Mediums of the mysterious noises at Rochester, Western New York / From a daguerreotype by Ap-

pleby, Rochester, N.Y. / Mrs. Margaretta Fox, Miss Catherine Fox, Mrs. Fish. / 8.10x11.10 (¾ length, oval in ornamental border.)
1852 S N.C.

4261 Mrs. George Jones, the Tragic Actress [in character] / Copyright by Linen & Fenell, 1838. F. S. Agate. (Melinda Jones, wife of the eccentric tragedian "The Count Joannes.")
1838 S N.C.

4262 Mrs. J. K. Polk / #448 / 11.12x8.9. From a daguerreotype by Plumbe. (Oval in conventional border, stars, etc.) 1846 S N.C.

4263 Mrs. Lucretia R. Garfield / Wife of James A. Garfield / Twentieth President of the United States / (Vignette.)
und M C&I

4264 Mrs. Lucy L. Bliss / Authoress of "Rock of Ages" new version / (Vignette.) und S C&I

4265 Muckross Abbey, Killarney /
und S C&I

4266 Mud S., De Great Record Buster / "Dar! she's done gone dat yer reckud again" / (Vignette, colored comic.)
1885 S C&I

4267 Mule Team on a Down Grade, A / "Clar de track for we's a comin" / Thos. Worth on stone. (Vignette.)
1881 S C&I

4268 Mule Team on an Up Grade, A / "Golly! Where is dis yere promis land?" / Thos. Worth on stone. (Vignette.) 1881 S C&I

Mulligan, Col. James See: No. 1197.

4269 Murder of Miss Jane McCrea, A.D. 1777 / #240 / 11.9x8.6 (3 additional lines, upright, round corners.)
1846 S N.C.

Murfreesboro, Tenn. See: No. 415.

Murphy, John See: No. 5708.

Murray, A. Alexander See: No. 4399.

Murray St. N.Y. See: "Life of a Fireman," No. 3517.

4270 Music / (Horse.)
1875 S C&I

Music (Horse) See: No. 2946.

4271 Music / Chestnut Mare, by Middletown, dam by Roe's Fiddler / Record 2:21½. Sept. 2nd, 1875 / Thos. Worth on stone. 16.12x25 (¾ view to left, stands in background.)
1875 L C&I

4272 Music Hath Charms! / 12.5x8.6 (2 cats playing banjo on roof, upright.) 1875 S C&I

4273 Mustang Team, The / (To left, Union Toll gate, toll keepers refusing cart "Bleeding Kansas" admittance. Beecher and lady in cart, Greeley of the "Tribune," Bennett of the "Herald," Raymond of the "Times" and Webb of the "Courier & Enquirer" also shown.) und M C&I

4274 My Absent Love / 11.11x9.4 (Portrait of girl, oval.) und S C&I

4275 My Boyhood Home / und S C&I

4276 My Boyhood's Home / 8.8x12.7 (Man with shovel, house in rear.) 1872 S C&I

4277 My Brother / (Oval, half length in ornamental border.) 1846 S N.C.

4278 My Charming Girl / (Vignette.) und S C&I

4279 My Child / #676 / 12.2x8.10 (Full length of child, doll in little wagon.) 1849 S N.C.

4280 My Child! My Child! / 12.4x8.2 (Woman overboard, holding child. Companion to "They're Saved" Etc. No. 6007.) und S C&I

4281 My Choice / (Vignette, girl's head.) und S C&I

4282 My Choice / und M N.C.

4283 My Cottage Home / F. F. Palmer, Del. 16.1x23.7 (Woman and dog at gate.) 1866 L C&I

4284 My Cottage Home / 2.11x4.3 (See: "Landscape Cards" No. 3438.) und V.S. C&I

4285 My Darling Boy / #482 / (Kissing own reflection in mirror.) und S N.C.

4286 My Darling Girl / #483 / (Full length.) und S N.C.

4287 My Darling Girl / #483 /(¾ length, looking at self in mirror.) und S N.C.

4288 My Darling Girl / Kiss Me Quick / und S C&I

4289 My Dear Little Pet / (Vignette, girl holding kitten.) 1877 S C&I

4290 My Favorite Horse / und S C&I

4291 My Favorite Pony / 11.14x8.8 (Boy feeding pony, upright, exterior scene.) 1871 S C&I

4292 My Father Land / A Favorite Swiss National Air / As sung by / Madam Otto / At the Park Theatre, etc. / 5 lines. Published by Millet's Music Saloon, N.Y. 1838. und S N.C.

4293 My Favorite / (Vignette, girl's head.) und S C&I

4294 My Favorite / (¾ length, young lady.) und S C&I

4295 My First Friend / #30 / (Oval in rectangle, girl with parrot.) und S N.C.

4296 My First Love / (Young lady putting love letter in knot hole in tree. Same composition as No. 3798.) und S N.C.

4297 My First Playmate / #620 / 11.10x 8.7 (Full length, mother, child and dog.) und S C&I

4298 My First Playmate / 11.10x8.9 (Full length, girl and spaniel.) und S C&I

4299 My Friend and I / #109 / 11.15x8.5 (¾ length, round corners.) 1846 S N.C.

4300 My Gentle Dove / (Vignette.) 1871 S C&I

4301 My Gentle Love / (Vignette, girl's head.) 1872 S C&I

4302 My Heart's Desire / und S C&I

4303 My Heart's Treasure / (Bust portrait.) und S C&I

4304 My Hero / 12x9.8. und S C&I

4305 My Highland Boy / (¾ length, vignette.) und S N.C.

4306 My Highland Boy / (Vignette.) und S C&I

4307 My Highland Girl / (Vignette.) und S C&I

4308 My Highland Girl / #298 / (Vignette.) und S N.C.

4309 My Highland Girl / 10.4x7.4. und S N.C.

4310 My Intended / #67 / 11.15x8.7 (Full length, striped dress, bustle, rose in hand.) 1847 S N.C.

4311 My Kitty and Canary / 12.6x8.2. 1871 S C&I

4312 "My Lips shall Praise Thee" / (Vignette of boy praying.) und S C&I

4313 My Little Drummer Boy / und S C&I

4314 My Little Favorite / und S C&I

4315 My Little Favorite / (Child holding dog.) und M C&I

4316 My Little Favorite / und M C&I

4317 My Little Friend / #283 / 11.11x8.5 (Full length, girl seated, flowers in lap.) 1845 S N.C.

4318 My Little Pet / 1845 S N.C.

4319 My Little Playfellow / #104 / 11.15 x8.10 (Oval in rectangle, girl with dog, brook in background. Title in plate.) 1847 S N.C.

4320 My Little Playfellow / 11.14x8.6 (Boy and dog.) und S N.C.

4321 My Little Playfellow / 9.6x7.7 (Oval, boy seated, dog on leash.) und S N.C.

4322 My Little Playfellow / #104 / (Vignette, girl with dog.) und S C&I

4323 My Little Playfellow / 9.8x7.8 (Oval in ornamental border, boy under tree with dog.) und S N.C.

4324 My Little Playfellow / und S C&I

4325 My Little Playmate / (Boy and dog.) und S C&I

4326 My Little White Bunnies / 8.6x 11.11 (Mother surrounded by young rabbits, dog at hole in background.) und S C&I

4327 My Little White Bunnies / Receiving a Visitor / 11.11x8.6 (Dog in background.) und S C&I

4328 My Little White Kittens / und S C&I

4329 My Little White Kittie / After the Goldfish / 12.11x7.15 (Slightly rounded corners.) und S C&I

4330 My Little White Kittie / Fishing / und S C&I

4331 My Little White Kittie / Its First Mouse / und S C&I

4332 My Little White Kitties / Into Mischief / und S C&I

4333 My Little White Kitties / Learning their A B C's / und S C&I

4334 My Little White Kitties / Playing Ball / 8x12.9 (Ball of wool on hassock.) 1870 S C&I

4335 My Little White Kitties / Playing Ball / 3 kittens, different composition, slightly rounded corners.) und S C&I

4336 My Little White Kitties / Playing Dominos / #344 / (Slightly rounded corners.) und S C&I

4337 My Little White Kitties / #520 / 12.2x8.3 (Playing with a miniature.) 1871 S C&I

4338 My Little White Kitties / Taking the Cake / #344 / (Slightly round top corners.) und S C&I

4339 My Little White Kitties / Taking the Cake / (Roses in pitcher on left, no round corners.) 1877 S C&I

4340 My Little White Kitties / Their First Mouse / 8x12.4. und S C&I

4341 My Little White Kitties / Their First Mouse / (Slightly rounded corners.) 1871 S C&I

4342 My Long Tail Blue / (Colored man in high hat and long tailed coat, music sheet.) und S N.C.

4343 My Love and I / 8.6x12.8 (2 portraits in locket — man and girl. Floral border.) 1872 S C&I

4344 My Own Mama / (Sleeping mother and child.) und S C&I

4345 My Own Sweet Pet / und S C&I

4346 My Own True Love / und S C&I

4347 My Pet Bird / und S C&I

4348 My Pet Bird / (Vignette.) und M C&I

4349 My Picture / J. Cameron on stone. (¾ length of girl, vignette.) 1856 L C&I

4350 My Pony and Dog / 8.4x12.4. (White pony in stable.) und S C&I

4351 My Pony & Dog / #497 / 8.12x11.8 (Exterior scene, piebald horse.) und S C&I

4352 My Pretty Irish Girl / und S C&I

4353 My Sister / #4 / (Oval in ornamental scroll border.)
1846 S N.C.

4354 My Sweetheart / (Vignette, girl's head.)
und S C&I

4355 My Sweetheart / (Girl's head.)
und L C&I

4356 My Three White Kittens /
und S C&I

4357 My Three White Kitties / Learning their A B C's / 8.2x12.8 (Slightly round corners.)
und S C&I

Myron Perry **See:** Fast Trotters No. 1907.

Mystery (Yacht) **See:** Regatta No. 5105.

Mystic Park Course **See:** Nos. 935, 983, 4250, 5571, 6221-2.

N

Namouna (Yacht) **See:** No. 5723.

4358 Nancy / 11.15 x 8.9 (¾ length, shawl draped over arms, marine view through window at left.)
und S N.C.

4359 Nancy / #255 / 12 x 8.8 (Half length, white dress, seated, writing.)
und S N.C.

4360 Nancy Hanks / J. Cameron, Del.
1892 S C&I

Nancy Hanks (Horse) **See:** Nos. 2531, 2539, 4360, 6193, 6200.

4361 Napoleon / (Vignette, body slightly to left, head turned slightly to right, military uniform.)
und M N.C.

4362 Napoleon / #174 / (Half length, vignette.)
und S N.C.

4363 Napoleon at St. Helena / 12.4x8.4 (Upright, standing on rock, sea in background.)
und S N.C.

4364 Napoleon at St. Helena /
und S C.C.

4365 Napoleon at Waterloo /
und S N.C.

4366 Napoleon Bonaparte / Emperor of France / (Half length.)
und M C&I

4367 Napoleon Crossing the Alps / 12x 8.10 (Vignette, upright, white horse to left.)
und S N.C.

4368 Napoleon Crossing the Alps / #78 / 12x8.8 (Upright, spirited troops in background.)
und S C.C.

4369 Napoleon, Emperor of France / #100 / 11.15x8.11 (Napoleon in Imperial robes seated on throne, full length.)
1847 S N.C.

4370 Napoleon / In the highest degree of his prosperity / #100 / 11.13x9 (Full length, military uniform.)
und S N.C.

4370A Napoleon / The Hero of 100 Battles / The celebrated horse, Euphrates, presented to him by the Emperor of Prussia / #62 / (Vignette, Napoleon in uniform mounted on white charger to right, sword in right hand, marching troops with bayonets.)
und S N.C.

4371 Napoleon / The Hero of 100 Battles / (To left, right arm extended, different composition from preceding.)
und S N.C.

4372 Napoleon's Strategy, or King William Out-generaled / (Vignette, cartoon showing Jules Favre, Crown Prince, King William all serving Napoleon at table.)
1870 S C&I

Napoleon **See:** Nos. 49, 1498, 3612, 3789, 5473, 5914, 6098-9, 6862-3.

4373 Napoleon Eugene Louis / Prince Imperial of France. Born 16th March 1856 / 11x9.
und S C&I

4374 Napoleon II — Duke Of Reichstadt /
1846 S N.C.

Napoleon II **See:** Nos. 6862-3.

4375 Napoleon III, Ubergabe der Kaiser /
1870 S C&I

Napoleon III **See:** Nos. 2371, 3789, 5914.

4376 Narragansett Steamship Co's Steamer "Bristol" of the Fall River Line Capt. A. G. Simmons, The / (1 additional line.)
und S C&I

4377 Narragansett Steamship Co's Steamer "Providence" of the Fall River Line, The / Capt. B. M. Simmons / 1 additional line. (Vignette. Same stone as preceding, name and Capt's initials changed.)
und S C&I

Narragansett (Steamboat) **See:** No. 5993.

Narragansett Park Course **See:** Nos. 5015, 6180, 6184-5, 6190.

4378 Narrow Way, The /
und S N.C.

4379 Narrows, The / From Fort Hamilton / #375 / 8.3x11.10.
und S N.C.

4380 Narrows, from Staten Island, The / #141 / 8.2x11.11 (2 female figures at right.) und S N.C.

4381 Narrows, New York Bay, The / From Staten Island / 7.15x12.7 (2 trees on each side, 8 people on hill in foreground.) und S C&I

4382 Narrows, New York Bay, from Staten Island, The / (4 people in foreground, trees smaller and changes in boats shown.) und S C&I

Nashville **See:** No. 6284.

4383 Nat Langham / Champion of the Middle Weights / 14.12x12.4 (1 additional line, 2 columns of 5 lines, upright.) und M C&I

Natchez (Mississippi Steamer) **See:** Nos. 2629-30, 2644, 4116, 5730.

4384 National Cadets 9th Regt. New York State Artillery / Henry U. Slipper — Col. Commandant / und S N.C.

4385 National Democratic Banner for 1860 / Hon. John C. Breckinridge of Kentucky for President, Hon. Joseph Lane of Oregon for Vice-President / (Upright.) 1860 S C&I

4386 National Democratic Banner, 1860 / Hon. Stephen A. Douglas of Illinois for President, Herschel V. Johnson of Georgia for Vice President / 12x8.10. (Upright.) 1860 S C&I

4387 National Democratic Banner of Victory, 1868. / Hon. Horatio S. Seymour of New York, Genl. Frank P. Blair of Missouri. Peace, Union and Constitutional Government / 12.11x8.10 (Upright.) 1868 S C&I

4388 National Game, The / Three "Outs" and one "Run" / Abraham Winning the Ball / (Left to right, Bell with bat marked "Fusion"; Douglas with bat marked "Non-Intervention"; Breckinridge with bat marked "Slavery Extension"; Lincoln with rail for bat marked "Equal Rights and Free Territory." Vignette.)
1860 M C&I

4389 National Union Republican Banner, 1860 / (Lincoln & Hamlin, upright.)
1860 S C&I

4390 National Union Republican Banner, 1868 / (Grant & Colfax, upright.)
1868 S C&I

4391 National Washington Monument /

In the City of Washington, D.C. / #273 / J.S. on stone. 12.2x8.8. 1 additional line, 2 columns. (Upright.)
und S N.C.

4392 National Washington Monument, The / Erected at the City of Washington, D.C. / By the Government and the people of the United States as a tribute to the glorious memory of George Washington / First in war. etc. 3 additional lines. The White House. U.S. Treasury. U.S. Capitol. 21.9x14.11 (Upright.) 1885 L C&I

4393 Natural and the Spiritual Man, The / #352 / 11x8.3 (Bust of Christ surrounded by 9 symbolical figures, upright.) und S N.C.

4394 Natural Bridge / In the "Blue Ridge" region, Rockbridge County, Va. / 8.8x12.8 (1 additional line height, etc.) und S C&I

4395 "Naughty Cat!" / (Upright, boy holding dead bird, cat at side.)
1874 S C&I

4396 Naval Bombardment of Vera Cruz/ March 1847 / #465 / 8.3x13.1.
1847 S N.C

4397 Naval Heroes of the United States/ #1 / (Battle of Lake Erie in center, surrounded by portraits of Perry, Lawrence, Decatur, Porter, Blakely, and Bainbridge.) 1846 S N.C.

4398 Naval Heroes of the United States/ #2 / (Battle of Lake Champlain in center, surrounded by portraits of McDonough, Hull, Stewart, Allen, Jones, and Barney.) 1846 S N.C.

4399 Naval Heroes of the United States/ #3 / No. 382 (Worships "Serapis" and "Bon Homme Richard" in center, surrounded by portraits of Alexander Murray, John Paul Jones, Richard Dale, Nicholas Biddle, Edward Preble, and John Barry.)
1846 S N.C.

4400 Naval Heroes of the United States/ #4 / (Center shows battle between Constitution and Guerriere, surrounded by 6 portraits.)

(I have never seen a copy of this print, and doubt if it was ever published. No record exists in the Copyright office.) 1846 S N.C.

4401 Nazareth of Galilee / N. D. de la Merci — Na sa del las merce des — Our Lady of Mercy / 8.8x12.8.
und S C&I

4402 Nearer my God to Thee / (Motto with flowers, vignette.)
und S C&I

4403 Nearest Way in Summer Time, The / Landscape by T. Creswick, R.A. 11.5 x15.14 (Couple with 4 horses and wagon fording stream.)
und M C&I

4404 Nearing the Finish Line / The American Sloop Yacht "Volunteer" winning her second & final Race for / The America's Cup against the Scotch Cutter "Thistle" over the outside course N.Y. Sept. 30, 1887 / Thistle. Volunteer. Scotland Lightship. Flagship Electra. 19.10x28.
1880 L C&I
Nebraska See: No. 2640.

4405 Neck and Neck to the Wire / Jay Eye See 2:10¾. Maud S 2:10¼. St. Juiien 2:11¼ / 18.4x27.14 (3 large heads, to left.)   1884 L C&I

4406 Necker /   und S N.C.
Needle Gun (Horse) See: No. 5436.

4407 Nellie / (Half length vignette portrait.)   und S C&I
Nellie Sontag (Horse) See: No. 1860.

4408 Nelson / (Top of print) / 2:10¾ (At bottom) / 7.12x10.8 (Oval, ¾ broadside, high-wheeled sulky to right.)   1891 S C&I
Nelson (Horse) See: Nos. 981-2, 6214-6.

4409 Nettie / By Rysdyk's Hambletonian, dam an American Star Mare / Winner of the first prize $2500 in the $5000 purse for 2:20 horses, at Beacon Park, Boston, Sept. 11th, 1874 / 2 additional lines. (High-wheeled sulky broadside to right.)   1874 S C&I

4410 Nettie — Record 2:18 / Driven by John E. Turner (Vignette.)
und S C&I
Nettie See: No. 923.

4411 New Brood, The / 8.2x12.8 (2 children feeding chickens.)
und S C&I
Newburn, N.C. See. No. 419.
New Brunswick, Canada See: Nos. 442, 2616, 3094, 3540, 5329, 5663, 5927.

4412 New Cachucha, The / El Jaleo de Jeres /   und S N.C.

4413 New "Confederate Cruiser," The / J. Cameron on stone. (Democratic Party in Greeley's hat in high sea, his coat used as a sail — vignette.)
1872 S C&I

4414 New England Beauty, A /
und S C&I

4415 New England Coast Scene, Off Boston Light /   und S C&I

4416 New England Coast Scene / 8.7x 12.8 (Rocky, moss-grown coast, ocean, fishermen and picnickers on rocks, numerous sailboats, islands, light house.)   und S C&I

4417 New England Home, A / 8x12.8.
und S C&I

4418 New England Homestead, A / 7.9x 12.8. From a daguerreotype by Cutting.
1852 S N.C.

4419 New England Scenery / F. F. Palmer, Del. 23.7x16.6 (Girl and boy on road at right, pantalettes.)
1866 L C&I

4420 New England Winter Scene / Painted by G. H. Durrie. 16.7x23.10 (Plain sky.)   1861 L C&I
(There is another state of this print which shows clouds in the sky.)

4421 New Excursion Steamer, The / Columbia / "Gem of the Ocean." / The largest Steamboat ever built for the Excursion business / Parsons & Atwater, Del. 19.5x34.8.
1877 L C&I

4422 New Fashioned Girl, The / (Vignette, full length.)
und S C&I

4423 New Fountain of Democracy, The / Swill Milk for Hungry Suckers. / J. Cameron on stone. (Vignette. Stream marked "Secession, Pro Slaver, Tammany and Corruption" running into tub at which Greeley is eating. Greeley's head is attached to body of cow, the "Suckers" are Democrats, shade of Jackson says. Shades of Jefferson: "Have the Democratic Party sunk as low as that?" "Tribune" Stables at left, building at rear marked "Cincinnati Slop Shop.")
1872 S C&I
New Hampshire See: Nos. 278, 536, 955, 1664-5, 2223, 3093, 3419, 3420, 4242, 4515, 5521.

4424 New Hat Man, The / (Figure made of hats, upright, vignette.)
1875 S C&I
New Haven See: Nos. 4790, 6429.

4425 New Jersey Fox Hunt, A / "Taking a Breath" / Thos. Worth on stone. (Vignette.)   1876 S C&I

4426 New Jersey Fox Hunt, A / "A Smoking Run" / Thos. Worth on stone. (Vignette.)   1876 S C&I
New Jersey See: Nos. 180, 1085,

3203, 4425-6, 4587, 6142, 6552-9, 6754-5.

New London See: No. 2095.

New Orleans, La. See: Nos. 417-8, 1099-1100, 3480.

4427 New Palace Steamer Pilgrim, of the Fall River Line / The Iron Monarch of Long Island Sound / 2 columns, 3 lines each of description, 8.10x14.8 (To right, no plate line.)
1883 M C&I

4428 New St. Patrick's Cathedral, The / Fifth Ave., New York / Corner stone laid Aug. 15th, 1858, by His Grace John Archbishop Hughes / 1 additional line. 12.8x9.1 (Upright.)
und S C&I

4429 New Steamship "Etruria," The, of the Cunard Line / 1 additional line of dimensions.
und S C&I

4430 New Steamship "Pavonia," The / of the Cunard Line / 1 additional line of dimensions.
und S C&I

4431 New Steamship "Umbria," of the Cunard Line, The / 1 additional line of dimensions. 8.4x14.
und S C&I

4432 New Suspension Bridge — Niagara Falls, The / 8.6x12.8 (View of falls, Suspension Bridge before completion; landscape, rocky cliffs, no train on bridge.)
und S C&I

4433 New York and Brooklyn / Sketched and drawn on stone by Parsons and Atwater. 103 references in 7 lines. 20.10 x32.12 (Bird's-eye view from Jersey City.)
1875 L C&I

4434 New York and Brooklyn / With Jersey City and Hoboken Water Front/ Parsons & Atwater on stone. 20.14x 32.14. 100 references in 7 lines (Bird's-eye view from Jersey City.)
1877 L C&I

4435 New York Bay / From Bay Ridge, L.I. / F. F. Palmer, Del. 8 references. 14.12x20.6 (New York, and New Jersey in background.)
1860 M C&I

4436 New York Bay, From Bay Ridge / Long Island / 5 references. 8.7x12.7.
und S C&I

4437 New York Bay / From the Telegraph Station / #376 / 8.3x11.9.
und S N.C.

4438 New York Beauty, The / (Vignette.)
und S C&I

New York City See: Nos. 251, 377, 531, 612, 1020, 1089, 1101-14, 1561-2, 1564, 1907, 1946, 2118, 2206, 2309, 2458, 2471, 2618-9, 2647, 2686, 2691-3, 3173, 3285, 3504-6, 3877, 3973, 4106, 4428, 4433-5, 4443-4, 4446, 4448, 4503, 4792, 4847, 4853, 5466, 5644, 6286, 6296, 6326, 6359, 6399-407, 6416-8, 6422-5, 6547, 6550, 6574.

New York City(Bartholdi's Statue) See: Nos. 373, 655, 2566-76.

New York City (Blackwell's Island) See: Nos. 532, 562.

New York City (Broadway) See: Nos. 697-9, 6430.

New York City (Castle Garden) See: Nos. 840, 1957.

New York City (Central Park) See: Nos. 508, 948-54, 1896, 2481, 5266.

New York City (City Hall) See: Nos. 739, 1086-8, 2522, 6422-4.

New York City (Crystal Palace) See: Nos. 743-4, 4440-2.

New York City (Custom House) See: Nos. 1334-5.

New York City (Great East River Bridge) See: Nos. 2471, 2479-80, 2584-2602, 2725-6.

New York City (Harbor) See: Nos. 2725-6, 3069, 4381-2, 4437, 4450, 4847-9, 5715, 5876, 6351, 6407.

New York City (Harlem River) See: Nos. 375, 6441-2, 6550, 6574.

4439 New York Clipper Ship "Challenge" / #475 / 8.12x12.12.
und S N.C.

4440 New York Crystal Palace For the Exhibition of the Industry of all Nations, etc., / F. F. Palmer, Del. 17.13x 26.
1853 L N.C.

4441 New York Crystal Palace / For the Exhibition of the Industry of all Nations. Constructed of Iron and Glass / The extreme length and breadth of the building are each 365 feet. Height of dome to top of lantern, 148 feet, entire / #110 / 7.14x12.6. 1 additional line dimensions. (Many people in foreground, horseman on extreme left, trolley in center.)
und S N.C.

4442 New York Crystal Palace / For the Exhibition, etc. (Title exactly same as preceding) / #110 / J. Schutz, Del. 7.14x12.6 (Fewer people in foreground, trolley on left, more of reservoir shown at right.)
und S N.C.

4443 New York Ferry Boat / 8.8x12.8 (No boats in background, ferry boat to right, flags to right, "Fulton" on boat.)
und S C&I

4444 New York Ferry Boat / 8x12.8 (Ships in background, boat to left, flags to right.)   und S C&I

4445 New York Fireman's Monument / Greenwood Cemetary, L.I. / 10.7x14.16 (7 columns, 6 lines.)
1855 M N.C.

4446 New York from Weehawken /
1835 S C.C.

4447 New York Light Guards Quick Step / Published by Hewitt & Jaques (Vignette, music sheet.)
1839 S N.C.

4448 New York, Looking North from the Battery /.   1860 S C&I

4449 New York / Pilot's Monument / In Greenwood Cemetery, L.I. / 10.4x14.15.
1855 M C&I

New York State See: Nos. 30, 191, 209-13, 1000, 1827, 3012, 3439, 4124, 4432, 4454-60, 4567, 4572, 4608, 4662-3, 5056, 5339, 5550-1, 5891-3, 5907, 5938-41, 6157, 6232, 6376, 6385, 6435, 6438.

New York State (Adirondacks) See: Nos. 323-4, 2865, 2982, 3070, 3086, 3091, 3406-8, 3413, 3439, 4787-8, 5049, 5275, 5395-8, 5627, 5895, 6419, 6435-6, 6573.

New York State (Brooklyn) See: Nos. 1262, 1297, 1299, 4433-4, 4568, 6402-3.

New York State (Catskills) See: Nos. 857-60, 1648, 1932-3, 3327, 5144, 5418-20, 6394, 6431.

New York State (Harlem River) See: Nos. 375, 2810-1, 6387, 6441-2.

New York State (Hudson River) See: Nos. 1277, 1315, 1751, 2971-9, 3010-1, 3021, 3026, 3153, 3439, 4123, 4245, 4601-2, 5421, 5891-3, 6282, 6350, 6377-81, 6383-4, 6421, 6428, 6433-4, 6438, 6444-8, 6453, 6457-8, 6617.

New York State (Long Island) See: Nos. 293, 1295-6, 3756, 3972, 4178, 4435-6, 4445, 4449, 4556, 4582, 4584, 4753, 5070, 6087-9, 6388, 6437.

New York State (West Point) See: Nos. 1277, 2972, 4245, 6104, 6325, 6378-80, 6383-4, 6428.

New York (U.S. Cruiser) See: Nos. 273, 6300, 6644.

New York (Horse) See: No. 6564.

New York (Steamer) See: No. 6405.

New York (Steamship) See: No. 3884.

Newark (Cruiser) See: No. 6644.

Newburn, N.C. See: No. 419.

4450 New York Yacht Club Regatta, The / The Start from the Stake Boat in the Narrows / Off the new club house and grounds, Staten Island, New York harbor / Parsons & Atwater, Del. Vesta, Henrietta, Dauntless, Phantom, Fleetwing, Palmer, Addie V, White Wing, Geraldine, Annie. 17.5x27.13.
1869 L C&I

4451 Newfoundland Dog /
und S C&I

4452 Newfoundland Dog / 8.3x11.3.
und S C&I

4453 Newport Beach / 8.8x12.
und S C&I

Newport, R.I. See: Nos. 2383, 5413, 6816.

4454 Niagara by Moonlight / (Same composition as No. 4458.)
und M C&I

4455 Niagara Falls / 8x10.2.
und S N.C.

4456 Niagara Falls / 14.12x20.1.
und M C&I

4457 Niagara Falls / From Goat Island/ 9.5x15.12 (Daylight.)
und M C&I

4458 Niagara Falls / From Goat Island / 9.5x15.12 (Same composition as preceding, but night scene—moon added.)
und M C&I

4459 Niagara Falls from Goat Island /
und S C&I

4460 Niagara Falls / From Table Rock / 8.4x11.11.   und S N.C.

4461 Niagara Falls / From the Canada Side / 7.15x12.7.
und S C&I

Niagara Falls See: Nos. 1827-9, 4432, 5056.

Niagara (Frigate) See: Nos. 4754, 6343-4.

4462 Nice and Tempting Oysters /
und S C&I

4463 Nice Family Party, A / J. Cameron on stone. (Political cartoon. Grant, center holding "Government Cake." Politicians reaching for it and saying "Let us have a piece," while Grant says "Let us have peace." Vignette.)
und M C&I

4464 Nigger in the Woodpile, The / (Young America, Horace Greeley, and Lincoln seated on woodpile marked "Republican Platform" under which is a negro. Vignette.)
1860 M C&I

4465 Nigh to Bethany /
und S C&I

4466 Nigh to Bethany /
und S N.C.

4467 Night / 8.4x11.2 (From original bas relief by Thorwaldsen.)
und S C&I

4468 Night After the Battle / Burying the Dead / #441 / 8.6x12.8 (Officer in center foreground, horse on left, 3 American and 1 Mexican dead shown.)
1846 S N.C.

4469 Night After the Battle, The / Burying the Dead / #441 / J. Cameron on stone / 8.4x12.7 (Nurse center foreground, many more dead and wounded shown than in preceding.)
1847 S N.C.

4470 Night After the Battle, The / 7.4x 12.8 (Soldier holding torch, while nurse and another soldier support wounded man.)
1862 S C&I

4471 Night Before the Battle / The Patriot's Dream /
1861 M C&I

4472 Night by the Camp-Fire / 10.6x 14.15 (3 hunters and dogs, lake in background.)
1861 M C&I

4473 Night Express, The / The Start /
8.8x12.12 (Engine, tender, and 4 coaches leaving station at left, moonlight.)
und S C&I

4474 Night on the Hudson, A / "Through at Daylight" / F. F. Palmer, Del. 18x 27.12 (Shows steamers "Isaac Newton" and "Francis Skiddy".)
1864 L C&I

4475 Night Scene at a Junction / 18x 27.11 (Locomotives in foreground have straight smoke stacks, 5 other engines in rear, 1 broadside — no moon.)
1881 L C&I

4476 Night Scene at an American Railway Junction / Lightning Express, Flying Mail and Owl Trains "On Time" / Parsons & Atwater, Del. (Train on right has 4 cars extending around curve to right, no locomotive broadside in rear, moon.) (Probably the 1st state of this print.)
1876 L C&I

4477 Night Scene at an American Railway Junction / Lightning Express, Flying Mail, and Owl Trains "On Time" / Parsons & Atwater, Del. (Train on right has only baggage car attached, no cars extending around curve at right, locomotive in rear broadside.)
1876 L C&I

NIGHT SCENE AT AN AMERICAN RAILWAY JUNCTION.

NIGHT SCENE AT A JUNCTION.

Nightingale, Florence, Home Of **See:** No. 2864.

Nightingale (Clipper Ship) **See:** No. 1159.

4478 Nightmare in the Sleeping Car, A/ "Oh, I was So-O-O dry! Chorus "Dry up and Bust" / Thos. Worth on stone. (Vignette.) 1875 S C&I

Nightshade (Horse) **See:** No. 880.

4479 Nills Tower, Naworth / und S C&I

4480 Ninety and Nine, The / 8.11x12.8. 3 columns and 6 lines of verse. (Christ returning sheep to fold.) 1875 S C&I

4481 Nip and Tuck! / Thos. Worth on stone. (Comic vignette, 3 sulkies racing.) 1878 S C&I

4482 "Nip and Tuck" Race, A / J. Cameron '92 on stone. 12x18.13 (4 horses under saddle, to right.) 1892 M C&I

4483 Nipped in the Ice / (Boat on right, figures center foreground.) und S C&I

4484 No Ma'am, I didn't come to shoot birds / 2.14x4.12 (Similar Composition to "Where do you buy your cigars?" No. 6637.) 1880 V.S. C&I

4485 No Ma'am, I don't Care to Shoot Birds / 1880 S C&I

4486 No, No, Fido / und V.S. C&I

4487 "No One to Love Me" / (Vignette, comic winter scene, mule out in snow.) 1880 S C&I

4488 No rose Without a Thorn / 12.7x 8.15 (Young man, kissing girl's hand, father about to strike him with rope, upright.) und S N.C. $25.

4489 No Slate Here / (Grant leaning over the counter of "The Washington Hotel, U. Sam — Proprietor" requesting a third term of Uncle Sam which is refused. Vignette.) 1874 S C&I

4490 No Tick Here / (Wall clock marked "Time is Money.") und S C&I

4491 No Time Here — Played Out / J. Cameron on stone (Broken-down horse is labelled "No Time Here — Played Out".) 1871 S C&I

[195]

4492 No You Don't / #264 / 11.7x8.12 (Upright, ¾ length, girl with rose, which young man tries to get.)
und S C&I

4493 No You Don't / 11.9x8.15 (Upright, half length, companion to "Kiss me Quick" No. 3348.)
und S C&I

4494 Noah's Ark / #20 / Sarony on stone. 8.4x12.9 (Gnarled tree on right, serpent entwined around 1 of 2 palm trees at left, no human figures in foreground.) und S N.C.

4495 Noah's Ark / 1 additional line Biblical quotation. (Ark to right, animals in foreground.)
und S N.C.

4496 Noah's Ark / 8.5x12.8 (Ark on left, pairs of animals entering, no human figures.) und S N.C.

4497 Noah's Ark / 8x12.8. 1 additional line. (Pairs of animals shown, 4 men in foreground.)
und S C&I

4498 Noah's Ark / 8.7x12.8. 2 additional lines. (3 men shown.)
und S C&I

4499 Nobby Tandem, A /
1879 V.S. C&I

4500 Noisy Pets / 8.15x12.12 (Child in chair, dog and cat at feet.)
und S C&I

4501 Noontide a shady spot /
und S C&I

Noordland (Steamship) See: Nos. 481, 5777.

Normandie (Steamship) See: No. 2310.

Norseman (Yacht) See: No. 6809.

4502 North American Indians / Osage warrior, Iroquois, Pawnee woman / Catlin, Del. 17.9x13.
und M C&I

North Carolina See: Nos. 386, 419, 589, 594, 810, 5908.

North Carolina (Steamship) See: Nos. 6327-30.

North Conway See: No. 278.

4503 North River Ferry Boat / (Vignette, no name on boat.)
und S C&I

4504 North Sea Whale Fishery / 8.12x 12.12 (Title in plate. Companion to "South Sea Whale Fishery" No. 5629.) (This print is usually marked "Pub-

lished at 33 Spruce St." and the publisher's name is not given. Nevertheless, it was definitely published by N. Currier.) und S N.C.

4505 North side view on the North Chincha Island / Sketched by H. Herryman, 1860. Published by William B. Colville, Callao.
und S C&I

4506 Northern Beauty, The / (Vignette, half length.) und S C&I

4507 Northern Scenery /
und V.S. C&I

Northern Scenery See: No. 2230.

4508 Nose Out of Joint, The / (Girl watching baby in bed, neglected dog nearby.) und S N.C.

4509 Nose Out of Joint, The / Buds of promise / #310 / 12x8 (Upright.)
und S N.C.

4510 Nosegay, The / #603 / (Upright, vignette, flowers in white vase.)
und S C&I

4511 Nosegay, The / #603 / (Upright, no vase.) und S N.C.

4512 Nosegay, The / (Upright, vignette, different composition.)
1870 S C&I

4513 Not Caught / There is many a slip between the cup and the lip / 13x20.12 (2 dogs after rat. Companion to "The First Lesson" No. 1973.)
und M N.C.

4514 Not Caught Yet / #592 / 8x12.8 (Fox beside trap baited with rabbit. Companion to No. 4189.)
und S N.C.

4515 Notch House, White Mountains, The / New Hampshire / #478 /
und S C&I

4516 Nothing Ventured Nothing Have /
und S C&I

4517 Notice to Smokers and Chewers / (Advertising card.)
und S C&I

4518 Notice to Smokers / and Chewers / #525 / (4 line rebus with small illustrations.) 1854 S N.C.

4519 Nova Scotia Scenery / 9.11x16.12.
1868 M C&I

Nova Scotia See: Nos. 442, 4519.

4520 Now and Then / (At top) or how to meet an old friend with a new face /

(2 views on 1 sheet showing Cass Kowtowing to high military officer and snubbing ordinary man.) Published by P. Smith.   1848 M N.C.

4521 Nuestra Senora de Guadalupe —

Our Lady of Guadalupe / #574 / 11.11 x8.5 (Oval within rectangle.)
    1848 S N.C.

Nutt, Commodore **See**: Nos. 2267, 2307.

O

4522 "O Dat Watermillion" / (Colored comic, 2 darkies caught in watermelon patch, vignette.)   1882 S C&I

4523 O! There's a Mousie! / 11.6 x 8.5 (Full length child in church, similar composition to "Little Ella.")   und S C&I

Oakland Park, Cal. Race Track **See**: No. 2534, 5334.

4524 Obdurate Mule, An / Going back on the Parson / "Now den all togedder and sumfin's bound to come" / (Mule refuses to move on railroad track even when fire is lighted under him, train approaching. Vignette, colored comic.)
    1890 S C&I

O'Brien, Wm. Smith **See**: No. 6704.

4525 Observations on the Cure of Strabismus / Alfred C. Post M.D. / Published by Charles S. Francis, 252 Broadway, N.Y. 7 Plates Dr. Westmacott, Delt. About 3 by 5 inches. (Vignette.)   1841 V.S. N.C.

4526 Occident / [Formerly "Wonder"] brown gelding, by pacing stallion St. Clair, dam's pedigree unknown. / Owned by Ex-Gov. Leland Stanford of California / Record 2:16¾, Sept. 17th, 1873 / Thos. Worth on stone. 16.6 x25 (High wheeled sulky to right, broadside.)   1876 L C&I

4527 Occident / By St. Clair — Record 2:16¾ / Owned by Leland Stanford /
    und S C&I

Occident (Horse) **See**: Nos. 769-70.

Ocean Express (Clipper Ship) **See**: 1160.

Ocean Monarch **See**: No. 745.

4528 Ocean Steamer in a Heavy Gale, An /   und S C&I

Oceanic (Steamship) **See**: No. 5778.

O'Connell, Daniel **See**: Nos. 1356-61, 1479, 2205, 3877.

4529 October Landscape /
    und M C&I

October Landscape **See**: No. 178.

4530 Odd Fellow / Friendship, Love and

Truth / #572 / (Full length figure in regalia.)   1848 S N.C.

4531 Odd Fellows / (Full length figures in regalia.)   und S C&I

4532 Odd Fellows / N.G. of a lodge. G.P. of an encampment / #572 / 11.13x 8.7 (2 figures, full length.)
    und S N.C.

4533 Odd Fellows Chart / 13.7x9.12.
    1877 S C&I

4534 Odd Fellows Chart / For colored people /   und S C&I

4535 "Odd Trick, The" / F.C. on stone. (Companion to "One for His Nob" No. 4613. Old maid with rose in one hand, other hidden hand holds aces, upright vignette.)   1884 S C&I

4536 Off a Lee Shore / 8.8x13.8 (Clipper ship with all sails set, rocky coast at right.)   und S C&I

4537 Off for the War / #198 / 11.7x8.7 (Officer with mustache, shown at right, upright.)   1861 S C&I

4538 Off for the War / 11.8x8.7 (Bearded officer at left, soldiers with flag in background, upright.)
    1861 S C&I

4539 Off for the War / The Soldier's Adieu / #190 / (Companion to No. 2858. Slightly rounded corners.)
    1861 S C&I

4540 Off His Nut / Gracious Massy, I'se struck de Comet! / Drawn by D. J. Murphy. (Darky with remains of sulky clinging to smoke stack of locomotive which hit him — Companion to 4597, vignette.)   1886 S C&I

4541 Off on The First Score / J. Cameron on stone. 12.2x19 (4 horses with high-wheeled sulkies passing the grandstand.)   1891 M C&I

4542 Off on the First Score / J. Cameron on stone. 12.2x18.15 (Same general composition as preceding, 1 horse and rig removed, and low-wheeled rigs with pneumatic tires substituted for the high-wheelers. (The new low-wheeled rigs with rubber tires supplanted the old style high-wheeled sulkies in 1892.) 1893 M C&I

4543 Off the Coast in a Snowstorm / Taking a Pilot / 8.14x12.14.
und S C&I

4544 Off the Port / 8.11 x 13.9 (Lighthouse at right.)
und S C&I
Off the Port See: No. 1162.

4545 Oh! How Fine / 8.9x12.10 (Friar with wine glass and carafe. Companion to "Lost" Nos. 3782, 6756.)
und S N.C.

4546 Oh! How Nice / #314 / 8.9x12.9 (Monkey eating oyster.)
und S N.C.

4547 Oh Sweetly We Will Sing Love / A favorite Ballad Rondo / as sung by Miss Shirreff, / Music by Auber / Written and arranged / by / William Clifton. 1839 S N.C.
Ohio See: Nos. 6101-2.
Ohio (Ship) See: No. 6333.

4548 Old Barn Floor, The / 15.14x23.14 (Pickaninny dancing, darky with banjo, farmer, girl and baby watching.)
1868 L C&I

4549 Old Blandford Church / Petersburg, Virginia / F.F.P. (Palmer) on stone. 8 x 12.8
und S C&I

4550 Old Bridge, The /
und S C&I

4551 Old Bull Dog on the Right Track, The / McClellan, Lincoln, Lee, Davis, Beauregard, Grant. (Vignette, political cartoon.) 1864 M C&I

4552 Old Castle, The / (Moonlight scene, ruins.)
und S C&I

4553 Old Credit Played Out / J. Cameron on stone. 2 columns of 2 lines. (Decrepit horse marked "No Time Here." Vignette.) 1871 S C&I

4554 Old Darby and Joan / Oh! For the days when we were young /
und S C&I

4555 Old Farm Gate, The / F. F. Palmer, Del. (Children playing on gate.)
1864 L C&I

4556 Old Farm House Williamsburg, L.I. / #473 / Crayon Studies.
und S N.C.

4557 Old Farm House, The / 8.7x12.8 (Winter scene.) 1872 S C&I

4558 Old Feudal Castle, The / (Shepherds with sheep, ruins in background.)
und S C&I

4559 Old Ford Bridge, The / 8.8x12.9.
und S C&I

OLD BARN FLOOR.

4560 Old General Ready for a "Movement", The / (Vignette.)
und M C&I

4561 Old Homestead, The / F. F. Palmer,
Del. 9.12x14.12.   1855 M N.C.

4562 Old Homestead, The / F. 'F. Palmer, Del. 10.13x15.7 (House more
prominent, barn nearly broadside, 2
large trees.)   und M C&I

4563 Old Homestead in Winter, The /
Painted by G. H. Durrie and signed on
stone. 18.10x26.8.
1864 L C&I

4564 Old Ironsides / 2 columns, 3 lines.
(Full length, sailor with American
flag.)   1861 S C&I

4565 Old Kentucky Home, De — Far
Away / 12x10. (Upright vignette, ¾
length of darky playing fiddle.)
1885 S C&I

4566 Old Lady who Lived in a Shoe, The
/ She had so many children, she didn't
know what to do /
und S C&I

4567 Old Manse, The / 8.8x12.8 (View of
the Vander Hayden Palace, Albany,
N.Y. (House on left, 5 figures to right.)
und S C&I

4568 Old Mansion House, Gowanus Road
/ Crayon Studies / #470 / 8.2x14.5
(Located at Fifth Avenue and Third St.
Bkln. Building to right is the Harrison
St. Church, water course is now Third
Avenue. Vignette. Same composition
as "Old Stone House" No. 4584.)
und S N.C.

4569 Old Mare the Best Horse, The /
Scott Leighton on stone. 15.13x23.13
(Winter scene, companion to "Waking
up the Old Mare" No. 6490.)
1881 L C&I

4570 Old Massa's Grave /
und S C&I

4571 Old Mill — in Summer, The / 8.7
x12.8.   und S C&I

4572 Old Mill-Dam, The / at Sleepy Hollow (New York) 8.8x12.6.
und S C&I

4573 Old Neptune, the Great Black Sea
Lion / the monarch of the ocean, the
only animal of the kind ever captured
alive; he was visited by over 600,000
persons during the few months he was
exhibited at Barnum's Museum, New
York. L.M. (Louis Maurer) on stone.
(Title repeated in Spanish, vignette.
upright.)   1860 S C&I

4574 Old Norman Castle, The /
und S C&I

4575 Old Norman Castle, The / F. F.
Palmer, Del.   und L N.C.

4576 Old Oaken Bucket, The / F. F. Palmer, Del. 15.4x22.8. 2 stanzas, 4 lines
of verse by Woodworth. (Rural scene,
house, barn, cattle, etc.)
1864 L C&I

4577 Old Oaken Bucket, The / 8.8x12.8.
2 columns, 2 lines of verse.
1872 S C&I

4578 Old Plantation Home, The / 8.7x
12.8 (Colored children dancing in yard,
darky playing banjo.)
1872 S C&I

Old Put (Horse) See: No. 5436.

4579 Old Ruined Castle, The / (River
in background.)   und S C&I

4580 Old Ruins, The / 8x12.8 (Ruins of
old church, cows, etc.)
und S C&I

4581 Old Ruins, The / #327 / (Vignette,
ruined castle, lake in foreground, 2
couples in boat.)
und S C&I

4582 Old Saw Mill, L.I. / #471 / (Vignette.)   und S N.C.

4583 Old Sledge / High-Low-Jack-Game
/ #675 / 11.12x9 (2 men playing cards,
upright.)   und S C&I

4584 Old Stone House L.I. 1699, The /
#470 / (Vignette, same stone as "Old
Mansion House" No. 4568. Title
changed.)   und S N.C.

4585 Old Suit and the New, The /
1879 S C&I

4586 Old Suit and the New, The / (Advertising card, 2 views about postcard
size.)   1880 V.S. C&I

4587 Old Tennant Parsonage, The / on
Monmouth Battlefield / Erected 1706 /
Published by William S. Potter, Free-
hold, N.J. 11.14x16.4.
1859 M C.C.

4588 Old Way, The / The New Way / I
Gave Credit — I Sell for Cash / 8.9x
12.14 (2 views on 1 sheet, showing 2
businessmen, 1 prosperous, 1 starving.)
1870 S C&I

4589 Old Virginny /
und S C&I

4590 Old Weir Bridge, The / Lakes of
Killarney /   und M C&I

4591 Old Windmill, The / F. F. Palmer,

Del. 10.8x14.15 (Cattle in foreground, village in background.)

und M C&I

O'Mahoney, Col. John **See:** No. 1196.

4592 On a Point / F. F. Palmer, Del. 9.14 x14.14 (2 dogs in wheat field, farm house in rear.)　　　1855 M N.C.

4593 On a Strong Scent! / (Vignette, hunting comic.)　　　1880 S C&I

4594 On Board the Great Western Steam Ship on her Voyage from Bristol to New York / W.K.H. (W. K. Hewitt) on stone. About 5x8.4 (Vignette, ship to right, music sheet.)

und S N.C.

4595 On de Haf Shell / (Vignette, darky opening oysters.)　　　1886 S C&I

4596 1876 — On Guard / Unceasing vigilance is the price of "Liberty" / 1876 S C&I

4597 On his style / "Take a Mity smart Lokymoty to cotch dis coon" / (Upright vignette, companion to No. 4540.) 1886 S C&I

4598 On the Coast of California / und S C&I

4599 On the Downs, at Epsom / und S C&I

4600 On the Homestretch / Thos. Worth on stone. (Companion to "Getting a Boost," No. 2363. Driver has fallen back through cover of wagon. Vignette.)　　　1882 S C&I

4601 On the Hudson / 8x12.8 (Shows steamer "St. John".)

1869 S C&I

4602 On the Hudson / 8x12.8 (Same as preceding, no name on boat.) 1869 S C&I

4603 On the Juniata / 9.11x16.15 (Picnic party on left.)　　　1869 M C&I

4604 On the Lake / 8.6x12.7 (Fisherman on shore, other figures in rowboat.) und S C&I

4605 On the Mississippi / 8x12.8 (Broadside of steamer "Mayflower.") 1869 S C&I

4606 On the Mississippi / 8x12.8 (Same as preceding, no name on boat.) 1869 S C&I

4607 On the Mississippi / Loading Cotton / 7.15x12.7 (Same stone as "Loading Cotton" No. 3745. Shows the New Orleans Packet boat "Eclipse.") 1870 S C&I

4608 On the Owago / 8.8 x 12.8 (Couple on bank at left.)　　　und S C&I

4609 On the St. Lawrence / Indian Encampment / 8.8 x 12.9　und S C&I

4610 On the Seine / About 5x7. Printed on Sheet with "View in Switzerland" No. 6386 (Vignette.)

und V.S. C&I

4611 Onconvanience of Single Life, The / Moral "It's never too late to mend" / (Same composition as "Miseries of a Bachelor" No. 4151. Upright.)　　　und S C&I

4612 One Flag — One Country — Zwei Lager / (2 soldiers drinking, vignette.) und S C&I

4613 "One for His Nob" / F.C. on stone. (Companion to "The Odd Trick" No. 4535. White man holding colored baby, upright, vignette.)

1884 S C&I

4614 One for His Pet / 1884 S C&I

4615 One of the Heavyweights / und S C&I

4616 Only Daughter, The / C.L. on stone. 10.1x7.12 (Upright.)

und S N.C.

4617 Only Daughter, The / #371 / (Full length, roses in hand.)

und S C&I

4618 Only Daughter, The / Pet of the Family / #371 / (Full length figure, roses at feet and in right hand, similar composition to preceding with slight changes in composition, upright.) und S N.C.

4619 Only Living Giraffes in America, The / Colossus 17 feet high, Cleopatra 15 feet high / #676 / (Upright, 2 Arab attendants.)　　　und S N.C.

4620 Only Son, The / und S N.C.

4621 Only Son, The / und S C&I

4622 Operatic Quadrilles / Selected and Arranged for the Piano Forte. From the most celebrated Operas. #1 — "La Dame Blanche" / William Martin, Boston. Pub. by Oliver Ditson 1839. (Interior view of opera house.) und S N.C.

4623 Orangemens Chart. O.B.L. / Holiness to the Lord / 10x13.11.

und S C&I

4624 Oregon / #402 / 7.12x13.2. (2 columns of 4 lines dimensions. (Hudson river steamer, Palisades in background.) und S N.C.

Oregon (Steamer) See: Nos. 5532-3, 5779-80.

O'Reilley, Miles See: No. 1550.

4625 Oriental Landscape / (Group with camels in foreground.)
und L C&I

4626 Origin of the Species, The / "There's a legend of yore, over which one might pore. That all the first babies were born of a flower, That Caesers and Catos were dug like potatoes, or dropped from the branches like juicy tomatoes / 8x12.11 (Shows Mephisto examining babies growing on plants like tomatoes.)
1874 S C&I

4627 Original "General Tom Thumb" as he appeared before Her Majesty, Queen Victoria, The / #680 / 8.8x12.8 (Central portrait of Tom Thumb surrounded by 9 small views of him in various characters. See Barnum's Gallery of Wonders #1. Upright.) 1860 S C&I

4628 Ormonde / Ridden by Fred Archer/ J. Cameron on stone. (Vignette, profile portrait to left, under saddle.)
1889 S C&I

4629 Ornamental Cards / (16 on the sheet.) und S C&I

4630 Osage Warrior / Iroquois. Pawnee Woman / North American Indians / Catlin, Del. 17.9x13 (Upright.)
und M C&I

Osborn, R. W. See: Nos. 3537, 4066.

4631 Oscar J. Dunn, Lieut. Govr. of Louisiana / 11.13x8.7 (Upright.)
und S C&I

4632 Ostend Doctrine, The / For sale at No. 2 Spruce St. (Buchanan held up by 4 robbers who justify themselves by quoting from the Ostend Doctrine, which is printed on a poster on wall at right. Vignette.)
und S N.C.

4633 O'Sullivan's Cascade / Lake of Killarney / 7.15x12.7 (Fishermen in foreground.) und S C&I

4634 Othello (Top of print) Trotting Stallion by Phil Sheridan, dam by Planet G. D. Haidee / G. G. D. Satan G. G. D. Pedlar Mare / 13.12x13.6 (Upright.) 1879 M C&I
Ottawa River See: Nos. 1826, 1830.

4635 "Ould Times" at Donnybrook Fair/

8.1x12.9 (Irish group dancing outside.)
und S C&I

4636 Our Boat sets lightly on the wave / A duet and trio / Written, composed and arranged / and respectfully dedicated to the / New York Boat Clubs / by / William Clifton / New York, Atwill, 201 Broadway / (Oval, boat race showing the Battery, N.Y. and Governor's Island. Music sheet.)
und S N.C.

4637 "Our Cabinet" / (President Grover Cleveland and 7 others, vignette, upright.) 1885 L C&I

4638 Our / Father / Who art in Heaven/ Hallowed, etc. / J. Cameron on stone (6 lines of prayer at top, vignette portrait of "Jesus" surrounded by people in center, and 8 more lines at bottom completing prayer. Upright vignette.)
und S C&I

4639 Our Father / Who Art / in Heaven/ 9.8x14.10 (Scroll with flowers, vignette.) 1876 M C&I

4640 Our Lady of Guadalupe /
und S C&I

Our Lady of Guadalupe See: "Nuestra Senora" etc. No. 4521.

4641 Our Lady of Knock / (Story under title.) und S C&I

4642 Our Lady of Lourdes /
und S C&I

4643 Our Lady of Mercy / Notre Dame de la Merci / 8.2x11.5 (Top corners slightly rounded.)
und S C&I

4644 Our Lady of Mount Carmel /
1859 S N.C.

4645 Our Lady of Mount Carmel /
und S C&I

4646 Our Lady of Refuge /
und S C&I

4647 Our Lady of the Light /
und S C&I

4648 Our Lady of the Rosary / 11.15x 8.15 (Mary, infant Jesus, rosary.)
und S C&I

4649 Our Lady of the Seven Sorrows /
und S C&I

4650 Our Pasture / #440 / (Sheep.)
und S N.C.

4651 Our Pasture / #441 / 8.3x13.2 (2 cows, 2 calves.) und S N.C.

4652 Our Pets / Fast Asleep / 11.2x9.1 (2 children.)
und S C&I

4653 Our Pets / Wide Awake / (Upright, 2 children, companion to above.)
und S C&I

4654 Our Redeemer / 2 additional lines. 8.8x12.1.   und S C&I

4655 Our Savior / The Agony in Gethsemane / 1 additional line of Biblical quotation. 8.4x11.12.   und S C&I

4656 Our Savior at Prayer /
und S C&I

4657 Our Savior / El Senor / 1 additional line of Biblical quotation. 8.9x12 (Full length, upright.)
und S N.C.

4658 Our Victorious Fleets in Cuban Waters / 18x30.15 (Showing 17 naval vessels under full steam, names in 2 lines.)   1898 L C&I

4659 Our Village Home / 2.8x4.11.
und V.S. C&I

4660 Out for a Day's Shooting / Off For the Woods / L. Maurer on stone. 17.14 x26. (Companion to "A Good Day's Sport," No. 2425 same stone as "Life in the Country" No. 3511.)
1869 L C&I

Note on No. 4661 — (Title changed, wagon enlarged, another man and dog added to composition, 1 dog alongside removed.)

4661 Outlet of Niagara River, The / 7.15 x 12.8 (No. second descriptive line, no figures.)   und S C&I

4662 Outlet of The Niagara River, The / Lake Ontario in the Distance / #839 / 8.6x12.10. (3 figures in left foreground.)   und S C&I

4663 Outward Bound / #377 / 8x12.9.
1845 S N.C.

4664 Outward Bound / #377 / 8.10 x 12.14 / 3-masted ship off Governor's Island, very similar composition to "The Gem of the Atlantic" No. 2228. (Only 1 copy known.)
und S N.C.

4665 Outward Bound /
1846 S N.C.

4666 Outward Bound / (Vignette, showing 1 of Grinnell Minturn California Clippers.)
und S C&I

4667 Outward Bound / (Religious scene, group in boat — from baby to old age.)
und S C&I

4668 Over the Garden Wall / (2 figures, man and woman, full length, upright.)   und M C&I

OUTWARD BOUND.

Oxford University See: Nos. 2623-4, 2968.

4669 Oyster Paddy / (Figure made of oyster shells, vignette, upright.)
1875 S C&I

4670 An Oyster Supper / "We won't

Get Home Until Morning" / 8.2x12.12. und S C&I

4671 Oysters In the Latest Style / (Figure made of oyster shells. Same as "Oyster Paddy," upright, vignette.)
1875 S C&I

P

4672 Pacific Coast Steamship Co.'s Steamer / State of California / Goodall Perkins & Co. General Agents, San Francisco, Cal. / C. R. Parsons on stone. 17.6x27.3 (Ship to left.)
1878 L C&I

4673 Pacific Mail Steamship Company's Steamer "Great Republic" / 1 additional line of dimensions. 7x13.12 (Vignette.)
und S C&I

Pacific (Steamship) See: Nos. 6234, 6323-4.

4674 Pacing a Fast Heat / J. Cameron '92 on stone. (3 horses and high-wheeled sulkies to right.)
1892 M C&I

4675 Pacing a Fast Heat / J. Cameron '92 on stone. 12x18.3 (3 horses and low-wheeled sulkies with pneumatic tires to right — very similar composition to preceding.)
1893 M C&I

4676 Pacing Champions on their Mettle/ J. Cameron on stone. (3 horses to high-wheeled sulkies.)
1889 S C&I

4677 Pacing for a Grand Purse / L. Maurer, N.Y. on stone. 20x28.5 (Companion to "Trotting for a Grand Stake" No. 6171. 4 horses and high-wheeled sulkies passing stand, to right.)
1890 L C&I

4678 Pacing for a Grand Purse / L. Maurer on stone.
und L C&I

4679 Pacing Horse "Billy Boyce" of St. Louis / As he appeared at Buffalo, N.Y. Aug. 1st, 1868 etc. 2 lines / 2:14¼ / Thos. Worth on stone. J. Cameron, Del. on stone. 16.14x26.8 (5 additional lines, under saddle to right, passing judges stand.)
1868 L C&I

4680 Pacing in the Latest Style / (Composition the same as "Grand Pacer Mascot" No. 2518 18.1x28. 3 horses and low-wheeled sulkies to right.)
1893 L C&I

4681 Pacing King, Hal Pointer, by Brown Hal, The / Record 2:04½ / L.M. (Louis Maurer) on stone. (Vignette, low-wheeled sulky, ¾ broadside to right.)
1891 S C&I

4682 Pacing King Robert J. Record 2:01½ / J. Cameron on stone. (Vignette.)
1894 S C&I

4683 Pacing King Robert J. Record 2:01½ / J. Cameron on stone. 18.5x27. Printed in oil colors by Currier & Ives. (¾ broadside, rubber-tired sulky to left.)
1894 L C&I

4684 Pacing King Robert J. in his Race with Joe Patchen, The / At Terre Haute, Ind. September 6th, 1894, winning the three heats in 2:03¾, 2:02½, 2:04¾. / J. Cameron on stone. (Above Title) Robert J. 2:01½ — Joe Patchen 2:04 (Low-wheeled sulkies, rubber tires, to right, vignette.)
1894 S C&I

4685 Pacing Wonder Little Brown Jug, of Chicago, Ills., The / Record 2:11¾ / Scott Leighton, Del. (Vignette, ¾ broadside, high-wheeled sulky to right.)
1882 S C&I

4686 Pacing Wonder Sleepy Tom, the Blind Horse, The / with Phillips, his driver coaxing him to "Go in and win" / Record 2:12¼ / 6 additional lines. (Vignette.)
1879 S C&I

4687 Pacing Wonder Sleepy Tom, the Blind Horse, The / With Phillips, his driver coaxing him to "Go in and Win" / Sired by Tom Rolf, son of Old Pocohantus / 6 additional lines. (¾ vignette, high wheeled-sulky to right.)
1879 S C&I

Packer, Governor, Pennsylvania, See: No. 2321.

4688 Paddle Wheel Steamship "Massachusetts", The /
und L C&I

Paddock, Tom See: No. 6093.

4689 Paddy and the Pigs / "Morrow Paddy — Where are ye going with the pigs?" "Whisht ye devil — they'll hear ye, it's to Cork I'm going but it's Kinsale they think I'm taking them to" / (Upright.) und M C&I

4690 Paddy Murphy's "Jantin Car" / 7.14 x12.10 (6 Irishmen and woman on 2-wheeled cart, to left.)
und S C&I

4691 Paddy Ryan / "The Trojan Giant" / 15.14x12.3. 3 additional lines (Upright, full length figure in fighting costume. und M C&I

4692 Page, The / 1846 S N.C.

4693 Pair of Nutcrackers, The / 12x8.8 (2 squirrels and bird in tree, upright, slightly rounded corners.)
und S C&I

Palisades See: Nos. 3823, 5155.

Palmer (Yacht) See: No. 4450.

Palo Alto See: Nos. 1494-5, 2296-8.

Palo Alto (Horse) See: No. 6217.

Pan Handle Scrap (Tobacco) See: No. 1618, 1808A, 5121.

4694 Pap, Soup, and Chowder / J. L. Magee on stone. (Left to right — Fillmore eating Government Pap, seated on the shoulders of the "Mirror"; Greeley of the "Tribune" carrying General Winfield Scott, who is spilling his soup down Greeley's neck; Webster eating while seated on the shoulders of Webb of the "Courier & Enquirer.") Entered according to act of Congress 1852 by P. Smith. For sale at No. 2 Spruce St., N.Y. 1852 S N.C.

4695 The Papal Benediction /
und S C&I

4696 Papa's Coming / 8.8x12 (Mother and baby waving greetings from window, upright.) 1872 S C&I

4697 Papa's Darlings / (Vignette, boy and girl.) 1877 S C&I

4698 Papa's Darlings / #356 / (Vignette, holding fruit and butterflies, etc.)
und S C&I

4699 Papa's New Hat / (Baby trying on father's high hat, one half length, vignette.) und S C&I

4700 Papa's Pet / (Vignette, upright, ¾ length, girl with cocker spaniels.)
und S C&I

Paris See: France.

Paris (Steamship) See: No. 3885.

Parke, General See: No. 2553.

Parker, Louisa See: No. 3795.

4701 A Parley / Prepared for an Emergency / J. Cameron, Del. 17.4x26.6

(Same stone as "Trappers on the Prairie," No. 6126. Title changed.)
und L C&I

Parnell, Charles Stuart See: Nos. 1007-8.

4702 Parole / Brown Gelding by Imp. Leamington, dam Maiden, by Lexington / The American Victor on the English Turf / 3 additional lines. E. Forbes on stone. (Vignette, broadside to right.) 1877 S C&I

4703 Parole / Brown Gelding By Imp. Leamington, dam Maiden by Lexington. / 2 additional lines. E. Forbes, on stone. (Same stone as preceding, vignette.) 1877 S C&I

4704 Parole / Brown Gelding by Imp. Leamington, dam Maiden, by Lexington / The American Victor on the English Turf / E. Forbes, Del. 17x 25.15 (Vignette, broadside to right.)
1879 L C&I

4705 Parole / 3.4x5.2.
1881 V.S. C&I

Parole See: Nos. 2642, 2764.

4706 Parson's Colt, The / Hears a trotter behind him and won't be stopped if it is Sunday / Thos. Worth on stone. (Vignette.) 1879 S C&I

4707 Parson's Colt, The /
1880 L C&I

4708 Parsons' Colt, The /
1880 V.S. C&I

4709 Part of the Battle of Shiloh /
und S C&I

4710 Parthenon of Athens / Plan of the Parthenon Restored by Alex J. Davis. Published by Stodart and Currier. (Vignette, plan of facade of Parthenon, 2 views on 1 sheet.)
und M N.C.

4711 Parting, The / or the Sailors Wife/ On stone by W. K. Hewitt, published by Hewitt, N. Currier's lithog. N.Y. (Music sheet.) und S N.C.

4712 Parting Hour, The / #673 / 12.6x9 (Full length, father bidding wife and child goodby.) 1849 S N.C.

4713 Parting Hour, The / (Full length, couple at tree, man carving entwined hearts, companion to No. 6653.)
und S C&I

4714 Partridge Shooting / From nature/ On stone by F. F. Palmer. 12.10x20.3 (Later altered to "Morning in the Woods," No. 4196, Palmer 1852 N.C., 2

hunters, 4 dogs, dead game on ground in center foreground.)
1852 M N.C.

4715 Partridge Shooting / 8.1x12.10 / #174 / Unquestionably by Palmer but unsigned. (2 dogs, left, hunter facing observer and 2 partridge in foreground.)
1855 S N.C.

4716 Partridge Shooting / 8x12.14 (Hunter left center, facing right, 3 dogs.)
und S N.C.

4717 Partridge Shooting / F. F. Palmer, Del. 12.13x20.6 (Hunter at left, shooting bird at right, 2 setters in center foreground, 6 other hunters in rear.)
1865 M C&I

4718 Partridge Shooting / 8.2x12.8 (2 dogs, to right, 2 birds, no hunter. Some prints marked "Patridge Shooting.")
1870 S C&I

4719 Partridge Shooting / 8.7x12.7 (Similar in composition to No. 4717, but only 1 hunter, other slight changes.)
und S C&I

4720 Past and Future / with verse by Moore and one by Shelley. W. Sabye, after a drawing by Miss Margret Gilles. (Large oval, portraits of 2 girls, companion to "Light and Shadow.")
und L C&I

4721 Pasture in Summer, The / The Drinking Trough / 16.11x24.15 (Cows at trough.)
1867 L C&I

4722 Pasture — Noontide, The /
und M C&I

4723 Path Through the Fields, The / 8.8x12.8.
und S C&I

4724 Path Through the Woods, The /
und S C&I

4725 Patriot of 1776, A / Defending His Homestead / 8.14x12.7 (Attacking a Dragoon on horse. 1 dead, 3 running away.)
1876 S C&I
Patron (Horse) See: Nos. 934, 6218.

4726 Pattern in Connemara / (Country dance.)
und S C&I

4727 Paul & Virginia / Lost in the Wood "Let us Pray" etc., / N. Sarony on stone. (Dome shape, in rectangle.)
und S C&I

4728 Paul and Virginia's Departure for France / "You are going, they tell me, in three days" / 11.13x8.6.
und S N.C.
Paulding, John See: Nos. 804-6.

4729 Pauline / (¾ length, seated at tree,

forget-me-nots in hand.)
und S N.C.

4730 Pauline / Forget Me Not / (¾ length, under tree, small bouquet in hand and locket with soldiers portrait.)
und S N.C.

4731 Pawle /
1881 S C&I
Pavonia (Steamship) See: Nos. 4430, 5781.
Pea Ridge, Ark. See: Nos. 420-1.

4732 Peace / #245 / 8.10x12.13 (Goats, sheep, etc.)
und S C&I

4733 Peace and Plenty / 9.15x16.13 (Cottage on right, wagon coming down road, barn, cattle, chickens, etc., on left.)
1871 M C&I

4734 Peace Be to This House / (Motto, bird, fruit, flowers, vignette.)
1872 S C&I

4735 Peaceful Lake, The /
und S C&I
Peaceful Lake, The See: Picturesque Landscapes No. 4778.

4736 Peaceful River, The / (Rustic bridge, man, woman, and child.)
und S C&I

4737 Peaches and Grapes / First Prize / (Vignette, upright, with butterfly.)
1870 S C&I
Pedee River See: No. 3995.
Pedestrian See: Nos. 1006, 1184, 2621, 2654-7, 3266.

4738 Peek-A-Boo! / 11.12x8.8 (Children playing about mother's skirts, slightly rounded corners, full length.)
1868 S C&I
Peekskill See: Nos. 2971, 2973-4, 6381.
Peerless (Horse) See: No. 6168.
Peerless (Steamboat) See: No. 5728.

4739 Peerless Beauty, The / (Girl's head.)
und S C&I

4740 Peerless Goldsmith Maid, Driven by Budd Doble, The / "The Queen of the Turf". Unrivaled in the World / J. Cameron, Del.
1871 S C&I

4741 Peerless Goldsmith Maid, Driven by Budd Doble, The / "The Queen of Trotters." Unrivalled in the World / Trotting in harness at East Saginaw, Mich., July 16th, 1874 etc. / and 2 additional lines (Vignette, ¾ broadside to right, high-wheeled sulky.)
1871 S C&I
Peers, Thos. F. See: No. 6067.

4742 Pelham / July 2nd, 1849, trotted one mile in harness, over the Centreville Course carrying 175 lbs. in / 2:28. Driven by Wm. Wheelan, Esq. / 12.13 x20.15 2 columns, 6 lines. (Broadside to left, high-wheeled sulky.)
1850 L N.C.

Pemberton, Gen. J. C. See: No. 2565.

Pendleton, G. H. See: Nos. 2497, 4824.

4743 Penitent Mule. The Parson on deck, The / "Nebber mind de sermon Parson we sees de point" / (Vignette, colored comic.) 1890 S C&I

Penn, Wm. See: Nos. 6697-9.

4744 Pennsylvania Hall, Bristol College (Front view) / Russell, Walker, and A. J. Davis, Architects, N.Y. 10.2x13.10 (On same sheet with "Clifton Hall," Bristol College, Pa.)
1835 M N.C.

Pennsylvania See: Nos. 1116, 1136, 1327, 1813, 2084, 2375, 2580-1, 2733, 2950, 3005, 3079, 4603, 4744-5, 5415, 5423, 5475, 6357, 6397, 6334-5, 6408, 6439-40, 6519, 6643.

4745 Pennsylvania Railroad Scenery / 8.8 x12.7. und S C&I

Pennsylvania (U.S. Ship of the Line) See: Nos. 753, 6334-5.

Penobscot (Steamboat) See: No. 5736.

Pensacola, Harbor See: No. 2088.

4746 People in the Tuileries, The / 24th February 1848 / #576 / 8.1x12.9. 4 additional lines. (Title repeated in French.) 1848 S N.C.

4747 People's Evening Line / (Shows steamers "Drew" and "St. John." Advertisement.) 1881 V.S. C&I

4748 People's Line. Hudson River / The Palace Steamers of the World / "Drew" "St. John" "Dean Richmond"/ Leaving New York etc. 2 columns, 9 lines (at left) and 3 lines (at right). Parsons & Atwater, Del. 19.13x35. Published by Endicott & Co., 52 Beekman St. 1877 L C&I

4749 Percheron Stallion Duc de Chartres imported by A. Rogy / Winner of first prize Grand Gold Medal at the Concours Hippique Regional held at Alencon, France in 1873 / 17.9x27 (Man holding horse to left, barn in rear.)
1883 L C&I

Peregrine (Horse) See: No. 3133.

4750 Perfect Bliss / 9.4x13.14 (Vignette,

Percheron Stallion DUC DE CHARTRES, Imported by A. Rogy. WINNER OF FIRST PRIZE, GRAND GOLD MEDAL, AT THE CONCOURS HIPPIQUE REGIONAL, HELD AT ALENCON, FRANCE, IN 1873.

man smoking cigar, ascending smoke spells "All Serene.")

1879 M C&I

4751 Perfect Bliss /

1880 S C&I

4752 Perfect Bliss / 4.7x7.3 (Cigar advertising card.)   1880 S C&I

Periere (Steamship) See: No. 5782.

4753 Permanent Fair Grounds of the / Queens County Agricultural Society / Mineola, L.I. / Lithographed and Published for Charles R. Bill, 747 Broadway, N.Y. — The grounds were laid out, and the buildings designed by the Secretary. Jno. Schutler, fct. 17.8x25.8.

1867 L C.C.

Perry, Oliver See: No. 4754.

4754 Perry's Victory on Lake Erie — Fought September 10th, 1813 / 3 additional lines and 1 line quotation by Perry. On stone by N. Sarony. "Lawrence" and "Niagara" keyed.

und S N.C.

Persia (Steamship) See: Nos. 3128, 5240.

4755 Persian Beauty / (Girl with greyhound.)   und S C&I

Persian Monarch (Steamship) See: Nos. 5783.

4756 Pet of the Family, The /

und S C&I

4757 Pet of the Family / on Christmas morning / (Vignette portrait, girl holding doll, toys, etc.)

und S C&I

4758 Pet of the Fancy / (Comic.)

1879 S C&I

4759 Pet of the Fancy /

und S C&I

4760 Pet of the Fancy / 4.7x7.3 (Cigar advertising card.)

1880 V.S. C&I

4761 Pet of the ladies, The /

und S C&I

Petersburg, Va. See: No. 422.

4762 Pets in Springtime / 8x12.7 (2 children with 3 sheep.)

und S C&I

4763 Peytona and Fashion / In their great match for $20,000 / Over the Union Course, L.I. May 13th, 1845. Won by Peytona / Peytona red chestnut, rider, blue jacket, black cap. Time 7:39¾, 7:45¼. Fashion light chestnut, rider, purple jacket, green cap / 2 columns, 11 lines. From Nature &

on stone by C. Severin. 17.13x28.10.

und L N.C.

4764 Phallas / by Dictator / Record 2:15½ / (Vignette, ¾ broadside, high-wheeled sulky to left.) (Some prints are labeled "Record 2:13½.")

1883 S C&I

4765 Phallas—Driven by E. D. Bithers—Record 2:15½ /

und L C&I

4766 Phallas — Record 2:13¾ / 2.12x 4.12.   1882 V.S. C&I

Phallas See: Nos. 5708, 6163, 6219.

Phantom (Yacht) See: No. 4450.

4767 Phebe / #393 / 11.13x8.3 (¾ length, seated on couch, left hand to head, roses in hair.)   1846 S N.C.

4768 Phebe / #393 / (Full length, red dress, fountain seen through window at left, same general composition as "Jane" No. 3178.)   1846 S N.C.

4769 Phenomenal Trotting Gelding Jay Eye See by Dictator, dam Midnight by Pilot, Jr., The / Driven by Edwin D. Bithers / Record 2:10¾ / 19.3x26.14 Printed in Oil Colors by Currier & Ives (¾ broadside, high-wheeled sulky to right.)   1884 L C&I

Philadelphia See: Nos. 529, 1116, 2375, 3079, 6085.

Philadelphia (Cruiser) See: Nos. 4964, 5807, 6644.

Philips, Miss S. See: No. 4156.

Phillips, Wendell See: No. 5050.

4770 Philosopher in Ecstasy, A / "By George! I've got it!! / (Greeley, jumping in air with hand upraised, holding copy of the "New York Tribune." Other hand holds butterfly labeled "The Nomination." Vignette, political cartoon.)

1872 S C&I

4771 Philosophy of Tobacco, The /

und S C&I

4772 Phoebe / #393 / 11.14x8.4 (¾ length, seated, red curtain, flowers on table at left.)   1846 S N.C.

4773 Photograph Marriage Certificate /.

und S C&I

4774 Pic-nic Party, The /

und M C&I

4775 Pic-nic Party, The /

1858 L C&I

4776 Picador / Weight 1950 lbs. / Winner of 1st prize grand gold medal and 500 Francs at the Concours Hippique Regional at Caen, France 1883 / Same

prize at same show held at St. Louis in 1882 / Imported July 1883 by A. Rogy, Pacific Farm, Seward, Nebraska. / Harry Lyman on stone. 11x15.7.
1883 M C&I
Pickens, Gov. of S.C. **See:** No. 5628.

4777 Pickerel / 8.7x12.8 (Still life, pond in left background.)
1872 S C&I

4778 Picturesque Landscapes / Cliff Castle — The Peaceful Lake — Falling Springs, Va. — In the Summer Time — Scottish Scenery — Early Autumn/ (6 small views on 1 sheet.)
und S C&I

4779 Piedmont / By Almond, dam by Mambrino Chief / Record 2:17¼ / Scott Leighton on stone. (¾ broadside, high-wheeled sulky to left.)
1882 S C&I
Pierce, Gen. Frank **See:** No. 536, 1245, 2126-7, 2252-3, 2482, 2493-4.

4780 Pigeon Shooting / "Playing the Decoy" / A. F. Tait, N.Y. on stone. 19x27.10 (2 hunters operating from blind.)
1862 L C&I
Pilgrim (Steamboat) **See:** Nos. 2516, 4427, 5737-8.

4781 Pilgrim's Progress, The / Christian and Hopeful arrive on the opposite sides of the river / #445 /
1853 S N.C.

4782 Pilot Boat in a Storm /
und S C&I

4783 Pilot Boat in a Storm / 7.14x12.6.
und S C&I

4784 Pinch Taken, The / #55 / (Half length male figure, top corners rounded. Companion to "Take a Pinch" No. 5945.)
und S N.C.

4785 Pioneer Cabin of the Yo-Se-mite Valley, The / 8.8x12.8.
und S C&I

4786 Pioneer's Home, The / On the Western Frontier / F. F. Palmer, Del. 18.12x26.14.
1867 L C&I
Pitcher, Molly **See:** Nos. 2802, 6754-5.
Pittsburgh, Pa. **See:** Nos. 2580-1.
Pittsburgh, Tenn. **See:** Nos. 423-5.
Place de la Concorde / (See "Courageous Conduct," etc. No. 1272.

4787 Placid Lake / Adirondacks / (Cottage and Carriage in foreground.)
und S C&I

4788 Placid Lake / Adirondacks / (Different composition.)
und S C&I

4789 Plan of Gilbert's Balance Floating Dry Dock / Connected with Basin and Railways / In course of construction for the U.S. Govt. at the / Navy Yard, Pensacola, Fla. and at the Navy Yard, Kittery, Me. / Under contract with / Gilbert & Secor / Drawn by Jno. R. Chapin, New York. 20x30.11.
1849 L N.C.

4790 Plan of New Haven, Conn. / A plan of the town of New Haven / with all the buildings in 1748 / 21.9x15.10 (Based on the 1st map of New Haven, by Amos Doolittle.)
und L C.C.

4791 Plan of School House / By A. J. Davis, Architect / Section from A to B / Side section — Section C to D / From "Rural Residences" by A. J. Davis, 1837. (Vignette.)
und S N.C.

4792 Plan of the City of New York, A / (The Bradford Map) A plan of the City of New York from an actual survey in the year 1728, with the addition of modern names. Shipping 10 Briggs, and 30 Sloops. Population 5800 / 17.1x21.10.
1849 L N.C.
Plantagenet (British Warship) **See:** No. 182.
Planter's Hotel, New Orleans **See:** No. 5254.

4793 Platner & Smith — Lee, Mass. / (Group of 4 under tree at right, flour mill in background. Evidently used as an advertisement.)
und S N.C.

4794 Played Out / J. Cameron on stone. (Decrepit horse Labeled "No Time Here." Vignette.)
1871 S C&I

4795 Playful / L. Maurer on stone.
und M C&I

4796 Playful Family, The / #248 / (Cat and kittens.)
und S N.C.

4797 Playful Family, The / 12.11x8.5 (Puppies, plate has slightly rounded corners, upright.)
und S C&I

4798 Playful Pets, The / #481 / (Arched top.)
und S N.C.

4799 Playful Pets, The / 11.13x8.10 (Little girl with dog and 3 puppies, upright.)
und S C&I

4800 Playing Dominoes /
und S C&I

4801 Playmates, The / (3 girls, oval in rectangle.)
und S N.C.

4802 Playmates, The / (Boy, girl and dog.)   und S C&I

4803 Playmates, The / #173 / 12x8.10 (3 girls, canary, kitten.)   und S C&I

4804 Please Give Me A Light, Sir / 1879 S C&I

4805 Please Give Me A Light Sir / (Cigar advertising card. Frog and owl.)   1880 V.S. C&I

4806 Pleasure / "Oh How Dinah Lubs dis Nigger." /   und S C&I

4807 Pleasure / A Freemonter Before the Election / (Upright, colored man facing observer, letter from New York in hand, ¾ length.)   und S N.C.

4808 Pleasures of the Country, The / Sweet Home / 9.14x16.14 (Family under tree in front yard.)   1869 M C&I

4809 Pleasures of the Country / Winter/ (Composition similar to "American Country Life, Pleasures of Winter," No. 123.)   und S C&I

4810 Pluck / One of the Right Sort / 10.13x15 (Dog with rat in mouth.)   und M N.C.

Plymouth Rock (Steamer) See: No. 6406.

4811 Po-can-teco, The / From Irving Park / 5.7x7.7 (Oval, printed on same sheet with "Buttermilk Falls.")   und V.S. C&I

Plymouth Rock, Mass. See: Nos. 3433-5.

4812 Pocahontas Boy [1790] Record 2:31 / Sired By Tom Rolf [3:06] Dam Fanny Benson, owned by J. H. Clark, Genesee Stock Farms Scio, N.Y. / 2 columns, 5 lines of Pacers and Trotters. Painted by T. J. Scott and signed on stone. 20x27. Reproduced in oil colors by C&I (Standing to left.)   und L C&I

Pocahontas (Horse) See: Nos. 200, 893, 2946.

Pocahontas (Yacht) See: No. 5560.

4813 Pocahontas Saving the Life of Capt'n John Smith /   und S N.C.

Pocahontas, Baptism of See: No. 361.

POINTERS.

[209]

4814 Point of the Joke, The / (Companion to #758.) 1879 S C&I

4815 Pointer, The / 12.13x9 (Title in plate, full length figure to left.) 1848 S N.C.

4816 Pointers / #443 / 8.7x12.14 ("P" on stone at left, group of 4 pointers in field. Taken from English sporting print published by Ackerman & Son, London.) 1846 S N.C.

4817 Pointing a Bevy / F. F. Palmer, Del. 24.13x19.10 (Close-up of dog, quail in right foreground. Companion to "Close Quarters" No. 1181.) 1866 L C&I

Police Gazette (Horse) See: Nos. 1862, 2664.

4818 Polished Off / "Golly — He's Licked" / (Vignette. Companion to 2399. Shows group following darky prizefighter.) 1888 S C&I

4819 Political Arena, The / und S C&I

4820 Political "Blondins" Crossing Salt River / (Shows Lincoln, Douglas, Buchanan, Breckinridge, Bell, Everett, and Greeley. Vignette.) 1860 M C&I

4821 Political Debate in the Darktown Club, A / Settling the Question / Thos. Worth on stone. (Vignette, 2 rivals talking at the same time for Blaine and Cleveland.) 1884 S C&I

4822 Political Debate in the Darktown Club, A / The Question Settled / Thos. Worth on stone. (2 darkies speaking for Blaine and Cleveland. Companion to preceding. Vignette.) 1884 S C&I

4823 Political Gymnasium, The / (Presidential candidates in gymnasium. Everett supporting Bell, seated on dumbbell; Greeley on horizontal bar marked "Nom. for Governor"; Lincoln on rail marked "President", Douglas and Breckinridge boxing. Vignette.) 1860 M C&I

4824 Political "Siamese" Twins, The / The offspring of Chicago Miscegenation / 10.12x14.8 (McClellan and Pendleton joined, Vallandingham, Seymour approving. Vignette.) 1864 M C&I

Polk, James K. See: Nos. 2490-1, 3157-67.

Polk, Mrs. James K. See: No. 4262.

4825 Polka, The / Pl. 1 / (At top.) und S N.C.

4826 Polka, The / Pl. 2 / (At top.) und S N.C.

4827 Polka, The / Pl. 3 / (At top) (Full length figures, Scottish Costume.) und S N.C.

4828 Polka, The / Pl. 4 / (At top.) und S N.C.

4829 Polly and Kitty / Roses Have Thorns / (Companion to "Kitty and Polly / Dividing The Spoils" No. 3359.) und M C&I

Polynia (Yacht) See: No. 5724.

4830 Pomona's Treasures / und S C&I

4831 Pompon Rose, The / Stodart & Currier's Lith. und V.S. N.C.

4832 Pond in the Woods, The / (Duck with young ducks.) und M C&I

4833 Ponto / (Boy and dog.) und S C&I

4834 Pony Team, The / 7.15x12.10 (Man pushing 4 children in cart.) und S C&I

4835 Pony Wagon, The / und S C&I

Pool (Game) See: Nos. 756, 1129. 5257.

4836 Pool, The / four rural scenes on one sheet / The Pool — The Windmill — Winter Morning — The Fisherman's Cot / (Vignette.) und S C&I

4837 Pool of Siloam, The / 8.6x12.5. 1846 S N.C.

4838 Poor Dolly / und S C&I

4839 Poor Trust is Dead / Bad Pay Killed Him / 12.14x9 (Title formed of human figures in eccentric positions. Dead dog in center (vignette) with "Trust" on collar. Upright.) 1868 S C&I

Pope, Genl. See: Nos. 380, 3919-20, 5452.

4840 Pope Leo XIII / Born March 2nd, 1810, Elected Supreme Pontiff Febr. 20th, 1878 / Bestowing Benediction, etc. / 11.15x8.6 (Vignette, upright.) 1878 S C&I

4841 Pope Pius IX / und S N.C.

4842 Pope Pius IX / (Bust portrait in ecclesiastic robes, vignette.) und S C&I

4843 Pope Pius IX / Anno Domine 1846/ #243 / (Vignette, half length, seated.) 1846 S N.C.

4844 Pope Pius IX / Bestowing the Papal benediction on all true Catholics throughout the world / on the twenty-fifth anniversary of his Pontificate June 16th, 1871 / #25 / 11.15x8.7 (¾ length portrait, seated, upright.) und S C&I

4845 Pope Pius IXth, Lying in State / 1878 S C&I

Pope Pius IX See: Nos. 583, 1499.

4846 Popping the Question / #505 / Entered by Sarony & Major. (Top corners rounded.) 1847 S N.C.

Porpoise (Brig) See: No. 6299.

Port Hudson, La. See: Nos 50, 5915.

4847 Port of New York, The / Bird's-Eye View from the Battery, Looking South / Parsons & Atwater, Del. 20.6x32.15 (52 references in 6 lines.) 1872 L C&I

4848 Port of New York, The / Bird's-Eye View from the Battery, Looking south / Parsons & Atwater, Del. 20.10 x33.4 (55 references in 6 lines.) 1878 L C&I

4849 Port of New York, The / Bird's Eye View from the Battery, Looking South / 20.9x33.4 (56 references in 5 lines.) 1892 L C&I

Port Royal, S.C. See: Nos. 678, 6373.

Porter, Admiral See: No. 51.

Porter, David See: No. 4397.

4850 Portrait of a girl / 1846 S N.C.

4851 Portuguese Mariner's Song, The / and / Trio / Arranged for one, two, or three Voices / On stone by J. H. Bufford. J. L. Hewitt & Co. Stodart & Currier's Lith. und S N.C.

4852 Positive Process from a Negative Result, A / "Try yer Funny Bizness on us, will yer?"/(Vignette, companion to "Dark Foreshading on a Flash Picture" No. 1369.) 1890 S C&I

4853 Post Office, The / New York / #610 / 8.4x12.8. und S N.C.

Post Office, N.Y. See: No. 6326.

4854 Pot Luck / #713 / 11.12x8.13 (Upright.) und S N.C.

Potomac, Va. See: Nos. 6395, 6449.

Potomac (Horse) See: No. 4249.

4855 Poultry Show on a Bust, A / Bad for the Dog / Scott Leighton on stone. (Vignette, chickens, ducks escaping from crates on wagon and invading fashionable carriage.) 1883 S C&I

4856 Poultry Show on the road, A / Fine Fun for the Pup / Scott Leighton on stone. (Vignette.) 1883 S C&I

4857 Poultry Yard, The / 11.14x15.15 (Interior scene.) 1870 M C&I

4858 Power of Music, The / #519 / (2 monkeys playing violins.) und S N.C.

4859 Prairie Fires of the Great West / 8.7x12.8 (Engine, tender, 7 coaches to left, buffalo running from fire in background.) 1871 S C&I

4860 Prairie Hens / 8.9x12.7. und S C&I

4861 Prairie Hunter, The / "One rubbed out" / Painted by A. F. Tait. O. Knirsch on stone. 14.8x20.10 (Companion to "A Check" No. 1021.) 1852 L N.C.

4862 Prairie on Fire / #489 / 8x11.4. und S N.C.

4863 Prairie Wolves Attacking a Buffalo Bull / "Taking breath." / Catlin, Del. und M C&I

4864 Praise / the Lord / O my soul (Vignette, floral scroll, motto.) 1875 S C&I

4865 Pray "God bless Papa and Mama" / 12.1x8.7 (Mother and child, upright.) und S N.C.

4866 Pray "God bless Papa and Mama"/. und S C&I

Preble, Edward See: No. 4399.

4867 Premium Fruit / (Vignette; pears, plums, grapes, apples, etc.) 1875 S C&I

4868 Premium Poultry / und S C&I

4869 Preparing for Congress / Thos. Worth on stone. (Upright, colored man dressing, Lincoln's picture on wall.) 1863 S C&I

4870 Preparing for Market / L. Maurer, Del. 18.16x27.4 (Child in doorway, no toy.) 1856 L N.C.

4871 Preparing for Market / L. Maurer, Del. 18.16x27.4 (Same stone as preceding, 2nd state, child holding toy horse by string.) 1856 L N.C.

4872 Preparing for Market / L. Maurer, Del. 18.16x27.4 (Same stone as preceding, 2nd state, child holding toy horse toy remains.) 1856 L N.C.
President (Steamship) **See:** Nos. 5784-6.

4873 President Cleveland and his Cabinet / (Vignette.) 1884 S C&I

4874 President Cleveland and his Cabinet / About 16x22 (Vignette, tinted background, 8 members keyed.) 1884 L C&I

4875 President Cleveland and His Cabinet / (Vignette, mottled background, 9 members keyed.) 1893 L C&I

4876 President Harrison and His Cabinet / (9 keys in 4 lines, vignette.) 1889 S C&I

4877 President Harrison and His Cabinet / 14.9x21.12 (Tinted background, 9 keys.) 1889 L C&I

4878 President Hayes and his Cabinet / J.C. on stone. 9x12.11 (8 keys in 4 lines.) 1877 S C&I

4879 President Lincoln and his Cabinet/ In council; Sept. 22nd, 1862. Adopting the Emancipation Proclamation, issued Jany. 1st, 1863 / Gideon Wells, Sec. of the Navy — Montgomery Blair, P.M. Genl. — Caleb B. Smith, Sec. of the Interior — Salmon P. Chase, Sec. of the Treasury — William H. Seward, Sec. of State — Edward Bales, Atty. Gen. — Edwin M. Stanton, Sec. of War — President Lincoln / (Vignette.) 1876 S C&I

4880 President Lincoln and Secretary Seward Signing / The Proclamation of Freedom, / January 1st, 1863 / "Upon this Act, I invoke, etc." / 1 additional line. 12.2x9.12 (Oval, upright.) 1865 S C&I

4881 President Lincoln at Genl. Grant's Headquarters / At City Point, Va. March 1865 / 10.4x13.10 (Lincoln — Sherman — Sheridan — Grant. Top corners rounded.) 1865 M C&I

4882 President Lincoln at Home / Reading the Scriptures to his wife and son/ 12.2x9.14 (Oval, names keyed above title, upright.) 1865 S C&I

4883 President Lincoln at Home / Reading the Scriptures to his wife and son/ 12.3x9.14 (Upright.) 1865 S C&I

4884 Presidential Fishing Party of 1848, The / Van Buren — Hale — Cass — Taylor / Published by Peter Smith, 2 Spruce St., N.Y. 16.3x10.8 (On opposite sides of stream fishing for delegates.) und S N.C.

4885 Presidential Reception in 1789, A / By General and Mrs. Washington / 8.13x12.4. 1876 S C&I

4886 Presidents of the United States, The / (Washington to Harrison, upright.) 1842 S N.C.

4887 Presidents of the United States, The / (Group of Presidents from Washington to Tyler. Washington, surmounted by Eagle and flags, "E Pluribus Unum" on banner — Eagle holding 9 arrows in right claw — 10 portraits in all — upright.) 1842 S N.C.

4888 Presidents of the United States, The / (Washington to Tyler. Washington surmounted by Eagle and flags— no arrows in Eagle's claw — minor changes in composition — 10 portraits in all — upright.) 1842 S N.C.

4889 Presidents of the United States, The / #190 (Washington to Polk. Portrait of Washington is marked "Washington", 13 stars surrounding portrait are white, "Declaration" below — 11 portraits in all — upright.) 1844 S N.C.

4890 Presidents of the United States, The / (Washington in center, to right. J. Q. Adams on right — Monroe at left. "Declaration" below — upright.) 1844 S N.C.

4891 Presidents of the United States, The / (Washington in center, to right. Monroe on left. "Declaration" below. Similar to preceding, slight changes in composition. Stars surrounding Washington are gray. Upright.) 1844 S N.C.

4892 Presidents of the United States, The / (Washington in center, to left. J. Q. Adams on left. "Declaration" below. Composition similar to preceding, but reversed — upright.) 1844 S N.C.

4893 Presidents of the United States, The / (Slight changes in composition.) 1844 S N.C.

4894 Presidents of the United States, The / (Upright.) 1845 S N.C.

4895 Presidents of the United States, The / (Upright.) 1846 S N.C.

4896 Presidents of the United States, The / #190 / 12.10x9.5 (11 portraits. Title at bottom in a straight line, no ribbon, black background, scroll border, portraits in straight lines — upright.) 1847 S N.C.

4897 Presidents of the United States, The / #584 (Lewis Cass in center, Washington to Polk, 12 portraits, upright.) 1848 S N.C.

4898 Presidents of the United States, The / From 1789 to 1850 / (Washington to Taylor, upright.) 1848 S N.C.

4899 Presidents of the United States, The / Zachary Taylor / The / People's choice for 12th President / #586 (Washington to Polk, 11 portraits, upright.) 1848 S N.C.

4900 Presidents of the United States, The / Washington 1789 to Fillmore 1850 / #719 (Washington in center in circle surmounted by flags, eagle, shield, cannon, etc., 13 portraits — upright.) 1850 S N.C.

4901 Presidents of the United States, The / (Washington to Polk — upright.) und S N.C.

4902 Presidents of the United States, The / (Washington to Tyler — upright.) und S N.C.

4903 Presidents, The / of the United States, from 1789 to 1861 / #80 / 11.12 x9 (Washington to Buchanan, 15 portraits — upright.) und S C&I

4904 Presidents, The / of the United States, from 1789 to 1869 / #80 / 11.13 x8.6 (Washington to Lincoln, 16 portraits with names and dates of administration — upright.) und S C&I

4905 Press Gang, The / (Children imitating England's "Press Gang," vignette.) und S N.C.

4906 Pretty American, The / (Vignette, portrait girl's head.) und S C&I

4907 Pretty Dolly / (Vignette, upright, girl in white dress.) 1873 S C&I

4908 Pretty Poll / La Perruche a Collier Rose / #6 (Upright.) und S N.C.

4909 Pretty Story, The / 7x5.1 (Young man and girl, rural scene, printed on same sheet with "Birdie and Pet.") und S C&I

4910 Pride of America, The / #508 (Full length, lady on white horse, upright.) und S N.C.

4911 Pride of America, The / #508 / 11.14x8.10 (Figure of "Liberty" draped in American flag, upright.) und S C&I

4912 Pride of Kentucky, The / (Vignette.) und S C&I

4913 Pride of Kildare, The / (Vignette portrait.) und S C&I

4914 Pride of the Garden, The / (Flowers in ornamental iron basket, upright, vignette.) 1873 S C&I

4915 Pride of the South, The / (Vignette, girl's head.) 1870 S C&I

4916 Pride of the West, The / #507 (Lady on horseback, upright.) und S N.C.

4917 Pride of the West, The / #507 / 11.10x8.8 (Lady on horseback, 2 dogs and other changes in composition, upright. Copyright 1847 by Sarony & Major.) 1847 S N.C.

4918 Pride of the West, The / (Vignette portrait.) 1870 S C&I
Prima Donna (Yacht) See: No. 5105.

4919 Primary Drawing Studies /(8 views on 1 sheet.) und S C&I

4920 Prime Tobacco / Tobacco Jack / (Upright, vignette, figure composed of tobacco leaves, clay pipe, cigars, and snuff.) 1875 S C&I
Prince (Horse) See: No. 6170.

4921 Prince Albert / #11 (Upright, full dress uniform on horseback, with mounted troops, vignette.) 1848 S N.C.

4922 Prince Albert / (¾ length portrait, upright.) und S N.C.

4923 Prince Albert / #11 / 12.1x8.11 (Full length, upright.) und S N.C.

4924 Prince Albert / 10.1x7.15 (¾ length, in uniform, upright.) und S N.C.

4925 Prince and Lantern / In their great match for $10,000. Two mile heats to wagons / Over the Union Course, L.I. Sept. 18th, 1856. / 6 additional lines. L. Maurer '56 on stone. 16.10x25.14 (¾, broadside to right.)

1857 L N.C.

4926 Prince and Princess of Wales, The/ #183 / |Photographed from life by Mayall, London.| 11.13x8.10 (Full length, top corners round.)
und S C&I

4927 Prince of the blood, A / 24.4x29.13 (Elephant folio head of horse.)
1893 L C&I

4928 Prince of Wales and Family / 8.3x 12.4 (2 lines of keys; Princess, Prince George, Albert Victor, Princess Louise and 2 small girls.)
und S C&I

4929 Prince of Wales, The / (Vignette, half length, Scots kilts.)
und S C&I

4930 Prince of Wales and Family, The / Photographed by Vernon Heath. 10.14 x8.8 (Prince, Princess and baby — slightly rounded corners, upright.)
und S C&I

4931 Prince of Wales at the Tomb of Washington, Oct. 1860, The / #77 (Upright, 8 figures shown.)
und S C&I

4932 Prince Wilkes Record 2:14¾ Driven by Crit Davis /(Similar composition to "Trotting Gelding Prince Wilkes," etc., No. 6176.   1889 S C&I

Prince Wilkes **See:** Nos. 5113, 6176.

Princess (Horse) **See:** Nos. 2019-20.

Princess (Steamboat) **See:** No. 6776.

Princess Louise **See:** No. 2970.

4933 Princess Royal of England / (In bridal robes, upright.)
und S C&I

Princeton (Frigate) **See:** Nos. 329, 6345-6.

Princeton, N.J. **See:** No. 6518.

Printing Press **See:** No. 4959.

Priscilla (Steamer) **See:** Nos. 3873, 5729.

4934 Prize "Black Hamburg" Grapes / "A Four Pound Bunch" / 17.13x14.12 (Companion to "First Premium Grapes" No. 1982 upright, and "First Premium Muscat Grapes" Nos. 1983 and 4939 and Prize Grapes, No. 4939.)
1865 M C&I

4935 Prize Boy, The / (Full-length figure seated, black background, probably for use as a fire screen.)
und L C&I

4936 Prize Boy, The. / 25.8x18.11 (Ele-

phant folio, tinted background, lace-trimmed trousers, round corners.)
1857 L C&I

4937 Prize Fat Cattle / (Vignette, standing to left.)
und S C&I

4938 Prize Fighter, The / "The Pet of the Fancy" / 14.8x11.8 (Oval, portrait of a dog.)
und M C&I

4939 Prize Grapes / A four pound bunch/ 17.15x14.13 (Upright.)
1865 M C&I

4940 Prize Herd, A / 17.12x26.8 (Longhorn cattle.)
und L C&I

4941 Prize Jersey Litchfield Bull /
und S C&I

4942 Prize Jersey "Niobe" / (Cattle.)
und S C&I

4943 Prize Setter, A / (Head of Irish setter with woodcock, vignette.)
und S C&I

4944 Prize Trotter, A /
1873 S C&I

4945 Prize Trotter, A / Clear the track! keep out of the way! / Talk is cheap and will not pay, / Attention to business brings the honey / and to men as to horses, time is money / J. Cameron on stone. (Shows Bonner in judge's stand offering $100,000 for the horse that beats Dexter's time — vignette.)
1873 S C&I

Proctor, J. **See:** No. 4252.

4946 Proctor Knott / By Luke Blackburn, dam Tallapoosa / Painted by Gean Smith, Chicago / (Vignette, under saddle to left.)
1888 S C&I

Proctor Knott **See:** No. 2209, 4946.

4947 Prodigal Son in Misery, The / #218 / 2 additional lines, Biblical quotation. 11.13x8.8 (Upright.)
und S N.C.

4948 Prodigal Son receiving his Patrimony, The / #216 / 2 additional lines Biblication. (Upright.)
und S N.C.

4949 Prodigal Son Returns to His Father, The / #219 / 2 additional lines Biblical quotation. (Upright.)
und S N.C.

4950 Prodigal Son wasting his substance, The / #217 / 2 additional lines Biblical quotation. 11.11x8.7 (Upright.)
und S N.C.

4951 Profit and Loss / Golly! What Luck! Where's dem Eeels? / (Colored fishing comic, 2 views on 1 sheet, 1 view showing full basket of eels, other showing eels escaping from basket — vignette.) 1880 S C&I

4952 Progress of Intemperance, The / 8.4x13.11 (4 views on 1 sheet entitled: Tempted — Persuaded — Hardened — Wrecked.) 1881 S C&I

4953 Progress of Intemperance, The / Plate 1 / The invitation to drink / 12.11x9.13 (Upright.)
1841 S N.C.

4954 Progress of Intemperance, The / Plate 2 / Sick and Repentant / 12.12x 9.13 (Upright.) 1841 S N.C.

4955 Progress of Intemperance, The / Plate 3 / The Relapse / 12.12x9.15 (Upright.) 1841 S N.C.

4956 Progress of Intemperance, The / Plate 4 / The Ruined Family / 12.12x 9.13 (Upright.) 1841 S N.C.

4957 Progress of Intemperance, The / Plate 5 / The Expectant Wife / 12.12x 9.14 (Upright.) 1841 S N.C.

4958 Progress of Intemperance, The / Plate 6 / The Robber / 12.12x9.13 (Upright.) 1841 S N.C.

4959 Progress of the Century, The / The Lightning Steam Press. The Electric Telegraph. The Locomotive. The Steamboat. / 8.14x12.6 (Composite view showing the items mentioned in secondary title.) 1876 S C&I

4960 Progressive Democracy — Prospect of a Smash Up / (Cart marked "Democratic Platform" with team and driver at each end and each team pulling in opposite direction. A squatter sovereign driving Douglas and Johnson to left, while "Old Buck" Buchanan drives Breckinridge and Lane to the right. The cart is halted on railroad track, while locomotive marked "Equal Rights" driven by Lincoln and Hamlin is about to run them down—vignette.)
1860 M C&I

4961 Promising Family, A / Black and Tan / 8.4x12.5 (Dog and 5 puppies, top corners slightly round.)
1868 S C&I

4962 Propagation Society, The — More freedom than welcome / Published by Peter Smith, 1853.
1853 V.S. N.C.

4963 Proposal, The / #524 (Full-length figures, upright.) und S N.C.
Prospect Fair Grounds, Bkln. See:

Nos. 903-4, 917, 2583, 3336, 3395, 5436, 6174, 6761.
Prospero (Horse) See: No. 910.

4964 Protected Steel Cruiser Philadelphia United States Navy / 10x15.
1893 M C&I

4965 Proteine / By Blackwood, dam by Mambrino Chorister / Record 2:18 / (Vignette.) 1878 S C&I

4966 Providence and Stonington Steamship Co's Steamer / Rhode Island / 2 columns, 3 lines. G. N. on stone. 8.5x13.6. und S C&I

4967 Providence and Stonington Steamship Co's Steamer / Rhode Island / New York and Boston via Providence / 1 additional line. Painted by C. R. Parsons. 1877 L C&I

4968 Providence and Stonington Steamship Co's Steamer Massachusetts / New York and Boston via Providence / Painted by C. R. Parsons.
1877 L C&I

4969 Providence and Stonington Steamship Co's Steamers / Massachusetts and Rhode Island / New York and Boston via Providence / 1 additional line and 2 columns, 6 and 3 lines. Parsons & Atwater, Del. 19.4x33.14 (Note: Despite title on this print, only one steamer is shown. Broadside to right.) 1877 L C&I
Providence (Steamer) See: Nos. 4377, 5731.

4970 Provisions Down / Oh! Oh! Oh! / 11.7x8.6 (Upright, delivery boy has slipped on ice, winter scene.)
und S N.C.
Public Park of Mexico, The See: La Alameda de Mexico No. 3368.
Pugilism See: Nos. 276, 525, 974, 2207-8, 2613, 3156, 3195, 3261-5, 3268, 3270, 3275, 4383, 4691, 4818, 4938, 6093-7, 6822.

4971 Puppies Nursery, The / 12.8x8.7 (Mother dog and 3 puppies.)
und S C&I

4972 Puppy / #39. und S N.C.
Purdy, Alexander See: No. 6067.

4973 Puritan and Genesta on the Homestretch, The / In their second and final International race for "The America's Cup," Sept. 16th, 1885 / Won by the Puritan / From the painting by Franklyn Bassford. 16.13x24.2 (Boats keyed.) 1885 L C&I
Puritan (Yacht) See: Nos. 110, 6810-1.

Puritan (Steamer) **See:** Nos. 3874-5, 5787.

4974 Pursuit, The / Painted by A. F. Tait. 18x25.10 (Companion to "The Last War-Whoop" Nos. 3457-8.)
1856 L N.C.

4975 Pursuit, The / 8.5x12.11 (Companion to "The Elopement" No. 1716—knight and lady.)
und S N.C.

4976 Pursuit of the Mexicans by the U. S. Dragoons / under the intrepid Col. Harney at the battle of Churubusco, August 20th, 1847 / #536 / 3 additional lines. J. Cameron on stone. (Officer on black horse, center, to left, sword in hand.) 1847 S N.C.

4977 Puss in Boots / 12.10x10 (Upright.)
und S C&I

4978 Pussy's Return / (Cat followed by litter of 6 kittens.)
und S C&I

4979 Put Up Job, A / Thos. Worth on stone. (Colored couple about to be snowballed — Companion to "A Fall from Grace" No. 1820—winter scene, vignette.) 1883 S C&I

Putnam, Israel **See:** Nos. 2276-9.

4980 Putting On His Airs / #149 (Companion to "Taking Off His Airs" No. 5960. Man on horseback, showing off to 2 young ladies in window, upright.)
und S C&I

4981 Puzzle / For a Winter's Evening / #63 / 10.3x13.15 (3 additional lines describing puzzle, 6 4-line and 1 2-line column.) 1840 S N.C.

4982 Puzzle For a Winter's Evening /
und S N.C.

4983 Puzzle Picture—Old Swiss Mill / 8.7x12.8 (Various animals and human heads hidden in picture.)
1872 S C&I

4984 Puzzled Fox, The / 8.7x12.7 (7 faces and animals hidden in drawing.)
1872 S C&I

4985 Puzzled Fox, The / Find the horse, lamb, wild boar, men's and women's faces / 8.8x12.8.
1872 S C&I

Puzzle. **See:** Nos. 513-4.

Q

4986 Quadrilles / from / Auber's Celebrated Opera / Le Dieu et La Bayadere / Respectfully dedicated to / Madlle. Augusta / by S. M. / Published by James L. Hewitt (Full length figure, vignette.) und S N.C.

4987 Quadrilles / from / Auber's Celebrated Opera / Le Dieu Et La Bayadere / Respectfully dedicated to / Madlle. Augusta / by S. M. / Published by Hewitt & Jaques, 239 Broadway. (Portrait of Madlle. Augusta, different from preceding.)
und S N.C.

4988 Quail / or Virginia Partridge / 8.8x12.7. 1871 S C&I

4989 Quail Shooting / from nature and on stone by F. F. Palmer. Setters the property of S. Palmer, Esq., Brooklyn, L. I. 13x20.6 (3 setters shown.)
1852 L N.C.

4990 Quail Shooting / 8.7x12.7 (Same location as shown in preceding view except with changes in costume and only 2 setters.) und S C&I

4991 Quails / #361 / 8.6x12.15 (Open scenery, no trees.)
1849 S N.C.

4992 Quails / #361 (Trees at right, different composition from preceding.)
und S N.C.

4993 Quarrel, The /
und S N.C.
Quebec. **See:** "Death of Montgomery" No. 1497.

4994 Queen of Angels /
und S N.C.

4995 Queen of Angels, The / La Reine des Anges—La Reina de Los Angeles / (Cherubs placing crown on Queen's head.) und S C&I

4996 Queen of Beauty / #108.
und S N.C.

4997 Queen of Beauty, The / (Vignette, portrait.) und S C&I

4998 Queen of Beauty, The / #108 (¾ length portrait, on balcony, moonlight scene.) und S C&I

4999 Queen of Cattle, The /
1876 M C&I

5000 Queen of Cattle, The—The Champion Steer / (2 views on same sheet.)
1886 L C&I

Queen of Clippers. **See:** "Clipper Ship" No. 1163.

5001 Queen of Hearts / (Vignette, ¾ portrait of girl holding bouquet.) 1857 L C&I

5002 Queen of Love, The / (Vignette, portrait.) und S C&I

5003 Queen of Love and Beauty / (Vignette, ½ length portrait.) 1870 S C&I

5004 Queen of Love and Beauty / ½ length portrait, different composition from preceding.) und S C&I

5005 Queen of the Amazons Attacked by a Lion / #6. und S N.C.

5006 Queen of the Angels, The / La Reine des Anges—La Reina de Los Angeles / Holy Angels pray for us / #289 / 8.8x12. und S N.C.

5007 Queen of the Ball, The / (Vignette, portrait.) 1870 S C&I

5008 Queen of the Blondes / (Upright.) und S C&I

5009 Queen of the Brunettes / 9.4x12.8. 1873 S C&I

5010 Queen of the Flowers /. und S C&I

5011 Queen of the Garden / (Vignette, bouquet of flowers in ornate iron basket.) 1873 S C&I

5012 Queen of the House, The / 9.6x 11.10 (Companion to "King of the House" No. 3335, child playing in bed.) 1875 S C&I

5013 Queen of the South / (Vignette portrait.) und S C&I

5014 Queen of the South, The / (Vignette.) und S C&I

5015 Queen of the Turf "Lady Thorn" driven by Daniel Pfifer, The / Trotting a Mile in Harness in 2:18¼ at Naragansett Park, Providence, October 8th, 1869 / J. Cameron on stone. (¾ view, high-wheeled sulky to right.) 1871 S C&I

5016 Queen of the Turf "Maud S." Driven by W. W. Bair, The / By Harold, dam Miss Russell by Pilot, Jr. / Record 2:08¾ / Scott Leighton on stone. 18.4x28 (High-wheeled sulky to left.

Prints of this same subject also show record as 2:10¾.) 1880 L C&I

5017 Queen of the West, The / und S C&I

Queen of the West — Mississippi River Steamer. See: Nos. 5223, 6102-3.

5018 Queen of the Woods / 11.6x14.11 (Not vignetted, tinted background.) und M N.C.

5019 Queen of the Woods, The / (Vignette.) und M C&I

5020 Queen Victoria / 10x7.12 (Upright.) und S C.C.

5021 Queen Victoria / #12 (Full length, imperial robe and crown, castle seen through window.) und S N.C.

5022 Queen Victoria / #12 (Vignette, equestrian portrait, troops in background.) 1848 S N.C.

5023 Queen Victoria / #12 (¾ portrait, vignette.) und S N.C.

5024 Queen Victoria / 8.8x12 (½ length, green curtain.) und S N.C.

5025 Queen Victoria / und S C&I

5026 Queen Victoria / (Vignette, printed on same sheet with Empress Eugenie.) und S C&I

5027 Queen Victoria's Court Quadrilles and the Grand Promenade Waltz / (Portrait of Queen Victoria.) und S N.C.

5028 Queen's Own, The! / Wimbledon Style / C. M. Vergnes—1875 on stone. 11x15.13 (Comic shooting print, companion to Nos. 1646, 1753, 2824.) 1875 M C&I

5029 Queen's Own, The / (Cigar advertising card.) 1880 V.S. C&I

5030 Queenstown Harbor / (People on wall at left of road.) und M C&I

5031 Queenstown Harbor / Cove of Cork, Ireland / (For other Irish Views look under "Ireland.") und S C&I

5032 Question Settled, The / (Political cartoon.) 1885 S C&I

A RACE FOR BLOOD!

R

5033 Raal Convanience, A / A Wife able and willing to help a man when he is bothered / (Same as "The Blessing of A Wife" No. 568.)
und S C&I

5034 Rabbit Catching / The Trap Sprung / 7.15x12.8 (2 boys about to inspect trap, winter scene.)
und S C&I

5035 Rabbit Hunt, The / All But Caught/ 8.6x12.6.   1849 S N.C.

5036 Rabbits in the Woods / 8.8x12.8.
und S C&I

5037 Race for the American Derby, The / [Belmont Stakes] Jerome Park, June 8th, 1878 / Spartan—Bramble—Duke of Magenta / 3 additional lines, and Time 2:43½. W. on stone. (Vignette, horses to right under saddle.)
1878 S C&I

5038 Race for Blood, A / L. Maurer on stone. 19.14x28.6 (3 horses head on, high-wheeled sulkies.)
1890 L C&I

5039 Race for Blood, A / 18.14x28.6 (This is the exact composition as the preceding print, except that small rubber-tired sulkies have been substituted and some foreground cut off and Maurer's name eliminated.)
1894 L C&I

5040 Race for the Queen's Cup, The / Between the American Yacht "Sappho" and the English Yacht "Livonia" in New York Harbor, October 23rd, 1871 / Won by the Sappho, Time 4 hours, 38 minutes, 5 seconds / 6 additional lines. 8.8x12.8.   1871 S C&I

5041 Race From the word "Go," A / 12.1x19.8 (4 horses to right, high-wheeled sulkies.)   1891 L C&I

5042 Race on the Mississippi, A / 7.14x 12.8 (Steamers "Eagle" and "Diana" shown, daylight scene.)
1870 S C&I

5043 Race to the Wire, A / J. Cameron on stone. 18.2x28.1 (10 horses passing grandstand.)   1891 L C&I

Racer (Clipper Ship) See: No. 1164.

A RACE FOR BLOOD!

5044 Rachel / 11.12x8.5 (¾ length, vase of flowers on table at right, green curtain.)　　　und S N.C.

5045 Racing Champions on their Mettle / 1889 L C&I

5046 Racing Cracks at the Starting Post / J. Cameron '85 on stone. 18x28. (7 horses under saddle.)　　1886 L C&I

5047 Racing King Salvator, Mile Record 1:35½ / By Prince Charlie, dam Salina by Lexington / (Profile to left, under saddle, standing, vignette.)　　1890 S C&I

5048 Racing King Salvator, Mile record 1:35½, The / By Prince Charlie / Dam Salina by Lexington / J. Cameron on stone. From life by Chas. L. Zellinsky. 20x27 (Profile to right, under saddle.)　　1891 L C&I

5049 Racquet River / "Adirondacks" / 8.8x12.7 (Man fishing from stepping stones, basket of fish on bank.)　　und S C&I

5050 Radical Party on a Heavy Grade, The / Sumner—Seymour—Grant / Colfax — Wilkes—Stanton—Wendell Phillips—Butler—Greeley—Stevens / Ben Wade / J. Cameron on stone. (Vignette.)　　1868 M C&I

5051 Rafting on the St. Lawrence / 9.15 x15.7.　　und M C&I

5052 Rail Candidate, The / (Negro and Greeley carrying a rail marked "Republican Platform," which Lincoln is stradling, vignette.)　　1860 M C&I

5053 Rail Shooting / 8.5x12.12 (2 in boat facing right.)　　und S C&I

5054 Rail Shooting / On the Delaware / From Nature and on stone by F. F. Palmer. 12.14x20.2.　　1852 L N.C.

5055 Rail Splitter at Work Repairing the Union, The /　　und S C&I

5056 Railroad Suspension Bridge, The / Near Niagara Falls / Length of Bridge 822 feet. Height above water 240 feet / John A. Roebling, Esq., Engineer. C. Parsons, Del. 10.4x15.7.　　1856 M N.C.

Railroad See: Nos. 32-3, 40, 68, 128-30, 185-9, 298, 496, 571-2, 1308-9, 1350-1, 1790-4, 2643, 2658, 3021, 3347, 3533-

6, 3542, 3771, 4190, 4473, 4475-7, 6049, 6051, 6491, 6664, 6792.

5057 Rally around the Flag / Victory at Last / (Full length, soldier in Zouave uniform.)   1861 S C&I

Rambler (Yacht) **See:** No. 6821.

Randolph, Edmund **See:** No. 6509.

5058 Rapids of Dunass / "On the Shannon" / 8.8.x12.10 (2 figures on right, castle on left.)   und S C&I

5059 Rarus / By Conklin's Abdallah, dam unknown / Record 2:20¾, Sept. 1st, 1875 / (Vignette, broadside to right, high-wheeled sulky.)
1876 S C&I

5060 Rarus / By son of Old Abdallah, dam by Telegraph / Record 2:13¼ / (Vignette, broadside to right, driver with beard and mustache.)
1877 S C&I

5061 Rarus / By son of Old Abdallah, dam by Telegraph / Record 2:13¼ (Sometimes 2:16) / (Composition similar to preceding but with slight changes and beardless driver.)
1877 S C&I

5062 Rarus, Record 2:13¼ / 2.12x4.12.
1881 V.S. C&I

5063 Rarus and Great Eastern / Crossing the Score in the third heat of their great match for $1,000 / At Fleetwood Park, N. Y., Sept. 22nd, 1877 / E. Forbes, Del. (Above title) Rarus, driven by John Splan. Great Eastern driven by C. S. Green. 3 additional lines. (Unusual race between Great Eastern under saddle and Rarus to sulky—vignette.)   1877 S C&I

Rarus **See:** Nos. 5071, 5708, 6163.

5064 Raspberries / #518 / 12.11x8.2 (Glass vase with roses and bluebells.)
1863 S C&I

5065 Raspberries / (Plate with raspberries, vase with flowers, basket and morning glories.)
1870 S C&I

5066 Raspberries / (Different composition from two preceding prints.)
und S C&I

5067 Rathgallan Head / Scene in the "Shaughraun" / 12.14x8.9.
und S C&I

5068 Rattling Heat, A / J. Cameron on stone. 12.1x18.14 (4 high-wheeled sulkies, ¾ view to left.)
1891 M C&I

5069 Rattling Heat, A / J. Cameron on stone. 12.1x18.14 (Same horses and drivers shown, small rubber-tired sulkies substituted for high-wheeled rigs.)
1893 M C&I

5070 Ravenswood / Long Island near Hallets Cove / M. Swett, Del. 11.4x50 (Showing the proposed layout of the grounds.)   und L N.C.

Rawlins, Gen. **See:** No. 2553.

Ray (Yacht) **See:** No. 5105.

Raymond, John T. **See:** No. 4273.

5071 R. B. Conklin's bay gelding Rarus, the "King of Trotters" / Driven by John Splan / Rarus by Conklin's Abdallah, dam by Telegraph was raised on Long Island by his present owner and his many victories / Over the best horses heretofore known on the track entitle him to be considered the fastest and most reliable trotter in the world / Record 2:16 / From life by E. Forbes. 16.11x26.1 (Broadside, high - wheeled sulky to right.)   1878 L C&I

5072 R. Cornell White's New Palatial Excursion Steamer "Columbia" / Sister ship of the "Grand Republic" built expressly for the Rockaway Route / Parsons & Atwater, Del.
1877 L C&I

5073 Reading the Bible / #292 / 1 additional line Biblical quotation. (Full length white dress, green curtain.)
1848 S N.C.

5074 Reading the Bible / #292 (¾ length.)   und S N.C.

5075 Reading the Scriptures /
und S N.C.

5076 Reading the Scriptures / "Search the scriptures," etc. 1 line. #247 / 12.6x8.2 (Couple shown, lamp on table.)
und S N.C.

5077 Reading the Scriptures / 12.5x7.15 (Family of 4, no lamp.)
1871 S C&I

5078 Ready for Battle / 8.6x12.6 (Stag and deer, mountain waterfall in rear.)
und S C&I

5079 Ready for a Frolic / 11.10x8.12 (Cat on sofa.)   1874 S C&I

5080 Ready for an Offer / 11.12x9.6 (Oval.)   und S C&I

5081 Ready for the Race / Sketched from life by Chas. L. Zellinsky. 18.2x 27.15 (2 horses under saddle, standing. Second state of "Mr. August Belmont's Potomac and Masher," etc. No. 4249.)
1891 L C&I

5082 Ready for the Signal / The Celebrated Running Horse Harry Bassett, by Lexington, dam Canary Bird / The property of Col. D. McDaniel's & Co. of Princeton, N. J. |James Roe, rider| / J. Cameron on stone. 5 additional lines. 17x25.13.   1872 L C&I

5083 Ready for the Start /
                          und S C&I

5084 Ready for the Trot / "Bring up your Horses" / Lith. by L. Maurer. Published by Heppenheimer & Maurer, 22 & 24 N. William St. Thos. Worth on stone. 18x27.
                          1877 L C&I

5085 Ready for the Trot / "Bring up· your Horses" / Printed in oil colors by Currier & Ives. L. Maurer, Lith. Thos. Worth on stone. 17.14x26.14.
                          1877 L C&I

5086 Rebecca / #133 (¾ length, white dress, bird on hand, exterior scene, waterfall in background.)
                          1846 S N.C.

5087 Rebecca / #133 (Full length, red dress, blue cape, different from preceding.)   1846 S N.C.

5088 Rebecca / #133 / 11.11x8.4 (Oval in ornamental border, ½ length.)
                          1846 S N.C.
     Rebecca (Yacht) See: No. 6812.

5089 Rechabite / Temperance, Fortitude, and Justice / #650 / 12.6x8.14 (Full length, male figure.)
                          1849 S N.C.

5090 Reconciliation, The / (Vignette.)
                          und S N.C.

5091 Re-Construction / Or a "White Man's Government" / Grant / (Vignette.)   1868 S C&I

5092 Record of Birth and Baptism / (Floral border, 4 lines verse.)
                          und S C&I

5093 Red Cloud / By Legal Tender, he by Davy Crockett |Pacer|, dam's pedigree unknown / Winner of the first prize $3,500 in the $7,500 purse for 2:20 horses at Buffalo, N. Y., Aug. 7th, 1874 / Winning the third, fourth, and fifth heats, beating Camors, Gloster, Nettie, Sensation, and St. James / Time 2:18, 2:18½, 2:21 / J. Cameron on on stone. 16.11x26.7 (Broadside to right, stands in background.)
                          1874 L C&I

5094 Red Cloud / By Legal Tender, etc. / (Same title as preceding) J. Cameron

on stone. (Vignette, broadside to left, high-wheeled sulky.)
                          1874 S C&I

5095 Red Hot Republicans on the Democratic Gridiron / "The San Domingo War Dance" / (Schurz, Sumner, Butler, and Greeley. Vignette.)
                          1872 S C&I
     Red Jacket (Clipper Ship) See: Nos. 1165-6.
     Red Virgil (Horse) See: No. 269.
     Red, White and Blue (Ship) See: Nos. 4137-8.

5096 Redeemer, The /
                          und S N. C.

5097 Redeemer, The / 1 line Biblical quotation.   und S C&I

5098 Redemption—Repudiation / 2 views on 1 sheet: Prosperity—man with gold. Other view—ruined man with bags filled with $1,000 green backs, inflation.
                          1875 S C&I

5099 Redpath / Scott Leighton on stone. (Vignette, profile to left—horse.)
                          1882 S C&I

5100 Redpath /   1875 S C&I

5101 Redpath /   1885 S C&I

5102 Refreshing Fountain, A / (2 small angels filling soda glass, flowers, etc.)
                          1879 S C&I

5103 Regatta of the New York Yacht Club, June 1st, 1854 / "Coming In" Rounding the Stake Boat / C. Parsons, Del. 17.13x28 (9 references.)
                          1854 L N.C.

5104 Regatta of the New York Yacht Club "Rounding the S. W. Spit" / J. E. Buttersworth on stone, C. Parsons, Del. 17.13x28 (9 references.)
                          1854 L N.C.

5105 Regatta of the New York Yacht Club, The Start / Prima Donna—Ceres — L'Esperance — Mystery — Alpha — Sibyl — Ray — Spray — Irene — Twilight — Una — Haze — Cornelia — Gertrude. J. E. Buttersworth on stone. C. Parsons, Del. 17.13x28.
                          1854 L N.C.

5106 Register for Colored People, A /
                          und S C&I

5107 Regular Hummer, A! / J. Cameron '79 on stone. (Horse outrunning 2 others, vignette to right.)
                          1879 S C&I

5108 Regular Hummer, A! / (Post card size.)   1880 V.S. C&I

Reid, Miss Elizabeth **See:** Nos. 4152-3.

5109 Reindeer Polka / G. E. Lewis, Del. Pub. by Jaques & Brother, 385 Broadway. 7.4x10.11 (Steamboat, reindeer.)
1850 S C.C.

5110 Rejected, The / #622 (Full length figure of man, vision of girl in background.) und S C&I

5111 Remember the Sabbath Day to Keep It Holy / und S N.C.

5112 Remember the Sabbath Day to Keep It Holy / 11.14x15.12 (Old man reading Bible, to group of 5, round top.) und M C&I

5113 Renowned Trotter "Prince Wilkes," Record 2:14¾, The / Owned by George A. Singerly of Philadelphia / Geo. A. Singerly 1888 on stone. 18x28.2 (Same composition as "Speeding to the Bike" No. 5645. High-wheeled sulky.)
1889 L C&I

5113A Republican Banner for 1860, The / Hon. Abraham Lincoln of Illinois— Hon. Hannibal Hamlin of Maine / 12x8.10. 1860 S C&I

5114 Republican Party going to the Right House, The / (Greeley carrying Lincoln on a rail to a building marked "Lunatic Asylum," vignette.)
1860 M C&I

Resaca de la Palma, Mexico **See:** Nos. 426, 808, 2299-300.

5115 Rescue, The / Sergeants Newton and Jasper of Marion's Brigade, rescuing American prisoners from a / British Guard, who had stacked their muskets while resting near a spring, South Carolina, 1779 / 8.14x12.7.
1876 S C&I

5116 Rescued / (Dog and children.) und S C&I

5117 Rescued / (Dog and boy.) und S C&I

5118 Residence of Lord Byron, The / Diodati, Italy. und S C&I

5119 Resignation / 11.11x8.13.
1847 S N.C.

Restigouche, New Brunswick **See:** "Black Bass Spearing" No. 543.

5120 Result in Doubt, The / "De one you's gets de water outen fust, am de winner" / King & Murphy, Dels., on stone. (Attempting to revive two colored men, companion to "A Fair Start" No. 1808, vignette.)
1884 S C&I

5121 Result in Doubt, The / (Identical title and composition used as ad for "Chew Pan Handle Scrap." Also see Nos. 1618, 1808A.)
1884 M C&I

5122 Resurrection, The / J. Cameron on stone. 18.5x13.2. Title repeated in French and Spanish. Published by N. Currier, Tract House, N. Y. (The only print I have seen with this address.)
1849 M N.C.

5123 Resurrection, The / 11.15x8.9.
und S C&I

5124 Resurrection of Christ, The / 12.1 x8.11. und S N.C.

5125 Return, The / F. P. on stone. 10.13 x8.10 (Oval, mother and son at sea wall, companion to "The Farewell" No. 1874.) und S C&I

5126 Return from Egypt, The / und S N.C.

5127 Return From Elba / In Judustrie— Comtoir in Hersfeld (Napoleon)/ Borninger & Manxler, Lithogr.
und L N.C.

5128 Return from the Pasture, The / F. F. Palmer, Del. (Cattle in stream, man and boy, woman standing in door of cottage.) und L C&I

5129 Return from the Pasture, The / F. F. Palmer, Del. (Changes in composition, cottage has been given thatched roof, woman and child outside.)
und L C&I

5130 Return from the Pasture, The / F. F. Palmer, Del. (Changes in composition, figure of man added, sitting at right of porch.) und L C&I

5131 Return from the Woods, The / F. F. Palmer, Del. 11.2x15.6 (2 hunters and dogs resting at edge of woods at right, wheat field and farm house at left.) und M C&I

5132 Re-Union on the Secesh-Democratic Plan / (Southerner offers to call it quits if Uncle Sam, burdened with Confederate debt of 650,000,000 and Federal debt of 1,500,000,000 and slaves will pay all expenses of war, vignette.)
1862 S C&I

5133 Revenge / #620 (2 dogs fighting, companion to "First Game" No. 1971.)
und S N.C.

5134 Rev. John Wesley / "Eighty-seven years have I sojourned on this earth endeavoring to do good" John Wesley. / 8.8x8. und S N.C.

5135 Rev. Richard Allen / Bishop of the First African Methodist Episcopal Church of the United States /
und S C&I

5136 Rev. William McAllister / J. Cameron on stone. 16.2x12.8 (Oval.)
und M C.C.

5137 Revd. Charles Wesley, A. M. / (Facsimile signature) "God Buries His workmen, but carries on his work" / Entered 1846 by H. R. Robinson. (Vignette.)
und S N.C.

5138 Revd. Christopher Rush, The / 2nd Superintendent of the Wesleyan Zion connection in America / Entered 1840 by T. Eato. Wm. Eiffe, Pinxt. J. M. McGee, Delt. 11.15x9.7 (½ length.)
1840 S N.C.

Rhine See: Germany.

5139 Rhode Island / 10x14.4 (Ship, no plate line but not vignetted—to right.)
1882 M C&I

Rhode Island See: Nos. 2383, 5413, 6816.
Rhode Island (Horse) See: No. 711.
Rhode Island (Steamer) See: Nos. 4967, 4969, 5139, 5788.
Rich, Charles C. See: No. 1986.
Richards, F. D. See: No. 1986.
Richball (Horse) See: No. 2519.
Richmond, Va. See: Nos. 1769, 1821-3.

5140 Ride to School, A / 7.14x4.14 (Printed on the same sheet with "Christmas Snow" No. 1081, boy pulling boy and girl on sled.)
und V.S. C&I

5141 Right Man for the Right Place, The / (Fremont, Fillmore and Buchanan. Fremont about to shoot Buchanan, Buchanan with dagger aimed at Fremont. Fillmore in center trying to separate combatants, vignette.)
und S N.C.

5142 Right Man for the Right Place, The /
und S C&I

5143 Right Revd. James T. Holly D.D. / First Bishop of the National Haitian Church / Consecrated in Grace Church, New York City, November 8th, 1874 / (½ length vignette.)
1875 S C&I

Ringgold, Major See: Nos. 1494-5, 3941.

5144 Rip Van Winkle's Cottage / In the Catskills /
und S C&I

5145 Ripe Cherries / 7.15x12.7 (White dish on side, cherries on table.)
1870 S C&I

5146 Ripe Fruit / (Watermelon, apples, grapes, bird's nest with 3 eggs, vignette.)
1875 S C&I

5147 Ripe Fruit /
und S C&I

5148 Ripe Fruits / (Oval, grapes, pears, blackberries, etc., printed on same sheet with "Choice Fruits" No. 1043.)
und V.S. C&I

5149 Ripe Strawberries /
und S C&I

5150 Ripton / July 19th, 1842. Beat Confidence, in a match for $500 a side, 2 mile heats in / Harness over Centreville Course, L. I., winning in 2 straight heats. Time 5:10, 5:14½, / 2 columns, 6 and 7 lines. 12.13x20.15 (Broadside to right, high-wheeled sulky.)
1850 L N.C.

5151 Rising Family, A / Painted by A. F. Tait. 18.4x23.12 (Snipe. Companion to "Cares of a Family" No. 814, and "The Happy Family," No. 2712.)
1857 L C&I

5152 Rival Charms / (Vignette, heads of 2 girls.)
und S C&I

5153 Rival Queens, The / Mary Queen of Scots defying Queen Elizabeth / 12.1 x8.6.
und S C&I

5154 Rival Roses, The / (Red and white rose growing in same pot, upright, vignette.)
1873 S C&I

5155 River Boat Passing the Palisades, A /
1869 S C&I

5156 River of Song / New York, Published by Horace Waters, 333 Broadway. G. E. Lewis, Del. (Identical composition to "Reindeer Polka," No. 5109.)
und S C.C.

5157 River Road, The /
und S C&I

River Road, The / 2.8x4.11. See "Gems of American Scenery" No. 2230.

5158 River Road, The / F. F. Palmer, Del. 11.1x15.8 (Same stone as "View near High Bridge, Harlem River" No. 6387.)
und M C&I

5159 River Shannon, The / From the Tower of Limerick Cathedral /
und S C&I

5160 River Side, The /
und S N.C.

5161 River Side, The / #142 (Mother and child on bank, 2 in row boat, cattle on opposite shore, vignette.)
und S C&I

5162 River Side, The / 7.15x12.6 (Couple on bank, 3 in rowboat, cows and house on opposite shore.)
und S C&I
River Side, The / (Printed on same sheet with "Sunnyside Hunter's Shanty," etc. See: No. 3439.

5163 River Side, The / 8.7x12.8 (2 figures on far bank, cows, castle in background.)
und S C&I

5164 Riverside, The / F. F. Palmer, Del. 15.10x11.4 (Fishermen on rock in center of stream.)
und M C&I

5165 Road—Summer, The / Painted by R. A. Clarke. 17.12x26.3 (Broadside to left, 4-wheeled rig, Hudson River in background, companion to "The Road —Winter" No. 5171.)
1853 L N.C.

5166 Road Team at a "Twenty Gait," A /
1880 S C&I

5167 Road Team at a "Twenty Gait," A / 2.12x4.12.
1883 V.S. C&I

5168 Road to the Holy Cross, The / Le Chemin de la tres Ste. Croix / 8.10x 11.13 (14 small scenes on sides.)
1845 S N.C.

5169 Road to the Holy Cross, The /
und S C&I

5170 Road to the Village, The / (Cattle in stream, village in rear.)
und M C&I

5171 Road—Winter, The / O. Knirsch on stone. 17.11x26.8 (Companion to "The Road—Summer" No. 5165.)
1853 L N.C.

5172 Road-Side, The / 11.5x14.15 (Oval in ornamental border, companion to "The Harvest Field" No. 2745.)
und M N.C.

5173 Roadside, The /
und S C&I

5174 Roadside Cottage / (Boy bringing sheep through gate, other children playing.)
und M C&I

THE ROAD.-SUMMER.

THE ROAD, - WINTER.

5175 Roadside Mill, The / 7.15x12.8.
1870 S C&I
Roanoke See: Nos. 810, 6375.

5176 Robert Blum / #651 / 9x11.12 (2 columns, 5 lines, ½ length portrait, execution scene through window at right.)   1849 S N.C.

5177 Robert Brown Elliott /
und S C&I

5178 Robt. Burns /
und M C&I

5179 Robert Burns and his Highland Mary / 2 columns, 4 lines verse. #181 / 11.11x8.10 (Full-length figures seated by stream with dog.)
1846 S N.C.

5180 Robert Burns and his Highland Mary / 2 columns, 4 lines of verse. (Similar to preceding, dog removed.)
und S C&I

5181 Robert Burns and his Highland Mary /(2 columns, 4 lines of verse, different composition from 2 preceding prints.)   und S N.C.

5182 Robert Burns and his Highland Mary / #71 / 11.12x8.12. 2 columns, 4 lines of verse. (Full length, seated under tree.)   und S C.C.

Robert E. Lee (Mississippi River Steamer) See: Nos. 746, 2629-30,2644.

5183 Robert Emmet (Above title) Dublin on the 19th of Sept., 1803. / (3 additional lines quotation. Full length courtroom scene, slightly rounded corners.)   und S N.C.

5184 Robert Emmet / Dublin on the 19th of Sept., 1803 / #725 / 3 line quotation. 11.11x8.5 (Full length, courtroom scene, lawyers, etc.)
und S C&I

5185 Robert Emmet / Ireland's "Martyr of Freedom" / 1 line quotation. 11.11 x8.8 (Lord Norbury on bench, full length of Robert Emmet in court.)
und S C&I

5186 Robert Emmet / Ireland's "Martyr of Freedom" / (Full length, 1 additional line quotation.)
und S C&I

5187 Robert Emmet's Betrothed /
und S C&I

[225]

Robert J. (Horse) See: Nos. 4682-4.

5188 Robert McGregor / By Major Edsall, dam by American Star / Record 2:18 / Scott Leighton on stone. (Vignette, ¾ view to right, high-wheeled sulky.) 1882 S C&I

5189 Robinson Crusoe and his man Friday / "Never had a man a more faithful servant, than Friday was to me, Etc." 12.11x8.12 (Crusoe and Friday walking, animals, boat, hut.) 1874 S C&I

5190 Robinson Crusoe and his Pets / 12.7x8.8 (Crusoe on porch of his house. Goats, dog, cat, turtles, wrecked vessel in background.) 1874 S C&I

5191 Robinson Crusoe and his Pets / "It would have Made a stoic smile," etc. (Different composition from preceding.) 1874 S C&I

5192 Robinson Crusoe and His Pets / und L C&I

Rochester Course See: Nos. 902, 923, 5339, 6211-12.

5193 Rochester Union Gray's Quick Step, The / By Henry Russell. J. T. Young, Del. und S N.C.

5194 Rock of Ages, The / 11.12x8.13 (3 lines verse.) 1873 S C&I

Rocket (Horse) See: No. 3383.

5195 Rocky Mountains, The / 8.8x12.8 (Buffalo herd in foreground.) und S C&I

5196 Rocky Mountains, The / Emigrants crossing the Plains / F. F. Palmer, Del. 17.7x25.13. 1866 L C&I

5197 Roll of Honor / 13x9 (For school children. Floral border, books, globe, etc.) 1874 S C&I

5198 Romeo and Juliet / #287 / (Act 3, Scene 5—2 columns, 4 lines of verse.) und S N.C.

Romer (Extraordinary Express Ship) See: No. 1798.

Roosevelt, Theodore See: No. 1202.

Rosamond (Horse) See: No. 3952.

5199 Rosanna / 1849 S N.C.

5200 Rosanna / (¾ length, seated with book, view through window shows a river boat.) und S N.C.

5201 Rosanna / #285 / 12.3x8.15 (¾ length, exterior scene, picking flowers, and flowers on arm.) und S N.C.

5202 Rose, The / (2 large roses, 2 buds, upright, vignette.) und S C&I

5203 Rose, The / #66 / (3 roses, 4 buds, bee and butterfly, upright vignette.) und S N.C.

5204 Rose, The / (2 roses, 3 buds.) und S C&I

5205 Rose / (Full length, girl's profile, reading under tree.) 1846 S N.C.

5206 Rose, The / (1 rose, 5 buds.) und S C&I

5207 Rose and Lily / 12.8x10 (½ length.) und S C&I

5208 Rose and Lily / (¾ length, vignette, 2 girls.) und S C&I

5209 Rose of Beauty / und S N.C.

5210 Rose of Beauty, The / (Vignette, girl's head.) und S C&I

5211 Rose of Killarney / und S C&I

5212 Rose of Killarney, The / Ballad. By / Miss Eliza Cook / Published by Hewitt & Jaques. und S N.C.

5213 Rose of May, The /#563 / 11.13x8.3 (Full length of girl on couch, holding roses.) 1847 S N.C.

5214 Rose of May, The / #563 (Full length, standing.) und S N.C.

5215 Roses of May / (6 large roses, 5 buds, buttetrfly, upright.) 1870 S C&I

5216 Rose / of May, The / #563 (5 roses 4 buds, butterfly on left upright, vignette.) und S C&I

5217 Rosebud and Eglantine / (Vignette, 2 girls' heads.) und S C&I

Rosecrans, Gen. W. S. See: Nos. 686, 2577, 3929-30.

5218 Roserk Abbey / (Ruins, Ireland.) und M C&I

5219 Roses, and Rosebuds / (Vignette, upright.) und M C&I

5220 Rosie / und S C&I

5221 Ross Castle—Lake of Killarney / Ireland. und M C&I

5222 Ross Trevor / 8.8x12.8. und S C&I

Rota (Steamship) See: No. 182.

ROUNDING THE LIGHT SHIP.

Rotterdam (Steamship) **See:** No. 5789.

5223 "Rounding a Bend" on the Mississippi / The Parting Salute / F. F. Palmer, Del. 18.4x27.14 (Shows the steamers "Queen of the West" and "Morning Star," and another unidentified steamer.)   1866 L C&I

5224 Rounding the Light Ship / 18.3x 27.15 (10 yachts shown, N. Y. scene, name on light ship "Sandy Hook.")
1870 L C&I

5225 Route to California, The / Truckee River Sierra Nevada / 8.7x12.8.
1871 S C&I

5226 Rowdy Boy / The Black Whirlwind of the Pacing Quartette of 1879 / Record 2:13¾ / J. C. on stone. (Vignette, ¾ to right, high-wheeled sulky.)
1879 S C&I

Rowing **See:** Nos. 92-4, 869, 973, 2095, 2620, 2623-4, 2650, 3153, 4164.

Rowell, Charles Pedestrian **See:** No. 1006.

5227 Rowing Him Up Salt River / (Cass in row boat.) Pub. by P. Smith.
1848 M N.C.

5228 Roy Wilkes / Record 2:14½ / J. Cameron on stone. (Vignette, high-wheeled sulky to right, printed in oil colors by Currier & Ives.)
1889 S C&I

5229 Roy Wilkes / Record 2:08¼ / (Vignette.)   und M C&I

5230 Roy Wilkes, Record 2:12¾ / L. M. on stone.   1890 S C&I

5231 Royal Beauty, The /
und S C&I

5232 Royal Family of England, The / Queen Victoria and her children / (2 additional lines.)   und S C&I

5233 Royal Family of Prussia, The /
und S C&I

5234 Royal Mail Steamship "Amsterdam" of the Netherlands Line /
und S C&I

5235 Royal Mail Steamship "Arabia" /
1853 L N.C.

5236 Royal Mail Steam Ship / "Asia" / F. Palmer, Del., and Lith. 13.14x22.2 (2 columns, 4 and 3 lines—broadside to right.)   1851 L N.C.

5237 Royal Mail Steam Ship "Austra-

lasian," The / 3100 Tons / To the British and North American Royal Mail Steamship Company / This Print is respectfully dedicated by the Publisher / 2 columns, 3 lines additional.
1861 L C&I

5238 Royal Mail Steam Ship / Bothnia / 1 additional line of dimensions.
und S C&I

5239 Royal Mail Steam Ship / "Europa" / 2 columns, 2 lines. 14.2x22.3 (Broadside to left.)   1849 L N.C.

5240 Royal Mail Steam Ship, The / "Persia" / C. Parsons, Del. 15.8x23.8.
1856 L N.C.

5241 Royal Mail Steam Ship / "Scotia"/ Off Cape Race. Throwing over the New York Associated Express Parcel / Painted by S. Walters. C. Parsons, Lith.   und L C&I

5242 Royal Mail Steamship "Scotia" / 2 columns, 1 line. 8x12.12.
und S C&I

5243 Royal Mail Steamship "Veendam" / Of the Netherlands Line /
und S C&I

5244 Royal Mail Steamship Zaandam of the Netherlands Line /
und S C&I

5245 R. T. Y. C. Schr. Cambria 199 Tons / James Asbury, Esq. London and Brighton Owner / Winner of the Great Ocean Yacht Race against the American Yacht "Dauntless" from Daunt Rock / Queenstown, Ireland, July 4th, to the Light Ship at Sandy Hook, July 27th, 1870 / Time 23 days beating the "Dauntless" 1 hour and 10 Minutes / Parsons & Atwater, Del. 19.8x27.12.
1870 L C&I

5246 Rubber, The / 11.11x8.14 (Man and woman playing cards.)
und S C&I

5247 Rubber, The / "Put to his Trumps" / L. Maurer on stone. 19.12x15.13 (4 card players, 2 onlookers, upright.)
und M N.C.

5248 Ruffed Grouse / Pheasant or Partridge / 8.8x12.8.   1871 S C&I
   Ruggles House, Newburgh See: Nos. 6421, 6433-4.

5249 Ruins, The / The Castle / (Printed on same sheet with "The Hillside — Cattskill Creek.")
und V.S. C&I
   Ruins in Sussex, England See: Landscape Cards No. 3438.

5250 Ruins of Chepstow Castle / South Wales / (Oval.)   und V.S. C&I
   Ruins of Lamphey Castle, England/ 2.11x4.3 (See: Landscape Cards No. 3438.)

5251 Ruins of the Abbey, The / F. F. Palmer, Del.   1856 M N.C.

5252 Ruins of the Abbey /
und S C&I

5253 Ruins of the Merchant's Exchange, N.Y. / After the Destructive Conflagration of Decbr. 16 & 17, 1835 / Sketched and drawn on stone by J. H. Bufford / Published by J. Disturnell. 156 Broadway & J. H. Bufford, 10 Beekman St. / Copyright by J. H. Bufford, 1835 / 9.7x12.5.
1835 S N.C.

5254 Ruins of the Planters Hotel, New Orleans, which fell at two o'clock on the morning of the 15th of May, 1835, burying 50 persons, 40 of which escaped with their lives / J. Bufford on stone. Printed by N. Currier, 1 Wall St., N.Y.   und S N.C.

5255 Run Down /   1877 S C&I

5256 Run Down / King & Murphy, Dels. (Companion to "Wound Up," No. 6783 colored comic.)   1884 S C&I

5257 Run of Luck, A / 10.7x15 (Monkey playing pool.)   1871 S C&I

5258 Running the "Machine" / (Fessenden turning a wheel marked "Chase Patent Greenback Mill." Lincoln, Stanton, Seward, and Welles shown, vignette.)   1864 M C&I

5259 Rural Architecture No. 1 / (Boy rolling hoop, lady with 2 children under tree, 2 on horseback, same as "Cottage Life — Summer." No. 1268.)
1856 M N.C.

5260 Rural Architecture No. 2 / (Same as "Cottage Life — Spring" No. 1266.)
1856 M N.C.

5261 Rural Lake, The / Painted by F. F. Palmer. 10.6x14.15 (Group of 3 in row boat.)   und M C&I

5262 Rural Scenery /
und S C&I

5263 Rush for the Heat, A / J. Cameron 1874 on stone. (¾ view, 2 horses and high-wheeled sulkies.)
1884 L C&I

5264 Rush for the Pole, A / J. Cameron on stone. (5 horses and high-wheeled sulkies to right, stand in rear, vignette.)   1877 L C&I
   Russia See: Nos. 599, 1825.

5265 Rustic Basket / (Vignette.)
und S C&I

5266 Rustic Bridge, Central Park / New York / 8.8x12.5.　und S C&I

5267 Rustic Stand of Flowers / (Upright, vignette.)　1875 S C&I

5268 Rutherford B. Hayes / Nineteenth President of the United States /
und S C&I

Ryan, Paddy See: No. 4691.

5269 Rysdyk's Hambletonian / Foaled May 5th, 1849 sired by "Old Abdallah" he by "Mambrino" and he by "Imported Messenger" dam the "Charles Kent" / Mare by Imported "Bell Founder" / Hambletonian is the sire of "Dexter" "George Wilkes" "Jay Gould" "Startle" "Aberdeen" "Bruno" and / Many other Famous Trotters and the Grand Sire of "Goldsmith Maid" / J. Cameron on stone. (Profile to left, standing, house in rear at left, vignette.)　1871 S C&I

5270 "Rysdyk's Hambletonian" / J. Cameron 1871 on stone. (Vignette.)
1871 S C&I

5271 Rysdyk's Hambletonian / Sired by Old Abdallah, etc. 12.3x8.11 (Standing in stall to left.)　1877 S C&I

5272 Rysdyk's Hambletonian / The Great Sire of Trotters / Painted from life by J. H. Wright, N.Y. (Profile to left, exterior, barn and house in background at left.)　1880 S C&I

5273 Rysdyk's Hambletonian / L. Maurer on stone at left. J. H. Wright — 1865 on stone at right. Reproduced by Heppenheimer & Maurer. 2 additional lines pedigree, and facsimile note from Rysdyk. 18.13x25.14 (Profile portrait to left in stable, also full-length portrait of Mr. Rysdyk — beside horse.)
1876 L C&I

5274 Rye and Rock / Thos. Worth on stone. (Colored man fishing and drinking rye, upright, vignette.)
1884 S C&I

S

Saale (Steamship) See: No. 5790.

5275 Sacandaga Creek / 5.6x7.6 (Oval. Companion to "Fawn's Leap, Catskills," No. 1933.)
und V.S. C&I

Sacandaga Creek See: "American Landscape / Sacandaga Creek" No. 177.

5276 Sacrament of St. James /
und S N.C.

5277 Sacred Heart / (Christ bearing heart.)　und S N.C.

5278 Sacred Heart of Jesus / Sacre Coeur de Jesus — Sacredo corazon de Jesus / #18 / 12.13x 8.10 (Full-length figure.)　1848 S N.C.

5279 Sacred Heart of Jesus / Title repeated in French and Spanish / #34 / 12.9x8.12 (Portrait of Jesus, robe held back to show heart surrounded by thorns.)　und S N.C.

5280 Sacred Heart of Jesus / #34 / 12.2 x8.12 (Same general composition as preceding, slightly rounded corners.)
und S C&I

5281 Sacred Heart of Jesus, The / 14.14 x11.5.　und M C&I

5282 Sacred Heart of Mary / Sacre Coeur de Marie — Sacredo Corazon de Maria / #19 / 12.13x8.10 (Full length.)
1848 S N.C.

5283 Sacred Heart of Mary / Title repeated in Spanish and Italian, #35 / 12.4 x8.13 (Half length.)
und S C&I

5284 Sacred Motto Tokens / 12.9x8.15 (9 small views: lambs, Bibles, flowers, crosses, etc.)　1874 S C&I

5285 Sacred to the Memory of ————/ 12.14x8.12 (Mother and daughter at right of tomb, upright.)
1847 S N.C.

5286 Sacred to the Memory of ———— / #191 (Father and 2 children, upright.)
1846 S N.C.

5287 Sacred to the Memory of ———— / #185 (Father and daughter at tomb in country church yard, weeping willow.)　1846 S N.C.

5288 Sacred to the Memory of ———— / #193 / 12.12x8.10 (Tomb on right, church yard and 3 people.)
1849 S N.C.

5289 Sacred to / the Memory / of ———— / (Floral scroll and wreath, vignette, upright.)　1872 S C&I

5290 Sacred Tomb of the Blessed Redeemer, The / 8.6x12.9 (Companion to following.)　und S C&I

5291 Sacred Tomb of the Blessed Virgin, The / 8.4x12.8 (Companion to preceding.) und S C&I

5292 Safe Sailing / (4 children playing in rowboat on land.) und S C&I

5293 Sage old Smoke, A / "Capital cigar, don't wonder de kids like 'em" / J. Cameron on stone. (Colored man smoking cigar he has taken from children, who had stolen them, vignette.) 1888 S C&I

5294 Sailor Boy, The / und S N.C.

5295 Sailor-Far-Far-At Sea, The / 11.14 x8.9 (2 columns, 4 lines verse — girl reading letter and looking at locket, upright.) 1845 S N.C.

5296 Sailor's Adieu, The / 11.15x8.6 (Ship to left.) und S N.C.

5297 Sailor's Adieu, The / 12x9 (Ship left, no shutter at window, frilled sleeves, side curls, sailor with sideburns, short hair ribbon, bow tie.) und S N.C.

5298 Sailor's Adieu, The / #15 (Upright, full length, no house shown, white picket fence in background.) und S N.C.

5299 Sailor's Adieu, The / 11.15x8.8 (Shutter at window, girl with different hair arrangement, tight sleeves, long hat ribbon, American flag on ship, ship at right. Companion to No. 5304.) und S N.C.

5300 Sailor's Adieu, The / #16 / 11.15x 8.5 (Couple at flower-covered door.) 1847 S N.C.

5301 Sailor's Adieu, The / 12.6x8.5. und S C&I

5302 Sailor's Bride, The / #667 / 11.12 x8.9 (Full length, deck scene, moonlight.) 1849 S N.C.

5303 Sailor's Return, The / #15 / 12x8.5 (Cottage at right, ship on left.) 1847 S N.C.

5304 Sailor's Return, The / 12x8.8 (Girl with tight sleeves, half of window shown, boat on right, companion to No. 5299.) und S N.C.

5305 Sailor's Return, The / #16 (No house shown, lady in red pleated dress.) und S N.C.

5306 Sailor's Return, The / 12.2x8.7 (Girl with leg-of-mutton sleeves, sailor with striped shirt, bundle on stick. Overhanging limb of tree.) und S N.C.

5307 Saint Anne / und S C&I St. Anthony, Minn. See: No. 5520.

5308 Sn. Anthony de Padua — St. Antoine de Padoue / #660 / 12.1x8.11 (Full length, surrounded by cherubs.) 1849 N.C.

5309 Sn. Benedict the Moor / und S C&I

5310 St. Bridget, Abbess of Kildare / 1848 S N.C.

5311 Saint Bridget — Sta. Brigida / (Full length, reading.) und S C&I

5312 St. Catherine / und S C&I

5313 St. Catherine of Sienna / und S C&I

5314 St. Cecelia / Sta. Cecelia — Ste. Cecile / (Full length of Saint with vision over head, cherubs in cloud.) und S C&I

5315 St. Charles Borromeo / und S C&I

5316 St. Clotilde / und S C&I

5317 St. Elizabeth / und S C&I

5318 Saa Emellia — Ste Emelie / #124 (Vignette, kneeling figure, profile.) 1846 S N.C.

5319 St. Emelie / (Half length, vignette.) und S N.C.

5320 St. Emily / 1846 S N.C.

5321 St. Ferdinand, The King / und S N.C.

5322 St. Fineen's Well, Ireland / und S C&I

5323 St. Francis of Assisi / und S C&I

5324 St. Francis of Paul / und S C&I

5325 Sn. Francisco-Xaverio — St. Francois Xavier / St. Francis Xavier / #657 / 12x8.11 (Full length.) 1849 S N.C.

5326 St. Ignatius of Loyola / und S C&I

5327 St. James / und S C&I

5328 St. Jean Baptiste Inspire — St. Juan Baptista Inspirata / St. John Baptist / und S N.C.
St. John (Hudson River Steamer) See: Nos. 196, 1626, 2541, 2981, 4601, 4747-8.

5329 St. John N.B. River / Indian Town/
          und S C&I
    St. John N.B. See: No. 2616.

5330 St. John the Baptist /
          und S C&I

5331 St. Joseph — Sn. Jose / #220 /
    12.12x8.11 (Round corners, ornamental
    border.)   1846 S N.C.

5332 St. Joseph (repeated in Spanish) /
    11.8x8 (St. Joseph holding Jesus.)
          und S C&I

5333 St. Juan Battista /
          und S C&I

5334 St. Julien / By Volunteer, dam by
    Sayre's Henry Clay / As he appeared
    at Oakland Park, Cal. Oct. 25th, 1879
    driven by Orrin A. Hickok, Trotting
    in harness for a purse of $850 / Con-
    ditioned to beat the best record of
    Rarus 2:13¼ winning in the unparal-
    leled time of / 2:12¾ / Thos. Worth on
    stone. 16.11x25.3 (Broadside to right.)
          1879 L C&I

5335 St. Julien / By Volunteer, etc. / Title
    same as preceding. J.C. on stone. (Vig-
    nette, ¾ to right, high-wheeled sulky.)
          1879 S C&I

5336 St. Julien /   1880 S C&I

5337 St. Julien / King of the Turf, driven
    by Orrin A. Hickok / Scott Leighton
    on stone.   1880 L C&I
    St. Julien (Horse) See: Nos. 433-4,
    1947-8, 2487-8, 2535, 3339, 3471, 4086,
    4405, 5384-7, 5708, 6163, 6177, 6182.

5338 St. Lawrence /
          und S C&I

5339 St. Lawrence / Rochester, Oct. 24th,
    1850 / Purse $300 mile heats best 3
    in 5 in harness / H. Delattre 1851 on
    stone. 2 additional lines, and 2 columns,
    5 lines. 12.12x20.11 (View of Rochester
    and Genesee Falls in background. To
    right, high wheel.)
          1852 L. N.C.
    St. Lawrence (U.S. Frigate) See:
    Nos. 6295, 6308-9.
    St. Lawrence River See: Nos. 2650,
    4609, 5051, 6452.

5340 St. Louis, The King / San Luis Rey
    — St. Louis Roi / #652.
          und S N.C.

5341 St. Louis the King / San Luis Rey
    — St. Louis Roi /
          und S C&I

5342 St. Louis Roi / St. Louis the King.
    San Luis Rey /   1849 S N.C.

    St. Louis (Great race) See: No.
5339.
    St. Louis (Steamship) See: No.
3886.
    St. Louis, Missouri See: No. 1117.

5343 St. A Madalena — St. E. Madeleine
    / 11.10x8.4 (Full length, kneeling, open
    book, cross, etc.)   und S N.C.

5344 St. Margaret /
          und S C&I

5345 St. Mary — Sta. Mary / #221 /
    12.12x8.11 (Ornamental border, round
    corners.)   1846 S N.C.

5346 St. Mary's Abbey / (Oval, on same
    sheet with "Highland Waterfall" (Eng-
    land) No. 2827.)   und V.S. C&I

5347 St. Michael /   und S C&I

5348 St. Michael — San Migoel / #326 /
    11.14x8.11 (Michael with opened wings,
    standing on head of Satan.)
          und S N.C.

5349 St. Michael — San Migoel / 11.10x
    8.7 (Full length of Michael with wings
    and sword.)   und S N.C.

5350 St. Nicholas / 12.1x8.10.
          und S N.C.

5351 St. Patrick / #9.
          und S N.C.

5352 St. Patrick — San Patrico / (Half-
    length vignette.)   und S C&I

5353 St. Patrick, The Apostle of Ireland/
    Born in the year 361, died in the year
    458 / 1 additional line. (Chasing
    snakes.)   und S C&I

5354 St. Paul /   und S C&I
    St. Paul (Steamship) See: No. 5791.
    St. Paul's Church, N.Y. See: Nos.
3065-8, 6071.

5355 Saint Peter / (Full length with
    keys to heaven.)   und S N.C.

5356 St. Peter — San Pedro /
          und S N.C.

5357 St. Peter receiving the Keys / San
    Pedro recibien do las llaves / 11.15x
    8.8 (Upright.)   und S C&I

5358 St. Philomena / 11.14x8.8 (Roses
    in hair, cherubs at her side, half-
    length, black background.)
          1845 S N.C.

5359 St. Philomena /
          und S C&I

5360 Sn. Ramon no-Nacido-S. Ramon
    non Nato / #650 / 12x8.8. A.W. on
    stone.   1849 S N.C.

5361 St. Raphael. San Rafael. /
und S C&I

5362 Sta Rita de Casia — Ste. Ritte de Casia / #659 / 11.12x8.11 (Full-length figure kneeling.) 1849 S N.C.

5363 Sta Rita de Casia /
und S C&I

5364 St. Rose of Lima /
und S C&I

5365 St. Theresa /
und S C&I

5366 St. Vincent de Paul /
und S C&I

5367 Sale of "Blooded Stock", A / (Vignette, auction sale.)
1880 S C&I

5368 Sale of the Pet Lamb, The / Painted by Wm. Collins, Esq. R.A. from an engraving by S. W. Reynolds. O. Knirsch on stone. 15x19.10 (2 columns, 4 lines of verse) Companion to "Sunday Morning" etc. No. 5884.
und M N.C.

5369 Sale of the Pet Lamb, The /
und S C&I

5370 Salmon Fishing / 8.8x12.8.
1872 S C&I

5371 Salmon Leap, near Ballyshannon / Ireland. und S C&I

5372 Salmon Leap / River Shannon / (Falls in background, fisherman left foreground.) und M C&I

Salvator (Horse) See: Nos. 1949, 2209, 2622, 5047-8.

5373 Sam Purdy / The Champion Trotting Stallion of the Pacific Slope / By George M. Patchen, Jr., otherwise called "California Patchen," dam Whiskey Jane by Illinois Medoc / Record 2:20½. und S C&I

5374 Samuel J. Tilden / (Vignette.)
und S C&I

5375 San Antonia de Padua / 1 additional line. (Upright.)
und S C&I

5376 San Antonio — Saint Anthony /
und S C&I

San Francisco, Cal. / See: Nos. 1118-20, 6409.

San Francisco (U.S. Cruiser) See: No. 6644.

San Francisco (Steamship) See: No. 5492.

5377 San Luis Rey — St. Louis the King — St. Louis Roi /
1849 S N.C.

5378 Sancho / A Celebrated Pointer / (Head of dog.) und S N.C.

5379 Sancho / A Celebrated Pointer / 9.13x11.13 (Dog with pheasant in mouth, to right, all of dog shown, no plate line.) und S N.C.

5380 Sancho / A Celebrated Pointer / Painted by Benj. Marshall, on stone after Fairland. 11.13x8.7 (Setter holding a pheasant in mouth, whole dog shown.) und S N.C.

5381 Sanctuary of our Lady of Guadalupe / und S C&I

Sankey, Ira See: No. 3126.

5382 Santa Anna's Messengers Requesting Genl. Taylor to surrender his forces at discretion, previous to the battle of Buena Vista / "General Taylor Never Surrenders" / #453 / 2 additional lines. 8.7x12.13 (Taylor on black horse, sword in right hand, right leg of horse raised.) 1847 S N.C.

5383 Santa Anna's Messengers Requesting Genl. Taylor, etc. (title identical to preceding) / #453 / 8.6x12.12 (Taylor's right hand extended, left leg of white horse raised, and other changes in composition.) 1847 S N.C.

5384 Santa Claus / 1882 S C&I
Santa Claus (Stallion) See: No. 6220.

5385 Santiago, Cuba /
und M C&I

5386 Sappho / (Head of girl.)
und V.S. C&I

Sappho (Yacht) See: Nos. 5040, 6813-5.

5387 Sara Bernhardt / (Vignette, ¾ length.) und S C&I

5388 Sarah / #50 / 11.10x8.1 (Winter costume, ¾ length.) und S C.C.

5389 Sarah / #50 / 11.12x8.6 (¾ length under tree, holding rose, and rose in hair.) und S N.C.

5390 Sarah / (Similar composition to preceding, no lace jabot.)
und S N.C.

5391 Sarah / #77 / 11.15x8.3 (Full length, seated, cloak over chair, poke bonnet.)
1848 S N.C.

5392 Sarah / 1876 S C&I

5393 Sarah / #50 (Half-length vignette.)
und S C&I

5394 Sarah Ann / #96 / 12x8.7 (Half length, curls and earrings, plate has round corners.) 1846 S N.C.

Saratoga **See:** "Surrender of Gen. Burgoyne" No. 5907.

Saratoga Racetrack **See:** Nos. 2734-6.

5395 Saratoga Lake / 2.13x3.15 (See "Landscape Views" No. 3439.)
und V.S. C&I

5396 Saratoga Lake / 8.8x12.8 (Couple in center foreground.)
und S C&I

5397 Saratoga Springs / 7.15x12.7 (Hotel to right, small circular park in foreground.) und S C&I

5398 Saratoga Springs, N.Y. / 8.2x12.10 (Circular park in left foreground, different buildings shown, entirely different from preceding, earlier view.)
und S C&I

5399 Satisfaction! / #512 / J. Schutz on stone. 7.6x12 (Companion to "Honour" No. 2927, dueling scene.)
und S N.C.

5400 Saucy Kate /
1847 S N.C.

5401 Saucy Kat / (Vignette.)
und S C&I

Savannah (U.S. Frigate) **See:** No. 6310.

5402 Saved! / Painted by E. Landseer. 14.14x19.12 (Child rescued by dog, companion to 6080.)
und M C&I

5403 Saviour of the World, The / #246 / 12.2x8.13 (Oval portrait in ornate border, 5 cartouches.)
1845 S N.C.

5404 Saviour of the World, The / Repeated in French and Spanish. 12x8.5.
und S N.C.

5405 Saviour of the World, The / El Salvador Del Mundo — La Sauveur Du Monde / #40 / 12.2x8.4.
und S C.C.

5406 Saviour's Invitation, The / 17.4x 11.13 (Preaching, 3 additional lines, round top.) 1866 M C&I

Sayers, Tom / **See:** Nos. 2613, 6094-7.

5407 Scales of Justice, The / 1 additional line from Aesop. (Monkey acting as judge, 2 cats fighting over cheese.) und S N.C.

5408 Scapular, The /
und S N.C.

5409 Scarlet Tanager / 7.14x4.14 (Printed on same sheet with "Baltimore Oriole" No. 355.)
und V.S. C&I

5410 Scene in Fairyland, A / 8.8x12.8.
und S C&I

5411 Scene in Old England, A /
und S C&I

5412 Scene in Old Ireland, A / (Castle in background, sunset.)
und S C&I

5413 Scene off Newport, A /
und S C&I

5414 Scene on the Lower Mississippi, A/.
und S C&I

5415 Scene on the Susquehanna, A / (Sheep in foreground, village on right.)
und S C&I

5416 Scenery of Connemara, Ireland / Ballynahinch Lake /
und S C&I

5417 Scenery of Ireland, The / Upper lake of Killarney / 9.14x16.15.
1869 M C&I

5418 Scenery of the Catskill / The Mountain House / 8x12.7 (Stagecoach at center, hotel on extreme right.)
und S C&I

5419 Scenery of the Catskills / 8.8x12.8 (Trees on each side extend to top of plate, group of 5 on rocks at left, hotel left center — "Mountain House".)
und S C&I

5420 Scenery of the Catskills / The Catskill Falls of the Catskill Mountains /
und S N.C.

5421 Scenery of the Hudson, The / View near "Anthony's Nose" / F. Palmer, Del. 15x20.4 ("Up the Hudson" No. 6350 shows the same locality, similar composition.) und L. C&I

5422 Scenery of the Upper Mississippi / An Indian Village / 8x12.8.
und S C&I

5423 Scenery of the Wissahickon / Near Philadelphia / 8.8 x 12.9. und S C&I

5424 Scenery of Wicklow, Ireland / The Devil's Glen / und S C&I

Schiller (Steamship) **See:** No. 6790.

Schoepff, Gen. **See:** No. 413.

Schofield, Gen. **See:** No. 5490.

5425 Scholar's Rewards / 12.11x9 (9 views, baskets of fruit with scroll bearing Biblical quotations.)
1874 S C&I

5426 School Rewards / 12.7x8.15 (9 small bouquets, rewards of merit for neatness and order, good conduct, punctuality, etc.)   1874 S C&I

5427 School Rewards / (8 views entitled Reward of Merit, Token of Honor, Certificate of Honor. Rural scenes surrounded by floral borders.)   und M C&I

5428 School's In /   und V.S. C&I

5429 School's Out / 5.8x7.8 (Full length, boy and dog, school and other children in background, winter scene.)   und V.S. C&I

5430 Schooner / #392 (Broadside to right.)   1846 S N.C.

5431 Schooner Yacht Cambria, 199 Tons / Winner of the great Ocean Race against the American Yacht "Dauntless' from Daunt Rock, Queenstown, Ireland, July 4 to the Light Ship / At Sandy Hook, July 27, 1870 / 1 additional line. Time, etc. 8.12x12.12.   und S C&I

5432 Schooner Yacht "Madeline" New York Yacht Club / owned and commanded by John S. Dickerson / 1 additional line.   und S C&I

5433 Schooner Yacht "Magic" of the N.Y. Yacht Club, The / Franklin Osgood, Esq., owner and commander / Winner of the Great International Yacht Race for the Queen's Cup at New York Aug. 8th, 1870 / 2 additional lines. 2 columns, 8 and 7 lines. 18.1x 27.3.   1870 L C&I

5434 Schooner Yacht "Magic" /(Identical to preceding, second line changed to: Lester Wallack owner and Commander.)   1870 L C&I

Schurz, Carl / See: Nos. 5095, 5664.

5435 Scientific Shaving on the Darktown Plan / "Nuffin but Fust class artist employed heah" / J. Cameron on stone. (Vignette, companion to Tonsorial Art, etc. No. 6114.)   1890 S C&I

5436 Scoring — Coming up for the Word / Little Fred, Needle Gun, Jessie Wales, Belle of Brooklyn, Old Put, and Lady Whitman / In their splendid trot on the Prospect Park Fair Grounds, May 29th, 1869 / 8 additional lines. J. Cameron, Del. on stone. 17.2x26.8 (Horses and drivers keyed above title, broadside to left.)   1869 L C&I

5437 Scoring for the First Heat / Ringing them back / Thos. Worth on stone.

SCORING FOR THE FIRST HEAT.

17.10x27 (8 horses shown, judge's stand in rear, high-wheeled sulkies.)
1877 L C&I

5438 Scotch Beauty, The /
und S C&I

5439 Scotch Cutter Madge, Captain Duncan, The / Length over all 45 ft. 8½ in. breadth of beam 7 ft. 9 in. / 8.14x 12.12.
1881 S C&I

5440 Scotch Laddie, The /
und S C&I

Scotia (Steamship) See: Nos. 5241-2.

Scotland See: Nos. 5, 87, 356, 607, 624-6, 754, 1630, 4103-5, 4778, 5441, 5967, 6253.

Scott, Chas. See: No. 1005.

Scott, Sir Walter See: No. 5.

Scott, Major Gen. Winfield See: Nos. 993, 2293, 2482, 2515, 3494-7, 3933-6, 3967, 4694, 6543, 6722-4.

5441 Scottish Border, The / (Castle on hill, fisherman asleep by stream.)
und M C&I

Scottish Scenery See: Picturesque Landscapes No. 4778.

Scud (Yacht) See: No. 1343.

Scythia (Steamship) See: No. 5792.

5442 Sea of Tiberias, The /
und S C&I

5443 Seal of Affection, The / #286 / 12.1 x8.12 (¾ length, at writing desk, making an impression of locket to be used as a seal, to right, colored band in hair.)
und S N.C.

5444 Seal of Affection, The / (Same general composition to left, round corners, rose in hair, to left.)
1846 S N.C.

Seal Rocks, California See: No. 768.

5445 Search the Scriptures / (¾ length, old man and daughter reading Bible.)
und S N.C.

5446 Search the Scriptures / 11.13x9.1.
und S N.C.

5447 Search the Scriptures /
und S C&I

5448 Season of Blossoms, The / 8.8x12.8.
und S C&I

5449 Season of Blossoms, The / F. F. Palmer, Del. 15.12x23.4.
1865 L C&I

5450 Season of Joy, The / 8.8x12.8 (4 children on lawn chasing butterfly.)
1872 S C&I

5451 "Secession Movement", The / (Figures representing different Southern states riding on pigs, mules, horses, and chasing a butterfly to edge of cliff, which they don't see — vignette.)
1861 S C&I

5452 Second Battle of Bull Run, Fought Augt. 29th, 1862, The / 2 additional lines. #800 / 8x12.9 (Union forces under Maj. Gen. John Pope at left and Rebel Army under Lee and Jackson.)
und S C&I

5453 See My Doggie? /
und S N.C.

5454 See My New Boots! /
1856 S N.C.

5455 See My New Boots! / (Vignette.)
1856 L C&I

5456 See / My New Boots / 11.14x8.8 (Full length.)
1870 S C&I

5457 See-Saw / (Group of 4).
und M C&I

5458 See-Saw / 11.7x8.5 (Upright, group of 3.)
und S C&I

5459 Selling Out Cheap / (Store card.)
und S C&I

5460 Selling Out Cheap! / (Sumner, with speeches against Grant on desk, telling the devil at his side, that he may have the country if he, Sumner, may have revenge, vignette.)
1870 S C&I

Seminary, Troy / See: No. 6157.

5461 Sensation / By Dixon's Ethan Allen, dam Indian Chief Record 2:22¼ / (Vignette.)
1876 S C&I

5462 Serenade /
1866 S C&I

5463 Sergeant Jasper of Charleston / Replacing the colors which had been shot away from Fort Moultrie during the combined attack of the British Fleet and / army upon Charleston, S.C., June 28th, 1776 /
1876 S C&I

Servia (Steamship) See: No. 1329, 5793.

5464 Servicable Garment, A / Or Reverie of a Bachelor / (Political cartoon of James Buchanan, vignette.)
und M N.C.

5465 Set of Eight, A /
und S C&I

5466 Set of Fashionable Quadrilles, The / From Auber's Celebrated Opera of Gustavus the Third, or the Masked Ball / (Interior of Niblo's Garden, N.Y.)
1840 S N.C.

5467 Set of the Queens Country Dances/
As performed at / The Court Balls /
Arranged for the / Piano Forte / By /
R'd Guinness / Principal Leader of the
Quadrille Band at the Royal Palace /
(Portrait of Queen Victoria, couples
dancing.)   und S N.C.

5468 Setter & Woodcock / (Vignette,
dog's head to left with bird in mouth.)
und S C&I

5469 Setters / #443 (Taken from an
English sporting print. Pub. by Ackerman & Sons. Companion to Nos. 2107,
4816, 5689.)
1846 S N.C.

5470 Settling the Question /(Same as "A
Literary Debate in the Darktown Club"
No. 3559.)   1885 S C&I

5471 Seven Churches of Clonmacnoise,
The / On the River Shannon, Ireland /
8x12.   und S C&I

5472 Seven Stages of Matrimony, The /
und S N.C.

Seward See: Nos. 3134, 3967, 4880,
5258, 6689.

Seymour See: Hon. Horatio Nos.
2905-6, 3962, 4387, 5050.

5473 Shade and Tomb of Napoleon, The
/ "The figure of Napoleon will be observed among the trees." /
und S C&I

5474 Shade and Tomb of Washington,
The / The Figure of Washington will
be observed among the trees / 8.8x12.7.
1876 S C&I

5475 Shakers near Lebanon / 8x12.12
(Interior meeting house showing shakers dancing.)   und S N.C.

5476 Shakespeare / (Vignette portrait.)
und M C&I

Shakespeare See: Nos. 538, 6703.

5477 Shall I? / 7.8x5.8 (Winter scene,
girl with snowball, companion to
"Throw if You Dare" No. 6052.)
und V.S. C&I

Shannon River See: Ireland.

5478 Shantying on the Lake Shore /(Second state of "Hunting, Fishing, and
Forest Scenes" No. 3002.)
1867 L C&I

5479 Sharp Brush on the Last Quarter,
A / Judge Fullerton-Goldsmith Maid
(Above title) / J. Cameron, Del. (¾
view to right, high-wheeled sulkies,
vignette.)   1884 S C&I

5480 Sharp Brush on the last Quarter,
A / J. Cameron on stone. (Same composition as preceding, no names of
horses given, vignette.)
1889 S C&I

(Note: 2 preceding titles, same
composition as "Best Time on Record,"
etc. No. 507.)

5481 Sharp Pace from Start to Finish,
A / 16.10x26.10 (5 horses under saddle to right, clubhouse in rear.)
1887 L C&I

5482 Sharp Pace from Start to Finish /
J. Cameron on stone. 18x26.10 (5
horses under saddle, no clubhouse in
rear.)   1884 L C&I

(Note: Composition of 2 preceding
prints same as "American Jockey Club
Races," etc. No. 175.)

5483 Sharp Rifle, A / With a Bulge on
the Shooter / Thos. Worth on stone.
(Gun backfiring, colored comic, vignette.)   1882 S C&I

5484 Sharpshooter, A / With a Bulge
on the Rifle / Thos. Worth on stone.
(Darky lying on mattress aiming rifle,
gun resting between toes, vignette.)
1882 S C&I

Sharpsburg, Md. See: No. 429.

Shattagee See: "American Winter
Sports" No. 209.

5485 Shaughraun, Act II, Scene I /
und M C&I

5486 "She Had So Many Children She
Didn't Know What To Do" / (Farm
scene, dog with 8 puppies.)
und S C&I

5487 Sheep Pasture, The / 8.7x12.7.
und S C&I

5488 Sheep Pasture, The / 10.14x14.14.
und M C&I

Sheepshead Bay See: Nos. 1949,
2209, 2622, 2628, 4249.

Shenandoah, Va. See: Nos. 2153,
6357.

Sheridan, Philip See: Nos 2553,
3897-8, 3925-6.

5489 Sheridan's Cavalry at the Battle
of Fisher's Hill /
und S C&I

5490 Sherman and his Generals / Distinguished Commanders, in the Atlanta
and Georgia Campaigns / McPherson—
Slocum — Blair — Thomas — Williams
— Howard — Sherman — Geary —
Schofield — Davis — Hazen — Kilpatrick — Logan.   1865 M C&I

Sherman, Roger See: No. 1530.

Sherman, W. T. See: Nos. 425, 678,

2327, 2653, 3493, 3931-2, 5490, 6544.

Shevanamon Mountains **See:** Ireland.

Shields (Gen.) **See:** No. 2294.

Shiloh **See:** No. 4709.

5491 Shing-Gaa-Ba-W'osin, or the Figured Stone / A Chippewa Chief / Taken at the Treaty of Fond du Lac / On Lake Superior / 1826 / J. O. Lewis, J. Cameron, Lith. (From Lewis' "Aboriginal Portfolio," vignette.)
und S C.C.

5492 Ships Antarctic Of New York, Capt. Stouffer, and Three Bells of Glasgow, Capt. Creighton rescuing the passengers and crew from / the wreck of the Steamship "San Francisco" / Disabled on her voyage from New York to San Francisco, Dec. 24th, 1853 and in a sinking condition / The Bark Kilby of Boston, Capt. Low had previously fallen in with the wreck and taken off a part of the passengers, but during a gale in the night was separated and could not regain it / Painted by J. E. Buttersworth. 17.3x24.12.
1854 L N.C.

(There is another state of this print without the last line — The Bark Kilby, etc.)

5493 Shoeing the Horse / #666 / 11.10x9 J. Schutz on stone. (Upright.)
und S N.C.

5494 Shoemaker, The / #507 / 11.14x8.7.
und S C&I

5495 Shoemaker's Circus, The / (2 views, on same sheet. Farmer: "Give me a roomy shoe" — Dandy: "I like a snug fit." Vignette.)
1882 S C&I

5496 Shooting on the Bay Shore / 9.12x 13.8.
1883 S C&I

5497 Shooting on the Beach / 8.7x12.7.
und S C&I

5498 Shooting on the Prairie / 8.8x12.9.
und S C&I

5499 Short Horned Bull, Grand Duke [10,284] at seven years old, The / Bred

SHOOTING ON THE BAY SHORE.

by the late Thomas Bates, Esq. Kirk-levington, England, etc. / F. M. Rotch, Del. (1 additional line, broadside to left.)   und M N.C.

5500 Short Stop at a Way Station, A / The Polite Conductor / Thos. Worth on stone. (Vignette.)
1875 S C&I

5501 Shrine of Our Lady of Lourdes /
und S C&I

Shunk, Gov. Francis of Penna. **See:** No. 2122.

5502 Shut the Door / (Companion to No. 608.)   1880 S C&I

Siamese Twins **See:** "Chang and Eng" No. 996.

Sibyl (Yacht) **See:** No. 5105.

5503 Sibyl's Temple, The /
und S C&I

5504 Sickness and Health / 10.7x14.13 (Boy with hand-organ, 2 children dancing, mother and invalid girl.)
und M N.C.

5505 Side Wheeler, A / "Bustin" a Trotter / (Vignette, comic.)
1879 S C&I

5506 Side Wheeler "Bustin" a Trotter,

A /   1880 V.S. C&I

5507 Siege and Capture of Vicksburg, Miss., July 4th, 1863 / 4 additional lines. 7.14x12.6.   und S C&I

5508 Siege of Charleston, The / Bombardment of Fort Sumter, and Batteries Wagner and Gregg, by the Union Batteries on Morris Island under command of General Gillmore—August 1863 / 8 x 12.10 (Sometimes this print is erroneously titled "Siege.")
und S C&I

5509 Siege of Constantine, The /
und S C&I

5510 Siege of Limerick from the 9th to 31st of August 1690, The / #569 / 3 additional lines. 8.2x12.11.
1848 S N.C.

5511 Siege of Limerick from the 9th to 31st of August 1690, The / 3 additional lines. (Similar to preceding with slight changes.)   und S C&I

5512 Seige (Sic) of Vera Cruz March 1847 / By the U.S. Army and Navy / #458 / 2 additional lines and 2 columns at side. J. Cameron on stone. (American Flag at right center.)
1847 S N.C.

SIGHTS AT THE FAIR GROUND.

5513 Seige (Sic) of Vera Cruz March 1847 / By the U.S. Army under Com. Perry / J. Cameron on stone. #462 / 8.5 x12.15 (American flag on left.)
1847 S N.C.

Sigel, Franz See: Nos. 674, 2254-5, 3895, 3904.

5514 Sights at the Fair Grounds / (General view showing cattle, etc., 2 oval portraits at top, left and right of Miss Hattie La France, high wire ascensionist, one half-length, the other full-length in costume.)
1888 L C&I

5515 Sights at the Fair Grounds / 18.11x 27.12 (Same as preceding, without portraits.) 1888 L C&I

5516 Sign of the Cross, The /
und S C&I

5517 Signal Fires of the Slievenaman Mountains, Ireland 1848 / #620 / J. Cameron on stone. 8.3x12.5.
1848 S N.C.

5518 Silas Wright, Jr. / 2.13x3 (From Jenkins' "History of Political Parties in the State of New York" 1846.)
und V.S. C.C.

5519 Silver Cascade / 2.8x4.10.
und V.S. C&I

5520 Silver Cascade / Near St. Anthony, Minnesota / (Couple fishing at base of falls.) und S C&I

5521 Silver Cascade / White Mountains / 8 x 12.9. und S C&I

Silver Cascade See: "Gems of American Scenery" No. 2230.

5522 Silver Creek — California / 8.8x 12.8. und S C&I

5523 Simply to Thy Cross I Cling / (Vignette, cross with acorns and oak leaves.) 1872 S C&I

5524 Simply to Thy Cross I Cling / (Vignette, cross with entwined flowers.)
1874 S C&I

5525 Simply to the Cross I Cling / 8.12x 21.2 (Lettered scroll, cross and flowers.). 1874 L C&I

5526 Single / 11.11x8.6 (Young man, fireplace, clock, hour-glass, boxing gloves, etc.)
1846 S N.C.

5527 Single / 12.1x8.9 (Young man at fireplace, long-stemmed pipes, no hour-glass, and other changes in composition.) 1845 S N.C.

5528 Single / #341 (Same general composition as 2 preceding, entered by Sarony & Major.)
1846 S N.C.

5529 Sinking of the British Battle Ship Victoria off Tripoli, Syria, June 22, 1893 / By collision with the Battle Ship Camperdown, etc. / 8.14x12.9.
1893 S C&I

5530 Sinking of the Cumberland by the Iron Clad "Merrimac" off Newport News, Va. March 8th, 1862 / Sketched by F. Newman, Newport News. Va. 7.14x12.8. 1863 S C&I

5531 Sinking of the Steamship Elbe of the North German Lloyd Line / By collision with the Steamship Crathie, in the North Sea off Lowestoft, January 30th, 1895, by which terrible disaster 335 persons were drowned, etc. / 9.2x 14.2. und M C&I

5532 Sinking of the Steamship Oregon of the Cunard Line / 2 additional lines.
1888 S C&I

5533 Sinking of the Steamship Oregon of the Cunard Line / By Collision with unknown schooner off the coast of Long Island, Sunday morning March 14, 1886 and rescued by S.S. Fulda / 8.11x15. 1886 S C&I

5534 Sinking of the Steamship Ville du Havre, The / 4 lines describing disaster. 8.8x12.11. 1873 S C&I

Sir Henry (Horse) See: No. 1666.

Sir Mohawk (Horse) See: No. 1860.

5535 Sir Moses Montefiore / The Great Hebrew Philanthropist and Benefactor of his People / Born in London Oct. 24th, 1784 — Died at Ramsgate, England July 28th, 1885 / aged 100 years 9 months and 4 days / (Facsimile signature above title, half length vignette.) und S C&I

5536 Sir Richard Sutton's Celebrated / Cutter Genesta / Modeled by J. Beaver Webb / 2 columns, 4 lines.
1885 S C&I

5537 Sister Jennie /
und S C&I

5538 Sisters, The / #3 / 12x8.12 (Full length, urn and flowers in background, white dress.) 1845 S N.C.

5539 Sisters, The / #3 (Full length, fountain in background and other changes in composition.)
1847 S N.C.

5540 Sisters, The / (2 figures, ¾ length, standing, curtain background.)
und S N.C.

[239]

5541 Sisters, The / #3 (Oval in rectangle, conventional border.)
1852 S N.C.

THE SISTERS.

5542 Sisters, The / 11.13x8.11 (Full length, sister at right has parasol up, urn at left, tree at right.)
1848 S N.C.

5543 Sister's Prayer, The /
und S C&I

5544 Six Moral Sentences / 13.10x9.13 (6 columns of characters, rebus.)
1875 S C&I

Sixty Ninth See: "Gallant Charge" No. 2213.

5545 Skating Carnival, The / (5 grotesque figures.)
und S C&I

5546 Skating Scene — Moonlight / 8x 12.9.
1868 S C&I

5547 Skin Game, A / "Dot ish French calf hand sewed" / V. Ostenbach on stone. 8.2x12.1
1884 S C&I

5548 Skinner Skinned, A / "Oh, mein gootness! der bottom is knocked out" / V. Ostenbach on stone. 7.13x12.
1884 S C&I

5549 Sleeping Beauty, The /
und S C&I

Sleepy George (Horse) See: No. 5931.

5550 Sleepy Hollow Bridge / Tarrytown, New York / 8.9 x 12.9 (Man fishing, church in background.)
und S C&I

5551 Sleepy Hollow Church / Near Tarrytown, N.Y. / F. F. Palmer, Del. 11.5 x16.4 (Group of 4 at left near path to church.)
1867 M C&I

Sleepy Hollow, N.Y. See. Nos. 4124, 4572.

5552 Sleepy Tom, Pacer Record 2:12¼ / 2.12x4.12.
und V.S. C&I

5553 Sleepy Tom, the Blind Horse, The Pacing Wonder driven by Phillips / Coaxing him to go on and win /
1879 S C&I

Sleepy Tom (Horse) See: Nos. 4686-7, 5552-3, 6163.

5554 Sleigh Race, The / #90 / 8.6x11.14 (2 sleighs, 4 people.)
1848 S N.C.

5555 Sleigh Race, The / (¾ view, 2 sleighs, team and single horse with couples to left, vignette, tinted background, title in white.)
1859 S C&I

5556 Sleigh Race, The / L. Maurer, Del.
1859 L C&I

5557 Sleigh Race, The / 8 8x12.6.
und S C&I

5558 Sleigh Race, The / #90 / (2 sleighs and 4 horses to right, nearest sleigh similar to The Road — Winter.)
und S C&I

Slocum, Genl. See: No. 5490.

5559 Sloop Yacht Mayflower / Modelled by Edward Burgess, Boston, Mass. Winner of the two races for the "America's Cup" 1866 / 2 columns of dimensions. 9.12x14 (To right.)
1866 M C&I

5560 Sloop Yacht Pocahontas of New York / Length of deck 73½ ft. Breadth of beam 21 ft. Depth of hold 7 ft. 10 ins. / Built by David Kirby, Rye, N.Y. / C.R. Parson, Del. 19.5x28.
1881 L C&I

5561 Sloop Yacht "Volunteer" / Modelled by Edward Burgess of Boston for Genl. C. T. Paine / P. on stone.
1887 S C&I

5562 Sloop Yachts Mischief and Atalanta in / The Race for the "America Cup" / At New York, Nov. 9th and 10th, 1881 / 2 columns, 4 & 5 lines. C. R. Parsons, Del. Printed in oil colors. 19.4x28 (Yachts keyed above title.)
1882 L C&I

5563 Slugged Out / "Better luck next time" / Thos. Worth on stone. (Vignette, battered prize fighter.)
1883 S C&I

THE SLEIGH RACE.

5564 Sluice Gate, The / (Printed on same sheet with "Hunter's Shanty" Riverside.)   und V.S. C&I

5565 Small Hopes and Lady Mac / E. Forbes, Del.   1878 L C&I
   Small Hopes See: Nos. 4258-9, 5565.

5566 Small Profits & Quick Sales / The Go Ahead Principle / (Vignette, cartoon.)   1870 S C&I

5567 Smelling Committee, The / Logan — Williams —/ Boutwell — Wilson — Weed — Butler — Thad Stevens — Bingham — Johnson. / J. Cameron on stone. (Vignette, holding noses. Dark horse "Impeachment", Johnson bringing forward "Wooley Friend, labeled 30,000.)   1868 S C&I

   Smith, Gen. A. See: No. 5824.

   Smith, Geo. A. See: No. 1986.

   Smith, Hiram See: No. 1986.

   Smith, Jos. See: No. 1986.

5568 Smoker's Promenade, The / Smoking is the Consolation / Of the Universal Nation / From the Hovel to the Palace / All enjoy tobacco's solace /

Thos. Worth on stone. 2 columns, 2 lines. (Vignette.)   1876 M C&I

5569 Smoking Him Out / (Cass leaving by roof, burning hut fired by Martin Van Buren and egged on by his son "Thats You, Dad, more free soil. We'll rat em out yet." Rats also leaving.) Pub. by P. Smith.   1848 S N.C.

5570 Smoking Run, A / (Postcard size, same composition as "A New Jersey Fox Hunt" No. 4426. Advertising card.)   1880 V.S. C&I

5571 Smuggler, Trotting Stallion owned by H. S. Russell, Milton, Mass. / Winner of the great stallion race for the Championship of the U.S. at Mystic Park, Medford, Mass. Sept. 15th. 1874/   1874 S C&I

5572 Smuggler, Record 2:15½ / Driven by Charles Marvin.
          1876 S C&I

5573 Smuggler /   1882 S C&I

5574 Smuggler and Judge Fullerton / In their grand competition for a special purse, $2000 at Belmont Park, Phila. July 15th, 1876, in which they

trotted a "dead heat" in 2:18 / J. Cameron on stone. 2 additional lines. (Vignette, ¾ to right, judge's stand in background. Republished later as "A Hot Race to the Wire" No. 2953.)
1876 S C&I

Smuggler (Horse) **See:** Nos. 935-6, 983-4, 1193, 5571-4, 6221-2.

5575 Snake in the Grass / 5.8x7.8.
und V.S. C&I

5576 Snap Apple Night/All Hallow Eve/ (After the painting by Daniel Maclise.)
und M C&I

5577 Snipe Shooting / From Nature and on stone by F. F. Palmer. 12.9x20.5.
1852 L N.C.

5578 Snipe Shooting / 8.8x12.8 (Hunter and dog, autumn foliage.)
und S C&I

Snow, Col. E. L. **See:** No. 1186.

Snow, Erastus **See:** No. 1986.

Snow, Lorenzo **See:** No. 1986.

5579 Snow-Shoe Dance, The / To Thank the Great Spirit for the First Appearance of Snow / Catlin, Del. 12.2x18.1.
und M C&I

5580 Snow Storm, The / 11x15.7 (Team of oxen hauling load of wood, 2 children snowballing in front of cottage.)
und M C&I

5581 Snowed up / Ruffed Grouse in Winter / 15x20.6.   1867 L C&I

Snowstorm (Horse) **See:** No. 1353.

5582 Snowy Morning, A / F. F. Palmer, Del. 11.9x16.6 (Man with pitchfork of hay on way to cattle on left, cottage on right.)   1864 M C&I

5583 Sociable Smoke, A / (2 men, dog on table smoking cigar.)
1880 S C&I

5584 Sociable Smoke, A / 4.7x7.3 (Advertising card.)
1880 V.S. C&I

5585 Social Cup, A / Give me another cup of that delightful tea / It keeps my spirits up and puts new strength in me / (3 old maids drinking tea, vignette.)   1883 M C&I

5586 Sofia /   1846 S N.C.

5587 Soft Thing on Snipe, A! / (Hunter and dog eaten by mosquitos, snipe amused, vignette.)
1880 S C&I

5588 Soldier Boy, The / "Off Duty" / #721 / 11.13x8.3 (Full length, camp

scene in background, slightly rounded corners.)   1864 S C&I

5589 Soldier Boy, The / "On Duty" / 11.12x8.5 (Full length, cannon in background, top corners slightly round.)
1864 S C&I

5590 Soldier Boys, The / The Last Defence / #842 / 11.14x8.11.
und S C&I

5591 Soldier's Adieu, The /
und S C.C.

5592 Soldier's Adieu, The / #14 (Interior scene.)   und S N.C.

5593 Soldier's Adieu, The / #14 / 11.11 x8.5 (Horse seen through window, different preceding.)
1847 S N.C.

5594 Soldier's Bride, The / #488 / 11.6 x8.13 (Portrait of young woman, white dress, belt with buckle.)
und S C&I

5595 Soldier's Dream of Home, The / #200 / 7.13x12.5 (Oval in rectangular border, 2 columns, 4 lines verse, companion to 5599.)   und S C&I

5596 Soldier's Dream of Honor /
und S C&I

5597 Soldier's Grave, The / 11.5x8.8.
1862 S C&I

5598 Soldier's Grave, The / #204 / 12.2 x8.11 (Woman at tomb, weeping willow, "In Memory of" on tomb, soldiers marching in rear.)
1865 S C&I

5599 Soldier's Home, The / The Vision / #201 / 12.5x7.13 (Oval in rectangle, woman asleep, vision of husband leading troops, companion to No. 5595.)
1862 S C&I

5600 Soldier's Memorial, The / In Memory of / 14.15x11.9 (Tombstone right, woman at left, marching soldiers in rear, top corners round.)
1863 M C&I

5601 Soldier's Memorial, The / 126th Regiment Company H — New York Volunteers / 18.7x14.1 (3 columns personnel and views of Capitol, Washington, bombing of Fort Sumter.)
1862 M C&I

5602 Soldier's Memorial, The / Third Regiment, Company B, Delaware Volunteers / (Portraits of Washington, Lincoln, McClellan, and Scott.)
1862 M C&I

5603 Soldier's Record, The / 5th Regi-

ment—Company E—New York Volunteer Artillery / 18.4x14.5.
1862 M C&I

5604 Soldier's Record, The / 150th Regiment—Company G—New York State Vols. / 18.14x14.5 (Capitol, Washington, and Bombardment of Fort Sumter)
1862 M C&I

5605 Soldier's Record, The / 18th Regiment—Company C—Conn. Volunteers / 18.4x14.5.
1862 M C&I

5606 Soldier's Return /
und S C.C.

5607 Soldier's Return, The / W. K. Hewitt Privent et Del. 12.4x9.
1840 S N.C.

5608 Soldier's Return, The / 12.3x8.10.
1845 S N.C.

5609 Soldier's Return, The /
1846 S N.C.

5610 Soldier's Return / #13 / 11.11x8.7 (Officer, plumed hat, green curtain.)
1847 S N.C.

5611 Soldier's Return, The /
1849 S N.C.

5612 Solomon's Temple /
und S N.C.

5613 Some Pumpkins / Trotting his mile in 2:10. Beating the locomotive "Lightning" by nearly 5 lengths, on a descending grade; and carrying 25 lbs. over weight / #236 (Same general composition reversed as "Blood will Tell" No. 571, vignette.)
1850 M N.C.

Somers, Brig. See: No. 6298.

5614 Son and Daughter of Temperance / E. L. Snow, Social Union / #711 / 11.10x8.7.
1850 S N.C.

5615 Son of Temperance / E. L. Snow, Social Union / #573 (Full length in regalia.)
1848 S N.C.

5616 Son of Temperance / No brother shall make, buy, sell liquor, etc. / 11.15x8.4(Full length, resting on scroll, left hand holding hat.)
1848 S N.C.

5617 Songs of Madame Anna Bishop / Published by Firth, Pond and Co. on stone by F. Davidson.
1847 S C.C.

5618 Sons of Temperance / Love, Purity, and Fidelity / #574 / 11.11 x 8.9.
und S N.C.

5619 Sons of Temperance /
und S C&I

5620 Sontag and Flora Temple / At the Half Mile Pole in 1:13 / In their Great Match for $2,000 over the Union Course, L. I., May 7th, 1855 / 4 additional lines. L. Maurer on stone. 17 x26.7 (Broadside to right, skeleton wagons, at ½ mile marker, grandstand in rear.)
1855 L N.C.

5621 Sophia / #137 / 11.11x8.7 (In arbor, black lace jacket, full length, holding bouquet.)
1846 S N.C.

5622 Sophia / #137 / 12x8.10 (¾ length, arm resting on table, vase of flowers, green curtain.)
und S N.C.

5623 Sophia / (Full length, holding bouquet.)
und M C&I

5624 Sorrel Dan, Pacer, Record 2:14 / (Postcard size.)
1881 V.S. C&I

Sorrel Dan See: Nos. 2638, 5624.

5625 Sorry Dog, A / "I shoot dot tog Bismark, he makes me much trouble" / (Vignette, ferryman hauling dog, cart, and child from water—missed ferry, companion to "The Jolly Jumper" No. 3289.)
1881 S C&I

5626 Sorry Her Lot Who Loves Too Well / (Scene from "Pinafore"—vignette.)
1879 S C&I

Soule, Pierce See: No. 4632.

5627 Source of the Hudson, The / In the

Indian Pass, Adirondacks / 8.8.x12.8.
und S C&I

South Carolina **See:** Nos. 596-7, 678, 802, 2089, 2210, 2611, 3118, 3995, 5508, 6373.

5628 South Carolina's "Ultimatum" / (Governor Pickens standing in front of mouth of cannon marked "Peace Maker," reaching forward to light powder with lighted torch, and saying he will fire it if Lincoln doesn't surrender Fort Sumter. Buchanan has hands above head, begging Pickens not to fire until he gets out of office. Fort Sumter in background—vignette.)
und M C&I

South Hadley, Mt. Holyoke Female Seminary **See:** No. 4240.

5629 South Sea Whale Fishery / #10. / 8.12x12.12 A boat destroyed by a wounded whale / The head of a large whale in the agonies of death / (Title in plate.)
und S N.C.

5630 Southern Beauty, The / (Vignette.)
und S C&I

5631 Southern Belle, The /
und S C&I

5632 Southern Cross, The / 11.13x8.15 (Full length of girl before Floral Cross, 2 columns, 4 lines of verse.)
1873 S C&I

5633 Southern River Scenery / 7.14x12.8.
1870 S C&I

5634 Southern Rose, The / (Girl's head.)
und S C&I

5635 Southern "Volunteers" / (Political cartoon.)
und S C&I

Sovereign of the Seas (Clipper Ship) **See:** No. 1167.

Spain (Steamship) **See:** No. 3887, 5794.

Spalding, Most Rev. M. J. **See:** No. 4227.

5636 Spaniel, The / #638 / 9x12.15 (Title in plate, profile to right.)
1848 S N.C.

5637 Spaniel, The / 8.14x12.13 (Spaniel by stream.)
1842 S N.C.

5638 Spanish Dance, The / [El Jaleo de Cadix] / #418.
und S N.C.

5639 Spanish Dance / [El Jaleo de Cadix] / 11.10x8.8
und S C&I

Spartan (Horse) **See:** No. 5037.

5640 Speak My Darling! / 11.10x9.4 (Woman and canary.)
und S C&I

SPEEDING ON THE AVENUE.

5641 Speak Quick / (Oval, ½ length of girl.)
und S C&I

5642 Speaking Likeness, A / und S C&I

5643 Speeding on the Darktown Track / "Go it fancy nebber mind de wherl, dere aint no rumatic tire to us" / Thos. Worth on stone. (Companion to "A Darktown Trotter" No. 1436.)
1892 S C&I

5644 Speeding on the Avenue / J. Cameron, Del. 18.5x28.15 (Harlem River, N. Y.)
1870 L C&I

5645 Speeding to the "Bike" / 18x28.1 (Same composition as "Renowned Trotter Prince Wilkes" No. 5113 except sulkies have small rubber tires and stone is not signed.)
1893 L C&I

5646 Spendthrift / (Postcard size.)
1881 V.S. C&I

5647 Spendthrift / By Imp. Australian, dam Aerolite, by Lexington / (Vignette, under saddle.)
1880 S C&I

5648 Sperm Whale "In a Flurry, The / #382 / 8.7x12.14 (Title in plate.)
1852 S N.C.

5649 "Spice" of the Trotting Track, The / Thos. Worth, N. Y., on stone. (Full length figure of Dan Mace with toy horse (Judge Fullerton) and sulky, 4 lines verse, vignette.)
1876 M C&I

5650 Spillout on the Snow, The /
1870 S C&I

5651 "Spill out" on the Snow, The / 16.6 x24.14 (9 horse-drawn sleighs, 2 colliding.)
1870 L C&I

5652 Spin on the Road, A / 2.12x4.12.
1880 V.S. C&I

5653 Spirit of '61, The / (Vignette, female figure, flag, eagle, etc. verses.)
1861 L C&I

5654 Spirit of '76, Stand By the Flag, The / The Young Continental /
und S C&I

5655 Spirit of the Union, The / #207 / Copyright 1860 by T. Duchoux. 2 columns, 4 lines each. 11.7x8.10 (Capitol, Mount Vernon, and Tomb at bottom. Vision of Washington in military uniform at top. Corners slightly round.)
1860 S C&I

5656 Spirit of the Union, The / 2 columns, 4 lines. 11.5x8.7 (Mount Vernon, and tomb of Washington at bottom.

Vision of Washington above. Changes in composition from preceding and no view of Capitol.)
1876 S C&I

5657 Spirit's Flight, The / 24x17.13 (White girl and colored girl flying through air, guided by angels, 6 lines of verse.)
1893 L C&I

5658 Spirit's Flight, The / (Same general composition as preceding.)
1874 S C&I

Splan, John See: No. 5708.

5659 Splendid Naval Triumph on the Mississippi, April 24th, 1862, The / Destruction of the Rebel Gunboats, Rams, and Iron Clad Batteries by the Union Fleet under Flag Officer Farragut / 3 additional lines, 15 keys.
1862 L C&I

5660 Splendid New Iron Steamer / Albany / of the Hudson River Day Line, The / (Broadside view.)
und S C&I

5661 Splendid Tea / (Vignette, old maid drinking tea, ½ length.)
1881 S C&I

5662 Splendid Steamship America of the National Line, The / "The Flying Eagle of the Atlantic" / 5 additional lines and 2 columns, 6 lines description.
und S C&I

5663 Split Rock, St. John River, N. B. / (2 on rock in foreground.)
und S C&I

5664 Splitting the Party / The Entering Wedge / J. Cameron on stone. (Greeley standing in cleft rock marked "Republican Party" and holding in hands papers marked "Free Trade" and "Protection." Schurz on right with upraised mallet marked "Cincinnati Nomination." Grant on left watching. Crouching on left are Hall, Sweeny, Tweed, Hoffman. On right, also crouching: Dana, Trumbull, Sumner, Gratz Brown—vignette.)
1872 S C&I

5665 Spoiling A Sensation / The Bicycle Boy on a Bull / Thos. Worth on stone. (Vignette, companion to "Creating a Sensation" No. 1301.)
1881 S C&I

5666 "Sponging" / Thos. Worth on stone. (Ragged hostler attending to horse of well-dressed driver, barroom in background, vignette.)
1880 S C&I

5667 Sports Who Came to grief, The /
Thos. Worth on stone. (Vignette.)
1881 S C&I

5668 "Sports" who lost their "Tin", The
/ Thos. Worth on stone. (Jockey, owner, handlers with horse and rig de-
jectedly returning from a race, companion to "The Crowd that Scooped
the Pools" No. 1312.)
1878 S C&I

5669 "Sports" Who Lost Their Tin, The
/ (Postcard size.)
1878 V.S. C&I

5670 Sportsman's Solace, The / (Still
life, tobacco, pipe, fishing flies, whisky,
wine, etc., vignette.)
1879 M C&I
Spottsylvania, Va. See: Nos. 430,
2388, 3937.
Sprague, Brig. Genl. W. See: No.
685.
Spray (Yacht) See: No. 5105.
Spree (Steamship) See: No. 5795.

5671 Spring / #687 / 8.5x12.9 (Group
of 7 beneath trees, companion to "Harvest" No. 2741.)
1849 S N.C.

5672 Spring / #453 / 7.14x12.8 (Horses,
colts, at outdoor drinking fountain,
from an English print, companion to
Nos. 311, 5849, 6729.
und S N.C.

5673 Spring / (Vignette, blond girl with
flowers in her hair and hand, companion to Nos. 312, 5851, 6732.)
1870 S C&I

5674 Spring / #453 (½ length portrait
of brunette, vignette, holding roses,
radically different from preceding,
companion to Nos. 313, 5849A, 6730.)
und S C&I

5675 Spring /
1870 M C&I

5676 Spring / 8x12.10 (6 children gathering flowers beside road.)
und S C&I

5677 Spring Flowers / (Tinted back-
ground, companion to "Summer Fruits"
No. 5857.)
1861 M C&I
Springbok, (Horse) See: No. 175.
Springfield, Ill. See: No. 6105.

5678 Spunk versus Science /
1879 V.S. C&I

5679 Squall off Cape Horn, A / 10.10
x15.6.
und M N.C.

5680 Squall off Cape Horn, A / 8.15
x12.7 (Broadside to right, sailing ves-

sel in a snow squall.)
und S C&I
Squam Lake, N. H. See: No. 3093.

5681 Squirrel Shooting / 8.8x12.8.
und S C&I

5682 Squirrel Shooting /
und V.S. C&I

5683 Stable No. 1, The / J. F. Herring,
Senr. Pinxt. O. Knirsch on stone. 15.5
x15.8 (Coach horse, shetland pony,
chickens, and cat, top corners round.)
und M N.C.

5684 Stable No. 2, The / J. F. Herring,
Senr. Pinxt. F. Venino on stone. 15.4
x15.6 (Dray horse harnessed in stable,
ducks, top corners round, upright.)
und M N.C.

5685 Stable Scenes, No. 1 / #241 / 8.8
x12.10.
und S N.C.

5686 Stable Scenes, No. 2 / J. Schutz on
stone. 8.8x12.10.
und S N.C.

5687 Stag at Bay, The / 7.14x12.6 (Stag
and 2 dogs, after the painting by
Landseer.)
und S C&I

5688 Stag at Bay, The / 14.8x20.10
(Same as preceding.)
und L C&I

5689 Stag Hounds / #445 (Group of 5
dogs, copied from the English print by
Ackerman.)
1856 S N.C.

5690 Stag Hunt, at Killarney, A / 10.6
x15.2 (Hunter and dogs following stag
through stream.)
und M C&I
Stamboul (Horse) See: No. 6223.

5691 Stanch Pointer, A / 8.12x12.6
(Light-colored dog to left. Have seen
copies of this print dated 1870.)
1871 S C&I

5692 Stanch Pointer, A / (Black and
white dog, left foreleg raised, different locale, to left.)
und S C&I
Stanton See: Nos. 5050, 5258.

5693 Star of Beauty, The / (Vignette,
girl's head.)
und S C&I

5694 Star of Love, The /
und S C&I

5695 Star of Love, The / #481 / 11.11
x8.10 (¾ length, red dress, lace shawl,
exterior scene.)
1847 S N.C.

5696 Star of the East, The / F. D. on
stone. (Reclining, full length, Harem
scene, not upright.)
1846 S N.C.

5697 Star of the Night, The / (Oriental girl, vignette.)   und S C&J

5698 Star of the North / #532 / 11.13 x8.1 (Woman on bed playing with dog.)   1847 S N.C.

5699 Star of the North, The / #532 (Vignette, woman playing with cat.)   und S C&I

5700 Star of the Opera, The / (Vignette, upright, ¾ length portrait.)   und S C&I

5701 Star of the Road, The / #686 / 8.5 x12.11 (Woman driving spirited team of white horses, country road.)
1849 S N.C.

5702 Star of the South / #533 / 8x11.12 (Turkish woman reclining on couch, smoking, not upright.)
1847 S N.C.

5703 Star of the South, The / #533 (Vignette, woman teasing parrot.)
und S C&I

5704 Star of the West, The / #422 / 8.9x12.12 (Full length, reclining figure, round corners.)   1846 S N.C.

5705 Star Pointer / Record 1:59¼ / J. C. (Cameron) on stone. (Vignette, ¾ view to right, small rubber-tired, low-wheel sulky.)   und S C&I

5706 Star Spangled Banner, The / #486 / 3 lines of verse. 11.11x8.10. (Allegorical female figure with flag.)
und S C&I

5707 Star Spangled Banner, The / #486 / 11.13x8.13 (Female figure with American Flag, burning ships, 3 lines of verse.)   und S C&I

5708 Stars of the Trotting Track / Famous American Trotters and Drivers / J. C. on stone. 21.14x28.8 (9 groups of horses: (1) Goldsmith Maid 2:14 (2) Dexter 2:17¼—Lady Suffolk 2:26 |saddle|—Lady Thorne 2:18¾ (3) Flora Temple 2:19¾ (4) St. Julien 2:11½ (5) Jay Eye See 2:10 [driven by E. D. Bither]—Maud S 2:08¾ |driven by W. W. Bair] (6) Phallas 2:13¾ (7) Rarus 2:13¼—Maxy Cobb 2:13¼ (8) Minnie R. 2:19—Fannie Witherspoon 2:16¼ [driven by W. H. McCarthy]—Harry Wilkes 2:15 [driven by Frank Van Ness]—Little Brown Jug-Pacer 2:11 — Johnston-Pacer 2:06¼ [driven by P. V. Johnston] (9) Ethan Allen 2:15 [with Running Mate] American Girl 2:16¼. 8 portraits: John E. Turner, John Splan, Hiram Woodruff, John Murphy, Dan Mace, Orrin Hickok, James Golden, Budd Doble. (Also used as an "Ad" by "The United States Mutual Accident Association.")   1886 L C&I

5709 Stars of the Turf—No. 1 /
1885 L C&I

5710 Stars of the Turf—No. 2 /
1885 L C&I

5711 Starting out on his Mettle / Thos. Worth on stone. (Vignette, fine rig and driver leaving stable.)
1878 S C&I

5712 Startling Announcement, A / (Negro boy awakening Jefferson Davis with the announcement that "Fort Donelson has been taken by the cinkum Bobolishunists." Davis refuses to believe it. Vignette.)
und S C&I

5713 Starucca Vale / N. Y. & Erie R. R. / 10.7x15.4.   und M C&I
State of California (Steamer) See: No. 4672.

5714 State Street, Boston / Massachusetts / #690 / 8.4x12.6.
1849 S N.C.

5715 Staten Island and the Narrows from Fort Hamilton / Fort Richmond -Fort Diamond-Fort Hamilton. F. F. Palmer, Del. 14.13x20.5 (This also appears with "Fort Diamond" altered to "Fort Lafayette.")
1861 L C&I
Staten Island See: Nos. 4380-2, 5715, 6407.

5716 Statue Unveiled, The / or the Colossus of Roads / (Commodore Vanderbilt in foreground "watering" the Hudson River R. R. and Jim Fisk "watering" the Erie R. R. Vignette.)
1859 S C&I

5717 Staunch Pointer, A /
1871 S C&I

5718 Staunch Pointer, A /
1870 S C&I

5719 Steadfast in the Faith /
und S C&I

5720 Steam Catamaran—H. W. Longfellow / 8.5x13.13 (Hudson River scene, broadside to right.)
und S C&I

5721 Steam Yacht Anthracite, owned by Mr. Richard Power of London, England / Built by Schlesinger, Davis & Co., Wallsend, England / 1 additional line of dimensions.
und S C&I

5722 Steam Yacht Corsair (Exact title is) To Charles J. Osborn, Esq. / This Print of his New and Elegant Steam Yacht "Corsair" is Respectfully Dedicated by / The Publisher / Built by William Cramp & Sons, Pa /
1881 L C&I

5723 Steam Yacht Namouna / The Property of James Gordon Bennett, Esq. / 2 columns, 3 and 5 lines. 17.2x27.
1882 L C&I

5724 Steam Yacht Polynia (Exact Title is) To James Gordon Bennett, Esq. / This Print of his New and Unrivalled Steam Yacht Polynia is with permission Respectfully dedicated by the Publisher / Built by Ward Stanton & Co., Newburgh, N. Y. / 17.2x26 (Broadside to left.)
1880 L C&I
Steamboat (Horse) See: No. 6224.

5725 Steamboat "Empire" / Built for Troy & New York Steamboat Co. S. R. Roe, Capt. / N. Sarony, Del. (3 additional lines and 2 columns, 4 and 5 lines, name on boat "Empire of Troy.")
1843 S N.C.

5726 Steamboat Isaac Newton / The Largest in the New or Old World / Capt W. H. Peck / #261 / 8.3x12.12 (2 columns, 4 lines. Broadside to right, Hudson River boat.)
1848 S N.C.

5727 Steam-Boat Knickerbocker / 8.4x13 (1 additional line, view of Albany in rear.)   und S N.C. $175.

5728 Steamboat Peerless / Lake Superior Line /   und L C&I

5729 Steamboat Priscilla /
und S C&I

5730 Steamboat Race on the Mississippi / Act IV, Scene III. Jarrett & Palmer's Revival of Uncle Tom's Cabin (Same as "Midnight Race on the Mississippi" No. 4117 names on boats changed to "Natchez" and "Eclipse." Also appears with "S. L. Thorp & Co., Cleveland, O., Publisher.")
1875 S C&I

5731 Steamboats Passing at Midnight on Long Island Sound / 8.8x12.8 (Steamers Bristol and Providence.)
und S C&I

5732 Steamer "Drew" / 8.14x14.2.
1883 S C&I

5733 Steamer "Drew" / 1 additional line dimensions. (Moonlight scene.)
und S C&I

5734 Steamer "Massachusetts" /
1882 S C&I

5735 Steamer Messenger No. 2 / Capt. J. C. Woodward / #684 / 8.4x13.1 (2 columns, 2 lines.)
und S N.C.

5736 Steamer Penobscot / One of the fleet forming the line between Boston, Bangor, and Mt. Desert / C. R. Parsons on stone. Printed in oil colors by Currier & Ives. 2 additional lines. 20x34.13.   1883 L C&I

5737 Steamer Pilgrim / One of the fleet forming the Fall River Line, the great Long Island Sound Route between New York and Boston via Newport & Fall River / 2 additional lines, and 4 columns, 3 lines.   1883 L C&I

5738 Steamer Pilgrim—Flagship of the Fall River Line /
1882 S C&I

5739 Steamer Tempest /
1882 S C&I

5740 Steamship Adriatic, 5,888 Tons, 1,350 Horse Power / George Steers Naval Constructor & Builder, Engines Built at Novelty Works, New York / To her commander Capt. Joseph I. Comstock this print is respectfully dedicated by the Publisher / C. Parsons, Del. 17x27.5 (2 columns, 3 lines, broadside to right.)
1860 L C&I

5741 Steamship Adriatic, White Star Line /   und S C&I

5742 Steamship Alaska of the Guion Line / "The Greyhound of the Atlantic" / (2 columns, 3 lines.)
und S C&I

5743 Steamship Aller /
und S C&I

5744 Steamship America /
und S C&I

5745 Steamship Anthracite /
und S C&I

5746 Steamship Assyrian Monarch of the Monarch Line /   und S C&I

5747 Steamship Augusta Victoria, Hamburg American Packet Co. /
1873 S C&I

5748 Steamship Belgenland of the Red Star Line /   und S C&I

5749 Steamship "Borussia" Regular Packet between Hamburg and New York /   und S C&I

5750 Steamship Bothnia of the Cunard Line, The /   und S C&I

5751 Steam Ship California of the Anchor Line / 1 additional line.
und S C&I

5752 Steamship Cephalonia /
und S C&I

5753 Steam Ship "City of Baltimore" 2367 Tons / Screw Propellor between New York & Liverpool / #353 (Vignette, broadside to left.)
und S C&I

5754 Steamship "City of Berlin" of the Inman Line /   und S C&I

5755 Steamship "City of Montreal" of the Inman Line /   und S C&I

5756 Steam Ship City of Washington / 1 additional line of dimensions. (Broadside to left.)   und S C&I

5757 Steamship Denmark /
und S C&I

5758 Steam Ship Egypt of the National Line / 1 additional line. (Vignette, to left.)   und S C&I

5759 Steamship "Egyptian Monarch" Wilson Line / Between New York and Hull /   und S C&I

5760 Steamship Eider /
und S C&I

5761 Steamship Etruria /
und S C&I

5762 Steamship Florida, Baltimore and Norfolk Line /   und S C&I

5763 Steamship "Franklin" / Sir O. W. Brierly, Del.   und S C&I

5764 Steamship Friesland /
und S C&I

5765 Steam Ship Frisia /
und S C&I

5766 Steamship Gaandam /
und S C&I

5767 Steamship "Galileo" Wilson Line / Between New York and Hull /
und S C&I

5768 Steamship Great Northern /
und S C&I

5769 Steamship Hammonia [Screw Propellor] / Regular Packet Between Hamburg and New York / (Vignette.)
und S C&I

5770 Steamship Hermann / Builders: Hull by Westervelt & Mackay; Engines by Stillman, Allen & Co. / #89 / 2 columns, 4 lines. 8.4x12.10.
und S N.C.

5771 Steam-Ship "Hermann" / Length 350 feet. Burthen 2774 Tons. Horse Power 700. 7.14x12.13.
und S C&I

5772 Steamship in a Gale, A /
und S C&I

5773 Steamship Lahn /
und S C&I

5774 Steamship Majestic, White Star Line /   und S C&I

5775 Steamship "Minnesota" of the Liverpool & Great Western Steam Co. / 1 additional line.   und S C&I

5776 Steamship Mississippi /
und S N.C.

5777 Steamship Noordland /
und S C&I

5778 Steam-Ship Oceanic / White Star Line / Length 438 feet. Tonnage 6000. Horse power 3000 / 8x12.6.
und S C&I

5779 S. S. Oregon of the Cunard Line, The / Between New York and Liverpool via Queenstown / 2 columns, 3 lines. 19.8x33.
1884 L C&I

5780 Steamship Oregon of the Cunard Line, The / "The Champion of the Atlantic" / 2 columns, 2 and 3 lines.
und S C&I

5781 Steamship Pavonia /
und S C&I

5782 Steam-Ship "Periere" / Length 371 feet. Burthen 3014 Tons. Horse Power 1250 /   und S C&I

5783 Steamship "Persian Monarch" /
und S C&I

5784 Steam Ship President |The Largest in the World| Lieut. Roberts R. N. Commander on her last voyage from New York to Liverpool / As last seen from the Packet Ship Orpheus, Capt. Cole in the terrific gale of March the 12th, 1841, at 5 o'clock P. M. Lat. 39.46-Long. 71, bearing N. E. by N. by compass steering E. / 4 additional lines. 2 columns, 3 lines. 8.7x13 (Black border.)   und S N.C.

5785 Steamship President, The / Lieut. Roberts R. N. Commander / The Largest in the World / Supposed to have struck an iceberg on her voyage from New York to Liverpool in March 1841, and sunk with all on board—by which heart-rending occurrence / 109 persons perished / 8.15x13.
und S N.C.

5786 Steamship President, The / The Largest in the World / J. M. McGee, Del. 2 columns, 1 line each (To right.) und S N.C.

5787 Steamship "Puritan" Fall River Line / und S C&I

5788 Steamship "Rhode Island" / 9x14. und S C&I

5789 Steamship Rotterdam / und S C&I

5790 Steamship "Saale" / und S C&I

5791 Steamship "St. Paul" / und S C&I

5792 Steamship Scythia, Cunard Line / und S C&I

5793 Steamship Servia / und S C&I

5794 Steamship "Spain" of the National Line / Running between New York, Queenstown and Liverpool. und S C&I

5795 Steamship Spree / und S C&I

5796 Steamship "Teutonic" of the White Star Line /. und S C&I

5797 Steamship Traave / und S C&I

5798 Steamship "Vanderbilt" 5,268 Tons, 2,500 Horse Power / J. Simonson, Naval Constructor and Builder. Engines built at the Allaire Works, New York / C. Parsons, Del. 16.14x26.12 (2 columns.) 1857 L C&I

5799 Steam Ship "Ville de Paris" / Capt. Surmont / 1 additional line of dimensions. und S C&I

5800 Steam Ship Washington / Belonging to the Ocean Navigation Company, Frederick Hewitt, Commander / #478 / 1 additional line, 2 columns, 3 lines. 8x12.13. (Broadside to right, New York City in background.) 1847 S N.C.

5801 Steamship Washington, The / The First American Ocean Mail Steamer / 8.10x13.2. und S N.C.

5802 Steamship "Washington," Capt. Fitch, The / Rescuing the passengers of the ship Winchester of Boston Tuesday, May 2nd, 1854 / From a sketch by Mr. Vincent, passenger on board the Washington / #363 / 8.3x12.15. 1854 S N.C.

5803 Steamship "Westernland" / und S C&I

5804 Steamship William Penn / und S C&I

5805 Steamship "Zeendam" / und S C&I

5806 Steam Yacht "Corsair" (Exact title is)—To Charles I. Osborn, Esq. / This print of his new and elegant steam yacht "Corsair" is respectfully dedicated by / The Publisher / 1 additional line of dimensions 17.6x26.12. (To left.) 1881 L C&I
    Stedding See: No. 6705.

5807 Steel Cruiser Philadelphia / 1893 S C&I

5808 Steeple Chase Cracks / 7.15 x 12.7 (6 monkeys as jockeys, riding dogs.) und S C&I

5809 Steeple-Chaser, A / Thos. Worth on stone. (Vignette, horse balking at jump, throwing rider.) 1880 S C&I

5810 Stella / (½ length vignette.) 1872 S C&I

5811 Stella and Alice Grey—Lantern and Whalebone / "Passing the Stand" / In Their Great Match for $2,000 in Double Harness over the Union Course, L. I., June 5th, 1855 / 4 additional lines. L. Maurer on stone. 17.2x27.13 (2 teams, skeleton wagons, ¾ view to right, judge's stand in rear.) 1855 L N.C.
    Stella (Horse) See: Nos. 3399, 5811.

5812 Stephen finding "His Mother"/(Columbia whipping Douglas with switch labelled "Maine Law" while Uncle Sam stands alongside, vignette.) 1860 M C&I

5813 Stephen Finding "His Mother" / (Columbia whipping Douglas with switch labelled "News From Maine." Uncle Sam stands alongside.) 1860 M C&I

5814 Stepping Stones, The / 11.6x15.11 (Woman and baby, cows in foreground, stream, and dog.) und M C&I
    Steve Maxwell (Horse) See: No. 6178.
    Stevens, T. See: Nos. 5050, 5567.
    Stewart, Charles See: No. 4398.
    Stiletto (Steam Yacht) See: No. 2814.

5815 Still Hunting on the Susquehanna/ (1st State. 2nd State—"Hunting on the Susquehanna" No. 3005.) und M C&I

5816 Stock Farm, The / 9x12.5 (Barnyard scene, horses, chickens, etc.)
und S C&I

5817 Stocks Down / #661 / 8.9x12.10.
1849 S N.C.

5818 Stocks Up / #662 / 8.9x12.11.
1849 S N.C.

5819 Stolen Interview, The / 8.10x11.9.
1872 S C&I

5820 Stolen Interview, The / 11.6x8.9
(Full-length figure of man below, and
woman on balcony.)
1872 S C&I

Stone St., N. Y. (Fire of 1845) See:
No. 6416.

Stoneman, Gen. See: No. 2295.

Stonington (Steamboat) See: No.
5993.

5821 "Stopping Place" on the Road, A /
The Horse Shed / Sketched by Thos.
Worth and on stone. 19.6x29.6
1868 L C&I

5822 Storming of Fort Donelson, The /
Terrific bayonet charge and capture of
the outer intrenchments by the Gallant
Soldiers of the West, Saturday, Feby.
15th, 1862 / 12.8x8.7.
1862 S C&I

5823 Storming of Fort Donelson, Tenn.,
Feb. 15th, 1862 / 4 additional lines.
1862 S C&I

5824 Storming of Fort Donelson, Tenn.,
Feby. 15th, 1862, The / 3 additional
lines of description. 16x22.8 (Gens.
Grant, Smith, McClernand.)
1862 L C&I

5825 Storming of the Bishop's Palace /
At the siege of Monterey, Sept. 22nd,
1846 / #472 / 12.12x8.5. J. Cameron
1847 on stone.   1847 S N.C.

5826 Storming of the Fortress of Chapultepec / At the city of Mexico,
Septr. 12th, 1847 / #548 / Cameron
1847 on stone. 8.10x12.14 (American
forces at left, fort at right.)
1847 S N.C.

5827 Storming the Castle / #312 (Children playing war.)
und S N.C.

5828 Storming the Castle / "Old Abe"
on guard / (Lincoln, Bell, Douglas.
Buchanan trying to help Breckinridge
climb in the window of the White
House. Douglas trying to unlock door
with keys marked "Regular Nom.,
Non-intervention, Nebraska Bill." Lincoln with lantern and rail.)
1860 M C&I

5829 Storming the Heights of Cerro
Gordo / April 18th, 1847 / #470 / 2
additional lines description. 8.4x12.10.
1847 S N.C.

5830 Storming of the Heights of Cerro
Gordo / April 18th, 1847 / #470 (2
additional lines and changes in composition, better drawing.)
1847 S N.C.

5831 Storming the Heights at Monterey
/ By the American Army Sept. 21st,
1846 / #424 / 12.5x8.11 (Officer in center with American flag, leading troops,
upright.)   1846 S N.C.

5832 Story of the Fight, The / 17.3x13.9
(2 columns, 6 lines of verse, vignette.)
1863 M C&I

5833 Story of the Fight, The / (2 columns, 6 lines of verse.)
1863 S C&I

5834 Story of the Great King, The /
und S C&I

5835 Story of the Revolution, The /
12.5x8.14 (Interior, old man with child
on knee, telling the story, upright.)
1876 S C&I

5836 Stratford on Avon / 8.3 x 12.11.
und S C&I

Stratton, Charles S. See: Tom
Thumb.

5837 Straw-Yard, Winter, The / 11.2x15.7
(2 horses center, pigs, pigeons, etc.)
und M C&I

5838 Strawberries / #517 / 8.3x12.12
(Berries in 2 baskets, dish with morning glories.)   1863 S C&I

5839 Strawberries / (Plate of strawberries, rose, pansies, tulip, blue lilies.)
1870 S C&I

5840 Strawberry Feast, A / (Chickens
eating strawberries.)
und S C&I

5841 Strawberry Season, The / 7.15x12.8
(Plate with berries.)
1870 S C&I

5842 Strictly Confidential / #109 / 11.12x
8.8.   und S C&I

5843 Stride of a Century, The / 11.15x
15.15 (Uncle Sam stretching over Main
building Pacific to Atlantic. 2 balloons,
railroad train, boats, etc., in background. Centennial Exhibition.)
1876 M C&I

5844 Striped Bass / 8.7x12.6 (Still life,
fish on bank, sea in back.)
1872 S C&I

Struve, Gustave See: No. 2683.

5845 Style Ob de Road, De / Thos. Worth on stone. (Colored couple in coach on way to the Casino, drawn by horse and mule, vignette, comic.)
1884 S C&I

5846 Suburban Gothic Villa, Murray Hill, The / Residence of W. C. Waddell. Drawn by A. J. Davis. On stone by F. F. Palmer.   1846 S N.C.

5847 Suburban Retreat, A / 8.7x12.9 (Group under tree at right, home on opposite bank, sailboats, probably Hudson River.)   und S C&I
Success (Horse) See: No. 881.

5848 Suffer little children to come unto Me / (Motto.)   und S C&I
Sullivan, John L. See: No. 3270.

5849 Summer / #454 / 8x12.8 (Horses, goats, sheep, taken from an English print. Companion to Nos. 311, 5672, 6729.   und S N.C.

5849A Summer / (Vignette, girl's head, companion to Nos. 313, 5674, 6730.)
und S C&I

5850 Summer /   1871 M C&I

5851 Summer / #451 (Portrait young woman, flowers in hand, and grain and flowers in hair, companion to Nos. 312, 5673, 6732. Vignette.)
1871 S C&I

5852 Summer Afternoon / 8x12.8 (Cattle in stream.)   und S C&I

5853 Summer Evening / 8x12.8 (Bridge in foreground, man driving cattle over it to right.)   und S C&I

5854 Summer Flowers / (Upright, vignette.)   und S C&I

5855 Summer Flowers /
1861 S C&I

5856 Summer Flowers / (Basket of roses, lilies, blue bells, hydrangea, dahlia, tinted background, companion to No. 317.)   1861 M C&I

5857 Summer Fruits / (Tinted background, companion to "Spring Flowers" No. 5677 and preceding. Vignette.)
1861 M C&I

SUMMER FLOWERS.

SUMMER FRUITS

5858 Summer Fruits /
1864 S C&I

5859 Summer Fruits and Flowers / 5.8x
7.8 (Oval, companion to "Autumn
Flowers" No. 320.)
und V.S. C&I

5860 Summer Gift, The / 7:15x12.8
(Peaches and pears.)
1870 S C&I

5861 Summer in the Country / 7.15x12.7
(2 equestrians on right, 2 dogs, no
fountain in yard or figures on porch,
group of 4 in front of house with slop-
ing roof.) und S C&I

5862 Summer in the Country / #267 /
8.8x12.10 (3 equestrians on left, 5 dogs,
farm hand, entirely different from preceding.) und S C&I

5863 Summer in the Country / 8.7x12.7
(Somewhat similar to preceding, house
with flat roof, flowers in right and left
foreground.) und S C&I

5864 Summer in the Country / F. F. Palmer, Del. 16.2x23.7 (Group on horseback on driveway, 3 dogs, group on
porch, 2 children at fountain in yard.)
1866 L C&I

5865 Summer in the Highlands / 15x20.7
(Mountain scene, 2 figures in carriage,
sailboats.) 1867 L C&I

5866 Summer in the Woods / 9.15x15.6
(Group of 5 under trees at stream. 1
fishing.) und S C&I

5867 Summer Landscape / After the
Painting by A. F. Bellows. (Also published as a Chromo, simulating an original oil painting.)
1869 L C&I

5868 Summer Landscape / Haymaking /
11.1x15.5. und S C&I

5869 Summer Morning / 7.14x12.7 (2
couples boating, mill in distance.)
und S C&I

5870 Summer Morning / F. F. Palmer,
Del. 10.6x14.12 (Children under trees,
river background.)
und M C&I

5871 Summer Night / 8.8x12.8 (Couple seated on log at edge of lake.)
und S C&I

5872 Summer Noon /
und S N.C.

5873 Summer Noon /
und S C&I

5874 Summer Ramble, A / (Couple and 2 children, round top.)
und M C&I

5875 Summer Retreat, A / 9.9x16.14 (Couple standing, cottage, rowboat, hills in distance.) 1869 M C&I

5876 Summer Scenes in New York Harbor / Parsons & Atwater, Del. 17.4x 27.10 (15 references of foreign and American steamers, frigates, yachts, etc. Race between 2 6-oared shells in foreground. 3 keys: Fort Lafayette — Staten Island — Jersey Shore.) 1863 L C&I

5877 Summer Shades / L. M. (Maurer) on stone. 15.2x22.12 (Round top.) 1859 L C&I

5878 Summer Time / Painted by F. F. Palmer. 17.11x14.7 (Thatched cottage, cattle and chickens under trees, upright.) und M C&I

5879 Summer Time, The / (3 children wading at foot of waterfall.)
und S C&I

5880 Summer's Afternoon, A (Sheep and cows on bank and in stream.)
und L C&I

5881 Summit of Happiness, The / #570 / 11.8x8.4 (Man standing on rain barrel, mandolin in hand, companion to "Depths of Despair" No. 1554.)
und S C&I

Sumner See: Nos. 403, 1474, 3479, 5050, 5095, 5460, 5664.

5882 Sunbeam, The /
und S C&I

5883 Sunday in the Olden Time / (Group leaving home for church.)
und S C&I

5884 Sunday Morning — In the Olden Time / Painted by William Collins, Esq. R.A. From an Engraving by S. W. Reynolds. 2 columns, 4 lines verse. 15.2x19.10 (Companion to "Sale of the Pet Lamb" No. 5368.)
und M N.C.

5885 Sunday School Certificate /
und S C&I

5886 Sunday School Emblems / 12.8x8.15

(9 vignetted views — crosses, harps, etc. Biblical quotations, upright.)
1874 S C&I

5887 Sunlight / 5.8x7.8 (Companion to No. 4173.) und V.S. C&I

5888 Sunny Hour, The /
und S C&I

5889 Sunny Morning /
und M C&I

5890 Sunny South, The / 7.14x12.7 (Brook with lush vegetation.)
1870 S C&I

5891 Sunnyside / (Published on sheet of landscape views No. 3439.)
und V.S. C&I

5892 Sunny Side / The Residence of the late Washington Irving, near Tarrytown, N.Y. / 14.13x20.8.
und L C&I

5893 Sunnyside — On the Hudson / 8x 12.8 (Similar composition to preceding.) und S C&I

5894 Sunol to Sulky Record 2:08¼ / (Postcard size.) und V.S. C&I

Sunol (Horse) See: Nos. 2473, 2475, 5894, 6194.

5895 Sunrise on Lake Saranac / 18.11x 27.4. 1860 L C&I

5896 Sunset Tree, The / F. F. Palmer, Del. (3 ladies under tree.)
und M C&I

Superb (Horse) See: Nos. 880-1.

5897 Sure horse for the First Money, A. / J. Cameron on stone. 18.1x28 (6 horses and sulkies, ¾ view, to left.)
1886 L C&I

5898 Sure of a Bite / "Golly! dis am a high old picnic" / Thos. Worth on stone. (Vignette, colored boy in rear of rowboat sampling liquor of fisherman in prow, crocodiles in water, companion to "Bustin' A Picnic" No. 755.)
1881 S C&I

5899 Sure Thing, A / "It's Picking up money backing dis yere pup" / King & Murphy, Dels. (Colored comic, companion to "All Broke Up" No. 77, vignette.) 1884 S C&I

5900 Surprise, The / L. Maurer on stone. 17.14x25.11 (Trapper on horse lassoing Indian.) 1858 L C&I

5901 Surprise Party, A / Parson: "Hab'nt I done tole you not to covert your neighbor's fowl?" / Thos. Worth on stone. (Vignette, winter scene, companion to #997.)
1883 S C&I

5902 Surrender of Cornwallis / At York-town, Va. Oct. 1781 / O'Hara — Corn-wallis — Tarleton — Lincoln — Wash-ington — Lafayette. / #366 / 12.10x 8.10 (American troops at right, fort and foot-soldiers in rear.)
1846 S N.C.

5903 Surrender of Cornwallis at York-town, Va., October 1781 /
und S N.C.

5904 Surrender of Cornwallis at York-town, Va. 1781 / (Above title) Lincoln — Hamilton — Lafayette — Washing-ton — Cornwallis — Tarleton — O'Hara — Chewton. 11.14x8.9 (Up-right in front of tent.)
1845 S N.C.

5905 Surrender of Cornwallis at York-town, Va. Cct. 1781 /
1848 S N.C.

5906 Surrender of Cornwallis at York-town, Va. Oct. 19th, 1781 / From the original painting by Colonel Trumbull in the Capitol at Washington. Painted by John Trumbull. F. Venino on stone. 15.13x24.15.   1852 L N.C.

5907 Surrender of General Burgoyne at Saratoga, N.Y. Oct. 17th, 1777 / From the original painting by Colonel Trum-bull in the Capitol at Washington. Painted by John Trumbull. O Knirsch on stone. 15.12x24.13.
1852 L N.C.

5908 Surrender of Genl. Joe Johnston near Greensboro, N.C. April 26th, 1865/ 8.2x12.8 Keyed: Genl. Johnston-Genl. Sherman.   1865 S C&I

5909 Surrender of Genl. Lee, at Ap-pomattox C.H. Va., April 9th, 1865 / Genl. Grant — Genl. Lee keyed above title. 11.15x8.14 (Upright, seated at table.)   1865 S C&I

5910 Surrender of General Lee at Ap-pomattox C.H., April 9, 1865 /
1868 S C&I

5911 Surrender of General Lee / At Ap-pomattox, C.H. Va., April 9th, 1865 / 8.6x12.5 (Genl. Lee — Genl. Grant keyed above title — soldiers seen through window.)   1873 S C&I

5912 Surrender of Lord Cornwallis / At Yorktown, Va. Oct. 19th, 1781 / 1 ad-ditional line quotation. 8.13x12.8 (Lin-coln — Washington — De Lauzon — L a f a y e t t e — Lord Cornwallis — O'Hara — Chewton [keyed].)
1876 S C&I

SURRENDER OF LORD CORNWALLIS AT YORKTOWN, VA.

5913 Surrender of Lord Cornwallis / At Yorktown, Va. Oct. 19th, 1781 / (Radically different composition, 3 officers keyed, Washington on horseback, 3 dismounted at his side.)
und S C&I

5914 Surrender of Napoleon III /
und L C&I

5915 Surrender of Port Hudson, La. July 8th, 1863 / To Maj. Gen. N. P. Banks / 2 additional lines. 7.15x12.8.
1863 S C&I

5916 Susan /   1844 S N.C.

5917 Susan / #46 / 11.10x8.8 (Full length, reading under tree, profile to right, round corners.)   1846 S N.C.

5918 Susan / #46 / 11.9x8.8 (Oval, ornamental border, ¾ length.)
1847 S N.C.

5919 Susan / #70 / 11.15x8.6 (Full length, seated, writing, red dress.)
1848 S N.C.

5920 Susan / 11.13x8.5 (Full length, red dress, green curtain.)
und S N.C.

5921 Susan / (Vignette, half length, rural scenery, exterior scene.)
und S N.C.

5922 Susan / #46 / 12.1x9.4 (Vignette, ¾ length.)   und S N.C.

5923 Susanna / #278 / 12.2x8.13 (Half length, lace shawl over head.)
1849 S N.C.

5924 Susanna / #278 / 12.2x8.14 (Full length, red dress.)
1849 S N.C.

5925 Susie / (Head of girl.)
und V.S. C&I

5926 Susie /   und S C&I
    Susquehanna See: Nos. 1537, 2733, 3005, 5415, 6358.
    Sussex, England See: "Landscape Cards" No. 3438.

5927 Sussex Vale / New Brunswick / 8.8x12.9.   und S C&I
    Swallow (Steamboat) See: No. 3779.
    Sweeny of Tammany Hall See: No. 5664.
    Sweepstakes (Clipper Ship) See: No. 1168.

5928 Sweet Sixteen /
und S C&I

5929 Sweet Spring Time / 11x15.6 (Rural scene, girl and boy feeding ducks.)   und S C&I

5930 Sweetser / The Pacing Whirlwind of the Buckeye State / Pacing at Cleveland, Ohio, October 3rd, 3 consecutive mile heats in 2:16, 2:16, 2:16¼ / E. Forbes on stone. (Vignette, ¾ view to left.)   1877 S C&I

5931 Sweetser — Sleepy George and Lucy / Pacing for a purse of $1000 at Hartford, Conn. Aug. 22nd, 1878 / Sweetser, Record 2:16, Sleepy George, Record 2:15, Lucy, Record 2:15 (Above title) / J. Cameron on stone. (Vignette, ¾ to right, high-wheeled sulkies.)   1878 S C&I

5932 Swell Smoker — Getting the Short End, A / J. Cameron on stone. (Vignette, dude gives bootblack long cigar for light, and gets a short butt in return.)   1888 S C&I

5933 Swell Smoker — Giving Long Odds, A / J. Cameron on stone. (Vignette, dude gives newsboy a light from long cigar.)   1888 S C&I

5934 Swell Sport on a Buffalo Hunt, A / "Aw-I say! I don't see any buffalo." / Thos. Worth on stone. (Comic vignette, "Sport" standing at edge of cliff about to be butted by buffalo.)
1882 S C&I

5935 Swell Sport Stampeded, A / "By Jove — I say! was that an Earthquake?" / Thos. Worth on stone. ("Sport" thrown from horse, buffalo herd in distance approaching, vignette.)   1882 S C&I

5936 Swift Pacer Arrow, by A. W. Richmond, The / Record 2:13¼ / (Vignette, broadside to right, high-wheeled sulky.)   1883 S C&I

5937 Swing of the First Heat, The /
1877 S C&I
    Switzerland See: Nos. 842-3, 3416-7, 3784, 3863, 6386, 6713.
    Swiveller (Horse) See: Nos. 622, 940, 1670, 4251.
    Sybil See: "Sibyl's Temple" No. 5503.
    Sylvan Grove (Steamer) See: No. 6388.
    Sylvan Lake See: "Landscape Cards" No. 3439.

5938 Sylvan Lake / New York / 8 x 12.8.
1868 S C&I

5939 Sylvan Lake / 7.15x12.8 (Couple in foreground, man in boat.)
und S C&I

5940 Sylvan Lake, The / #195 (Radically different composition, man fishing in foreground.)   und S C&I

5941 "Table D'Hote, The / A Comic Song / 5 additional lines. Published by James L. Hewitt & Co. (Dining scene.) und S N.C.

5942 Tacony / Union Course, L.I. July 14th, 1853 / 17.14x26.6 (4 additional lines, 2 columns.) 1853 L N.C.

5943 Tacony and Mac / Hunting Park Course, Phila. June 2nd, 1853 / Purse $1,500 mile heats, best 3 in 5 under the saddle / 5 additional lines. L. Maurer on stone. 17.5x26.8 (To left under saddle, broadside.) 1853 L N.C.
Taglioni, Madlle **See:** Nos. 3371, 3854, 3860, 6034.

5944 Take a Peach ? / und S C&I

5945 Take a Pinch / #54 (Companion to "The Pinch Taken," No. 4784.) und S N.C.

5946 "Take Back the Heart that Thou Gavest"/(Butcher boy returning heart to servant girl, vignette.) 1875 S C&I

5947 Take Care! / (Half length, vignette of girl's head.) und S C&I

5948 Take Your Choice / 11.10x8.11 (Half length of 2 girls' heads.) und S C&I

5949 Take Your Choice / (Vignette. 3 girls' heads.) und S C&I

5950 Taking a breath / und S C&I

5951 Taking a Rest / 1894 S C&I

5952 Taking a Smash / und S C&I

5953 Taking a "Smile" / #448 / L.M. on stone (Maurer). 8.2x12.6 (2 old soaks having drink with bartender.) 1854 S N.C.

5954 Taking Breath / (Postcard size, cigar ad. Same composition as "A New Jersey Fox Hunt" No. 4425. 1880 V.S. C&I

5955 Taking Comfort / 3.7x4.8 (Man smoking cigar, smoke forming the words "Perfect Bliss" — oval.) 1880 V.S. C&I

5956 Taking Comfort / 4.7x7.3 (Man

TAKING THE BACK TRACK.

[257]

smoking cigar, smoke forming words "Perfect Bliss.")
1880 V.S. C&I

5957 Taking Comfort / (Man smoking cigar, smoke forming words "Perfect Bliss.")
1879 S C&I

5958 Taking Comfort / F. F. Palmer, Del. 9.14x14 (Hen surrounded by brood of chicks.)
1866 M C&I

5959 Taking it Easy / (Postcard size, cigar ad.)
und V.S. C&I

5960 Taking Off His Airs / (Man showing off, falling off horse, 2 girls in window laughing. Companion to "Putting on his Airs," No. 4980.)
und S C&I

5961 Taking the Back Track / A Dangerous Neighborhood / J. Cameron on stone. 17.6x26.6 (Same as "The Life of a Trapper / A Sudden Halt," No. 3526.)
1866 L C&I

5962 "Taking the Stump" or Stephen in search of his Mother / Bell — Governor Wise of Virginia — Douglas with peg leg — Buchanan — Breckinridge — Lincoln. (Vignette.)
1860 M C&I

5963 Talked to Death /
1873 S C&I

Tallahassee See: Lafayette Lake No. 3404.

5964 Tallyrand / (Frontispiece to "A Letter to Pius VII," lith. by Stodart & Currier.)
und V.S. N.C.

5965 Tallulah Falls, Georgia / 8.8x12.7 (Group on path to left of Falls.)
und S C&I

5966 Tambourine Dance, The / #508 (Full length, exterior scene.)
und S N.C.

5967 Tantallon Castle / Coast of Scotland / 11.1x15.6 (Cart and figures on beach.)
und M C&I

Tarrytown, N.Y. See: Nos. 804-6, 4124, 4572, 5550-1, 5892-3.

5968 Taste for the Fine Arts, A / (Cow licking picture while artist flirts with farm girl.)
und S C&I

Taylor, John See: No. 1986.

Taylor, Zachary See: Nos. 389-90, 1485, 2296-300, 2329-31, 2513-4, 3364, 3679-80, 3938-9, 4884, 5382-3, 6495, 6874-9.

5969 Tea Party, The /
und S C&I

5970 Tea with Dolly /
und S C&I

5971 Team Fast to the Pole, A / Thos. Worth on stone. (Comic, wrecked sleigh, couple hanging on pole, winter scene, vignette.)
1883 S C&I

5972 Team Fast on the Snow, A / Thos. Worth on stone. (Colored comic, couple in crude sleigh pulled by mule, vignette.)
1883 S C&I

5973 Team on the Snow, A / Thos. Worth on stone. 13.8x17.8.
1883 M C&I

5974 Team that Takes no Dust, A / J. Cameron on stone. (Light 4-wheeled wagon to left, vignette.)
1875 S C&I

Tecumseh See: Nos. 1507-11.

5975 Tee-To-Tal Society, The /
und S N.C.

5976 Telasco and Amarilli / Burning of the Palace of the Incas, Conquest of Mexico / #376 / 12.12x9.6 (Full length of warrior and girl.)
und S N.C.

Telegraph See: Progress of the Century No. 4959.

Telegraph Station, New York Bay See: No. 4437.

Tell, William See: Nos. 6706-13.

Temperance See: Nos. 517-20, 1453, 2194-5, 2432, 3541, 5089, 5614-5, 5618-9, 5975, 6139-40, 6476, 6753.

Tempest (Steamship) See: No. 5739.

5977 Temple of Jupiter, Aegina /
und S C&I

5978 Temple of Solomon / 2 columns, 14 lines description.
und S C&I

5979 Temple of Solomon, The / El Templo de Salomon / 2 columns, 14 lines description. 8.9x12.14.
1846 S N.C.

5980 Temple of Christ, The / 2 line Biblical quotation. F.N. on stone. 12x8.9 (Full length Christ on the Mount, Satan alongside.)
und S C&I

5981 Tempted / 8.8x12.8 (Companion to "Hooked," No. 2928.)
1874 S C&I

5982 Tempting Fruit / 8.4x12.8.
1875 S C&I

5983 Tempting Lunch, A / 7.15x12.8 (Oranges, nuts, raisins.)
1870 S C&I

5984 Tempting the Baby / (Grandmother holding out apple as inducement to make child walk, mother and older child in doorway.) 1868 M C&I

5985 Ten Broeck / By imp. Phaeton, dam Fanny Holton by Lexington / The Fastest Race Horse in the World / Time 1 mi. 1:39¾. 3 mi. 5:26½. 4 mi. 7:15¾ / J. Cameron on stone. (Vignette, under saddle to right.) 1877 S C&I

Ten Broeck (Horse) See: Nos. 2642, 5985.

5986 Ten / Commandments / The / #177 / (Wording with illustrations interspersed, rebus.) und S N.C.

5987 Ten Commandments, The / (2 columns.) 13.5x10.1. und S C&I

5988 Ten Virgins, The / "While the Bridegroom tarried they all slumbered and slept. And at midnight there was a cry made, Behold, the bridegroom cometh; go ye out to meet him" / 12.7x7.15. und S C&I

Tennessee See: Nos. 396, 415, 590, 2577, 3771, 5822-4.

Tennis See: Nos. 3463-4.

5989 Tenny / By Rayon D'Or, dam Belle of Maywood / (Vignette, standing, profile to left, running horse.) 1891 S C&I

5990 Tenny / By Rayon D'Or, dam Belle of Maywood / Sketched from life by Chas. L. Zellinsky. J. Cameron on stone. 19.11x28.2 (Standing, profile to left, under saddle, colored jockey.) 1892 L C&I

5991 Tenny / 1892 S C&I

Tenny (Horse) See: Nos. 1949, 2622.

5992 Terra Cotta / By Harry O'Fallon, dam Laura B. by Bay Dick. J.C. on stone. (Vignette, under saddle.) 1881 S C&I

5993 Terrible Collision Between the Steamboats Stonington and Narragansett / At 11:30 P.M. of Friday June 11th, 1880 off Cornfield Light, Long Island Sound / 3 additional lines description. 8.7x13.8. 1880 S C&I

5994 Terrific Collision between the Steamboats Dean Richmond and C. Vanderbilt / Near Rondout, on the Hudson River, Sept. 19th, 1867 / By which the Dean Richmond was sunk,

and several lives lost / 7.13x12.5 (Moonlight scene.) und S C&I

5995 Terrific Combat between the Monitor 2 guns, & Merrimac 11 guns / In Hampton Roads March 9th, 1862 / 1 additional line. 1862 S C&I

5996 Terrific Combat between the Monitor 2 guns & Merrimac 11 guns / In Hampton Roads March 9th, 1862 / in which the little "Monitor" whipped the "Merrimac" and the whole "School" of Rebel Steamers / 7.10x12.2 (Monitor on left, gunboats in rear firing.) 1862 S C&I

5997 Terrific Combat between the Monitor 2 guns & Merrimac, 10 guns / In Hampton Roads March 9th, 1862 / The First Fight between Iron Clad Ships of War / 7.13x12.12 (2 keys above title —Minnesota — Rebel Steamer.) 1862 S C&I

5998 Terrific Engagement between "Monitor" 2 guns and "Merrimac" 10 guns in Hampton Roads, March 9th, 1862 / "The First Fight between Iron Ships of War in which the Merrimac was crippled and the whole Rebel Fleet driven back to Norfolk" / F. F. Palmer, Del. 1862 L C&I

Teutonic (Steamship) See: No. 5796.

5999 Text with Modern Improvements, A / 1881 S C&I

Thames, (Death of Tecumseh) See: Nos. 1507-11.

Thames River, England (Boat Race) See: Nos. 2623-4.

6000 That Blessed Baby / und S C&I

6001 That Blessed Baby / #624 / (Father walking floor with baby while mother sleeps.) und S C&I

6002 Thatched Cottage, The / 8.8x12.8. und S C&I

6003 Thatched Roof, The / und S C&I

That's So! See: "Life in New York," No. 3506.

6004 "That's What's the Matter" / "Hello Friend; Pretty bad looking smash up." "Yes, confound it, it comes from buying a poor wagon" / Moral: Buy your wagons from a reliable source / Thos. Worth on stone. (Vignette, evidently published to be used as an ad.) 1882 S C&I

6005 Theodore Frelinghuysen / Hurrah! Hurrah! the Country's risin' for Henry Clay and Frelinghuysen / 11.9x8.12.
und S N.C.

6006 Theodore Frelinghuysen / Nominated for / Vice-President of the United States / From a daguerreo'ype by Chilton. 11.9x8.12 (Right hard on book, green curtain.)
1844 S N.C.
Theoxena (Bark) See: No. 371.

6007 They're Saved! They're Saved! / 8.4x12.6 (Woman and child saved from sea. Companion to "My Child! My Child!" No. 4280.)   und S C&I

6008 Third day of the Siege of Monterey, Sept. 23rd, 1846 / #494 / 8.4x12.13.
1846 S N.C.

6009 Third Heat in Two Sixteen, A / Judge Fullerton and Goldsmith Maid in their trot at East Saginaw, Mich. July 16th, 1874 / J. Cameron on stone. 4 additional lines. 16.12x26.14 (¾ view to right, high-wheeled sulkies passing stand.)   1874 L C&I

6010 This Certifies that . . . has been a member . . . /   1889 S C&I

6011 This certifies that . . . has been a member of / Fire Department / of . . . for a period of . . . years / 20x15.6 (Tinted background.)
1889 L C&I

6012 This Certifies / That . . . / is a member / of . . . / company . . . / No. . . . / Fire Department / 20x14.13 (Fire scenes at sides and bottom, fireman returning rescued baby to mother at top.   1877 L C&I

6013 This Certifies / that . . . is a member / of . . . company / No. . . . / Fire Department / 20x15 (Surrounded by various fire scenes, tinted background.)   1889 L C&I

6014 This Certifies / That . . . / is a member of / the Ladies Loyal Union League / of . . . (6 war scenes, & portraits of Martha Washington & Florence Nightingale.)
1863 S C&I

6015 This Certifies / That . . . / is a member of . . . / the loyal Union League / of . . . / (Portraits of Washington and Jackson and 6 small scenes — railroad train, Mississippi steamer, 2 Civil War scenes, commerce, and farming.)   1863 S C&I

6016 This Certifies / That . . . / is a member of the . . . / Sunday School /

of . . . / 12.14x9 (Rural scene at top, religious scenes at sides and bottom.)
und S C&I

6017 This Certifies / That . . . / is a member of the . . . / Sunday school / of . . . / "Suffer Little Children to Come Unto Me" etc. / 13.14x10.6 (Portrait of Christ.)   1877 S C&I

6018 This Certifies that / the Rite of / Holy Matrimony / was celebrated between . . . / Engraved by J. C. McRae. (Vignette, view of marriage in center.)
1857 S C&I

6019 This Man forgot to / Shut the door / (Vignette, man being hit over the head.)   1880 M C&I

6020 This Man was / Talked to death / J. Cameron on stone. (Vignette, 2 men carrying dead man on stretcher.)
1873 S C&I

6021 "Thistle" / Cutter Yacht, Designed by G. L. Watson, built by D. W. Henderson & Co. Glasgow. Owned by Mr. James Bell, Glasgow, Scotland / 1 additional line dimensions. Printed in oil colors by Currier & Ives. 20x28.1.
1887 L C&I
Thistle (Yacht) See: Nos. 1344, 4404, 6021.

6022 Thomas Corwin / The Wagon Boy of Ohio / The People's Choice for Twelfth President of the United States / #469 / 11.15x8.7 (¾ length, standing at table, covered wagon seen through window.)   1847 S N.C.

6023 Thomas F. Meagher / 11.2x8.5 (¾ length, oval in rectangle, green curtain.)   1852 S N.C.

6024 Thomas F. Meagher / #621 / 6 additional lines. 11.6x8.5 (¾ length portrait, seated, profile, boat scene through window.)
1848 S N.C.

6025 Thomas Francis Meagher / (¾ length in uniform, vignette.)
und S C&I
Thomas, Genl. See: Nos. 413, 5490.

6026 Thomas Jefferson / Third President of the United States / 11.13x9.5.
und S N.C.

6027 Thomas Jefferson / "The Black Whirlwind of the East" / Black stallion by Toronto Chief, dam Gipsey Queen by Wagner / Owned by W. B. Smith, Esq. of Hartford, Conn. foaled 1863 bred by T. J. Vail of Hartford / Record 2:23 Sept. 20th, 1875 / Thos.

Worth on stone. 16.11x25 (Broadside to right, high-wheeled sulky, passing judge's stand.)   1875 L C&I

6028 Thomas Jefferson / "The Black Whirlwind of the East" / 4 additional lines. J. Cameron on stone. (Broadside to right, vignette.)
1880 S C&I

6029 Thomas Wildey / Father of the Order of Odd Fellowship in this country / and Past Grand Sire of the Order /   und S N.C.

6030 Thou Gav'st Me a Bright Sword, Lady /   und S N.C.

6031 Thou Hast Learned to Love Another / (Policeman kissing governess in park, vignette, comic.)
1875 S C&I

6032 Thou Shalt / Not Steal / (Motto, scroll with flowers, vignette.)
und S C&I

Three Bells (Steamship) See: No. 5492.

Three Brothers (Clipper Ship) See: Nos. 1169-70.

6033 Three Favorites, The / #490 / 8.7x 12.13 (Portraits of 3 horses at drinking trough.)   und S N.C.

6034 Three Graces, The / Cerito — Elssler — Taglioni / #416 / 12.5x8.15 (Standing inside wreaths, lying on ground, round corners.)
und S N.C.

6035 Three Greedy Kitties / After the Feast / (Bottle of cream, sardines, water glass.)   1871 S C&I

6036 Three Greedy Kitties, The / At the Feast /   1871 S C&I

6037 Three Holy Women, The /
und S C&I

6038 Three Jolly Kittens, The / After the Feast / 8.3x12.6.
1871 S C&I

6039 Three Jolly Kittens, The / At the Feast / 8.3x12.7 (Liquor, sardines, etc.)   1871 S C&I

6040 Three Little Maids from School (Mikado) / (Full length, upright.)
und L C&I

6041 Three Little Sisters, The / (Vignette.)   1862 M C&I

6042 Three Little White Kitties / Fishing / 8.4x12.4.   1870 S C&I

6043 Three Little White Kitties / Fishing / (Goldfish Bowl.)
1871 S C&I

6044 Three Little White Kitties / Their First Mouse /.   1871 S C&I

6045 Three Sisters, The / (2 older have arms around youngest.)
1871 S C&I

6046 Three Sorry Kitties, The / After the Feast / (All sick.)
und S C&I

6047 Three White Kittens, The / Peace / O. St. (Starck) on stone.
und M C&I

6048 Three White Kittens, The / War /
und M C&I

Throop See: No. 1750.

6049 Through Express, The / (Locomotive, 4 coaches approaching from right, vignette.)   und S C&I

6050 Through the Bayou by Torchlight /
und S C&I

6051 Through to the Pacific / 7.15x12.9 (Rear view of train passing town on right, ocean in distance.)
1870 S C&I

6052 Throw if you dare! / 7.8x5.8 (Winter scene, boy carrying books, school house in background. Companion to No. 5477.)   und V.S. C&I

Thumb, Tom See: Nos. 2302-9, 4627.

6053 Thy Kingdom Come / (Vignette; harp, crown, and flowers.)
1872 S C&I

6054 Thy Will be Done / 12.8x8.7 (Scroll, cross, flowers, black background.)
1872 S C&I

6055 Thy Word is a Light Unto my Path / 8.7x12.8 (Title in plate, Bible on cushion.)   1872 S C&I

Tiberias See: Foreign Views, misc.

6056 Tick-Tick-Tickle / (Vignette, girl holding watch to ear.)
1873 S C&I

6057 Tickle! Tickle! /
und S C&I

Tidal Wave (Yacht) See: No. 6821.
Tilden, Samuel See: Nos. 2460, 2498, 5374, 6349.
Tillman, Wm. See: No. 6714.

6058 Time is Money /
1873 S C&I

6059 Time is Precious / 8.7x12.7 (Motto, scythe, Holy Bible, hour glass, roses, sun rising, etc.)   1872 S C&I

6060 Time Worn Abbey, The /
und S C&I

6061 Tip-Top / Thos. Worth on stone (Man smoking, smoke forming the words "Try One," vignette.)
1879 S C&I

6062 Tip-Top / 1880 S C&I

6063 Tip-Top / (Postcard size, cigar ad.)
1880 V.S. C&I

Tippecanoe See: Genl. Wm. H. Harrison Nos. 2322-5.

6064 Tired Soldier, The /
und S C&I

Titus See: Foreign Views, misc.
Tivoli, Italy See: Italy.

6065 T. J. Jackson (Facsimile signature) Lieut. Genl. Stonewall Jackson / (Vignette.)
und S C&I

6066 To Avoid a Smash / We sell for Cash / J. Cameron on stone. 10.5x 14.12 (Vignette, man tripping over bag marked "Credits," bag on his back marked "Debts," falling and breaking pitcher.)
1875 M C&I

6067 To the Governor's Guard 2nd Regt. N.Y. State Artillery, Thos. F. Peers Col. Comdt. / This Plate is most respectfully dedicated by Alexander Purdy / Lith. of N. Currier 2 Spruce St. & 169 Broadway / 9.15x12.12.
1842 S N.C.

6068 To the Grand Army of the Republic / This Print of / Our Old Commander / General U. S. Grant / is Respectfully dedicated / (Vignette, full length of Grant on horseback.)
1885 L C&I

6069 To the / Memory of / . . . / #370 / 13.2x8.14 (Woman kneeling at left of tomb, 2 children, tree at left, river in background.)
1845 S N.C.

6070 To the / Memory / of . . . / 12.10x 8.9 (Tomb in center, weeping willow directly behind tomb, lady at left, church in right background.)
und S N.C.

6071 To the Memory of . . . / 12.15x9.12 (2 women at tombstone, St. Paul's Churchyard, N.Y.)
und S N.C.

6072 To the Memory of . . . / 12.14x8.12 (Tomb in center, lady on right, entire church in background.)
1845 S N.C.

6073 To the Memory of . . . / (2 children and widow kneeling, costumes of the 1830's. Very early print.)
und S N.C.

6074 To the Memory of . . . / #78 / 12.10x8.9 (Church, church yard, and stream, lady leaning on tomb.)
1846 S N.C.

6075 To the Memory of . . . /
1846 S N.C.

6076 To the Memory of . . . / 12.10x8.11.
und S C&I

6077 To the / Memory of / W. H. Harrison / Born February 9th, 1773 / Inaugurated President of the United States, March 4th, 1841/Died April 4th, 1841 / Age 68 "Then shall the dust return / to the earth as it was / And the Spirit shall return / Unto God who gave it" / W. K. Hewitt on stone. 9.4x 13.1 (Tomb of Harrison, mourning band around print.)
und S N.C.

6078 To the memory of Wm. H. Harrison, born February 9th, 1773 / Inaugurated President of the United States March 4th, 1841 / Died April 4th, 1841 / At 68 / #135 / 4 lines of poetry. 13.1x8.2.
und S N.C.

6079 To the Rescue / 7.13x12.7.
und S C&I

6080 To the Rescue! / 14.14x19.10 (Companion to "Saved," No. 5402.)
und M C&I

6081 To Thy Cross I Cling /
und S C&I

Tobacco See: Nos. 503-4, 613, 784, 790, 1044, 1330-1, 1686, 1782, 1808A, 2436, 2476, 2815-8, 3290-4, 3369, 3845, 4517-8, 4750-2, 4758-60, 4771, 4804-5, 4920, 5029, 5293, 5568, 5583-4, 5670, 5932-3, 5954-6, 6061-3, 6116, 6636-7, 6819, 6820, 6842.

6082 Toboganning in the Alps /
und S C&I

6083 Toboganning on Darktown Hill — Getting a Hist / "Dar, I knowed it" / (Toboggan overturned after hitting pig, vignette.)
1890 S C&I

6084 Toboganning on Darktown Hill — An Untimely Move / "Clar de track" / (Pigs running in front of toboggan, vignette.)
1890 S C&I

6085 Tocsin of Liberty, The / Rung by the State House Bell [Independence Hall] Philadelphia July 4th, 1776 / 1 additional line proclamation. 9x12.6.
1876 S C&I

6086 Toilette, The / 11.2x9 (Oval.)
und S C&I

6087 Toll-Gate, Jamaica Plank Road / Crayon Studies.　und S N.C.

6088 Toll-Gate, Jamaica Plank Road /. und S N.C.

6089 Toll Gate, Jamaica, L.I. / #472 / (2 oxen drawing cart, vignette.) und S N.C.

6090 Tom Bowling / (Vignette.) 1881 V.S. C&I

6091 Tom Bowling / by Lexington, dam Lucy Fowler, by Imp. Albion, bred by H. P. McGrath, Lexington, Ky. / J. Cameron on stone. 4 additional lines. (Vignette, under saddle to right.) 1873 S C&I

Tom Bowling (Horse) See: No. 175, 6090-1.

Tom Moore (Horse) See: No. 6225.

6092 Tom Ochiltree / By Lexington, out of Katona / Winner of the Westchester Cup at Jerome Park, June 5 and the $1000 purse at same Course June 18, 1877 / and of numerous other stakes, etc. / (Vignette, under saddle to left.) 1877 S C&I

Tom Ochiltree (Horse) See: No. 2642, 6092.

6093 Tom Paddock / Born 1824. Height 5 feet 10½ inches, weight 12 stone. 2 columns, 6 lines. 14.2x12.4. und S C&I

6094 Tom Sayers / Champion of England / 1 additional line and 3 columns (Full length in fighting position, slightly to right, vignette.) 1860 S C&I

6095 Tom Sayers / Champion of England / Born at Pimlico, Brighton, Sussex, 1826. Height 5 feet 8 inches. Lowest Fighting Weight, 10 stone, 10 lbs. / 2 columns records. L.M. on stone. 14.13x12.6 (Full length.) und M C&I

6096 Tom Sayers / Champion of England / 3 columns records. (Half length, vignette, fighting togs, full face.) 1860 S C&I

6097 Tom Sayers / Champion of England / 3 columns records. (Half length vignette, fighting togs, profile to left.) 1860 S C&I

Tom Thumb See: Nos. 2302-8, 4627.

6098 Tomb and Shade of Napoleon, The / From a natural curiosity at St. Helena / 10.4x8.3 (Oval in rectangle.) und S N.C.

6099 Tomb and Shade of Napoleon, The / Find the figure of Napoleon among the trees / #214 / 10.14x8.2 (Different composition from preceding.) und S N.C.

6100 Tomb and Shade of Washington, The / Find the Figure of Washington among the trees / (Upright.) und S C&I

6101 Tomb of Genl. W. H. Harrison, The / North Bend, Ohio / 8.3x12.15 (Steamboat "Queen of the West" shown in rear, 3 figures under trees at left.) 1842 S N.C.

6102 Tomb of Genl. W. H. Harrison, The/ North Bend, Ohio / Drawn on the spot by J. Leslie, of Cincinnati, Ohio, 1841 / Published by W. A. Moyston, Wheeling, Va. 15x18.9. 1841 M N.C.

6103 Tomb of Kosciusko, The / West Point / #234 / und S N.C.

6104 Tomb of Kosciusko, The / West Point / #234 / 8x12.7 (2 male figures in left foreground, 6 boats in river, changes in composition from preceding.) und S C&I

6105 Tomb of Lincoln, The / Springfield, Illinois / und S C&I

6106 Tomb of Napoleon, St. Helena, The / 10.4x8.3 (Oval.) und S N.C.

6107 Tomb of Washington, Mount Vernon, Va., The / H. Macaire, Del. 7.8 x13.10. und S N.C.

6108 Tomb of Washington, The / Mount Vernon, Va. 1840 / 8.4x12.12. und S N.C.

6109 Tomb of Washington, Mt. Vernon, Va., The / und S C&I

6110 Tomb of Washington, The / Mount Vernon, Va. / 11.8x16.1 (6 figures, round top corners.) und M C&I

6111 Tomb of Washington, Mount Vernon, Va., The / 14.15x20.5. und L C&I

6112 Tomb of Washington, The / Mount Vernon, Va. / 8.8x12.8. und S C&I

6113 Tommy Tateish Onejero / Interpreter to the Japanese Embassy / 12 x9.2. und S C&I

Tompkins, Daniel D. See: No. 1352.

Tonquin (Ship) See: No. 299.

6114 Tonsorial Art in the Darktown Style / "Go to de next shop. We done dont handle common niggahs" / J. Cameron on stone. (Vignette, companion to "Scientific Shaving, etc.," No. 5435.) 1890 S C&I

THE TRAPPERS CAMP-FIRE.

6115 Too Sweet For Anything /
und S C&I

6116 Top of the Heap / (Vignette, man smoking, smoke forming "The Boss.")
1880 S C&I

Torbay **See:** No. 6700.

Toronto **See:** Nos. 2319, 6352, 6396, 6420.

6117 Toronto Chief, General Butler and Dexter / In their great race under saddles, over the Fashion Course, L.I. July 19th, 1866 / J Cameron on stone. 5 additional lines. 17x27.4 (Broadside to right, under saddle.)
1866 L C&I

6118 Tower of Solomon, The /
1846 S N.C.

Town Moor (Iroquois) Winning **See:** No. 3133.

6119 Toy Bridge, The /
und S C&I

Traave (Steamship) **See:** Nos. 3039, 5797.

6120 Training a Trotter / 2.12x4.12.
1881 V.S. C&I

6121 Training Day / (Children playing war, mother and grandmother watching.)
1866 M C&I

6122 Transfiguration, The /
und S N.C.

6123 Trapper's Camp Fire, The / F. F. Palmer, Del. 17x25.8 (Night scene.)
1866 L C&I

6124 Trapper's Camp Fire, The / A Friendly Visitor / F. F. Palmer, Del. 17x25.14 (Daylight scene, similar to preceding but with an Indian seated at fire.)
1866 L C&I

6125 Trapper's Last Shot, The / 11x15.9.
und M C&I

6126 Trappers on the Prairie / Peace or War? / J. Cameron on stone. 17.3x26.5 (Same as "A Parley," No. 4701.)
1866 L C&I

6127 Traveling on his Beauty /
und S C&I

Tree, Ellen **See:** Nos. 1713-5.

6128 Tree of Death, The / 1 additional line Biblical quotation.
und S C&I

6129 Tree of Death, The / The Sinner / #399 / 12.9x9 (Companion to "The Tree of Life," No. 6138.)
und S N.C.

6130 Tree of Evil, The /
und S N.C.

6131 Tree of Good, The /.
und S N.C.

6132 Tree of Intemperance, The / #147 / 12.6x8.12. 2 line Biblical quotation (Saloon left background, ruined house on right.) 1849 S N.C.

6133 Tree of Intemperance, The / (Different composition from preceding.)
und S C&I

6134 Tree of Life, The / #21 / 1 line Biblical quotation. (Devil in background.)
und S N.C.

6135 Tree of Life, The / 2 lines of verse. 9.5x12.3. und S C.C.

6136 Tree of Life, The / On each side of the river was a tree of life which / Bare twelve manner of fruits / 11.15x 8.7 (2 angels, glittering castle in background, no devil.)
1870 S C&I

6137 Tree of Life, The / 1 additional line Biblical quotation.
1892 L C&I

6138 Tree of Life, The — The Christian/ #398 / 12.8x8.15. 1 additional line Biblical quotation. (Angel watering tree, and repulsing devil. Companion to "Tree of Death — the Sinner," No. 6129.) und S N.C.

6139 Tree of Temperance, The / 12x8.14. 3 additional lines (4 limbs on tree, 4 on way to church on left, farmer ploughing on right.)
1849 S N.C.

6140 Tree of Temperance, The / 12.14x 8.12. 3 additional lines. (Family of 4 on way to church, tree trunk labeled "Health-Strength of Body," fruits marked "Success" "Morality" "Honesty" etc. 4 limbs on tree, different from preceding.) 1872 S C&I
Trenton, N.J. See: Nos. 6521-4, 6526, 6552-9.
Trenton Falls See: Landscape Cards, No. 3438.

6141 Trenton Falls, New York / 8.8x12.7 (Close view, 4 on ledge.)
und S C&I
Trenton Falls See: Nos. 6142, 6376.

6142 Trenton High Falls / New Jersey / 8.3x12.6 (6 figures on the left.)
und S C&I

6143 Trial By Jury—The Judge's Charge / "Gemmen of de jury if dem chickens cant be counted for, dat cullud pusson must be foun guilty" / (Vignette, comic.) 1887 S C&I

6144 Trial by Jury — The Verdict / "We finds de prisnur not guilty cos dem chickens am couted for" / (Shows rear of jury box, and each juror has chickens hidden in pockets. (Vignette, colored comic.) 1887 S C&I

6145 Trial of Effie Deans, The / Painted by R. S. Lander, R.S.A. From an Engraving by Fred'k K. Bromley. 14.6x 23.13 (Scene from "The Heart of Midlothian" by Sir Walter Scott) (Currier evidently made arrangements with the English publisher to use their own imprint on this engraving.)
und L C&I

6146 Trial Of Patience, The / (Boy holding skein of wool for grandmother, 2 boys in doorway.)
und M C&I

6147 Trial of the Irish Patriots at Clonmel, Oct. 22nd, 1848 / Thomas F. Meagher, Terence B. McManus, Patrick Donohue receiving their sentence/ #642 / 3 additional lines. 7.15x12.9.
1848 S N.C.

6148 Tribute Money /
und S N.C.

6149 Tribute of Autumn, The / 7.14x12.7 (Apples and grapes.)
1870 S C&I

6150 Trinket / 1881 S C&I

6151 Trinket, Record 2:10¾ / (Postcard size.) 1881 V.S. C&I

6152 Trinket / By Princeps, dam Ouida, by Rysdyk's Hambletonian / Record 2:14. 18.4x27.11 (Broadside to right, spectators in background, vignette.)
1879 S C&I

6153 Trinket / Record 2:14 / (Broadside to right, passing judge's stand.)
1879 S C&I

6154 Trinket / By Princeps, dam Ouida, by Rysdyk's Hambletonian / Record 2:14 / 18.4x27.11 (Broadside to right, high-wheeled sulky.)
1884 L C&I
Tripoli, Bombardment Of See: No. 600.

6155 Triumph of Faith, The / 10.6x13.6 (Christ walking on the sea and rescuing another man.)
1874 M C&I

6156 Triumph of the Cross, The / (Cross resting on ferns and leaves, crown "Victory" below, vignette.)
1874 S C&I

6157 Trojan Quick Step / (Showing the Court House and Seminary, Troy, N.Y.) und S N.C.

6158 Trolling For Blue Fish / F. F. Palmer, Del. 18.8x27.14 (4 in small sloop.)
1866 L C&I

6159 Tropical and Summer Fruits / 15x 20.4 (Bananas, cherries, etc., scarlet tanager, tinted background.)
1867 L C&I

6160 Tropical and Summer Fruits /
1867 S C&I

6161 Trot "For the Gate Money," A / 16.6x24.14 (Entrance to the track.)
1869 L C&I

6162 Trot, with Modern Improvements, A / Thos. Worth on stone. (Comic, horse and driver with pillows as protectors, vignette.)
1881 S C&I

6163 Trotters / (Miniature views of celebrated horses on 1 sheet as follows: Mattie Hunter, 2. Phallas, 2. Goldsmith Maid, 2. Johnston, 2. Sleepy Tom, 2. Majolica, 5. Maud S, 5. A Road Team, 12. Maxy Cobb, 2. Harry Wilkes, 7. St. Julien, 2. Jay Eye See, 5. Director, 2. Training a Trotter, 2. Rarus, 2. A Spin on the Road, 2.) 29x34.4.
und L C&I

6164 Trotter's Burial, The / The Dearest spot on Earth for Me / 9.1x12.12 (Same composition as "Dearest Spot on Earth," No. 1470.)
1878 S C&I

6165 Trotters on the Grand Circuit / Warming Up / Thos. Worth on stone. 17.8x27.
1877 L C&I

6166 Trotters on the Snow /
und V.S. C&I

6167 Trotters on the Snow / J. Cameron on stone. (Vignette.)
und S C&I

Trotting, at the Fair Grounds **See:** Nos. 294-5.

6168 "Trotting Cracks" at Home / A Model Stable / Peerless — Dexter — The Auburn Horse / Sketched and on stone by Thos. Worth. 19.4x29.15 (Companion to following.)
1868 L C&I

6169 "Trotting Cracks" at the Forge / Mountain Boy — Grey Eagle — Lady Thorn / 19.6x29.5 (Companion to preceding.)
1869 L C&I

6170 "Trotting Cracks" on the Snow / (Above Title) Pocohantus, Lancet, Prince, Grey Eddy, General Darcy, Flora Temple, Lantern, Lady Wood-

"TROTTING CRACKS" AT THE FORGE.

ruff, Brown Dick, Alice Grey, Stella / L. Maurer, fct. on stone. 16.11x27.15.
1858 L C&I

6171 Trotting for a Great Stake / L. Maurer, N.Y., on stone. 20x28.5 (3 high-wheeled sulkies to right, judge's stand in background, companion to "Pacing for a Grand Purse" No. 4677.)
1890 L C&I

6172 Trotting Gelding Billy D with Running Mate, The / owned by J. B. Barnaby, driven by John Murphy / Record 2:14¾ / Painted by J. Mc-Auliffe and signed on stone. 18.6x29.2 (To skeleton wagon.)
1881 L C&I

6173 Trotting Gelding Clingstone, Record 2:14 / (Vignette.)
1882 S C&I

6174 Trotting Gelding Frank with J. O. Nay his Running Mate, The / As they appeared at Prospect Park, L.I. Nov. 15th, 1883 / Driven by John Murphy / Making the fastest mile ever trotted in any way of going; and reducing the record to / 2:08½ / Printed in oil colors by Currier & Ives. 19x30.2 (Skeleton wagon, ¾ view to left, horses keyed above title.)
1884 L C&I

6175 Trotting Gelding Harry Wilkes, by George Wilkes / Record 2:14¾ / J. Cameron 1885 on stone. (Vignette, broadside to right, high-wheeled sulky.)
1885 S C&I

6176 Trotting Gelding Prince Wilkes, by Red Wilkes / Record 2:14¾ / (Vignette, high-wheeled sulky to left.)
1889 S C&I

6177 Trotting Gelding St. Julien, Record 2:11¼ / Scott Leighton on stone.
1881 S C&I

6178 Trotting Gelding Steve Maxwell, by Ole Bull, Jr. / Driven by John Murphy / Record 2:21½, 2 miles 4:48½ / Scott Leighton on stone. (¾ view, high wheeled sulky to left.)
1881 S C&I

6179 Trotting Horse Darby, by Delmonico / Champion of the Grand Circuit of 1879 / Record 2:16½ / (Vignette, to right.)
1879 S C&I

6180 Trotting Horse George Palmer driven by C. Champlin, The / Winning the third heat in the trot for a purse Of $5000 mile heats best 3 in 5 in harness / At Naragansett Park, R.I. Oct. 8th, 1869 / against Lady Thorn,

Goldsmith Maid, Lucy and American Girl / Time 2:19¼ / 2 additional lines. J. Cameron on stone. 16.14x26.3 (Stands in background, high wheeled sulky, broadside to right.)
1870 L C&I

6181 Trotting Horse Judge Fullerton, driven by Dan Mace / 11.8x20.
1874 M C&I

6182 Trotting King St. Julien, Record 2:11¾ / 2.12x4.12.
1881 V.S. C&I

6183 Trotting Mare American Girl / J. Cameron on stone.
1870 L C&I

6184 Trotting Mare "American Girl," driven by M. Rodin / As she appeared at Narragansett Park, Providence, R.I. June 26, 1869, winning in three straight heats the first prize   , beating "Lady Thorn" / "Goldsmith Maid" "Lucy" and "George Palmer" mile heats best 3 in 5 in harness. Time 2:22½, 2:19, 2:20½ / J. Cameron on stone. (Vignette, ¾ to right.)
1871 S C&I

6185 Trotting Mare "American Girl," driven by M. Rodin / by Cassius Clay Jr. Mr. Travis Virginia Mare, pedigree unknown / Winning in three straight heats the first prize $2000 of the $3000 purse at Narragansett Park, Providence, R.I. June 26, 1869 beating Lady Thorn, Goldsmith Maid, Lucy and George Palmer / 1 additional line and time. 16.13x26. J. Cameron on stone. (Broadside to right.)
1870 L C&I

6186 Trotting Mare Belle Hamlin, Record 2:12¾ / L.M. on stone. (¾ view to right, high-wheeled sulky, vignette.)
1889 S C&I

6187 Trotting Mare Belle Hamlin, Record 2:12¾ / Scott Leighton on stone. (Vignette, high-wheeled sulky to left.)
1889 S C&I

6188 Trotting Mare Belle Hamlin, Record 2:12¾ / (Changes in composition from preceding, vignette, high-wheeled sulky to left.) 1889 S C&I

6189 Trotting Mare Goldsmith Maid, driven by Budd Doble, The / By Edsall's Hambletonian, dam by Old Abdallah / Winning in three straight heats the first prize $5000 of the $10,000 purse / At the Buffalo Fair Grounds, Buffalo, N.Y. August 11th, 1869 / Beating American Girl, George Palmer, and Lucy / 2 additional lines. J.

Cameron on stone. 16.14x26.6 (Broadside to left, high-wheeled sulkies. Also used as an ad for "The Celebrated Vacuum Oil Blacking.")
1870 L C&I

6190 Trotting Mare "Lucy" as she appeared / Trotting in harness at Narragansett Park, R.I. Oct. 15, 1868 / 2 additional lines. J. Cameron on stone. (¾ view to right, high-wheeled sulky.)
1868 S C&I

6191 Trotting Mare Martha Wilkes, Record 2:08 / J. Cameron on stone. (Vignette, low rubber-tired sulky to right.)
1892 S C&I

6192 Trotting Mare Nancy Hanks by Happy Medium / Record 2:09 / (Vignette, broadside to right, high-wheeled sulky.)
1891 S C&I

6193 Trotting Mare Nancy Hanks, Record 2:04 / Driven by Budd Doble to a bicycle sulky built by the Chas. S. Caffrey Co. Camden, N.J. / J. Cameron on stone.(¾ view to right, low-wheeled sulky, different from preceding.)
1892 S C&I

6194 Trotting Mare Sunol, Record 2:08¼ / L.M. on stone. (¾ to left, high-wheeled sulky, vignette.)
1889 S C&I

6195 Trotting on the Road / Swill against Swell / Thos. Worth on stone. J.C. on stone. (Vignette, man driving cart, passed by garbage cart and being splashed.)
1873 S C&I

6196 Trotting Queen Alix, Record 2:03¾ / J. Cameron on stone. 18.10x27.2 (Low-wheeled, rubber-tired sulky to left.)
1894 L C&I

6197 Trotting Queen Alix, by Patronage / Record 2:03¾ / L.M. on stone. (Vignette to left, low-wheeled sulky.)
1893 S C&I

6198 Trotting Queen Maud S., Record 2:08¾ / Scott Leighton on stone. (Vignette.)
1881 S C&I

6199 Trotting Queen Maud S, Record 2:10¾, The / 2.12x4.12 (Also used as an ad for "Mueller's German Liniment and Condition Powder.)
1881 V.S. C&I

6200 Trotting Queen Nancy Hanks, Record 2:04 /
1892 L C&I

6201 Trotting Stallion Alcryon, by Alcyone / Record 2:15¼ / L.M. on stone. (Vignette, ¾ to right, high-wheeled sulky.)
1889 S C&I

6202 Trotting Stallion Commodore Vanderbilt, driven by Dan Mace / Trotted a heat in harness in 2:25 over the Union Course, L.I., June 12th, 1866 / Now at the stables of J. E. Adams, Stamford, Conn. / J. Cameron 1865 on stone. 12.15x21 (Skeleton wagon to left, stands in left rear.)
1871 L C&I

6203 Trotting Stallion Dan Rice, owned by T. M. Lynn, Portsmouth, O. / Washington Park, Providence, R.I. Oct. 25th, 1866, purse $1000 mile heats best 3 in 5 in harness / 2 columns, 6 lines. J. Cameron on stone. 16.10x26.3 (Skeleton wagon, broadside to right.)
1866 L C&I

6204 Trotting Stallion Directum by Director / Record 2:05¼ / J. Cameron '93 on stone. 18.8x27.14(Small-wheeled, rubber-tired sulky to right.)
1894 L C&I

6205 Trotting Stallion George M. Patchen Jr. of California / By George M. Patchen, dam by Bellfounder. Bred and raised by Joseph Regan, Mount Holly, New Jersey / As he appeared in his great match with Commodore Vanderbilt / Over the Fashion Course, L.I., May 23rd, 1866, purse and stake $1500 mile heats best 3 in 5 in harness / additional lines / Time 2:30, 2:30, 2:27¾ / J. Cameron on stone. 16.10x 25.8 (Broadside to right.)
1866 L C&I

6206 Trotting Stallion Gray Eagle of Kentucky / By Gray Eagle, dam by Trustee. Cincinnati, Ohio, Nov. 10th, 1865, purse $2000 best 2 in 3, 2 mile heats to wagons / J. Cameron on stone. 16.12x26.4.
1866 L C&I

6207 Trotting Stallion / Hambletonian Mambrino / The Property of Montgomery and Rossell, Phila. / 3 additional lines. J.C. (Cameron) on stone. (¾ to right, high wheel.)
1879 S C&I

6208 Trotting Stallion Hannis driven by John E. Turner / By Relf's Mambrino Pilot / Record 2:17¾ / J. Cameron on stone. (To right, high-wheeled sulky.)
1881 S C&I

6209 Trotting Stallion Hannis driven by John E. Turner / By Relf's Mambrino Pilot / Record 2:19¼ / E. Forbes on stone. (Vignette, ¾ view to right, changes in composition from preceding.)
1877 S C&I

6210 Trotting Stallion Mambrino Champion, owned by M.F. Foote / Beekman,

Dutchess Co., N.Y. / 2 additional lines of pedigree. J. Cameron 1867 on stone. 18.10x25.4 (Standing in barn to left.)
1867 L C&I

6211 Trotting Stallion Mambrino Gift, owned by Messrs. Nye & Foster / By Relf's Mambrino Pilot, dam Waterwitch by Alexander's Pilot, Jr. / Winner of the first prize of $2750 of the $6000 purse for 2:26 horses at Rochester, N.Y. Aug. 13th, 1873 / 2 additional lines. J. Cameron on stone. (Vignette, broadside to right, high-wheeled sulky. 1874 S C&I

6212 Trotting Stallion Mambrino Gift, etc. / (Title exactly same as preceding, changes in composition from preceding.) und S C&I

6213 Trotting Stallion Monroe Chief, by Jim Monroe / Driven by Peter V. Johnston / Record 2:18¼ / Scott Leighton on stone. (Vignette, ¾ view to left.) 1881 S C&I

6214 Trotting Stallion Nelson by Young Rolfe / Record 2:14¼ / L.M. on stone. 1889 M C&I

6215 Trotting Stallion Nelson, Record 2:10 / (Vignette, ¾ to left.) 1889 S C&I

6216 Trotting Stallion Nelson by Young Rolfe / Record 2:10 / L.M. on stone (Vignette, ¾, low-wheeled sulky to left.) 1893 M C&I

6217 Trotting Stallion Palo Alto, by Electioneer / Record 2 / L.M. on stone (High-wheeled sulky to right, vignette.) 1890 S C&I

6218 Trotting Stallion Patron, Record 2:14¼ / (Vignette.) 1887 S C&I

6219 Trotting Stallion Phallas, driven by E. D. Bithers / by Dictator, dam Betsy Trotwood, by Black Chief / Record 2:15½ / Jno. Cameron on stone. 17.10x27. Printed in oil colors by Currier & Ives. (¾ view to right, high-wheeled sulky.) 1883 L C&I

6220 Trotting Stallion Santa Claus, by Strathmore / Record 2:17½/(Vignette, high-wheeled sulky to right, broadside.) 1881 S C&I

6221 Trotting Stallion Smuggler owned by H. S. Russell [Milton, Mass.] / By Blanco, dam by Herod's Tuckahoe / Winner of the Great Stallion Race for the Championship of the United States at Mystic Park, Medford, Mass. Sept. 15th, 1874 / 3 additional lines. J. Cam-

eron on stone. (Vignette, broadside, driver with beard.) 1875 S C&I

6222 Trotting Stallion Smuggler, owned by H. S. Russell, etc. / Title exactly as preceding. (¾ view, driver with mustache and other changes in composition.) 1874 S C&I

6223 Trotting Stallion Stamboul, by Sultan / Record 2:12¼ / L.M. on stone. (Vignette, ¾ view to right, high wheel.) 1890 S C&I

6224 Trotting Stallion Steamboat / 1890 S C&I

6225 Trotting Stallion Tom Moore, driven by Dan'l. Mace / Sired by Hambletonian, dam Townsend Mare raised by John Minchin, Goshen, Orange County, N.Y. / Trotted on the Fashion Course, L.I. Nov. 4th, 1869, in harness a mile against time 2:35, won in 2:31 / 1 additional line. J. Cameron '70 on stone. 17.2x26.8 (High wheel, broadside to right, grand- and judge's stands in background.) 1870 L C&I

6226 Trotting Stallion Wedgewood by Belmont / Record 2:19 / Scott Leighton on stone. (¾ view to left, high-wheeled sulky, vignette.) 1881 S C&I

6227 Trout Brook, The / F. F. Palmer, Del. 11.3x15.8. 1862 M C&I

6228 Trout Fishing / From nature and on stone by F. F. Palmer. 12.8x20.3. 1852 L N.C.

6229 Trout Pool, The / 8.8x12.7 (Fisherman on left bank, cider mill in background.) und S C&I

6230 Trout Stream, The / From nature and on stone by F. F. Palmer. 14.11x20.2 1852 L C&I

6231 Trout versus Gout / #164 / J. Schutz on stone. (Same as "Waiting for a Bite" No. 6488. Copied from the painting "The Enthusiast" by Theodore Lane.) und S N.C.

6232 Troy Fire Company / (View of fire in John C. Andrews Music Store, Troy, N.Y.) und S N.C.

Truckee River, Route to California See: No. 5225.

6233 True Daughter of the North, The / 1870 S C&I

6234 True Daughter of the South, The / (Half length vignette.) 1870 S C&I

6235 True Friends, The / (Girl, asleep, head pillowed on black dog.)
und S C&I

6236 True Issue, or "That's Whats the Matter," The / (Lincoln and Jeff Davis tearing a map of the United States apart, McClellan trying to bring them together, vignette.)
1864 S C&I

6237 True Peace Commissioner, The /
und S C&I

6238 True Portrait of / our Blessed Saviour, The / Sent by Publius Lentullus to the Roman Senate / 11.15x8.8.
und S C&I

6239 True Portrait of our Virgin Mary, The /
und S C&I

6240 True Yankee Sailor, The /
und S N.C.

Trumbull, Lyman See: No. 5664.

6241 Trust / in the / Lord / (Vignette, scroll surrounded by flowers.)
1872 S C&I

6242 Trust Me Till I Sell My Dog? / (Sign says) "Tods are cash." / 8x12.3 (Poorly dressed man asking bartender for a drink.)
1873 S C&I

Trustee (Horse) See: No. 911.

6243 Try Our Clams / (Vignette, figure made of clams, evidently intended as an ad for a restaurant.)
1875 S C&I

6244 Trying It On / (Vignette, Grant in barroom asking "Uncle Sam" for another turn, Uncle Sam refusing. Sign says "The Washington Hotel — U. Sam, Proprietor.")
1874 S C&I

6245 Tshu-Gue-Ga / A Celebrated Chief, half Winnebago and half French / Sketched at Green Bay Treaty 1827 by J. O. Lewis. J. Cameron, Lith. N.Y. (From Lewis' "Aboriginal Portfolio." Vignette.)
und S C.C.

6246 Tug ob War, De! / Thos. Worth on stone. (Vignette, colored comic, companion to "Done Gone Busted" No. 1604.)
1883 S C&I

6247 "Tumbled To it" / Thos. Worth on stone. (White man, Indian and lion clinging to overturned canoe, vignette, companion to "Got the Drop On Him" No. 2455.)
1881 S C&I

6248 Turn of the Tune, The / Traveller playing the "Arkansas Traveller" / 2 additional lines. Cameron on stone. 7.14 x12.8 (Companion to "The Arkansas Traveller" No. 270.)
1875 S C&I

Turner, John E. See: No. 5708.

6249 'Twas a calm Still Night /
1880 V.S. C&I

6250 'Twas a Calm Still Night / (Vignette, midnight serenade by cats in backyard.)
1875 S C&I

6251 T. W. Dorr / Inaugurated Governor of Rhode Island, May 3, 1842 /
und S N.C.

Tweed, Wm. See: Nos. 614, 5664.

6252 "Twere vain to tell thee all I feel" / 2 additional lines. (Vignette, doctor at bedside of patient.)
und S C&I

Twilight (Yacht) See: No. 5105.

6253 Twilight Hour, The / "When the Kye Come Hame" / 11.4x15.8 (Couple seated by stream, cattle going home.)
und S C&I

6254 Twin Brother, The /
und S C&I

6255 Twin Monkeys, The /
und S C&I

6256 Twin Monkeys, The / "Darwin's Theory" / 11.5x7.14 (Full-length, monkey, full face.)
und S C&I

6257 Twin Screw S.S. Kensington / of the Red Star Line /
und S C&I

6258 Twin Screw Steamer Campania of the Cunard Line / 2 additional lines.
und S C&I

6259 Twin Screw Steamer Deutschland of the Hamburg American Line / 2 additional lines. (To left.)
und S C&I

6260 Twin Screw Steamer Lucania of the Cunard Line / 2 additional lines. 8.9x 14.15 (Broadside to right.)
und S C&I

6261 Two Beauties, The / (Upright, vignette.)
und S C&I

6262 Two Little "Fraid Cats" /
1863 S C&I

6263 Two little Fraid Cats / 8.4x12.10 (Mouse and 2 white kittens.)
und S C&I

6264 "Two Minute Clip, A" / 12.1x19 (3 horses to right, low-wheeled sulkies.)
1893 M C&I

6265 Two Pets, The / #31 (2 girls at dressing table, upright, full length.)
und S N.C.

6266 Two Pets, The / #561 / 11.12x8.9 (Full length, girl with pantalettes, dog on table, exterior scene, top corners round.) 1848 S N.C.

6267 Two Pets, The / (Girl with young deer, full length.)
und M C&I

6268 Two pets, The / 12.1x8.13 (Woman and children.) und S C&I

6269 Two Sisters, The / #159 / 12.3x8.7 (¾ length, seated in open window.)
1845 S N.C.

6270 Two Sisters, The / 10x8 (Half length, oval in rectangle.)
und S N.C.

6271 "Two Souls with but a Single Thought" / 9.12x13.8 (Colored couple on porch, moonlight, eating 1 large slice of watermelon, vignette.)
1889 S C&I

6272 Two to Go! / Thos. Worth on stone. (Comic Billiard print, vignette, companion to "Got Em Both" Nos. 2453-4.)
1882 S C&I

6273 Two to Go! / 22.4x37 (Same composition as preceding.)
1892 L C&I

6274 Two to Go / 1892 S C&I

6275 "Two Twenty" on the Road / J. Cameron on stone. (Vignette, fine rig and driver.) 1875 S C&I

6276 Two Watchers, The / (Small boy asleep, dog on guard, slightly rounded corners.) und S C&I

Tyler, John **See:** No. 3281.

U

6277 Uebergabe des Kaisers Napoleon III, an den Konig Wilhelm von Preussen zu Sedan, Frank Reich 2 Sept. 1870 / 8.3x12.8 (3 additional lines — Surrender of the French at Sedan.)
1870 S C&I

Umbria (Steamship) **See:** No. 4431.
Una (Yacht) **See:** No. 5105.

6278 Unbolted / Thos. Worth on stone. (Horse running away, driver standing on axle of 2 remaining wheels of 4-wheeled rig.) und S C&I

6279 "Uncle Sam" Making new Arrangements / (Uncle Sam standing on steps of White House, holding a "Wanted" sign; in other hand a bill reading "This is to certify that I have hired A. Lincoln for 4 years from March 1st, 1861. Lincoln with satchel and axe. Buchanan seen about to leave with bag marked "Dirty Linen". Bell, Breckinridge, and Douglas applying for the position. Vignette.)
1860 S C&I

Uncle Sam **See:** Nos. 2769, 3555-6, 4489, 5843, 6244.

6280 Uncle Tom and Little Eva / Eva Gayly Laughing, was hanging a wreath of roses round his neck / "Oh, Tom, you look so funny" / #511.
und S N.C.

6281 Unconscious Sleeper, The / (Child asleep, while kittens eats food on her plate.) und S C&I

6282 Under Cliff — on the Hudson / 8.8x12.8. und S C&I

6283 Under the Rose / (Vignette, half length, girl smelling bouquet.)
1872 S C&I

Union Course, L.I. **See:** Nos. 555-6, 897, 911, 932, 938, 1666, 1758-9, 2344, 2420, 3146, 3168, 3382-3, 3399, 3847, 3952, 4763, 4925, 5620, 5811, 5942, 6202.

6284 Union Iron Clad Monitor "Montauk", The / Destroying the Rebel Steamship "Nashville" on the Ogeechee River near Savannah, Ga. Feby. 27th, 1863 / 8.1x12.9.
und S C&I

6285 Union League of America Certificate / 9x12.7 (Portraits of Washington and Jackson.) 1863 S C&I

6286 Union Place Hotel, / Union Square, New York / South East corner of Broadway & 14th Street / This hotel is situated in the most fashionable and elegant quarter of the city, and is unsurpassed in all it's departments for convenience, quietness and luxury / J. C. Wheeler, John Wheeler, Proprietors. F. F. Palmer, Del. 8.11x11.14.
und S N.C.

6287 Union Soldier's Discharge Certificate, The / 15x11.8 (Portraits of Sherman, Grant, Sheridan, and Lincoln, battle scenes at top and bottom.)
1865 S C&I

6288 Union Volunteer, The / (4 lines of verse in 2 columns.)
1861 S C&I

6289 Union Volunteer, The / Home from the War / 13.9x17.12.
1863 L C&I

6290 Union Volunteer, The / Off for the War / 1863 L C&I

6291 United American / Patriotism, Charity & Harmony / #653 / 8.15x11.13 (Full-length figure in regalia.) 1849 S N.C.

6292 United States Army leaving the Gulf Squadron 9th March 1847, The / Drawn by J. M. Ladd, Esq. U.S. Navy. 7.15x13. 1847 S N.C.

6293 United States Capitol, The / On Capitol Hill, Washington, D.C. / Congress-Senate / The Capitol is Built of Yellow Sandstone / In the Southern Extension / 3 additional lines. 9x14.4. und S C&I

6294 United States Capitol / Washington, D.C. / #593 / 7.15x12.7 (¾ view from left.) und S N.C.

6295 United States Frigate "St. Lawrence" 50 guns, The / #295 / Title in plate. (Broadside to right, sails furled.) und S N.C.

6296 United States, late Holt's Hotel / J. H. Colin, Del. 13.12x17.8. und M N.C.

6297 United States Mail Steamship / "Baltic" / Collins Line / Builders, hull by Brown and Bell, N.Y. / Engines by Allaire Works, N.Y. / 12 additional lines of dimensions. 1851 L N.C.

6298 U.S. Brig-of-War Somers, The / A mutiny was discovered on board this vessel Novr. 26th, 1842 while on her homeward voyage from the coast of Africa, and the three ringleaders, Philip Spencer, Midshipman, Samuel Cromwell, Boatswain's Mate, and Elijah Small, Seaman, were hung at the yard arm Dec. 1st, 1842 which completely suppressed the mutiny / (Broadside view of ship showing men hanging from yard arm.) und S N.C.

6299 U.S. Brig Porpoise in a Squall, The / und S N.C.

6300 U.S. Cruiser "New York" / und L C&I

6300A U.S. Dragoons / Cutting their way through a Mexican Ambuscade / #428 / 8.8x12.12 (Dragoon in foreground on white horse facing left, holding reins in left hand.) 1846 S N.C.

6301 U.S. Dragoons / Cutting their way through a Mexican Ambuscade / #428/ 8.6x 12.10 (Dragoon on white horse facing left, holding pistol in left hand, other changes in composition.) 1847 S N.C.

6302 U.S. Dragoons / Cutting their way through a Mexican Ambuscade / Guerillas — Guerilla Chief / #428 / 8.7x 12.10 (Dragoon on white horse to right. Much better drawing than preceding 2. Other changes in composition.) 1847 S N.C.

6303 U.S. Frigate Constitution / 3 additional lines of description. und S N.C.

6304 U.S. Frigate Constitution / #88 (Broadside to right. Ship occupies more space on plate.) und S N.C.

6305 U.S. Frigate Cumberland, 54 guns/ The Flagship of the Gulf Squadron, Comm. Perry / #89 / 8.12x12.12 (New York City in background, title in plate.) 1848 S N.C.

6306 U.S. Frigate Cumberland, 54 guns/ The Flag Ship of the Gulf Squadron, Comm. Perry / #607 / 8.11x12.11 (New York City in background, title in plate.) 1848 S N.C.

6307 U.S. Frigate Independence, 64 guns / (New York City and Governor's Island in background.) 1841 S N.C.

6308 U.S. Frigate "St. Lawrence", 50 guns, The / 1847 S N.C.

6309 U.S. Frigate "St. Lawrence", 50 Guns, The / #295 (Title in plate, sails furled, to right.) und S N.C.

6310 U.S. Frigate "Savannah" 60 guns / 1843 S N.C.

6311 U.S. Frigate United States capturing H.B.M. Frigate Macedonian, The / Fought Octr. 25th, 1812 / 8.2x12.15 Lith. & Pub. by N. Currier, 2 Spruce St. & 169 Broadway, N.Y. und S N.C.

6312 U.S. Mail Steamship "Adriatic" / 1350 Horse Power / 1856 S N.C.

6313 U.S. Mail Steamship "Arctic" / 1850 M N.C.

6314 U.S. Mail Steam Ship / Arctic / Collins Line / Builders Hull by Wm. H. Brown, Engines by Stillman Allen & Co. Novelty Works N.Y. / 2 columns of 2 lines. 13.12x21.13 (Broadside to left.) 1850 L N.C.

6315 U.S. Mail Steam Ship / Atlantic / 8.6x12.15. 1850 S N.C.

THE UNITED STATES FRIGATE "ST. LAWRENCE." 50 GUNS.

6316 U.S. Mail Steam Ship Atlantic / Collins Line / Builders Hull by Wm. H. Brown, N.Y., Engines by Stillman Allen & Co. Novelty Works, N.Y. / 2 columns of 3 lines. #457 (Sail and flag at stern, broadside to right.)
1852 S N.C.

6317 U.S. Mail Steam Ship Atlantic / Collins Line / Builders Hull by Wm. H. Brown, N.Y., Engines by Stillman Allen & Co. Novelty Works, N.Y. / 2 columns of 3 lines. #458 / 8.2x12.13 (Second state, composition same as above except sail and flag eliminated.)
1852 S N.C.

6318 U.S. Mail Steam Ship Atlantic / Builders, Hull by Wm. H. Brown, N.Y., Engines by Stillman Allen & Co. Novelty Works, N.Y. / 2 columns of 6 lines. (Broadside to right.)
1850 M N.C.

6319 U.S. Mail Steam Ship Atlantic / Balance of title same as preceding. 14.2x21 (Broadside to right.)
1850 L. N.C.

6320 U.S. M. Steam Ship Baltic / Collins Line / Brown and Bell, N.Y., Builders / #460 / 2 columns of 4 lines.

8.5x12.14 (Broadside to left.)
1852 S N.C.

6321 U.S. Mail Steam Ship / Baltic / Collins Line / Builders, Hull by Brown & Bell, N.Y. Engines by Allaire Works N.Y. / 2 columns of 7 and 6 lines. 13.12x21.12 (Broadside to right.)
1850 L N.C.

6322 U.S. Mail Steam Ship "California" /   und S C&I

6323 U.S. Mail Steam Ship / Pacific Collins Line / Builders, Hull by Brown & Bell, N.Y. Engines by Allaire Works, N.Y. / 2 columns of 6 lines. 14.1x21.12 (Broadside to left.)
1850 L N.C.

6324 U.S. Mail Steam Ship / Pacific Collins Line /   1850 S N.C.

6325 U.S. Military Academy, West Point / From the opposite shore / F. F. Palmer, Del. 11.2x15.10 (Group of 4 in foreground. Shows river steamer.)
1862 M C&I

6326 U.S. Post Office, New York / 9.2x 12.14.   und S C&I

6327 U.S. Ship North Carolina, 102 guns / Title in plate. 9x12.14 (New York in

background, Castle Garden on right.)
1843 S N.C.

6328 U.S. Ship North Carolina / Title in plate. 9.12x13.2.
1843 S N.C.

6329 U.S. Ship North Carolina, 102 Guns / H. Diss, pinx. (Castle Garden and battery at right.)
1843 S N.C.

6330 U.S. Ship North Carolina, 102 guns / 9.12x13.2 (Skyline of New York and Castle Garden in background.)
1844 S N.C.

6331 U.S. Ship of the Line "Delaware" / #587 / 8.12x12.12.
und S N.C.

6332 U.S. Ship of the Line in a Gale / #557 / 8.5x12.13.   1847 S N.C.

6333 U.S. Ship of the Line Ohio, 104 guns / #546 / 8.12x12.15. Title in plate. (Sailing to right, Governor's Island in background.)   1847 S N.C.

6334 U.S. Ship cf the Line Pennsylvania, 140 Guns / #404 / 1 additional line of dimensions. Title in plate. 8.12x13 (1 ship in background, broadside.)
und S N.C.

6335 U.S. Ship of the Line Pennsylvania, 140 guns / #404 (Changes in composi-

tion, ships in background, bow on.)
und S N.C.

6336 U.S. Sloop of War Albany, 22 guns / Title in plate. #291 / 9.1x13.3.
und S N.C.

6337 U.S. Sloop of War in a Gale / 9.4 13.4.   und S N.C.

6338 U.S. Sloop of War "Kearsarge" 7 guns, sinking the Pirate "Alabama", 8 guns; / Off Cherbourg, France, Sunday, June 19th, 1864 / 2 additional lines description. 8x12.8.
1864 S C&I

6339 U.S. Sloop of War "Kearsarge" 7 guns, Sinking the Pirate "Alabama" 8 guns / Off Cherbourg, France, Sunday, June 19th, 1864 / (2 additional lines of description. "Kearsarge" in foreground, 2 American flags shown. Entirely different composition from preceding.)   1864 S C&I

6340 U.S. Sloop of War Vincennes, 20 guns / Title in plate. #815 / 8.15x12.15.
1845 S N.C.

6341 U.S. Steam Frigate "Mississippi" / In the Gulf of Mexico, March, 1847 / #588 / 8.12x12.12 (Scene shows frigate in heavy weather, waves breaking over bow.)   1848 S N.C.

U. S. SHIP OF THE LINE OHIO, 104 GUNS.

6342 U.S. Steam Frigate "Mississippi" in a Typhoon, The / On her passage from Samoa, Japan to the Sandwich Islands Oct. 7th, 1854 Lat. 35' 59" N. Long. 153' 47" E. / E Brown, Jr., Del. 15.15x20.14.   1857 L C&I

6343 U.S. Steam Frigate "Niagara" / Modeled by George Steers, Built at the Navy Yard, Brooklyn, N.Y. / #467 / 1 additional line and 2 columns of 3 and 4 lines. 7.12x13 (Vignette, sailing to left.)   und S C&I

6344 U.S. Steam Frigate "Niagara" / Modeled by George Steers, Built at the Navy Yard, Brooklyn, New York / 1 additional line and 2 columns of 3 and 4 lines. C. Parsons, Del. 17.4x26.11.
                                 1857 L C&I

6345 U.S. Steam Frigate, Princeton / N. Sarony on stone. Title in plate.
                                 1844 S N.C.

6346 U. S. Steam Frigate "Princeton" /
                                 1845 S N.C.

6347 U.S. Steam Frigate "Wabash" 60 guns / Off Cape Hatteras 7th of January, 1857 / #292 / 8.8x12.14.
                                 und S C&I

6348 "Unser Karl" / Prinz Friedrich Karl / Von Preussen / (Vignette portrait.)   und S C&I

6349 Up in a Balloon / (Tilden and Hendricks burning rags to inflate balloon entitled "Tammany Gasbag". Basket entitled "Democratic Platform manufactured at St. Louis, 1876." Hendricks suggests that specie be thrown out in order to keep bag up.)
                                 1876 S C&I

6350 Up the Hudson / (View near Anthony's Nose. Composition similar to "Scenery of the Hudson" No. 5421.)
                                 und S C&I

6351 Upper and Lower Bay of New York / From the Battery looking South West / 8.8x12.8 (Castle Garden — Bedloes Island—Bergen Point keyed above title.)   und S C&I

6352 Upper Canada College / Dedicated by permission to the Revd. I. H. Harris, D.D. Principal of Upper Canada Colledge, by His Obt. Hb'le Servt, Thomas Young. T Young, Arct. Delt. Toronto, U.C. 1835, J. H. Bufford on stone. 11.14 x17.14.   und M N.C.

6353 Upper Lake of Killarney, The / Kerry County, Ireland.
                                 und S C&I

Utah See: No. 2649.

Utica Race Course See: Nos. 909, 3304.

V

6354 Valkyrie / Challenger for the America's Cup, October 1893 / 10x13.9.
                                 und S C&I

Valkyrie (Yacht) See: No. 6454.

Vallandingham, C. L. See: Nos. 1028, 4824.

6355 Valley Falls, Virginia / 8x12.8 (Man fishing in foreground.)
                                 und S C&I

Valley Forge See: No. 6519.

6356 Valley of the Black Water, Ireland /   und S C&I

6357 Valley of the Shenandoah, The / F. F. Palmer, Del. 14.15x20.1 (Showing an army encampment.)
                                 1864 L C&I

6358 Valley of the Susquehanna, The / E. Blummer on stone. 14.12x20.10 (Group of 3 in foreground.)
                                 und L C&I

6359 Van Amberg & Co's Triumphal Car / Passing the Astor House, Apr. 20th, 1846 / #417 / 8x13.
                                 1846 S N.C.

Van Buren, Martin See: Nos. 2478, 4013, 4028-35, 4165, 4884, 5569.

Vanderbilt, Commodore See: Nos. 612, 732, 897, 1907, 2643, 2946, 4256-9, 5716.

Vanderbilt (Steamship) See: Nos. 1169-70, 5798.

Vander Hayden Palace, Albany, N.Y. See: No. 4567.

Van Ness, Frank See: No. 5708.

6360 Vantile Mack, the infant Lambert, or / Giant Baby!! / 7 years old, weighs 257 pounds! / Measures 61 inches around the chest!!. 36 inches around the leg!! / with his mother only 24 years of age / Now appearing at Barnum's American Museum / (Fulllength figure, upright, vignette.)
                                 und S C&I

Van Wart, Isaac See: "Capture of Andre" 804-6.

6361 Vase of Flowers, The / #536 (Upright, vignette.)   1847 S N.C.

6362 Vase of Flowers, The / (Different composition and type of vase, upright, vignette.) 1870 S C&I

6363 Vase of Flowers, The / #536 (Roses, lilies, etc. in ornamental vase.)
und S C&I

6364 Vase of Fruit, The /
1864 M C&I

Vassar College **See:** No. 4123.

Veendam (Steamship) **See:** No. 5243.

6365 Velocipede, The / "We can beat the swiftest steed, / With our new Velocipede" / (Race between horse and sulky and velocipede.) 1869 S C&I

6366 Venice / From the Canal of the Guidecca / J. M. W. Turner, R. A. Pinxt. 14.14x20.3 (Moonlight scene.)
und L C&I

6367 Venice / From the Canal of the Guidecca / J. M. W. Turner, R. A. Pinxt. 14.14x20.3 (Identical composition to preceding except daylight scene.) und L C&I

Venice **See:** Foreign Views, Misc.

Vera Cruz **See:** Nos. 601-2, 797, 1194, 3432, 3933, 4113, 4396, 5512-3.

Vermont **See:** No. 670.

6368 Very Rev. Father Thos. N. Burke C.P. / The Champion of Irish History/ (Vignette, half length portrait.)
und S C&I

6369 Very Reverend, The / Theobold Mathew / #122 / 8.15x11.3.
1848 S N.C.

6370 Very Reverend, The / Father Theobold Mathew / (Changes in composition from preceding.)
und S C&I

6371 Very Warm Corner, A / Thos. Worth on stone. (Vignette, hunter and dog caught in traps, comic.)
1883 S C&I

Vesta (Yacht) **See:** Nos. 2634- 4450, 6817.

Vesta (French Steamship) **See:** No. 6791.

Vestris, Madlle. **See:** Nos. 3852.

Vicksburg **See:** Nos. 51, 3489, 5507.

Victoria, Queen **See:** Nos. 1799, 4012, 5020-7.

Victoria (Steamship) See: No. 5529.

6372 Victorious Attack on Fort Fisher, N.C. Jan. 15th, 1865 / By the U.S. Fleet under Rear Admiral D. D. Porter,

And troops under Major General A. H. Terry / F.F. Palmer, Del. 15.11x22.13.
1865 L C&I

6373 Victorious Bombardment of Port Royal, S.C., Nov. 7th, 1861 / By the United States Fleet under command of Commodore Dupont / 8.4x11.15.
und S C&I

6374 Victory Doubtful / 8.2x12.8 (Children laughing at window, as wife pushes husband out of door, companion to "Blue Monday" No. 579.)
und S C&I

6375 Victory of Roanoke, Feb. 8th, 1862, The / The brilliant and decisive bayonet charge of the New York 9th. Hawkin's Zouaves /
und S C&I

6376 View down the Ravine / At Trenton Falls, N.Y. / 10.7x15.3 (Moonlight scene, 5 figures on ledge in right foreground.) und M C&I

6377 View down the river / (1 of 9 landscape views of N.Y. State printed on 1 sheet **See:** No. 3439.)
und V.S. C&I

6378 View from Fort Putnam / West Point, Hudson River. / #239 (Soldier in foreground.) und S N.C.

6379 View from Fort Putnam / West Point, Hudson River, N. Y. / 8x12.5 (Man and dog in foreground, other slight changes.) und S C&I

6380 View from Fort Putnam / West Point, Hudson River, N.Y. / 8x12.8 (Sound Steamer shown, no figures in foreground.) und S C&I

6381 View from Peekskill, Hudson River, N.Y. / F. F. Palmer, Del.
1862 M C&I

6382 View from the Rock of Gibraltar of the burning of the / U.S. Steam Frigate Missouri / On the evening of August 26th, 1843 /
und S N.C.

6383 View from West Point /
und S C.C.

6384 View from West Point / Hudson River / #518. und S N.C.

6385 View in Dutchess County, N.Y. / F. F. Palmer, Del.
und L C&I

6386 View in Switzerland / Pl. 2 (Vignette, road with several figures, farm buildings, etc. Printed on same sheet with "On the Seine" No. 4610.)
und S C&I

[276]

6387 View near Highbridge / Harlem River, N.Y. / 10.14x15.8. F. F. Palmer, Del. (Sometimes erroneously marked F. F. Pamer. Later the title was changed to "The Riverroad" No. 5158.)
und M C&I

6388 View of Astoria L.I. / From the New York side / F. F. Palmer, Del. 11x15.10 (Steamer Sylvan Grove and 6 sailboats shown.)
1862 M C&I

6389 View of Baltimore / Vue de Baltimore — Ansicht von Baltimore / #598 / 8.1x12.11.   1848 S N.C.

6390 View of Boston / Title repeated in French and German / #627.
1848 S N.C.

6391 View of Bunker Hill & Monument June 17, 1843 / Pub. by J. Fisher, Boston. 8.7x12.1 (Shows ceremony at monument during Webster's speech.)
und S N.C.

6392 View of Chapultepec and Molino Del Rey [After the battle] / City of Mexico in the distance / where Worth's division of the United States Army 3100 strong met and defeated the whole Mexican Army 14000 strong under Genl. Santa Anna Sept. 8th, 1847 / From a sketch taken from Casa Del Mata by H. Meendez and forwarded by Lieut. Larkin Smith U.S.A. / #553 / 8.6x12.8.   1847 S N.C.

6393 View of Chicago / (Published also as "Chicago As It Was.")
und S C&I

6394 View of Esopus Creek / (N.Y.)
und S C&I

6395 View of Harper's Ferry, Va. / From the Potomac Side / 14.11x20.5.
und L C&I

6396 View of King Street City of Toronto, N.C. / T. Young Archt. Delt. Toronto, N.C. 1835. J. H. Bufford, Del. on stone. 11.14x17.14. N. Currier's Lith., N.Y.   und S N.C.

6397 View of Mauch Chunk from the Narrows / E. Valois. 4.14x7.
und S C.C.

6398 View of Madison the Capital of Wisconsin / Taken from the Water Cure / South side of Lake Menona, 1855 / S. H. Donnel, Del. C. Currier's Lith, 33 Spruce St., N.Y.
und M C.C.

6399 View of New York / 8.8x13 (Bird's eye view from south.)
1860 S C&I

6400 View of New York / #626 / 8.8x 12.15 (Bird's eye view from south, slight changes in composition from preceding.)   1869 S C&I

6401 View of New York / 8.7x12.15 (Bird's eye view from point over Governor's Island.)   und S C&I

6402 View of New York / From Brooklyn Heights / Palmer, Del. 11.9x17.2 16 references (First state.)
1849 M N.C.

6403 View of New York / From Brooklyn Heights / Palmer, Del. 18 references. 12.9x17.2 (1 inch added to height of stone, 2 additional references are "Delmonico's, Broadway" and "Brick Church" to which spire has been added.)   1849 M N.C.

6404 View of New York / From Weehawken / Title repeated in French and German / #626 / 8.3x12.11.
1848 S N.C.

6405 View of New York / From Weehawken / F. F. Palmer, Del. 25 references. 12.11x21.6 (Shows Steam Boats "New York" and "Isaac Newton.")
1849 L N.C.

6406 View of New York / Jersey City, Hoboken and Brooklyn / Sketched and on stone by C. Parsons. 19.11x33.4 (Steamboats Commonwealth, Metropolis, and Plymouth Rock shown — Similar to "City of New York" No. 1103.)   1858 L C&I

6407 View of New York Bay / From Staten Island /   und S C&I

6408 View of Philadelphia / (Bird's eye view.)   1875 S C&I

6409 View of San Francisco, California/ Taken from Telegraph Hill April 1850 by Wm. B. McMurtrie, draughtsman of the U.S. Surveying Expedition / Published by N. Currier N. Y. — Wm. B. McMurtrie San Francisco. Clarkes Point — Rincon Point — Happy Valley — Long Wharf Building — Pacific St. Wharf (Building) — Apollo Warehouse — Niantic Warehouse — Sansome St. — Portsmouth Square keyed above title. On stone by F. Palmer. 14.14x29.14(Top corners rounded.)
1851 L N.C.

6410 View of Santiago / Cuba /
und S C&I

6411 View of the Distributing Reservoir / On Murray's Hill — City of New York / 2 columns, 3 lines each. 8.1x 12.12.   1842 S N.C.

6412 View of the Federal Hall of the City of New York, A / As appeared in the year 1797; with the adjacent buildings thereto / From the original drawing by George Holland. Drawn expressly for D. T. Valentine's Manual. 14.1x20.10.   und M C.C.

6413 View of the Great Conflagration of Dec. 16th and 17th, 1835; From Coenties Slip / Sketched and drawn on stone by J. H. Bufford / Published by J. Disturnell 156 Broad Way & J. H. Bufford, 10 Beekman St. / N. Currier's Lith. No. 1 Wall St. 9.6x12.7.
               und M N.C.

6414 View of the Great Conflagration of Dec. 16th and 17th, 1835, etc. / (Same as preceding except N. Currier's Lith. N.Y. 1st line under title.) Entered by Act of Congress by J. H. Bufford.
               1836 M N.C.

6415 View of the Great Conflagration at New York July 19th, 1845. / From the Bowling Green / Nearly 300 buildings destroyed — Estimated loss of property, $7,000,000. / 8.3x12.12 (Companion to following, view looking up Broadway. Also see No. 6425.)
               1845 S N.C.

6416 View of the Great Conflagration at New York July 19th, 1845. / Nearly 300 buildings destroyed — From Cor.

Broad & Stone Sts. — Estimated loss of property $7,000,000. / 8.3x12.7 (Also see No. 6425.)   1845 S N.C.

6417 View of the Great Receiving Reservoir, / Yorkville, City of New York / 8.4x12.14. 2 columns, 4 lines each.
               1841 S N.C.

6418 View of the Great Receiving Reservoir, / Yorkville, City of New York. / 8.4x12.14. 2 columns, 3 lines each.
               1842 S N.C.

6419 View of the High Falls at Trenton/ West Canada Creek, N.Y. /
               und S C&I

6420 View of the Houses of Parliament and Government Offices, City of Toronto, N.C. / T. Young, Archt. Delt. Toronto, N.C. 1835. J. H. Bufford, Del. on stone. 11.14x17.14. N. Currier's Lith., N.Y.   und S N.C.

6421 View of the Hudson River / From Ruggles House, Newburgh / #256 / 8.3 x11.11 (Porch in right foreground, 1 male figure, arbor on left. Sailboats shown, no steamboats. See Nos. 6433-4.)   1846 S N.C.

6422 View of the Park, Fountain & City Hall / #401 / 8.1x11.10 (Wall on left, awnings over sidewalk, 2 flags on City Hall, 1 flag on Park Row.)
               und S N.C.

VIEW OF THE TERRIFIC EXPLOSION AT THE GREAT FIRE IN NEW YORK.

6423 View of the Park, Fountain and City Hall, New York. / #401 / 8x11.10 (Wall of Astor House and awnings over sidewalk at left, flags to left, view from higher elevation than preceding and less of Park Row shown.) 1847 S N.C.

6424 View of the Park, Fountain and City Hall, N.Y. 1851 / 8.2x12.13 (Similar to preceding except more traffic on street in foreground. 3 flags to right.)

6425 View of the terrific explosion at the great fire in New York / Engine No. 22 destroyed and several lives lost. From Broad St., July 19th, 1845. 17 stores blown up / 8.2x12.6. (Companion to Nos. 6415-6.) 1845 S N.C.

6426 View of Waterbury Conn. / From West Side Hill / W. H. Hewitt, Del. Published by Lucien I. Bisbee, Waterbury, 1837. 15.1x22.9. 1837 L N.C.

6427 View of West End, St. Croix West Indies / F. Scholten Fec. 1838. 8.6x16.4. und S N.C.

6428 View of West Point / und S C.C.

6429 View of West Rock / Near New Haven, Conn. / Painted by J. Smith. 15.11x23.7. 1864 L C&I

6430 View on Broadway, N.Y. / Showing the Building of / The United States Mutual Accident Association / (320 & 322 Broadway) 25.14x19.11. 1886 L C&I

6431 View on Esopus Creek / (Cattle in foreground.) und S C&I

6432 View on Fulton Avenue, Brooklyn, L.I. / #464 (Vignette, same composition as Crayon Studies No. 1299.) und S N.C.

6433 View on Hudson River / From Ruggles House, Newburgh / 8.8x12.7 (2 women, 2 children on vine-covered porch, tree on left, sailing boats on river.) und S C&I

6434 View on Hudson River / From Ruggles House, Newburgh / 8.7x12.7 (Man, woman and child on porch, no large tree at left, river steamer and yachts more prominent, other changes in composition, see also No. 6421.) und S C&I

6435 View on Lake George, N.Y. / F. F. Palmer, Del. 15x20.6 (Only life shown is deer swimming.) 1866 L C&I

6436 View on Lake George / F. Palmer, Del. (Changes in composition.) und S C&I

6437 View on Long Island, N.Y. / F. Palmer, Del. 14.12x20.8 (Location shown is Spinney Hill, near Manhasset. Strange as it may seem this is the only large folio decorative view published by the firm marked Long Island.) 1857 L C&I

6438 View on Montgomery Creek / Near the Hudson / (Boathouse on left.) und S C&I

6439 View on the Delaware / Near Easton, Pennsylvania / (Row boat in foreground, rainbow in background.) und S C&I

6440 View on the Delaware / "Water Gap" in the distance. / Painted by Geo. Inness. 14.12x22.9. (Railroad train in background.) 1860 L C&I

6441 View on the Harlem River, N.Y. / The High Bridge in the distance / From nature and on stone by F. F. Palmer. 14.12x20.2 (Same stone as "Bass Fishing at Macomb's Dam," No. 375. Height increased by adding more sky. Foliage thickened on trees at left.) 1852 L C&I

6442 View on the Harlem River, N.Y. / The High Bridge in the distance /. und L C&I

6443 View on the Housatonic / Painted by C. H. Moore. 13.10x20.4 (A very attractive rural scene, and the only subject by this artist.) 1867 L C&I

6444 View on the Hudson / F. F. Palmer, Del. (Shows the "Crow's Nest.") und L C&I

6445 View on the Hudson / F.F. Palmer, Del. / 15 x 20.11 (Same view as preceding, with slight changes in composition and showing many more boats in river.) und L C&I

6446 View on the Hudson / (1 of 9 views of New York State. See: Landscape Cards No. 3439.) und V.S. C&I

6447 View on the Hudson / Crow's Nest / (Man sitting on rock, few small sailboats on river.) und S C&I

6448 View on the Hudson / Crow's Nest / (Changes in composition from preceding.) und S C&I

6449 Views on the Potomac / Near Harper's Ferry / F. F. Palmer, Del. 15x 20.3. 1866 L C&I

VIEW ON BROADWAY, NEW YORK.
Showing the Building of
THE UNITED STATES MUTUAL ACCIDENT ASSOCIATION.

6450 View on the Rhine / 8.8x12.8 (Castle in right background, pedestrians and wagons.) und S C&I

6451 View on the Rondout / F. F. Palmer, Del. / 10.3 x 15.7. und M C&I

6452 View on the St. Lawrence / Indian Encampment / 8x12.8 (Camp on left shore, 3 canoes in stream.) und S C&I

6453 View up the River / (1 of 9 views of New York State. See Landscape Cards No. 3439.) und V.S. C&I

6454 Vigilant and Valkyrie in a "Thrash to Windward" / In their International Race for "The America's Cup" Oct. 7th, 9th, and 13th, 1893 / Won by the Vigilant / 16x24.1. 1893 L C&I

6455 "Vigilant" / Defender of the "America's Cup" / 9.15 x 13.6. und S C&I

Vigilant (Yacht) See: Nos. 6454-5.

6456 Villa, Designed for Dav. Codwise, Esq. / By A. J. Davis, Arc't / 6.5x8.1 (From "Rural Residences" by A. J. Davis 1837.) und S N.C.

6457 Villa on the Hudson, A. / 9.14x17. 1869 M C&I

6458 Villa on the Hudson, A / 1870 S C&I

6459 Village Beauty, The / und S C&I

6460 Village Blacksmith, The / F. Palmer, Del. 9.13x14.15 (Smith at anvil, shop has wing, chimney on left side of building.) und M C&I

6461 Village Blacksmith, The / 9.15x 14.15 (Smith at forge, no wing on shop, large tree at left, chimney in center, and other slight changes.) und M C&I

6462 Village Blacksmith, The / F. F. Palmer, Del. 15.16x23.5 (6 lines of Longfellow's verse in 2 columns, entirely different composition from 2 preceding prints.) 1864 L C&I

6463 Village Chapel, near Paris / 2.11x 4.3 (1 of 9 views on Landscape Cards No. 3438.) und V.S. C&I

6464 Village Street, The / F. Palmer, Del. 10.7x14.14 (2 children in foreground feeding ducks in pond.) 1855 M C&I

6465 Village Street, The / 9.14x14.14 (More houses on street, no children in foreground.) und M C&I

A VILLA ON THE HUDSON.

Ville de Paris (Steamship) **See:** No. 5799.

Ville du Havre (Steamship) **See:** No. 5534.

Vincennes (Sloop) **See:** No. 6340.

6466 Viola / (Vignette, ¾ length.)
und L C&I

6467 Violet and Daisy / (Girls' heads.)
und S C&I

6468 Virgin & Child / #250 (Top corners of plate slightly round.)
und S C&I

6469 Virgin & Child, The / La Vierge et Enfant / La Virgen E Hijo / #259 (Ornamental scroll border.)
1848 S N.C.

6470 Virgin Mary, The / Le Virgine Hijo / #90 / 8.8x12.11 (Upright, full length figure holding Christ, ornamental border.)
1848 S N.C.

6471 Virgin Mary, The /
1849 S N.C.

6472 Virginia / (¾ length, roses each side, plain background.)
und S N.C.

6473 Virginia / (Vignette, half length.)
und S N.C.

6474 Virginia Home in the olden time, A / 8.7x12.8.
1872 S C&I

Virginia **See:** Nos. 380-2, 391-2, 395, 400, 402-3, 405, 410, 430, 435-6, 438-9, 528, 537, 539, 592, 1769, 1821-4, 2213, 2294, 2388, 2653, 2870-4, 4778, 4881, 5904-6, 5909-13, 6107-12, 6355, 6357, 6375, 6395, 6474, 6449.

6475 Virginia Water, Windsor Park. / 8.8x12.8.
und S C&I

6476 Virtue, Love and Temperance. / Love, Purity and Fidelity / (Female figure at side of man swearing off drink, table at left with cards, dice and drink.)
1851 S N.C.

6477 Vision, The /
und S N.C.

Vision (Brig) **See:** No. 687.

6478 Voltaire / By Tattler, dam Young Portia, by Mambrino Chief / Record 2:21¼ / J. Cameron on stone. (Vignette, ¾ view to right, high-wheeled sulky.)
1879 S C&I

Voltigeur (Horse) **See:** No. 2073.

6479 Voluntary manner in which some of the Southern volunteers enlist, The. / Thos. Worth on stone. (Volunteer forced to enlist at the point of a bayonet.)
und S C&I

6480 Volunteer Crossing the Finish Line / Proclaimed the victor by the guns of the flagship "Electra" in her second and final race for the "America's Cup" against the Scotch Cutter "Thistle" / over the outside course, from the Scotch Light Ship 20 miles to windward and return Sept. 30th, 1887 / Franklyn Bassford '87 on stone. 19.10x 28.
1887 L C&I

Volunteer (Yacht) **See:** Nos. 194, 4404, 5561, 6818.

Volunteer (Horse) **See:** No. 6482.

6481 Volunteer / Modelled by Edward Burgess of Boston for Genl. C. J. Paine / 2 additional lines of data and 2 columns of 5 lines each.
1887 L C&I

6482 Volunteer / The great Sire of Trotters / J. Cameron 1880 on stone. (Vignette, profile portrait to right.)
1880 S C&I

6483 Volunteer / 3 additional lines and 2 columns of 5 lines each.
1887 S C&I

6484 Waa-Na-Taa, or the foremost in battle / Chief of the Sioux Tribe / Painted by J.O. Lewis, at the treaty of Prairie du Chien, 1825. J. Cameron, Lith. (From Lewis' "Aboriginal Portfolio.")
und S C.C.

Wabash (Frigate) **See:** No. 6347.

6485 Wacht am Rhine, Die / Das Deutsche Schwert an dem Beschutzt de Deutschen Rhein / 12x8.8 (Full-length figure with sword and shield.)
und S C&I

Wade **See:** Nos. 3030, 5050.

6486 Wait for Me! / (Young girl stopping to pull up stocking.)
und S C&I

6487 Wait Your Turn / (Vignette, boy eating, while dog waits expectantly, full length.)
und S C&I

6488 Waiting for a Bite / #164 / 8x11.14. J. Schutz on stone. (Same composition as "Trout versus Gout" No. 6231, from the painting "The Enthusiast" by Theodore Lane.)
und S N.C.

6489 Waiting for a Drink / #651 (3 men outside "Liquidary" Club Room, 1 drinking from bottle. Another man, waiting says "I don't want to hurry you friend, but when you are done I'd thank you for the bottle." Third man says "O bountiful nature what a neck the fellow's got.")
und S N.C.

6490 Waking Up the Old Mare / Scott Leighton on stone. 15.12x24. Printed in oil colors. (Companion to "The Old Mare, the Best Horse" No. 4569.)
1881 L C&I

6491 Waking Up the Wrong Passenger/ "I say, old man keep your hooks out of my trousers" / Thos. Worth on stone. (Comic, railroad scene, vignette.)
1875 S C&I

Wales, South See: No. 1022.

6492 Walked home on his ear! / 11.15x9 (Mother leading boy by ear, after swimming.) 1878 S C&I

6493 Walk In! / und S C&I

Wall Street See: Nos. 1334-5, 5253.

Wamba (Horse) See: No. 896.

Wanderer (Yacht) See: No. 6821.

6494 War / #246 (Scene after battle, 2 men and horse dead at ruined bridge.)
und S C&I

6495 War President, A / Progressive Democracy / Entered by Peter Smith 1848 (Cartoon of Zachary Taylor.)
1848 S N.C.

6496 Warming Up / und S C&I

Wallace, Genl. See: No. 425.

6497 Warming Up / Thos. Worth on stone. (Vignette, group around stove in saloon, drinking.)
1884 S C&I

6498 Warming Up / L. Maurer on stone. 18.2x28.10 (Group of horses in front of grandstand, low-wheeled rubber-tired sulkies.) 1893 L C&I

Warren, Genl. Joseph See: Nos. 1515, 2955.

Warren, Genl. See: No. 2553.

6499 Warren Miller / (Facsimile signature) 19x16.8. und M C&I

Warren, Minnie See: No. 2307.

6500 Warwick Castle, / On the Avon / F. F. Palmer, Del. 11.12x15.9 (2 row-boats in foreground, castle right background.) und M C&I

Washington See: Nos. 539, 1516-22,

1975, 2232, 2261-2, 2337, 3396-8, 4022-7, 4392, 4885-91, 4897-4904, 5474, 6100, 6107-12.

6501 Washington / 23.4x13.7 (Half length, upright, slightly to right.)
und L C&I

6502 Washington / #187 / 11.13x8.4 (Slightly rounded corners, full length portrait, white horse, upright.)
und S N.C.

6503 Washington / 12x8.8 (Full length standing beside horse, right hand holding hat, left arm on horse.)
und S N.C.

6504 Washington / 12.2x8.12 (Full length, right hand on rock at side, orderly with horse in right background.) und S N.C.

6505 Washington / 1880 S C&I

6506 Washington / (¾ length in uniform, to right.) und M C&I

6507 Washington / (Bust to right, lace jabot.) und M C&I

6508 Washington / (Approximately 5x7, printed on same sheet with Martha Washington.) und V.S. C&I

6509 Washington and his Cabinet / George Washington; Genl. Henry Knox, Secy. of War; Alexander Hamilton, Secy of the Treasury; Thomas Jefferson, Secy of State; Edmund Randolph, Attorney General. (Vignette.) 1876 S C&I

6510 Washington and Lincoln / The Father and Saviour of our country / 14.15x10.15 (Upright, full length figures, corners slightly rounded.)
1865 M C&I

6511 Washington, Appointed Commander-in-Chief / 8.13x12.11 (3 lines description.) 1876 S C&I

6512 Washington As A Mason / 12x8.
und S C&I

6513 Washington As A Mason / 11.13x 8.6 (Full length figure, in Masonic regalia, top corners slightly rounded.)
1868 S C&I

6514 Washington at Home / Geo. Washn. Parke Custis, Genl. Washington, Eleanor Parke Custis, Mrs. Washington. / 16.12x23.15 (Composition similar to Washington Family — picture of Mount Vernon on wall.)
1867 L C&I

6515 Washington at Mount Vernon 1789/ "Agriculture is the most healthy, the most useful, and the most noble employment of man" Washington / #367 12.7x8.3 (Washington on horseback, inspecting work of 2 colored men, upright.)   1852 S N.C.

6516 Washington at Prayer /
          und S C&I

6517 Washington at Prayer / #90 / 11.13 x8.7 (Upright, scene in tent, hand on Bible.)   und S N.C.

6518 Washington at Princeton, January 3rd, 1777 / #386 / 8.8x13. H.B. on stone, copied by permission of Graham's Magazine. 2 additional lines.
          1846 S N.C.

6519 Washington at Valley Forge, Dec. 1777-8 / 11.9x8.9.
          und S N.C.

6520 Washington Columns, The / Yo-Semite Valley / 8.7x12.8 (Rowboat in foreground, no human figures.)
          und S C&I

6521 Washington / Crossing the Delaware / W. K. Hewitt on stone. (Upright, vignette, Washington to right, troops and boats in background.)
          und S N.C.

6522 Washington Crossing the Delaware / Evening previous to the battle of Trenton, Dec. 25, 1776 / #224 (Washington on horseback, river in background.)   und S N.C.

6523 Washington Crossing the Delaware / Evening previous to the battle of Trenton, Decemr. 25, 1776 / #69 / 8.5 x 12.5 (Washington and soldiers in boat.)
          und S C&I

6524 Washington Crossing the Delaware / Evening previous to the battle of Trenton, Decemr. 25, 1776 / J. Cameron on stone.   und S C&I

6525 Washington Crossing the Delaware / On the evening of Dec. 25th, 1776, previous to the battle of Trenton / 8.15x12.6 (Washington on white horse, on heights above river.)
          1876 S C&I

6526 Washington / Driven by Joel Conklin, in training for his match with Kemble Jackson, trotted to a 250 lb. wagon, in 2:43-2:44. Centreville Course L.I., Oct. 1st, 1855, match for $2000, mile heats to harness / L. Maurer on stone. 16.15x26.5 (2 columns, 2 lines.)
          1855 L N.C.

Washington, D.C. See: Nos. 792-4, 1122-3, 3548, 4391-4, 6541.

6527 Washington Family, The / George

and Martha Washington, G. W. P. Custis, Eleanor Custis, Wm. Lee / 8.8x12.4.   und S C&I

6528 Washington Family / Washington, his Lady & Two Grandchildren by the name of Custis / 9x12.15 (No word "America" on map, Washington looking to right.)   und S N.C.

6529 Washington Family / Washington, his lady & two grandchildren by the name of Custis / 8.7 x 12.15 (Practically the same composition as preceding, but less top ground and foreground.)
          und S N.C.

6530 Washington Family, The / Washington, Geo. Washn Parke Custis, Eleanor, Lady Washington / 8.1x12.7 (Same composition as previous but with some changes.)
          1867 S C&I

6531 Washington Family, The / George Washington Parke Custis, General George Washington, Eleanor Washington, William Lee / (Globe and map on table.)   und S C&I

6532 Washington Family / Nephew, Genl. Washington, Niece, Lady Washington / #70 / 8.5x12.11 (Globe at left, map of America on table, red curtain, and marine scene through window, Washington looking at observer.)
          und S N.C.

6533 Washington. / First in valor, wisdom and virtue /
          und S N.C.

6534 Washington / First in valor, wisdom and virtue / 11.14x8.12 (Full-length portrait beside horse, cannon, etc.)   und S C&I

6535 Washington / First in War, First in Peace, and First in the hearts of his Countrymen / #34 / 12.2x8.14 (Seated, full length.)   1846 S N.C.

6536 Washington / First in War, First in Peace, and First in the hearts of his Countrymen / #265 / 12x8.10 (Interior, right hand extended, left hand resting on sword, full length, upright. River scene and Indian village seen through window at right.)
          und S N.C.

6537 Washington / First in War, First in Peace, And First in the hearts of his Countrymen / 12x8.10 (Composition similar to preceding but no river scene shown through window.)
          und S C.C.

6538 Washington / First in War, First in Peace, and First in the hearts of

his Countrymen / #71 / 12.1x8.9.
und S N.C.

6539 Washington / First in War, First in Peace, and First in the hearts of his Countrymen / 12x8.8 (Full-length figure, after Stuart, sword in left hand, right arm extended.)
und S N.C.

6540 Washington / First in War, First in Peace, and First in the hearts of his Countrymen / 11.13x8.5 (Full-length in uniform, standing beside horse.) und S C.C.

6541 Washington / From the President's House / 8x12.8 (Title also in French and German.) 1848 S N.C.

6542 Washington in the Field /
und S N.C.

6543 Washington, McClellan, and Scott —Three-in-one Picture / (This picture is made by taking 3 separate portraits of Washington, McClellan, and Scott. The 1 of Washington is kept intact; the portraits of McClellan and Scott are pasted back to back, cut into strips of equal width and placed over the portrait of Washington at right angles and at regular intervals apart. When these are mounted in a special deep rabbeted frame and the observer stands to the left he sees a portrait of Mc-Clellan; when directly in front a portrait of Washington, and to the right a portrait of Scott. Currier made a number of these novelty pictures with various combinations, See Nos. 3549-50.)
und M C&I

6544 Washington, Sherman, and Grant— Three-in-one Picture /
und M C&I

6545 Washington Taking Command of the American Army / At Cambridge, Mass. July 3rd, 1775 / 8.15x12.6 (Washington at left on white horse, troops at right.) 1876 S C&I

6546 Washington Taking Command of the American Army, at Cambridge, Mass. July 3rd, 1775 /
1848 S N.C.

6547 Washington Taking Leave of the Officers of his Army / At Francis's (sic) Tavern, Broad Street, New York, Decr. 4th, 1783 / Steuben — Knox — Washington — Gov. Clinton — Hamilton / #547 / 8.10x12.7 (Almost identical composition to "Washington's Farewell," etc. No. 6550. Washington holding wine glass in hand, decanter on table.) 1848 S N.C.

Washington (Horse) See: No. 6526.
Washington (Steamship) See: Nos. 5800-2.
Washington Park, Providence, R.I. See: No. 6203.

6548 Washington's Dream / L. Maurer on stone. 20.15x16 (Round top, ornamental design in upper corners.)
1857 L C&I

6549 Washington's Entry into New York / On the evacuation of the city by the British, Nov. 25th, 1783 / 10.8x15.
1857 M C&I

6550 Washington's Farewell to the Officers of his Army / at the Old Tavern, corner Broad and Pearl Sts. Dec. 4th, 1783 / 8.12x12.1 (2 additional lines, similar composition to "Washington Taking Leave," etc. No. 6547 except wine glass and decanter removed.)
1876 S C&I

6551 Washington's Headquarters, at Newburgh, on the Hudson / 8.8x12.8.
und S C&I

6552 Washington's Reception on the Bridge at Trenton, in 1789 / On his way to be inaugurated 1st President of the United States / 12.8x8.5.
und S N.C.

6553 Washington's Reception on the Bridge at Trenton, in 1789 / On his way to be inaugurated 1st President of the United States / Pub. at 33 Spruce St., New York. Isaac J. Oliver, Printer. 8.4x12.6 (The heading to "Carrier's Address of the American Patriot, 1846.") und S N.C.

6554 Washington's Reception by the Ladies, on passing the/Bridge at Trenton, N.J. April 1789, on his way to New York to be inaugurated First President of the United States / 12.1x8.12 (Upright, star and monogram at top.)
1845 S N.C.

6555 Washington's Reception by the Ladies, on passing the / Bridge at Trenton, N.J. April 1789 / On his way to New York to be inaugurated First President of the United States / #365 / 12.2x8.13 (Upright shield at top, no monogram, 2 officers at left.)
1845 S N.C.

6556 Washington's Reception by the Ladies, on passing the / Bridge at Trenton, N.J. April 1789 / On his way to New York to be inaugurated First President of the United States / 12.2 x8.12 (Shield and monogram at top, 1 officer and horse at left of Washington, upright.) 1845 S N.C.

THE WATER JUMP.

6557 Washington's Reception by the Ladies, on passing the / Bridge at Trenton, N.J. April 1789 / on his way to New York to be inaugurated First President of the United States / #365/ 11.15x8.10 (Upright, small girl facing observer, strewing flowers. Eagle at top with outstretched wings.)
1845 S N.C.

6558 Washington's Reception by the Ladies, on passing the / Bridge at Trenton, N.J. April 1789 / On his way to New York to be inaugurated first president of the United States / 11.14 x8.9 (Upright.)   1848 S N.C.

6559 Washington's reception by the Ladies / On the bridge at Trenton, N.J. April, 1789. / On his way to New York to be inaugurated First President of the United States. / 9.4x12.8 (Washington in center, woman strewing flowers in front of him.)
1889 S C&I

6560 Watch on the Rhine, The /
und S C&I

6561 Watchers, The / (Boy and dog.)
und S C&I

6562 Water Fowl Shooting / #175 / 8x12 (2 hunters and 2 dogs in boat, another hunter on shore at right.)
und S N.C.

6563 Water Jump, The / J. Cameron on stone. Printed in oil colors. 18.11x26.14 (3 horses to left, top corners slightly rounded.)   1884 L C&I

6564 Water Jump at Jerome Park, The / Dandy, purple and red. New York, blue, white spots. Deadhead green, black cap. In the handicap steeple chase purse $600, of which $100 to second, Nov. 6th, 1877, won by Deadhead; New York second. E.F. (E. Forbes) on stone.   und S C&I

6565 Water Lily, The / 10.5x14.12 (Female figure resting on water among lilies, top corners round.)
und M N.C.

6566 Water Nymph, The /
und S C&I

6567 Water Rail Shooting / #176 / 8.2x 12.11.   1855 S N.C.

6568 Water-Rail Shooting / 8.2x12.8 (2 in boat center, shooting to right.)
1870 S C&I

6569 Water-Rail Shooting / 8.2x12.8.
und S C&I

6570 Waterfall — Moonlight / (Upright.) und L C&I

6571 Waterfall, The / 5.8x7.8 (Printed on same sheet with "The Abbey" No. 2) und VS C&I

6572 Waterfall — Tivoli, Italy / 8.8x12.8. und S C&I

Waterloo See: Nos. 437, 4365.

6573 Watkin's Glen / New York / 12 x 9 (Group on right bank of gorge, hotel at top of cliff, upright.) und S C&I

6574 Waverly House / Martens, Delt. N. Currier's Lith. 15x18.8 (¾ front view, hotel was located at 52 Broadway.) und M N.C.

6575 Way they come from California, The / 10.15x17.6 (Group on shore with bags of gold, begging to be taken aboard boats.) 1849 M N.C.

6576 Way they cross "The Isthmus", The / 11x17.5 (Riding on mules.) 1849 M N.C.

6577 Way they get Married in California, The / 1849 M N.C.

6578 Way they go to California, The / 10.15x17.7 (Group of ships, "For California", rocket ship, air liner, etc.) 1849 M N.C.

6579 Way They Raise a California Outfit, The / Here saay, take the pair fur four shillin—you won't?, well / what'll you give? say I'm bound to sell um / cause I'm off for Kaliforny / (Ragged man selling pair of turkeys, wagon "Overland Route to Kaliforny" in background.) 1849 M N.C.

6580 Way they wait for "The Steamer" at Panama, The / J. Cameron on stone. 10.14x17.6 (Fighting on dock.) 1849 M N.C.

6581 Way to grow Poor, The — The way to grow rich / 7.15x12.10 (2 views on same sheet, 1 showing gambling, pools, betting, etc., industry on the other.) 1875 S C&I

6582 Way to Happiness, The / McGee, Del. 9.13x12 (Circle in rectangle girl reading Bible, upright.) und S N.C.

6583 Way to Happiness, The / 9.12x11.12 (Similar composition to preceding, upright.) und S N.C.

6584 Way to happiness, The / 11.13x8.12 (Similar to preceding, slight changes and size.) und S N.C.

THE WAY THEY GO TO CALIFORNIA.

6585 Way to happiness, The / #120 / 12x8.10 (Upright, ¾ length portrait of girl reading Bible, exterior scene, cottage in background.)
und S N.C.

6586 Way to Happiness, The / 11.13x9.9 (¾ length portrait.)
und S N.C.

6587 Wayside Inn, The / F. F. Palmer, Del. 15.14x23.6 (6 lines of verse at each end of title.) 1864 L. C&I

6588 "We met by chance; Or waiting for the swell" / (Bathing scene, comic, vignette.) 1875 S C&I

6589 "We Parted on the Hillside" / 1881 V.S. C&I

6590 "We Parted on the Hillside" / "Amid the Winter's snow" / Thos. Worth on stone. (White comic, vignette, winter scene.)
1880 S C&I

6591 We praise Thee, O Lord / (Vignette.) und S C&I

6592 We Sell For Cash / (Clerk pointing over shoulder.) 1875 S C&I

6593 We Trust / (Clerk pointing over left shoulder, vignette, comic. Probably published for use in stores. Upright.)
1881 S C&I

6594 Wearing of the Green / 2 additional lines of poetry. (¾ length, upright.)
und S C&I

Webb See: Nos. 4273, 4694, 4823.

Weber, Col. Max See: No. 1198.

Webster, Daniel See: Nos. 1362-6, 2898.

6595 Wedding, The / #589 / 11.14x8.12 (Upright.) und S N.C.

6596 Wedding Day, The / (Full length, couple about to enter church, upright.)
und S N.C.

6597 Wedding day, The / J. McGee, Del. 7.2x8.14 (Exterior scene, companion to No. 1529.) und S N.C.

6598 Wedding day, The / (Full length, couple in front of church, upright.)
und S C.C.

6599 Wedding day, The / #106 (¾ length, upright, round corners.)
und S N.C.

6600 Wedding day, The / 12.1x8.6 (¾ length, changes in composition from preceding, upright.)
1846 S N.C.

6601 Wedding Evening, The /
und S C&I

6602 Wedding Morning, The / #344 (Full length of couple kneeling in church, upright.) und S N.C.

6603 Wedgewood Record 2:19 /
1881 V.S. C&I

Wedgewood (Horse) See: No. 6226.

Weed, Thurlow See: Nos. 2641, 5567.

Weehawken See: Nos. 4446, 6404.

Weitzel, Genl. See: No. 2553.

6604 Welcome / (Motto—surrounded by flowers, vignette.)
1873 S C&I

6605 Welcome Home / (Motto.)
und S C&I

6606 Welcome / Take a drink / #335 (¾ length figure man facing observer, upright.) und S N.C.

6607 Welcome to Our Home / (Motto with flowers, vignette.)
1874 S C&I

6608 Well-Bred Setter, A / (Dog to right, bird in mouth.)
1871 S C&I

6609 Well-Bred Setter, A / (Same as preceding.) 1870 S C&I

6610 Well-Bred Setter, A / (Entirely different composition and dog from preceding. No bird in dog's mouth.)
und S C&I

6611 Well-broken Retriever, A / (Same composition as "A Well-Bred Setter" No. 6608.) 1870 S C&I

6612 Well Bunched at the Last Hurdle / J. Cameron, Del. on stone. 18.8x28.3 (9 horses head-on, under saddle.)
1887 L C&I

6613 Well — I'm Blowed! / Thos. Worth on stone (Horse comic, vignette, horse winded after race.)
1883 S C&I

6614 "Well Together at the First Turn"/ J. Cameron 1873 on stone. 17.1x26.6 (Same composition as following print but poorer paper and printing. Only 1 line in title and no grandstand shown in rear. 3 horses and high-wheeled sulkies to right.) 1886 L C&I

6615 "Well Together at the First Turn"/ J. Cameron 1873 on stone. 17.1x26.7 (Same composition as preceding but better printing and grandstand shown in rear.) 1886 L C&I

6616 "Well Together at the First Turn"/ W. H. Allen driven by Peter Manee, Huntress driven by John Trout, and

John W. Conley driven by W. H. Crawford. Trotting at Fleetwood Park, Morrisania, N.Y. May 28th, 1873 / J. Cameron 1873 on stone. 16.14x25.15.
1873 L C&I

Welles, Gideon **See:** No. 5258.

Wells, Daniel **See:** No. 1986.

Wellesley Boy (Horse) **See:** No. 2946.

Werra (Steamship) **See:** No. 3040.

Wesley, John **See:** Nos. 3282-3.

West Indies **See:** No. 6427.

6617 West Point Foundry, Cold Spring / Hudson River, New York / F. F. Palmer, Del. 1862 M C&I

West Point **See:** Nos. 1277, 2972, 4245, 6103-4, 6325, 6378-80, 6383-4.

West Rock **See:** New Haven, Conn. No. 6429.

West Virginia **See:** No. 6449.

6618 Western Beauty, The / (Upright, vignette.) und S C&I

6619 Western Farmer's Home, The / 8.8 x12.8. 1871 S C&I

6620 Western River Scenery / 11.8x16.9 (Group on shore in foreground, paddlewheel steamer in the distance.)
1866 M C&I

Westernland (Steamship) **See:** Nos. 480, 5803.

Weston, Edward Payson — Pedestrian **See:** Nos. 1184, 2654-7.

6621 We've Had a Healthy Time! / (Vignette, woman returning to home wrecked by pets — monkey, dog, parrot, and cats.) 1880 S C&I

6622 Whale Fishery / Attacking a right whale / (Same general composition as large Folio "The Whale Fishery. Attacking a right whale.")
und S C&I

6623 Whale Fishery, The / Attacking a right whale — and "Cutting In" 16.3x 23.12 (Companion to No. 6627.)
und L C&I

6624 Whale Fishery, The. Cutting in /
und S C&I

6625 Whale Fishery, The. "In a flurry" / #382. 1852 S N.C.

6626 Whale Fishery, The. "Laying on" / (2 rowboats in foreground about to attack whale, ship in background, title in plate.) 1852 S N.C.

6627 Whale Fishery, The / The sperm whale in a flurry / 16x24 (Companion to No. 6623.) und L C&I

6628 Whale Fishery, The. Sperm whale "in a flurry" / 9.8x12.11.
und S C&I

Whalebone (Horse) **See:** No. 5811.

W. H. Allen (Horse) **See:** No. 6616.

Whaling **See:** Nos. 204-5, 812, 4504, 5629, 5648, 6622-8.

6628A What is it? or "Man Monkey" on exhibition at Barnum's Museum, New York / "This is the most singular animal with many of the features and other characteristics of the human and brute species, etc. He is as playful as a kitten, etc." / (At Top) Barnum's Gallery of Wonders No. 26. 9.8x8.8.
und S C&I

6629 What Shall the Harvest Be? /
1886 S C&I

6630 What's Sauce for the Goose is Sauce for the Gander / E.W.C. on stone. Entered by E. W. Clay 1851. 11.9x17.6 (2 views on same sheet, 1 showing southerner trying unsuccessfully to recover his runaway slave from northern merchant. Other view shows merchant trying unsuccessfully to get his goods back from southerner.)
1851 M N.C.

6631 Wheat Field, The /
und S N.C.

6632 Wheat Field, The /
und S C&I

6633 "Wheelmen in a Red Hot Finish" / J. Cameron on stone. 12.6x18.14 (7 bicyclists passing judge's stand.)
1894 M C&I

Wheeler, Wm. A. **See:** Nos. 2504, 2925.

Wheelock, Ark. **See:** No. 4159.

6634 When Shall We Three Meet Again? / 8.12x12.7 (2 donkey heads.)
und S C&I

6635 When the Flowing Tide Comes In / (Vignette, group in row boat stranded on mud flat.) 1879 S C&I

6636 Where Do You Buy Your Cigars? /
1879 S C&I

6637 Where Do You Buy Your Cigars? / (Similar composition to "No, Ma'am, I Don't Care to Shoot Birds" No. 4484. Postcard size, advertising card.)
1880 V.S. C&I

6638 Which Donkey Will I Take? / (Girl at seashore, fop with pair of donkeys, vignette.) 1881 S C&I

6639 Which Of Us Will You Marry? / #433 / 11.10x8.11 (Upright, ¾ length

WHEELMEN IN "A RED HOT FINISH."

of blonde and brunette.)
1846 S N.C.

6640 White Doggies Into Mischief /
und S C&I

6641 White Dog's Got Him, De! / (Vignette, colored comic, companion to "De brack dog wins" No. 645.)
1889 S C&I

6642 White Fawn, The /
1868 S C&I

6643 White Hall, Bristol College, Pa. / Plan of White Hall, Bristol Co., Pa. / Alex. J. Davis, Architect, N.Y. / N. Currier's lithog. 1835. 10.2x13.10 (Vignette.)
1835 S N.C.

White Mountains **See:** Nos. 1664-5, 2223, 4242, 4515, 5521.

6644 White Squadron, U.S. Navy, The / Armored Steel Battle Ship Massachusetts. Cruiser Chicago. Armored Steel Cruiser New York. Cruiser San Francisco. Cruiser Philadelphia. Cruiser Newark. / 19x34.8.
1893 L C&I

White Wing (Yacht) **See:** No. 4450.

6645 Who comes here! / 8.6x12.10.
und S N.C.

6646 Who Goes There / Que vive! / #718 (2 alert dogs.)
und S N.C.

6647 Who Speaks First? / 11.11x8.10 (Girl with 2 dogs.)
und S C&I

6648 Who's Afraid Of You? / 8.6x12.5 (4 puppies and rat, slightly rounded corners, companion to "Going For Him" No. 2400.)
1868 S C&I

6649 Who Said Rats? / 8.10x10.12 (Oval, portrait of dog.)
und S C&I

6650 Who Will Love Me? / (Vignette, girl's head.)
und S C&I

6651 Whose Chick Are You? /
und S C&I

6652 Why Don't He Come? / 11.12x8.15 (Girl by tree, entwined hearts cut in bark. Copied from engraving "In Memoriam," companion to "The parting hour" No. 4713, upright.)
und S C&I

6653 Why Don't He Come? / First At the Rendezvous / 12.10x8.8 (Lady on white horse, dog and whip on ground.)
und S C&I

6654 Why Don't Yer Come Along? / Thos. Worth on stone. (1 horse and rig outdistancing 4 others, vignette.)
1883 S C&I

6655 Why Don't You Take It? /
und S C&I

6656 Wicklow — Ireland /
und M C&I

6657 Wide Awake / (Companion to "Little Sleepy" No. 3718.)
und S C&I

6658 Wide Path, The /
und S N.C.

Widow McChree (Horse) See: Nos. 202, 924.

6659 Widow's Son, The /
und S C&I

6660 Widow's Treasure, The / 12.2x8.14 (Mother and child.)
und S N.C.

6661 Widower's Treasure, The / 12.2x 8.14 (Man and child in mourning, seated before easel showing portrait of wife. Companion to preceding.)
und S N.C.

6662 Wi-Jun-Jon — The Pigeon's Egg Head / Going to Washington, and Returning to his home / Catlin, Del. 12.11 x18.3 (2 views on same sheet: 1st shows full length figure Indian in his native costume, second shows him returning home in military uniform with whisky bottles in his pockets, and carrying fan and umbrella.)
und M C&I

6663 Wild Cat Banker, A, or A "Circulating Medium" / Secured by / "Public Stocks" / #159 (Tramp, bearded and unkempt, locked in stocks. See: "A Circulating Medium.")
1853 S N.C.

6664 Wild Cat Train, A / No Stop-overs / Thos. Worth on stone. (Vignette, railroad comic.) 1884 S C&I

6665 Wild Duck Shooting / (Taken from an English print.)
und S C.C.

6666 Wild Duck Shooting / 8.14x12.14 (2 hunters at right, 3 dogs in water, bare trees. Taken from an English print by Ackerman & Son entitled "Flapper Shooting.") und S N.C.

6667 Wild Duck Shooting / 7.8x12.12 (Similar to preceding.)
und S N.C.

6668 Wild Duck Shooting / #53 / 8.7x 12.11 (2 hunters on left facing right, 2 dogs taking to water after ducks. English type.) 1846 S N.C.

6669 Wild Duck Shooting / From nature and on stone by F. F. Palmer. 12.15x 20.5. 1852 L N.C.

6670 Wild Duck Shooting / A Good Day's Sport / A. F. Tait N.Y. 1854 and O. Knirsch on stone. 18.7x25.12 (2 hunters and 2 dogs. Rowboat on shore well filled with ducks.)
1854 L N.C.

6671 Wild Duck Shooting / On the Wing/ 8.3x12.7 (Bareheaded hunter, hat on ground with powder horn in it, birds on wing over opposite shore to right, oar in row boat.)
1870 S C&I

6672 Wild Duck Shooting / On the Wing/ 7.15x12.7 (Composition somewhat similar to preceding, hunter has hat on, no powderhorn, or dead ducks on ground, but several in rowboat. This print was copied from the painting "On the Wing" by Ranney. Ducks on wing to right.) und S C&I

6673 Wild Duck Shooting / On the Wing / 8x12.6 (Hunter is wearing bandanna, several dead ducks on ground, no hat or powder horn, no birds on wing to right, no birds in rowboat.)
und S C&I

6674 Wild Flowers /
und S C&I

6675 Wild Horses at Play on the American Prairies / The Rocky Mountains in the distance / Catlin, Del. 12.2x17.14.
und M C&I

6676 Wild Irishman / By Glencoe, dam Mary Morris, by Medoc / From the original painting in possession of his owner R. P. Fields, Esq. to whom / This print is respectfully dedicated by the Publisher / Painted by R. A. Clarke. O. Knirsch on stone. 19.5x26.5 (Title in foreground of plate, profile to left.) 1854 L N.C.

6677 Wild Turkey Shooting / 8.6x12.8 (2 hunters at left.) 1871 S C&I

6678 Wild West in Darktown, The / Attack on the Deadhead Coach / (Vignette.) 1893 S C&I

6679 Wild West in Darktown, The / The Buffalo Chase / (Vignette.)
1893 S C&I

Wilderness, Va. See: Nos. 435-6.

Wildey, See: "Thomas, Founder of Odd Fellows" No. 6029.

Wildflower (Horse) See: No. 2474.

6680 Wilhelm I / Konig von Preussen / (Upright, vignette.)
und S C&I

Wilkes, Capt. Charles See: No. 5050.

6681 Will he bite? / Chromo in oil colors from the original painting by / Miss Juliana Oakley / 14.1x17.1.
1868 M C&I

6682 Will You Be True? / (¾ length, girl, oval.)   und S C&I

6683 William / #344 / 12.3x8.9 (Upright, ¾ length, cane in right hand, letter in left, flower background.)
und S N.C.

6684 William A. Graham / Whig Candidate for / Vice-President of the United States / 11.6x9 (Upright, ¾ length, seated, right hand on book.)
1852 S N.C.

6685 William and Susan / #102 (Upright, ¾ length vignette.)
und S N.C.

6686 William Bigler / Governor of Pennsylvania / #329 / 11.7x8.11. Published by Fisher & Brother, 15 North 6th St. Phila. (Upright.)   und S N.C.

6687 William C. Bouck / 2.13x3 (From Jenkins "History of Political Parties in the State of New York" Auburn, N.Y.)   und V.S. C.C.

6688 William F. Johnston / Governor of Pennsylvania / #329 / Pub. by Turner & Fisher, 15 North 6th St. Phila. 11.12 x8.12 (Facsimile signature, ¾ length figure, farm scene through window at left, upright.)   1848 S N.C.

6689 Wm. H. Seward / 2.13x3 (From Jenkins "History of Political Parties in the State of New York" Auburn, N.Y. 1846.)   und V.S. C.C.

6690 William Henry Harrison / J. McGee.   und S N.C.

6691 William Henry Harrison / Ninth President of the United States / #27 / 11.7x9 (Upright, quill in right hand, sword hilt shown over left hand.)
und S N.C.

6692 William Henry Harrison / Ninth President of the United States / 13x9 (2 lines: dates of birth and death, upright, full length, black border.)
und S N.C.

6693 William Henry Harrison / Ninth President of the United States / 11.11 x9.4 (Upright, quill in right hand, sword hilt under left hand.)
und S N.C.

Wm. J. Romer, (Extraordinary Express) See: No. 1798.

6694 Wm. L. Marcy / 2.13x3 (From Jenkins "History of Political Parties

in the State of New York", Auburn, N.Y.)   und V.S. C.C.

6695 Wm. O. Butler / Democratic Candidate for / Vice-President of the United States / #591 / 11.10x9 (Upright, military uniform seated, ¾ length.)   1848 S N.C.

6696 Wm. P. Dewees, M.D. / Drawn on stone by M. E. D. Brown from the portrait painted by John Neagle. 11.11 x9.8 (The earliest dated Currier.)
1834 S N.C.

William Penn (Steamship) See: No. 5804.

6697 Wm. Penn's Treaty with the Indians when he founded the Province of Pennsa, 1661 / The only treaty that never was broken / N. Sarony on stone. 8.4x12.9 (River on the right.)
und S N.C.

6698 Wm. Penn's Treaty with the Indians when he founded the Province of Pennsa / 1661 / The only treaty that never was broken / (River on the left, composition reversed.)
und S N.C.

6699 Wm. Penn's treaty with the Indians when he founded the Province of Pennsa, 1661 / 8.3x12.10 (Different composition from preceding, water on the left.)   und S N.C.

6700 William Prince of Orange Landing at Torbay, England / November 5th, 1688 / 12.10x8.7 (Upright.)
und S C&I

6701 William R. King / Democratic Candidate for Vice-President of the United States / From a daguerreotype by Brady / 11.8x8.13(Upright, half length seated.)   1852 S N.C.

6702 William R. King / Vice-President of the United States / From a daguerreotype by Brady / 11.8x8.13 (Same stone as preceding, title changed.)   1852 S N.C.

6703 William Shakespeare / (Vignette, upright.)   und M C&I

6704 Wm. Smith O'Brien / Ireland's Patriot, 1848 / #618 / 3 lines of verse. 11.6x8.15 (Seated, holding rolled scroll, battle scene through window.)
1848 S N.C.

6705 William Stedding. The German sailor who captured the schooner "S. J. Waring" with Tillman, the colored steward. / (Exhibited at Barnum's Museum.)   und S C&I

6706 William Tell / Death of Gessler / #584 / 8.3x12.5 (2 columns, 4 lines of verse.)
und S C&I

6707 William Tell / Escaping from the Tyrant / #583 / 8.5x12.8 (2 columns, 4 lines of verse.)
und S C&I

6708 William Tell Escaping from the Tyrant /
und S N.C.

6709 William Tell / Replying to Gessler/ #582 / 8x12.5 (2 columns, 4 lines of verse.)
und S C&I

6710 William Tell / Replying to the Governor / 9.2x12.1.
und S C&I

6711 William Tell / Shooting the Apple On His Son's Head /
und S N.C.

6712 William Tell / Shooting the Apple On His Son's Head / #581 / 8.3x12.7 (2 columns, 4 lines of verse.)
und S C&I

6713 William Tell's Chapel / Lake of Geneva / 7.8x5.8 (Upright, oval.)
und V.S. C&I

6714 Wm. Tillman, the colored steward/ of the schooner S. J. Waring which was captured by the piratical Brig Jeff Davis / and recaptured by Tillman and Wm. Stedding the German sailor after killing three / of the pirates in charge of her / Receiving visitors daily at Barnum's Museum, New York. (Vignette, upright, ¾ length.)
und S C&I

6715 William W. Brown / (Colored orator.)
und S C&I

Williams, Gen. See: Nos. 5490, 5567.

Williams, David See: "Capture of Andre" Nos. 804-6.

Williams, George (Historian) See: No. 2345.

Williamsburg, Va. See: Nos. 438-9.

6716 Willie and Mary / (Upright, full-length figures.)
und S C&I

6717 Willie and Rover / (On dog's back.)
und S C&I

6718 Willie's Little Pets / 8.2x12.9 (Barnyard scene.)
und S C&I

Wilson, Henry See: Nos. 5567, 6782.

Wilson's Creek See: "Death of Gen. Lyon" No. 1483.

Winchester See: "Genl. Shields" No. 2294.

6719 Windmill, The / (Published on 1 sheet with "The Pool," "Winter Morn-

ing," and "The Fisherman's Cot" — vignette.)
und S C&I

6720 Windsor Castle and Park / (Deer in foreground.)
und M C&I

Windsor Park See: "Virginia Water" No. 6475.

6721 Wine Tasters, The /
und S N.C.

6722 Winfield Scott / (Fascimilie signature, head and shoulders slightly to left, vignette.)
und M C&I

6723 Winfield Scott / The People's Choice for / Thirteenth President of the United States / #477 / 11.7x8.10 (Upright, half length, military uniform, red curtain in back.)
1847 S N.C.

6724 Winfield Scott / Whig Candidate for / Fourteenth President of the United States / From a daguerreotype. 11.8x8.8 (Upright, half length, civilian clothes, red curtain.)
1852 S N.C.

6725 Winning Card, The / L. Maurer on stone. (Identical to "The Rubber.")
und L C&I

6726 Winning "Hands Down" With a Good Second / 18.8x28.3 (30 horses under saddle passing stand.)
1887 L C&I

6727 Winning Horses of the American Turf /
1889 L C&I

6728 Winning in Style / L. Maurer on stone. 16x12.12 (Horse with low-wheeled sulky passing judge's stand.)
1893 M C&I

6729 Winter / 8x12.8 (Horses and mules under shed, companion to Nos. 311, 5672, 5849.)
und S N.C.

6730 Winter / (Half length upright vignette, girl with mask. Companion to Nos. 313,, 5674, 5849A.)
und S C&I

6731 Winter / (Half length upright vignette, girl with mask.)
und L C&I

6732 Winter / (Companion to Nos. 312, 5673, 5851.)
1870 S C&I

6733 Winter / (Vignette, girl's head.)
1870 S C&I

6734 Winter Evening / 10.6x15 (Skating pond, group at fire on bank at right, moonlight scene.)
1854 M N.C.

6735 Winter Evening /
1856 M N.C.

6736 Winter in the Country / A cold morning / Painted by G. H. Durrie. 18.5x27. 1864 L C&I

6737 Winter in the Country / Getting Ice / Painted by G. H. Durrie. 18.8x27.1. 1864 L C&I

6738 Winter in the Country / The Old Grist Mill / Painted by G. H. Durrie. 18.6x26.15. 1864 L C&I

6739 Winter Moonlight / F. F. Palmer, Del. 17.12x14.7 (Top corners rounded, upright.) 1866 M C&I

6740 Winter Morning / F. F. Palmer, Del. 11.5x15.5 (Sleigh and pair of horses approaching house at right, barnyard on left.) 1861 M C&I

Winter Morning — 1 of 4 scenes on 1 sheet **See:** No. 4836.

6741 Winter Morning / Feeding the Chickens / Painted by G. H. Durrie. 14.14x20.10. 1863 L C&I

6742 Winter Morning in the Country / 8.7x12.7. (Similar composition to Large folio "American Farm Scenes, Winter" No. 136.) 1873 S C&I

(This print is sometimes found with 1872 date.)

6743 Winter Pastime / F. F. Palmer, Del. 10.7x14.15 (Skating pond on right, group of children on bank on left, sleigh with 2 horses on left.) 1855 M N.C.

6744 Winter Pastime / 10.6x14.15 (Portion of composition similar to "Frozen Up." Grist mill in left rear, skating pond, skaters, and group of 4 on bank in right foreground.) 1870 M C&I

6745 Winter Scene / 5.8x7.8. und V.S. C&I

6746 Winter Scene in the Country / und L C&I

6747 Winter Sports — Pickerel Fishing/ 8.7x12.8 (Composition somewhat similar to Large Folio "American Winter Sports," No. 210. 3 men fishing through holes in the ice, skaters in background.) 1872 S C&I

6748 Winter Twilight / 2.5x4.12. und V.S. C&I

Wisconsin **See:** Nos. 3853, 3974, 6398.

Wise, H. A. Gov., Va. **See:** No. 5962,

WINTER PASTIME.

6749 Wise Child, A /
1884 S C&I

Witch of the Wave **See:** American Clipper Ship, etc. No. 114.

6750 With Malice toward none / With charity for all / (Rustic letters, scroll and flowers. Motto.)
1875 S C&I

6751 Wizard's Glen, The / 14.12x14.12 (Similar to "The Magic Lake," "Magic Grottoes," etc.) 1868 M C&I

6752 Woman Taken in Adultery / Jesus Christ et la femme adultere / #428 / 12.7x8.15 (Upright.)
und S N.C.

6753 Woman's Holy War / Grand Charge on the Enemy's Works / 11.3x8.10 (Women in armor on horseback, breaking barrels of beer, gin, whisky, etc. Upright.) 1874 S N.C.

6754 Women of '76 / The / "Molly Pitcher" the Heroine of Monmouth / 1848 S N.C.

6755 Women of '76, The / "Molly Pitcher" the Heroine of Monmouth / 2 columns of 2 lines (Molly serving cannon at which her husband was killed.)
und S C&I

6756 Won! / #671 / 12.11x8.11 (Upright, domino holding 4 aces. Companion to "Lost," No. 3782.)
und S N.C.

6757 Won by a Dash / J. Cameron on stone. (5 horses under saddle passing stand to right.) 1892 M C&I

6758 Won by a Foot / Kemble, Del. (Man with big feet winning race, vignette.)
1883 S C&I

6759 Won by a Neck / J. Cameron on stone. (Composition same as No. 6761 but all of the background removed and a board fence substituted. Horses not named.) 1889 L C&I

6760 Won by a Neck / (5 horses passing judge's stand, no similarity in composition to preceding.)
1892 M C&I

6761 Won by a Neck / Lady Thorn, Goldsmith Maid, and American Girl / In the first heat of their great trotting contest on the Prospect Park Fair Grounds, August 28th, 1869 / J. Cameron 1869 on stone. 16.13x26.12 (8 additional lines pedigrees and time. Horses and drivers keyed above title. ¾ broadside, high-wheeled sulkies to right.)
1869 L C&I

6762 Wonderful Albino Family, The / Rudolph Lucasie, wife and children

from Madagascar / 1 additional line (Sometimes has Barnum's Gallery of Wonders No. 14 at top. Upright.)
und S C&I

6763 Wonderful Albino Family, The / Rudolph Lucasie wife and child from Madagascar / they have pure white skin silken white hair and pink eyes / though born of perfectly black parents / now exhibiting at Barnum's American Museum, New York / (At top) Barnum's Gallery of Wonders No. 14. (Round top.)
und S C&I

6764 Wonderful Eliophobus Family Rudolph Lucasie, wife and son from Madagascar, The / They have pure white skin and pink eyes / Taken March 1870 / 8x12.8 (Top corners round, not upright.)
1870 S C&I

6765 Wonderful Mare Maud S. Record 2:10¾, The / Bred by A. J. Alexander, Woodburn, Ky. Foaled March 28th, 1874. Sired by Harold, dam Miss Russell, by Pilot, Jr. / As she appears at speed, driven by her celebrated driver W. W. Bair / Scott Leighton on stone. (Vignette, ¾ broadside, high-wheeled sulkies to right.) 1880 S C&I

6766 Wonderful Mare Maud S. Record 2:10¼, The / Second and third lines exactly as preceding. Scott Leighton on stone. (Vignette, high-wheeled sulky to left.) 1881 S C&I

6767 Wonderful Mare Maud S. the property of Wm. H. Vanderbilt, Esq. / 4 additional lines (Vignette, high-wheeled sulky to left.)
1878 S C&I

6768 Wonderful story, The / "The naughty wolf leaped upon the good woman and ate her up"/12.12x8.4 (Upright, girl reading to younger children.) und S C&I

6769 Wood Ducks / 8.8x12.8.
und S C&I

Wood, Fernando **See:** Nos. 1028, 1550.

6770 Woodcock / 8.8x12.8 (1 with bill in sand.) 1871 S C&I

6771 Woodcock / Scolopax Minor / 8.6 x12.10 (Both birds with heads up, different from preceding.)
1849 S N.C.

6772 Woodcock Shooting / 8x12 (Hunter at left shooting, another at right, 3 dogs in center. English type.)
und S N.C.

6773 Woodcock Shooting / #175 / 8x12.10 (Hunter at right center, back to ob-

server, shooting birds at left. 2 dogs.)
1855 S N.C.

6774 Woodcock Shooting / From nature and on stone by F. F. Palmer. 13.1x 20.5.   1852 L N.C.

6775 Woodcock Shooting / 8.2x12.7 (Hunter at left under trees, shooting birds at left. 2 dogs left center.)
1870 S C&I

Woodford Mambrino (Horse) **See:** No. 937.

6776 "Wooding up" on the Mississippi / F. F. Palmer, Del. 18.4x27.13 (Steamer "Princess" at dock, another coming around the bend.)
1863 L C&I

6777 Woodland Gate / W. Collins, R. A. Painter.   und M N.C.

6778 Woodlands in Summer, The / (Group of people on path. Companion to following.)   und S C&I

6779 Woodlands in Winter / (Boy and girl on lane, wolves at side.)
und S C&I

Woodruff, Hiram **See:** No. 5708.

6780 Woods in Autumn, The / 11.7x16.6.
und M C&I

Wool, Col. John E. **See:** Nos. 993, 2284, 3917-8.

6781 Word and the Sign, The / (Upright vignette, cross, Bible and flowers.)
1877 S C&I

Work, Frank **See:** Nos. 622, 4251.

6782 Working Men's Banner, The / For President. For Vice President. Ulysses S. Grant "The Galena Tanner" Henry Wilson "The Natick Shoemaker"/ 12.10 x9 (Upright, full length figures.)
1872 S C&I

Worth, Gen. Wm. J. **See:** No. 2326.

6783 "Wound Up"/ King & Murphy, Del. on stone. (Colored comic, companion to "Run Down," No. 5256.)
1884 S C&I

6783A Wound Up /   1877 S C&I

6784 Wounded Bittern, The / 8x12.8 (Bittern attacked by dog.)
und S N.C.

6785 Wreath of Flowers, A / 12.8x10 (Upright vignette.)
und S C&I

6786 Wreck of the Atlantic, The / The

splendid Steamship of the White Star Line / 2 additional lines. 8.8x12.8 (Rope in foreground on which passengers are coming ashore.)
1873 S C&I

6787 Wreck of the Atlantic, The / The Splendid, etc. (Same as preceding.) 8x12.9 (Entirely different composition, more of steamship shown, rockets in air and buoy in background.)
1873 S C&I

6788 Wreck of the Ship "John Minturn"/ Capt. Stark, on the coast of New Jersey in the terrible gale of Feby. 15th, 1846. 3 o'clock A.M. with 51 persons on board / 2 additional lines. 7.13x12.6.
1846 S N.C.

6789 Wreck of the Steamship "Cambria" / on her voyage from Hamburg to New York, January 19th, 1883 /
1883 S C&I

Wreck of the Steam Ship "San Francisco" **See:** Ships Antarctic, etc. No. 5492.

6790 Wreck of the Steamship "Schiller"/ On her voyage from New York to Hamburg, May 7th, 1875 / 2 columns, 5 lines each in English and German. 8.5x13 (Above title) Bishop's light half a mile distant visible half an hour after the steamer struck.
1875 S C&I

6791 Wreck of the U.S.M. Steamship "Arctic" off Cape Race, Wednesday, Sept. 27, 1854. / In collision with the French iron propeller "Vesta" in which nearly 300 persons perished. Lith. by N. Currier from a sketch made by a passenger. Buttersworth and Parsons, Del. 17.4x25.4.   1854 L N.C.

6792 Wrecked by a Cow Catcher / (Cow has butted engine and 1 coach off the track. Colored comic, vignette.)
1885 S C&I

Wright, Genl. **See:** No. 2553.
Wright, Silas **See:** No. 5518.

6793 Wrong Way — Right Way / I get trusted — I pay as I go / 8.8x12.14 2 views on 1 sheet (1 shows man worried about unpaid bills, other view shows a happy man with well-filled pocketbook.)   1872 S C&I

6794 W. W. Brown / Colored author / (Upright, vignette.)   und S C&I

Y

6795 Yacht "Countess of Dufferin" of the Royal Canadian Yacht Club, The / 9x13.2.   und S C&I

6796 Yacht "Dauntless" of N.Y. 268 tons, The / Owned and commanded by Vice Commodore Jas. G. Bennett, Jr. / Arriving at Queenstown, Ireland in 12 days, 19 hours, and 6 minutes from New York /. und S C&I

6797 Yacht "Dauntless" of New York, The / Off Queenstown, July 13th, 1869 / Owned and commanded by Jas. G. Bennett, Jr. / Parsons & Atwater, Del. 19.2x28. 1 additional line and 2 columns, 5 and 6 lines. (Sailing to right.) 1869 L C&I

6798 Yacht "Fleetwing" of New York, 212 tons / Owned by Messrs. Osgood, competitor in the great ocean yacht race, from New York to Cowes, December 1866 / Making the run in 14 days, 6 hours mean time / 8x12.7.
und S C&I

6799 Yacht "Haze" 87 tons, The / Built by George Steers New York / To her owner Wm. B. Duncan, Esq. This print is with permission respectfully / Dedicated by / The publisher / C. Parsons, Del. 16.12x27.8. 2 columns, 7 and 6 lines. (Skyline of New York in background.) 1861 L C&I

6800 Yacht "Henrietta" 195 tons, The / Modelled by Mr. Wm. Tooker N.Y. Built by Mr. Henry Steers, Greenpoint, L.I. / Owned by Mr. James Gordon Bennett, Jr. / Winner of the great ocean yacht race with the "Fleetwing" and "Vesta" from New York to Cowes, England for $90,000 Dec. 25th, 1866. Making the run in 13 days 22¾ hours mean time / C. Parsons Del. 2 columns 6 and 7 lines. 17.12x27.13.
1867 L C&I

6801 Yacht "Henrietta" 205 tons, The / (Balance of title same as preceding.)
1867 L C&I

6802 Yacht "Henrietta" 205 tons, The / Owned by Mr. James Gordon Bennett, Jr. / 2 additional lines. und S C&I

6803 Yacht "Madeleine" N.Y. Yacht Club, The / Owned and commanded by Commodore John S. Dickerson / 3 additional lines and 2 columns, 3 and 2 lines. 9.5x13.1. und S C&I

6804 Yacht "Mallory" 44 tons, The / Built by Chas. H. Mallory at Mystic, Conn. 1858 / To her owner James T. Bache, Esq. this print is with permission respectfully dedicated by / The publisher / C. Parsons, Del. 2 columns, 5 lines. 1861 L C&I

6805 Yacht "Maria" 216 tons, The / Modelled by R. L. Stevens, built by Mr. Capes 1844 and owned by Messrs. J.C., R.L., & E.A. Stevens of Hoboken, N.J. / To E.A. Stevens, Esq. This print

is with permission respectfully dedicated by / The publisher / C. Parsons on stone. 2 columns, 7 and 8 lines. 17.8 x27.10. (Yacht "Irene" keyed.)
1861 L C&I

6806 Yacht "Meteor" of N.Y. 293 Tons / Owned by G. L. Lorillard, Esq. of the New York Yacht Club / 8.8x12.10.
und S C&I

6807 Yacht "Meteor" of New York, The/ Leaving Sandy Hook Augst. 1869 bound to Europe / To her owner and commander George L. Lorillard, Esq, member of the N.Y. Yacht Club / This print is with permission respectfully dedicated by / The publisher / Parsons & Atwater, Del. 2 columns, 6 and 7 lines. 19x27.10 1869 L C&I

6808 Yacht "Mohawk" of New York, The / Parsons & Atwater, Del. (Broadside to left.) 1877 L C&I

6809 Yacht "Norseman" of New York / 1 additional line. 19x28.
1882 L C&I

6810 Yacht "Puritan" of Boston / C. Parsons on stone. 15.3x21.
1885 L C&I

6811 Yacht "Puritan" / Winner of the two races for the American Cup /
1885 M C&I

6812 Yacht "Rebecca" 75 tons, The / Modelled by Mr. Wm. Tooker, built by Mr. E. H. White N.Y. / To her owner James G. Bennett, Esq. this print is respectfully dedicated / C. Parsons, Del. 2 columns, 5 and 4 lines.
1861 L C&I

6813 Yacht "Sappho" of N.Y. 210 tons / Owned and commanded by W. P. Douglas, Esq. Rear Commodore N.Y. Yacht Club / 8.8x12.10.
und S C&I

6814 Yacht "Sappho" of N.Y. 310 tons / (Balance same as preceding.)
und S C&I

6815 Yacht "Sappho" of New York, The/ Leaving Sandy Hook July 28th, 1869 bound to Europe / To her owner and commander William Douglas, Esq. Rear Admiral of the New York Yacht Club / This print is respectfully dedicated by the publisher / Parsons & Atwater, Del. 1 additional line of dimensions and 2 columns, 10 and 6 lines. 18.8x28. 1869 L C&I

6816 Yacht Squadron at Newport, The / 16.8x27.16 (14 boats keyed in 5 lines.)
1872 L C&I

6817 Yacht "Vesta" of N.Y. 210 tons, The / Owned by Mr. Lorillard / Competitor in the Great Ocean Yacht from

New York to Cowes, December 1866 / Making the run in 14 days, 7½ hours, mean time / und S C&I

6818 Yacht "Volunteer" / Modelled by Edward Burgess of Boston for Gen. C. J. Raine / (Printed in oil colors.) 1887 L C&I

6819 Yachtsman's Solace, The / When the Breeze dies out, and near and far / The lazy craft on the listless waves / Rock to and fro; a good cigar / Is the only solace my spirit craves / (Group on yacht, smoking, vignette.) 1883 S C&I

6820 Yachtsman's Delight, The / A Sociable Smoke / (Tobacco advertising card.) 1879 S C&I

6821 Yachts on a Summer Cruise / (Above title) Tidal Wave — Dreadnought — Wanderer — Columbia — Rambler. 16.12x27.10. 1871 L C&I

Yale See: No. 2095.

6822 Yankee Doodle on his Muscle / or the way the Benicia Boy astonished the English Men / (J. C. Heenan) (Vignette.) und S C&I

Yankee Doodle See: No. 2607.

6823 Yankee Locke / The Distinguished Yankee Comedian / As he appeared at all the principal theatres of the Union / From a daguerreotype by L. K. Warren, J. L. Magee, Del. (Central portrait of G. E. Locke surrounded by six character parts: Solomon Swop, Moderation Easterbrook, Jonathan Ploughboy, Lob Sap Sago, Curtis Chunk, and Jedediah Homebred.) und L C.C.

6824 Yankee Tar, The / und S C.C.

Yates, Joseph See: No. 3296.

6825 Year after Marriage, A / #114 / 8.5x11.11 (Full length of mother, child in cradle. Companion to No. 1459.) 1847 S N.C.

6826 Year after Marriage, A / The Mother's Jewel / 8.8x11.9 (Same general composition as preceding. Companion to No. 1461.) und S C&I

6827 Year Before Marriage / The Bride's Jewel / 8.5x11.9. und S C&I

6828 Yes or No? / 8.11x12.2 (Girl holding picture of man in back of her.) und S C&I

Yorktown, Va. — Surrender of Cornwallis / See: Nos. 5904-6, 5912-3.

6829 Yosemite Falls / California / 8.8x 12.7. und S C&I

6830 Yosemite Valley — California / The Bridal Veil Fall / F. F. Palmer, Del. 17.10x25.12 (Indians in camp in foreground.) 1866 L C&I

Yosemite Valley See: Nos. 659, 1681, 3767, 4785, 6520.

6831 You Don't Mean It? / (Vignette, half length.) 1872 S C&I

6832 You Will! Will you? / J.C. on stone. (Also published with title changed to "Going for Him," No. 2400.) 1868 S C&I

6833 Young African, The / On stone by G. Kramm. (Upright vignette, half length figure.) und S N.C.

6834 Young America / #550 / (Vignette, ¾ figure of boy.) und S C&I

6835 Young America / (Vignette, half length figure of boy.) 1873 S C&I

Young America (Clipper Ship) See: No. 1171.

6836 Young America / "Celebrating the Fourth" / 8x11.8 (Full length boy shooting fire crackers, top corners of plate slightly rounded.) 1867 S C&I

6837 Young America "Celebrating" / Fourth of July / 1857 L C&I

6838 Young America / The Child of Liberty / (Vignette, half length figure of boy with shield and helmet.) 1876 S C&I

6839 Young Blood in an old Body / 8.7x 12.7 (4 boys pulling an old stage coach filled with children, railroad train in background.) 1874 S C&I

Young, Brigham & Jr. See: No. 1986.

6840 Young Brood, The / 7.15x12.8 (Children feeding ducks in stream.) 1870 S C&I

6841 Young Brood, The / (Hen with chickens.) 1860 L C&I

6842 Young Cadets, The / (Tobacco advertising card.) und V.S. C&I

6843 Young Cavalier, The / #308 / (Vignette.) und S C&I

6844 Young Chieftain, The / 8.7x11.12 (Upright, young boy in Scotch costume.) und S N.C.

6845 Young Chieftain, The / #560 / 8.8x 11.15 (¾ length figure of Scotch girl, seated.) 1848 S N.C.

6846 Young Circassian, The / #714 / und S N.C.

6847 Young Circassian, The / #714 / (¾

length figure, minaret seen through window.) und S C&I

6848 Young Companions, The / #170 / 8.11x11.12 (Young girl with basket of flowers, dog on lap.)
und S N.C.

6849 Young Companions, The / 8.12x 11.13 (Children in orchard.)
und S C&I

6850 Young Continental, The / The Spirit of '76 / #484 / "Stand by the Flag" (Top of print.) 2 columns, 2 lines of verse. 9x11.11 (Full length figure in military uniform.)
und S N.C.

6851 Young England /
und S C&I

6852 Young Fullerton [3528] Record 2:20¾ / Owned by Judson H. Clark, Genesee Valley Stock Farm, Elmira, N.Y. / By Edward Everett [81] dam Flora by Jupiter [46] / Dam of Electra Rec 2:20 / 2 columns, 2 lines each. Oleographed by Currier & Ives. 16x23 (¾ view to left, high-wheeled sulky.)
1888 L C&I

6853 Young Georgian /
1868 S C&I

6854 Young Georgian, The / 8.9x12.12 (Plate corners rounded. Full length female figure, reclining.)
1846 S N.C.

6855 Young Hopeful / (Upright vignette, full length boy seated.)
1874 S C&I

6856 Young Housekeepers, The / 8.13x 11.14 (Full length figures.)
und S N.C.

6857 Young Housekeepers, The / A Year after Marriage / #608 / 8.12x11.14 (Upright, couple with baby, standing at window.) 1848 S N.C.

6858 Young Housekeepers, The / The Day after Marriage / #222 / 8.9x12.1 (Upright, couple standing at window.)
1848 S N.C.

6859 Young Lovers, The / #265 / (Upright, boy teaching girl to play flute.)

Z

Zaandam (Steamship) See: No. 5244.

Zachary Taylor See: Nos. 325, 1485, 1938, 2231, 2296-300, 2329-31, 2513-4, 3679-80, 3938-9, 4884, 4899, 5382-3, 6495.

Zachary Taylor (Horse) See: No. 3848.

und S N.C.

6860 Young Mother, The / #277 / (¾ length.) und S N.C.

6861 Young Mother, The / #277 / 9x11 (Oval. Holding baby in arms, another child on chair with dog.) (This is also printed rectangularly.)
und S C&I

6862 Young Napoleon / 8.12x11.4.
und S N.C.

6863 Young Napoleon / Contemplating his Father's Sword / 8.9x11.1 (¾ length portrait.) und S N.C.

6864 Young Navigator / L. Maurer on stone. 10.10x14.10 (Full length boy sailing an old shoe.)
1858 M C&I

6865 Young Protector, The / (Boy standing at side of younger girl seated on rustic bench.) und S N.C.

6866 Young Ruffed Grouse / 9.10x12.6. A. F. Tait '56 N.Y. on stone. (Oval, same composition as "The Infant Brood," No. 3100.)
1865 S C&I

6867 Young Sailor, The / #691 / 8.12x 12.2 (Full length figure on shore, full rigged boat in right background.)
1849 S N.C.

6868 Young Scotland / #711 /(Vignette.)
und S C&I

6869 Young Shepherdess, The /
und S C&I

6870 Young Soldier, The / #319 / 8.12x 11.15 (Full length, interior scene, portrait of Washington on wall.)
und S N.C.

6871 Young Students, The / #619 / 8.12x 11.8 (Small girl sewing while mother is teaching boy.) und S C&I

6872 Young Volunteer, The /
und S N.C.
Young Woful (Horse) See: No. 939.

6873 "Your Plan and Mine" / (Vignette, political portraits of McClellan, Jeff, Lincoln.) 1864 S C&I

6874 Zachary Taylor / The Nation's Choice for / Twelfth President of the United States / #476 / (Profile to right, hand resting on map of Mexico, military uniform.) 1847 S N.C.

6875 Zachary Taylor / The Nation's Choice for / Twelfth President of the United States / #476 / 11.7x8.10 (Half length, hand resting on sword, red curtain.) 1847 S N.C.

6876 Zachary Taylor / People's Candidate for / President / Millard Fillmore / Whig Candidate for Vice-President / #593 / 12.9x8.6 (2 oval portraits on same sheet.) 1848 S N.C.

6877 Zachary Taylor / People's Candidate for / Twelfth President of the United States / #586 / 11.15x8.14 (Right hand resting on map of Mexico, military uniform.)
1848 S N.C.

6878 Zachary Taylor / The People's Choice for / Twelfth President of the United States / From life and on stone by Risso of New Orleans. #617 / (Vignette, half length, full face, military coat.) 1848 S N.C.

6879 Zachary Taylor / Twelfth President of the United States / #30 / 11.4x8.14 (¾ length, full face, hand resting on letter, no military uniform.)
1849 S N.C.

Zeendam (Steamship) See: No. 5805.

ADDENDA

Mr. Conningham's check list is the most comprehensive record of Nathaniel Currier, Charles Currier, and Currier & Ives prints ever compiled. During the twenty years since its publication, only a few unrecorded items have come to light. They are listed below. It is not unlikely that in future years a few more previously unknown prints will turn up.

C.S.

American Railroad Scene
1872 S C&I
American Railroad Scene
1874 S C&I
American Winter Scene—The Falls oval 5.8x7.8 und VS C&I
Bird's Eye View of the Great Suspension Bridge, connecting the cities of New York and Brooklyn. Looking Southeast
1883 L C&I
Circular Pleasure Railway. In Hoboken, N.J. und S N.C.
Gov. Benj. Gratz Brown of Missouri Liberal Republican candidate for Vice-President of the United States
und S C&I
Great Race on the Mississippi, The / From New Orleans to St. Louis 1210 miles / Between the Steamers Robt. E. Lee, Capt. J. W. Cannon and Natchez, Capt. T. P. Leathers, won by the R. E. Lee—Time 3 days, 18 hours, 30 minutes. (Night scene) 1870 L C&I
Hon. Henry Wilson, National Republican and Workingman's candidate for Vice-President of the U.S. 1872 S C&I
Il Grande Ponte Sospeso Dell "East River" (Great East River Suspension Bridge—in Italian) 1886 L C&I
Johnny and Bessie. A Brother's Help
und S C&I
Neptune House, New Rochelle, Westchester County, New York. This splendid establishment is delightfully situated on Long Island Sound, about a mile from the Village of New Rochelle, and eighteen miles from New-York. In point of salubrity and picturesque scenery it is not surpassed by any in America. The accommodations are of the

most excellent description; warm and cold, salt and fresh water baths ready at all times; and nothing is spared to promote the amusement and comfort of the inmates. Pleasure and fishing boats for aquatic excursions, and vehicles and horses for driving or riding provided at a moment's notice. The Steam-Boat American Eagle leaves New Rochelle early every morning and the foot of Fulton St. East River every afternoon, landing at the dock. The Harlem Railroad cars will convey passengers to Fordham from whence stages run twice a day to New Rochelle. July 1st, 1842 C. F. Rice und L N.C.

Sailor's Return, The (ship on the right)
und S C&I
Steam Ship Royal William on her first Voyage to New York on the 14th of July 1838. From painting by Samuel Walters. On stone by Fleetwood.
1838 L N.C.

View of the High Falls of Trenton—West Canada Creek, N. Y. 15x21½ Aquatint engraved by W. J. Bennett. Published by Currier & Ives 152 Nassau Street.
und L C&I
View on the Rondout. und S C&I
Vista de la Ciudad de New York, Mostrando el Edificio de la EQUITA— Broadway 120 (View of New York City published for Equitable Life Insurance Company—in Spanish)
1876 L C&I

West Point, from Phillipstown 15¾x21¾ Aquatint engraving by W. J. Bennett, published by Currier & Ives, 152 Nassau St. und L C&I